Moreton Morrell Site

Research Methods for Business Students

Visit the *Research Methods for Business Students*, Fifth Edition Companion Website at **www.pearsoned.co.uk/saunders** to find valuable student learning material including:

- Multiple choice questions to test your learning.
- Tutorials on Excel, NVivo and SPSS.
- Updated research datasets to practice with.
- Updated additional case studies with accompanying questions.
- Smarter Online Searching Guide – how to make the most of the Internet in your research.

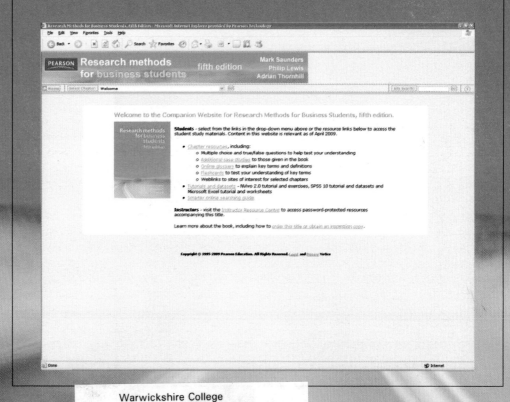

PEARSON
Education

We work with leading authors to develop the strongest educational
materials in business strategy, bringing cutting-edge thinking and best
learning practice to a global market.
Under a range of well-known imprints, including Financial Times Prentice
Hall, we craft high quality print and electronic publications which help
readers to understand and apply their content, whether studying or at
work.
To find out more about the complete range of our publishing please visit
us on the World Wide Web at: **www.pearsoned.co.uk**

Research Methods
for Business
Students

Fifth edition

Mark Saunders

Philip Lewis

Adrian Thornhill

FT Prentice Hall
FINANCIAL TIMES

An imprint of Pearson Education
Harlow, England • London • New York • Boston • San Francisco • Toronto • Sydney • Singapore • Hong Kong
Tokyo • Seoul • Taipei • New Delhi • Cape Town • Madrid • Mexico City • Amsterdam • Munich • Paris • Milan

Pearson Education Limited
Edinburgh Gate
Harlow
Essex CM20 2JE
England
and Associated Companies throughout the world

Visit us on the World Wide Web at:

www.pearsoned.co.uk

First published under the Pitman Publishing imprint in 1997
Second edition 2000
Third edition 2003
Fourth edition 2007
Fifth edition 2009

ISBN: 978-0-273-71686-0

British Library Cataloguing-in-Publication Data
A catalogue record for this book is available from the British Library
Library of Congress Cataloging-in-Publication Data
Saunders, Mark, 1959-
   Research methods for business students / Mark Saunders, Philip Lewis, Adrian Thornhill. —5th ed.
      p. cm.
   Includes bibliographical references and index.
   ISBN 978-0-273-71686-0 (pbk. : alk. paper) 1. Business—Research. 2. Business—Research—Data processing. I. Lewis, Philip, 1945- II. Thornhill, Adrian. III. Title.
   HD30.4.S28 2009
   650.072—dc22

                                                                                          2008054877

10 9 8 7 6 5 4
13 12 11 10

Typeset in ITC Slimbach Std 9.5/12.5 by 73

Printed and bound by Rotolito Lombarda, Italy

Brief Contents

Contents

11   Collecting primary data using questionnaires   360

12   Analysing quantitative data   414

Appendices

Supporting resources

Visit www.pearsoned.co.uk/saunders to find valuable online resources:

Companion Website for students
- Multiple choice questions to test your learning.
- Tutorials on Excel, NVivo and SPSS.
- Updated research datasets to practice with.
- Updated additional case studies with accompanying questions.
- Smarter Online Searching Guide – how to make the most of the Internet in your research.

For instructors
- Complete, downloadable Instructor's Manual.
- PowerPoint slides that can be downloaded and used for presentations.

Also – the regularly maintained Companion Website provides the following features:
- Search tool to help locate specific items of content.
- E-mail results and profile tools to send results of quizzes to instructors.
- Online help and support to assist with website usage and troubleshooting.

For more information please contact your local Pearson Education sales representative or visit **www.pearsoned.co.uk/saunders**

How to use this book

This book is written with a progressive logic, which means that terms and concepts are defined when they are first introduced. One implication of this is that it is sensible for you to start at the beginning and to work your way through the text, various boxes, self-check questions, review and discussion questions, case studies and case study questions. You can do this in a variety of ways depending on your reasons for using this book. However, this approach may not necessarily be suitable for your purposes, and you may wish to read the chapters in a different order or just dip into particular sections of the book. If this is true for you then you will probably need to use the glossary to check that you understand some of the terms and concepts used in the chapters you read. Suggestions for three of the more common ways in which you might wish to use this book are given below.

As part of a research methods course or for self-study for your research project

If you are using this book as part of a research methods course the order in which you read the chapters is likely to be prescribed by your tutors and dependent upon their perceptions of your needs. Conversely, if you are pursuing a course of self-study for your research project, dissertation or consultancy report, the order in which you read the chapters is your own choice. However, whichever of these you are, we would argue that the order in which you read the chapters is dependent upon your recent academic experience.

For many students, such as those taking an undergraduate degree in business or management, the research methods course and associated project, dissertation or consultancy report comes in either the second or the final year of study. In such situations it is probable that you will follow the chapter order quite closely (see Figure P.1). Groups of chapters within which we believe you can switch the order without affecting the logic of the flow too much are shown on the same level in this diagram and are:

- those chapters associated with data collection (Chapters 8, 9, 10 and 11);
- those associated with data analysis (Chapters 12 and 13).

In addition, you might wish to read the sections in Chapter 14 on writing prior to starting to draft your critical review of the literature (Chapter 3).

Alternatively, you may be returning to academic study after a gap of some years, to take a full-time or part-time course such as a Master of Business Administration, a Master of Arts or a Master of Science with a Business and Management focus. Many students in such situations need to refresh their study skills early in their programme, particularly those associated with critical reading of academic literature and academic writing. If you feel the need to do this, you may wish to start with those chapters that support you in

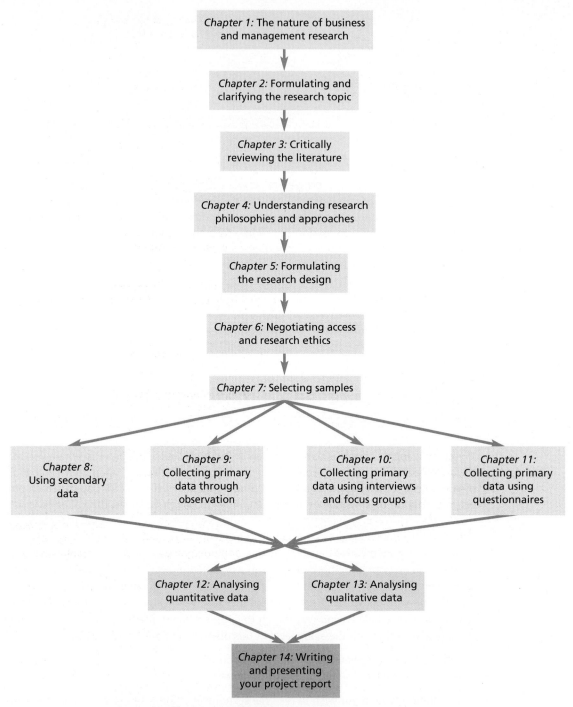

Figure P.1 Using this book in your second or final year of study

developing and refining these skills (Chapters 3 and 14), followed by Chapter 8, which introduces you to the range of secondary data sources available that might be of use for other assignments (Figure P.2). Once again, groups of chapters within which we believe you can switch the order without affecting the logic of the flow too much are shown on

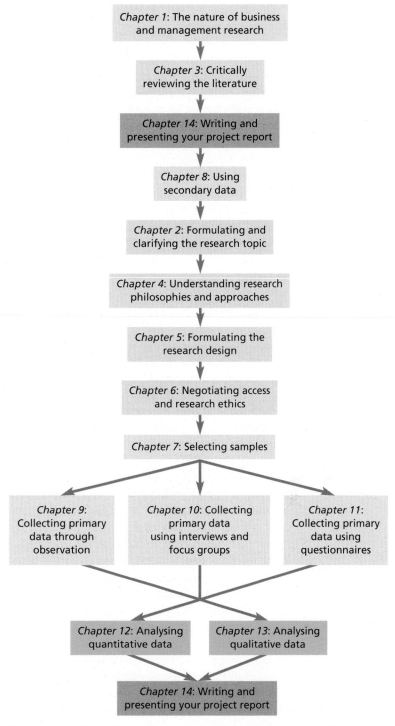

Figure P.2 Using this book as a new returner to academic study

the same level in the diagram and are:

- those chapters associated with primary data collection (Chapters 9, 10 and 11);
- those associated with data analysis (Chapters 12 and 13).

In addition, we would recommend that you re-read Chapter 14 prior to starting to write your project report, dissertation or consultancy report.

Whichever order you choose to read the chapters in, we would recommend that you attempt all the self-check questions, review and discussion questions and those questions associated with the case studies. Your answers to the self-check questions can be self-assessed using the answers at the end of each chapter. However, we hope that you will actually have a go at each question prior to reading the answer! If you need further information on an idea or a technique, then first look at the references in the further reading section.

At the end of Chapters 2–14 the section headed 'Progressing your research project' lists a number of tasks. Such tasks might involve you in just planning a research project or, alternatively, designing and administering a questionnaire of your own. When completed, these tasks will provide a useful *aide-mémoire* for assessed work and can be used as the basis for the first draft of your project report. It is worth pointing out here that many consultancy reports for organisations do not require you to include a review of the academic literature.

As a guide through the research process

If you are intending to use this book to guide you through the research process for a research project you are undertaking, such as your dissertation, we recommend that you read the entire book quickly before starting your research. In that way you will have a good overview of the entire process, including the range of techniques available, and will be better able to plan your work.

After you have read the book once, we suggest that you work your way through the book again following the chapter order. This time you should attempt the self-check questions, review and discussion questions and those questions associated with each case study to ensure that you have understood the material contained in each chapter prior to applying it to your own research project. Your responses to self-check questions can be assessed using the answers at the end of each chapter.

If you are still unsure as to whether particular techniques, procedures or ideas are relevant, then pay special attention to the 'focus on student research', 'focus on management research' and 'focus on research in the news' boxes. 'Focus on student research' boxes are based on actual students' experiences and illustrate how an issue has been addressed or a technique or procedure used in a student's research project. 'Focus on management research' boxes discuss recent research articles in established refereed academic journals, allowing you to see how research is undertaken successfully. These articles are easily accessible via online databases. 'Focus on research in the news' boxes provide topical news stories of how particular research techniques, procedures and ideas are used in the business world. You can also look in the 'further reading' for other examples of research where these have been used. If you need further information on an idea, technique or procedure then, again, start with the references in the further reading section.

Material in some of the chapters is likely to prove less relevant to some research topics than others. However, you should beware of choosing techniques because you are happy with them, if they are inappropriate. Completion of the tasks in the section headed 'Progressing your research project' at the end of Chapters 2–13 will enable you to generate all the material that you will need to include in your research project, dissertation or consultancy report. This will also help you to focus on the techniques and ideas that are most appropriate to your research. When you have also completed these tasks for Chapter 14 you will have written your research project, dissertation or consultancy report.

As a reference source

It may be that you wish to use this book now or subsequently as a reference source. If this is the case, an extensive index will point you to the appropriate page or pages. Often you will find a 'checklist' box within these pages. 'Checklist' boxes are designed to provide you with further guidance on the particular topic. You will also find the contents pages and the glossary useful reference sources, the latter defining over 400 research terms. In addition, we have tried to help you to use the book in this way by including cross-references between sections in chapters as appropriate. Do follow these up as necessary. If you need further information on an idea or a technique then begin by consulting the references in the further reading section. Wherever possible we have tried to reference books that are in print and readily available in university libraries.

Guided tour

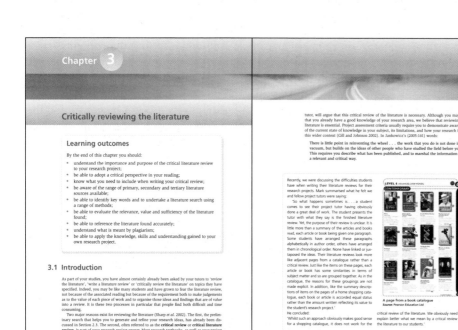

Chapter openers provide a clear and concise introduction to the topics to be covered, together with a list of **Learning outcomes** that you should have achieved by the end of the chapter.

Practical illustrations bring to life some of the issues and challenges you will encounter during your course and beyond. These include short **Focus on student research** and longer **Cases**.

Explore recent articles and up-to-date issues in research practice through the **Focus on management research** and **Research in the news** features.

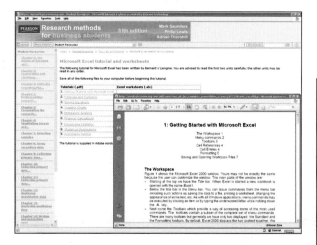

Save time and improve your research results by using the **Tutorials** on Excel, NVivo and SPSS, and the **Smarter Online Searching Guide**. Both of these valuable resources are accessible at **www.pearsoned.co.uk/saunders**.

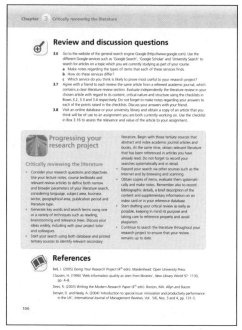

You will be given lots of opportunities to review your progress! Every chapter includes handy **Checklists**, tips on **Progressing your research project,** as well as Self-check questions (at the end of the chapter). There are additional interactive **Multiple choice questions** on the Companion Website.

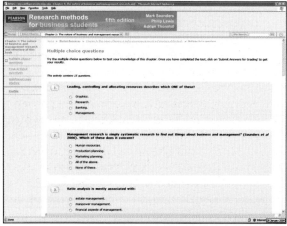

A **Summary, Self-check questions** and **Review and discussion questions,** and recommended **Further reading** at the end of each chapter enable you to reflect upon key points and pursue topics in more depth.

Preface

In writing the fifth edition of *Research Methods for Business Students* we have responded to the many comments we have received regarding previous editions. In particular, this has led us to substantially revise Chapter 4 'Understanding research philosophies and approaches', Chapter 5 'Formulating the research design' and discuss consultancy projects where appropriate (e.g. in Chapter 14 'Writing and presenting your project report'). We have also revised Chapter 13 'Analysing qualitative data' to reflect the variety of types of processes to analyse these data. In our revisions throughout the book and our sourcing of all new cases we have taken into account the growing importance of the Internet as a means of accessing academic literature and research data sets. This has necessitated substantial updating for Chapter 3, 'Critically reviewing the literature', and Chapter 8, 'Using secondary data'. We have also taken the opportunity to check and revise the tables of Internet addresses fully and to further develop our discussions regarding issues associated with the use of email, Internet chat rooms in interviewing (Chapter 10) and Internet and intranet-mediated questionnaires (Chapter 11).

The reality of relatively inexpensive and easily accessible computer processing power for almost all students has had significant implications for business and management students' research. As in previous editions, we have taken a predominantly non-software-specific approach in our writing. By doing this, we have been able to focus on the general principles needed to utilise a range of analysis software and the Internet effectively for research. However, recognising that many students have access to sophisticated data-analysis software and may need help in developing these skills, we continue to provide access to 'teach yourself' guides to SPSS™, Excel™, NVivo™ and Internet searching via the book's website (www.pearsoned.co.uk/saunders). Where appropriate, these guides are provided with data sets. In the preparation of the fifth edition we were fortunate to receive considerable feedback from colleagues in universities throughout the world. We are extremely grateful to all the reviewers who gave their time and shared their ideas.

Inevitably, the body of knowledge of research methods has developed further since 2006, and we have revised the chapters accordingly. Our experiences of teaching and supervising students and working through the methods in classes have suggested alternative approaches and the need to provide additional material. Consequently, we have taken the opportunity to update and refine existing worked examples and develop new ones where appropriate. The new case studies at the end of each chapter have been developed with colleagues, providing up-to-date scenarios through which to illustrate issues associated with undertaking research. However, the basic structure remains much the same as the previous four editions.

Other minor changes and updating have been made throughout. Needless to say, any errors of omission and commission are our responsibility.

As with previous editions, much of our updating has been guided by comments from students and colleagues, to whom we are most grateful. We should like to thank students from Oxford Brookes University and on the Research Methods' Summer Schools for their comments on all of the chapters. Colleagues in both our own and other universities have continued to provide helpful comments and advice. We are particularly grateful to Levent Altinay (Oxford Brookes University), Murray Clark (Sheffield Hallam University), Joanne Duberley (Birmingham University), David Hart (Northumbria University), Tracey Panther (Oxford Brookes University) and Christine Williams (University of Gloucestershire). Colleagues and friends again deserve thanks for their assistance in providing examples of research across the spectrum of business and management, co-authoring chapters, writing case studies and in reviewing parts of this book, in particular, Mohammad Al-Kilani (Al-Hussein Bin Talal University, Jordan), Peter Bolan (University of Ulster), David Coghlan (Trinity College, Dublin), Mridula Dwivedi (Institute for International Management and Technology, Gurgaon, India), Karen Handley (Oxford Brookes University), Peter Harris (Oxford Brookes University), Bill Lee (University of Sheffield), Liz Lee-Kelley (Cranfield University), Stephanie Macht (Northumbria University), Michael Savvas (Aberystwyth University), Richard Slack (Northumbria University), Mike Wallace (Cardiff University and Advanced Institute of Management Research), Catherine Wang (Royal Holloway, University of London), Alison Wray (Cardiff University), Anil Yadav (Institute for International Management and Technology, Gurgaon, India) and Deli Yang (Bradford University).

The contributions of Lynette Bailey, Darren Bolton and Martin Jenkins to Chapters 3 and 8 and of Andrew Guppy to Chapter 12 in earlier editions of this book are gratefully acknowledged.

We would also like to thank all of the staff at Pearson Education (both past and present) who supported us through the process of writing the fifth edition. Our thanks go, in particular, to Matthew Walker, our commissioning editor, for his support and enthusiasm throughout the process and to Stuart Hay for his insightful comments. We would also like to express our thanks to Elizabeth Rix as desk editor.

Once again, our thanks are due to Jane, Jenny, Jan, Jemma, Ben, Andrew and Katie, who still allow us the time to absent ourselves to think and write.

MNKS
PL
AT
July 2008

Contributors

Mark N.K. Saunders BA, MSc, PGCE, PhD, FCIPD, is Professor of Business Research Methods in the School of Management at the University of Surrey. He was formerly professor of Business Research Methods and Assistant Dean (Director of Research and Doctoral Programmes) at Oxford Brookes University Business School. He is a visiting professor at Newcastle Business School, University of Northumbria. He teaches research methods to masters and doctoral students as well as supervising masters dissertations and research degrees. Mark has published articles on research methods, service quality, and trust and organisational justice perspectives on the management of change. He is co-author with Phil and Adrian of *Employee Relations: Understanding the Employment Relationship*; with Phil, Adrian, Mike Millmore and Trevor Morrow of *Strategic Human Resource Management* and with Adrian, Phil and Mike Millmore of *Managing Change: A Human Resource Strategy Approach*, all published by Financial Times Prentice Hall. He has also co-authored two books on business statistics, the most recent being *Statistics: What You Need to Know* co-authored with Reva Berman-Brown. He continues to undertake consultancy in the public, private and not-for-profit sectors. Prior to becoming an academic, he had a variety of research jobs in local government.

Philip Lewis BA, PhD, MSc, MCIPD, PGDipM, Cert Ed, began his career in HR as a training adviser with the Distributive Industry Training Board. He then taught HRM and research methods in three UK universities. He studied part-time for degrees with the Open University and the University of Bath, from which he gained an MSc in industrial relations and a PhD for his research on performance pay in retail financial services. He is co-author with Adrian and Mark of *Employee Relations: Understanding the Employment Relationship* and *Managing Change: A Human Resource Strategy Approach*; with Mark, Adrian, Mike Millmore and Trevor Morrow of *Strategic Human Resource Management* and with Adrian, Mark and Mike Millmore of *Managing Change: A Human Resource Strategy Approach*, all published by Financial Times Prentice Hall. He has undertaken consultancy in both public and private sectors.

Adrian Thornhill BA, PhD, PGCE, FCIPD, was formerly Head of the Department of Human Resource Management at Gloucestershire Business School, University of Gloucestershire. He has taught HRM and research methods to postgraduate, undergraduate and professional students, and supervised research degrees. Adrian has published a number of articles principally associated with employee and justice perspectives related to managing change and the management of organisational downsizing and redundancy. He is co-author with Phil and Mark of *Employee Relations: Understanding the Employment Relationship;* with Phil, Mark, Mike Millmore and Trevor Morrow of *Strategic Human Resource Management* and with Phil, Mark and Mike Millmore of *Managing Change: A Human Resource Strategy Approach*, all published by Financial Times Prentice Hall. He has also co-authored a book on downsizing and redundancy and undertaken consultancy in both public and private sectors.

Dr Mohammad H. Al-Kilani is an Assistant Professor in Organisational Behaviour and Organisation Theory at the Faculty of Business and Economics, Al-Hussein Bin Talal University.

Peter Bolan is Director of International Travel and Tourism at the University of Ulster School of Hospitality and Tourism Management.

Dr David Coghlan is a Lecturer in Organisational Development and Action Research at Trinity College Dublin School of Business Studies.

Dr Mridula Dwivedi is Assistant Professor at the Institute for International Management and Technology, Gurgaon, India.

Dr Karen Handley is a Senior Lecturer in Human Resource Management and Organisational Behaviour at Oxford Brookes University Business School.

Professor Peter Harris is Professor of Management Accounting in the Department of Hospitality, Leisure and Tourism Management at the Business School, Oxford Brookes University

Dr Bill Lee is a Senior Lecturer in Accounting and Financial Management at the Management School, University of Sheffield.

Dr Liz Lee-Kelley is a Senior Lecturer in Programme and Project Management at Cranfield School of Management, Cranfield University.

Stephanie Macht is a Lecturer in Strategic Management at Newcastle Business School, Northumbria University.

Dr Michael Savvas is a Visiting Lecturer in International and Human Resource Management at the School of Management and Business, Aberystwyth University.

Richard Slack is Reader in Accounting and Programme Director for Research Development PhD at Newcastle Business School, Northumbria University.

Professor Mike Wallace is a Professor of Public Management at Cardiff Business School and Associate Director for Capacity Building, Advanced Institute of Management Research.

Catherine L. Wang is a Senior Lecturer in Strategy at the School of Management, Royal Holloway, University of London.

Professor Alison Wray is a Research Professor of Language and Communication at Cardiff University.

Anil Yadav is Registrar at Institute for International Management and Technology, Gurgaon, India.

Dr Deli Yang is Reader in International Business, Bradford University School of Management.

Publisher's acknowledgements

Reviewers

We would like to express thanks to the reviewers who have been involved in the development of the fifth edition of this book. We are grateful for their insight and helpful recommendations.

Ragnhild Silkoset, BI Norwegian School of Management
Kristian Nielsen, Rotterdam Business School
Poul Houman Andersen, The Aarhus School of Business
Frits Wijbenga, Durham Business School, Durham University
Loic Ple, IESEG School of Management
Judith Thomas, Oxford Brookes University
David Douglas, Staffordshire University
Angela Byrne, Manchester Met University
Aileen Corley, Liverpool John Moores University
Jeff Newall, University of Derby

Publisher's acknowledgements

We are grateful to the following for permission to reproduce copyright material:

Illustrations

Figure 1.2 Mark Saunders, Philip Lewis and Adrian Thornhill 2009; Figure 3.1 Mark Saunders, Philip Lewis, Adrian Thornhill and Martin Jenkins 2003; Figure 3.3 Mark Saunders, Philip Lewis, Adrian Thornhill and Martin Jenkins 2003; Figure 4.1 Mark Saunders, Philip Lewis and Adrian Thornhill 2008; Figure 5.1 Mark Saunders, Philip Lewis and Adrian Thornhill 2008; Figure 8.1 Mark Saunders, Philip Lewis and Adrian Thornhill 2006; Figure 9.2 from Management and Organisational Behaviour, 6e Financial Times Prentice Hall; (Mullins, L.J., 2002); Chapter 11 unnumbered screenshot, page 361: Extract from Nando's online questionnaire (2008), reproduced with permission; Figure 11.2 from Constructing Questions for Interviews and Questions, Cambridge University Press, Foody, W., 1993); Chapter 11 unnumbered screenshot, page 383: Question layout created by SurveyMonkey.com (2008), reproduced with permission; Chapter 11 unnumbered screenshot, page 386: Question layout created by SurveyMonkey.com (2008), reproduced with permission.

Tables

Table 1.1 from Realigning the stakeholders in management research: lessons form industrial, work and organizational psychology in British Journal of Management Vol. 12 Special issue, pp. 41–8, Blackwell Publishing, (Hodgkinson, G.P., Herriot, P. and Anderson, N., 2001; Table 3.1 Mark Saunders, Philip Lewis and Adrian Thornhill 2008; Table 7.2 Mark Saunders, Philip Lewis and Adrian Thornhill 2008; Table 9.3 from Real WorldResearch: A Resource for Social Scientists and Practitioner – Researchers, 2e Blackwell Publishing, (Robson 2002); Table 11.4 from Translation techniques for questionnaires in International and Cross-Cultural Management Research, Sage Publications, (Usunier, 1998); Table 12.2 Mark Saunders, Philip Lewis and Adrian Thornhill 2008; Table 12.4 Mark Saunders, Philip Lewis and Adrian Thornhill 2008; Table 12.5 Mark Saunders, Philip Lewis and Adrian Thornhill 2008; Table 14.1 from How to Write and Publish a Scientific Paper 5e, Phoenix. AZ: Oryx Press, Greenwood Publishing Group Inc., Westport CT, (Day, R., 1998:160).

Photos

3 Mark Saunders;17 Alamy Images: Baron Bratby; 21 Alamy Images: Nicholas Linton (b); 52 Alamy Images: Anthony Kay; 102 Alamy Images: Rob Judges/Oxford; 107 Science Photo Library Ltd: Astrid & Hanns-Frieder Michler; 132 Alamy Images: David Hoffmann Photo Library; 137 Philip Lewis; 163 Getty Images/Lifestock; 164 Alamy Images: Paul Repson; 205 Alamy Images: Freddie Jones; 211 Rex Features: Giuseppe Aresu; 248 Corbis: Leif Skoogtors; 257 Philip Lewis, 284 Corbis: E Streichan/Zefa; 289 Philip Lewis, 313 Mridula Dwivedi; 319 Getty Images: Eamonn McCormack; 355 Corbis: Gregor Schuster/Zefa; 407 Mohammad Al Kilani; 415 Mark Saunders; 481 Alamy Images: Marshall Ikonography; 520 Mark Saunders; 527 Ben Saunders; 558 Alamy Images: Alex Segre.

Text

Box 3.5 from Structure of the literature review, Taylor & Francis Ltd (Williams, C.S, and Saunders M.N.K, 2006); Box 3.15 from Microsoft reveals answer to Google Scholar Candace Lombardi, ZDNet News, 12th April 2006, The YGS Group; Box 14.2 from How to . . . . write an abstract from http://www.emeraldinsight.com; Box 14.3 from The changing travel behaviour of Austria's ageing population and its impact on tourism in Tourism Review. 62 (3/4): 15–20, Emerald Group Publishing, (Moller, C, Weiermair, K and Wintersberger, E 2008); Box 14.5 from Real World Research 2e, Blackwell Publishing, (Robson, 2002).

We are also grateful to the Financial Times Limited for permission to reprint the following material:

Box 1.1 Research that aids publicists but not the public, © FT.com, 30 October 2007; Box 2.6 Many workers feel too qualified for jobs, © Financial Times, 29th October 2007; Box 2.9 The e-sport revolution Korean-style, © Financial Times, 15 September 2007; Box 3.6 Biofuel targets in EU will outweigh benefits, © Financial Times, 18 January 2008; Box 3.9 Google in challenge to Wikipedia, © Financial Times, 15 December 2007; Box 6.3 Star performers on back of the Internet, © Financial Times, 14 April 2007; Box 6.16 Watchdog in call for criminal sanctions, © Financial Times, 22 November 2007; Box 7.1 You don't need to be a mechanical engineer to drive a car, © Financial Times, 12 February 2007; Box 7.15 'How I did it' books give me a sinking feeling, © Financial Times, 28 August 2007; Box 10.13 Sir Adrian's thorn, © Financial Times, 29 May 2008; Box 10.18 BT keeps an eye on surfing habits in quest for better advert targeting, © Financial Times, 24 May 2008; Box 11.6 George Lucas is a god in Britain. Literally, © Financial Times, 14 February 2003; Box 11.8 TNS warns over reliability of data collected online, © Financial Times, 4 September 2007; Box 12.21 Rock faces FTSE 100 exit, © Financial Times, 12 December 2007; Box 13.1 Wide range of weapons in analysts' armoury, © Financial Times, 16 May 2008; Box 13.10 Sales Manager wins 'Apprentice', © Financial Times, 12 June 2008; Box 12.10 FSA warns on derivatives dangers, © Financial Times, 11 February 2008.

In some instances we have been unable to trace the owners of copyright material and we would appreciate any information that would enable us to do so.

Chapter 1

The nature of business and management research and structure of this book

Learning outcomes

By the end of this chapter you should:

- be able to outline the purpose and distinct focus of management research;
- be able to place your research project on a basic-applied research continuum according to its purpose and context;
- understand the stages you will need to complete (and revisit) as part of your research process;
- have an overview of this book's purpose, structure and features;
- be aware of some of the ways you can use this book.

1.1 Introduction

This book is designed to help you to undertake your research project, whether you are an undergraduate or postgraduate student of business and management or a manager. It provides a clear guide on how to undertake research as well as highlighting the realities of undertaking research, including the more common pitfalls. The book is written as an introductory text to provide you with a guide to the research process and with the necessary knowledge and skills to undertake a piece of research from thinking of a research topic to writing your project report. As such, you will find it useful as a manual or handbook on how to tackle your research project.

After reading the book you will have been introduced to and explored a range of approaches, strategies and methods with which you could tackle your research project. Of equal importance, you will know that there is no one best way for undertaking all research. Rather you will be aware of the choices you will have to make and how these choices will impact upon what you can find out. This means you will be able to make an informed choice about the approaches, strategies and methods that are most suitable to your own research project and be able to justify this choice. In reading the book you will have been introduced to the more frequently used techniques and procedures for collecting and analysing different types of data, have had a chance to practise them, and be able to make a reasoned choice regarding which to use. When selecting and using these techniques you will be aware of the contribution that the appropriate use of information technology can make to your research.

However, before you continue, a word of caution. In your study, you will inevitably read a wide range of books and articles. In many of these the terms 'research method' and 'research methodology' will be used interchangeably, perhaps just using methodology as a more verbose way of saying method. In this book we have been more precise in our use of these terms. Throughout the book we use the term **methods** to refer to techniques and procedures used to obtain and analyse data. This, therefore, includes questionnaires, observation and interviews as well as both quantitative (statistical) and qualitative (non-statistical) analysis techniques and, as you have probably gathered from the title, is the main focus of this book. In contrast, the term **methodology** refers to the theory of how research should be undertaken. We believe that it is important that you have some understanding of this so that you can make an informed choice about your research. For this reason, we also discuss a range of philosophical assumptions upon which research can be based and the implications of these for the method or methods adopted.

The Post-it® note is one of the best known and most widely used office products in the world. Yet, despite the discovery of the repositionable adhesive that made the Post-it® note possible in 1968, it was not until 1980 that the product was introduced to the market (Lemelson-MIT Program 2007). In the 1960s 3M research scientist, Spence Silver, was looking for ways to improve the adhesive used in tapes. However, he discovered something quite different from what he was looking for, an adhesive that did not stick strongly when coated onto the back of tapes! What was unclear was how it might be used. Over the next five years he demonstrated and talked about his new adhesive to people working within the company.

Most people working for 3M know the story of what happened next and how the Post-it® note concept came about. A new product development researcher working for 3M, Art Fry, was frustrated by how the scraps of paper he used as bookmarks kept falling out of his church choir hymn book. He realised that Silver's adhesive would mean his bookmarks would not fall out. Soon afterwards the Post-it® note concept was developed and market research undertaken. This was extremely difficult as the product was revolutionary and was, in effect, designed to replace pieces of torn scrap paper! However, despite some initial scepticism within the company, Post-it® notes were launched in 1980. One year after their launch, they were named 3M's outstanding new product.

Whilst your research project will be within the business

Post-it® notes in use
Source: © Mark Saunders 2006

and management discipline rather than natural science (such as developing a new adhesive), our introductory example still offers a number of insights into the nature of research and in particular the business and management research you will be undertaking. In particular, it highlights that when undertaking research we should be open to finding the unexpected and how sometimes the applicability of our research findings may not be immediately obvious. It also emphasises the importance of discussing your ideas with other people.

1.2 The nature of research

When listening to the radio, watching the television or reading a daily newspaper it is difficult to avoid the term 'research'. The results of 'research' are all around us. A debate about the findings of a recent poll of people's opinions inevitably includes a discussion of 'research', normally referring to the way in which the data were collected. Politicians often justify their policy decisions on the basis of 'research'. Newspapers report the findings of research companies' surveys (Box 1.1). Documentary programmes tell us about 'research findings', and advertisers may highlight the 'results of research' to encourage you to buy a particular product or brand. However, we believe that what these examples really emphasise is the wide range of meanings given to the term 'research' in everyday speech.

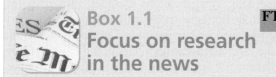

Box 1.1
Focus on research in the news

FT

Research that aids publicists but not the public

This is the age of the bogus survey. I woke up recently to the news that 95 per cent of children in Britain had been victims of crime. Of course they had. From a legal perspective, pushing a classmate or taking a pencil without the intention of returning it is a crime. School playgrounds are hotbeds of crime and always have been.

The difference between the bogus survey and real research is that real research has the objective of yielding new information, while bogus surveys are designed to generate publicity. The organisation that had undertaken this bogus survey – I forbear from mentioning its name – did not disguise that it had done so in order to draw attention to the problem of abuse of children.

Statistics about the incidence of real criminal activity against and among children are hard to come by and hard to interpret. We do not really know whether things are getting better or worse, or by how much – at least not without careful research and analysis, which would be hard to explain on television. Programme producers will not ask you to appear to spell out these complexities, but will allow you to horrify viewers and listeners with alarming news.

Public relations professionals understand these triggers, to such an extent that commissioning a bogus survey is now a standard element in the pitch they present to potential clients and conducting these surveys is an increasingly large part of the activity of market research organisations.

There is even a term for this kind of activity. It is called 'thought leadership'. That term illustrates the problem. It probably does not matter much that the bogus survey is used to generate spurious news. The danger is that opinion polls designed to produce eye-catching answers displace serious thought and analysis. The organisation that announced that 95 cent of children had been victims of crime judged, correctly, that its survey better served its needs than serious research into the problems with which it was concerned, that had not been done.

The study of business is afflicted by confusion between the results of a survey of what people think about the world and a survey of what the world is really like. At another recent meeting I heard a platform speaker announce that 40 per cent of books would be electronically published by 2020. A pesky academic asked exactly what this number meant and what evidence it was based on. The speaker assured the audience that the number had been obtained in a survey by eminent consultants of the opinions of the industry's thought leaders.

Newspapers, broadcasters and consultants will start to distinguish bogus surveys from substantive knowledge only when their audience demonstrates that it knows the difference. When you are asked for your opinion in your role as thought leader, put the phone down. You will be serving the public interest as well as saving your time.

Source: article by John Kay, *Financial Times*, FT.Com site. 30 Oct. 2007. Copyright © 2007 The Financial Times Ltd.

Walliman (2005) argues that many of these everyday uses of the term 'research' are not research in the true meaning of the word. As part of this, he highlights ways in which the term is used wrongly:

- just collecting facts or information with no clear purpose;
- reassembling and reordering facts or information without interpretation;
- as a term to get your product or idea noticed and respected.

The first of these highlights the fact that, although research often involves the collection of information, it is more than just reading a few books or articles, talking to a few people or asking people questions. While collecting data may be part of the research process, if it is not undertaken in a systematic way, on its own and, in particular, with a clear purpose, it will not be seen as research. The second of these is commonplace in many reports. Data are collected, perhaps from a variety of different sources, and then assembled in a single document with the sources of these data listed. However, there is no interpretation of the data collected. Again, while the assembly of data from a variety of sources may be part of the process of research, without interpretation it is not research. Finally, the term 'research' can be used to get an idea or product noticed by people and to suggest that people should have confidence in it. In such instances, when you ask for details of the research process, these are either unclear or not forthcoming.

Based upon this brief discussion we can already see that research has a number of characteristics:

- Data are collected systematically.
- Data are interpreted systematically.
- There is a clear purpose: to find things out.

We can therefore define **research** as something that people undertake in order to find out things in a systematic way, thereby increasing their knowledge. Two phrases are important in this definition: 'systematic way' and 'to find out things'. 'Systematic' suggests that research is based on logical relationships and not just beliefs (Ghauri and Grønhaug 2005). As part of this, your research will involve an explanation of the methods used to collect the data, will argue why the results obtained are meaningful, and will explain any limitations that are associated with them. 'To find out things' suggests there are a multiplicity of possible purposes for your research. These may include describing, explaining, understanding, criticising and analysing (Ghauri and Grønhaug 2005). However, it also suggests that you have a clear purpose or set of 'things' that you want to find out, such as the answer to a question or number of questions.

1.3 The nature of business and management research

Using our earlier definition of research it would seem sensible to define business and management research as undertaking systematic research to find out things about business and management.

Easterby-Smith *et al.* (2008) argue that four things combine to make business and management a distinctive focus for research:

- the way in which managers (and researchers) draw on knowledge developed by other disciplines;

- the fact that managers tend to be powerful and busy people. Therefore, they are unlikely to allow research access unless they can see personal or commercial advantages.
- The fact that managers are educated. Many now have undergraduate and postgraduate degrees and, as such, tend often to be as well educated as those conducting research about them.
- The requirement for the research to have some practical consequence. This means it either needs to contain the potential for taking some form of action or needs to take account of the practical consequences of the findings.

Ongoing debate within the British Academy of Management has explored the status of management research. One feature, which has gained considerable support, is the *trans-disciplinary* nature of such research. While this has similarities to Easterby-Smith *et al.*'s (2008) point regarding the use of knowledge from other disciplines, it also emphasises that the research 'cannot be reduced to any sum of parts framed in terms of contributions to associated disciplines' (Tranfield and Starkey 1998:352). In other words, using knowledge from a range of disciplines enables management research to gain new insights that cannot be obtained through all of these disciplines separately. Another feature of management research highlighted in the debate is a belief that it should be able to develop ideas and to relate them to practice. In particular, that research should complete a virtuous circle of theory and practice (Tranfield and Starkey 1998) through which research on managerial practice informs practically derived theory. This in turn becomes a blueprint for managerial practice, thereby increasing the stock of relevant and practical management knowledge. Thus, business and management research needs to engage with both the world of theory and the world of practice. Consequently, the problems addressed should grow out of interaction between these two worlds rather than either on their own.

In the past decade debate about the nature of management research has focused on how it can meet the *double hurdle* of being both theoretically and methodologically rigorous, while at the same time embracing the world of practice and being of practical relevance (Hodgkinson *et al.* 2001). Much of this debate has centred around the work by Gibbons *et al.* (1994) on the production of knowledge and, in particular, the concepts of Mode 1 and Mode 2 knowledge creation. **Mode 1** knowledge creation emphasises research in which the questions are set and solved by academic interests, emphasising a fundamental rather than applied nature, where there is little if any focus on utilisation of the research by practitioners. In contrast, **Mode 2** emphasises a context for research governed by the world of practice, highlighting the importance of collaboration both with and between practitioners (Starkey and Madan 2001) and the need for the production of practical relevant knowledge. Based upon this, Starkey and Madan (2001) observe that research within the Mode 2 approach offers a way of bringing the supply side of knowledge represented by universities together with the demand side represented by businesses and overcoming the double hurdle.

Drawing from these debates, it could be argued that business and management research not only needs to provide findings that advance knowledge and understanding, it also needs to address business issues and practical managerial problems. However, this would negate the observation that Mode 2 practices develop from Mode 1. It might also result in business and management research that did not have obvious commercial benefit not being pursued. This, Huff and Huff (2001) argue, could jeopardise future knowledge creation as research that is currently not valued commercially might have value in the future. Building upon these ideas Huff and Huff, rather like Fukami (2007) who found a third road in addition to the two academic career roads of research and teaching, highlight a further form of knowledge production: Mode 3. **Mode 3** knowledge production focuses on an appreciation of the human condition as it is and as it might become, its purpose being to 'assure survival and promote the common good at various levels of social aggregation' (Huff and Huff 2001:53). This emphasises the importance of broader issues of human relevance of research. Consequently, in addition to research that satisfies your intellectual curiosity for its own sake, the findings of business and management research might also contain practical implications, and these findings may have societal consequences far broader and complex than perhaps envisaged by Mode 2.

Tranfield and Denyer (2004) draw attention to concerns resulting from the separation of knowledge producers from knowledge users. This had the effect of introducing a schism, or what (Starkey and Madan 2001) call the 'relevance gap' which, they argue, has become more marked over recent years. More encouragingly, academic management research can be seen as a design science (Huff *et al.* 2006), its mission being to develop valid knowledge to support thoughtful, designing practitioners. From the design science perspective, the main purpose of academic management research is to develop valid knowledge to support organisational problem solving in the field. That support can be direct, instrumental or more indirect – giving general enlightenment on the type of problem at hand.

Rousseau (2006) has drawn attention to ways of closing what she terms the prevailing 'research-practice gap' – the failure of organisations and managers to base practices on best available evidence. She extols the virtues of 'evidence-based management', which derives principles from research evidence and translates them into practices that solve organisational problems. Rousseau's argument is that research findings do not appear to have transferred well to the workplace. Instead of a scientific understanding of human behaviour and organisations, managers, including those with MBAs, continue to rely largely on personal experience, to the exclusion of more systematic knowledge.

However, perhaps the most telling comment on the so-called 'relevance gap' is from Tranfield and Denyer (2004:13) who assert that ignoring such a gap would be 'unthinkable in other professional fields, such as medicine or engineering, where a national scandal would ensue if science base and practice were not inextricably and necessarily interlinked'. The article by Hodgkinson *et al.* (2001) offers a useful four-fold taxonomy for considering this in relation to managerial knowledge. Using the dimensions of theoretical and methodological rigour and of practical relevance they identify four quadrants (see Table 1.1).

Hodgkinson *et al.* argue that pedantic science is characterised by a focus on increasing methodological rigour at the expense of results that are relevant and can sometimes be found in refereed academic journals. In contrast, populist science is characterised by a focus on relevance and usefulness whilst neglecting theoretical and methodological rigour, examples being found in some books targeted at practising managers. Consequently, whilst findings might be useful to managers, the research upon which they are based is unlikely to be valid or reliable. Puerile science both lacks methodological rigour and is of limited practical relevance and, although unlikely to be found in refereed

Table 1.1 A taxonomy for considering the 'relevance gap' in relation to managerial knowledge

Theoretical and methodological rigour	Practical relevance	Quadrant
Higher	Lower	Pedantic science
Lower	Higher	Populist science
Lower	Lower	Puerile science
Higher	Higher	Pragmatic science

Source: developed from Hodgkinson *et al.* (2001).

Box 1.2
Focus on management research

In an *Academy of Management Review* article Van De Ven and Johnson (2006) examine three related ways in which the gap between theory and practice has been framed. One approach views it as a knowledge transfer problem. Practitioners fail to adopt the findings of research in fields, such as management because the knowledge is produced in a form that cannot be readily applied in practical contexts.

A second approach views knowledge of theory and practice as distinct kinds of knowledge. Each reflects a different fundamental approach for addressing different questions. To say that the knowledge of theory and practice are different is not to say that they are in conflict, or that they substitute for each other; rather, they complement one another.

This leads to a third view – namely, that the gap between theory and practice is a knowledge-production problem which questions the traditional mode of research practised in business and professional schools and has led to the proposal that a key defining characteristic of management research is its applied nature.

Having reviewed the problems and assumptions of the first two approaches, Van De Ven and Johnson propose a method of *engaged scholarship* in which researchers and practitioners coproduce knowledge that can advance theory and practice in a given domain.

academic journals, can be found in other media. Finally, pragmatic science is both theoretically and methodologically rigorous and relevant.

Within these boundaries of advancing knowledge, addressing business issues, solving managerial problems and promoting the common good, the purpose and the context of your research project can differ considerably. For some research projects your purpose may be to understand and explain the impact of something, such as a particular policy. You may undertake this research within an individual organisation and suggest appropriate action on the basis of your findings. For other research projects you may wish to explore the ways in which various organisations do things differently. In such projects your purpose may be to discover and understand better the underlying processes in a wider context, thereby providing greater understanding for practitioners. For yet other research projects you may wish to place an in-depth investigation of an organisation within the context of a wider understanding of the processes that are operating.

Despite this variety, we believe that all business and management research projects can be placed on a continuum (Figure 1.1) according to their purpose and context. At one extreme of the continuum is research that is undertaken purely to understand the processes of business and management and their outcomes. Such research is undertaken largely in universities and largely as the result of an academic agenda. Its key consumer is the academic community, with relatively little attention being given to its practical applications. This is often termed **basic, fundamental** or **pure research**. Given our earlier discussion it is unlikely that Mode 2 and Mode 3 business and management research would fulfil these criteria due to at least some consideration being made of the practical consequences. Through doing this, the research would start to move towards the other end of the continuum (Figure 1.1). At this end is research that is of direct and immediate relevance to managers, addresses issues that they see as important, and is presented in ways that they understand and can act on. This is termed **applied research**. In our view applied research is very similar to consultancy in many cases, particularly when the latter is conducted in a thorough manner.

Basic research ⟵⟶	Applied research
Purpose:	**Purpose:**
• Expand knowledge of processes of business and management	• Improve understanding of particular business or management problem
• Results in universal principles relating to the process and its relationship to outcomes	• Results in solution to problem
	• New knowledge limited to problem
• Findings of significance and value to society in general	• Findings of practical relevance and value to manager(s) in organisation(s)
Context:	**Context:**
• Undertaken by people based in universities	• Undertaken by people based in a variety of settings including organisations and universities
• Choice of topic and objectives determined by the researcher	• Objectives negotiated with originator
• Flexible time scales	• Tight time scales

Figure 1.1
Basic and applied research
Sources: authors' experience; Easterby-Smith *et al.* 2008; Hedrick *et al.* 1993.

Research by Shapiro *et al.* (2007) indicates that many managers and academics do perceive a problem with a gap between basic, fundamental or pure research and applied research. Clearly this has implications for the take up of research findings. Echoing the work of Van De Ven and Johnson (2006) (see Box 1.1 above), Shapiro *et al.* (2007:250) argue that if managers and academics believe that there is problem in which management research is 'lost in translation', then proposed solutions might focus on changes in the way research findings are disseminated. Alternatively, if the belief is that there is a knowledge production problem, so that any chance for impact on practice is 'lost before translation' (Shapiro *et al.* 2007:250), then proposed solutions might focus on ways to foster more researcher practitioner collaboration as research programs are developed and carried out.

Wherever your research project lies on this basic–applied continuum, we believe that you should undertake your research with rigour. To do this you will need to pay careful attention to the entire research process.

Inevitably, your own beliefs and feelings will impact upon your research. Although you might feel that your research will be value neutral (we will discuss this in greater detail later, particularly in Chapter 4), it is unlikely that you will stop your own beliefs and feelings influencing your research. Your choice of what to research is also likely to be influenced by topics that excite you, and the way you collect and analyse your data by the skills you have or are able to develop. Similarly, as we discuss in Chapter 2, practical considerations such as access to data and the time and resources you have available will also impact upon your research process.

1.4 The research process

Most research textbooks represent research as a multi-stage process that you must follow in order to undertake and complete your research project. The precise number of stages varies, but they usually include formulating and clarifying a topic, reviewing the literature, designing the research, collecting data, analysing data and writing up. In the majority of these the research process, although presented with rationalised examples, is described as a series of stages through which you must pass. Articles you have read may also suggest that the research process is rational and straightforward. Unfortunately, this is very rarely true, and the reality is considerably messier, with what initially appear as great ideas sometimes having little or no relevance (Saunders and Lewis 1997). While research is often depicted as moving through each of the stages outlined above, one after the other, this is unlikely to be the case. In reality you will probably revisit each stage more than once. Each time you revisit a stage you will need to reflect on the associated issues and refine your ideas. In addition, as highlighted by some textbooks, you will need to consider ethical and access issues during the process.

This textbook also presents the research process as a series of linked stages and gives the appearance of being organised in a linear manner. However, as you use the book you will see from the text, extensive use of cross-referencing, examples of research by well-known researchers and how research is reported in the news, examples of student research and case studies that we have recognised the iterative nature of the process you will follow. As part of this process, we believe that it is vital that you spend time formulating and clarifying your research topic. This we believe should be expressed as one or more research questions that your research must answer, accompanied by a set of objectives that your research must address. However, we would also stress the need to reflect on your ideas continually and revise both these and the way in which you intend to progress your research. Often this will involve revisiting stages (including your research question(s) and objectives) and working through them again. There is also a need to plan ahead, thereby ensuring that the necessary preliminary work for later stages has been undertaken. This is emphasised by Figure 1.2, which also provides a schematic index to the remaining chapters of the book. Within this flow chart (Figure 1.2) the stages you will need to complete as part of your research project are emphasised in the centre of the chart. However, be warned: the process is far messier than a brief glance at Figure 1.2 suggests!

1.5 The purpose and structure of this book

The purpose

As we stated earlier (Section 1.1), the overriding purpose of this book is to help you to undertake research. This means that early on in your research project you will need to be clear about what you are doing, why you are doing it, and the associated implications of what you are seeking to do. You will also need to ensure that you can show how your ideas relate to research that has already been undertaken in your topic area and that you have a clear research design and have thought about how you will collect and analyse your data. As part of this you will need to consider the validity and reliability of the data you intend to use, along with associated ethical and access issues. The appropriateness and suitability of the analytical techniques you choose to use will be of equal importance. Finally, you will need to write and present your research project report as clearly and precisely as possible.

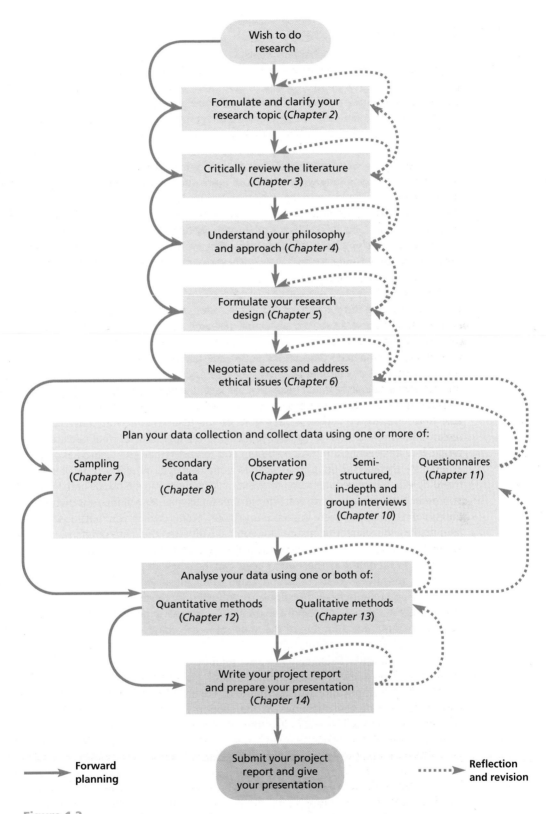

Figure 1.2
The research process
Source: © Mark Saunders, Philip Lewis and Adrian Thornhill 2009.

The structure of each chapter

Each of the subsequent chapters deals with part of the research process outlined in Figure 1.2. The ideas, techniques and methods are discussed using as little jargon as is possible. Where appropriate you will find summaries of these, using tables, checklists or diagrams. When new terms are introduced for the first time they are shown in **bold**, and a definition or explanation follows shortly afterwards. They are also listed with a brief definition in the glossary. The application of appropriate information technology is considered in most instances as an integral part of the text. Discussion of information technology is not software specific but is concerned with general principles. However, we recognise that you may wish to find out more about how to use data analysis software packages and so have included tutorials for the quantitative data analysis software SPSS™, the spread sheet Excel™ and the qualitative data analysis software NVivo™ (with practice data sets) on this book's Companion Website. These will enable you to utilise whatever software you have available most effectively. We have also included the Smarter Online Searching Guide to help you with your Internet searches. Chapters have been cross-referenced as appropriate, and an index is provided to help you to find your way around the book.

Included within the text of each chapter is a series of boxes which are called *Focus on student research*. These are based on actual research projects, undertaken by students, in which points made in the text are illustrated. In many instances these examples illustrate possible pitfalls you may come across while undertaking your research. Further illustrations are provided by *Focus on management research* and *Focus on research in the news* boxes. *Focus on management research* boxes discuss recent research in business and management. These are normally derived from refereed academic journal articles and you are likely to be able to download the actual articles from online databases at your university. *Focus on research in the news* boxes provide topical newspaper articles that illustrate pertinent research-related issues. All these will help you to understand the technique or idea and to assess its suitability or appropriateness to your research. Where a pitfall has been illustrated, it will, it is hoped, help you to avoid making the same mistake. There is also a series of boxed *Checklists* to provide you with further focused guidance for your own research. At the end of each chapter there is a *Summary* of key points, which you may look at before and after reading the chapter to ensure that you have digested the main points.

To enable you to check that you have understood the chapter a series of *Self-check questions* is included at the end. These can be answered without recourse to other (external) resources. *Answers* are provided to all these self-check questions at the end of each chapter. Self-check questions are followed by *Review and discussion questions*. These suggest a variety of activities you can undertake to help you further develop your knowledge and understanding of the material in the chapter, often involving discussion with a friend. Self-test multiple choice questions are available on this book's Companion Website. Each chapter also includes a section towards the end headed *Progressing your research project*. This contains a series of questions that will help you to consider the implications of the material covered by the chapter for your research project. Answering the questions in the section *Progressing your research project* for each chapter will enable you to generate all the material that you will need to include in your project report. Each chapter's questions involve you in undertaking activities that are more complex than self-check questions, such as a library-based literature search or designing and piloting a questionnaire. They are designed to help you to focus on the techniques that are most appropriate to your research. However, as emphasised by Figure 1.2, you will almost certainly need to revisit and revise your answers as your research progresses.

Each chapter is also accompanied by *References*, *Further reading* and a *Case study*. Further reading is included for two distinct reasons:

- to direct you to other work on the ideas contained within the chapter;
- to direct you to further examples of research where the ideas contained in the chapter have been used.

The main reasons for our choice of further reading are therefore indicated.

The new case studies at the end of each chapter are drawn from a variety of business and management research scenarios and have been based on the case study's authors' and students' experiences when undertaking a research project. They have been written to highlight real issues that occur when undertaking business and management research. To help to focus your thoughts or discussion on some of the pertinent issues, each case is followed by evaluative questions. Additional case studies relating to each chapter are available from the book's companion website. A case study follows every chapter.

An outline of the chapters

The book is organised in the following way.

Chapter 2 is written to assist you in the generation of ideas, which will help you to choose a suitable research topic, and offers advice on what makes a good research topic. If you have already been given a research topic, perhaps by an organisation or tutor, you will need to refine it into one that is feasible, and should still therefore read this chapter. After your idea has been generated and refined, the chapter discusses how to turn this idea into clear research question(s) and objectives. (Research questions and objectives are referred to throughout the book.) Finally, the chapter provides advice on how to write your research proposal.

The importance of the critical literature review to your research is discussed in Chapter 3. This chapter outlines what a critical review needs to include and the range of primary, secondary and tertiary literature sources available. The chapter explains the purpose of reviewing the literature, discusses a range of search strategies, and contains advice on how to plan and undertake your search and to write your review. The processes of identifying key words and searching using online databases and the Internet are outlined. It also offers advice on how to record items and to evaluate their relevance.

Chapter 4 addresses the issue of understanding different research philosophies, including positivism, realism, interpretivism, objectivism, subjectivism and pragmatism. Within this the functionalist, interpretive, radical humanist and radical structuralist paradigms are discussed. Deductive and inductive approaches to research are also considered. In this chapter we challenge you to think about your own values and how you view the world and the impact this will have on the way you undertake your research.

These ideas are developed further in Chapter 5 which explores formulating your research design. As part of this, a range of research strategies are discussed and the difference between quantitative and qualitative methods explained. The use of multiple methods is explored and consideration given to the implications of design choices for the credibility of your research findings and conclusions.

Chapter 6 explores issues related to gaining access and to research ethics. It offers advice on how to gain access both to organisations and to individuals. Potential ethical issues are discussed in relation to each stage of the research process and different data collection methods. Issues of data protection are also introduced.

A range of the probability and non-probability sampling techniques available for use in your research is explained in Chapter 7. The chapter considers why sampling is necessary, and looks at issues of sample size and response rates. Advice on how to relate your choice of sampling techniques to your research topic is given, and techniques for assessing the representativeness of those who respond are discussed.

Chapters 8, 9, 10 and 11 are concerned with different methods of obtaining data. The use of secondary data is discussed in Chapter 8, which introduces the variety of data that are likely to be available and suggests ways in which they can be used. Advantages and disadvantages of secondary data are discussed, and a range of techniques for locating these data, including using the Internet, is suggested. Chapter 8 also offers advice on how to evaluate the suitability of secondary data for your research.

In contrast, Chapter 9 is concerned with collecting primary data through observation. The chapter examines two types of observation: participant observation and structured observation. Practical advice on using each is offered, and particular attention is given to ensuring that the data you obtain are both valid and reliable.

Chapter 10 is also concerned with collecting primary data, this time using semi-structured, in-depth and group interviews. The appropriateness of using these interviews in relation to your research strategy is discussed. Advice on how to undertake such interviews is offered, including the conduct of focus groups, Internet-mediated (including online) and telephone interviews. Particular attention is given to ensuring that the data collected are both reliable and valid.

Chapter 11 is the final chapter concerned with collecting data. It introduces you to the use of both self-administered and interviewer-administered questionnaires, and explores their advantages and disadvantages. Practical advice is offered on the process of designing, piloting and administering Internet-mediated, postal, delivery and collection, and telephone questionnaires to enhance their response rates. Particular attention is again given to ensuring that the data collected are both reliable and valid.

Analysis of data is covered in Chapters 12 and 13. Chapter 12 outlines and illustrates the main issues that you need to consider when preparing data for quantitative analysis and when analysing these data by computer. Different types of data are defined, and advice is given on how to create a data matrix and to code data. Practical advice is also offered on the analysis of these data using computer based analysis software. The most appropriate diagrams to explore and illustrate data are discussed, and suggestions are made about the most appropriate statistics to use to describe data, to explore relationships and to examine trends.

Chapter 13 outlines and discusses the main approaches available to you to analyse data qualitatively both manually and using computer aided qualitative data analysis software (**CAQDAS**). The nature of qualitative data and issues associated with transcription are discussed. Following an overview of the analysis process, the use of deductively based and inductively based analytical procedures is discussed. These include pattern matching, explanation building, data display and analysis, template analysis, analytic induction, grounded theory, discourse analysis and narrative analysis.

Chapter 14 helps you with the structure, content and style of your final project report and any associated oral presentations. Above all, it encourages you to see writing as an intrinsic part of the research process that should not be left until everything else is completed.

Appendices and glossary

This book contains four appendices designed to support you at different stages of your research project. In the early stages, as you begin to read, you will need to keep a reference of what you have read using a recognised system, the most frequently used of which are detailed in Appendix 1. When selecting your sample you may need to calculate the minimum sample size required and use random sampling numbers (Appendices 2 and 3). Finally, when designing your data collection tools and writing your project report you will need to ensure that the language you use is non-discriminatory. Guidelines for these are given in Appendix 4. A separate glossary of over 400 research-methods-related terms is also included for quick reference.

1.6 Summary

- This book is designed to help you to undertake a research project whether you are an undergraduate or postgraduate student of business and management or a manager. It is designed as an introductory text and will guide you through the entire research process.
- Business and management research involves undertaking systematic research to find out things. It is transdisciplinary, and engages with both theory and practice.
- All business and management research projects can be placed on a basic–applied continuum according to their purpose and context.
- Wherever your research project lies on this continuum, you should undertake your research with rigour. To do this you will need to pay careful attention to the entire research process.
- In this book, research is represented as a multi-stage process; however, this process is rarely straightforward and will involve both reflecting on and revising stages already undertaken and forward planning.
- The text of each chapter is supported through a series of boxed examples. These include, focus on student research and focus on research in the news. In addition, there are checklists, self-check questions and review and discussion questions, an assignment and a case study with questions. Answers to all self-check questions are at the end of the appropriate chapter.
- Answering the questions in the section 'Progressing your research project' for Chapters 2–13 will enable you to generate all the material that you will need to include in your project report. When you have also answered the questions in this section for Chapter 14, you will have written your research report.

Self-check questions

Help with these questions is available at the end of the chapter.

1.1 Outline the features that can make business and management research distinctive from research in other disciplines.

1.2 What are the key differences between basic and applied research (and consultancy)?

1.3 Examine Figure 1.2. What does this suggest about the need to plan and to reflect on and revise your ideas?

Review and discussion questions

1.4 Agree with a friend to each read a different quality newspaper. Make a note of at least 10 articles in your newspaper that mention the word 'research'. Now examine the articles one at a time. As you examine each article, does the reference to research . . .
  - . . . refer to the collection of facts or information with no clear purpose?
  - . . . refer to the reassembling and reordering of facts or information without interpretation?
  - . . . provide a means of getting the reader to respect what is being written?
  - . . . refer to the systematic collection and interpretation of data with a clear purpose? Discuss your answers with your friend.

1.5 Obtain a copy of one or two of the articles referred to in Section 1.3. Read the article carefully. To what extent do you believe that business and management research should always meet the twin requirements of rigour and relevance? Give reasons for your answer.

References

Easterby-Smith, M., Thorpe, R. Jackson, P. and Lowe, A. (2008) *Management Research* (3rd edn). London: Sage.

Fukami, C. (2007) 'The third road', *Journal of Management Education,* Vol. 31, pp. 358–64.

Ghauri, P. and Grønhaug, K. (2005) *Research Methods in Business Studies: A Practical Guide* (3rd edn). Harlow: Financial Times Prentice Hall.

Gibbons, M.L., Limoges, H., Nowotny, S., Schwartman, P., Scott, P. and Trow, M. (1994) *The New Production of Knowledge: The Dynamics of Science and Research in Contemporary Societies.* London: Sage.

Hedrick, T.E., Bickmann, L. and Rog, D.J. (1993) *Applied Research Design.* Newbury Park, CA: Sage.

Hodgkinson, G.P., Herriot, P. and Anderson, N. (2001) 'Re-aligning the stakeholders in management research: Lessons from industrial, work and organizational psychology', *British Journal of Management,* Vol. 12, Special Issue, pp. 41–8.

Huff, A.S. and Huff, J.O. (2001) 'Re-focusing the business school agenda', *British Journal of Management,* Vol. 12, Special Issue, pp. 49–54.

Huff, A., Tranfield, D. and van Aken, J. (2006) 'Management as a design science mindful of art and surprise. A conversation between Anne Huff, David Tranfield, and Joan Ernst van Aken', *Journal of Management Inquiry,* Vol. 15. No. 4, pp. 413–24.

Lemelson-MIT Program (2007) 'Art Fry and Spencer Silver'. Available at: http://web.mit.edu/invent/iow/frysilver.html [Accessed 19 December 2007.]

Rousseau, D. (2006) 'Is there such a thing as "evidence-based management?"', *Academy of Management Review,* Vol. 31, No. 2, pp. 256–69.

Saunders, M.N.K. and Lewis, P. (1997) 'Great ideas and blind alleys? A review of the literature on starting research', *Management Learning,* Vol. 28, No. 3, pp. 283–99.

Shapiro, D., Kirkman, B. and Courtney, H. (2007) 'Perceived causes and solutions of the translation problem in management research', *Academy of Management Journal,* Vol. 50, No. 2, pp. 249–66.

Starkey, K. and Madan, P. (2001) 'Bridging the relevance gap: aligning stakeholders in the future of management research', *British Journal of Management,* Vol. 12, Special Issue, pp. 3–26.

Tranfield, D. and Starkey, K. (1998) 'The nature, social organization and promotion of management research: towards policy', *British Journal of Management,* Vol. 9, pp. 341–53.

Tranfield, D. and Denyer, D. (2004) 'Linking theory to practice: a grand challenge for management research in the 21st century?', *Organization Management Journal,* Vol. 1, No. 1, pp. 10–14.

Van De Ven, A. and Johnson, P. (2006) 'Knowledge for Theory and Practice', *Academy of Management Review,* Vol. 31, No. 4, pp. 802–21.

Walliman, N. (2005) *Your Research Project: A Step by Step Guide for the First-Time Researcher* (2nd edn). London: Sage.

Further reading

Easterby-Smith, M., Thorpe, R. Jackson, P. and Lowe, A. (2008). *Management Research.* **(3rd edn). London: Sage. Chapter 1** provides a very clear and readable introduction to management research and how it is distinct from other forms of research.

Starkey, K. and Madan, P. (2001) 'Bridging the relevance gap: aligning stakeholders in the future of management research', *British Journal of Management,* **Vol. 12, Special Issue, pp. 3–26.** This paper argues the need for relevant management research within a Mode 2 framework, emphasising a need for research partnership.

Case 1
Isabelle's research dilemma

Source: Baron Bratby/Alamy

Isabelle was very thoughtful. She had a puzzled look on her face. The dilemma she had was one experienced by many students in conducting research for a dissertation. Her research was concerned with managers and how they coped with pressure in the workplace. She particularly wanted to find out the coping strategies they used. This required consideration of theory and method and whether the research would have practical relevance. After her preliminary reading around the topic she decided that it was necessary to engage in both the world of theory and the world of practice and that the problems addressed would develop out of the interaction between these two worlds.

Theory in management could be seen as problematic, because for some researchers management is not a discipline. It is perceived as multi-disciplinary with many of its early practitioners receiving their training in the social sciences (Pettigrew 2001). Isabelle thought this could be advantageous in that it enables management research to gain new insights that may not be obtained through a number of disciplines separately. She also considered that a topic on pressure and coping could be understood at a number of levels of analysis from an individual to a structural level. In doing this she would be considering theoretical ideas and attempting to perceive them in a pragmatic way. It also meant looking at them anew which would provide some imaginative and original insights for her dissertation.

Isabelle found that more traditional research on managing pressure focused on positivistic approaches with an emphasis on being scientific and rigorous. This approach often uses quantitative methods with an emphasis on measuring and the use of factor analysis. Researchers hope this allows them to find statistical correlations between two variables and demonstrate some relationship between sources of pressure and possible physical, psychological or even physiological outcomes, if coping strategies were not successful. Research of this kind can be found in the work of Sadri and Marcoulides (1997) and Wheatley (2000).

Isabelle decided she would not use this approach. She felt that a number of students' dissertations had already used this approach and she wanted to get away from statistical analysis and examining pressure on managers using a positivistic approach. She also thought that this traditional research ignored the managers' biography which could prove to be important in understanding how the manager coped with pressure. The more traditional approach seems to perceive the individual as passive and playing little part in making and constructing his/her reality. It was as if the researcher with questions asked in the questionnaire had already structured the reality. However, people working in organisations do have histories, futures and expectations and pursue their individual goals. For example, long-term sources of a person's distress may be traced back to experiences at work many years before. To study this would require Isabelle to use a different method. She decided to adopt in-depth interviews as primary sources so that she could study the turning-points in the lives of her participants over a period of time. This may indicate why they took particular decisions and the consequences of making those decisions.

In terms of method Isabelle decided that the approach she would adopt would be qualitative rather than quantitative. This would involve using in-depth interviews. She would also use life stories and family histories because this kind of biographical approach was more holistic

(Miller 2007). This holistic viewpoint manifested itself in two ways. Firstly, biographical data range across time. Hence, 'a biographical approach is indicated where the area of interest is either the effect of change across time, historical events as these events have impinged upon the individual, or his or her movement along their life course' (Miller 2007:74). Secondly, the biographical approach is a bridge between social structure and the individual. Social structure is a complex concept in which there was some disagreement among social scientists. But it can be understood to mean a relative enduring pattern of social arrangements within a particular society, group or social organisation. Thus, social structures may constrain the individual's behaviour and expectations. Discussing your biography means telling about the constraints and opportunities, and turning-points that were available in the past and how one dealt with them. The biographical approach is about the intersection between the individual and social structure.

In conducting such research Isabelle knew she had to deal with complex issues with the subject-matter and the method she wanted to adopt. The relationship between the interviewee and interviewer is central to this type of research. She felt she had the emotional maturity to manage the process. Most importantly she felt that the research was rigorous, systematic and relevant to managers in the workplace.

References

Miller, R.L. (2007) *Researching Life Stories and Family Histories.* London: Sage Publications.

Pettigrew, A.M. (2001) 'Management research after modernism', *British Journal of Management*, Vol. 12, pp. 61–70.

Sadri, G. and Marcoulides, G.A. (1997) 'An examination of academic and occupational stress in the USA', *International Journal of Educational Management*, Vol. 11, No. 1, pp. 32–43.

Wheatley, R. (2000) *Taking the Strain. A Survey of Managers and Workplace Stress.* London: Institute of Management.

Questions

1 How do you think Isabelle's understanding of theory and method changed in adopting the approach she chose?
2 What particular knowledge and skills did she develop in preparing this research?
3 What problems do you think she would have anticipated in conducting research into pressure and coping among managers that her literature review may not have identified?

Self-check answers

1.1 The features you outline are likely to include the:
- transdisciplinary nature of business and management research;
- development of ideas that are related to practice and in particular the requirement for the research to have some practical consequence;
- need for research to complete the virtuous circle of theory and practice;
- addressing of problems that grow out of the interaction between the worlds of theory and practice.

1.2 The key differences between basic and applied research relate to both the purpose and the context in which it is undertaken. They are summarised in Figure 1.1.

1.3 Figure 1.2 emphasises the importance of planning during your research project. Forward planning needs to occur at all stages up to submission. In addition, you will need to reflect on and to revise your work throughout the life of the research project. This reflection needs to have a wide focus. You should both consider the stage you have reached and revisit earlier stages and work through them again. Reflection may also lead you to amend your research plan. This should be expected, although large amendments in the later stages of your research project are unlikely.

Get ahead using resources on the Companion Website at:
www.pearsoned.co.uk/saunders
- Improve your SPSS and NVivo research analysis with practice tutorials.
- Save time researching on the Internet with the Smarter Online Searching Guide.
- Test your progress using self-assessment questions.
- Follow live links to useful websites.

Chapter 2

Formulating and clarifying the research topic

Learning outcomes

By the end of this chapter you should be able to:

- generate ideas that will help in the choice of a suitable research topic;
- identify the attributes of a good research topic;
- turn research ideas into a research project that has clear research question(s) and objectives;
- draft a research proposal.

2.1 Introduction

Many students think that choosing their research topic is the most exciting part of their course. After all, this is something that they get to decide for themselves rather than having to complete a task decided by their tutors. We will stress in this chapter that it is important to choose something that will sustain your interest throughout the months that you will need to complete it. You may even decide to do some research that is something that forms part of your leisure activities!

Before you start your research you need to have at least some idea of what you want to do. This is probably the most difficult, and yet the most important, part of your research project. Up until now most of your studies have been concerned with answering questions that other people have set. This chapter is concerned with how to formulate and clarify your research topic and your research question. Without being clear about what you are going to research it is difficult to plan how you are going to research it. This reminds us of a favourite quote in *Alice's Adventures in Wonderland*. This is part of Alice's conversation with the Cheshire Cat. In this Alice asks the Cat (Carroll 1989:63–4):

> 'Would you tell me, please, which way I ought to walk from here?'
> 'That depends a good deal on where you want to get to', said the Cat.
> 'I don't much care where', said Alice.
> 'Then it doesn't matter which way you walk', said the Cat.

Formulating and clarifying the research topic is the starting point of your research project (Ghauri and Grønhaug 2005; Smith and Dainty 1991). Once you are clear about this, you will be able to choose the most appropriate research strategy and data collection and analysis techniques. The formulating and clarifying process is time consuming and will probably take you up blind alleys (Saunders and Lewis 1997). However, without spending time on this stage you are far less likely to achieve a successful project (Raimond 1993).

In the initial stages of the formulating and clarifying process you will be generating and refining research ideas (Section 2.3). It may be that you have already been given a research idea, perhaps by an organisation or tutor. Even if this has happened you will still need to refine the idea into one that is feasible. Once you have done this you will need to turn the idea into research questions and objectives (Section 2.4) and to write the research proposal for your project (Section 2.5).

Mobile phone operators have high hopes that, following the success of text messaging, 'picture messaging', using camera phones will establish photos as a new genre in mobile communication. Although sales figures are good for camera phones, it's not clear to what extent people are using camera phones, to send picture messages. Recent media reports have described early results as disappointing. Possible explanations include obstacles such as cost, reliability and interface complexity. Alternatively, a camera phone's value might not lie in sending images but in using the captured images for other activities.

A team of researchers (Kindberg *et al.* 2005) decided to establish what users actually do with their camera phones. The research had two main objectives. The first was to explore the range and diversity of use to help broaden the team's outlook on current and future camera phone use. The second was to elucidate the characteristics and context of use for different activities to learn how such activities may be better supported.

The team recruited 34 subjects: 19 in the UK and 15 in the USA. The study consisted of two interviews with each subject, conducted two to five weeks apart. During each interview, researchers asked the subjects to show five images (photos or videos) from their camera phones. The images may have been either taken or received by the research subject.

Source: Nicholas Linton/Alamy

The data collected enabled the research team to develop a six-part taxonomy that describes how people use camera phone images for social and personal purposes and affective and functional purposes. Reviewing the taxonomy reveals implications for future products and services.

However, before you start the formulating and clarifying process we believe that you need to understand what makes a good research topic. For this reason we begin this chapter with a discussion of the attributes required for a good research topic.

2.2 Attributes of a good research topic

The attributes of a business and management research topic do not vary a great deal between universities (Raimond 1993), although there will be differences in the emphasis placed on different attributes. If you are undertaking your research project as part of a course of study the most important attribute will be that it meets the examining body's requirements and, in particular, that it is at the correct level. This means that you must choose your topic with care. For example, some universities require students to collect their own data as part of their research project whereas others allow them to base their project on data that have already been collected. Alternatively, some ask you to undertake an organisation-based piece of applied research, whilst others simply say that it must be within the subject matter of your course or programme. You, therefore, need to check the assessment criteria for your project and ensure that your choice of topic will enable you to meet these criteria. If you are unsure, you should discuss any uncertainties with your project tutor.

In addition, your research topic must be something you are capable of undertaking and one that excites your imagination. Capability can be considered in a variety of ways. At the personal level you need to feel comfortable that you have, or can develop, the skills that will be required to research the topic. We hope that you will develop your research skills as part of undertaking your project. However, some skills, for example foreign languages, may be impossible to acquire in the time you have available. As well as having the necessary skills we believe that you also need to have a genuine interest in the topic. Most research projects are undertaken over at least a six-month period. A topic in which you are only vaguely interested at the start is likely to become a topic in which you have no interest and with which you will fail to produce your best work.

Your ability to find the financial and time resources to undertake research on the topic will also affect your capability. Some topics are unlikely to be possible to complete in the time allowed by your course of study. This may be because they require you to measure the impact of an intervention over a long time period (Box 2.1). Similarly, topics that are likely to require you to travel widely or need expensive equipment should also be disregarded unless financial resources permit.

Capability also means you must be reasonably certain of gaining access to any data you might need to collect. Gill and Johnson (2002) argue that this is usually relatively straightforward to assess. They point out that many people start with ideas where access to data will prove difficult. Certain, more sensitive topics, such as financial performance or decision making by senior managers, are potentially fascinating. However, they may present considerable access problems. You, therefore, should discuss this with your project tutor after reading Chapter 6.

For most topics it is important that the issues within the research are capable of being linked to theory (Raimond 1993). Initially, theory may be based just on the reading you have undertaken as part of your study to date. However, as part of your assessment criteria you are almost certain to be asked to set your topic in context (Section 3.2). As a consequence you will need to have a knowledge of the literature and to undertake further reading as part of defining your research questions and objectives (Section 2.4).

Most project tutors will argue that one of the attributes of a good topic is clearly defined research questions and objectives (Section 2.4). These will, along with a good

Box 2.1
Focus on student research

Turning ideas into a viable project

Zaynab was not short of ideas for her research. But she was much less sure about how she would move from a topic of interest for her research to a question that could be answered for her research project. It was emphasised to her by her tutors that ideas were easy, turning them into viable research projects was another matter altogether.

Having explored various websites and looked at some publications in the library, she drew up a plan of action which she was sure would give her the material necessary to write her research proposal.

Charting the ideas

At the start her project, Zaynab got a huge sheet of paper to make a map of all of her ideas, questions, associations, sources and leads. She marked her most compelling thoughts in a red. Then she marked the main links to those ideas in that red too. She was careful not to throw out the weaker or isolated thoughts. She felt this map would help her know the place of all her thoughts. She thought that she could make another map later in the project if she felt there was too much information.

Archive the questions

Next Zaynab recorded who originally asked the question and left a space by each one to record answers or places to look for answers. Then she highlighted the questions that she found most challenging, the ones that really grabbed her attention. She thought that archiving questions would encourage her to articulate them well. Forming thoughts as questions helped her to be clear about what she needed to research.

Blog it

Zaynab was a keen blogger so she posted summaries of her ideas and questions on a weblog. She asked for site visitors to suggest further reading, new research methods or for answers to answer her questions. She received a healthy amount of feedback from which she made real progress in turning favourite idea into question that could be answered for her research project.

Thinking about the application of the findings

Zaynab knew that she would be expected to comment on the practical implications of her findings when writing up her research. Therefore, an important part of her plan of action at the outset was to ask herself what would be the implications for practice for the various outcomes that might be expected.

knowledge of the literature, enable you to assess the extent to which your research is likely to provide fresh insights into the topic. Many students believe this is going to be difficult. Fortunately, as pointed out by Phillips and Pugh (2005), there are many ways in which such insight can be defined as 'fresh' (Section 2.5).

If you have already been given a research idea (perhaps by an organisation) you will need to ensure that your questions and objectives relate clearly to the idea (Kervin 1999). It is also important that your topic will have a **symmetry of potential outcomes**: that is, your results will be of similar value whatever you find out (Gill and Johnson 2002). Without this symmetry you may spend a considerable amount of time researching your topic only to find an answer of little importance. Whatever the outcome, you need to ensure you have the scope to write an interesting project report.

Finally, it is important to consider your career goals (Creswell 2002). If you wish to become an expert in a particular subject area or industry sector, it is sensible to use the opportunity to develop this expertise.

It is almost inevitable that the extent to which these attributes apply to your research topic will depend on your topic and the reasons for which you are undertaking the

Box 2.2
Checklist

Attributes of a good research topic

Capability: is it feasible?

✔ Is the topic something with which you are really fascinated?

✔ Do you have, or can you develop within the project time frame, the necessary research skills to undertake the topic?

✔ Is the research topic achievable within the available time?

✔ Will the project still be current when you finish your project?

✔ Is the research topic achievable within the financial resources that are likely to be available?

✔ Are you reasonably certain of being able to gain access to data you are likely to require for this topic?

Appropriateness: is it worthwhile?

✔ Does the topic fit the specifications and meet the standards set by the examining institution?

✔ Does your research topic contain issues that have a clear link to theory?

✔ Are you able to state your research question(s) and objectives clearly?

✔ Will your proposed research be able to provide fresh insights into this topic?

✔ Does your research topic relate clearly to the idea you have been given (perhaps by an organisation)?

✔ Are the findings for this research topic likely to be symmetrical: that is, of similar value whatever the outcome?

✔ Does the research topic match your career goals?

research. However, most of these attributes will apply. For this reason it is important that you check and continue to check any potential research topic against the summary checklist contained in Box 2.2.

2.3 Generating and refining research ideas

Some business and management students are expected both to generate and to refine their own research ideas. Others, particularly those on professional and post-experience courses, are provided with a research idea by an organisation or their university. In the initial stages of their research they are expected to refine this to a clear and feasible idea that meets the requirements of the examining organisation. If you have already been given a research idea we believe you will still find it useful to read the next subsection, which deals with generating research ideas. Many of the techniques which can be used for generating research ideas can also be used for the refining process.

Generating research ideas

If you have not been given an initial **research idea** there is a range of techniques that can be used to find and select a topic that you would like to research. They can be thought of as those that are predominantly **rational thinking** and those that involve more **creative thinking** (Table 2.1). The precise techniques that you choose to use and the order in which you use them are entirely up to you. However, like Raimond (1993), we believe you should use both rational and creative techniques, choosing those that you believe are going to be of most use to you and which you will enjoy using. By using one or more creative techniques you are more likely to ensure that your heart as well as your head is in your research project. In our experience, it is usually better to use a variety of techniques. In order to do this you will need to have some understanding of the

Table 2.1 More frequently used techniques for generating and refining research ideas

Rational thinking	Creative thinking
• Examining your own strengths and interests	• Keeping a notebook of ideas
• Looking at past project titles	• Exploring personal preferences using past projects
• Discussion	• Relevance trees
• Searching the literature	• Brainstorming
• Scanning the media	

techniques and the ways in which they work. We therefore outline the techniques in Table 2.1 and suggest possible ways they might be used to generate research ideas. These techniques will generate one of two outcomes:

- one or more possible project ideas that you might undertake;
- absolute panic because nothing in which you are interested or which seems suitable has come to mind (Jankowicz 2005).

In either instance, but especially the latter, we suggest that you talk to your project tutor. Box 2.3 illustrates how ideas are at the heart of business and management life.

Examining own strengths and interests

It is important that you choose a topic in which you are likely to do well and, if possible, already have some academic knowledge. Jankowicz (2005) suggests that one way of doing this is to look at those assignments for which you have received good grades. For most of these assignments they are also likely to be the topics in which you were interested (Box 2.1). They will provide you with an area in which to search and find a research idea. In addition, you may, as part of your reading, be able to focus more precisely on the sort of ideas about which you wish to conduct your research.

As noted in Section 2.2, there is the need to think about your future. If you plan to work in financial management it would be sensible to choose a research project in the financial management field. One part of your course that will inevitably be discussed at any job interview is your research project. A project in the same field will provide you with the opportunity to display clearly your depth of knowledge and your enthusiasm.

Looking at past project titles

Many of our students have found looking at past projects a useful way of generating research ideas. For undergraduate and taught masters degrees these are often called **dissertations**. For research degrees they are termed **theses**. A common way of doing this is to scan your university's list of past project titles for anything that captures your imagination. Titles that look interesting or which grab your attention should be noted down, as should any thoughts you have about the title in relation to your own research idea. In this process the fact that the title is poorly worded or the project report received a low mark is immaterial. What matters is the fact that you have found a topic that interests you. Based on this you can think of new ideas in the same general area that will enable you to provide fresh insights.

Scanning actual research projects may also produce research ideas. However, you need to beware. The fact that a project is in your library is no guarantee of the quality of the arguments and observations it contains. In many universities all projects are placed in the library whether they are bare passes or distinctions.

Box 2.3
Focus on management research

What every leader needs to know about followers

Management studies courses and books usually contain plenty of material on leadership. Seemingly, everyone wants to understand just what makes a good leader. Followership, by contrast, is the stuff of the rarely mentioned. Most of the limited research and writing on subordinates has tended either to explain their behaviour in the context of leaders' development rather than followers', or mistakenly assume that followers are amorphous, all one and the same. As a result, we hardly notice, for example, that followers who follow mindlessly are altogether different from those who are deeply committed.

In a *Harvard Business Review* article Kellerman (2007) explores the behaviour of those in organisations whose role it is to follow. She argues that in an era of flatter, networked organisations and cross-cutting teams of knowledge workers, it's not always obvious who exactly is following (or, for that matter, who exactly is leading) and how they are going about it.

Kellerman develops a typology of followers using one metric – level of engagement of the follower. She categorises all followers according to where they fall along a continuum that ranges from 'feeling and doing absolutely nothing' to 'being passionately committed and deeply involved'.

Kellerman's typology specifies five types of followers: isolates, bystanders, participants, activist and diehards.

Isolates are completely detached. These followers are scarcely aware of what's going on around them. Moreover, they do not care about their leaders, know anything about them, or respond to them in any obvious way. Their alienation is, nevertheless, of consequence. By knowing and doing nothing, these types of followers passively support the status quo and further strengthen leaders who already have the upper hand. As a result, isolates can drag down their groups or organisations.

Bystanders observe but do not participate. These free riders deliberately stand aside and disengage, both from their leaders and from their groups or organisations. They may go along passively when it is in their self-interest to do so, but they are not internally motivated to engage in an active way. Their withdrawal also amounts to tacit support for whoever and whatever constitutes the status quo.

Participants are engaged in some way. Regardless of whether these followers clearly support their leaders and organisations or clearly oppose them, they care enough to invest some of what they have (time or money, for example) to try to make an impact.

Activists feel strongly one way or another about their leaders and organisations, and they act accordingly. These followers are eager, energetic and engaged. They invest heavily in people and processes, so they work hard either on behalf of their leaders or to undermine and even unseat them.

Diehards are prepared to go down for their cause – whether it's an individual, an idea, or both. These followers may be deeply devoted to their leaders, or they may be strongly motivated to oust their leaders by any means necessary. They exhibit an all-consuming dedication to someone or something they deem worthy.

Kellerman concludes by asserting that this typology has critical implications for the way leaders should lead and managers should manage.

It should be borne in mind that this article does not report a piece of original research. Kellerman points out in the piece that she has developed the typology 'after years of study and observation'. You may argue that this is worth little as it is based on impressions which are not substantiated by careful and systematic fieldwork. However, in our view this is just the sort of article that may stimulate ideas for a research project on, for example, differing patterns of 'followership' within different occupational groups.

Discussion

Colleagues, friends and university tutors are all good sources of possible project ideas. Often project tutors will have ideas for possible student projects, which they will be pleased to discuss with you. In addition, ideas can be obtained by talking to practitioners and professional groups (Gill and Johnson 2002). It is important that as well as discussing possible ideas you also make a note of them. What seemed like a good idea in the coffee shop may not be remembered quite so clearly after the following lecture!

Searching the literature

As part of your discussions, relevant literature may also be suggested. Sharp *et al.* (2002) discuss types of literature that are of particular use for generating research ideas. These include:

- articles in academic and professional journals;
- reports;
- books.

Of particular use are academic **review articles**. These articles contain both a considered review of the state of knowledge in that topic area and pointers towards areas where further research needs to be undertaken. In addition, you can browse recent publications, in particular journals, for possible research ideas (Section 3.5). For many subject areas your project tutor will be able to suggest possible recent review articles, or articles that contain recommendations for further work. Reports may also be of use. The most recently published are usually up to date and, again, often contain recommendations that may form the basis of your research idea. Books by contrast are less up to date than other written sources. They do, however, often contain a good overview of research that has been undertaken, which may suggest ideas to you.

Searching for publications is only possible when you have at least some idea of the area in which you wish to undertake your research. One way of obtaining this is to re-examine your lecture notes and course textbooks and to note those subjects that appear most interesting (discussed earlier in this section) and the names of relevant authors. This will give you a basis on which to undertake a **preliminary search** (using techniques outlined in Sections 3.4 and 3.5). When the articles, reports and other items have been obtained it is often helpful to look for unfounded assertions and statements on the absence of research (Raimond 1993), as these are likely to contain ideas that will enable you to provide fresh insights.

Scanning the media

Keeping up to date with items in the news can be a very rich source of ideas. The stories which occur everyday in the 'broadsheet' or 'compact' newspapers (e.g. *The Times*, *Financial Times*, *Guardian* and the *Daily Telegraph*), in both traditional print and online versions, may provide ideas which relate directly to the item (e.g. the extent to which items sold by supermarkets contravene the principles of 'green consumerism' by involving excessive 'food miles' in order import them). The stories may also suggest other ideas which flow from the central story (e.g. the degree to which a company uses its claimed environmental credentials as part of its marketing campaign).

Keeping a notebook of ideas

One of the more creative techniques that we all use is to keep a **notebook of ideas**. All this involves is simply noting down any interesting research ideas as you think of them and, of equal importance, what sparked off your thought. You can then pursue the idea using more rational thinking techniques later. Mark keeps a notebook by his bed so he can jot down any flashes of inspiration that occur to him in the middle of the night!

Exploring personal preferences using past projects

Another way of generating possible project ideas is to explore your personal preferences using past project reports from your university. To do this Raimond (1993) suggests that you:

1 Select six projects that you like.
2 For each of these six projects, note down your first thoughts in response to three questions (if responses for different projects are the same this does not matter):
   a What appeals to you about the project?
   b What is good about the project?
   c Why is the project good?
3 Select three projects that you do not like.
4 For each of these three projects, note down your first thoughts in response to three questions (if responses for different projects are the same, or cannot be clearly expressed, this does not matter; note them down anyway):
   a What do you dislike about the project?
   b What is bad about the project?
   c Why is the project bad?

You now have a list of what you consider to be excellent and what you consider to be poor in projects. This will not be the same as a list generated by anyone else. It is also very unlikely to match the attributes of a good research project (Box 2.2). However, by examining this list you will begin to understand those project characteristics that are important to you and with which you feel comfortable. Of equal importance is that you will have identified those that you are uncomfortable with and should avoid. These can be used as the parameters against which to evaluate possible research ideas.

Relevance trees

Relevance trees may also prove useful in generating research topics. In this instance, their use is similar to that of mind mapping (Buzan 2006), in which you start with a broad concept from which you generate further (usually more specific) topics. Each of these topics forms a separate branch from which you can generate further, more detailed sub-branches. As you proceed down the sub-branches more ideas are generated and recorded. These can then be examined and a number selected and combined to provide a research idea (Sharp *et al.* 2002). This technique is discussed in more detail in Section 3.4, which also includes a worked example of a relevance tree.

Brainstorming

The technique of **brainstorming** (Box 2.4), taught as a problem-solving technique on many business and management courses, can also be used to generate and refine research ideas. It is best undertaken with a group of people, although you can brainstorm on your own. To brainstorm, Moody (1988) suggests that you:

1 Define your problem – that is, the sorts of ideas you are interested in – as precisely as possible. In the early stages of formulating a topic this may be as vague as 'I am interested in marketing but don't know what to do for my research topic'.
2 Ask for suggestions, relating to the problem.

Box 2.4
Focus on student research

Brainstorming

George's main interest was football. When he finished university he wanted to work in marketing, preferably for a sports goods manufacturer. He had examined his own strengths and discovered that his best marks were in marketing. He wanted to do his research project on some aspect of marketing, preferably linked to football, but had no real research idea. He asked three friends, all taking business studies degrees, to help him brainstorm the problem.

George began by explaining the problem in some detail. At first the suggestions emerged slowly. He noted them down on the whiteboard. Soon the board was covered with suggestions. George counted these and discovered there were over 100.

Reviewing individual suggestions produced nothing that any of the group felt to be of sufficient merit for a research project. However, one of George's friends pointed out that combining the suggestions of Premier League football, television rights and sponsorship might provide an idea which satisfied the assessment requirements of the project.

They discussed the suggestion further, and George noted the research idea as 'something about how confining the rights to show live Premiership football to paid-for satellite TV channels would impact upon the sale of Premiership club-specific merchandise'.

George arranged to see his project tutor to discuss how to refine the idea they had just generated.

3 Record all suggestions, observing the following rules:
- No suggestion should be criticised or evaluated in any way before all ideas have been considered.
- All suggestions, however wild, should be recorded and considered.
- As many suggestions as possible should be recorded.
4 Review all the suggestions and explore what is meant by each.
5 Analyse the list of suggestions and decide which appeal to you most as research ideas and why.

Refining research ideas
The Delphi technique

An additional approach that our students have found particularly useful in refining their research ideas is the **Delphi technique** (Box 2.5). This involves using a group of people who are either involved or interested in the research idea to generate and choose a more specific research idea (Robson 2002). To use this technique you need:

1 to brief the members of the group about the research idea (they can make notes if they wish);
2 at the end of the briefing to encourage group members to seek clarification and more information as appropriate;
3 to ask each member of the group, including the originator of the research idea, to generate independently up to three specific research ideas based on the idea that has been described (they can also be asked to provide a justification for their specific ideas);
4 to collect the research ideas in an unedited and non-attributable form and to distribute them to all members of the group;
5 a second cycle of the process (steps 2 to 4) in which individuals comment on the research ideas and revise their own contributions in the light of what others have said;

Box 2.5
Focus on student research

Using a Delphi Group

Tim explained to the group that his research idea was concerned with understanding the decision-making processes associated with mortgage applications and loan advances. His briefing to the three other group members, and the questions that they asked him, considered aspects such as:

- the influences on a potential first-time buyer to approach a specific financial institution;
- the influence on decision making of face-to-face contact between potential borrowers and potential lenders.

The group then moved on to generate a number of more specific research ideas, among which were the following:

- the factors that influenced potential first-time house purchasers to deal with particular financial institutions;
- the effect of interpersonal contact on mortgage decisions;
- the qualities that potential applicants look for in mortgage advisers.

These were considered and commented on by all the group members. At the end of the second cycle Tim had, with the other students' agreement, refined his research idea to:

- the way in which a range of factors influenced potential first-time buyers' choice of lending institution.

He now needed to pursue these ideas by undertaking a preliminary search of the literature.

---

6 subsequent cycles of the process until a consensus is reached. These either follow a similar pattern (steps 2 to 4) or use discussion, voting or some other method.

This process works well, not least because people enjoy trying to help one another. In addition, it is very useful in moulding groups into a cohesive whole.

The preliminary study

Even if you have been given a research idea, it is still necessary to refine it in order to turn it into a research project. Some authors, such as Bennett (1991), refer to this process as a **preliminary study**. For some research ideas this will be no more than a review of some of the literature, including news items (Box 2.6). This can be thought of as the first iteration of your critical literature review (see Figure 3.1 later). For others it may include revisiting the techniques discussed earlier in this section as well as informal discussions with people who have personal experience of and knowledge about your research ideas. In some cases **shadowing** employees who are likely to be important in your research may also provide insights. If you are planning on undertaking your research within an organisation it is important to gain a good understanding of your host organisation (Kervin 1999). However, whatever techniques you choose, the underlying purpose is to gain a greater understanding so that your research question can be refined.

At this stage you need to be testing your research ideas against the checklist in Box 2.2 and where necessary changing them. It may be that after a preliminary study, or discussing your ideas with colleagues, you decide that the research idea is no longer feasible in the form in which you first envisaged it. If this is the case, do not be too downhearted. It is far better to revise your research ideas at this stage than to have to do it later, when you have undertaken far more work.

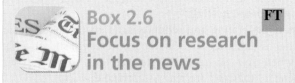

Box 2.6
Focus on research in the news

FT

Many workers feel too qualified for jobs

More than half the workers in a huge swath of occupations think they are overqualified, research commissioned by the *Financial Times* shows. The figures reopen the debate about whether Britain is spending too much taxpayer money on churning out graduates. They could also be used against employers, accused by many economists of failing to adapt their business models to reap full benefit from the graduates in their workforces.

Two-thirds of people in 'customer service occupations', which include call centre workers, think their qualifications are more elevated than their job requires. For example, university graduates would count themselves overqualified if they were doing work they believed called for nothing more than A-levels.

Almost two-thirds of people in sales occupations also think they are overqualified, and more than 60 per cent in 'elementary administration and service occupations', which include junior clerical workers and postmen, feel this way.

Francis Green, an economist at Kent University who carried out the research, said the high figures were not surprising, since graduates were 'absolutely pouring into the labour market'. Professor Green said the proportion of workers who thought they were overqualified had increased by about five percentage points nationwide in five years.

Prime Minister Gordon Brown believes that Britain needs still more graduates to turn the country into a higher-skills economy, closing its productivity gap with competitors such as the USA. More than 35 per cent of young people already have graduate-level qualifications in higher or further education, but the government's target is 50 per cent. However, critics regard the growth in graduate places, under both Labour and Conservative governments, as primarily designed to woo middle-class voters.

John Philpott, economist at the Chartered Institute of Personnel and Development, said that many people with qualifications were not being used well by employers 'still operating in low-quality, low-value markets that don't require high-quality people'. But Alex Bryson, research director at the Policy Studies Institute, said the high overqualification figures might partly reflect a 'trade-off' between convenience and salary. He pointed out that the occupations at the top of the list were 'customer-facing', with working hours designed to accommodate customers. By the same token, this wide variety of hours would also suit employees with other commitments, such as mothers.

Professor Green said the figures did not prove Britain was producing too many graduates. 'If someone goes to university and studies Picasso or Shakespeare', they make society better. 'We economists can't measure that, but it's absolutely absurd to discount it just because we can't do so'.

Professor Green's UK-wide figures are based on interviews with thousands of workers as part of long-term research into Britain's skills, part-financed by the former Department for Education and Skills.

Source: article by Turner, David (2007) *Financial Times*, 29 Oct.

Integrating ideas

The integration of ideas from these techniques is essential if your research is to have a clear direction and not contain a mismatch between objectives and your final project report. Jankowicz (2005:34–6) suggests an integrative process that our students have found most useful. This he terms 'working up and narrowing down'. It involves classifying each research idea first into its area, then its field, and finally the precise aspect in which you are interested. These represent an increasingly detailed description of the research idea. Thus your initial area, based on examining your course work, might be accountancy. After browsing some recent journals and discussion with colleagues this becomes more focused on the field of financial accounting methods. With further reading, the use of the Delphi technique and discussion with your project tutor you decide to focus on the aspect of activity-based costing.

You will know when the process of generating and refining ideas is complete as you will be able to say 'I'd like to do some research on . . .'. Obviously there will still be a big gap between this and the point when you are ready to start serious work on your research. Sections 2.4 and 2.5 will ensure that you are ready to bridge that gap.

Refining topics given by your employing organisation

If, as a part-time student, your manager gives you a topic, this may present particular problems. It may be something in which you are not particularly interested. In this case you will have to weigh the advantage of doing something useful to the organisation against the disadvantage of a potential lack of personal motivation. You, therefore, need to achieve a balance. Often the research project your manager wishes you to undertake is larger than that which is appropriate for your course. In such cases, it may be possible to complete both by isolating an element of the larger organisational project that you find interesting and treating this as the project for your course.

One of our students was asked to do a preliminary investigation of the strengths and weaknesses of her organisation's pay system and then to recommend consultants to design and implement a new system. She was not particularly interested in this project. However, she was considering becoming a freelance personnel consultant. Therefore, for her course project she decided to study the decision-making process in relation to the appointment of personnel consultants. Her organisation's decision on which consultant to appoint, and why this decision was taken, proved to be a useful case study against which to compare management decision-making theory.

In this event you would write a larger report for your organisation and a part of it for your project report. Section 14.4 offers some guidance on writing two separate reports for different audiences.

Other problems may involve your political relationships in he organisation. For example, there will be those keen to commission a project which justifies their particular policy position and see you as a useful pawn in advancing their political interests. It is important to have a clear stance with regards to what you want to do, and your personal objectives, and to stick to this.

Finally, perhaps the biggest potential problem may be one of your own making: to promise to deliver research outcomes to your employer and not do so.

2.4 Turning research ideas into research projects

Writing research questions

Much is made in this book of the importance of defining clear **research questions** at the beginning of the research process. The importance of this cannot be overemphasised. One of the key criteria of your research success will be whether you have a set of clear conclusions drawn from the data you have collected. The extent to which you can do that will be determined largely by the clarity with which you have posed your initial research questions (Box 2.7).

Defining research questions, rather like generating research ideas (Section 2.3), is not a straightforward matter. It is important that the question is sufficiently involved to generate the sort of project that is consistent with the standards expected of you (Box 2.2). A question that prompts a descriptive answer, for example 'What is the proportion of graduates entering the civil service who attended the old, established UK universities?', is far

Box 2.7
Focus on student research

Defining the research question

Imran was studying for a BA in Business Studies and doing his placement year in an advanced consumer electronics company. When he first joined the company he was surprised to note that the company's business strategy, which was announced in the company newsletter, seemed to be inconsistent with what Imran knew of the product market.

Imran had become particularly interested in corporate strategy in his degree. He was familiar with some of the literature that suggested that corporate strategy should be linked to the general external environment in which the organisation operated. He wanted to do some research on corporate strategy in his organisation for his degree dissertation.

After talking this over with his project tutor Imran decided on the following research question: 'Why does [organisation's name] corporate strategy not seem to reflect the major factors in the external operating environment?'

easier to answer than: 'Why are graduates from old, established UK universities more likely to enter the civil service than graduates from other universities?' More will be said about the importance of theory in defining the research question later in this section. However, beware of research questions that are too easy.

It is perhaps more likely that you fall into the trap of asking research questions that are too difficult. The question cited above, 'Why are graduates from old, established UK universities more likely to enter the civil service than graduates from other universities?' is a case in point. It would probably be very difficult to gain sufficient access to the inner portals of the civil service to get a good grasp of the subtle 'unofficial' processes that go on at staff selection which may favour one type of candidate over another. Over-reaching yourself in the definition of research questions is a danger.

Clough and Nutbrown (2002) use what they call the '**Goldilocks test**' to decide if research questions are either 'too big', 'too small', 'too hot' or 'just right'. Those that are too big probably need significant research funding because they demand too many resources. Questions that are too small are likely to be of insufficient substance, while those that are too 'hot' may be so because of sensitivities that may be aroused as a result of doing the research. This may be because of the timing of the research or the many other reasons that may upset key people who have a role to play, either directly or indirectly, in the research context. Research questions that are 'just right', note Clough and Nutbrown (2002:34), are those that are 'just right for investigation at *this* time, by *this* researcher in *this* setting'.

The pitfall that you must avoid at all costs is asking research questions that will not generate new insights (Box 2.2). This raises the question of the extent to which you have consulted the relevant literature. It is perfectly legitimate to replicate research because you have a genuine concern about its applicability to your research setting (for example, your organisation). However, it certainly is not legitimate to display your ignorance of the literature.

McNiff and Whitehead (2000) make the point that the research question may not emerge until the research process has started and is therefore part of the process of 'progressive illumination'. They note that this is particularly likely to be the case in practitioner action research (Section 4.3).

It is often a useful starting point in the writing of research questions to begin with one **general focus research question** that flows from your research idea. This may lead to

Table 2.2 Examples of research ideas and their derived focus research questions

Research idea	General focus research questions
Advertising and share prices	How does the running of a TV advertising campaign designed to boost the image of a company affect its share price?
Job recruitment via the Internet	How effective is recruiting for new staff via the Internet in comparison with traditional methods?
The use of aromas as a marketing device	In what ways does the use of specific aromas in supermarkets affect buyer behaviour?
The use of Internet banking	What effect has the growth of Internet banking had upon the uses customers make of branch facilities?

several more detailed questions or the definition of research objectives. Table 2.2 has some examples of general focus research questions.

In order to clarify the research question Clough and Nutbrown (2002) talk of the Russian doll principle. This means taking the research idea and 'breaking down the research questions from the original statement to something which strips away the complication of layers and obscurities until the very essence – the heart – of the question can be expressed . . . just as the Russian doll is taken apart to reveal a tiny doll at the centre' (Clough and Nutbrown 2002:34).

Writing your research questions will be, in most cases, your individual concern but it is useful to get other people to help you. An obvious source of guidance is your project tutor. Consulting your project tutor will avoid the pitfalls of the questions that are too easy or too difficult or have been answered before. Discussing your area of interest with your project tutor will lead to your research questions becoming much clearer.

Prior to discussion with your project tutor you may wish to conduct a brainstorming session with your peers or use the Delphi technique (Section 2.3). Your research questions may flow from your initial examination of the relevant literature. As outlined in Section 2.3, journal articles reporting primary research will often end with a conclusion that includes the consideration by the author of the implications for future research of the work in the article. This may be phrased in the form of research questions. However, even if it is not, it may suggest pertinent research questions to you.

Writing research objectives

Your research may begin with a general focus research question that then generates more detailed research questions, or you may use your general focus research question as a base from which you write a set of **research objectives**. Objectives are more generally acceptable to the research community as evidence of the researcher's clear sense of purpose and direction. It may be that either is satisfactory. Do check whether your examining body has a preference.

We contend that research objectives are likely to lead to greater specificity than research or investigative questions. Table 2.3 illustrates this point. It summarises the objectives of some research conducted by one of our students. Expression of the first research question as an objective prompted a consideration of the objectives of the

Table 2.3 Phrasing research questions as research objectives

Research question	Research objective
1 Why have organisations introduced team briefing?	**1** To identify organisations' objectives for team briefing schemes
2 How can the effectiveness of team briefing schemes be measured?	**2** To establish suitable effectiveness criteria for team briefing schemes
3 Has team briefing been effective?	**3** To describe the extent to which the effectiveness criteria for team briefing have been met
4 How can the effectiveness of team briefing be explained?	**4a** To determine the factors associated with the effectiveness criteria for team briefing being met
	b To estimate whether some of those factors are more influential than other factors
5 Can the explanation be generalised?	**5** To develop an explanatory theory that associates certain factors with the effectiveness of team briefing schemes

organisations. This was useful because it led to the finding that there often were no clear objectives. This in itself was an interesting theoretical discovery.

The second and third objectives **operationalise** the matching research questions by introducing the notion of explicit effectiveness criteria. In a similar way the fourth objective (parts a and b) and the fifth objective are specific about factors that lead to effectiveness in question 4. The biggest difference between the questions and objectives is illustrated by the way in which the fifth question becomes the fifth objective. They are similar but differ in the way that the objective makes clear that a theory will be developed that will make a causal link between two sets of variables: effectiveness factors and team briefing success.

This is not to say that the research questions could not have been written with a similar amount of specificity. They could. Indeed, you may find it easier to write specific research questions than objectives. However, we doubt whether the same level of precision could be achieved through the writing of research questions alone. Research objectives require more rigorous thinking, which derives from the use of more formal language.

Maylor and Blackmon (2005) recommend that personal objectives may be added to the list of research objectives. These may be concerned with your specific learning objectives from completion of the research (e.g. to learn how to use a particular statistical software package or improve your word processing ability) or more general personal objectives such as enhancing your career prospects through learning about a new field of your specialism.

Maylor and Blackmon suggest that such personal objectives would be better were they to pass the well-known SMART test. That is that the objectives are:

- *Specific*. What precisely do you hope to achieve from undertaking the research?
- *Measurable*. What measures will you use to determine whether you have achieved your objectives? (e.g. secured a career-level first job in software design).
- *Achievable*. Are the targets you have set for yourself achievable given all the possible constraints?

- *Realistic.* Given all the other demands upon your time, will you have the time and energy to complete the research on time?
- *Timely.* Will you have time to accomplish all your objectives in the time frame you have set?

The importance of theory in writing research questions and objectives

Section 4.1 outlines the role of theory in helping you to decide your approach to research design. However, your consideration of theory should begin earlier than this. It should inform your definition of research questions and objectives.

Theory (Box 2.8) is defined by Gill and Johnson (2002:229) as 'a formulation regarding the cause and effect relationships between two or more variables, which may or may not have been tested'.

In a similar contribution to that of Sutton and Staw (1995), Whetten (1989) contends that if the presence of theory is to be guaranteed, the researcher must ensure that what is passing as good theory includes a plausible, coherent explanation for why certain relationships should be expected in our data.

Box 2.8
Focus on management research

Clarifying what theory is not

Sutton and Staw (1995) make a useful contribution to the clarification of what theory is by defining what it is not. In their view theory is not:

1 *References.* Listing references to existing theories and mentioning the names of such theories may look impressive. But what is required if a piece of writing is to 'contain theory' is that a logical argument to explain the reasons for the described phenomena must be included. The key word here is 'why': why did the things you describe occur? What is the logical explanation?

2 *Data.* In a similar point to the one above, Sutton and Staw argue that data merely describe which empirical patterns were observed: theory explains why these patterns were observed or are expected to be observed. 'The data do not generate theory – only researchers do that' (Sutton and Staw 1995:372).

3 *Lists of variables.* Sutton and Staw argue that a list of variables which constitutes a logical attempt to cover the determinants of a given process or outcome do not comprise a theory. Simply listing variables which may predict an outcome is insufficient: what is required for the presence of theory is an explanation of why predictors are likely to be strong predictors.

4 *Diagrams.* Boxes and arrows can add order to a conception by illustrating patterns and causal relationships but they rarely explain why the relationships have occurred. Indeed, Sutton and Staw (1995:374) note that 'a clearly written argument should preclude the inclusion of the most complicated figures – those more closely resembling a complex wiring diagram than a comprehensible theory'.

5 *Hypotheses or predictions.* Hypotheses can be part of a sound conceptual argument. But they do not contain logical arguments about why empirical relationships are expected to occur.

Sutton and Staw (1995:375) sum up by stating that 'theory is about the connections between phenomena, a story about why events, structure and thoughts occur. Theory emphasises the nature of causal relationships, identifying what comes first as well as the timing of events. Strong theory, in our view, delves into underlying processes so as to understand the systematic reasons for a particular occurrence or non-occurrence'.

There is probably no word that is more misused and misunderstood in education than the word 'theory'. It is thought that material included in textbooks is 'theory', whereas what is happening in the 'real world' is practice. Students who saw earlier drafts of this book remarked that they were pleased that the book was not too 'theoretical'. What they meant was that the book concentrated on giving lots of practical advice. Yet, the book is full of theory. Advising you to carry out research in a particular way (variable A) is based on the theory that this will yield effective results (variable B). This is the cause and effect relationship referred to in the definition of theory cited above and is very much the view of Kelly (1955). Kelly argues that the individual who attempts to solve the daily problems which we all face goes about this activity in much the same way as the scientist. Both continuously make and test hypotheses and revise their concepts accordingly. Both organise their results into what are called schemata and then into a system of broader schemata which are called theories. Kelly asserts that we need such schemata and theories in order to make sense of the complexity of the world in which we live. Without these organising frameworks we would be overwhelmed by the unconnected detail we would have to recall.

The definition demonstrates that 'theory' has a specific meaning. It refers to situations where, if A is introduced, B will be the consequence. Therefore, the marketing manager may theorise that the introduction of loyalty cards by a supermarket will lead to customers being less likely to shop regularly at a competitor supermarket. That is a theory. Yet, the marketing manager would probably not recognise it as such. He or she is still less likely to refer to it as a theory, particularly in the company of fellow managers. Many managers are very dismissive of any talk that smacks of 'theory'. It is thought of as something that is all very well to learn about at business school but bears little relation to what goes on in everyday organisational life. Yet, the loyalty card example shows that it has everything to do with what goes on in everyday organisational life.

Section 4.1 notes that every purposive decision we take is based on theory: that certain consequences will flow from the decision. It follows from this that every managers' meeting that features a number of decisions will be a meeting that is highly **theory dependent** (Gill and Johnson 2002). All that will be missing is a realisation of this fact. So, if theory is something that is so rooted in our everyday lives it certainly is something that we need not be apprehensive about. If it is implicit in all our decisions and actions, then recognising its importance means making it explicit. In research the importance of theory must be recognised: therefore it must be made explicit.

Kerlinger and Lee (2000) reinforce Gill and Johnson's definition by noting that the purpose of examining relationships between two or more variables is to explain and predict these relationships. Gill and Johnson (2002:33) neatly tie these purposes of theory to their definition:

> . . . it is also evident that if we have the expectation that by doing A, B will happen, then by manipulating the occurrence of A we can begin to predict and influence the occurrence of B. In other words, theory is clearly enmeshed in practice since explanation enables prediction which in turn enables control.

In our example, the marketing manager theorised that the introduction of loyalty cards by a supermarket would lead to customers being less likely to shop regularly at a competitor supermarket. Following Gill and Johnson's (2002:33) point that 'explanation enables prediction which in turn enables control', the supermarket would be well advised to conduct research that yielded an explanation of why loyalty cards encourage loyalty. Is it a purely economic rationale? Does it foster the 'collector' instinct in all of us? Does it appeal to a sense of thrift in us that helps us cope with an ever more wasteful world? These explanations are probably complex and interrelated. Reaching a better understanding of them would help the marketing manager to predict the outcome of any changes to the scheme. Increasing the amount of points per item would be effective if the economic explanation was valid. Increasing the range of products on which extra points were offered might appeal to the 'collector' instinct. More accurate prediction would offer the marketing manager increased opportunities for control.

The explanations for particular outcomes are a concern for Mackenzie (2000a, 2000b). His argument is that much research (he used the example of employee opinion surveys) yield ambiguous conclusions because they only ask questions which reveal the state of affairs as they exist (in his example, the thinking of employees in regard to, say, their pay). What they do not ask is questions which help those using the research results to draw meaningful conclusions as to why the state of affairs is as it is. If meaningful conclusions cannot be drawn, then appropriate actions cannot be taken to remedy such deficiencies (or improve upon the efficiencies) that the research reveals. Usually such additional questions would involve discovering the key implementation processes (in the case of pay these may be the way in which managers make and communicate pay distribution decisions) which may shed light on the reasons why such deficiencies (or efficiencies) exist.

Mackenzie used the metaphor of the knobs on an old-fashioned radio to illustrate his argument. If the radio is playing a station and you are unhappy with what is being received, you will turn the volume knob to alter the volume or the tuning knob to change the station. He argues that the typical questionnaire survey is like the radio without knobs. You cannot make the results more useful, by knowing more about their causes, because you have no means to do so. All you have for your results is a series of what Mackenzie (2000a:136) terms 'knobless items', in which you are asking for respondents' opinions without asking for the reasons why they hold these opinions. What Mackenzie advocates is including '**knobs**' in the data collection process so that the causal relationship between a process and an outcome can be established.

Phillips and Pugh (2005) distinguish between research and what they call **intelligence gathering**, using what Mackenzie (2000a, 2000b) calls 'knobless items'. The latter is the gathering of facts (Box 2.9). For example, what is the relative proportion of undergraduates to postgraduates reading this book? What is the current spend per employee on training in the UK? What provision do small businesses make for bad debts? This is often called descriptive research (Section 4.2) and may form part of your research project. Descriptive research would be the first step in our example of supermarket loyalty card marketing. Establishing that there had been a change in customer behaviour following the introduction of supermarket loyalty cards would be the first step prior to any attempt at explanation.

Phillips and Pugh contrast such 'what' questions with 'why' questions. Examples of these 'why' questions are as follows: Why do British organisations spend less per head on training than German organisations? Why are new car purchasers reluctant to take out extended warranties on their vehicles? Why do some travellers still prefer to use cross-channel ferries as opposed to the Channel Tunnel? Such questions go 'beyond description and require analysis'. They look for 'explanations, relationships, comparisons, predictions, generalisations and theories' (Phillips and Pugh 2005:48).

It is a short step from the 'why' research question to the testing of an existing theory in a new situation or the development of your own theory. This may be expressed as a hypothesis that is to be tested (Section 4.1), or the eventual answer to your research question may be the development or amendment of a theory (Box 2.10).

Although intelligence gathering will play a part in your research, it is unlikely to be enough. You should be seeking to explain phenomena, to analyse relationships, to compare what is going on in different research settings, to predict outcomes and to generalise; then you will be working at the theoretical level. This is a necessary requirement for most research projects.

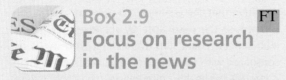

Box 2.9
Focus on research in the news

FT

The e-sport revolution Korean-style

As Lee Yun-yeol limbered up in his tracksuit for the match of the year, hundreds of screaming girls in the Seoul stadium went wild. Against deafening heavy metal music, the fans screeched his name in high-pitched unison and waved signs proclaiming 'I want to cook you rice' – the Korean equivalent of 'Will you marry me?!' The commentators ran through the players' game histories and TV cameras panned across the audience. At home, some 10 million people were watching one of the eight cable channels ready to broadcast the match live. In this high-octane atmosphere – somewhere between a rock concert and a soccer cup final – Mr Lee took his place. But he did not step into a boxing ring or on to a tennis court. He sat down before a computer screen, donned headphones, and prepared to bomb his opponent into oblivion in a computer game called Starcraft.

South Korea is the world's most wired country. Computer gaming has become mainstream and 'pro-gamers' are treated like pop stars and come armed with ultra-trendy hairstyles, lucrative sponsorship deals, burly bodyguards, and groupies. E-sports are not a niche pursuit in Korea. Being a pro-gamer was named the most desired occupation in one survey of 1150 teenagers, and some private institutes even offer courses in online game strategies. Business also wants part of the action. Top companies such as Samsung Electronics, SK Telecom and Shinhan Bank all sponsor e-sports.

'Korea's great internet infrastructure has played a really big role in making e-sports so huge here', Je Hunho, general manager of the Korean E-sports Association, says. But he sees global potential: 'E-sports have started to spread across the world and we hope that one day it will be an Olympic sport.'

But the e-sports revolution has its darker side. In 2005 a South Korean man died after reportedly playing an online computer game for 50 hours with few breaks (BBC News Online 2005). The 28-year-old man collapsed after playing the game at an Internet café. The man had not slept properly, and had eaten very little during his marathon session, said police. The man

only paused playing to go to the toilet and for short periods of sleep, said the police. 'We presume the cause of death was heart failure stemming from exhaustion', a provincial police official told the Reuters news agency. He was taken to hospital following his collapse, but died shortly after, according to the police. It is not known whether he suffered from any previous health conditions. They added that he had recently been dismissed from his job because he kept missing work to play computer games.

Players can easily get immersed in computer games and feel compelled to play for hours at a stretch, particularly in massively multiplayer online role playing games (MMORPGs) in which thousands of gamers play and interact in shared fantasy or science fiction worlds. Reports of gamers spending 10 to 15 hours a day in front of video games are becoming more frequent. Experts say gamers should take regular screen breaks.

According to the research of psychologist Professor Mark Griffiths, playing excessively is not problematic in any shape or form for the majority of gamers. However, his view is that online gaming addiction for a small minority is a real phenomenon and people suffer the same symptoms as traditional addictions. But this only applies to a small minority of gamers.

In one detailed survey of 540 gamers, Professor Griffiths and his team found that there were four playing more than 80 hours a week, which is considered 'excessive'. He explained many people liked to play MMORPGs for long periods of time because of the social aspect of the games. He explained that these are the types of games that completely engross the player. They are not games that you can play for 20 minutes and stop. 'If you are going to take it seriously, you have to spend time doing it', he said.

But he warned there was a difference between 'healthy enthusiasm' and 'unhealthy addiction'. People who sacrificed jobs, partners and loved ones were considered 'extreme players'. Unlike help for traditional addictions, such as gambling, there is very little help for computer game addiction, he said. 'It is not taken seriously yet – it is the same for internet addiction', he said. More than 15 million people, or 30% of the population, are registered for online gaming in South Korea. The country also host the annual World Cyber Games.

Sources: article by Fifield, Anna (2007) *Financial Times*, 15 Sept.; BBC News Online (2005).

Box 2.10
Focus on student research

Writing a research question based on theory

Justine was a final-year marketing undergraduate who was interested in the theory of cognitive dissonance (Festinger 1957). She wanted to apply this to the consumer purchasing decision in the snack foods industry (e.g. potato crisps) in the light of the adverse publicity that the consumption of such foods was having as a result of the 'healthy eating' campaign.

Justine applied Festinger's theory by arguing in her research project proposal that a consumer who learns that snack over-eating is bad for her health will experience dissonance, because the knowledge that snack over-eating is bad for her health is dissonant with the cognition that she continues to over-eat snacks. She can reduce the dissonance by changing her behaviour, i.e., she could stop over-eating. (This would be consonant with the cognition that snack over-eating is bad for her health.) Alternatively, she could reduce dissonance by changing her cognition about the effect of snack over-eating on health and persuade herself that snack over-eating does not have a harmful effect on health. She would look for positive effects of snack over-eating, for example by believing that snack over-eating is an important source of enjoyment which outweighs any harmful effects. Alternatively, she might persuade herself that the risk to health from snack over-eating is negligible compared with the danger of car accidents (reducing the importance of the dissonant cognition).

Justine's research question was 'How does the adverse "healthy eating" campaign publicity affect the consumer's decision to purchase snack foods?'

You may still be concerned that the necessity to be theory dependent in your research project means that you will have to develop a ground-breaking theory that will lead to a whole new way of thinking about management. If this is the case you should take heart from the threefold typology of theories summarised by Creswell (2002) (see Figure 2.1). He talks of 'grand theories', usually thought to be the province of the natural scientists (e.g. Darwin and Newton). He contrasts these with 'middle-range theories', which lack the capacity to change the way in which we think about the world but are nonetheless of significance. Some of the theories of human motivation well known to managers would be in this category. However, most of us are concerned with 'substantive theories' that are restricted to a particular time, research setting, group or population or problem (Creswell 2002). For example, studying the reasons why a total quality initiative in a particular organisation failed would be an example of a substantive theory. Restricted they may

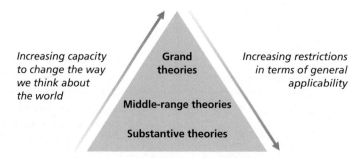

Figure 2.1 Grand, middle-range and substantive theories

be, but a host of 'substantive theories' that present similar propositions may lead to 'middle-range theories'. By developing 'substantive theories', however modest, we are doing our bit as researchers to enhance our understanding of the world about us. A grand claim, but a valid one!

This discussion of theory does assume that a clear theoretical position is developed prior to the collection of data (the **deductive approach**). This will not always be the case. It may be that your study is based on the principle of developing theory after the data have been collected (the **inductive approach**). This is a fundamental difference in research approach, and will be discussed in detail in Section 4.3.

2.5 Writing your research proposal

At the start of all courses or modules we give our students a plan of the work they will be doing. It includes the learning objectives, the content, the assessment strategy and the recommended reading. This is our statement of our side of the learning contract. Our students have a right to expect this.

However, when we insist on a proposal for a research project that is often the equivalent of at least two other modules, there is often a marked reluctance to produce anything other than what is strictly necessary. This is unsatisfactory. It is unfair to your project tutor because you are not making entirely clear what it is you intend to do in your research. You are also being unfair to yourself because you are not giving yourself the maximum opportunity to have your ideas and plans scrutinised and subjected to rigorous questioning.

Writing a research proposal is a crucial part of the research process. If you are applying for research funding, or if your proposal is going before an academic research committee, then you will know that you will need to put a great deal of time into the preparation of your proposal. However, even if the official need for a proposal is not so vital it is still a process that will repay very careful attention.

The purposes of the research proposal
Organising your ideas

Section 14.1 notes that writing can be the best way of clarifying our thoughts. This is a valuable purpose of the proposal. Not only will it clarify your thoughts but it will help you to organise your ideas into a coherent statement of your research intent. Your reader will be looking for this.

Convincing your audience

However coherent your ideas and exciting your research plan, it counts for little if the proposal reveals that what you are planning to do is simply not possible. As part of research methods courses many tutors ask students to draft a research proposal. This is then discussed with a tutor. What usually happens is that this discussion is about how the proposed research can be amended so that something more modest in scope is attempted. Initially work that is not achievable in the given timescale is proposed. The student's task is to amend initial ideas and convince the module tutor that the proposed research is achievable within the time and other resources available.

Contracting with your 'client'

If you were asked to carry out a research project for a commercial client or your own organisation it is unthinkable that you would go ahead without a clear proposal that you would submit for approval. Acceptance of your proposal by the client would be part of the contract that existed between you.

So it is with your proposal to your project tutor or academic committee. It may be necessary to obtain clearance from the relevant research ethics committee. For example, in one university the university's code of practice states that ethics committee perusal in necessary for all research involving human participants. It is important for all work that will be made public – for example, undergraduate dissertations, theses for higher degrees, externally funded research and 'unfunded' research (including undergraduate and postgraduate research) which produces reports or other publications. In another UK university, researchers have an obligation to spell out exactly what they mean by anonymity and confidentiality to research participants in advance of the research taking place. In this context anonymity refers to concealing the identity of the participants in all documents resulting from the research; and confidentiality is concerned with to the right of access to the data provided by individual participants and, in particular, the need to keep these data secret or private. In addition, researchers should clarify the steps they will take to ensure protection of respondents' identities and ensure that the information collected is stored securely.

Acceptance implies that your proposal is satisfactory. While this is obviously no guarantee of subsequent success, it is something of comfort to you to know that at least you started your research journey with an appropriate destination and journey plan. It is for you to ensure that you do not get lost!

The content of the research proposal

Title

This may be your first attempt at the title. It may change as your work progresses. At this stage it should closely mirror the content of your proposal.

Background

This is an important part of the proposal. It should tell the reader why you feel the research that you are planning is worth the effort. This may be expressed in the form of a problem that needs solving or something that you find exciting and has aroused your curiosity. The reader will be looking for evidence here that there is sufficient interest from you to sustain you over the long months (or years) ahead.

This is also the section where you will demonstrate your knowledge of the relevant literature. Moreover, it will clarify where your proposal fits into the debate in the literature. You will be expected to show a clear link between the previous work that has been done in your field of research interest and the content of your proposal. In short, the literature should be your point of departure. This is not the same as the critical literature review (Section 3.2) you will present in your final project report. It will just provide an overview of the key literature sources from which you intend to draw.

Research questions and objectives

The background section should lead smoothly into a statement of your research question(s) and objectives. These should leave the reader in no doubt as to precisely what it is that your research seeks to achieve. Be careful here to ensure that your objectives are precisely written and will lead to observable outcomes (look again at Table 2.3, e.g., 'to describe the extent to which the effectiveness criteria specified for the team briefing scheme have been met'). Do not fall into the trap of stating general research aims that are little more than statements of intent (e.g. 'to discover the level of effectiveness of the team briefing scheme').

Method

This and the background sections will be the longest sections of the proposal. It will detail precisely how you intend to go about achieving your research objectives. It will also justify your choice of method in the light of those objectives. These two aims may be met by dividing your method section into two parts: research design and data collection.

In the part on research design you will explain where you intend to carry out the research. If your earlier coverage has pointed out that your research is a single-organisation issue, perhaps a part of a piece of organisational consultancy, then this will be self-evident. However, if your research topic is more generic you will wish to explain, for example, which sector(s) of the economy you have chosen to research and why you chose these sectors. You will also need to explain the identity of your research population (e.g. managers or trade union officials) and why you chose this population.

This section should also include an explanation of the general way in which you intend to carry out the research. Will it be based, for example, on a questionnaire, interviews, examination of secondary data or use a combination of data collection techniques? Here again it is essential to explain why you have chosen your approach. Your explanation should be based on the most effective way of meeting your research objectives.

The research design section gives an overall view of the method chosen and the reason for that choice. The data collection section goes into much more detail about how specifically the data are to be collected. For example, if you are using a survey strategy you should specify your population and sample size. You should also clarify how the survey instrument such as a questionnaire will be distributed and how the data will be analysed. If you are using interviews, you should explain how many interviews will be conducted, their intended duration, whether they will be audio-recorded, and how they will be analysed. In short, you should demonstrate to your reader that you have thought carefully about all the issues regarding your method and their relationship to your research objectives. However, it is normally not necessary in the proposal to include precise detail of the method you will employ, for example the content of an observation schedule or questionnaire questions.

You will also need to include a statement about how you are going to adhere to any ethical guidelines. This is particularly important in some research settings, such as those involving medical patients or children (Sections 6.4 and 6.5).

Timescale

This will help you and your reader to decide on the viability of your research proposal. It will be helpful if you divide your research plan into stages. This will give you a clear idea as to what is possible in the given timescale. Experience has shown that however well the researcher's time is organised the whole process seems to take longer than anticipated (Box 2.11).

As part of this section of their proposal, many researchers find it useful to produce a schedule for their research using a **Gantt chart**. Developed by Henry Gantt in 1917, this provides a simple visual representation of the tasks or activities that make up your research project, each being plotted against a time line. The time we estimate each task will take is

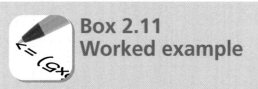

Box 2.11
Worked example

Louisa's research timescale

As part of the final year of her undergraduate business studies degree, Louisa had to undertake an 8000–10 000-word research project. In order to assist her with her time management, she discussed the following outline timescale, developed using Microsoft Outlook's project planning tools 'Tasks', with her tutor.

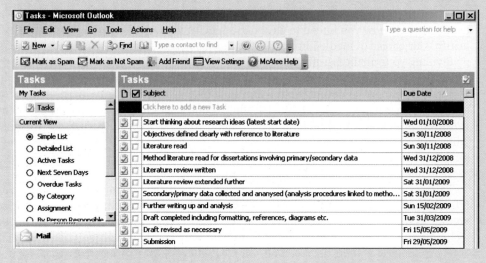

represented by the length of an associated horizontal bar, whilst the task's start and finish times are represented by its position on the time line. Figure 2.2 (opposite) shows a Gantt chart for a student's research project. As we can see from the first bar on this chart, the student has decided to schedule in two weeks of holiday. The first of these occurs over the Christmas and New Year period, and the second occurs while her tutor is reading a draft copy of the completed project in April. We can also see from the second and fourth bar that, like many of our students, she intends to begin to draft her literature review while she is still reading new articles and books. However, she has also recognised that some activities must be undertaken sequentially. For example, bars 9 and 10 highlight that before she can administer her questionnaire (bar 10) she must complete all the revisions highlighted as necessary by the pilot testing (bar 9).

Resources

This is another facet of viability (Box 2.2). It will allow you and the reader to assess whether what you are proposing can be resourced. Resource considerations may be categorised as finance, data access and equipment.

Conducting research costs money. This may be for travel, subsistence, help with data analysis, or postage for questionnaires. Think through the expenses involved and ensure that you can meet these expenses.

Assessors of your proposal will need to be convinced that you have access to the data you need to conduct your research (Sections 6.2 and 6.3). This may be unproblematic if you are carrying out research in your own organisation. Many academic committees

Activity	October				November				December				January				February				March				April				May					
Week number:	1	2	3	4	5	6	7	8	9	10	11	12	13	14	15	16	17	18	19	20	21	22	23	24	25	26	27	28	29	30	31	32	33	34	35	36
Holiday													■														■									
Read literature																																				
Finalise objectives																																				
Draft literature review																																				
Read methodology literature																																				
Devise research approach																																				
Draft research strategy and method																																				
Develop questionnaire																																				
Pilot test and revise questionnaire																																				
Administer questionnaire																																				
Enter data into computer																																				
Analyse data																																				
Draft findings chapter																																				
Update literature read																																				
Complete remaining chapters																																				
Submit to tutor and await feedback																																				
Revise draft, format for submission																																				
Print, bind																																				
Submit																																				
KEY DATES					1														2				3					4						5		

KEY DATES:
1. Nov 1st: Submit proposal to tutor.
2. Jan 20th: Begin fieldwork.
3. March 1st: Complete fieldwork.
4. April 20th: Complete draft and hand in.
5. May 20th: Final submission.

Figure 2.2 Gantt chart for a research project

wish to see written approval from host organisations in which researchers are planning to conduct research. You will also need to convince your reader of the likely response rate to any questionnaire that you send.

It is surprising how many research proposals have ambitious plans for large-scale data collection with no thought given to how the data will be analysed. It is important that you convince the reader of your proposal that you have access to the necessary computer hardware and software to analyse your data. Moreover, it is necessary for you to demonstrate that you have either the necessary skills to perform the analysis or can learn the skills in an appropriate time, or you have access to help.

References

It is not necessary to try to impress your proposal reader with an enormous list of references (Robson 2002). A few key literature sources to which you have referred in the background section and which relate to the previous work that is directly informing your own proposal should be all that is necessary.

Criteria for evaluating research proposals
The extent to which the components of the proposal fit together

Your rationale for conducting the research should include a study of the previous published research, including relevant theories in the topic area. This study should inform your research question(s) and objectives. Your proposed method should flow directly from these research question(s) and objectives (Box 2.12). The time that you have allocated should be a direct reflection of the methods you employ, as should the resources that you need.

Box 2.12
Focus on student research

Fitting together the various components of the research proposal

Jenny was a middle manager in a large insurance company. She was very interested in the fact that electronic forms of communication meant that organisations could move information-based administrative work round different locations. Her company was scanning paper applications for insurance policies onto its computer system and delivering these into a central electronic bank of work. The company had employees in three different locations in the UK, and work was drawn from the bank on the basis of workload existing in each particular location. Recently, senior management had been considering developing work locations in South Asian cities, where it felt the standard of English meant that such functions could be fulfilled effectively. Jenny anticipated that this would pose certain logistical problems, for example, staff training and communications. Knowledge of these problems would give her a clear picture of the limit of complexity of the work that could be done. This was particularly important since the complexity range went from the simple to the technically complex. Research into the literature on cross-cultural training justified Jenny's concern. As a consequence of her thought and reading, she developed her research question as: 'What cross-cultural problems may be posed by international electronic work transfer in the insurance industry, and how may these problems limit the complexity of the work that may be transferred?'

Through her reading of the practitioner journals, Jenny was aware that some other financial-services organisations had been sending their work to Asia for some time. She decided that approaching these companies and interviewing their key personnel would be a fruitful approach. The main problem that Jenny would have with this research would be the time that the interview work would take, given that such companies were located all over the UK and North America. She was unsure how many interviews would be necessary. This would become clearer as she progressed in the research. However, it was unlikely that fewer than 10 companies would yield sufficient valuable data. She thought that she could collect the necessary data in a four-month period, which fitted in with her university deadline. There were no specific resources that Jenny needed other than finance and time. Since her research would be of immediate benefit to her employer she thought that neither would pose a problem.

The viability of the proposal

This is the answer to the question: 'Can this research be carried out satisfactorily within the timescale and with available resources?'

Box 2.13
Focus on student research

A written research proposal

Puvadol was a student from Thailand who returned home from the UK to complete his MA dissertation. His proposed dissertation concerned the applicability of Western methods of involving employees in decision-making in Thai organisations.

An abbreviated version of Puvadol's proposal follows:

Title

The influences of Thai culture on employee involvement.

Background

Involving employees in the decision making of their employing organisations has been increasingly popular in Europe and North America in recent years. The influx of American organisations into Thailand has meant that similar approaches are being adopted. However, this assumes that Thai employees will respond to these techniques as readily as their European and American counterparts.

Doubts about the validity of these assumptions derive from studies of Thai national culture (Komin 1990). Using Rokeach's (1979) conceptual framework, Komin characterised Thai culture in a number of ways. I have isolated those that relate to employee involvement. These are that Thais wish to:

a save face, avoid criticism and show consideration to others;

b exhibit gratitude to those who have shown kindness and consideration;

c promote smooth, conflict-free interpersonal relations;

d interpret 'rules' in a flexible way with little concern for principles;

e promote interdependent social relations;

f be seen to be achieving success through good social relations rather than individual success.

I intend to demonstrate in this section that these six cultural values contradict the values of employee involvement (e.g. employee involvement may involve employees in openly criticising managers, which directly contradicts **a** above).

Research objectives

1 To examine the assumptions behind the management technique of employee involvement.

2 To establish the characteristics of the Thai national culture.

3 To identify the opinions of Thai employees and their managers, working in American-owned organisations in Thailand, towards values underpinning employee involvement.

4 To draw conclusions about the applicability of employee involvement to Thai employees.

Method

1 Conduct a review of the literatures on employee involvement and Thai national culture in order to develop research hypotheses.

2 Carry out primary research in three American-owned petrochemical and manufacturing organisations in Thailand to assess the opinions of Thai employees and their managers towards values underpinning employee involvement. Informal approval has been gained from three organisations. American-owned organisations are relevant because it is in these that employee involvement is most likely to be found and values underpinning employee involvement exhibited. Petrochemical and manufacturing organisations are chosen because the occupations carried out in these organisations are likely to be similar, thus ensuring that any differences are a function of Thai national culture rather than of occupational culture.

A questionnaire will be developed with questions based on the Thai values **a–f** in the Background section above. Each value will lead to a hypothesis (e.g. employee involvement may not be appropriate to Thai culture because it may mean that employees openly criticise their managers). The questions in the questionnaire will seek to test these hypotheses. The questionnaire will be distributed to a sample (size to be agreed) of employees and of managers across all three organisations.

Data analysis will use the SPSS software. Statistical tests will be run to ensure that results are a function of Thai cultural values rather than of values that relate to the individual organisations.

Timescale

January–March 2008: review of literature

April 2008: draft literature review

May 2008: review research methods literature and agree research strategy

June 2008: agree formal access to three organisations for collection of primary data

July–August 2008: compile, pilot and revise questionnaire

September 2008: administer questionnaire

October–November 2008: final collection of questionnaires and analysis of data

November 2008–February 2009: completion of first draft of project report

March–May 2009: final writing of project report

Resources

I have access to computer hardware and software. Access to three organisations has been negotiated, subject to confirmation. My employer has agreed to pay all incidental costs as part of my course expenses.

References

Komin, S. (1990) *Psychology of the Thai People: Values and Behavioral Patterns.* Bangkok, Thailand: National Institute of Development Administration (in Thai).

Rokeach, M. (1979) *Understanding Human Values: Individual and Society.* New York: The Free Press.

The absence of preconceived ideas

Your research should be an exciting journey into the unknown. Do not be like the student who came to Phil to talk over a research proposal and said, 'Of course, I know what the answer will be'. When asked to explain the purpose of doing the research if he already knew the answer, he became rather defensive and eventually looked for another supervisor and, probably, another topic.

If it is absolutely crucial that your proposal is of the highest quality then you may wish to use an **expert system** such as Peer Review Emulator™. This software is available either on its own or as part of the Methodologist's Toolchest™ suite of programs. It asks you a series of questions about your proposed research. The program then critiques these answers to ensure that common research standards are achieved (Idea Works 2008).

2.6 Summary

- The process of formulating and clarifying your research topic is the most important part of your research topic.
- Attributes of a research topic do not vary a great deal between universities. The most important of these is that your research topic will meet the requirements of the examining body.
- Generating and refining research ideas makes use of a variety of techniques. It is important that you use a variety of techniques, including those that involve rational thinking and those that involve creative thinking.
- The ideas generated can be integrated subsequently using a technique such as working up and narrowing down.

- Clear research questions, based on the relevant literature, will act as a focus for the research that follows.
- Research can be distinguished from intelligence gathering. Research is theory dependent.
- Writing a research proposal helps you to organise your ideas, and can be thought of as a contract between you and the reader.
- The content of the research proposal should tell the reader what you want to do, why you want to do it, what you are trying to achieve, and how you to plan to achieve it.

Self-check questions

Help with these questions is available at the end of the chapter.

2.1 For the workplace project for her professional course, Karen had decided to undertake a study of the effectiveness of the joint consultative committee in her NHS Trust. Her title was 'An evaluation of the effectiveness of the Joint Consultative Committee in Anyshire's Hospitals NHS Foundation Trust'. Draft some objectives which Karen may adopt to complement her title.

2.2 You have decided to search the literature to 'try to come up with some research ideas in the area of Operations Management'. How will you go about this?

2.3 A colleague of yours wishes to generate a research idea in the area of accounting. He has examined his own strengths and interests on the basis of his assignments and has read some review articles, but has failed to find an idea about which he is excited. He comes and asks you for advice. Suggest two techniques that your colleague could use, and justify your choice.

2.4 You are interested in doing some research on the interface between business organisations and schools. Write three research questions that may be appropriate.

2.5 How may the formulation of an initial substantive theory help in the development of a research proposal?

2.6 How would you demonstrate the influence of relevant theory in your research proposal?

Review and discussion questions

2.7 Together with your colleagues, decide on the extent to which a set of research topics constitute a 'good research topic' according to the checklist in Box 2.2. The set of topics you choose may be past topics obtained from your tutor which relate to your course. Alternatively, they may be those which have been written by you and your colleagues as preparation for your project(s).

2.8 Look through several of the academic journals which relate to your subject area. Choose an article which is based upon primary research. Assuming that the research question and objectives are not made explicit, infer from the content of the article what the research question and objectives may have been.

2.9 Watch the news on television. Most bulletins will contain stories on research which has been carried out to report the current state of affairs in a particular field. Spend some time investigating news sites on the Internet (e.g. http://www.news.google.com) in order to learn more about the research which relates to the news story. Study the story carefully and decide what further questions the report raises. Use this as the basis to draft an outline proposal to seek answers to one (or more) of these questions.

Progressing your research project

From research ideas to a research proposal

☐ If you have not been given a research idea, consider the techniques available for generating and refining research ideas. Choose a selection of those with which you feel most comfortable, making sure to include both rational and creative thinking techniques. Use these to try to generate a research idea or ideas. Once you have got some research ideas, or if you have been unable to find an idea, talk to your project tutor.

☐ Evaluate your research ideas against the checklist of attributes of a good research project (Box 2.2).

☐ Refine your research ideas using a selection of the techniques available for generating and refining research ideas. Re-evaluate your research ideas against the checklist of attributes of a good research project (Box 2.2). Remember that it is better to revise (and in some situations to discard) ideas that do not appear to be feasible at this stage. Integrate your ideas using the process of working up and narrowing down to form one research idea.

☐ Use your research idea to write a general focus research question. Where possible this should be a 'why?' or a 'how?' rather than a 'what?' question.

☐ Use the general focus research question to write more detailed research questions and your research objectives.

☐ Write your research proposal making sure it includes a clear title and sections on:
  ☐ the background to your research;
  ☐ your research questions and objectives;
  ☐ the method you intend to use;
  ☐ the timescale for your research;
  ☐ the resources you require;
  ☐ references to any literature to which you have referred.

References

BBC News Online (2005) 'South Korean dies after games session'. Available at: http://news.bbc.co.uk/1/hi/technology/4137782.stm [Accessed 21 May 2008.]

Bennett, R. (1991) 'What is management research?', in N.C. Smith and P. Dainty (eds) *The Management Research Handbook*. London: Routledge: pp. 67–77.

Buzan, T. (2006) *The Ultimate Book of Mind Maps*. London: Harper Thorsons.

Carroll, L. (1989) *Alice's Adventures in Wonderland*. London: Hutchinson.

Clough, P. and Nutbrown, C. (2002) *A Student's Guide to Methodology*. London: Sage.

Creswell, J. (2002) *Qualitative, Quantitative, and Mixed Methods Approaches* (2nd edn). Thousand Oaks, CA: Sage.

Festinger, L. (1957) *A Theory of Cognitive Dissonance*. Stanford, CA: Stanford University Press.

Ghauri, P. and Grønhaug, K. (2005) *Research Methods in Business Studies: A Practical Guide* (3rd edn). Harlow: Financial Times Prentice Hall.

Gill, J. and Johnson, P. (2002) *Research Methods for Managers* (3rd edn). London: Sage.

Idea Works (2008) 'Methodologist's Toolchest features'. Available at: http://www.ideaworks.com/mt/index.html [Accessed 19 May 2008.]

Jankowicz, A.D. (2005) *Business Research Projects* (4th edn). London: Thomson Learning.

Kellerman, B. (2007) 'What Every Leader Needs to Know About Followers', *Harvard Business Review*, Vol. 85, No. 12. pp. 84–91.

Kelly, G.A. (1955) *The Psychology of Personal Constructs*. New York: Norton.

Kerlinger, F. and Lee, H. (2000) *Foundations of Behavioral Research* (4th edn). Fort Worth, TX: Harcourt College Publishers.

Kervin, J.B. (1999) *Methods for Business Research* (2nd edn). New York: HarperCollins.

Kindberg, T., Spasojevic, M., Fleck, R. and Sellen, A. (2005) *The Ubiquitous Camera: An In-Depth Study of Camera Phone Use*. Available at: http://www.informatics.sussex.ac.uk/research/groups/interact/publications/ubiquitousCamera.pdf [Accessed 19 May 2007.]

Mackenzie, K.D. (2000a) 'Knobby analyses of knobless survey items, part I: The approach', *International Journal of Organizational Analysis*, Vol. 8, No. 2. pp. 131–54.

Mackenzie, K.D. (2000b) 'Knobby analyses of knobless survey items, part II: An application', *International Journal of Organizational Analysis*, Vol. 8, No. 3, pp. 238–61.

Maylor, H. and Blackmon, K. (2005) *Researching Business and Management*. Basingstoke: Palgrave Macmillan.

McNiff, J. with Whitehead, J. (2000) *Action Research in Organizations*. London: Routledge.

Moody, P.E. (1988) *Decision Making: Proven Methods for Better Decisions* (2nd edn). Maidenhead, McGraw-Hill.

Phillips, E.M. and Pugh, D.S. (2005) *How to get a PhD* (4th edn). Maidenhead: Open University Press.

Raimond, P. (1993) *Management Projects*. London: Chapman & Hall.

Robson, C. (2002) *Real World Research* (2nd edn). Oxford: Blackwell.

Saunders, M.N.K. and Lewis, P. (1997) 'Great ideas and blind alleys? A review of the literature on starting research', *Management Learning*, Vol. 28, No. 3, pp. 283–99.

Sharp, J., Peters, J. and Howard, K. (2002) *The Management of a Student Research Project* (3rd edn). Aldershot: Gower.

Smith, N.C. and Dainty, P. (1991) *The Management Research Handbook*. London: Routledge.

Sutton, R. and Staw, B. (1995) 'What theory is not', *Administrative Science Quarterly*, Vol. 40, No. 3, pp. 371–84.

Whetten, D. (1989) 'What constitutes a theoretical contribution?', *Academy of Management Review*, Vol. 14, No. 4, pp. 490–5.

Further reading

Fisher, C. (2007) *Researching and Writing a Dissertation for Business Students* (2nd edn), Harlow: Financial Times Prentice Hall. Chapter 1 has some very practical tips on choosing your research topic.

Maylor, H. and Blackmon, K. (2005) *Researching Business and Management*. Basingstoke: Palgrave Macmillan. Chapter 3 covers similar ground to this chapter and has some useful ideas on generating research topics and some very interesting examples of student topics.

Sutton, R. and Staw, B. (1995) 'What theory is not', *Administrative Science Quarterly*, Vol. 40, No. 3, pp. 371–84. This is an excellent article which makes very clear what theory is by explaining what theory is not. The authors draw on their experience as journal editors who constantly have to examine articles submitted for publication. They report that the reason for refusals is usually that there is no theory in the article. This leads to some very clear and practical advice for us all to follow.

Whetten, D. (1989) 'What constitutes a theoretical contribution?', *Academy of Management Review*, Vol. 14, No. 4, pp. 490–5. Whetten also comments as a journal editor and covers similar ground to Sutton and Staw. Again, this is clear and straightforward advice and, read together with Sutton and Staw, gives a pretty clear idea of how to avoid criticisms of a lack of theory in research writing.

Case 2
Media climate change reporting and environmental disclosure patterns in the low-cost airline industry in the twenty-first century

Source: Anthony Kay/Alamy

Emma was now at the start of her final year of her business and accounting degree. This was a four-year degree, with a placement year in the third year. Emma had been on placement in the finance and administration function of a budget airline company. Now, back at university, she was concerned that the project proposal form was due for submission in three weeks' time. The project proposal comprised a draft title, outline of the research topic including research question, aims and objectives, introduction to academic literature including the proposed theoretical base, research method and consideration of ethical issues, likely timescale and an assessment of the resources that would be needed. The proposal was the first formally assessed part of the research project and was the key document that would be used to allocate an appropriate project supervisor.

Emma reflected on her second year and final year modules and also what she had been involved with on her placement. During her placement Emma had mainly been helping in the production of the monthly management accounts and was responsible for checking the landing charges levied by airports against each inbound flight. The placement year had been very busy as the airline had enjoyed rapid growth and now flew to 24 destinations compared to 14 just two years ago. Emma thought about all of these but could only feel that this was a job and how could she turn any aspect of that into a research project. Emma now wished that she had done something different during that year that would give her a topic area. Although she knew people at the airline that she could interview or who would fill in questionnaires for her, the problem remained about what? Again, when she thought about her course and the modules she had studied, Emma could not really think of an area to turn into a suitable project and panic began to set in. Three weeks to think about and write a proposal now seemed impossible. She had performed very well in her second year modules, but all of the accounting modules focused on technical aspects of accounting and financial reporting. Whilst Emma knew she was good at these aspects of accounting she wanted to try and identify a topic that was more in the news, and one that would link to both her placement experience and her course. She wanted to use the project in presentations for a job and was hoping to work in the airline or travel industry as a trainee accountant.

One of the final year modules that Emma was studying, 'Contemporary Issues in Accounting' covered aspects of corporate governance, social responsibility, whistle-blowing and ethics. There was a guest lecture that week given by a professor of ethics examining the issue of environmental accounting. The lecture highlighted the increased environmental disclosure that had taken place over the last decade as public companies sought to reassure stakeholders who were concerned about the adverse environmental impact caused by business. The lecture went into specific details, citing Deegan *et al.* (2000 and 2002), who had examined the oil and mining industries. This research showed how environmental disclosures had increased following adverse events such as oil spillages or pollution that had been widely reported in the media. The professor ended the lecture raising the issue of global warming and business responsibility, with the news that Prince Charles had not attended the World Future Energy Summit in Abu Dhabi due to the level of carbon waste from the associated flights for him and his entourage.[1]

Emma was pleased that she had attended the lecture, an obvious research topic was right in front of her! She thought of the airline industry and the problem of global warming and carbon omissions and wondered what companies in that industry were saying about those issues in their annual reports. She immediately looked up the annual reports for her placement company for the last five years which were all available as pdf documents on their corporate website. Quickly looking at the environmental section it was clear that there had been a significant increase in its content over that period. Emma was not surprised there had been an increase in disclosure as this was a common and already well observed trend. However it was a good starting point. She read the articles that the professor had referred to in his lecture, Deegan *et al.* (2000) and Deegan *et al.* (2002). From these articles she also referred to Patten (1992) and Gray *et al.* (1995). Looking on the electronic journal search she also found more recent articles on environmental disclosure such as Campbell *et al.* (2006) and Murray *et al.* (2006). They was certainly plenty of literature in the area. Emma focused on the earlier articles by Deegan *et al.* and Patten and arranged an appointment with one of the accounting tutors to discuss these and her ideas for the research proposal. The meeting was scheduled for the week before the proposal was due to be submitted, so Emma prepared some outline notes to take to the meeting from which she hoped to finalise her own proposal.

Emma had the following main points listed for the meeting:

- Increase in her placement company's environmental disclosure over the past five years.
- Look for same trends in all airline companies.
- Quantify levels of environmental disclosure.
- Relate to increase in disclosure trends from literature.
- Get news stories about omissions and carbon foot-printing.
- Interview placement company employees about their views.

The meeting with the tutor went well and the tutor was supportive of the general topic area, but Emma was surprised by how much further work she had still to do to formulate the proposal. Emma had told her tutor about the guest lecture, the annual report disclosures she already had identified, the articles and the link between the increased disclosure and global warming issues. The tutor asked Emma how she would be able to link the disclosure with the press stories and show that it was not just a coincidence. The only news stories Emma had so far collected all related to the past 12 months. Emma needed to think about this aspect in more depth. The tutor also asked Emma if she had any ideas about a possible theoretical base that could be relevant for the research. From the articles, Emma said that legitimacy theory would be used as this had been the theoretical framework within the articles. Again, the tutor raised concerns for Emma to think about to clearly establish that a legitimacy problem existed that could then be used to explain the increase in associated disclosure. Towards the end of the meeting the tutor also questioned Emma as to why she wanted to carry out interviews.

---

[1]Borland, S. (2008) 'Prince Charles beamed all the way to Dubai', 23 Jan., www.telegraph.co.uk/news

Emma felt that having worked in the industry, she could get access to some of the management and that it would be useful for her research. The tutor acknowledged the possible access but questioned whether the interviews were really needed for the research and what value they were adding.

Over the next week, Emma tried to address the issues raised by the tutor. To show the increase in news stories associated with airlines and global warming, Emma had found out how to use one of the online media databases that would allow her to search for news stories by year by key words and groups of key words. Emma had already read one month's coverage and had coded the content into good, bad or neutral news. She had also started to collate the increased number of flights and destinations covered by the low-cost airlines over the years of her study. Emma had decided to narrow her focus onto this part of the industry rather than the whole airline industry. The biggest issue related to the need for interviews. It surprised her that she did not need to carry them out as she had always thought that doing this would be better for her research. She decided not to do them and to rely on desk-based research using the media coverage and annual report disclosures.

The topic area was now clear in her mind to investigate the change in environmental disclosure over time by low cost airlines. She was pleased to narrow the focus rather than have to research the whole industry, and due to the growth of such airlines this seemed a sensible approach. The most pleasing part of the process was that Emma also knew why she was looking at the disclosure and how she would try and explain its change over time. Having some idea of the theory base also filled Emma with confidence to proceed and she was now really looking forward to getting started for real.

The research topic and the proposal were handed in. The proposal was titled: Media Climate Change Reporting and Environmental Disclosure Patterns in the Low-Cost Airline Industry in the Twenty-First Century.

Questions

1 Why is it important that your research can be related to a relevant theory base, and when during the project does the theoretical framework need to be identified?
2 Do you think that Emma is right to restrict her project to only low-cost airlines, rather than the whole industry or a comparison with another sector? Give reasons for your answer.
3 Do you think Emma was correct in her decision not to carry out interviews? Give reasons for your answer.

If she were to change her mind, are there any ethical issues that would need to be addressed? (Hint: you may find Section 6.4 helpful in thinking about this question.)

References

Campbell, D.J., Moore, G. and Shrives, P.J. (2006) 'Cross-sectional effects in community disclosure', *Accounting, Auditing and Accountability Journal*, Vol. 19, No. 1, pp. 96–114.

Deegan, C., Rankin, M. and Voght, P. (2000) 'Firms' disclosure reactions to major social incidents: Australian evidence', *Accounting Forum*, Vol. 24, No. 1, pp. 101–30.

Deegan, C., M. Rankin and Tobin J. (2002) 'An examination of the corporate social and environmental disclosures of BHP from 1983–1997: A test of legitimacy theory', *Accounting, Auditing and Accountability Journal*, Vol. 15, No. 3, pp. 312–43.

Gray, R.H., Kouhy, R. and Lavers, S. (1995) 'Corporate social and environmental reporting: a review of the literature and a longitudinal study of UK disclosure', *Accounting, Auditing & Accountability Journal*, Vol. 8, No. 2, pp. 47–77.

Murray, A., Sinclair, D. Power, D. and Gray, R. (2006) 'Do financial markets care about social and environmental disclosure? Further evidence from the UK', *Accounting, Auditing & Accountability Journal*, Vol. 19, No. 2, pp. 228–55.

Patten, D.M. (1992) 'Intra-industry environmental disclosure in response to the Alaskan oil spill: a note on legitimacy theory', *Accounting, Organisations and Society*, Vol. 17, pp. 471–75.

Additional case studies relating to material covered in this chapter are available via the book's Companion Website, **www.pearsoned.co.uk/saunders**. They are:

- The use of internal and word of mouth recruitment methods
- Strategic issues in the brewing industry
- Catherine Chang and women in management.

Self-check answers

2.1 These may include:
  a Identify the management and trade union objectives for the Joint Consultative Committee and use this to establish suitable effectiveness criteria.
  b Review key literature on the use of joint consultative committees.
  c Carry out primary research in the organisation to measure the effectiveness of the Joint Consultative Committee.
  d Identify the strengths and weaknesses of the Joint Consultative Committee.
  e Where necessary, make recommendations for action to ensure the effective function of the Joint Consultative Committee.

2.2 One starting point would be to ask your project tutor for suggestions of possible recent review articles or articles containing recommendations for further work that he or she has read. Another would be to browse recent editions of operations management journals such as the *International Journal of Operations & Production Management* for possible research ideas. These would include both statements of the absence of research and unfounded assertions. Recent reports held in your library or on the Internet may also be of use here. You could also scan one or two recently published operations management textbooks for overviews of research that has been undertaken.

2.3 From the description given, it would appear that your colleague has considered only rational thinking techniques. It would therefore seem sensible to suggest two creative thinking techniques, as these would hopefully generate an idea that would appeal to him. One technique that you could suggest is brainstorming, perhaps emphasising the need to do it with other colleagues. Exploring past projects in the accountancy area would be another possibility. You might also suggest that he keeps a notebook of ideas.

2.4 Your answer will probably differ from that below. However, the sorts of things you could be considering include:
  a How do business organisations benefit from their liaison with schools?
  b Why do business organisations undertake school liaison activities?
  c To what degree do business organisations receive value for money in their school liaison activities?

2.5 Let us go back to the example used in the chapter of the supermarket marketing manager who theorises that the introduction of a loyalty card will mean that regular customers are less likely to shop at competitor supermarkets. This could be the research proposal's starting point, i.e. a hypothesis that the introduction of a loyalty card will mean that regular customers are less likely to shop at competitor supermarkets. This prompts thoughts about the possible use of literature in the proposal and the research project itself. This literature could have at least two strands. First, a practical strand which looks at the research evidence which lends credence to the hypothesis. Second, a more abstract strand that studies human consumer behaviour and looks at the cognitive processes which affect consumer purchasing decisions.

This ensures that the proposal and resultant research project are both theory driven and also ensures that relevant theory is covered in the literature.

2.6 Try including a subsection in the background section that is headed 'How the previous published research has informed my research questions and objectives'. Then show how, say, a gap in the previous research that is there because nobody has pursued a particular approach before has led to you filling that gap.

Get ahead using resources on the Companion Website at:
www.pearsoned.co.uk/saunders
- Improve your SPSS and NVivo research analysis with practice tutorials.
- Save time researching on the Internet with the Smarter Online Searching Guide.
- Test your progress using self-assessment questions.
- Follow live links to useful websites.

Critically reviewing the literature

3.1 Introduction

As part of your studies, you have almost certainly already been asked by your tutors to 'review the literature', 'write a literature review' or 'critically review the literature' on topics they have specified. Indeed, you may be like many students and have grown to fear the literature review, not because of the associated reading but because of the requirement both to make judgements as to the value of each piece of work and to organise those ideas and findings that are of value into a review. It is these two processes in particular that people find both difficult and time consuming.

Two major reasons exist for reviewing the literature (Sharp *et al.* 2002). The first, the preliminary search that helps you to generate and refine your research ideas, has already been discussed in Section 2.3. The second, often referred to as the **critical review** or **critical literature review**, is part of your research project proper. Most research textbooks, as well as your project tutor, will argue that this critical review of the literature is necessary. Although you may feel that you already have a good knowledge of your research area, we believe that reviewing the literature is essential. Project assessment criteria usually require you to demonstrate awareness of the current state of knowledge in your subject, its limitations, and how your research fits in this wider context (Gill and Johnson 2002). In Jankowicz's (2005:161) words:

> There is little point in reinventing the wheel . . . the work that you do is not done in a vacuum, but builds on the ideas of other people who have studied the field before you. This requires you describe what has been published, and to marshal the information in a relevant and critical way.

Recently, we were discussing the difficulties students have when writing their literature reviews for their research projects. Mark summarised what he felt we and fellow project tutors were saying:

'So what happens sometimes is . . . a student comes to see their project tutor having obviously done a great deal of work. The student presents the tutor with what they say is the finished literature review. Yet, the purpose of their review is unclear. It is little more than a summary of the articles and books read, each article or book being given one paragraph. Some students have arranged these paragraphs alphabetically in author order, others have arranged them in chronological order. None have linked or juxtaposed the ideas. Their literature reviews look more like adjacent pages from a catalogue rather than a critical review. Just like the items on these pages, each article or book has some similarities in terms of subject matter and so are grouped together. As in the catalogue, the reasons for these groupings are not made explicit. In addition, like the summary descriptions of items on the pages of a home shopping catalogue, each book or article is accorded equal status rather than the amount written reflecting its value to the student's research project.'

He concluded:

'Whilst such an approach obviously makes good sense for a shopping catalogue, it does not work for the critical review of the literature. We obviously need to explain better what we mean by a critical review of the literature to our students.'

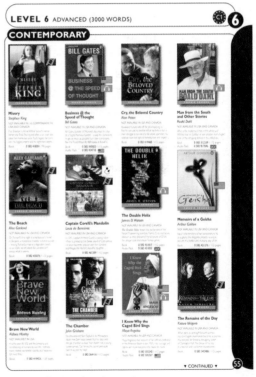

A page from a book catalogue
Source: Pearson Education Ltd

The significance of your research and what you find out will inevitably be judged in relation to other people's research and their findings. You, therefore, need both to 'map and assess the existing intellectual territory' (Tranfield *et al.* 2003:208), establishing what research has been published in your chosen area, and, if possible, to try to identify any other research that might currently be in progress. Consequently, the items you read and write about will enhance your subject knowledge and help you to clarify your research question(s) further. This process is called 'critically reviewing the literature'.

For most research projects, your literature search will be an early activity. Despite this early start, it is usually necessary to continue searching throughout your project's life. The process can be likened to an upward spiral, culminating in the final draft of a written critical literature review (Figure 3.1). In the initial stage of your literature review, you will start to define the parameters to your research question(s) and objectives (Section 3.4). After generating key words and conducting your first search (Section 3.5), you will have a list of references to authors who have published on these subjects. Once these have been obtained, you can read and evaluate them (Section 3.6), record the ideas (Section 3.7) and start drafting your review. After the initial search, you will be able to redefine your parameters more

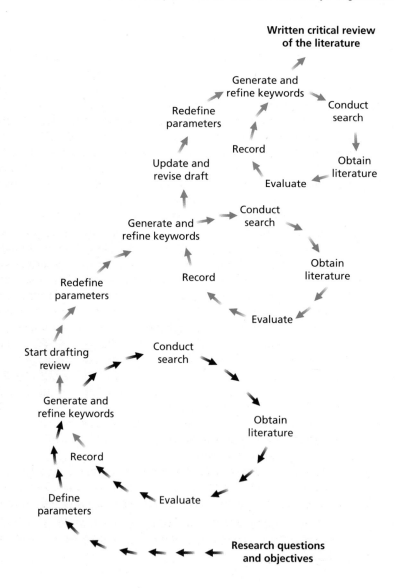

Figure 3.1
The literature review process
Source: © Mark Saunders, Philip Lewis, Adrian, Thornhill and Martin Jenkins 2003

precisely and undertake further searches, keeping in mind your research question(s) and objectives. As your thoughts develop, each subsequent search will be focused more precisely on material that is likely to be relevant. At the same time, you will probably be refining your research question(s) and objectives in the light of your reading (Section 2.4).

Unlike some academic disciplines, business and management research makes use of a wide range of literature. While your review is likely to include specific business disciplines such as finance, marketing and human resource management, it is also likely to include other disciplines. Those most frequently consulted by our students include economics, psychology, sociology and geography. Given this, and the importance of the review to your research, it is vital for you to be aware of what a critical literature review is and the range of literature available before you start the reviewing process. For these reasons, we start this chapter by outlining the purpose of your critical review of the literature, its content and what we mean by 'critical' (Section 3.2) and then discussing those literature resources available (Section 3.3).

3.2 The critical review

The purpose of the critical review

Reviewing the literature critically will provide the foundation on which your research is built. As you will have gathered from the introduction, its main purpose is to help you to develop a good understanding and insight into relevant previous research and the trends that have emerged. You would not expect a scientific researcher inquiring into the causes of cot death to start his or her research without first reading about the findings of other cot death research. Likewise, you should not expect to start your research without first reading what other researchers in your area have already found out.

The precise purpose of your reading of the literature will depend on the approach you are intending to use in your research. For some research projects you will use the literature to help you to identify theories and ideas that you will test using data. This is known as a **deductive approach** (Section 4.3) in which you develop a theoretical or conceptual framework, which you subsequently test using data. For other research projects you will be planning to explore your data and to develop theories from them that you will subsequently relate to the literature. This is known as an **inductive approach** (Section 4.3) and, although your research still has a clearly defined purpose with research question(s) and objectives, you do not start with any predetermined theories or conceptual frameworks. We believe such an approach cannot be taken without a competent knowledge of your subject area. It is, however, impossible to review every single piece of the literature before collecting your data. The purpose of your literature review is not to provide a summary of everything that has been written on your research topic, but to review the most relevant and significant research on your topic. If your analysis is effective, new findings and theories will emerge that neither you nor anyone else has thought about (Strauss and Corbin 1998). Despite this, when you write your critical review, you will need to show how your findings and the theories you have developed or are using relate to the research that has gone before, thereby demonstrating that you are familiar with what is already known about your research topic.

Your review also has a number of other purposes. Many of these have been highlighted by Gall *et al.* (2006) in their book for students undertaking educational research and are, we believe, of equal relevance to business and management researchers:

- to help you to refine further your research question(s) and objectives;
- to highlight research possibilities that have been overlooked implicitly in research to date;

- to discover explicit recommendations for further research. These can provide you with a superb justification for your own research question(s) and objectives;
- to help you to avoid simply repeating work that has been done already;
- to sample current opinions in newspapers, professional and trade journals, thereby gaining insights into the aspects of your research question(s) and objectives that are considered newsworthy;
- to discover and provide an insight into research approaches, strategies (Section 4.3) and techniques that may be appropriate to your own research question(s) and objectives.

Adopting critical perspective in your reading

Harvard College Library (2006) provides for its students a useful check list of skills to be practised for effective reading. These skills include:

Previewing, which is looking around the text before you start reading in order to establish precisely its purpose and how it may inform your literature search;

Annotating; that is conducting a dialogue with yourself, the author, and the issues and ideas at stake.

Here the Harvard advice, we think, is very useful. It urges readers to be 'thinking-intensive' (see Box 3.1).

Summarising. The best way to determine that you've really got the point is to be able to state it in your own words. Outlining the argument of a text is a version of annotating, and can be done quite informally in the margins of the text.

Box 3.1
Checklist

Annotating your critical reading. Advice on how to read in a 'thinking-intensive' way

✔ First of all: throw away the highlighter in favour of a pen or pencil. Highlighting can actually distract from the business of learning and dilute your comprehension. It only seems like an active reading strategy; in actual fact, it can lull you into a dangerous passivity.

✔ Mark up the margins of your text with words: ideas that occur to you, notes about things that seem important to you, reminders of how issues in a text may connect with your research questions and objectives. This kind of interaction keeps you conscious of the reason you are reading. Throughout your research these annotations will be useful memory triggers.

✔ Develop your own symbol system: asterisk a key idea, for example, or use an exclamation point for the surprising, absurd, bizarre . . . Like your margin words, your hieroglyphs can help you reconstruct the important observations that you made at an earlier time. And they will be indispensable when you return to a text later in the term, in search of a particular passage that you may want to include in your project report.

✔ Get in the habit of hearing yourself ask questions – 'what does this mean?' 'why is he or she drawing that conclusion?' Write the questions down (in your margins, at the beginning or end of the reading, in a notebook, or elsewhere). They are reminders of the unfinished business you still have with a text: to come to terms with on your own, once you've had a chance to digest the material further, or have done further reading.

Comparing and Contrasting. Ask yourself how your thinking been altered by this reading or how has it affected your response to the issues and themes your research?

The Harvard College Library advice above suggests that you should get in the habit of hearing yourself ask questions of your reading. Wallace and Wray (2006) recommend the use of **review questions**. These are specific questions you ask of the reading, which will be linked either directly or, at least, indirectly, to your research question. So you may, for example, address a piece of reading with the view to it answering the question: 'what does research suggest are the main reasons why customers are likely to change car insurance provider?'

The word 'critical' has appeared in this chapter a number of times so far. It is vital in your reading of the literature that a critical stance should be taken. So what is meant by critical reading? Wallace and Wray (2006) sum this up rather succinctly by saying that 'the lengthy list if critical skills (required for critical reading) boil down to just two: the capacity to evaluate what you read and the capacity to relate what you read to other information'.

More specifically Wallace and Wray advocate the use of five critical questions to employ in critical reading. These are:

1 Why am I reading this? (The authors argue that this is where the review question in particularly valuable. It acts as a focusing device and ensures that you stick to the purpose of the reading and not get sidetracked too much by the author's agenda.)
2 What is the author trying to do in writing this? (The answer to this may assist you in deciding how valuable the writing may be for your purposes.)
3 What is the writer saying that is relevant to what I want to find out?
4 How convincing is what the author is saying? (In particular, is the argument based on a conclusion which is justified by the evidence?)
5 What use can I make of the reading?

The content of the critical review

As you begin to find, read and evaluate the literature, you will need to think how to combine the academic theories and ideas about which you are reading to form the critical review that will appear in your project report. Your review will need to evaluate the research that has already been undertaken in the area of your research project, show and explain the relationships between published research findings and reference the literature in which they were reported (Appendix 1). It will draw out the key points and trends (recognising any omissions and bias) and present them in a logical way which also shows the relationship to your own research. In doing this you will provide readers of your project report with the necessary background knowledge to your research question(s) and objectives and establish the boundaries of your own research. Your review will also enable the readers to see your ideas against the background of previous published research in the area. This does not necessarily mean that your ideas must extend, follow or approve those set out in the literature. You may be highly critical of the earlier research reported in the literature and seek to discredit it. However, if you wish to do this you must still review this literature, explain clearly why it is problematic, and then justify your own ideas.

In considering the content of your critical review, you will therefore need:

• to include the key academic theories within your chosen area of research;
• to demonstrate that your knowledge of your chosen area is up to date;
• through clear referencing, enable those reading your project report to find the original publications which you cite.

Box 3.2
Checklist

Evaluating the content of your critical literature review

✔ Have you ensured that the literature covered relates clearly to your research question and objectives?

✔ Have you covered the most relevant and significant theories of recognised experts in the area?

✔ Have you covered the most relevant and significant literature or at least a representative sample?

✔ Have you included up-to-date literature?

✔ Have you referenced all the literature used in the format prescribed in the assessment criteria?

In addition, by fully acknowledging the research of others you will avoid charges of plagiarism and the associated penalties (Section 3.8). The content of your critical review can be evaluated using the checklist in Box 3.2.

What is really meant by being 'critical' about the content

Within the context of your course you have probably already been asked to take a critical approach for previous assignments. However, it is worth considering what we mean by critical within the context of your literature review. Mingers (2000:225–6) argues that there are four aspects of a critical approach that should be fostered by management education:

- critique of rhetoric;
- critique of tradition;
- critique of authority;
- critique of objectivity.

The first of these, the 'critique of rhetoric', means appraising or evaluating a problem with effective use of language. In the context of your critical literature review, this emphasises the need for you, as the reviewer, to use your skills both of making reasoned judgements and of arguing effectively in writing. The other three aspects Mingers identifies also have implications for being critical when reading and writing about the work of others. This includes you questioning, where justification exists to do so, the conventional wisdom, the 'critique of tradition' and the dominant view portrayed in the literature you are reading, the 'critique of authority'. Finally, it is likely also to include recognising in your review that the knowledge and information you are discussing are not value free, the 'critique of objectivity'.

Being critical in reviewing the literature is, therefore, a combination of your skills and the attitude with which you read. In critically reviewing the literature, you need to read the literature about your research topic with some scepticism and be willing to question what you read. This means you need to be constantly considering and justifying with clear arguments your own critical stance. You, therefore, will have to read widely on your research topic and have a good understanding of the literature. Critically reviewing the literature for your research project, therefore, requires you to have gained topic-based

Box 3.3
Checklist

Evaluating whether your literature review is critical

✔ Have you shown how your research question relates to previous research reviewed?

✔ Have you assessed the strengths and weaknesses of the previous research reviewed?

✔ Have you been objective in your discussion and assessment of other people's research?

✔ Have you included references to research that is counter to your own opinion?

✔ Have you distinguished clearly between facts and opinions?

✔ Have you made reasoned judgements about the value and relevance of others' research to your own?

✔ Have you justified clearly your own ideas?

✔ Have you highlighted those areas where new research (yours!) is needed to provide fresh insights and taken these into account in your arguments? In particular:

✔ where there are inconsistencies in current knowledge and understanding?

✔ where there are omissions or bias in published research?

✔ where research findings need to be tested further?

✔ where evidence is lacking, inconclusive, contradictory or limited?

✔ Have you justified your arguments by referencing correctly published research?

background knowledge, understanding, the ability to reflect upon and to analyse the literature and, based on this, to make reasoned judgements that are argued effectively. When you use these skills to review the literature, the term 'critical' refers to the judgement you exercise. It, therefore, describes the process of providing a detailed and justified analysis of, and commentary on, the merits and faults of the key literature within your chosen area. This means that, for your review to be critical, you will need to have shown critical judgement.

Part of this judgement will inevitably mean being able to identify the most relevant and significant theories and recognised experts highlighted in Box 3.3. In addition, Dees (2003) suggests that this means you should:

- refer to and assess research by recognised experts in your chosen area;
- consider and discuss research that supports and research that opposes your ideas;
- make reasoned judgements regarding the value of others' research, showing clearly how it relates to your research;
- justify your arguments with valid evidence in a logical manner;
- distinguish clearly between fact and opinion.

These points are developed in Box 3.3, which contains a checklist to evaluate the extent to which your literature review is critical. The more questions to which you can answer 'yes', the more likely your review will be critical!

The structure of the critical review

The **literature review** that you write for your project report should therefore be a description and critical analysis of what other authors have written (Jankowicz 2005). When drafting your review you, therefore, need to focus on your research question(s) and objectives. One way of helping you to focus is to think of your literature review as discussing how far existing published research goes in answering your research question(s). The shortfall in the literature will be addressed, at least partially, in the remainder of your project report. Another way of helping you to focus is to ask yourself how your review relates to your objectives. If it does not, or does only partially, there is a need for a clearer focus on your objectives. The precise structure of the critical review is usually your choice, although you should check, as it may be specified in the assessment criteria. Three common structures are:

- a single chapter;
- a series of chapters;
- throughout the project report as you tackle various issues.

In all project reports, you should return to the key issues from the literature in your discussion and conclusions (Section 14.3).

Within your critical review, you will need to juxtapose different authors' ideas and form your own opinions and conclusions based on these. Although you will not be able to start writing until you have undertaken some reading, we recommend that you start drafting your review early (Figure 3.1). What you write can then be updated and revised as you read more.

A common mistake with critical literature reviews, highlighted at the start of this chapter, is that they become uncritical listings of previous research. Often they are little more than annotated bibliographies (Hart 1998), individual items being selected because they fit with what the researcher is proposing (Greenhalgh 1997). Although there is no single structure that your critical review should take, our students have found it useful to think of the review as a funnel in which you:

1 start at a more general level before narrowing down to your specific research question(s) and objectives;
2 provide a brief overview of key ideas and themes;
3 summarise, compare and contrast the research of the key writers;
4 narrow down to highlight previous research work most relevant to your own research;
5 provide a detailed account of the findings of this research and show how they are related;
6 highlight those aspects where your own research will provide fresh insights;
7 lead the reader into subsequent sections of your project report, which explore these issues.

In addition, some writers argue that, in order to improve the transparency of your review process, you should explain precisely how you searched for selected the literature you have included in your review, outlining your choice of key words and of databases used (Tranfield *et al.* 2003). Within the 'funnel' we have just proposed, this can be thought of as step 0! This is discussed in more detail in Sections 3.4 and 3.5.

Whichever way you structure your review you must demonstrate that you have read, understood and evaluated the items you have located. The key to writing a critical literature review is therefore to link the different ideas you find in the literature to form a coherent and cohesive argument, which sets in context and justifies your research. Obviously, it should relate to your research question and objectives. It should show a clear link from these as well as a clear link to the empirical work that will follow. Box 3.4 provides a checklist to help you ensure that the structure of your literature review supports this. Subsequent parts of your project report (Section 14.3) must follow on from this.

Box 3.4
Checklist

Evaluating the structure of your literature review

✔ Does your literature review have a clear title which describes the focus of your research rather than just saying 'literature review'?

✔ Have you explained precisely how you searched the literature, and the criteria used to select those studies included?

✔ Does your review start at a more general level before narrowing down?

✔ Is your literature review organised thematically around the ideas contained in the research being reviewed rather than the researchers?

✔ Are your arguments coherent and cohesive – do your ideas link in a way that will be logical to your reader?

✔ Have you used sub-headings within the literature review to help guide your reader?

✔ Does the way you have structured your literature review draw your reader's attention to those issues which are going to be the focus of your research?

✔ Does your literature review lead your reader into subsequent sections of your project report?

Box 3.5
Focus on management research

Structure of the literature review

An article published by Christine Williams and Mark Saunders in the *Service Industries Journal* (Williams and Saunders 2006:582–3) includes a review of the literature on problems associated with traditional approaches to measuring service quality. The following extract is taken from this review. Although your literature review will be longer than this, the extract illustrates:

- the overall structure of starting at a more general level before narrowing down;
- the provision of a brief overview of the key ideas;
- the linking of ideas;
- narrowing down to highlight that work which is most relevant to the research reported.

In their paper, Williams and Saunders subsequently review, in more detail, research involving the development of an alternative approach, the Service Template Process.

Traditional Approaches to measuring service quality

Traditional survey-based approaches to measuring service quality or customer satisfaction such as SERVQUAL (Parasuraman *et al.* 1985) measure the gap between service users' perceptions and expectations across a series of standardised dimensions characterising the service. Notwithstanding shortcomings of conceptualising service quality in this manner, recognised for example in the SERVQUAL debates (Carman 1990; Cronin and Taylor 1992), the use of the disconfirmation approach is reported widely in the literature (Parasuraman 1995; Robinson 1999).

Carman (1990) argues that constructs representing service quality are a function of a particular service and the industry within which it is located. Carman (2000) also confirms that different users of a service may assign different levels of importance to the same quality dimension. Furthermore, the use of generic constructs to measure a particular service's quality may not provide the details necessary to define the specific causes of a problem rather than its symptoms (Kilmann 1986). Generic constructs, therefore,

▶ **Box 3.5**
Focus on management research (continued)

may fail to account for the uniqueness and realities of specific services, and how these are expressed and interpreted by the parties involved. Furthermore, where these measures are used only from the perspective of service user or deliverer, any problems identified are unlikely to reflect fully the dyadic nature of service encounters (Svensson 2001).

If the measurement of service quality is to lead to improvement, data collected must be useful. In this context, usefulness can be viewed from three interrelated perspectives. The first emphasises the suitability of the constructs used to capture perceptions of reality considered important by each party involved within the specific service (Chi Cui *et al.* 2003), in other words, construct validity. The second perspective relates to the implications of the sufficiency of detail in respect of a clear understanding of the particular service situation. Kilmann (1986:131) summarises this as the need to 'define problem causes rather than just symptoms'. The third is concerned with the extent to which these data enable meanings to be understood and explored and quality improvement agendas derived.

Problems of second order interpretation (Yin 2003) can occur when data collected using measures of service quality are subject to interpretation by third parties, such as consultants or managers. The meanings ascribed to the data by the interpreter may differ from those given by service users or deliverers, leading to inconsistency in interpretation. A person undertaking an inquiry may have filtered and added her or his own understanding to the language used and emphases placed by respondents, rather than it being understood and interpreted as intended (Foddy 1994). Consequently, meanings in the data may be lost, or at best, mis-reported. Furthermore, traditional approaches do not normally require respondents to indicate the relative importance of quality constructs (Pitt *et al.* 1995). Such analyses usually involve the person undertaking the inquiry judging what is important, concentrating attention on those areas that she or he believes are of critical concern (Foddy 1994; Krueger 1994). Consequently, her or his judgement about which characteristics are key to the quality of service forms the basis for analysis and future action.

Source: Williams, C.S. and Saunders, M.N.K. (2006). Copyright © Taylor & Francis. Reproduced by permission of the publisher.

3.3 Literature sources available

An overview

The literature sources available to help you to develop a good understanding of, and insight into, previous research can be divided into three categories: primary (published and unpublished), secondary, and tertiary (Figure 3.2). In reality these categories often overlap: for example, primary literature sources, including conference proceedings, can appear in journals, and some books contain indexes to primary and secondary literature.

The different categories of literature resources represent the flow of information from the original source. Often as information flows from primary to secondary to tertiary sources it becomes less detailed and authoritative but more easily accessible. Recognising this information flow helps you to identify the most appropriate sources of literature for your needs. Some research projects may access only secondary literature sources whereas others will necessitate the use of primary sources.

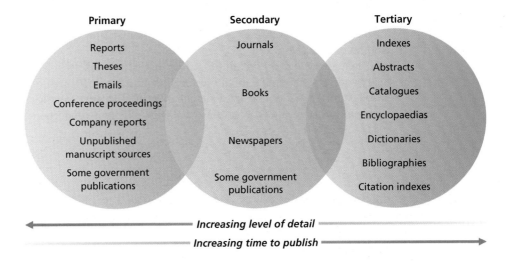

Figure 3.2
Literature sources available

The nature of this information flow is typical of traditional printed publications. However, the Internet is changing this situation, providing a more direct means of both publishing and accessing information. Alongside this, moves toward 'freedom of information' mean that what were traditionally 'grey literature', such as some government publications, are increasingly being made available, usually via the Internet. The majority of academic publications still exhibit this information flow, although the final place of publication is increasingly the Internet.

Figure 3.2 also illustrates the reduced currency of secondary literature sources, which are utilising information already published in primary sources. Because of the time taken to publish, the information in these sources can be dated. Your literature review should reflect current thinking as far as possible, so the limitations of such sources must be recognised.

Primary literature sources are the first occurrence of a piece of work. They include published sources such as reports and some central and local government publications such as White Papers and planning documents. They also include unpublished manuscript sources such as letters, memos and committee minutes that may be analysed as data in their own right (Section 8.2). It is because primary literature sources can be difficult to trace that they are sometimes referred to as **grey literature**.

Secondary literature sources such as books and journals are the subsequent publication of primary literature. These publications are aimed at a wider audience. They are easier to locate than primary literature as they are better covered by the tertiary literature.

Tertiary literature sources, also called 'search tools', are designed either to help to locate primary and secondary literature or to introduce a topic. They, therefore, include indexes and abstracts as well as encyclopaedias and bibliographies.

Your use of these literature sources will depend on your research question(s) and objectives, the need for secondary data to answer them (Section 8.3) and the time available. For some research projects you may use only tertiary and secondary literature; for others you may need to locate primary literature as well. Most research projects will make the greatest use of secondary literature, and so it is this we consider first, followed by the primary literature. Tertiary literature sources are not discussed until Section 3.5, as their major use is in conducting a literature search.

Secondary literature sources

The number of secondary literature sources available to you is expanding rapidly, especially as new resources are developed or made available via the Internet. Your university's librarians are likely to be aware of a wide range of secondary literature in business and management that can be accessed from your library, and will keep themselves up to date with new resources.

The main secondary literature sources that you are likely to use, along with those primary sources most frequently used for a literature review, are outlined in Table 3.1. The most important when placing your ideas in the context of earlier research are refereed academic journals. Books are, however, likely to be more important than professional and trade journals in this context.

Journals

Journals are also known as 'periodicals', 'serials' and 'magazines', and are published on a regular basis. While most are still produced in printed form, many additionally provide online access, via a subscription service. Journals are a vital literature source for any research. The articles are easily accessible. They are well covered by tertiary literature, and a good selection can be accessed from most university libraries either in print, for reference purposes, or via their online services. This online access is usually restricted to members of the university (Table 3.1). Trade and some professional journals may be covered only partially by the tertiary literature (Table 3.2). You, therefore, need to browse these journals regularly to be sure of finding useful items. Many journals' content pages can also be browsed via the Internet (Section 3.5).

Articles in **refereed academic journals** (such as the *Journal of Management Studies*) are evaluated by academic peers prior to publication, to assess their quality and suitability. They are usually written by recognised experts in the field. There will be usually be detailed footnotes; an extensive bibliography; rigorous attention to detail; and verification of information. Such articles are written for a more narrow audience of scholars with a particular interest in the field. The language used may be technical or highly specialised as a prior knowledge of the topic will be assumed. Often, an accepted article will still need to undergo several serious revisions, based on the referees' comments, before it actually appears in print.

These are usually the most useful for research projects as they will contain detailed reports of relevant earlier research. Not all academic journals are refereed. Most *non-refereed academic journals* will have an editor and possibly an editorial board with subject knowledge to select articles. The relevance and usefulness of such journals varies considerably, and occasionally you may need to be wary of possible bias (Section 3.6).

Professional journals (such as *People Management*) are produced for their members by organisations such as the Chartered Institute of Personnel and Development (CIPD), the Association of Chartered Certified Accountants (ACCA) and the American Marketing Association (AMA). They contain a mix of news-related items and articles that are more detailed. However, you need to exercise caution, as articles can be biased towards their author's or the organisation's views. Articles are often of a more practical nature and more closely related to professional needs than those in academic journals. Some organisations will also produce newsletters or current awareness publications that you may find useful for up-to-date information. Some professional organisations now give access to selected articles in their journals via their web pages, though these may be only accessible to members (see Table 8.2 and Section 3.5). Trade journals fulfil a similar function to professional journals. They are published by trade organisations or aimed at particular industries or trades such as catering or mining. Often they focus on new products or services and news items. They rarely contain articles based on empirical research, although some provide summaries of research. You should therefore use these with considerable caution for your research project.

Table 3.1 Main secondary and primary literature sources

Source	Frequency of publication	Format of publication	Coverage by abstracts and indexes (tertiary sources)	Likely availability
Refereed academic journal, non-refereed academic journal	Mainly monthly or quarterly		Well covered. In addition, content pages often available for searching via publishers' websites	Kept as reference in most university libraries; with many accessible via the Internet through various subscription services. Those not available locally can usually be obtained using inter-library loans. Professional organisations may also provide access to their journals via their own web pages
Professional journal		Mainly printed, vast majority now available via the Internet. Can be also available on CD-ROM	Increasingly well covered by services such as ABI/Inform and Business Source Premier. In addition, content pages often available for searching via publishers' websites	Not as widely available in university libraries as academic and refereed journals. Can be obtained using inter-library loans. Most trade associations will have an associated website
Trade journal	Mainly weekly or monthly			
Books	Once; subsequent editions may be published	Mainly printed, increasingly available via the Internet including some text reproduced on line. Can also be available on CD-ROM	Well covered by abstracts and indexes. Searches can be undertaken on remote university OPACs* via the Internet	Widely available. Those not available locally can be obtained using interlibrary loans
Newspapers	Mainly daily or weekly	'Quality' newspapers now available on the Internet or through subscription online databases. Also available on CD-ROM and microfilm (for older back-runs)	Specialised indexes available. CD-ROM and Internet format easy to search using key words	Home nation 'quality' newspapers kept as reference in most university libraries. Internet access to stories, often with additional information on the websites, for most national and international 'quality' newspapers
Conference proceedings	Dependent on the conference, sometimes as part of journal	As for refereed academic journals. May be published in book form (e.g. Index to Conference Proceedings). Some conference proceedings or abstracts are published on the Internet	Depends on conference, although often limited. Specialist indexes sometimes available	Not widely held by university libraries. May be possible to obtain using inter-library loans
Reports	Once	As for refereed academic journals. Government reports increasingly accessible via the Internet	Poor compared with most secondary sources, although some specialised indexes exist	
Theses	On the awarding of the research degree	Mainly printed	Good for PhD and MPhil research degrees, otherwise poor	Usually obtained using inter-library loans. Often only one copy

*OPAC, Online Public Access Catalogue.

Source: © Mark Saunders, Philip Lewis and Adrian Thornhill 2008.

Table 3.2 Tertiary literature sources and their coverage

Name	Format	Coverage
ABI Inform	Internet, CD-ROM	Indexes approximately 100 international business and management journals. Also contains a wide range of trade and professional titles. Covers additional subjects such as engineering, law and medicine. Full text of selected articles from 500 journals may be available depending on subscription (CD-ROM updated monthly)
British National Bibliography (BNB)	CD-ROM, print	Bibliographic information for books and serials (journals) deposited at the British Library by UK and Irish publishers since 1950
British Library Integrated Catalogue	Internet	Gives access to British Library catalogues including reference collections and document supply collections (books, journals, reports, conferences, theses)
Wilson Business Periodicals Index	Internet	Indexes English language business periodicals (articles and book reviews). North American focus. Selection for indexing is by subscriber preference and has altered over time (since 1959)
EBSCO Business Source Premier	Internet	Full-text articles from over 2000 management, business, economics and information technology journals, over 600 of which are refereed. Also contains a wide range of trade and professional titles
EMERALD Fulltext	Internet	801 full-text journals from MCB University Press
Emerald Management Xtra	Internet	Provides access to 160 full text journals and reviews from 300 management journals.
Global Books in Print	Internet	English language bibliographic information for books in print from most of the world
Helecon	Internet	Combined indexes from seven European databases on business and management. European focus
Index to Conference Proceedings	Internet	Proceedings of all significant conferences held worldwide. Annual cumulation available via the website as part of the Document Supply Conference File from the British Library Integrated Catalogue
Index to Theses	Internet	A comprehensive listing of theses with abstracts accepted for higher degrees by universities in Great Britain and Ireland since 1716
Ingenta	Internet	Journals contents page service, updated daily
ISI Web of Science	Internet	Includes access to a wide range of services, including citation indexes
Key Note Reports	Internet	Key Note market information reports
Lexis Nexis Executive	Internet	News coverage from approximately 12 000 publications, national and local newspapers, press releases, transcripts of TV broadcasts, newswires, statistical bulletins, magazines and trade journals
MINTEL	Internet, CD-ROM	Mintel reports plus short business press articles used in the compilation of the reports
Research Index	Internet, print	Indexes articles and news items of financial interest that appear in the UK national newspapers, professional and trade journals (updated frequently)
Sage Publications/ SRM Database of Social Research Methodology	Internet CD-ROM	Abstracts of methodological literature published in English, German, French and Dutch since 1970
Social Science Citation Index	Internet	Access to current and retrospective bibliographic information, author abstracts, and cited references found in over 1700 social sciences journals covering more than 50 disciplines. Also covers items from approximately 3300 of the world's leading science and technology journals
UK Official Publications (UKOP)	Internet	UKOP is the official catalogue of UK official publications since 1980. Containing 450 000 records from over 2000 public bodies

Books

Books and monographs are written for specific audiences. Some are aimed at the academic market, with a theoretical slant. Others, aimed at practising professionals, may be more applied in their content. The material in books is usually presented in a more ordered and accessible manner than in journals, pulling together a wider range of topics. They are, therefore, particularly useful as introductory sources to help clarify your research question(s) and objectives or the research methods you intend to use. Some academic text-books, such as this one, are now supported by web pages providing additional information. However, books may contain out-of-date material even by the time they are published.

Newspapers

Newspapers are a good source of topical events, developments within business and government, as well as recent statistical information such as share prices. They also sometimes review recent research reports (Box 3.6). The main 'quality' newspapers have websites

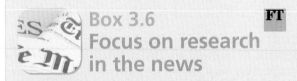

Box 3.6
Focus on research in the news

FT

Biofuel targets in EU 'will outweigh benefits'

A plan to increase the use of biofuels in Europe may do nothing to help fight climate change and incur costs that outweigh the benefits, says an internal European Union report. The unpublished study by the Joint Research Centre, the European Commission's in-house scientific institute, may complicate the Commission's plans to set a new biofuels target so that by 2020 they account for 10 per cent of transport fuels in the 27-member EU.

'The costs will almost certainly outweigh the benefits', says the report, a copy of which has been obtained by the *Financial Times*. 'The decrease in welfare caused by imposing a biofuels target' is between €33 bn ($48 bn, £25 bn) and €65 bn, the study says. 'The uncertainty is too great to say whether the EU 10 per cent biofuel target will save greenhouse gas or not', it adds.

EU leaders called for the target last year as part of a move to cut greenhouse gas emissions by 20 per cent of 1990 levels by 2020.

However, some commissioners have expressed concern about the knock-on effects of using plants for fuel. Indonesia has seen mass street protests this week over record soyabean prices triggered by US farmers opting to grow corn to supply the biofuel industry. Green

groups are also concerned that forests could be cleared for food crops that have been displaced by biofuel plantations. Corn and palm oil are among the most popular biofuel sources, though only sugar from Brazil is considered sufficiently 'green' by the Joint Research Centre as it grows quickly and produces a lot of energy.

A Commission spokeswoman said the centre's report had not been peer reviewed. She said: 'It is a contribution to the debate. We are looking at the whole picture and we will have sustainability criteria'.

In the draft directive, only those biofuel sources grown on land that was not forest or peat bog can be counted. There would also be a minimum level of greenhouse-gas saving, as some require more carbon to make than fossil fuels burn. Countries would have to monitor imports to check their origin. However, since the World Trade Organisation governs trade in biofuels, it is not possible to block them on environmental grounds.

The Joint Research Centre suggests that it would be more efficient to use biomass to generate power and that the separate transport target be scrapped. It is even doubtful of the merits of using waste products, such as straw, since transporting large quantities to biofuel factories itself requires fuel.

Adrian Bebb, of Friends of the Earth, said: 'The report has a damning verdict on the EU policy. It should be abandoned in favour of real solutions to climate change.'

Source: article by Bounds, Andrew (2008) *Financial Times*, 18 Jan. Copyright 2008 The Financial Times Limited Ltd.

carrying the main stories and supporting information. Back copies starting in the early 1990s are available on CD-ROM or online via a full-text subscription service, such as *Proquest Newspapers* (Table 3.1). Current editions of newspapers can usually be found via the Internet. Most newspapers have a dedicated website and provide access to a limited full-text service free of charge. Items in earlier issues are more difficult to access, as they are usually stored on microfilm and need to be located using printed indexes. However, you need to be careful, as newspapers may contain bias in their coverage, be it political, geographical or personal. Reporting can also be inaccurate, and you may not pick up any subsequent amendments. In addition, the news presented is filtered depending on events at the time, with priority given to more headline-grabbing stories (Stewart and Kamins, 1993).

Primary literature sources

Primary literature sources are more difficult to locate, although an increasing number are now being made available via the Internet (Table 3.1). The most accessible, and those most likely to be of use in showing how your research relates to that of other people, are reports, conference proceedings and theses.

Reports

Reports include market research reports such as those produced by Mintel and Keynote, government reports and academic reports. Even if you are able to locate these, you may find it difficult to gain access to them because they are not as widely available as books (Section 8.4). Reports are not well indexed in the tertiary literature, and you will need to rely on specific search tools such as the *British National Bibliography for Report Literature* and the British Library Public Catalogue (see Table 3.2).

The move toward 'freedom for information' by many Western governments has resulted in more information being made available via the web, for example the European Union's (EU) European Commission website and the Commission's Statistics website Eurostat. These and other governmental websites are listed in Table 8.3. European 'grey literature', including reports, conference proceedings, and discussion and policy papers, has been covered since 1980 by SIGLE (System for Information on Grey Literature in Europe) and is available from the publisher OVID.

Individual academics are also increasingly publishing reports and their research on the Internet. These can be a useful source of information. However, they may not have gone through the same review and evaluation process as journal articles and books. It is therefore important to try to assess the authority of the author, and to beware of personal bias.

Conference proceedings

Conference proceedings, sometimes referred to as symposia, are often published as unique titles within journals or as books. Most conferences will have a theme that is very specific, but some have a wide-ranging overview. Proceedings are not well indexed by tertiary literature so, as with reports, you may have to rely on specific search tools such as *Index to Conference Proceedings* and the British Library Public Catalogue (Table 3.2) as well as more general search engines such as Google. If you do locate and are able to obtain the proceedings for a conference on the theme of your research, you will have a wealth of relevant information. Many conferences have associated web pages providing abstracts and occasionally the full papers presented at the conference.

Theses

Theses are unique and so for a major research project can be a good source of detailed information; they will also be a good source of further references. Unfortunately, they can be difficult to locate and, when found, difficult to access as there may be only one copy at the awarding institution. Specific search tools are available, such as *Index to Theses* (see Table 3.2). Only research degrees such as PhD and MPhil are covered well by these tertiary resources. Research undertaken as part of a taught masters degree is not covered as systematically.

3.4 Planning your literature search strategy

It is important that you plan this search carefully to ensure that you locate relevant and up-to-date literature. This will enable you to establish what research has been previously published in your area and to relate your own research to it. All our students have found their literature search a time-consuming process, which takes far longer than expected. Fortunately, time spent planning will be repaid in time saved when searching the literature. As you start to plan your search, you need to beware of information overload! One of the easiest ways to avoid this is to start the main search for your critical review with a clearly defined research question(s), objectives and outline proposal (Sections 2.4 and 2.5). Before commencing your literature search, we suggest that you undertake further planning by writing down your search strategy and, if possible, discussing it with your project tutor. This should include:

- the parameters of your search;
- the key words and search terms you intend to use;
- the databases and search engines you intend to use;
- the criteria you intend to use to select the relevant and useful studies from all the items you find.

Whilst it is inevitable that your search strategy will be refined as your literature search progresses, we believe that such a planned approach is important as it forces you to think carefully about your research strategy and justify, at least to yourself, why you are doing what you are doing.

Defining the parameters of your search

For most research questions and objectives you will have a good idea of which subject matter is going to be relevant. You will, however, be less clear about the parameters within which you need to search. In particular, you need to be clear about the following (Bell 2005):

- language of publication (e.g. English);
- subject area (e.g. accountancy);
- business sector (e.g. manufacturing);
- geographical area (e.g. Europe);
- publication period (e.g. the last 10 years);
- literature type (e.g. refereed journals and books).

One way of starting to firm up these parameters is to re-examine your lecture notes and course textbooks in the area of your research question. While re-examining these, we suggest you make a note of subjects that appear most relevant to your research question and the names of relevant authors. These will be helpful when generating possible key words later.

For example, if your research was on the marketing benefits of arts sponsorship to UK banking organisations you might identify the subject area as marketing and sponsorship. Implicit in this is the need to think broadly. A common comment we hear from students

Box 3.7
Focus on student research

Defining parameters for a research question

Simon's research question was 'How have green issues influenced the way in which manufacturers advertise cars?' To be certain of finding material, he defined each parameter in narrow and, in most instances, broader terms:

Parameter	Narrow	Broader
Language	UK (e.g. car)	UK and USA (e.g. car and automobile)
Subject area	Green issues	Environmental issues
	Motor industry	Manufacturing
	Advertising	Marketing
Business sector	Motor industry	Manufacturing
Geographical area	UK	Europe and North America
Publication period	Last 5 years	Last 15 years
Literature type	Refereed journals and books	Journals and books

who have attempted a literature search is 'there's nothing written on my research topic'. This is usually because they have identified one or more of their parameters too narrowly (or chosen key words that do not match the control language, Section 3.5). We, therefore, recommend that if you encounter this problem you broaden one or more of your parameters to include material that your narrower search would not have located (Box 3.7).

Generating your key words

It is important at this stage to read both articles by key authors and recent review articles in the area of your research. This will help you to define your subject matter and to suggest appropriate key words. Recent review articles in your research area are often helpful here as they discuss the current state of research for a particular topic and can help you to refine your key words. In addition, they will probably contain references to other work that is pertinent to your research question(s) and objectives (Box 3.8). If you are unsure about review articles, your project tutor should be able to point you in the right direction. Another potentially useful source of references is dissertations and theses in your university's library.

After re-reading your lecture notes and textbooks and undertaking this limited reading you will have a list of subjects that appear relevant to your research project. You now need to define precisely what is relevant to your research in terms of key words.

The identification of **key words** or 'search' terms is the most important part of planning your search for relevant literature (Bell 2005). Key words are the basic terms that describe your research question(s) and objectives, and will be used to search the tertiary literature. Key words (which can include authors' surnames identified in the examination of your lecture notes and course textbooks) can be identified using one or a number

Box 3.8
Focus on management research

Using an archival research method in the framework for conducting and evaluating research

In one of the most recently read articles from the *International Journal of Management Reviews*, Srivastava (2007) uses a sophisticated method of literature review in a review of supply chain management. The article argues that there is a growing need for integrating environmentally sound choices into supply-chain management research and practice. The author peruses the literature and concludes that a broad frame of reference for green supply-chain management (GrSCM) is not adequately developed and that a succinct classification to help academicians, researchers and practitioners in understanding integrated GrSCM from a wider perspective is needed.

Srivastava covers the literature on GrSCM exhaustively from its conceptualisation, primarily taking a 'reverse logistics angle'. Using the rich body of available literature, including earlier reviews that had relatively limited perspectives, the literature on GrSCM is classified on the basis of the problem context in supply chain's major influential areas. It is also classified on the basis of methodology and approach adopted. Various mathematical tools/techniques used in literature *vis-à-vis* the contexts of GrSCM are mapped. A timeline indicating relevant papers is also provided as a ready reference.

The literature research is driven by theoretical preconsiderations and may be classified as an archival research method in the framework for conducting and evaluating research suggested by Searcy and Mentzer (2003). The process of analysis comprises the following steps:

- *Defining unit of analysis:* the unit of analysis was defined as a single research paper/book.
- *Classification context:* the classification context to be applied in the literature review to structure and classify the material was selected and defined. There were two contexts: the problem context and methodology/approach context.

- *Material evaluation:* the material was analysed and sorted according to the classification context. This allowed identification of relevant issues and interpretation of the results. Problem context and related methodology/approaches allowed classification of the reviewed literature. Srivastava argues that this can be derived deductively or inductively.
- *Collecting publications and delimiting the field:* Srivastava's literature review focuses upon books, edited volumes and journal articles only, from 1990. Library databases were used where a keyword search using some important keywords such as 'green supply chain', remanufacturing', 'green purchasing', 'green design', 'industrial ecology', 'industrial ecosystems', 'RL', 'remanufacturing' and 'waste management' were conducted.

To delimit the number of publications, empirical papers mainly addressing firm-level or specific operational issues were excluded from the review. Similarly, highly technical work on topics such as life-cycle assessment, inventory, pollution prevention and disassembly were also excluded from the review. Research with a highly ecological rather than supply chain perspective (green purchasing, industrial ecology and industrial ecosystems) was also excluded. Srivastava used the published literature from 1990 onwards to go back to other papers by cross-referencing. As the published literature is interlinked to a considerable degree, one paper (stem) leads to others (branches). So, one thread, leads to others. As references accumulated, it was found that some of them were more central and useful than others. Srivastava considered such references as seminal papers. These were also found to be generally referenced a number of times in subsequent literature. Thus, within the defined objective, this work integrates and takes forward the literature on GrSCM since its conceptualisation. About 1500 books, articles from journals and edited volumes were covered and generated a list of 227 cited references which are given at the end of the article.

References

Searcy, D.L. and Mentzer, J.T. (2003) 'A framework for conducting and evaluating research', *Journal of Accounting Literature*, 22, pp. 130–67.

Srivastava, S. (2007) 'Green supply-chain management: A state-of-the-art literature review', *International Journal of Management Reviews*, 9(1), pp. 53–80.

of different techniques in combination. Those found most useful by our students include:

Discussion

We believe you should be taking every opportunity to discuss your research. In discussing your work with others, whether face to face, by email or by letter, you will be sharing your ideas, getting feedback and obtaining new ideas and approaches. This process will help you to refine and clarify your topic.

Initial reading, dictionaries, encyclopaedias, handbooks and thesauruses

To produce the most relevant key words you may need to build on your brainstorming session with support materials such as dictionaries, encyclopedias, handbooks and thesauruses, both general and subject specific. These are also good starting points for new topics with which you may be unfamiliar and for related subject areas. Initial reading, particularly of recent review articles, may also be of help here. Project tutors, colleagues and librarians can also be useful sources of ideas.

It is also possible to obtain definitions via the Internet. The online search engine Google offers a 'define' search option (by typing 'Define:[enter term]') that provides links to websites providing definitions. Definitions are also offered in free online encyclopaedias such as Wikipedia (see Box 3.9).[1] These are often available in multiple languages and, although

---

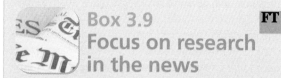

Box 3.9
Focus on research in the news   **FT**

Google has taken direct aim at Wikipedia with a project designed to supplant the collectively produced encyclopedia as the primary source for basic information on the web. Known as 'Knol', and currently restricted to a limited test, the service is a highly ambitious attempt to collect and organise 'user-generated information' in all fields of knowledge.

The move echoes other Google efforts to transform online behaviour. With Google's service, anyone will eventually be able to write a web page about any topic they want, and have it indexed by Google and other search engines. Authors will also be able to benefit from any advertising placed on the page. Google has given few details about how it would rank submissions to highlight the most accurate or useful, but said user ratings would be important.

'A Knol on a particular topic is meant to be the first thing someone who searches for this topic for the first time will want to read', Udi Manber, a Google engineer, wrote on a blog post that announced the project. That role is often taken by Wikipedia entries, which frequently appear high on Google's and other search engines' results, making the collective encyclopedia one of the 10 most visited sites.

The design of the Google project seeks to address some of the fundamental issues that have hampered the controversial Wikipedia. Entries in the encyclopedia are anonymous and often lead to heated 'edit wars', as people with rival opinions compete to change items. By contrast, Google plans to identify its writers and avoid the collective editing process altogether. 'The key idea behind the Knol project is to highlight authors', Mr Manber said. He added Google expected rival notes to appear on many topics: 'Competition of ideas is a good thing'. That approach will avoid the 'problems of governance that come from trying to run a collaborative community' like Wikipedia, said Larry Sanger, a founder of the website who split with that project over its failure to apply stricter editing policies.

Source: article by Waters, Richard (2007) *Financial Times*, 15 Dec.

---

[1] The Internet address for Wikipedia is http://www.wikipedia.org/.

anyone is allowed to edit the entries, inappropriate changes are usually removed quickly (Wikipedia 2008). However, whilst these websites may be useful for a quick reference or in helping to define keywords, your university will almost certainly expect you to justify the definitions in your research project using refereed journal articles or textbooks.

Brainstorming

Brainstorming has already been outlined as a technique for helping you to develop your research question (Section 2.3). However, it is also helpful for generating key words. Either individually or as part of a group, you write down all the words and short phrases that come to mind on your research topic (Box 3.10). These are then evaluated and key words (and phrases) selected.

Box 3.10
Focus on student research

Generating key words

Han's research question was 'How do the actual management requirements of a school pupil record administration system differ from those suggested by the literature?' She brainstormed this question with her peer group, all of whom were teachers in Hong Kong. The resulting list included the following key words and phrases:

schools, pupil records, administration, user requirements, computer, management information system,

access, legislation, information, database, security, UK, Hong Kong, theories

The group evaluated these and others. As a result, the following key words (and phrases) were selected:

pupil records, management information system, computer, database, user requirement

Dictionaries and encyclopaedias were used subsequently to add to the choice of key words:

student record, MIS, security

Han made a note of these prior to using them in combination to search the tertiary literature sources.

Relevance trees

Relevance trees provide a useful method of bringing some form of structure to your literature search and of guiding your search process (Sharp *et al.* 2002). They look similar to an organisation chart and are a hierarchical 'graph-like' arrangement of headings and subheadings (Box 3.11). These headings and subheadings describe your research question(s) and objectives and may be key words (including authors' names) with which you can search. Relevance trees are often constructed after brainstorming. They enable you to decide either with help or on your own (Jankowicz 2005):

- which key words are directly relevant to your research question(s) and objectives;
- which areas you will search first and which your search will use later;
- which areas are more important – these tend to have more branches.

To construct a relevance tree:

1 Start with your research question or objective at the top level.
2 Identify two or more subject areas that you think are important.
3 Further subdivide each major subject area into sub-areas that you think are of relevance.
4 Further divide the sub-areas into more precise sub-areas that you think are of relevance.

5 Identify those areas that you need to search immediately and those that you particularly need to focus on. Your project tutor will be of particular help here.

6 As your reading and reviewing progress, add new areas to your relevance tree.

Computer software to help generate relevance trees, such as Inspiration (2008) and MindGenius (2008), is also increasingly available in universities. Using this software also allows you to attach notes to your relevance tree and can help generate an initial structure for your literature review.

3.5 Conducting your literature search

Your literature search will probably be conducted using a variety of approaches:

- searching using tertiary literature sources;
- obtaining relevant literature (Section 3.6) referenced in books and journal articles you have already read;
- scanning and browsing secondary literature in your library;
- searching using the Internet.

Eventually it is likely you will be using a variety of these in combination. However, we suggest that you start your search by obtaining relevant literature that has been referenced in books and articles you have already read. Although books are unlikely to give adequate up-to-date coverage of your research question, they provide a useful starting point and usually contain some references to further reading. Reading these will enable you to refine your research question(s), objectives and the associated key words prior to

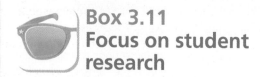

Box 3.11
Focus on student research

Using a relevance tree

Sadie's research question was 'Is there a link between benchmarking and Total Quality Management?' After

brainstorming her question, she decided to construct a relevance tree using the key words and phrases that had been generated.

Using her relevance tree Sadie identified those areas that she needed to search immediately (underlined) and those that she particularly needed to focus on (starred*):

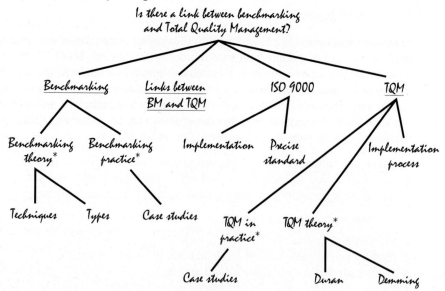

searching using tertiary literature sources. It will also help you to see more clearly how your research relates to previous research, and will provide fresh insights.

Tertiary literature sources

A variety of tertiary literature is available to help you in your search. Most of these publications are called indexes and abstracts, and a selection will be accessible via the Internet or held by your university library. It is very tempting with easy access to the Internet to start your literature search with an Internet search engine. Whilst this can retrieve some useful information it must be treated with care. Your project report is expected to be an academic piece of work and hence must use academic sources. Therefore it is essential that you use tertiary sources that provide access to academic literature. Many of these can now be easily accessed via the Internet anyway. An index will, as its name suggests, index articles from a range of journals and sometimes books, chapters from books, reports, theses, conferences and research. The information provided will be sufficient to locate the item – for example, for journal articles:

- author or authors of the article;
- date of publication;
- title of the article;
- title of the journal;
- volume and part number of the journal issue;
- page numbers of the article.

Most index searches will be undertaken to find articles using key words, including the author's name. Occasionally you may wish to search by finding those authors who have referenced (cited) a key article after it has been published. A citation index enables you to do this as it lists by author the other authors who have cited that author's publications subsequent to their publication.

An **abstract** provides the same information as an index but also includes a summary of the article, hence the term abstract. This abstract can be useful in helping you to assess the content and relevance of an article to your research before obtaining a copy. You should beware of using abstracts, as a substitute for the full article, as a source of information for your research. They contain only a summary of the article and are likely to exclude much of relevance.

Indexes and abstracts are produced in printed and electronic (computerised) formats, the latter often being referred to as online databases. This is the term we shall use to refer to all electronic information sources. With the increasing amount of information available electronically, printed indexes and abstracts are often overlooked. Yet, they can still provide a valuable resource, providing a varied and sometimes more specific range of information. An increasing number of online databases contain full-text articles. This has helped both to simplify literature searching and to make it a more seamless process, with the searching and retrieval of the full text available from the same source. Most of these online databases will allow you to print, save or email your results. The latter two options will obviously help save you printing costs.

Access to the majority of databases that you will use via the Internet will be paid for by a subscription from your university. There are, however, some pay-as-you-use databases, where the cost of the search is passed on to the user. Online databases provide a wealth of information. Whilst many online databases are intuitive to use, it is still advisable to obtain a librarian's help or to attend a training session prior to your search to find out about the specific features available. It is also vital that you plan and prepare your search in advance so your time is not wasted. For many databases, password protected access is now possible from remote sites such as home or work as well as from your university. Your librarian should have more information on this. An additional source of information via the Internet, which our students have found useful, is publishers' web pages. These often include journals' content pages (see Table 3.4).

Most university library OPACs (online public access catalogues) are now accessible via the Internet (see Table 3.5 on p. 87). These provide a very useful means of locating resources. If you identify useful collections of books and journals, it is possible to make use of other university libraries in the vacations. Within the UK, the SCONUL Vacation Access Scheme gives details of access policies of the libraries in UK higher-education institutions.[2]

To ensure maximum coverage in your search you need to use all appropriate abstracts and indexes. One mistake many people make is to restrict their searches to one or two business and management tertiary sources rather than to use a variety. The coverage of each abstract and index differs in both geographical coverage and type of journal (Section 3.3). In addition, an abstract or index may state that it indexes a particular journal yet may do so only selectively. This emphasises the importance of using a range of databases to ensure a wide coverage of available literature. Some of those more frequently used are outlined in Table 3.2. However, new databases are being developed all the time so it is worth asking a librarian for advice.

Searching using tertiary literature

Once your key words have been identified, searching using tertiary literature is a relatively straightforward process. You need to:

1 ensure that your key words match the controlled index language (unless you can use free text searching);
2 search appropriate printed and database sources;
3 note precise details, including the search strings used, of the actual searches you have undertaken for each database;
4 note the full reference of each item found; this can normally be done by cutting and pasting the references.

Tranfield *et al.* (2003), in their article on **systematic review**, emphasise the importance of reporting your literature search strategy in sufficient detail to ensure that your search could be replicated (Boxes 3.12, 3.13). Your review will be based on the subset of those items found which you consider are relevant.

Printed sources

Although they are increasingly rare, printed indexes and abstracts require a different searching technique from electronic databases. The coverage of printed indexes tends to be smaller and possibly more specialised than that of databases. Unlike databases, it is normally only possible to search by author or one broad subject heading, although some cross-references may be included. Because they are paper based, each issue or annual accumulation must be searched individually, which can be time consuming.

Databases

Most databases, in contrast, allow more precise searches using combinations of search terms. These can include indexed key words, which will need to match the database's **controlled index language** of pre-selected terms and phrases or 'descriptors'. These can include specified subject words, author names, and journal titles. If your key words do

---

[2]Details of these can be found on the Internet at: http://www.sconul.ac.uk/use_lib/vacation.html.

Box 3.12
Focus on management research

Conducting a review of the literature through the process of systematic review

Tranfield *et al.* (2003) emphasise that undertaking a review of the literature is an important part of any research project. The researcher maps and assesses the relevant intellectual territory in order to specify a research question which will develop knowledge of the topic. In their view, however, traditional 'narrative' reviews frequently lack thoroughness, and in many cases are not undertaken as genuine pieces of investigatory science. Consequently, they can lack a means for making sense of what the collection of studies is saying. These reviews can suffer from researcher bias and a lack of rigour. In addition, Tranfield *et al.* assert that the use of reviews of the available evidence to provide insights and guidance for intervention into operational needs of practitioners and policymakers has largely been of secondary importance. For practitioners, making sense of a mass of often-contradictory evidence has become more difficult. Inadequate or incomplete evidence seriously impedes policy formulation and implementation.

In their article Tranfield *et al.* explore ways in which evidence-informed management reviews might be achieved through the process of systematic review used in the medical sciences. Over the last 15 years, medical science has attempted to improve the review process by synthesising research in a systematic, transparent, and reproducible manner with the twin aims of enhancing the knowledge base and informing policymaking and practice.

According to Tranfield *et al.* and Denyer and Neely (2004) systematic review includes:

- the development of clear and precise aims and objectives for the literature review;
- pre-planned search methods;
- a comprehensive search of all potentially relevant articles;
- the use of clear assessment criteria in the selection of articles for review;
- assessment of the quality of the research in each article and of the strength of the findings;
- synthesising the individual studies using a clear framework;
- presenting the results in a balanced, impartial and comprehensive manner.

Both Tranfield *et al.* and Denyer and Neely (2004) outline how the review was undertaken. This includes how the key words used in the search were identified, and what they were; how the key words were combined into search strings using Boolean operators; the databases searched and the total numbers of articles found; and appendices that list the relevance criteria used to exclude and include articles in the review. Denyer and Neely argue that this should enable readers to determine the reasonableness of the decisions taken by the reviewers when writing their reviews as well as the appropriateness of the conclusions in each review.

not match those in the controlled index language, your search will be unsuccessful. You, therefore, need to check your key words with the 'index' or 'browse' option prior to searching. This is especially useful to establish how an author is indexed or whether hyphens should be used when entering specific terms. Some databases will also have a 'thesaurus' which links words in the controlled index language to other terms. Some thesauruses will provide a definition of the term used as well as indicating other broader subject areas, more specific subject areas or subjects related to the original term. Despite using these tools, your searches may still be unsuccessful. The most frequent causes of failure are summarised in Box 3.13 as a checklist.

Once individual key words have been checked, subsequent searches normally use a combination of key words linked using **Boolean logic**. These are known as **search strings** and enable you to combine, limit or widen the variety of items found using 'link terms' (Table 3.3). Boolean logic can also be used to construct search strings using dates, journal

Box 3.13
Checklist

Minimising problems with your key words

✔ Is the spelling incorrect? Behaviour is spelt with a 'u' in the UK but without in the USA.

✔ Is the language incorrect? Chemists in the UK but drug stores in the USA.

✔ Are you using incorrect terminology? In recent years some terms have been replaced by others, such as 'redundancy' being replaced by 'downsizing'.

✔ Are you using recognised acronyms and abbreviations? For example, UK for United Kingdom or ICI instead of Imperial Chemical Industries.

✔ Are you avoiding jargon and using accepted terminology? For example, downsizing rather than redundancy.

✔ Are you avoiding words that are not in the controlled index language?

Table 3.3 Common link terms that use Boolean logic

Link term	Purpose	Example	Outcome
AND	Narrows search	Recruitment AND interviewing AND skills	Only articles containing all three key words selected
OR	Widens search	Recruitment OR selection	Articles with at least one key word selected
NOT	Excludes terms from search	Recruitment NOT selection	Selects articles containing the key word 'recruitment' that do not contain the key word 'selection'
***(truncation)**	Uses word stems to pick up different	Motivat*	Selects articles with: Motivate Motivation Motivating
? (wild card)	Picks up different spellings	behavio?r	Selects articles with: Behavior Behaviour

titles and names of organisations or people. Initially it may be useful to limit your search to journal titles to which your university subscribes. It may also be valuable to narrow your search to specific years, especially if you are finding a wealth of items and need to concentrate on the most up to date. By contrast, searching by author allows you to broaden your search to find other work by known researchers in your area.

You can also search just one or more specified fields in the database such as the author, title or abstract. This may be useful if you wish to find articles by a key author in your subject area. Alternatively, many databases allow you to search the entire database rather than just the controlled vocabulary using **free text searching**. Free text searching is increasingly common for electronic publications both on CD-ROM and accessed via the Internet, in particular quality newspapers and journals. These may not have a controlled index language. There are, however, problems with using a free text search. In particular, the context of a key word may be inappropriate, leading to retrieval of numerous irrelevant articles and information overload.

Scanning and browsing

Any search will find only some of the relevant literature. You will therefore also need to scan and browse the literature. New publications such as journals are unlikely to be indexed immediately in tertiary literature, so you will need to browse these publications to gain an idea of their content. In contrast, scanning will involve you going through individual items such as a journal article to pick out points that relate to your own research. It is particularly important that you browse and scan trade and professional journals, as these are less likely to be covered by the tertiary literature.

To make browsing and scanning easier you should:

- identify when those journals that are the most relevant are published and regularly browse them;
- browse new book displays in libraries;
- scan new book reviews in journals and newspapers;
- scan publishers' new book catalogues where available;
- discuss your research with your project tutor and librarians, who may be aware of other relevant literature.

Internet access to resources now allows you to browse journals that may not be held in, or accessible from, your university library. Many publishers make the contents pages of their journals available without charge on the web (Table 3.4) and may offer an article alert service where they will provide a regular email update of articles in your area of interest. Alternatively, databases such as Ingenta provide access to thousands of journals' contents pages (Table 3.2). Professional journals may also be accessible through the web page of the professional organisation (Table 8.2). Many publishers make their current book catalogues available on the Internet, and these can be accessed either directly (Table 3.4) or through the publishers' catalogues' home page (see Table 3.5). In addition, websites of bookshops such as Amazon, Blackwell and the Internet Book Shop provide access to catalogues of books in print. These can usually be searched by author, title and subject, and may have reviews attached (Table 3.4). In addition, some bookseller websites (and Google Books) have a facility whereby you can view selected pages from the book. However, as when using electronic indexes and abstracts, it is important that you keep full details of the literature you have scanned and browsed (Box 3.14). As well as enabling you to outline the method you used for your literature review, it will also help prevent you repeating searches you have already undertaken.

Searching the Internet

The development of the Internet has revolutionised information gathering, including searching for literature. It will provide you with access to resources that may be of use either for your literature review or as secondary data (Chapter 8). However, you should beware, as these resources may be difficult to locate and the quality of the material is highly variable. This is emphasised by Clausen (1996:4), who likens the Internet to:

> . . . a huge vandalized library where someone has destroyed the catalogue and removed the front matter and indexes from most of the books. In addition thousands of unorganized fragments are added daily by a myriad of cranks, sages and persons with time on their hands who launch their unfiltered messages into cyberspace.

Table 3.4 Selected publishers' and bookshops' Internet addresses

Name	Internet address	Contents
Publishers		
Blackwell Publishers	http://www.blackwellpublishing.com	Books and journals
Cambridge University Press	http://www.cup.cam.ac.uk	Books and journals; links to other university presses and publishing-related services
Pearson Education Limited	http://www.pearsoned.co.uk	Business and management books for practitioners and students. Links to book-specific web pages
Office of Public Sector Information	http://www.opsi.gov.uk	OPSI publications, including full text of Statutory Instruments and Public Acts
Emerald	http://www.emeraldinsight.com	Over 100 professional and academic management journals
Open University Press	http://www.openup.co.uk	Books and journals
Oxford University Press	http://www.oup.co.uk	Books and journals, including full-text online journals, a database of abstracts
Prentice Hall	http://www.pearsoned.co.uk	Books and other study materials
Routledge	http://www.routledge.com	Books
Sage	http://www.sagepub.co.uk	Books, journals, software, CD-ROMs
Cengage (previously Thomson)	http://www.cengagelearning.co.uk	Books, and other study materials
Bookshops		
Amazon	http://www.amazon.co.uk	Searchable database principally of books (UK site)
	http://www.amazon.com	Searchable database principally of books (USA site)
Blackwell	http://www.blackwell.co.uk	Searchable database principally of books
Internet Book Shop UK	http://www.ibuk.com	Searchable database principally of books
Abe Books	http://www.abebooks.co.uk	New, second-hand, rare, or out-of-print, through 13 500 independent booksellers.
The Book Depository	http://www.bookdepository.co.uk/	
The Book Place	http://www.thebookplace.co.uk	Searchable database principally of books
TSO (The Stationery Office)	http://www.tsoshop.co.uk	Searchable database of UK books in print. Especially useful for UK government reports

NB: All services in this table were free at the time of writing.

Table 3.5 Selected Internet search tools and their coverage

Name	Internet address	Comment
General search engines		
Alta Vista Search	http://www.altavista.com	Searches web and Usenet newsgroups
Google	http://www.google.com	Access to over 3 billion documents
Google UK	http://www.google.co.uk	
Google Scholar	http://scholar.google.com/	Access to academic journals, theses, books, journals and abstracts from a limited number of academic and professional organisations. Access to the full text is often dependent on an institution's subscription to a journal or service
HotBot	http://www.hotbot.co.uk/	Searches web; useful features include sorting by date and media type
Lycos	http://www.lycos.com	Searches web, gopher and ftp sites; offers both key word and subject searching
Specialised search engines		
UK government	http://www.direct.gov.uk	Searches central and local government websites and government agencies
Information gateways		
Biz/Ed	http://www.bized.co.uk	Information service, links economics and business students and teachers and information providers
BUBL subject tree	http://bubl.ac.uk	Links to a vast range of Internet resources by alphabetical subject list or by class (subject) number order
Human Resource Management Resources on the Internet	http://www.nbs.ntu.ac.uk/research//depts/hrm/links.php	Annotated list of links. List split into sub-categories, and provides short description of content
HERO (UK Universities and Colleges OPACs)	http://www.hero.ac.uk	Links to UK university and college online public access (library) catalogues (OPACs)
Pinakes	http://www.hw.ac.uk/libWWW/irn/pinakes/pinakes.html	Links to major information gateways to Internet resources (especially UK based)
Publishers' catalogues homepage	http://www.lights.ca/publisher/	Links to major publishers' websites, listed alphabetically by country
Resource Discovery Network	http://www.rdn.ac.uk/	Subject-based information and Internet tutorials
SOSIG UK Business and Industrial Management Resource	http://www.sosig.ac.uk/roads/subject-listing/roads/subject-listing/	Detailed descriptions and links to UK business and industrial and industrial management sites
Subject directories		
Yahoo	http://dir.yahoo.com/	Subject-based directory
Yahoo UK	http://uk.yahoo.com	Optionally limits searches to just UK and Ireland
	http://uk.dir.yahoo.com/news_and_media/newspapers	Comprehensive listing of newspapers available on the Internet, worldwide
Yellow Pages UK	http://www.yell.co.uk	Telephone yellow pages with useful links to UK companies' home pages

There is a variety of approaches you can use for searching the Internet. These are summarised in Figure 3.3. Printed guides are available and can be a useful starting point for information. However, because of the rate at which the Internet is growing and the fact that material can literally disappear overnight, these guidebooks are likely to

Box 3.14
Focus on student research

Searching electronic indexes and abstracts

Matthew described his research project using the key words 'small business' and 'finance'. Unfortunately, he encountered problems when carrying out his search using one of the online databases of full text and abstracts for business, management and economics journals to which his university subscribed:

- When he entered the key word 'small business', he retrieved references to over 162 000 items many of which were in trade magazines.
- He was unsure how to combine his key words into search strings to make his search more specific.
- Full-text versions were not available for the many of the most recent items retrieved.

After discussing the problem, the librarian showed Matthew how to use the advanced search option of the online database. Using this, Matthew first searched using the terms 'small business' and 'finance' combined as a search string. This still resulted in over 500 items being highlighted.

He then refined his search further by limiting it to the collection of scholarly (peer reviewed) journals. This resulted in just over 200 items being retrieved. Matthew made a note of the details of his search:

Database:	Business Source Complete
Collection:	Scholarly (peer reviewed) journals
Dates:	1980 to 2008
Search:	small business AND finance
Fields searched:	Abstract
Date of search:	38 June 2008
Total items retrieved:	219

He then copied the references for these items (articles) onto his MP3 player. As Matthew scrolled through these, he noted that some of them had direct links to copies of the full text stored as a .pdf file. For many of the others, the librarian informed him that he could access the full text using different online databases. However, he still needed to assess each article's relevance to his research before obtaining full copies.

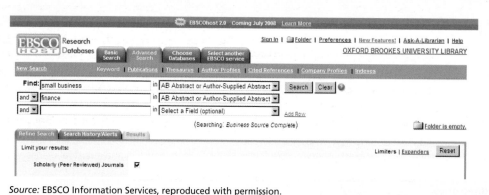

Source: EBSCO Information Services, reproduced with permission.

become out of date extremely quickly. Alternatively, you can use websites dedicated to providing support information on searching the Internet. One such example that our students have found useful is that provided by Phil Bradley, an information expert.[3] This contains information on different search engines, articles on Internet searching and web page and website design and is regularly updated. Another useful site is hosted by RBA Information Services.[4] This contains an excellent directory of business-related websites

---

[3]The Internet address of the home page of this site is http://www.philb.com/.
[4]The Internet address of the home page of this site is http://www.rba.co.uk.

as well as a wealth of more generic information on searching the Internet. Once again, we recommend that you keep full details of the Internet searches you have undertaken, making a note of:

- the search engine used;
- the precise search undertaken;
- the date when the search was undertaken;
- the total number of items retrieved.

Home pages

Addresses of Internet sites or home pages (such as http://www.surrey.ac.uk) can be the quickest and most direct method of accessing these resources. Addresses can be obtained from many sources, the most frequently used of which are guidebooks (e.g. Hahn 2008), newspaper reviews, articles in journals, librarians and lecturers. Home pages, which can have multiple linked pages and hypertext links whereby pointing and clicking on the screen takes you to another website, are similar to a title or contents page. Although home pages often contain publicity for a company or institution, they are an excellent way of navigating around the Internet, as they bring a selection of Internet site addresses and search tools together (Table 3.5). A problem with going directly to one address is that your search is constrained by other people's ideas. Similarly, hypertext links are limited by other people's ideas and the way they have linked pages.

Search tools

Search tools, often referred to as **search engines**, are probably the most important method of Internet searching for your literature review as they will enable you to locate most current and up-to-date items. Although normally accessed through home pages, each search tool will have its own address (Table 3.5).

Most search tools search by key words or subject trees. A *subject tree* is similar to a contents page or index. Some are in the form of alphabetical subject lists, whereas others are in hierarchical groups of subjects that are then further subdivided with links to more narrowly focused subject groups. It is vital that you do not rely on one search tool but use a variety, noting and evaluating each as you use them. Each search tool will have different interfaces, ways of searching and methods of displaying information. They will search different areas of the Internet and are likely to display different results.

Search tools can be divided into four distinct categories (Figure 3.3, Table 3.5):

- general search engines;
- meta search engines;
- specialised search engines and information gateways;
- subject directories.

Most search engines index every separate document. In contrast, subject directories index only the 'most important' Internet documents. Therefore, if you are using a clear term to search for an unknown vaguely described document, use a search engine. If you are looking for a document about a particular topic, use a subject directory (Habrakan *et al.* 2008).

General search engines such as Google and Google Scholar (Box 3.15) normally search parts of the Internet using key words and Boolean logic (Table 3.3) or a phrase. Each search engine uses an automated computer process to index and search, often resulting in a very large number of sites being found. As people have not evaluated these sites, many are usually inappropriate or unreliable. As no two general search engines search in precisely the same way it is advisable (and often necessary) to use more than one. In contrast, meta

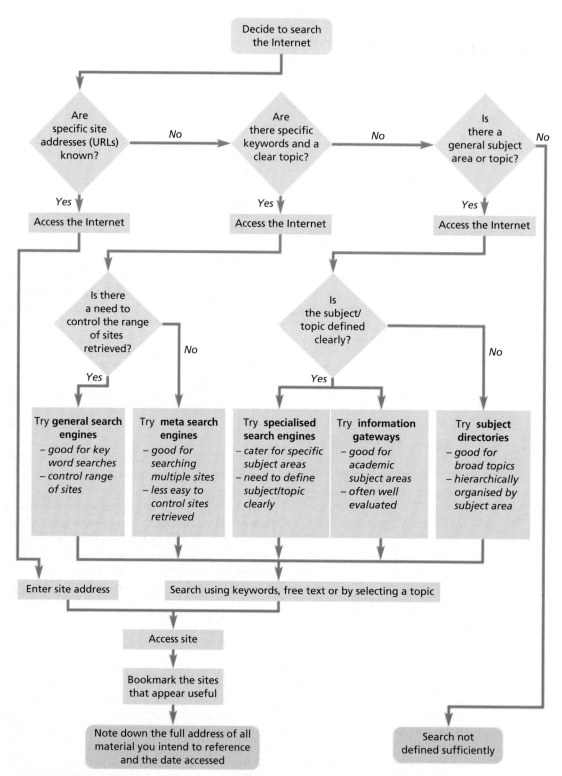

Figure 3.3 Searching the Internet

Source: © Mark Saunders, Philip Lewis, Adrain Thornhill and Martin Jenkins 2003.

search engines allow you to search using a selection of search engines at the same time, using the same interface. This makes searching easier, and the search can be faster. Unfortunately, it is less easy to control the sites that are retrieved. Consequently, meta search engines often generate more inappropriate or unreliable sites than general search engines.

Specialised search engines cater for specific subject areas. To use these it is necessary to define your general subject area prior to your search. Information gateways also require you to define your subject area. Information gateways are often compiled by staff from departments in academic institutions. Although the number of websites obtained is fewer, they can be far more relevant, as each site is evaluated prior to being added to the gateway.

Subject directories are hierarchically organised indexes categorised into subject areas, and are useful for searching for broad topics. As people normally compile them, their content has been partly censored and evaluated. Consequently, the number of sites retrieved is fewer but they usually provide material that is more appropriate. Most of the subject directories now offer some form of key word search and links to other search tools.

Search tools are becoming more prolific and sophisticated all the time. Be careful: their use can be extremely time consuming. Your search will probably locate a mass of resources, many of which will be irrelevant to you. It is also easy to become sidetracked to more interesting and glossy websites not relevant to your research needs! There are an increasing number of web-based tutorials to help you learn to search the web. One of these, Marketing Insights' *Smarter Online Searching Guide*, is available via this book's web page. This highlights using search tools, including Advanced search in Google and online e-business resources.

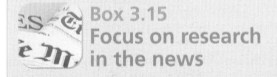

Box 3.15
Focus on research in the news

Microsoft reveals answer to Google Scholar

Microsoft has announced the release of an English-language beta version of Windows Live Academic Search, a service for searching academic journals. The release is available in Australia, Germany, Italy, Japan, Spain and the United Kingdom, as well as in the United States, and is marketed as an alternative to Google Scholar or SciFinder Scholar.

Academic Search indexes library-subscribed content and supports OpenURL, the library standard currently used for linking to subscription-based content. To operate Academic Search, libraries or research facilities must provide Microsoft with information on their OpenURL link resolver, a vendor that creates and manages the customized links to content. Academic search can then provide direct access links to the full text materials, based on their institutions' subscriptions.

Academic Search includes the expected sorting and citation-compiling features common to academic-journal searching. Researchers can control the amount of immediate information that comes up in search results in a variety of ways. Search results link directly to full articles from the publisher, if the user is researching from an institution that subscribes to that publishers' content.

Material that is not subscribed to by the searching institution still comes up in a search, with abstract and all relevant publication information available.

Microsoft announced that Academic Search currently covers only physics, electrical engineering and computer science, but it is working with publishers to expand content access. Upon testing, however, the system does seem to link to humanities journal portals such as the Oxford Journals' Forum for Modern Languages Studies.

In addition to academic returns, the current version of Academic Search provides search results for portals named 'Web', 'News', 'Local' and 'Feeds'. The service is undoubtedly a direct attempt to compete with Google Scholar. Academic Search can also be integrated into Windows Live, the new online Microsoft desktop service.

Source: article by Lombardi, Candace (2006) ZDNet News, 12 Apr. (http://news.zdnet.com/2100-9588_22-6060314.html). Used with permission of ZDNET.com copyright © 2008. All rights reserved.

Bookmarking

Once you have found a useful Internet site, you can note its address electronically. This process is termed 'bookmarking' or 'add to favourites' depending on the Internet browser you use. It uses the software to note the Internet address, and means that you will be able to access it again directly. The vast amount of resources available, and the fact that resources, home pages and sites can be added and deleted by their producers, means it is vital to keep a record of the addresses and a note of the date you accessed it (Section 3.7). These will be needed to reference your sources when you write your critical review (Section 3.2). When sufficient sites have been bookmarked, it is possible to arrange them in whatever hierarchical way you wish.

3.6 Obtaining and evaluating the literature

Obtaining the literature

After your initial search of books and journal articles, tertiary literature will provide you with details of what literature is available and where to locate it. The next stage (Figure 3.1) is to obtain these items. To do this you need to:

1 Check your library catalogue to find out whether your library holds the appropriate publication. Remember many libraries now, rather than holding publications such as journals and newspapers in paper form or CD-ROM, provide access via the Internet;
2 (For those publications that are held by your library or available via the Internet) note their location; and
   a Find the publication and scan it to discover whether it is likely to be worth reading thoroughly – for articles it is often possible to make a reasonable assessment of relevance using the abstract; or
   b Browse other books and journals with similar class marks to see whether they may also be of use;
3 (For those items that are not held by your library or available via the Internet) order the item from another library on **inter-library loan**. This is not a free service so make sure you really need it first. Our students have found that, in general, it is only worthwhile to use inter-library loan for articles from refereed journals and books.

Evaluating the literature

Two questions frequently asked by our students are 'How do I know what I'm reading is relevant?' and 'How do I know when I've read enough?' Both of these are concerned with the process of evaluation. They involve defining the scope of your review and assessing the value of the items that you have obtained in helping you to answer your research question(s). Although there are no set ways of approaching these questions, our students have found the following advice helpful.

You should, of course, read all the literature that is closely related to your research question(s) and objectives. The literature that is most likely to cause problems is that which is less closely related (Gall *et al*. 2006). For some research questions, particularly for new research areas, there is unlikely to be much closely related literature and so you will have to review more broadly. For research questions where research has been going on for some years you may be able to focus on more closely related literature.

Assessing relevance and value

Assessing the relevance of the literature you have collected to your research depends on your research question(s) and objectives. Remember that you are looking for relevance, not critically assessing the ideas contained within. When doing this, it helps to have thought about and made a note of the criteria for inclusion and exclusion prior to assessing each item of literature. In contrast, assessing the value of the literature you have collected is concerned with the quality of the research that has been undertaken. As such it is concerned with issues such as methodological rigour and theory robustness as well as the quality of the arguments. For example, you need to beware of managerial autobiographies, where a successful entrepreneur's or managing director's work experiences are presented as the way to achieve business success (Fisher 2007) and articles in trade magazines. The knowledge presented in such books and articles may well be subjective rather than based upon systematic research.

Box 3.16 provides a checklist to help you in this process.

Remember to make notes about the relevance of each item as you read it and the reasons why you came to your conclusion. You may need to include your evaluation as part of your critical review.

Assessing sufficiency

Your assessment of whether you have read a sufficient amount is even more complex. It is impossible to read everything, as you would never start to write your critical review, let alone your project report. Yet you need to be sure that your critical review discusses what research has already been undertaken and that you have positioned your research project in the wider context, citing the main writers in the field (Section 3.2). One clue that you have achieved this is when further searches provide mainly references to items you have already read. You also need to check what constitutes an acceptable amount of reading, in terms of both quality and quantity, with your project tutor.

Box 3.16
Checklist

Evaluating the relevance and value of literature to your research

Relevance

✔ How recent is the item?

✔ Is the item likely to have been superseded?

✔ Are the research questions or objectives sufficiently close to your own to make it relevant to your own research (in other words, does the item meet your relevance criteria for inclusion)?

✔ Is the context sufficiently different to make it marginal to your research question(s) and objectives (in other words, is the item excluded by your relevance criteria)?

✔ Have you seen references to this item (or its author) in other items that were useful?

✔ Does the item support or contradict your arguments? For either it will probably be worth reading!

Value

✔ Does the item appear to be biased? For example, does it use an illogical argument, emotionally toned words or appear to choose only those cases that support the point being made? Even if it is, it may still be relevant to your critical review!

✔ What are the methodological omissions within the work (e.g. sample selection, data collection, data analysis)? Even if there are many it still may be of relevance!

✔ Is the precision sufficient? Even if it is imprecise it may be the only item you can find and so still of relevance!

✔ Does the item provide guidance for future research?

Sources: authors' experience; Bell (2005); Fisher (2007); Jankowicz (2005); McNeill (2005).

3.7 Recording the literature

The literature search, as you will now be aware, is a vital part of your research project, in which you will invest a great deal of time and effort. As you read each item, you need to ask yourself how it contributes to your research question(s) and objectives and to make *notes* with this focus (Bell 2005). When doing this, many students download and print copies of articles or photocopy articles and pages from books to ensure that they have all the material. We believe that, even if you print or photocopy, you still need to make notes. The process of note making will help you to think through the ideas in the literature in relation to your research.

In addition to making notes, Sharp *et al.* (2002) identify three sets of information you need to record. These are:

- bibliographic details;
- brief summary of content;
- supplementary information.

Until the advent of inexpensive microcomputers it was usual to write this information on *index cards*. Database software such as Microsoft's Access™ or specialist bibliographic software such as Reference Manager for Windows™ or EndNote™ provide a powerful and flexible alternative method for recording the literature, although they will probably mean noting it down and transferring it to your database later. Recording can seem very tedious, but it must be done. We have seen many students frantically repeating searches for items that are crucial to their research because they failed to record all the necessary details in their database of references.

Box 3.17
Focus on student research

Undertaking an Internet search

Ceinwen's research question was reasonably defined, if somewhat broad. She wanted to assess the impact of European enlargement on small to medium-sized organisations. As part of her search strategy she decided, in addition to the academic databases of business and management journals, also to search the Internet using a general search engine. Her first key word 'European enlargement' revealed that there were over 505 000 sites and displayed the first 10. Of these, although in the broad topic area, none appeared to be relevant as they were not related specifically to small to medium-sized enterprises (SMEs):

▶ Box 3.17
Focus on student research

She decided to refine her search using the advanced search features of the search engine. Although the search engine still found over 1200 sites, the content of the first 10 appeared more relevant to her research question:

Ceinwen looked at the second site and found that it contained details of a conference entitled 'Challenges for Entrepreneurship and Small Business Development in the Context of European Enlargement' hosted by a University School of Management. She made a note of the keynote speakers so that she could search for academic articles written by them using her university's online databases. She then proceeded to look at the next site in her list.

Bibliographic details

For some project reports you will be required to include a **bibliography**. Convention dictates that this should include all the relevant items you consulted for your project, including those not referred to directly in the text. For others, you will be asked to include only a list of **references** for those items referred to directly in the text. The **bibliographic details** contained in both need to be sufficient to enable readers to find the original items. These details are summarised in Table 3.6.

Table 3.6 Bibliographic details required

Journal	Book	Chapter in an edited book
• Author(s) – surname, first name initials	• Author(s) – surname, first name initials	• Author(s) – surname, first name initials
• Year of publication (in parentheses)	• Year of publication (in parentheses)	• Year of publication (in parentheses)
• Title of article	• Title and subtitle of book (underlined)	• Title of chapter
• Title of journal (underlined)	• Edition	• Author(s) of book – surname, first name initials
• Volume	• Place of publication	• Title and subtitle of book (underlined)
• Part/issue	• Publisher	• Edition
• Page numbers (preceded by 'p.' for page or 'pp.' for pages)		• Place of publication
		• Publisher
		• Page numbers of chapter

If an item has been taken from an electronic source you need to record as much of the information in Table 3.6 as is available along with details of format (e.g. CD-ROM). If you located the item via the Internet, you need to record the full address of the resource and the date you accessed the information as well (Appendix 1). This address is often referred to as the URL, the unique resource location or universal/uniform resource locator.

Most universities have a preferred referencing style that you must use in your project report. This will normally be prescribed in your assessment criteria. Three of the most common styles are the Harvard system (a version of which we have used in this book), the American Psychological Association (APA) System and the Vancouver or footnotes system. Guidelines on using each of these are given in Appendix 1.

Brief summary

A brief summary of the content of each item in your reference database will help you to locate the relevant items and facilitate reference to your notes and photocopies. This can be done by annotating each record with the key words used, to help locate the item and the abstract. It will also help you to maintain consistency in your searches.

Supplementary information

As well as recording the details discussed earlier, other information may also be worth recording. These items can be anything you feel will be of value. In Table 3.7 we outline those that we have found most useful.

Table 3.7 Supplementary information

Information	Reason
ISBN	The identifier for any book, and useful if the book has to be requested on inter-library loan
Class number (e.g. Dewey decimal)	Useful to locate books in your university's library and as a pointer to finding other books on the same subject
Quotations	Always note useful quotations in full and with the page number of the quote; if possible also take a photocopy or save entire document as a PDF file.
Where it was found	Noting where you found the item is useful, especially if it is not in your university library and you could only take notes
The tertiary resource used and the key words used to locate it	Useful to help identify resources for follow-up searches
Evaluative comments	Your personal notes on the value of the item to your research in relation to your relevance and value criteria
When the item was consulted	Especially important for items found via the Internet as these may disappear without trace
Filename	Useful if you have saved the document as a PDF file.

3.8 Plagiarism

There is no doubt that plagiarism has become an enormously important topic in academic institutions in recent years, largely as a result of the ease with which material can be copied from the Internet and passed of as the work of the individual student. It is a serious topic as the consequences of being found guilty of plagiarism can be severe as the example in Box 3.18 from a UK university shows.

Neville (2007) argues that plagiarism is an issue that runs parallel to a debate with recurring questions about the purpose of higher education in the twenty-first century. He notes that, on the one hand, there is the argument that an insistence on 'correct' referencing is supporting a system and a process of learning that is a legacy of a different time and society. This argument holds that universities are enforcing upon you an arcane practice of referencing that you will probably never use again outside higher education. On the other hand, there is the argument that plagiarism is an attack upon values of ethical, proper, decent behaviour: values consistent with a respect for others. These are ageless societal values that universities should try to maintain.

So what precisely is plagiarism? Easterby-Smith *et al.* (2008:50) define it is 'presenting the work and ideas of other people and passing them off as your own, without acknowledging the original source of the ideas used'. The same authors cite Park's (2003) list of four common forms of plagiarism which are commonly found in universities. These are listed below.

1 Stealing material from another source and passing it off as your own, for example:
   • buying a paper from a research service, essay bank or term-paper mill (either specially written for the individual or pre-written);
   • copying a whole paper from a source text without proper acknowledgement;
   • submitting another student's work with or without that student's knowledge (e.g. by copying a computer disk);
2 submitting a paper written by someone else (e.g. a peer or relative) and passing it off as your own;

Box 3.18
Focus on student research

Penalties for being found guilty of plagiarism

Overview of the penalties

There is a range of penalties that can be applied in cases of plagiarism. The penalty is chosen either by the School or the Committee on Applications and will depend on the seriousness of the offence and on whether there are any mitigating circumstances. Example penalties are:

1 only the sections of the assignment determined not to be plagiarised are marked;
2 academic year is failed and must be retaken;
3 student is excluded from the University.

The seriousness of the offence is related to issues such as:

• whether the student has committed offences previously;
• the magnitude of the plagiarism;
• the number of marks and the level of the assignment involved.

Source: University of Leeds. Available online at: http://www.lts.leeds.ac.uk/plagiarism/penalties.php?PHPSESSID=4582f0d02aa8927c671b34ddb8c4f459

3 copying sections of material from one or more source texts, supplying proper documentation (including the full reference) but leaving out quotation marks, thus giving the impression that the material has been paraphrased rather than directly quoted;

4 paraphrasing material from one or more source texts without supplying appropriate documentation;

It is tempting to think that all cases of plagiarism are a consequence of students either being too idle to pursue their research and writing diligently, or wishing to appear cleverer that they really are. But the fact is that plagiarism is an extremely complex issue and the reasons for it may owe as much to student confusion as willful negligence. That said, there is little excuse for confusion. All universities have ample guidance for students on the topic of plagiarism and will emphasise that it the responsibility of the individual student to become aware of the university's regulations surrounding its conduct. In addition, there is no shortage of excellent websites with guidance for students (e.g. the University of Alberta Libraries site at: http://www.library.ualberta.ca/guides/plagiarism/index.cfm).

In addition, an increasing number of universities ask students to check their own work using plagiarism detection software.

3.9 Summary

- A critical review of the literature is necessary to help you to develop a thorough understanding of, and insight into, previous research that relates to your research question(s) and objectives. Your review will set your research in context by critically discussing and referencing work that has already been undertaken, drawing out key points and presenting them in a logically argued way, and highlighting those areas where you will provide fresh insights. It will lead the reader into subsequent sections of your project report.
- There is no one correct structure for a critical review, although it is helpful to think of it as a funnel in which you start at a more general level prior to narrowing down to your specific research question(s) and objectives.
- Literature sources can be divided into three categories: primary, secondary and tertiary. In reality, these categories often overlap. Your use of these resources will depend on your research question(s) and objectives. Some may use only tertiary and secondary literature. For others, you may need to locate primary literature as well.
- When planning your literature search you need to:
  - have clearly defined research question(s) and objectives;
  - define the parameters of your search;
  - generate key words and search terms;
  - discuss your ideas as widely as possible.
  Techniques to help you in this include brainstorming and relevance trees.
- Your literature search is likely to be undertaken using a variety of approaches in tandem. These will include:
  - searching using tertiary sources and the Internet;
  - following up references in articles you have already read;
  - scanning and browsing secondary literature in your library.
  Don't forget to make precise notes of the search processes you have used and their results.
- Once obtained, the literature must be evaluated for its relevance to your research question(s) and objectives using clearly defined criteria. This must include a consideration of each item's currency. Each item must be read and noted. Bibliographic details, a brief description of the content and appropriate supplementary information should also be recorded.
- Care should be taken when writing your literature review not to plagiarise the work of others.

Self-check questions

Help with these questions is available at the end of the chapter.

3.1   The following extract and associated references are taken from the first draft of a critical literature review. The research project was concerned with the impact of direct insurers on the traditional motor insurer.
List the problems with this extract in terms of its:
  a content;
  b structure.

Jackson (1995) suggests that businesses must be developed from a customer rather than a product perspective. Lindesfarne (1994) demonstrates that direct selling gives the consumer increased control as it is up to them when and if they wish to respond to adverts or direct mail. MacKenzie (1995) comments that free gifts are useful for getting responses to adverts, which is ultimately what all direct insurers need. Bowen (1995) suggests that this type of company can be split into three equally important parts: marketing, insurance and information technology. Motor insurance is particularly price sensitive because of its compulsory nature and its perception by many to have no real 'value' to themselves.

Bowen, I. (1994) 'Short cut to success', *Post Magazine* 2, 26 July.
Jackson, D.R. (1995) 'Prudential's prudent parochialism', *Direct Marketing*, 26–29 April.
Lindisfarne, I. (1995) 'Death of a salesman', *Post Magazine* 15, 30–31 June.
MacKenzie, G. (1995) 'Rise of the freebie', *Post Magazine* 2, 5–6 February.

3.2   Outline the advice you would give a colleague on:
  a how to plan her search;
  b which literature to search first.

3.3   Brainstorm at least one of the following research questions, either on your own or with a colleague, and list the key words that you have generated.
  a How effective is profit-related pay as a motivator?
  b How do the opportunities available to a first-time house buyer through interpersonal discussion influence the process of selecting a financial institution for the purposes of applying for a house purchase loan?
  c To what extent do new methods of direct selling of financial services pose a threat to existing providers?

3.4   You are having considerable problems with finding relevant material for your research when searching online databases. Suggest possible reasons why this might be so.

3.5   Rewrite the following passage as part of a critical literature review using the Harvard system of referencing:

From what I've read, the English Language Teaching market, which this company serves, remains attractive for publishers despite a decline in growth as this quote shows: 'Overall, the ELT materials market has continued to show growth, because, globally, the demand for English learning persists, albeit on a lower growth track than in the 1980s'.[1] The latest published statistics that I've been able to find (1999) tell us that there are 1,300 million ELT learners worldwide.[2] I therefore think that the need for good ELT authors is growing and, as Francis says: 'the name of the author remains a critical success factor, and an important sub-brand in many cases'.[3]

[1]R. Francis, 'Youngsters drive ELT growth', Bookseller, 23 May 2003, p. 26.
[2]Gasson, C. (ed.), Book Publishing in Britain (London: Bookseller Publications, 1999).
[3]R. Francis 'ELT Publishing', p. 93 in C. Gasson (ed.), Book Publishing in Britain (London: Bookseller Publications, 1999) pp. 86–104.

Review and discussion questions

3.6 Go to the website of the general search engine Google (http://www.google.com). Use the different Google services such as 'Google Search', 'Google Scholar' and 'University Search' to search for articles on a topic which you are currently studying as part of your course.

    a Make notes regarding the types of items that each of these services finds.

    b How do these services differ?

    c Which service do you think is likely to prove most useful to your research project?

3.7 Agree with a friend to each review the same article from a refereed academic journal, which contains a clear literature review section. Evaluate independently the literature review in your chosen article with regard to its content, critical nature and structure using the checklists in Boxes 3.2, 3.3 and 3.4 respectively. Do not forget to make notes regarding your answers to each of the points raised in the checklists. Discuss your answers with your friend.

3.8 Visit an online database or your university library and obtain a copy of an article that you think will be of use to an assignment you are both currently working on. Use the checklist in Box 3.16 to assess the relevance and value of the article to your assignment.

Progressing your research project

Critically reviewing the literature

- Consider your research questions and objectives. Use your lecture notes, course textbooks and relevant review articles to define both narrow and broader parameters of your literature search, considering language, subject area, business sector, geographical area, publication period and literature type.

- Generate key words and search terms using one or a variety of techniques such as reading, brainstorming and relevance trees. Discuss your ideas widely, including with your project tutor and colleagues.

- Start your search using both database and printed tertiary sources to identify relevant secondary literature. Begin with those tertiary sources that abstract and index academic journal articles and books. At the same time, obtain relevant literature that has been referenced in articles you have already read. Do not forget to record your searches systematically and in detail.

- Expand your search via other sources such as the Internet and by browsing and scanning.

- Obtain copies of items, evaluate them systematically and make notes. Remember also to record bibliographic details, a brief description of the content and supplementary information on an index card or in your reference database.

- Start drafting your critical review as early as possible, keeping in mind its purpose and taking care to reference properly and avoid plagiarism.

- Continue to search the literature throughout your research project to ensure that your review remains up to date.

References

Bell, J. (2005) *Doing Your Research Project* (4th edn). Maidenhead: Open University Press.

Clausen, H. (1996) 'Web information quality as seen from libraries', *New Library World* 97: 1130, pp. 4–8.

Dees, R. (2003) *Writing the Modern Research Paper* (4th edn). Boston, MA: Allyn and Bacon.

Denyer, D. and Neely, A. (2004) 'Introduction to special issue: innovation and productivity performance in the UK', *International Journal of Management Reviews*, Vol. 5/6, Nos. 3 and 4, pp. 131–5.

Easterby-Smith, M., Thorpe, R. Jackson, P. and Lowe, A. (2008) *Management Research* (3rd edn). Sage: London.

Fisher, C. (2007) *Researching and Writing a Dissertation for Business Students* (2nd edn). Harlow: Financial Times Prentice Hall.

Gall, M.D., Gall, J.P. and Borg, W. (2006) *Educational Research: An Introduction* (8th edn). New York: Longman.

Gill, J. and Johnson, P. (2002) *Research Methods for Managers.* (3rd edn). London: Paul Chapman.

Greenhalgh, T. (1997) 'Papers that summarize other papers (systematic reviews and meta-analyses)', *British Medical Journal,* Vol. 315, pp. 672–5.

Habrakan, A., Schmitz, R. and van Tilberg, P. (2008) 'Searching the World Wide Web: a basic tutorial', available at: http://www.tilburguniversity.nl/services/library/instruction/www/onlinecourse [Accessed 21 May 2008.]

Hahn, H. (2008) 'Harley Hahns Internet Yellow Pages', available at: http://www.harley.com/yp/home.html [Accessed 20 May 2008.]

Hart, C. (1998) *Doing a Literature Review.* London: Sage.

Harvard College Library (2006) 'Interrogating texts: 6 reading habits to develop in your first year at Harvard'. Available at: http://hcl.harvard.edu/research/guides/lamont_handouts/interrogatingtexts.html [Accessed 20 May 2008.]

Inspiration (2008) Inspiration homepage. Available at: http://www.inspiration.com [Accessed 21 May 2008.]

Jankowicz, A.D. (2005) *Business Research Projects* (4th edn). London: Thomson Learning.

McNeill, P. (2005). *Research Methods.* (3rd edn). London: Routledge.

MindGenius (2008) MindGenius homepage. Available at: http://www.mindgenius.com/website/presenter.aspx?type=doc&uri=/home.htm#topofpage [Accessed 21 May 2008.]

Mingers, J. (2000) 'What is it to be critical? Teaching a critical approach to management undergraduates', *Management Learning,* Vol. 31, No. 2, pp. 219–37.

Neville, C. (2007) *The complete guide to referencing and plagiarism*. Maidenhead: Open University Press.

Park, C. (2003) 'In other (people's) words: plagiarism by university students – literature and lessons', *Assessment & Evaluation in Higher Education*, Vol. 28, No. 5, pp. 471–88.

Searcy, D.L. and Mentzer, J.T. (2003) 'A framework for conducting and evaluating research', *Journal of Accounting Literature*, Vol. 22, pp. 130–67.

Sharp, J.A., Peters, J. and Howard, K. (2002) *The Management of a Student Research Project* (3rd edn). Aldershot: Gower.

Srivastava, S. (2007) 'Green supply-chain management: A state-of-the-art literature review', *International Journal of Management Review,* Vol. 9, No. 1, pp. 53–80.

Stewart, D.W. and Kamins, M.A. (1993) *Secondary Research: Information Sources and Methods* (2nd edn). Newbury Park: CA, Sage.

Strauss, A. and Corbin, J. (1998) *Basics of Qualitative Research* (2nd edn). Newbury Park, CA: Sage.

Tranfield, D., Denyer, D. and Smart, P. (2003) 'Towards a methodology for developing evidence-informed management knowledge by means of systematic review', *British Journal of Management*, Vol. 14, No. 3, pp. 207–22.

Wallace, M. and Wray, A. (2006) *Critical Reading and Writing for Postgraduates.* London: Sage.

Wikipedia (2008) Wikipedia home page. Available at: http://www.wikipedia.org [Accessed 21 May 2008.]

Williams C.S. and Saunders M.N.K. (2006) 'Developing the service template: From measurement to agendas for improvement', *Service Industries Journal*, Vol. 26, No. 5, pp. 1–15.

Further reading

Bell, J. (2005). *Doing Your Research Project.* (4th edn). Maidenhead: Open University Press. **Chapter 6** provides a good introduction to the process of reviewing the literature. The section on the critical review of the literature is especially helpful.

Habrakan, A., Schmitz, R. and van Tilberg, P. (2008) 'Searching the World Wide Web: a basic tutorial'. Available at: http://www.tilburguniversity.nl/services/library/instruction/www/onlinecourse [Accessed 21 May 2008.] This website provides an introduction to, and history of, the Internet and WWW along with an interactive tutorial. The tutorial offers an explanation of different types of information that you can find on the Internet and how to access them. It also contains a common-sense guide to searching for particular websites.

Neville, C. (2007). *The Complete Guide to Referencing and Plagiarism.* Maidenhead: Open University Press. **Chapter 4** is a very helpful guide on what constitutes plagiarism and how it can be avoided. The chapter ends with some useful exercises designed to ensure that the reader does not fall into some common traps.

Sharp, J.A., Peters, J. and Howard, K. (2002) *The Management of a Student Research Project.* (3rd edn). Aldershot: Gower. **Chapter 4** contains a useful in-depth discussion of the use of relevance trees in your literature search.

Tranfield, D., Denyer, D. and Smart, P. (2003) 'Towards a methodology for developing evidence-informed management knowledge by means of systematic review', *British Journal of Management,* Vol. 14, No. 3, pp. 207–22. This paper provides an excellent introduction to the process of systematic review. Although a full systematic review as outlined in this paper may be too time consuming for your research project, there are many useful points made regarding how to plan your search strategy and explain in your project report how your review was undertaken.

Case 3
Complexity theory and emergent change

Source: Rob Judges/Oxford/Alamy

Sarah was in the final year of her undergraduate business studies degree course. She was starting on her research project, and had been thinking about what to investigate. The module 'Organisational Change' that she had taken in her second year particularly interested her. Some of the ideas she had learned about related very clearly to an aspect of her university experience. At the beginning of her first year she had joined the university drama society, and since then she had been very actively involved. Sarah had noticed how different groups would form spontaneously among drama-society members from time to time. Those who became enthusiastic about a particular activity would work together to run workshops or put on plays. Meanwhile, other groups would get themselves organised to lobby forcefully for changes in the way the society was run. As a result, the drama society had gone from strength to strength. Membership was increasing and more adventurous productions were being staged, to great acclaim from other students.

Of the theories she had come across in the 'Organisational Change' module, complexity theory was the one that seemed intuitively to explain this success. Sarah was especially fascinated by the idea of 'self-organisation', where members collaborate spontaneously in responding to environmental demands and bring about desired change. It applied perfectly to her drama club experience – encouraging self-organisation must be a key to successful management of change anywhere. Sarah had a hunch that what she'd observed would happen in other societies and clubs in the university. She hit on the idea of using complexity theory as the conceptual framework for her research project, which would be an investigation of how members in other university societies and clubs worked together to run their activities and make change happen.

Her project tutor approved of what she proposed and invited her to begin by carrying out a review of literature on complexity theory and organisational change. The aim was to inform her research design and data collection methods. The question she chose to frame her review was: 'How does complexity theory suggest that organisational change should be managed?' Her literature search had soon produced plenty of texts. She started with the book by McMillan (2004), *Complexity, Organizations and Change*. This and each text she read afterwards reinforced her hunch that complexity theory showed how change could be managed effectively in any organisation. She did stumble on one text arguing against the application of complexity theory to organisational change, but she couldn't see much point in including it. The authors of the texts she did use explained what complexity theory was, showed how it applied to organizational change – occasionally reporting their own research – and offered prescriptions for managing change. It was easy to write her draft review because she agreed with so much of what the authors were saying.

But when she presented the draft review to her project tutor, she got a shock. The feedback was: 'This is a good summary of what you've read, but not critical enough. Your review question shows how you've assumed that complexity can be used to prescribe practice. How can you be sure? You've simply confirmed the prejudices you had before you started the review! You need to challenge what authors are saying, not just accept every claim they make. You've ignored the literature by authors who don't like the application of complexity theory for prescribing practice, when you could learn something from their criticisms. They might lead you to question your assumptions.'

Sarah was confused. What did the project tutor mean? Challenging authors sounded like being negative about everything she had just interpreted so positively. Her project tutor also recommended that she read the textbook by Wallace and Wray (2006), *Critical Reading and Writing for Postgraduates*, to help her become a more critical reader. She had a flick through the book, dubious because it was aimed at postgraduates, but quickly seized on the 'critical analysis' ideas about evaluating authors' claims. She realised she had never thought to check, say, whether authors had enough evidence to make their generalised claims convincing. Or whether they all meant the same thing by terms such as 'self-organisation'. Or whether their values as researchers coloured their claims in ways that others might find contentious. Sarah could now see that she had selected for inclusion in her review only those texts which supported her hunch – where authors were positive about applying complexity theory to organisational change. She had accepted all their claims without question and had ignored the one text that challenged them. Further, she had never thought to search for a published review on the topic. Could she learn from an expert reviewer, who might have examined more texts than she had? Why not include such a review article in her own effort?

So Sarah searched for reviews, locating one by Burnes (2005). He had included various texts whose authors were more sceptical about complexity theory. He had not just described the claims of complexity theory enthusiasts. Rather, he had described and evaluated all the claims – positive and negative – in a manner consistent with the advice offered by Wallace and Wray. Amongst the limitations he pointed to was the lack of empirical studies on organisational change using complexity theory. Yet, such research evidence would help to justify prescriptions about good practice in managing change. Without evidence, how could anyone know that prescriptions really worked? Sarah went back to the texts she had reviewed previously, looking for what was wrong with claims she had previously accepted. She completely changed her mind about the usefulness of complexity theory. Sarah promised herself that there would be no doubt about the second draft of her literature review being critical enough. She set herself a new review question: 'What are the weaknesses of using complexity theory to prescribe how change should be managed?' She would demonstrate how the complexity theory enthusiasts had simply confirmed their pre-existing prejudices, failing to acknowledge the limitations of their work and building their prescriptions more on wishful thinking than on hard research evidence.

When she handed in the second draft of her literature review to her project tutor she received another shock. The feedback this time was: 'A great improvement over your under- critical first draft. But it's now over-critical. Your new review question shows how you've now assumed that complexity theory can't be used to prescribe practice. How can you be sure? Try to adopt a more balanced approach to your critical review.' Sarah was now even more confused. What did the project tutor mean by 'balance'? And what were the implications for writing the third draft of her literature review?

References

Burnes, B. (2005) 'Complexity theories and organizational change', *International Journal of Management Reviews*, Vol. 7, No. 2, pp. 73–90.

McMillan, E. (2004) *Complexity, Organizations and Change*. London: Routledge.

Wallace, M. and Wray, A. (2006) *Critical Reading and Writing for Postgraduates*. London: Sage.

Questions

1 Why is it important for your research investigation that you be critical when reviewing the literature?

2 What might Sarah's project tutor mean by suggesting that a critical literature review should be 'balanced'?

3 What does Sarah need to do to develop a literature review which is sufficiently critical, yet also sufficiently balanced?

Additional case studies relating to material covered in this chapter are available via the book's Companion Website, **www.pearsoned.co.uk/saunders**. They are:

- The development of discount warehouse clubs;
- The problems of valuing intellectual capital;
- National cultures and management styles.

Self-check answers

3.1 There are numerous problems with the content and structure of this extract. Some of the more obvious include:

a The content consists of predominantly trade magazines, in particular *Post Magazine*, and there are no references of academic substance. Some of the references to individual authors have discrepancies: for example, was the article by Lindisfarne (or is it Lindesfarne?) published in 1994 or 1995?

b The items referenced are from 1994 and 1995. It is certain that more recent items are available.

c There is no real structure or argument in the extract. The extract is a list of what people have written, with no attempt to critically evaluate or juxtapose the ideas.

3.2 This is a difficult one without knowing her research question! However, you could still advise her on the general principles. Your advice will probably include:

a Define the parameters of the research, considering language, subject area, business sector, geographical area, publication period and literature type. Generate key words and search terms using one or a variety of techniques such as reading, brainstorming or relevance trees. Discuss her ideas as widely as possible, including with her tutor, librarians and you.

b Start the search using tertiary sources to identify relevant secondary literature. She should commence with those tertiary sources that abstract and index academic journal articles and books. At the same time she should obtain relevant literature that has been referenced in articles that she has already read.

3.3 There are no incorrect answers with brainstorming! However, you might like to check your key words for suitability prior to using them to search an appropriate database. We suggest that you follow the approach outlined in Section 3.5 under 'searching using the tertiary literature'.

3.4 There is a variety of possible reasons, including:

- One or more of the parameters of your search are defined too narrowly.
- The key words you have chosen do not appear in the controlled index language.
- Your spelling of the key word is incorrect.
- The terminology you are using is incorrect.
- The acronyms you have chosen are not used by databases.
- You are using jargon rather than accepted terminology.

3.5 There are two parts to this answer: rewriting the text and using the Harvard system of referencing. Your text will inevitably differ from the answer given below owing to your personal writing style. Don't worry about this too much as it is discussed in far more detail in Section 14.5. The references should follow the same format.

Writing in the trade literature, Francis (2003:26) emphasises that the English Language Teaching (ELT) market remains attractive for publishers. He states: 'Overall, the ELT materials market has continued to show growth, because, globally, the demand for English learning persists, albeit on a lower growth track than in the 1980s'. This assertion is supported by published statistics (Gasson 1999), which indicate that there are 1,300 million ELT learners worldwide. Alongside this, the need for good ELT authors is growing, Francis (1999:93) asserting: 'the name of the author remains a critical success factor, and an important sub-brand in many cases'.

Gasson, C. (ed.) (1999) *Book Publishing in Britain*, London, Bookseller Publications.

Francis, R. (1999) 'ELT Publishing', in Gasson C. (ed.), *Book Publishing in Britain*, London, Bookseller Publications, 86–104.

Francis, R. (2003) 'Youngsters drive ELT growth', *Bookseller*, 23 May, p. 26.

Get ahead using resources on the Companion Website at:
www.pearsoned.co.uk/saunders

- Improve your SPSS and NVivo research analysis with practice tutorials.
- Save time researching on the Internet with the Smarter Online Searching Guide.
- Test your progress using self-assessment questions.
- Follow live links to useful websites.

Chapter 4

Understanding research philosophies and approaches

Learning outcomes

By the end of this chapter you should be able to:

- define the key terms ontology, epistemology and axiology and explain their relevance to business research;
- explain the relevance for business research of philosophical perspectives such as positivism, realism, pragmatism and interpretivism;
- understand the main research paradigms which are significant for business research;
- distinguish between main research approaches: deductive and inductive;
- state your own epistemological, ontological and axiological positions.

4.1 Introduction

Much of this book is concerned with the way in which you collect data to answer your research question. You are not unusual if you begin thinking about your research by considering whether you should, for example, administer a questionnaire or conduct interviews. However, thoughts on this question belong in the centre of the research 'onion', by which means we have chosen to depict the issues underlying the choice of data collection techniques and analysis procedures in Figure 4.1. Before coming to this central point we argue that there are important layers of the onion that need to be peeled away.

Indeed, some writers, such as Guba and Lincoln (1994:105), argue that questions of research methods are of secondary importance to questions of which paradigm is applicable to your research (we deal with paradigms later in this chapter). They note:

> both qualitative and quantitative methods may be used appropriately with any research paradigm. Questions of method are secondary to questions of paradigm, which we define as the basic belief system or world view that guides the investigation, not only in choices of method but in ontologically and epistemologically fundamental ways.

This chapter is concerned principally with the first two of the onion's layers: research philosophy (Section 4.2) and research approach (Section 4.3). In the next chapter we examine what we call research strategy, choices and time horizons. The sixth layer, data collection techniques and analysis procedures, is dealt with in Chapters 7–13.

4.2 Understanding your research philosophy: why research philosophy is important

In this first part of the chapter we examine **research philosophy** (Figure 4.1). This over-arching term relates to the development of knowledge and the nature of that knowledge. At first reading this sounds rather profound. But the point is that this is precisely what you are doing when embarking on research – developing knowledge in a particular field. The knowledge development you are embarking upon may not be as dramatic as a new theory of human motivation. But even if the purpose has the relatively modest ambition of answering a specific problem in a particular organisation it is, nonetheless, developing new knowledge.

Our values can have an important impact on the research we decide to pursue and the way in which we pursue it. This may not lead to any form of discord, but it may mean that some observers accuse us of untoward bias. In 2003 the *British Medical Journal* reported that the leading independent medical journal *The Lancet* had taken the unprecedented step of accusing a major European pharmaceutical company of sponsoring biased research into its new anticholesterol drug.

In his editorial in *The Lancet*, Richard Horton, the journal's editor, said the company's tactics 'raise disturbing questions about how drugs enter clinical practice and what measures exist to protect patients from inadequately investigated medicines'. He accused the clinical trials, which investigated the efficacy of the new drug, of including 'weak data', 'adventurous statistics', and 'marketing dressed up as research'. The editorial argued 'physicians must tell their patients the truth about the drug, that, compared with competitors, it has an inferior evidence base supporting its safe use'.

In the same edition of *The Lancet* the company issued a furious response. 'Regulators, doctors, and

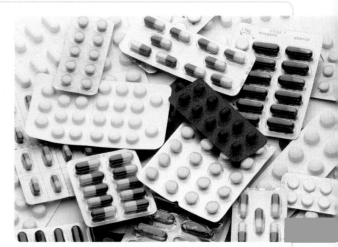

Source: Science Photo Library

patients as well as my company have been poorly served by your flawed and incorrect editorial', wrote the CEO. He said that he deplored the fact that a respected scientific journal should make such an outrageous critique of a serious, well studied, and important medicine.'

Source: Dyer (2003:1005)

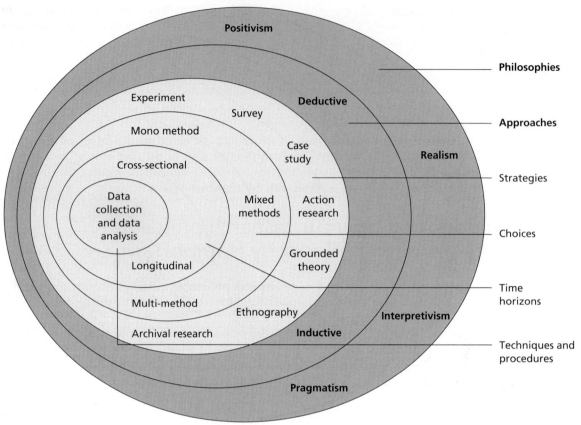

Figure 4.1
The research 'onion'
Source: © Mark Saunders, Philip Lewis and Adrian Thornhill 2008

The research philosophy you adopt contains important assumptions about the way in which you view the world. These assumptions will underpin your research strategy and the methods you choose as part of that strategy. As Johnson and Clark (2006) note, as business and management researchers we need to be aware of the philosophical commitments we make through our choice of research strategy since this has significant impact not only on what we do but we understand what it is we are investigating.

In part, the philosophy you adopt will be influenced by practical considerations. However, the main influence is likely to be your particular view of the relationship between knowledge and the process by which it is developed. The researcher who is concerned with facts, such as the resources needed in a manufacturing process, is likely to have a very different view on the way research should be conducted from the researcher concerned with the feelings and attitudes of the workers towards their managers in that same manufacturing process. Not only will their strategies and methods probably differ considerably, but so will their views on what is important and, perhaps more significantly, what is useful.

In summary we agree with Johnson and Clark (2006) who argue that the important issue is not so much whether our research should be philosophically informed, but it is how well we are able to reflect upon our philosophical choices and defend them in relation to the alternatives we could have adopted.

Within this section it would be easy to fall into the trap of thinking that one research philosophy is 'better' than another. This would miss the point. They are 'better' at doing different things. As always, which is 'better' depends on the research question(s) you are seeking to answer. Of course, the practical reality is that a particular research question rarely falls neatly into only one philosophical domain as suggested in the 'onion' (Figure 4.1). Indeed, later in this chapter we shall also be encouraging you to think in a more flexible way about the research approach and methods you adopt.

You may ask what practical use is an understanding of your philosophical position? Is it as much use as the outer layer on a real onion, which is cast aside, with only the inner layers retained? We think that it is of practical benefit to understand the taken-for-granted assumptions that we all have about the way the world works. Only if we have such an understanding can we examine these assumptions, challenge them if we think it appropriate, and behave in a different way.

In this discussion we examine two major ways of thinking about research philosophy: ontology and epistemology. Each contains important differences which will influence the way in which you think about the research process. This is the purpose of this chapter. It is not to offer a shopping list from which you may wish to choose that philosophy or approach that suits you best. It is to enhance your understanding of the way in which we approach the study of our particular field of activity.

Having said all this by way of introduction to this section on research philosophies, maybe it is best to start with the pragmatist's philosophy: that in designing your research method the most important consideration is your research question. Subsequently, we will consider the role of assumptions we make about the way in which the world works; what different philosophies consider to be acceptable knowledge; the role of our own values and research paradigms.

Pragmatism: do you have to adopt one position?

It is unavoidable that the debate on ontology and epistemology which follows has a competitive ring. The debate is often framed in terms of a choice between either the positivist or the interpretivist research philosophy. Even if you accept the Guba and Lincoln (1994) argument we noted earlier, that questions of method are secondary to questions of epistemology, ontology and axiology, you would still be excused for thinking that choosing between one position and the other is somewhat unrealistic in practice. If this is your view then you would be adopting the position of the pragmatist. **Pragmatism** argues that the most important determinant of the epistemology, ontology and axiology you adopt is the research question – one may be more appropriate than the other for answering particular questions. Moreover, if the research question does not suggest unambiguously that either a positivist or interpretivist philosophy is adopted, this confirms the pragmatist's view that it is perfectly possible to work with variations in your epistemology, ontology and axiology. This mirrors a theme which recurs in this book – that mixed methods, both qualitative and quantitative, are possible, and possibly highly appropriate, within one study (see Section 5.4). Tashakkori and Teddlie (1998) suggest that it is more appropriate for the researcher in a particular study to think of the philosophy adopted as a continuum rather than opposite positions. They note that 'at some points the knower and the known must be interactive, while at others, one may more easily stand apart from what one is studying' (Tashakkori and Teddlie 1998:26).

Tashakkori and Teddlie (1998) contend that pragmatism is intuitively appealing, largely because it avoids the researcher engaging in what they see as rather pointless debates about such concepts as truth and reality. In their view you should 'study what interests you and is of value to you, study in the different ways in which you deem appropriate, and use the results in ways that can bring about positive consequences within your value system' (Tashakkori and Teddlie 1998:30).

Ontology: what assumptions do we make about the way in which the world works?

Ontology is concerned with nature of reality. This raises questions of the assumptions researchers have about the way the world operates and the commitment held to particular views. The two aspects of ontology we describe here will both have their devotees among business and management researchers. In addition, both are likely to be accepted as producing valid knowledge by many researchers.

The first aspect of ontology we discuss is **objectivism**. This portrays the position that social entities exist in reality external to social actors concerned with their existence. The second aspect, **subjectivism**, holds that social phenomena are created from the perceptions and consequent actions of those social actors concerned with their existence.

Objectivism: how social entities exist independent of social actors

This represents the position that social entities exist in reality external to social actors. An example of this may be management itself (Box 4.1). You may argue that management is an objective entity and decide to adopt an objectivist stance to the study of particular aspects of management in a specific organisation. In order to substantiate your view you would say that the managers in your organisation have job descriptions which prescribe their duties, there are operating procedures to which they are supposed to adhere, they are part of a formal structure which locates them in a hierarchy with people reporting to them and they in turn report to more senior managers. This view emphasises the structural aspects of management and assumes that management is similar in all organisations. Aspects of the structure in which management operates may differ but the essence of the function is very much the same in all organisations. Insofar as management does differ in organisations it is a function of the different objective aspects of management.

Box 4.1
Focus on student research

A management exodus at On Tology

As part of a major organisational change all the managers in the marketing department of the chemical manufacturer On Tology left the organisation. They were replaced by new managers who were thought to be more in tune with the more commercially aggressive new culture that the organisation was trying to create. The new managers entering the organisation filled the roles of the managers who had left and had essentially the same job duties and procedures as their predecessors.

John wanted to study the role of management in On Tology and in particular the way in which managers liaised with external stakeholders. He decided to use the new managers in the marketing department as his research subjects.

In his research proposal he decided to write a little about his research philosophy. He defined his ontological position as that of the objectivist. His reasoning was that management in On Tology had a reality that was separate from the managers that inhabit that reality. He pointed to the fact that the formal management structure at On Tology was largely unchanged from that which was practised by the managers that had left the organisation. The process of management would continue in largely the same way in spite of the change in personnel.

However, for your approach to the study of management you may prefer to take the view that the objective aspects of management are less important than the way in which the managers themselves attach their own individual meanings to their jobs and the way they think that those jobs should be performed. This approach would be very much more akin to the subjectivist view.

Subjectivism: understanding the meanings that individuals attach to social phenomena

The subjectivist view is that social phenomena are created from the perceptions and consequent actions of social actors. What is more, this is a continual process in that through the process of social interaction these social phenomena are in a constant state of revision.

Remenyi *et al.* (1998:35) stress the necessity to study 'the details of the situation to understand the reality or perhaps a reality working behind them'. This is often associated with the term constructionism, or **social constructionism**. This follows from the interpretivist philosophy that it is necessary to explore the subjective meanings motivating the actions of social actors in order for the researcher to be able to understand these actions. Social constructionism views reality as being socially constructed. Social actors, such as the customers you may plan to study in your organisation, may place many different interpretations on the situations in which they find themselves. So individual customers will perceive different situations in varying ways as a consequence of their own view of the world. These different interpretations are likely to affect their actions and the nature of their social interaction with others. In this sense, the customers you are studying not only interact with their environment, they also seek to make sense of it through their interpretation of events and the meanings that they draw from these events. In turn their own actions may be seen by others as being meaningful in the context of these socially constructed interpretations and meanings. Therefore, in the case of the customers you are studying, it is your role as the researcher to seek to understand the subjective reality of the customers in order to be able to make sense of and understand their motives, actions and intentions in a way that is meaningful (Box 4.2). All this is some way from the position that customer service in an organisation has a reality that is separate from the customers that perceive that reality. The subjectivist view is that customer service is produced through the social interaction between service providers and customers and is continually being revised as a result of this. In other words, at no time is there a definitive entity called 'customer service'. It is constantly changing.

This objectivist–subjectivist debate is somewhat similar to the different ways in which the theoretical and practical approaches to organisational culture have developed in the past 25 years. Smircich (1983) noted that objectivists would tend to view the culture of an organisation as something that the organisation 'has'. On the other hand, the subjectivist's view would be that culture is something that the organisation 'is' as a result as a process of continuing social enactment. Management theory and practice has leaned towards treating organisation culture as a variable, something that the organisation 'has': something that can be manipulated, changed in order to produce the sort of state desired by managers. The subjectivist viewpoint would be to reject this as too simplistic and argue that culture is something that is created and re-created through a complex array of phenomena which include social interactions and physical factors such as office layout to which individuals attach certain meanings, rituals and myths. It is the meanings that are attached to these phenomena by social actors within the organisation that need to be understood in order for the culture to be understood. Furthermore, because of the continual creation and re-creation of an organisation's culture it is difficult for it to be isolated, understood and then manipulated.

Box 4.2
Focus on research in the news **FT**

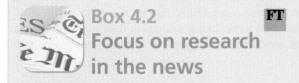

Royal Opera reaches out to 'cool crowd'

There are few areas of social activity that are as defined by social grouping as attendance at musical events, as a visit to any major opera house or rock concert will confirm. So the challenge for those businesses wishing to expand their market appeal is to convince under-represented social groups that the activity of that business is 'for them'.

For example, London's Royal Opera House is the ultimate high culture experience. But while the ROH's pampering of its audience ensures that its core supporters remain loyal, it may also be putting off young professionals, who are instead engaging with what they regard as newer and livelier forms of culture. That is one of the results of market research by the consultancy Dunnhumby, famous for its demographic analysis of Tesco Clubcard customers. It has analysed box office and other spending habits at the ROH to find that although it appealed strongly to its core audience of opera and ballet lovers, and to young people in education using its student standby scheme, it was failing to attract enough people in their 20s and 30s.

As a direct result of the research, the ROH plans to put on a three-day cultural festival featuring some of the coolest names in town: art by Julian Opie, famous for his paintings of Blur; a club night by electronics star Scanner and digital games by the performance group Blast Theory. The festival will attempt to bring a new, cooler audience to the ROH, said Tony Hall, chief executive of the Royal Opera House. 'It is about working out ways to get young professionals excited, between their student years and their 40s, when they discover opera and ballet for themselves. We want to get that buzzy, cool crowd to come in. It is all about the Royal Opera House reaching outwards and bringing new people in.'

The festival, which will be spread over a long weekend in September, is being backed by the financial services company Deloitte for the next five years. Its senior partner and chief executive John Connolly said that the pairing was a logical one. 'The partnership particularly appealed because it brings together our appetite for innovation and focus on young people with a commitment to widening access to the arts', he said. Mr Hall said the use of Dunnhumby's research, which separated the ROH's audience into different segments, made it possible to find out more than ever about its responses and habits, and enabled the ROH to fine-tune its artistic policy accordingly.

Source: article by Aspden, Peter (2008) *Financial Times*, 1 Mar.

Epistemology: what is acceptable knowledge in a particular field of study?

Epistemology concerns what constitutes acceptable knowledge in a field of study. The most important distinction is one hinted at the start of Section 4.2 in our example of two researchers' views of what they consider important in the study of the manufacturing process. The researcher (the 'resources' researcher) who considers data on resources needed is likely to be more akin to the position of the natural scientist. This may be the position of the operations management specialist who is comfortable with the collection and analysis of 'facts'. For that researcher, reality is represented by objects that are considered to be 'real', such as computers, trucks and machines. These objects have a separate existence to that of the researcher and for that reason, this researcher would argue that the data collected are far less open to bias and therefore more 'objective'. The 'resources' researcher would place much less authority on the data collected by the 'feelings' researcher, who is concerned with the feelings and attitudes of the workers towards their managers in that same manufacturing process. The 'resources' researcher would view the objects studied by the 'feelings' researcher – feelings and attitudes – as social phenomena which have no external reality. They cannot be seen, measured and modified like computers, trucks and machines. You may argue, of course, that human feelings can be, and frequently are, measured. Indeed, the 'resources' researcher may place more authority on such data were it to be presented in the form of a table of statistical data. This would lend the data more objectivity in the view of the 'resources' researcher. But this raises the question of whether those data presented in statistical form are any more deserving of authority than those presented in a narrative, which may be the choice of the 'feelings' researcher.

The 'resources' researcher is embracing what is called the positivist philosophy to the development of knowledge whereas the 'feelings' researcher is adopting the interpretivist philosophy. We deal with both in this sub-section on epistemology, as well as the stance of the researcher embracing the realist and interpretivist philosophies.

Positivism: working in the tradition of the natural scientist

If your research reflects the philosophy of **positivism** then you will probably adopt the philosophical stance of the natural scientist. You will prefer 'working with an observable social reality and that the end product of such research can be law-like generalisations similar to those produced by the physical and natural scientists' (Remenyi *et al.* 1998:32).

Like the 'resources' researcher earlier, only phenomena that you can observe will lead to the production of credible data. To generate a research strategy to collect these data you are likely to use existing theory to develop hypotheses. These hypotheses will be tested and confirmed, in whole or part, or refuted, leading to the further development of theory which then may be tested by further research.

The hypotheses developed, as in Box 4.3, lead to the gathering of facts that provide the basis for subsequent hypothesis testing. Both the examples we have cited so far, that of

Box 4.3
Focus on student research

The development of hypotheses

Brett was conducting a piece of research for his project on the economic benefits of working from home for software developers. He studied the literature on home working in general and read in detail two past dissertations in his university library that dealt with the same phenomenon, albeit that they did not relate specifically to software developers. As a result of his reading, Brett developed a number of theoretical propositions, each of which contained specific hypotheses. Listed below is that which Brett developed in relation to potential increased costs, which may negate the economic gains of home working.

THEORETICAL PROPOSITION: *Increased costs may negate the productivity gains from home working.*

Specific hypotheses:

1 Increased costs for computer hardware, software and telecommunications equipment will negate the productivity gains from home working.
2 Home workers will require additional support from on-site employees, for example technicians, which will negate the productivity gains from home working.
3 Work displaced to other employees and/or increased supervisory requirements will negate the productivity gains from home working.
4 Reduced face-to-face access by home workers to colleagues will result in lost opportunities to increase efficiencies, which will negate the productivity gains from home working.

Source: developed from Westfall (1997).

the 'resources' researcher and Brett in Box 4.3, will be concerned with facts rather than impressions. Such facts are consistent with the notion of 'observable social reality' similar to that employed by the physical and natural scientists to which we referred in Remenyi *et al.*'s (1998) definition earlier.

Another important component of the positivist approach to research is that the research is undertaken, as far as possible, in a value-free way. At first sight this is a plausible position, particularly when one contrasts the perspective of the 'resources' researcher with the 'feelings' researcher in our earlier example. The 'resources' researcher would claim to be external to the process of data collection in the sense that there is little that can be done to alter the substance of the data collected. The assumption is that 'the researcher is independent of and neither affects nor is affected by the subject of the research' (Remenyi *et al.* 1998:33). After all, the 'resources' researcher cannot change the fact that there are five trucks and 10 computers. In Box 4.3 Brett would collect data that would facilitate the estimation of quantitative cost estimates and allow the hypotheses to be tested. The 'resources' researcher's claim to be value free is, on the face of it, rather stronger than that of the 'feelings' researcher. It may be argued that the 'feelings' researcher is part of the data collection process. It would be normal for at least part of the process of data collection on the feelings and attitudes of the workers towards their managers to include the personal involvement of the 'feelings' researcher with those workers. A personal interview, for example, will involve the 'feelings' researcher framing the questions to ask and interpreting the respondent's examples. It is hard to imagine that the 'feelings' researcher would ask every respondent exactly the came question in exactly the same way and interpret every response with computer-like consistency.

You may argue, of course, that complete freedom from the inclusion of our own values as researchers is impossible. Even the researcher seeking to adopt a decided positivist stance exercises choice in the issue to study, the research objectives to pursue and the data to collect. Indeed, it could be argued that the decision to adopt a seemingly value-free perspective suggests the existence of a certain value position.

It is frequently advocated that the positivist researcher will be likely to use a highly structured methodology in order to facilitate replication (Gill and Johnson 2002). Furthermore, the emphasis will be on quantifiable observations that lend themselves to statistical analysis. However, as you read through this chapter and the next you will note that this may not necessarily be the case since it is perfectly possible to adopt some of the characteristics of positivism in your research, for example hypothesis testing, using data originally collected in in-depth interviews.

Realism: do objects exist independently of our knowledge of their existence?

Realism is another philosophical position which relates to scientific enquiry. The essence of realism is that what the senses show us as reality is the truth: that objects have an existence independent of the human mind. The philosophy of realism is that there is a reality quite independent of the mind. In this sense, realism is opposed to idealism, the theory that only the mind and its contents exist. Realism is a branch of epistemology which is similar to positivism in that it assumes a scientific approach to the development of knowledge. This assumption underpins the collection of data and the understanding of those data. This meaning (and in particular the relevance of realism for business and management research) becomes clearer when two forms of realism are contrasted.

The first type of realism is direct realism. **Direct realism** says that what you see is what you get: what we experience through our senses portrays the world accurately. The second kind of realism is called **critical realism**. Critical realists argue that what we experience are sensations, the images of the things in the real world, not the things directly. Critical realists point out how often our senses deceive us. For example, when you next watch an international rugby or cricket match on television you are likely to see an advertisement for the sponsor in a prominent position on the actual playing surface. This looks like it is standing upright on the field. However, this is an illusion. It is in fact painted on the grass. So what we really see are sensations, which are representations of what is real.

The direct realist would respond to the critical realist by arguing that what we call illusions are actually due to the fact that we have insufficient information. We do not perceive the world in television images. We move around, move our eyes and ears, use all our senses. In the case of the television advertisement, the complete experience of it would include seeing it from all directions and angles.

A simple way to think about the difference between direct and critical realism is as follows. Critical realism claims that there are two steps to experiencing the world. First, there is the thing itself and the sensations it conveys. Second, there is the mental process-ing that goes on sometime after that sensation meets our senses. Direct realism says that the first step is enough. To pursue our cricket (or rugby) example, the umpire who is the critical realist would say about his umpiring decisions: 'I give them as I see them!' The umpire who is a direct realist would say 'I give them as they are!'

Business and management research is concerned with the social world in which we live. So you may agree with writers such as Bhaskar (1989) who identify with the episte-mology of critical realists. Their argument is that as researchers we will only be able to understand what is going on in the social world if we understand the social structures that have given rise to the phenomena that we are trying to understand. In other words, what we see is only part of the bigger picture. Bhaskar (1989) argues that we can identify what we do not see through the practical and theoretical processes of the social sciences.

Thus, the critical realist's position is that our knowledge of reality is a result of social conditioning (e.g. we know that if the rugby player runs into the advertisement that is standing up he will fall over!) and cannot be understood independently of the social actors involved in the knowledge derivation process (Dobson 2002).

A further important point needs to be made about the distinction between direct and critical realism, both of which are important in relation to the pursuit of business and man-agement research. The first relates the capacity of research to change the world which it studies. The direct realist perspective would suggest the world is relatively unchanging: that it operates, in the business context, at one level (the individual, the group or the organisation). The critical realist, on the other hand, would recognise the importance of multi-level study (e.g. at the level of the individual, the group and the organisation). Each of these levels has the capacity to change the researcher's understanding of that which is being studied. This would be the consequence of the existence of a greater variety of struc-tures, procedures and processes and the capacity that these structures, procedures and processes have to interact with one another. We, therefore, would argue that the critical realist's position that the social world is constantly changing is much more in line with the purpose of business and management research which is too often to understand the reason for phenomena as a precursor to recommending change.

Interpretivism: understanding differences between humans as social actors

You may be critical of the positivist tradition and argue that the social world of business and management is far too complex to lend itself to theorising by definite 'laws' in the same way as the physical sciences. Those researchers critical of positivism argue that rich insights into this complex world are lost if such complexity is reduced entirely to a series of law-like generalisations. If you sympathise with such a view your research philosophy is likely to be nearer to that of the interpretivist.

Interpretivism advocates that it is necessary for the researcher to understand differences between humans in our role as social actors. This emphasises the difference between conducting research among people rather than objects such as trucks and computers. The term 'social actors' is quite significant here. The metaphor of the theatre suggests that as humans we play a part on the stage of human life. In theatrical productions, actors play a part which they interpret in a particular way (which may be their own or that of the director) and act out their part in accordance with this interpretation. In the same way we interpret our everyday social roles in accordance with the meaning we give to these roles. In addition, we interpret the social roles of others in accordance with our own set of meanings.

The heritage of this strand of interpretivism comes from two intellectual traditions: **phenomenology** and **symbolic interactionism** (Chapter 9). Phenomenology refers to the way in which we as humans make sense of the world around us. In symbolic interactionism we are in a continual process of interpreting the social world around us (Box 4.4, opposite) in that we interpret the actions of others with whom we interact and this interpretation leads to adjustment of our own meanings and actions.

Crucial to the interpretivist philosophy is that the researcher has to adopt an empathetic stance. The challenge here is to enter the social world of our research subjects and understand their world from their point of view. Some would argue that an interpretivist perspective is highly appropriate in the case of business and management research, particularly in such fields as organisational behaviour, marketing and human resource management. Not only are business situations complex, they are also unique. They are a function of a particular set of circumstances and individuals coming together at a specific time.

Axiology: what roles do our values play in our research choices?

Axiology is a branch of philosophy that studies judgements about value. Although this may include values we posess in the fields of aesthetics and ethics, it is the process of social enquiry with which we are concerned here. The role that your own values play in all stages of the research process is of great importance if you wish your research results to be credible. This is why we think it is worth noting this important topic here, particularly through the example in Box 4.5.

Heron (1996) argues that our values are the guiding reason of all human action. He further argues that researchers demonstrate axiological skill by being able to articulate their values as a basis for making judgements about what research they are conducting and how they go about doing it. After all, at all stages in the research process you will be demonstrating your values. The example in Box 4.5 illustrates the relevance of values in research topic selection. Choosing one topic rather than another suggests that you think one of the topics is more important. Your choice of philosophical approach is a reflection of your values, as is your choice of data collection techniques. For example, to conduct a study where you place great importance on data collected through interview work suggests that you value personal interaction with your respondents more highly than their views expressed through an anonymous questionnaire.

An interesting idea which comes from Heron's (1996) discussion of axiology is the possibility of writing your own statement of personal values in relation to the topic you are studying. This may be more evidently applicable to some research topics than others.

Box 4.4
Focus on management research

Understanding consumer adoption of Internet banking: an interpretive study in the Australian banking context

Lichtenstein *et al.* (2006) report in the *Journal of Electronic Commerce Research* key findings from an interpretive study of Australian banking consumer experiences on the adoption of Internet banking. The paper provides an understanding of how and why specific factors affect the decision by Australian consumers whether or not to bank on the Internet.

The main findings were:

- convenience – particularly in terms of time savings – is the main motivator for consumer adoption of internet banking;
- security, privacy and trust concerns dominated consumer concerns about Internet banking in Australia;
- there is a need for extensive and deep levels of consumer support from banks;
- some banking consumers may still be unaware of the existence, features, relative advantages and benefits of Internet banking;
- phone banking was the main method of banking used by people who might otherwise have attempted Internet banking;
- some people still do not feel confident about their ability to use the Internet, and view using the Internet for applications such as Internet banking as too difficult;
- Internet-proficient consumers found difficulty with the initial set-up procedure for Internet banking.

The authors argue that the findings highlight increasing risk acceptance by consumers in regard to Internet-based services and the growing importance of offering deep levels of consumer support for such services. Finally, the paper suggests that banks will be better able to manage consumer experiences with moving to Internet banking if they understand that such experiences involve a process of adjustment and learning over time, and not merely the adoption of a new technology.

Lichtenstein *et al.* were interested in reasons why some groups, such as older people and those on lower incomes, are slow to adopt Internet banking, They, therefore, designed a sample which included those groups; Internet and non-Internet as well as Internet banking and non-Internet banking users; a range of age and income groups; people from rural and city areas, and males and females. Thirty-two participants were recruited through community groups and libraries.

To collect the data, the researchers used a combination of individual and focus group interviews. A series of five individual interviews provided the opportunity to construct complete profiles for each interviewee, given that in group interviews, multiple views and opinions can gravitate to a group view as a result of social influences. All interviews were semi-structured, allowing new issues to emerge for exploration. The interviews were of approximately one and a half hours' duration for focus groups and one hour for individual interviews. Interview questions covered demographics and banking method choices, as well as key motivators and inhibitors in the use of Internet banking as suggested by literature. Deeper issues were explored as they emerged.

The research project was conducted in two phases. In the first phase, data were collected from interviews of Australian banking consumers and analysed using only a grounded theory approach. The results were then interpreted using theories of innovation and the digital divide in order to highlight related issues. In the second phase, a comprehensive literature review was conducted which provided extensive theoretical understandings that helped inform the second data analysis.

The data were analysed by qualitative content analysis where coded categories discovered in the interview transcripts were inductively developed according to grounded theory techniques but also drawing on the theoretical concepts wherever they appeared in the data. The categories evolved to conclusive states over iterative readings and were grouped into themes at the end of analysis. The themes were then reviewed and key findings developed including findings regarding major influences and new trends and a theoretical framework conceptualising key factors in consumer Internet banking adoption.

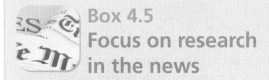

Box 4.5
Focus on research in the news

Yahoo gives $1 million to Georgetown University

The Internet giant, Yahoo has been criticised for giving information to the Chinese government that led to a journalist to be jailed for 10 years. The company has been working with Google, Microsoft, human rights organisations, investors and legal experts to hammer out a code of conduct to protect online free speech and privacy. As part of this programme, Yahoo is giving $1 million to Georgetown University, Washington DC, to study the relationship between international values and Internet communications technologies. The fund will be known as the Yahoo International Values, Communications, Technology, and Global Internet Fellowship Fund.

Georgetown's Yahoo Fellow in Residence and Junior Yahoo Fellows begun their work in the autumn of 2007. They will examine the use of communication technologies and how regulation of the Internet affects privacy and freedom of expression issues internationally. The fellowship fund will focus their efforts on countries that are growing quickly in the marketplace such as China, India, Russia and Brazil. Besides doing research, Yahoo Fellows will work with faculty to enhance curricular activities such as contributing to guest lectures, seminars and case studies.

Source: derived from article by Sachoff, Mike (2007) WebPro News, 13 Apr. Available at: http://www.webpronews.com/topnews/2007/04/13/yahoo-gives-1-million-to-georgetown-university

Those topics concerned with personal career development, for example, may be obvious candidates for this process. For example, it would be an issue of personal value that it is the responsibility of the individual to take charge of their own career development. In areas of finance it may be a strongly held value of the researcher that as much information as possible should be available to as many stakeholders as possible.

A statement of values may be of use both to you as the researcher and those parties with whom you have contact in your research. The use to you would be a result of your 'being honest with yourself' about quite what your values are. This would, for example, heighten your awareness of value judgements you are making in drawing conclusions from your data. These value judgements may lead to the drawing of conclusions which may be different from those drawn by researchers with other values. Other relevant parties connected with your research may include any fellow researchers, your supervisor and the university research ethics committee. This latter body may be of particular relevance to thoughts about the role of values in research topic choice and ways of pursuing research. Being clear about your own value position may help you in deciding what is appropriate ethically and arguing your position in the event of queries about decisions you have made. Sections 6.3 and 6.4 go into more detail about research ethics.

Research paradigms

To draw this section on research philosophies together we explore research philosophy further through the concept of research paradigms. **Paradigm** is a term frequently used in the social sciences, but one which can lead to confusion because it tends to have multiple meanings. The definition we use here is that a paradigm is a way of examining social phenomena from which particular understandings of these phenomena can be gained and explanations attempted.

Table 4.1 Comparison of four research philosophies in management research

	Positivism	Realism	Interpretivism	Pragmatism
Ontology: *the researcher's view of the nature of reality or being*	External, objective and independent of social actors	Is objective. Exists independently of human thoughts and beliefs or knowledge of their existence (realist), but is interpreted through social conditioning (critical realist)	Socially constructed, subjective, may change, multiple	External, multiple, view chosen to best enable answering of research question
Epistemology: *the researcher's view regarding what constitutes acceptable knowledge*	Only observable phenomena can provide credible data, facts. Focus on causality and law like generalisations, reducing phenomena to simplest elements	Observable phenomena provide credible data, facts. Insufficient data means inaccuracies in sensations (direct realism). Alternatively, phenomena create sensations which are open to misinterpretation (critical realism). Focus on explaining within a context or contexts	Subjective meanings and social phenomena. Focus upon the details of situation, a reality behind these details, subjective meanings motivating actions	Either or both observable phenomena and subjective meanings can provide acceptable knowledge dependent upon the research question. Focus on practical applied research, integrating different perspectives to help interpret the data
Axiology: *the researcher's view of the role of values in research*	Research is undertaken in a value-free way, the researcher is independent of the data and maintains an objective stance	Research is value laden; the researcher is biased by world views, cultural experiences and upbringing. These will impact on the research	Research is value bound, the researcher is part of what is being researched, cannot be separated and so will be subjective	Values play a large role in interpreting results, the researcher adopting both objective and subjective points of view
Data collection techniques most often used	Highly structured, large samples, measurement, quantitative, but can use qualitative	Methods chosen must fit the subject matter, quantitative or qualitative	Small samples, in-depth investigations, qualitative	Mixed or multiple method designs, quantitative and qualitative

In our view the work of Burrell and Morgan (1982) is particularly helpful in summarising and clarifying the epistemologies and ontologies we have covered above. In addition, these writers have offered a categorisation of social science paradigms which can be used in management and business research to generate fresh insights into real-life issues and problems.

In Figure 4.2 we illustrate the four paradigms: functionalist; interpretive; radical humanist; and radical structuralist.

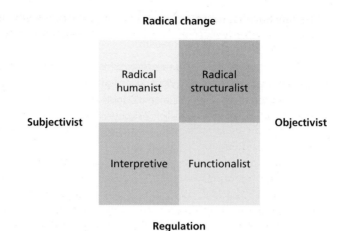

Figure 4.2
Four paradigms for the analysis of social theory
Source: developed from Burrell and Morgan (1982) *Sociological Paradigms and Organisational Analysis.*
Reproduced with permission of Ashgate Publishing Company

Figure 4.2 shows that the four paradigms are arranged to correspond to four conceptual dimensions: **radical change** and regulation and subjectivist and objectivist. The
latter two terms are familiar to you from our discussion of ontology in the previous
section. In relation to business and management, radical change relates to a judgement
about the way organisational affairs should be conducted and suggests ways in which
these affairs may be conducted in order to make fundamental changes to the normal
order of things. In short, the radical change dimension adopts a critical perspective on
organisational life. The **regulatory perspective** is less judgemental and critical.
Regulation seeks to explain the way in which organisational affairs are regulated and offer
suggestions as to how they may be improved within the framework of the way things are
done at present. In other words, the radical change dimension approaches organisational
problems from the viewpoint of overturning the existing state of affairs; the regulatory
dimension seeks to work within the existing state of affairs.

Burrell and Morgan (1982) note that the purposes of the four paradigms are:

- to help researchers clarify their assumptions about their view of the nature of science
  and society;
- to offer a useful way of understanding the way in which other researchers approach
  their work;
- to help researchers plot their own route through their research; to understand where it
  is possible to go and where they are going.

In the bottom right corner of the quadrant is the **functionalist paradigm**. This
is located on the objectivist and regulatory dimensions. Objectivism is the ontological
position you are likely to adopt if you are operating with this paradigm. It is regulatory in
that you will probably be more concerned with a rational explanation of why a particular
organisational problem is occurring and developing a set of recommendations set within
the current structure of the organisation's current management. This is the paradigm
within which most business and management research operates. Burrell and Morgan
(1982) note that it is often problem-oriented in approach, concerned to provide practical
solutions to practical problems. Perhaps the key assumption you would be making here is
that organisations are rational entities, in which rational explanations offer solutions to
rational problems. A typical example of a management research project operating within

the functionalist paradigm would be an evaluation study of a communication strategy to assess its effectiveness and make recommendations as to the way in which it may be made more effective.

Contained in the bottom left corner of the quadrant is the **interpretive paradigm**. As has been noted, the philosophical position to which this refers (interpretivism) is the way we as humans attempt to make sense of the world around us (Box 4.6). The concern you would have working within this paradigm would be to understand the fundamental meanings attached to organisational life. Far from emphasising rationality, it may be that the principal concern you have here is discovering irrationalities. Concern with studying an organisation's communication strategy may soon turn to understanding the ways in which the intentions of management become derailed for completely unseen reasons, maybe reasons which are not apparent even to those involved with the strategy. This is likely to take you into the realm of organisation politics and the way in which power is used. Burrell and Morgan (1982) note that everyday life is accorded the status of a miraculous achievement. Your concern here would not be to achieve change in the order of things, it would be to understand and explain what is going on.

In the top left corner the **radical humanist paradigm** is located within the subjectivist and radical change dimensions. As we said earlier, the radical change dimension adopts a critical perspective on organisational life. As such, working within this paradigm you would be concerned with changing the status quo, or in Burrell and Morgan's (1979:32) words 'to articulate ways in which humans can transcend the spiritual bonds and fetters which tie them into existing social patterns and thus realise their full potential'. The ontological perspective you would adopt here, as in the interpretive paradigm, would be subjectivist.

Finally, in the top right corner of the quadrant is the **radical structuralist paradigm**. Here your concern would be to approach your research with a view to achieving fundamental change based upon an analysis of such organisational phenomena as power relationships and patterns of conflict. The radical structuralist paradigm is involved with structural patterns with work organisations such as hierarchies and reporting relationships and the extent to which these may produce dysfunctionalities. It adopts an objectivist perspective because it is concerned with objective entities, unlike the radical humanist ontology which attempts to understand the meanings of social phenomena from the subjective perspective of participating social actors.

Box 4.6
Focus on management research

A paper by Burke (2007) in *Library Review* examines research choices in information management and suggests a way of applying the research paradigms to information management research. This was achieved by an examination of research approaches which may be useful in information management research. As a background to this discussion the importance of communication, competition, and change in information management was highlighted. Each of the research paradigms were examined for relevance and although there were possibilities of usefulness in different contexts, Burke generally considered that the interpretive is the most useful and the one that will give the richest results. The decision was justified by taking a particular example of information management research deconstructing epistemological assumptions of interpretivism.

Box 4.6
Focus on management research *(continued)*

The central theme of Burke's paper is that research which deals primarily with people and information in a world of change, competition and fluid communications technology should take into account and allow for an understanding of human behaviour. This understanding helps to highlight different contexts, backgrounds and cultures and therefore provides assistance in making appropriate choices concerning research paradigms and information management, which in turn will ensure thoughtful method choices and justifiable research results.

Burke argues that the way in which information professionals undertake research is of paramount importance as they need to react to what can be termed the three 'C's', i.e. communications, competition and change. In particular, communications have radically altered since the impact of technology, for example the immediacy of communication and the accessibility of all time zones mean that business can thrive 24/7 in an international arena.

The example of information management research upon which Burke based the conclusion took place over a number of years and was conducted in three countries by ethnographic means using participant observation within an interpretivist philosophy. The study examined the relationship between the design of an organisation's structure and information fulfilment. Information fulfilment was defined as a final stage of information seeking behaviour which ensures that the user has gained all the information needed to fully complete a task, beyond initial satisfaction. The research was conducted in higher education institutions in Poland, Russia and the UK. The deconstruction of the interpretive paradigm view shows that this stance is justified as providing the best way of collecting social phenomena in natural settings, which is so important in the field of information management and which was vital to the success of the research project. While the application of the interpretive paradigm to the information field is well documented, it is still relatively unusual to apply these principles to the field of information management and thus demonstrate the usefulness of this paradigm to the information fulfilment research project.

Box 4.7
Focus on student research

An outline research proposal on corporate social responsibility using integrated paradigms

The purpose of Krista's research is to understand how corporations implement corporate social responsibility (CSR) codes of conduct. Inherent in this exploration is an understanding of the following:

- what role corporations believe they have in society;
- how this impacts the types of CSR commitments they make in their codes of conduct;
- how these commitments are operationalised;
- how these actions are communicated to those who are asked or required to conduct them;

- how these individuals feel about their new responsibilities;
- how the actions were in fact carried out;
- what the targeted groups feel about the actions carried out;
- the successes and failures experienced during these processes.

Integrated research paradigm

Krista anticipates using both qualitative and quantitative techniques to collect data. However, she points out that the approach will not be from a positivist perspective, as she believes there is no truth or absolute reality to be discovered. She argues that codes of conduct are a human construct and the success or failure of implementing the code is dependent upon the perspective of the individuals or groups affected. Krista contends that this suggests a likely approach of interpretivist/social constructivism/interactionism (Mertens

1998; Denzin 2001; Aram and Salipante 2003). She notes that the individuals or groups affected by the codes of conduct are also situated in historical and cultural contexts, which impact on how they perceive the actions of the corporation and its value to them.

The focus of Krista's research will be on the corporation and what it has learned and has yet to learn about successful implementation of its code as defined by all affected groups, including the marginalised, oppressed and least powerful.

Krista's research is likely to be approached from primarily an interpretivist or social constructionist perspective in that there are multiple realities to be understood and all impact the overall success or failure of the code implementation efforts. Identifying and understanding the relationships between multiple realities of code implementation will start to reveal the 'underlying patterns and order of the social world' (Morgan 1980:609) with regard to this phenomenon. She argues that the patterns and order themselves can provide insight into more successful or unsuccessful code implementation techniques and considerations. The end goals of Krista's research are twofold. The first goal is to help the corporation with its efforts to improve its social responsibilities to society as are appropriate to its unique context. The second goal is to empower stakeholder representatives to better communicate with the corporation in consensus-building activities regarding needs and wants for both parties. Krista notes that the quantitative element of this research will be used solely to determine the generalisability of this information for other corporations around the world and will not impact on the overall perspective taken.

Owing to the exploratory and descriptive nature of this research (Robson 2002), data collection, organisation and analysis will be guided primarily by a grounded theory, or inductive perspective, whereby the collection, examination and process of continual re-examination of data will determine the research findings.

As the social constructivist perspective is considered to be an integrated perspective, Krista contends that it is appropriate also to use mixed methods. She will use qualitative methods in the form of case studies to create an in-depth, rich account (Yin 2003; Scholz and Tietje 2002; Rubin and Rubin 1995) of

how corporations implement their codes of conduct and what stakeholders think about their efforts. The second phase of research will be used to determine whether the code implementation practices identified in the case studies can be used to describe successful or unsuccessful implementation of CSR codes within a more general group of corporations. A survey strategy will be used to determine whether the information found is more generalisable or specific to certain unique corporations.

Bridging the relevance gap

Krista argues in her outline proposal that her research will attempt to help bridge the 'relevance gap' between researchers and practitioners on CSR code implementation (Aram and Salipante 2003; Tranfield and Starkey 1998), by ensuring the research strategies (decided on in advance with the case study companies) and the outcomes are both rigorous and appropriate to solve the unique corporation's questions. Therefore, her research strategy will need to allow her to provide both context-specific recommendations and conclusions the corporation can use and data that is potentially generalisable to a wider range of corporations.

Krista points out that it is difficult at the earliest stages of her research to predict whether the data collected from the study will be generalisable and that it is certain that the data will not be reproducible. Tsoukas (1994) discusses the inherent nature of change in all human activity and thus the expectation that change will occur in all systems, groups or individuals under study. Therefore, Krista argues, conducting research as an interpretivist assumes that the research will be virtually impossible to reproduce.

Thus, Krista's research is likely to be conducted from a social constructionist or interpretivist perspective, integrating qualitative and quantitative data collection techniques and analysis procedures to strengthen the validity and quality of data analysis and research findings. The purpose is to understand the different perspectives or realities that are constructed during the implementation of social issues, how history and culture impact these realities and how they impact the overall 'success' of implementation through revealing underlying social patterns and order.

▶ **Box 4.7**
Focus on student
research (continued)

References

Aram, J.D. and Salipante, P.F. (2003) 'Bridging scholarship in management: epistemological reflections', *British Journal of Management*, Vol. 14, pp. 189–205.

Denzin, N.K. (2001) *Interpretive Interactionism* (2nd edn). London: Sage.

Mertens, D.M. (1998) *Research Methods in Education and Psychology: Integrating Diversity with Quantitative and Qualitative Approaches*. London: Sage.

Morgan, G. (1980) 'Paradigms, metaphors and puzzle solving in organization theory', *Administrative Science Quarterly*, Vol. 25, pp. 605–22.

Robson, C. (2002) *Real World Research: A Resource for Social Scientists and Practitioner-Researchers* (2nd edn). Oxford: Blackwell.

Rubin. H.J. and Rubin, I.S. (1995) *Qualitative Interviewing: The Art of Hearing Data*. London: Sage.

Scholz, R.W. and Tietje, O. (2002) *Embedded Case Study Methods: Integrating Quantitative and Qualitative Knowledge*. London: Sage.

Tranfield, D. and Starkey, K. (1998) 'The nature, social organization and promotion of management research: towards policy', *British Journal of Management*, Vol. 9, pp. 341–53.

Tsoukas, H. (1994) 'Refining common sense: types of knowledge in management studies', *Journal of Management Studies*, Vol. 31, pp.761–80.

Yin, R.K. (2003) *Case Study Research: Design and Methods* (3rd edn). London: Sage.

4.3 Research approaches

Chapter 2 notes that your research project will involve the use of theory. That theory may or may not be made explicit in the design of the research (Chapter 5), although it will usually be made explicit in your presentation of the findings and conclusions. The extent to which you are clear about the theory at the beginning of your research raises an important question concerning the design of your research project. This is whether your research should use the deductive approach, in which you develop a theory and hypothesis (or hypotheses) and design a research strategy to test the hypothesis, or the inductive approach, in which you would collect data and develop theory as a result of your data analysis. Insofar as it is useful to attach these **research approaches** to the different research philosophies, deduction owes more to positivism and induction to interpretivism, although we believe that such labelling is potentially misleading and of no real practical value.

The next two sub-sections of this chapter explain the differences between these two approaches and the implications of these differences.

Deduction: testing theory

As noted earlier, deduction owes much to what we would think of as **scientific research**. It involves the development of a theory that is subjected to a rigorous test. As such, it is the dominant research approach in the natural sciences, where laws present the basis of explanation, allow the anticipation of phenomena, predict their occurrence and therefore permit them to be controlled (Collis and Hussey 2003).

Robson (2002) lists five sequential stages through which deductive research will progress:

1 deducing a **hypothesis** (a testable proposition about the relationship between two or more concepts or variables) from the theory;

2 expressing the hypothesis in operational terms (that is, indicating exactly how the concepts or variables are to be measured), which propose a relationship between two specific concepts or variables;

3 testing this operational hypothesis (this will involve one or more of the strategies detailed in Chapter 5);

4 examining the specific outcome of the inquiry (it will either tend to confirm the theory or indicate the need for its modification);

5 if necessary, modifying the theory in the light of the findings.

An attempt is then made to verify the revised theory by going back to the first step and repeating the whole cycle.

Deduction possesses several important characteristics. First, there is the search to explain causal relationships between variables. It may be that you wish to establish the reasons for high employee absenteeism in a retail store. After studying absence patterns it occurs to you that there seems to be a relationship between absence, the age of workers and length of service. Consequently, you develop a hypothesis that states that absenteeism is more likely to be prevalent among younger workers who have worked for the organisation for a relatively short period of time. To test this hypothesis you utilise another characteristic, the collection of quantitative data. (This is not to say that a deductive approach may not use qualitative data.) It may be that there are important differences in the way work is arranged in different stores: therefore you would need to employ a further important characteristic of deduction approach, **controls to allow the testing of hypotheses**. These controls would help to ensure that any change in absenteeism was a function of worker age and length of service rather than any other aspect of the store, for example the way in which people were managed. Your research would use a highly **structured methodology** to facilitate replication (Gill and Johnson 2002), an important issue to ensure reliability, as we shall emphasise in Section 5.6.

In order to pursue the principle of scientific rigour, deduction dictates that the researcher should be independent of what is being observed. This is easy in our example because it involves only the collection of absence data. It is also unproblematic if a postal questionnaire is being administered, although the high level of objectivity this suggests appears less convincing when one considers the element of subjectivity in the choice of questions and the way these are phrased (Section 11.3).

An additional important characteristic of deduction is that concepts need to be **operationalised** in a way that enables facts to be measured quantitatively. In our example above, the obvious one is absenteeism. Just what constitutes absenteeism would have to be strictly defined: an absence for a complete day would probably count, but what about absence for two hours? In addition, what would constitute a 'short period of employment' and 'younger' employees? What is happening here is that the principle of **reductionism** is being followed. This holds that problems as a whole are better understood if they are reduced to the simplest possible elements.

The final characteristic of deduction is **generalisation**. In order to be able to generalise statistically about regularities in human social behaviour it is necessary to select samples of sufficient numerical size. In our example above, research at a particular store would allow us only to make inferences about that store; it would be dangerous to predict that worker youth and short length of service lead to absenteeism in all cases. This is discussed in more detail in Section 5.6.

Induction: building theory

An alternative approach to conducting research on DIY store employee absenteeism would be to go on to the shopfloor and interview a sample of the employees and their supervisors about the experience of working at the store. The purpose here would be to get a feel of what was going on, so as to understand better the nature of the problem. Your task then would be to make sense of the interview data you had collected by analysing those data. The result of this analysis would be the formulation of a theory. This may be that there is a relationship between absence and relatively short periods of employment. Alternatively, you may discover that there are other competing reasons for absence that may or may not be related to worker age or length of service. You may end up with the same theory, but you would have gone about the production of that theory using an inductive approach: theory would follow data rather than vice versa as with deduction.

We noted earlier that deduction has its origins in research in the natural sciences. However, the emergence of the social sciences in the 20th century led social science researchers to be wary of deduction. They were critical of an approach that enabled a cause–effect link to be made between particular variables without an understanding of the way in which humans interpreted their social world. Developing such an understanding is, of course, the strength of an inductive approach. In our absenteeism example we would argue that it is more realistic to treat workers as humans whose attendance behaviour is a consequence of the way in which they perceive their work experience, rather than as if they were unthinking research objects who respond in a mechanistic way to certain circumstances.

Followers of induction would also criticise deduction because of its tendency to construct a rigid methodology that does not permit alternative explanations of what is going on. In that sense, there is an air of finality about the choice of theory and definition of the hypothesis. Alternative theories may be suggested by deduction. However, these would be within the limits set by the highly structured research design. In this respect, a significant characteristic of the absenteeism research design noted above is that of the operationalisation of concepts. As we saw in the absenteeism example, age was precisely defined. However, a less structured approach might reveal alternative explanations of the absenteeism–age relationship denied by a stricter definition of age.

Research using an inductive approach is likely to be particularly concerned with the context in which such events were taking place. Therefore, the study of a small sample of subjects might be more appropriate than a large number as with the deductive approach. As can be seen in Chapter 10, researchers in this tradition are more likely to work with qualitative data and to use a variety of methods to collect these data in order to establish different views of phenomena (Easterby-Smith *et al.* 2008).

At this stage you may be asking yourself: So what? Why is the choice that I make about my research approach important? Easterby-Smith *et al.* (2008) suggest three reasons. First, it enables you to take a more informed decision about your research design (Chapter 5), which is more than just the techniques by which data are collected and procedures by which they are analysed. It is the overall configuration of a piece of research involving questions about what kind of evidence is gathered and from where, and how such evidence is interpreted in order to provide good answers to your initial research question.

Second, it will help you to think about those research strategies and choices that will work for you and, crucially, those that will not. For example, if you are particularly interested in understanding why something is happening, rather than being able to describe what is happening, it may be more appropriate to undertake your research inductively rather than deductively.

Third, Easterby-Smith *et al.* (2008) argue that knowledge of the different research traditions enables you to adapt your research design to cater for constraints. These may be practical, involving, say, limited access to data, or they may arise from a lack of prior knowledge of the subject. You simply may not be in a position to frame a hypothesis because you have insufficient understanding of the topic to do this.

Combining research approaches

So far we have conveyed the impression that there are rigid divisions between deduction and induction. This would be misleading. Not only is it perfectly possible to combine deduction and induction within the same piece of research, but also in our experience it is often advantageous to do so.

We return to the topic of using multiple methods in Section 5.6. Table 4.2 summarises some of the major differences between deduction and induction.

At this point you may be wondering whether your research will be deductive or inductive. Creswell (2002) suggests a number of practical criteria. Perhaps the most important of these are the emphasis of the research (Box 4.8) and the nature of the research topic. A topic on which there is a wealth of literature from which you can define a theoretical framework and a hypothesis lends itself more readily to deduction. With research into a topic that is new, is exciting much debate, and on which there is little existing literature, it may be more appropriate to work inductively by generating data and analysing and reflecting upon what theoretical themes the data are suggesting.

The time you have available will be an issue. Deductive research can be quicker to complete, albeit that time must be devoted to setting up the study prior to data collection and analysis. Data collection is often based on 'one take'. It is normally possible to predict the time schedules accurately. On the other hand, inductive research can be much more protracted. Often the ideas, based on a much longer period of data collection and analysis, have to emerge gradually. This leads to another important consideration, the extent to which you are prepared to indulge in risk. Deduction can be a lower-risk strategy, albeit that there are risks, such as the non-return of questionnaires. With induction you have constantly to live with the fear that no useful data patterns and theory will emerge. Finally, there is the question of audience. In our experience, most managers are familiar with deduction and much more likely to put faith in the conclusions emanating from this approach. You may also wish to consider the preferences of the person marking your research report. We all have our preferences about the approach to adopt. You may be wise to establish these before nailing your colours too firmly to one mast.

This last point suggests that not all the decisions about the research approach that you make should always be so practical. Hakim (2000) uses an architectural metaphor to

Table 4.2 Major differences between deductive and inductive approaches to research

Deduction emphasises	Induction emphasises
• scientific principles • moving from theory to data • the need to explain causal relationships between variables • the collection of quantitative data • the application of controls to ensure validity of data • the operationalisation of concepts to ensure clarity of definition • a highly structured approach • researcher independence of what is being researched • the necessity to select samples of sufficient size in order to generalise conclusions	• gaining an understanding of the meanings humans attach to events • a close understanding of the research context • the collection of qualitative data • a more flexible structure to permit changes of research emphasis as the research progresses • a realisation that the researcher is part of the research process • less concern with the need to generalise

Box 4.8
Focus on student research

Deductive and inductive research

Sadie decided to conduct a research project on violence at work and its effects on the stress levels of staff. She considered the different ways she would approach the work were she to adopt:

- the deductive approach;
- the inductive approach.

If she decided to adopt a deductive approach to her work, she would have to:

1 start with the hypothesis that staff working with the public are more likely to experience the threat or reality of violence and resultant stress;
2 decide to research a population in which she would have expected to find evidence of violence, for example, a sizeable social security office;

3 administer a questionnaire to a large sample of staff in order to establish the extent of violence (either actually experienced or threatened) and the levels of stress experienced by them;
4 be particularly careful about how she defined violence;
5 standardise the stress responses of the staff, for example, days off sick or sessions with a counsellor.

On the other hand, if she decided to adopt an inductive approach she might have decided to interview some staff who had been subjected to violence at work. She might have been interested in their feelings about the events that they had experienced, how they coped with the problems they experienced, and their views about the possible causes of the violence.

Either approach would have yielded valuable data about this problem (indeed, both may be used in this project, at different stages). Neither approach should be thought of as better than the other. They are better at different things. It depends where her research emphasis lies.

illustrate the choice of approach. She introduces the notion of the researcher's preferred style, which, rather like the architect's, may reflect '. . . the architect's own preferences and ideas . . . and the stylistic preferences of those who pay for the work and have to live with the final result' (Hakim 2000:1). This echoes the feelings of Buchanan *et al.* (1988:59), who argue that 'needs, interests and preferences (of the researcher) . . . are typically overlooked but are central to the progress of fieldwork'. However, a note of caution: it is important that your preferences do not lead to your changing the essence of the research question, particularly if it has been given to you by an organisation as a consultancy project.

4.4 Summary

- The term research philosophy relates to the development of knowledge and the nature of that knowledge.
- Your research philosophy contains important assumptions about the way in which you view the world.
- There are three major ways of thinking about research philosophy: epistemology, ontology and axiology. Each contains important differences which will influence the way in which you think about the research process.
- Pragmatism holds that the most important determinant of the epistemology, ontology and axiology adopted is the research question.
- Ontology is a branch of philosophy which is concerned with the nature of social phenomena as entities.

- Objectivism is the ontological position which holds that social entities exist in reality external to social actors whereas the subjectivist view is that social phenomena are created from the perceptions and consequent actions of social actors.
- Epistemology concerns what constitutes acceptable knowledge in a field of study.
- Positivism relates to the philosophical stance of the natural scientist. This entails working with an observable social reality and the end product can be law-like generalisations similar to those in the physical and natural sciences.
- The essence of realism is that what the senses show us is reality, is the truth: that objects have an existence independent of the human mind.
- Interpretivism is an epistemology that advocates that it is necessary for the researcher to understand the differences between humans in our role as social actors.
- Axiology is a branch of philosophy that studies judgements about value.
- Social science paradigms can be used in management and business research to generate fresh insights into real-life issues and problems. The four paradigms explained in the chapter are: functionalist; interpretive; radical humanist; and radical structuralist.
- There are two main research approaches: deduction and induction. With deduction a theory and hypothesis (or hypotheses) are developed and a research strategy designed to test the hypothesis. With induction, data are collected and a theory developed as a result of the data analysis.

Self-check questions

Help with these questions is available at the end of the chapter.

4.1 You have decided to undertake a project and have defined the main research question as 'What are the opinions of consumers to a 10 per cent reduction in weight, with the price remaining the same, of "Snackers" chocolate bars?' Write a hypothesis that you could test in your project.

4.2 Why may it be argued that the concept of the manager is socially constructed rather than 'real'?

4.3 Why are the radical paradigms relevant in business and management research given that most managers would say that the purpose of organisational investigation is to develop recommendations for action to solve problems without radical change?

4.4 You have chosen to undertake your research project following a the deductive approach. What factors may cause you to work inductively, although working deductively is your preferred choice?

Review and discussion questions

4.6 Visit an online database or your university library and obtain a copy of a research-based refereed journal article that you think will be of use to an assignment you are currently working on. Read this article carefully. What research philosophy do you think the author has adopted? Use Section 4.2 to help you develop a clear justification for your answer.

4.7 Think about the last assignment you undertook for your course. In undertaking this assignment, were you predominantly inductive or deductive? Discuss your thoughts with a friend who also undertook this assignment.

4.8 Agree with a friend to watch the same television documentary.

    a To what extent is the documentary inductive or deductive in its use of data?

    b Have the documentary makers adopted a positivist, realist, interpretivist or pragmatist philosophy?

Do not forget to make notes regarding your reasons for your answers to each of these questions and to discuss your answers with your friend.

Progressing your research project

Diagnosing your research philosophy[1]

Please indicate your agreement or disagreement with each of these statements. There are no wrong answers.

	Strongly agree	Agree	Slightly agree	Slightly disagree	Disagree	Strongly disagree
1 For the topic being researched there is one single reality, the task of the researcher is to discover it	❑	❑	❑	❑	❑	❑
2 The reality of the topic being researched exists separately from the researcher	❑	❑	❑	❑	❑	❑
3 Management research is value laden	❑	❑	❑	❑	❑	❑
4 A researcher can not be separated from what is being researched and so will inevitably be subjective	❑	❑	❑	❑	❑	❑
5 A variety of data collection techniques should be used in research, both quantitative and qualitative	❑	❑	❑	❑	❑	❑
6 The reality of what is being researched exists independently of people's thoughts, beliefs and knowledge of their existence	❑	❑	❑	❑	❑	❑
7 Researchers must remain objective and independent from the phenomena they are studying, ensuring that their own values do not impact on data interpretation	❑	❑	❑	❑	❑	❑
8 Management research should be practical and applied	❑	❑	❑	❑	❑	❑
9 Management research should integrate different perspectives to help interpret the data	❑	❑	❑	❑	❑	❑
10 Management researchers need to employ methods that allow in-depth exploration of the details behind a phenomenon	❑	❑	❑	❑	❑	❑

Now discuss your answers with your colleagues. To guide your discussion you need to think about:

1 What do you consider to be the nature of reality? Why

2 To what extent do your own values influence your research? Why?

3 What is your relationship with what you research? Why?

[1]Developed with help from Judith Thomas and Joanne Duberley.

References

Bhaskar, R. (1989) *Reclaiming Reality: A Critical Introduction to Contemporary Philosophy*, London: Verso.

Buchanan, D., Boddy, D. and McAlman, J. (1988) 'Getting in, getting on, getting out and getting back', in A. Bryman (ed.) *Doing Research in Organisations*. London: Routledge, pp. 53–67.

Burke, M. (2007) 'Making choices: research paradigms and information management: practical applications of philosophy in IM research', *Library Review*, Vol. 56, No. 6, pp. 476–84.

Burrell, G. and Morgan, G. (1982) *Sociological Paradigms and Organisational Analysis*. London: Heinemann.

Collis, J. and Hussey, R. (2003) *Business Research: A Practical Guide for Undergraduate and Postgraduate Students* (2nd edn). Basingstoke: Palgrave Macmillan.

Creswell, J. (2002) *Research Design: Quantitative and Qualitative Approaches* (2nd edn). Thousand Oaks, CA: Sage.

Dobson, P. (2002) 'Critical realism and information systems research: why bother with philosophy? Available at http://informationr.net/ir/7-2/paper124.html [Accessed 27 May 2008.]

Dyer, O. (2003) 'Lancet accuses AstraZeneca of sponsoring biased research', *British Medical Journal*, Vol. 327, No. 1, p. 1005.

Easterby- Smith, M., Thorpe, R. Jackson, P. and Lowe, A. (2008) *Management Research* (3rd edn). Sage: London.

Gill, J. and Johnson, P. (2002) *Research Methods for Managers*. (3rd edn). London: Sage.

Guba, E. and Lincoln, Y. (1994) 'Competing paradigms in qualitative research', in N.K. Denzin and Y.S. Lincoln (eds) *Handbook of Qualitative Research*. London: Sage, pp. 105–17.

Hakim, C. (2000) *Research Design: Successful Designs for Social and Economic Research* (2nd edn). London: Routledge.

Heron, J. (1996) *Co-operative Inquiry: Research into the Human Condition*. London: Sage.

Johnson, P. and Clark, M. (2006) 'Mapping the terrain: an overview of business and management research methodologies', in P. Johnson and M. Clark. (eds) *Business and Management Research Methodologies*. London: Sage.

Lichtenstein, S., Williamson, K. and Sturt, C. (2006) 'Understanding consumer adoption of Internet banking: an interpretive study in the Australian banking context', *Journal of Electronic Commerce Research*, Vol. 7, No. 2, pp. 50–66.

Remenyi, D., Williams, B., Money, A. and Swartz, E. (1998) *Doing Research in Business and Management: An Introduction to Process and Method*. London: Sage.

Robson, C. (2002) *Real World Research* (2nd edn). Oxford: Blackwell.

Smircich, L. (1983) 'Concepts of culture and organisational analysis', *Administrative Science Quarterly*, Vol. 28, No. 3, pp. 339–58.

Tashakkori, A. and Teddlie, C. (1998) *Mixed Methodology: Combining Qualitative and Quantitative Approaches*. Thousand Oaks, CA: Sage.

Westfall, R.D. (1997) 'Does telecommuting really increase productivity? Fifteen rival hypotheses', AIS Americas Conference, Indianapolis, IN, 15–17 August.

Further reading

Burrell, G. and Morgan, G. (1982) *Sociological Paradigms and Organisational Analysis*. London: Heinemann. This is an excellent book on paradigms which goes into far more detail than space has allowed in this chapter.

Maylor, H. and Blackmon, K. (2005) *Researching Business and Management*. Basingstoke: Palgrave Macmillan. Chapter 5 is a very approachable account of the major research philosophies.

Tashakkori, A. and Teddlie, C. (1998) *Mixed Methodology: Combining Qualitative and Quantitative Approaches*. Thousand Oaks, CA: Sage. There is some useful discussion relating to pragmatism in Chapter 2 of this book.

Case 4
Consultancy research for a not-for-profit organisation

Source: David Hoffman Photo Library/Alamy

Thomas's work placement is at a management consultancy firm, Spectrum, which provides strategic and financial advice to organisations in the UK not-for-profit (NFP) sector. The NFP sector has different segments, the largest of which includes organisations which have a public-interest objective, and which are known as charities. These are typically organisations dedicated to improving the quality of life for specific groups or individuals (e.g. children or the elderly), or focused on relieving poverty or distress. NFP organisations are growing in importance in the UK economy, and have an increasing role in the provision of public services (Brandsen and Pestoff 2008).

One of Spectrum's clients is the Association for Voluntary Organisations for the Elderly (AVOE), a UK organisation providing a range of services to charity members who give care and support to the elderly. AVOE is traditionally known as providing information (e.g. a monthly newsletter on developments in the elderly-care sector); representation (e.g. at government consultations on matters relating to the elderly, including pensions); and support (e.g. advice on changes in statutory law; and networking opportunities through regional conferences and workshops). The main source of income for AVOE is membership fees. It also receives a fixed annual government grant to support its work.

In the past year it has become apparent that the cost of providing membership services is rising more quickly than income from membership fees. Jill Baxter, AVOE's Chief Executive, recently asked Spectrum to conduct an internal operational review to identify ways of generating additional income. Jennifer, Thomas's work-placement supervisor, managed this project which was completed last week.

The internal review identified several opportunities as well as potential problems for AVOE. An important finding was that AVOE currently provides more services to its members than was the case several years ago, even though all members pay a flat fee which has not increased in the past five years. For example, AVOE hosts some of its members' websites. The review also identified that although all large charities supporting the elderly are members of AVOE, some of the medium-sized charities and many of the small, regional and local charities are not (or in some cases have recently cancelled their membership).

Following the review, AVOE asked Spectrum to undertake a research project to investigate what its members really want from the umbrella body, and how it can attract new members. Jill Baxter, Jennifer and Thomas met in AVOE's Manchester offices, and agreed that the principal research question would be:

Why do charities supporting the elderly decide to join (or not) or leave an umbrella organisation such as AVOE?

The answer to this exploratory question should enable AVOE to develop strategic options for increasing membership revenues at a reasonable cost. Jennifer has asked Thomas to prepare a research proposal for the new project.

Thomas is now considering how to design the research so that he can answer the agreed question. He wonders how the research is situated in relation to the two 'paradigms' of research in the social sciences, which are traditionally labelled *positivist* and *interpretivist*. Thomas has read a great deal about the 'paradigm wars', but feels that the arguments about whether there is or is not an 'external reality' are tiresome and unproductive. On the one hand he believes that these metaphysical debates are relevant to a philosophical understanding of research, and how we 'come to know' what we claim to know (and what we claim to have found out from research). But on the other hand, he worries that some researchers spend so long debating the metaphysical questions that they fail to 'get on' and do research which is useful to society. He suspects that some researchers feel constrained believing that the paradigm prescribes the method: the positivist paradigm prescribes quantitative methods; the interpretivist paradigm prescribes qualitative methods; and each paradigm rejects the methods used by the 'other side'.

Thomas wants to focus on what is pragmatically useful to answer the research question. He also wants his research design to be robust and useful to AVOE. As he reads more about research design, he comes to realise that in fact the distance between post-positivists and interpretivists is not as great as it might seem (after all, he argues, is anyone really a 'pure' positivist these days?). There are important points of agreement: for example, post-positivists and interpretivists agree that our understanding of reality is constructed, and that research is influenced by the values of the researchers and the theoretical frameworks they use (Reichardt and Rallis 1994:85–91).

Reading further, Thomas is delighted to find that there really is a third way, which is the pragmatic tradition developed by American scholars such as John Dewey and William James in the late nineteenth century and early twentieth century. Pragmatists are driven by the problems which people face, and want to find out 'what works'. They also argue (e.g. Howe 1988) that qualitative and quantitative methods are compatible, and that good research design often involves mixed methods. This means that the decision about whether to use qualitative or quantitative methods (or both) depends on the research question and on the current stage of the research cycle (e.g. using inductive or deductive reasoning).

Thomas realises, however, that the pragmatic approach is no 'easy' option. He can't just 'do what he likes'. Instead, he has to think hard: first about the research question; and then about which methods are appropriate to answer it. After reading some of the literature on mixed methodology, such as Tashakkori and Teddlie (1998), he writes a research proposal recommending a *parallel mixed model design*. The proposed design combines qualitative and quantitative data collection, analysis and interference processes.

- All existing members (approximately 80) will be asked to respond to an interviewer-administered questionnaire with closed questions (e.g. eliciting members' perceptions of the utility of a range of services already provided or proposed), and open questions (e.g. asking for members' opinions about the value of membership). Questionnaire interviews will be conducted by telephone. The questionnaire will gather categorical information about members' size (e.g. measured by revenue); service provided (e.g. residential homes, home care, in-hospital support, networking and support facilities); and geographic coverage (e.g. national, regional or local).

- During the same time period, Thomas will organise focus groups with a sample of members and non-members, as well as other stakeholders such as government officials who interact with AVOE and with UK elderly-care organisations.
- Data will be analysed using quantitative and qualitative techniques. Questionnaire data will be analysed using correlation, cross-tabulation and other descriptive and statistical techniques. The focus group and open-question survey data will be analysed to look for key themes and patterns. Particular attention will be given to respondents' comments on perceived benefits of different services. In addition, some of the qualitative interview data will be quantified – for example, by counting the frequency with which specific services are mentioned.

Later that week, Thomas emails the draft proposal to Jennifer. He wonders if she will accept the argument for a research design based on pragmatist principles, especially as she is known as a qualitative researcher with an interpretivist philosophy.

References

Brandsen, T. and Pestoff, V. (2008) 'Co-production, the third sector and the delivery of public services', *Public Management Review*, Vol. 8, No. 4, pp. 493–501.

Howe, K. (1988) 'Against the quantitative-qualitative incompatibility thesis – or dogmas die hard', *Educational Researcher*, Vol. 17, No. 8, pp. 10–16.

Reichardt, C. and Rallis, S. (1994) 'Qualitative and quantitative inquiries are not incompatible: a call for a new partnership', in C. Reichardt and S. Rallis (eds) *The Qualitative-Quantitative Debate: New Perspectives*. San Francisco: Jossey-Bass.

Tashakkori, A. and Teddlie, C. (1998) *Mixed Methodology: Combining Qualitative and Quantitative Approaches*. London: Sage.

Questions

1 How does pragmatism differ from post-positivism and interpretivism, and are there some shared beliefs?
2 How can Thomas respond if Jennifer insists on a 'pure' qualitative method?
3 If pragmatism argues that the research questions should drive the choice of research methods, how can Thomas be sure of the quality of the research?

An additional case study relating to material covered in this chapter is available via this book's Companion Website **www.pearsoned.co.uk/saunders**. It is:

- Marketing music products alongside emerging digital music channels.

Self-check answers

4.1 Probably the most realistic hypothesis here would be 'consumers of "Snackers" chocolate bars did not notice the difference between the current bar and its reduced weight successor'. Doubtless that is what the Snackers' manufacturers would want confirmed!

4.2 Although you can see and touch a manager, you are only seeing and touching another human being. The point is that the role of the manager is a socially constructed concept. What a manager is will differ between different national and organisational cultures and will differ over time. Indeed, the concept of the manager as we generally understand it is a relatively recent human invention, arriving at the same time as the formal organisation in the past couple of hundred years.

4.3 The researcher working in the radical humanist or structuralist paradigms may argue that it is predictable that managers would say that the purpose of organisational investigation is to develop recommendations for action to solve problems without radical change because radical change may involve changing managers! Radicalism implies root and branch investigation and possible change and most of us prefer 'fine tuning' within the framework of what exists already, particularly if change threatens our vested interests.

4.4 The question implies an either/or choice. But as you work through this chapter and, in particular, the next on deciding your research design, you will see that life is rarely so clear cut! Perhaps the main factor that would cause you to review the appropriateness of the deductive approach would be that the data you collected might suggest an important hypothesis, which you did not envisage when you framed your research objectives and hypotheses. This may entail going further with the data collection, perhaps by engaging in some qualitative work, which would yield further data to answer the new hypothesis.

Get ahead using resources on the Companion Website at:
www.pearsoned.co.uk/saunders
- Improve your SPSS and NVivo research analysis with practice tutorials.
- Save time researching on the Internet with the Smarter Online Searching Guide.
- Test your progress using self-assessment questions.
- Follow live links to useful websites.

Formulating the research design

5.1 Introduction

In Chapter 4 we introduced the research onion as a way of depicting the issues underlying your choice of data collection method or methods and peeled away the outer two layers – research philosophies and research approaches. In this chapter we uncover the next three layers: research strategies, research choices and time horizons. These three layers can be thought of as focusing on the process of research design, that is, turning your research question into a research project (Robson 2002). As we saw, the way you choose to answer your research question will be influenced by your research philosophy and approach. Your research question will subsequently inform your choice of research strategy, your choices of collection techniques and analysis procedures, and the time horizon over which you undertake your research project.

Your *research design* will be the general plan of how you will go about answering your research question(s) (the importance of clearly defining the research question cannot be over-emphasised). It will contain clear objectives, derived from your research question(s), specify the sources from which you intend to collect data, and consider the constraints that you will inevitably have (e.g. access to data, time, location and money) as well as discussing ethical issues. Crucially, it should reflect the fact that you have thought carefully about why you are employing your particular research design. For example, it would be perfectly legitimate for your assessor to ask you why you chose to conduct your research in a particular organisation, why you chose the particular department, and why you chose to talk to one group of staff rather than another. You must have valid reasons for all your research design decisions. The justification should always be based on your research question(s) and objectives as well as being consistent with your research philosophy.

Hakim (2000) compares a researcher designing a research project with an architect designing a building. This analogy is particularly useful when thinking about your research project. Like an architect, your research design will need to fulfil a particular purpose within the practical constraints of time and money. The way in which you design your research will depend upon your own preferences, your research philosophy, and your ideas as to the most appropriate strategy and choices of methods for conducting your research. In addition, if you are undertaking your research project for an organisation, it may also be influenced by the preferences of those who are paying for the work! This can be likened to architects designing visually impressive buildings at their clients' requests. However, like the architect, you will undoubtedly be aiming to produce the best possible design guided by these constraints and influences. For small-scale research projects, such as the one you are likely to do as part of your taught course, the person who designs the research is nearly always the same as the person who undertakes the data collection, data analysis and subsequently writes the project report. Continuing with our analogy, this can be likened to the architect and builder being the same person. It also emphasises the need for you to spend time on

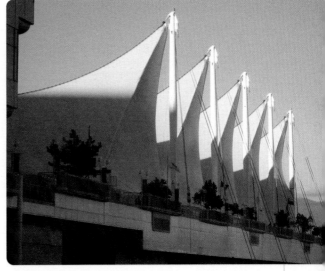

Canada Place, Vancouver
Source: © Philip Lewis 2007

ensuring that you have a good research design in order to avoid what Robson (2002:80) describes as 'the research equivalent of the many awful houses put up by speculative builders without the benefit of architectural experience'. This is essential because good research, like a good building, is attributed to its architect.

At this point we should make a clear distinction between design and tactics. The former is concerned with the overall plan for your research; the latter is about the finer detail of data collection and analysis, the centre of the research onion. Decisions about tactics will involve your being clear about the different quantitative and qualitative data collection techniques (e.g. questionnaires, interviews, focus groups, secondary data) and subsequent quantitative and qualitative data analysis procedures, which will be dealt with in detail in subsequent chapters.

In this chapter we commence with a brief review of the purpose of research (Section 5.2). This has clear links with our earlier discussion of the need to have a clear research question in Section 2.4. Subsequently we consider possible research strategies (Section 5.3). After defining quantitative and qualitative data, different research choices combining one or more data collection techniques and analysis procedures are outlined (Section 5.4). We then examine the time horizons you might apply to your research (Section 5.5), the issues of research credibility (Section 5.6) and the ethics of research design (Section 5.7). The data collection and analysis centre of the research-process onion (Figure 5.1) will be dealt with in Chapters 7–11 and 12–13 respectively.

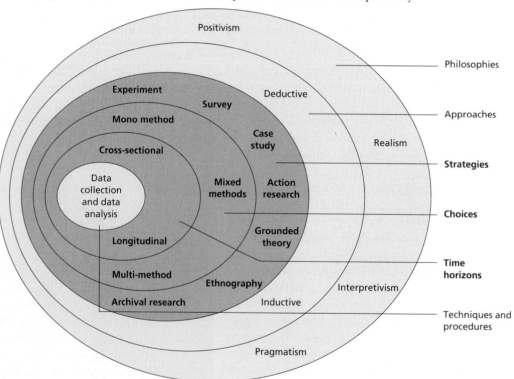

Figure 5.1
The research 'onion'
Source: © Mark Saunders, Philip Lewis and Adrian Thornhill 2008

5.2 The purpose of your research

In Chapter 2 we encouraged you to think about your research project in terms of the question you wished to answer and your research objectives. Within this we highlighted how the way in which you asked your research question would result in either descriptive, descriptive and explanatory, or explanatory answers. In thinking about your research question, you inevitably have begun to think about the purpose of your research.

The classification of research purpose most often used in the research methods' literature is the threefold one of exploratory, descriptive and explanatory. However, in the same way as your research question can be both descriptive and explanatory, so your research project may have more than one purpose. Indeed, as Robson (2002) points out, the purpose of your enquiry may change over time.

Exploratory studies

An **exploratory study** is a valuable means of finding out 'what is happening; to seek new insights; to ask questions and to assess phenomena in a new light' (Robson 2002:59). It is particularly useful if you wish to clarify your understanding of a problem, such as if you are unsure of the precise nature of the problem (Box 5.1). It may well be that time is well spent on exploratory research, as it may show that the research is not worth pursuing!

Box 5.1
Focus on management research

Exploring how the employee–organisation relationship affects the linkage between perception of developmental HRM practices and employee outcomes

Contemporary research on 'best practice', high-performance, high-commitment, high involvement, progressive, and human-capital-enhancing human resource management (HRM) suggests that such practices (e.g. training opportunities, career development) lead to organisations offering resources and opportunities that improve the motivation, skills, attitudes and behaviours of their employees. Most of these models suggest that human resource (HR) practices or systems deliver performance through the effect they have on employees, but some studies conclude that the positive implications for employees are at best uncertain. For example, one influential review (Wright and Boswell 2002) argues that the dearth of research aimed at understanding how multiple (or systems of) HR practices impact individuals certainly suggests an opportunity for future research.

This theoretical position was the point of departure for an exploratory study by Kuvaas (2008), the results of which were published in *Journal of Management Studies*. The purpose of Kuvaas's study was to examine whether and how the quality of the employee–organisation relationship (EOR) influences the relationship between employee perception of developmental human resource (HR) practices and employee outcomes (e.g. work performance and intention to leave the organisation).

Kuvaas conducted the study using data collected from 593 employees representing 64 local savings banks in Norway in 2003 using structured questionnaires which were distributed using a web-based tool.

The study found a strong and direct negative relationship between perception of developmental HR practices and employee turnover intention, but perceived procedural and interactional justice moderated this linkage. No support was found for a mediating role of the EOR indicators in the relationship between perception of developmental HR practices and employee outcomes.

Kuvaas concludes that even though employees perceive HR practices to be developmental, this may not translate into higher work performance. The results suggest that without a high quality employee–organisation relationship, developmental HR practices may actually reduce work performance. Therefore, investments in HR practices should not be viewed as a way to compensate for a poorly managed employee–organisation relationship. However, as long as HR practices (especially training and career development activities) are perceived as developmental, they can be very important in reducing turnover intention and thus voluntary turnover

There are three principal ways of conducting exploratory research:

- a search of the literature;
- interviewing 'experts' in the subject;
- conducting focus group interviews.

Exploratory research can be likened to the activities of the traveller or explorer (Adams and Schvaneveldt 1991). Its great advantage is that it is flexible and adaptable to change. If you are conducting exploratory research you must be willing to change your direction as a result of new data that appear and new insights that occur to you. A quotation from the travel writer V.S. Naipaul (1989:222) illustrates this point beautifully:

> I had been concerned, at the start of my own journey, to establish some lines of enquiry, to define a theme. The approach had its difficulties. At the back of my mind was always a worry that I would come to a place and all contacts would break down . . . If you travel on a theme the theme has to develop with the travel. At the beginning your interests can be broad and scattered. But then they must be more focused; the different stages of a journey cannot simply be versions of one another. And . . . this kind of travel depended on luck. It depended on the people you met, the little illuminations you had. As with the next day's issue of fast-moving daily newspapers, the shape of the character in hand was continually being changed by accidents along the way.

Adams and Schvaneveldt (1991) reinforce this point by arguing that the flexibility inherent in exploratory research does not mean absence of direction to the enquiry. What it does mean is that the focus is initially broad and becomes progressively narrower as the research progresses.

Descriptive studies

The object of **descriptive research** is 'to portray an accurate profile of persons, events or situations' (Robson 2002:59). This may be an extension of, or a forerunner to, a piece of exploratory research or, more often, a piece of explanatory research. It is necessary to have a clear picture of the phenomena on which you wish to collect data prior to the collection of the data. One of the earliest well-known examples of a descriptive survey is the Domesday Book, which described the population of England in 1085.

Often project tutors are rather wary of work that is too descriptive. There is a danger of their saying 'That's very interesting . . . but so what?' They will want you to go further and draw conclusions from the data you are describing. They will encourage you to develop the skills of evaluating data and synthesising ideas. These are higher-order skills than those of accurate description. Description in management and business research has a very clear place. However, it should be thought of as a means to an end rather than an end in itself. This means that if your research project utilises description it is likely to be a precursor to explanation. Such studies are known as **descripto-explanatory studies**.

Explanatory studies

Studies that establish causal relationships between variables may be termed **explanatory research**. The emphasis here is on studying a situation or a problem in order to explain the relationships between variables (Box 5.2). You may find, for example, that a cursory analysis of quantitative data on manufacturing scrap rates shows a relationship between scrap rates and the age of the machine being operated. You could go ahead and subject the data to statistical tests such as correlation (discussed in Section 12.5) in order to get a

Box 5.2
Focus on student research

An explanatory study

Declan wanted to study the relationship between the written accounts of environmental policies which organisations present in their annual report and the actual practices of organisations. He wanted to establish the closeness of the match between the public face of organisations and practical reality. In particular, he wanted to know the extent to whether it was the public statements which were the key influence upon practice or whether written accounts were based on careful research about what went on in the organisation.

This research adopted a case study strategy. Declan examined three organisations in some detail. The data collected were mainly qualitative, although some secondary quantitative data were used. What emerged was that the written accounts of environmental policies had little effect on what happened on the ground. Actual practice was a function largely of pressure from external sources (e.g. legislation) and a combination of internal and external sources (e.g. 'good' practice).

clearer view of the relationship. Alternatively, or in addition to, you might collect qualitative data to explain the reasons why customers of your company rarely pay their bills according to the prescribed payment terms.

5.3 The need for a clear research strategy

The different research strategies

In this section we turn our attention to the **research strategies** you may employ. Each strategy can be used for exploratory, descriptive and explanatory research (Yin 2003). Some of these clearly belong to the deductive approach, others to the inductive approach. However, often allocating strategies to one approach or the other is unduly simplistic. In addition, we must emphasise that no research strategy is inherently superior or inferior to any other. Consequently, what is most important is not the label that is attached to a particular strategy, but whether it will enable you to answer your particular research question(s) and meet your objectives. Your choice of research strategy will be guided by your research question(s) and objectives, the extent of existing knowledge, the amount of time and other resources you have available, as well as your own philosophical underpinnings. Finally, it must be remembered that these strategies should not be thought of as being mutually exclusive. For example, it is quite possible to use the survey strategy as part of a case study.

In our discussion of research strategies we start with the experiment strategy. This is because, although in their purest form experiments are infrequently used in management research, their roots in natural science laboratory-based research and the precision required mean that the 'experiment' is often the 'gold standard' against which the rigour of other strategies is assessed. The strategies that we consider subsequently in this section are:

- experiment;
- survey;
- case study;
- action research;
- grounded theory;
- ethnography;
- archival research.

This is followed by a brief discussion of the role of practitioner-researcher. This is particularly important if you are a part-time student, or intend to undertake the research for your project using an organisation for whom you are working.

Experiment

Experiment is a form of research that owes much to the natural sciences, although it features strongly in much social science research, particularly psychology. The purpose of an experiment is to study causal links; whether a change in one independent variable produces a change in another dependent variable (Hakim 2000). The simplest experiments are concerned with whether there is a link between two variables. More complex experiments also consider the size of the change and the relative importance of two or more independent variables. Experiments therefore tend to be used in exploratory and explanatory research to answer 'how' and 'why' questions. In a **classic experiment** (Figure 5.2), two groups are established and members assigned at random to each. This means the two groups will be exactly similar in all aspects relevant to the research other than whether or not they are exposed to the planned intervention or manipulation. In the first of these groups, the **experimental group**, some form of planned intervention or manipulation, such as a 'buy two, get one free' promotion, is made subsequently. In the other group, the **control group**, no such intervention is made. The dependent variable, in this example purchasing behaviour, is measured before and after the manipulation of the independent variable (the use of the 'buy two, get one free' promotion) for both the experimental group and the control group. This means that a before and after comparison can be undertaken. On the basis of this comparison, any difference between the experimental and control groups for the dependent variable (purchasing behaviour) is attributed to the intervention, in our example the 'buy two, get one free' promotion.

In assigning the members to the control and experimental groups at random and using a control group, you try to control (that is, remove) the possible effects of an alternative explanation to the planned intervention (manipulation) and eliminate threats to internal validity. This is because the control group is subject to exactly the same external influences as the experimental group other than the planned intervention and, consequently, this intervention is the only explanation for any changes to the dependent variable. By assigning the members of each group at random, changes cannot be attributed to differences in the composition of the two groups. Therefore, in minimising threats to internal validity, you are minimising the extent to which the findings can be attributed to any flaws in your research design rather than the planned interventions.

Often experiments, including those in disciplines closely associated with business and management such as organisational psychology, are conducted in laboratories rather than in the field. This means that you have greater control over aspects of the research process such as sample selection and the context within which the experiment occurs. However,

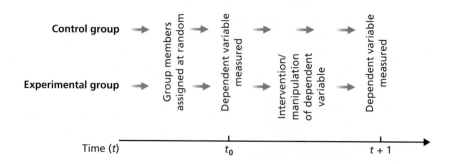

Figure 5.2
A classic experiment strategy

whilst this improves the **internal validity** of the experiment, that is, the extent to which the findings can be attributed to the interventions rather than any flaws in your research design, **external validity** is likely to be more difficult to establish (we discuss issues of validity in Section 5.6). Laboratory settings, by their very nature, are unlikely to be related to the real world of organisations. As a consequence, the extent to which the findings from a laboratory experiment are able to be generalised to all organisations is likely to be lower than for an organisation (field)-based experiment (Box 5.3).

In summary, an experiment will involve typically:

- definition of a theoretical hypothesis (in our discussion: the introduction of a promotion will result in a change in the number of sales);
- selection of samples of individuals from known populations;

Box 5.3
Focus on management research

Using an experimental strategy in project management research

In a *Journal of Operations Management* article, Bendoly and Swink (2007) reported experimental research which they had carried out into the topic of effective project management. Their starting position was that effective project management relies on the timely exchange of information regarding appropriate resource availability, associated scheduling options, and related costs and benefits. At the same time, information, or lack of it, can also impact the behaviour of project managers in ways that do not directly focus on work objectives but nevertheless affect performance. For example, a project manager's decisions may be based on more than simply his/her 'rational' understanding of the task at hand. Decisions may also be influenced his/her beliefs regarding the motivations of other decision makers upon whom he/she is dependent. The authors argue that it is valuable to recognise that the actions of individuals charged with complex tasks (such as project management) may be motivated by both task specific (i.e. locally or globally rational) objectives as well as non-task interests (e.g. social). Actions based on non-task social interests may not necessarily contribute positively to the task objective of the individual. They may in fact degrade such performance, as they may be more directed towards either positive or negative impacts on other parties.

Bendoly and Swink designed and executed a series of interviews and experiments involving MBA students in order to examine evidence of support for their hypothesis. The method included a number of pre-experiment, during experiment, and post-experiment procedures and measurements, which are described in detail in the article. The study included pre- and post-experimental perceptual scales addressing resource sharing, information visibility, and project priority, in addition to measures of subjects' managerial experiences, predispositions and perceptions.

Phase 1 of the experiment consisted of preliminary data collection for use as controls. Phase 2 involved providing each subject with a case reading based on the specific treatment-combination exposure assigned to that subject. Phase 3 required the subjects to participate in three project management simulation scenarios, with project dynamics and decision-making interactions all conducted in an Excel-based simulation environment. In Phase 4 of the experiment participants were asked in interviews to respond to a set of follow-up questions. These questions were designed to capture impressions developed by the participants regarding the task environment as well as more general views of the firm associated with the case experiment. While some of these items were strictly used for the purpose of testing the effectiveness of the treatments, others provided perceptual measures key to several of the authors' hypotheses.

Bendoly and Swink conclude that the effects of information availability upon performance may extend beyond immediate task-related outcomes. It not only affects immediate project timeliness, it also impacts decision makers' perceptions of the actions and priorities of other organisational actors.

- random allocation of samples to different experimental conditions, the experimental group and the control group;
- introduction of planned intervention or manipulation to one or more of the variables (in our discussion, the introduction of the promotion);
- measurement on a small number of dependent variables (in our discussion, purchasing behaviour);
- control of all other variables.

Inevitably, an experimental strategy will not be feasible for many business and management research questions. For example, you could not, for ethical reasons, assign employees to experience redundancy or small and medium-sized enterprises owners to experience their banks foreclosing on business loans. Similarly, it may be considered unfair to carry out experiments in relation to beneficial interventions such as providing additional support to research project students only on the basis of them being selected for the experimental group! Some people are not willing to participate in experiments and so those who volunteer may not be representative. Because of this, the experiment strategy is often used only on captive populations such as university students, employees of a particular organisation and the like. As discussed earlier, the design requirements of an experiment often mean that samples selected are both small and atypical, leading to problems of external validity. Whilst you may be able to overcome this with a large and representative sample (Section 7.2), Hakim (2000) advises that this is likely to be both costly and complex.

Survey

The **survey** strategy is usually associated with the deductive approach. It is a popular and common strategy in business and management research and is most frequently used to answer who, what, where, how much and how many questions. It therefore tends to be used for exploratory and descriptive research. Surveys are popular as they allow the collection of a large amount of data from a sizeable population in a highly economical way. Often obtained by using a questionnaire administered to a sample, these data are standardised, allowing easy comparison. In addition, the survey strategy is perceived as authoritative by people in general and is both comparatively easy to explain and to understand. Every day a news bulletin or a newspaper reports the results of a new survey that indicates, for example, that a certain percentage of the population thinks or behaves in a particular way (Box 5.4).

The survey strategy allows you to collect quantitative data which you can analyse quantitatively using descriptive and inferential statistics (Sections 12.4 and 12.5). In addition, the data collected using a survey strategy can be used to suggest possible reasons for particular relationships between variables and to produce models of these relationships. Using a survey strategy should give you more control over the research process and, when sampling is used, it is possible to generate findings that are representative of the whole population at a lower cost than collecting the data for the whole population (Section 7.2). You will need to spend time ensuring that your sample is representative, designing and piloting your data collection instrument and trying to ensure a good response rate. Analysing the results, even with readily available analysis software, will also be time consuming. However, it will be your time and, once you have collected your data, you will be independent. Many researchers complain that their progress is delayed by their dependence on others for information.

The data collected by the survey strategy is unlikely to be as wide-ranging as those collected by other research strategies. For example, there is a limit to the number of questions that any questionnaire can contain if the goodwill of the respondent is not to be presumed

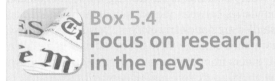

Box 5.4
Focus on research in the news

Indians forge ahead in online shopping

Online shopping has caught up with the net savvy Indians in a big way.

Seventy-eight per cent of the Indian respondents (those accessing the Internet) surveyed in a recent Nielsen Survey on global Internet shopping habits, have used the Internet to make a purchase and more than half of the respondents (55 per cent) have made at least one online purchase in the past one month. The survey concluded that the Internet is no longer a niche technology as far as socio-economic Class A and perhaps even B is concerned. Almost all strata of Indian society are influenced by online media.

Online shopping has opened up new commercial avenues in India. For example, 73 per cent of Indians have purchased airline tickets/reservations in the past three months, this percentage being the highest for any country in Asia Pacific. By comparison, more than 60 per cent of Irish and UAE Internet users bought airline tickets/reservations on the Internet in the last three months, making travel the fourth most popular shopping category on the web globally.

Books (46 per cent), Electronic Equipment (29 per cent), Tours and Hotel Reservations (24 per cent), DVDs/Games (23 per cent), Event Tickets (23 per cent), Clothing/Accessories/Shoes (21 per cent), and Music (20 per cent) are some other popular purchases made online by Indians.

A credit card is the most common method of payment for online purchases made by Indians with 84 per cent opting for that payment option over others. It is also the highest percentage for any country in Asia Pacific for payments made through credit cards for online purchases. Debit cards (29 per cent), bank transfers (24 per cent) and cash on delivery (13 per cent) are some other methods of payment that are popular amongst Indians.

Turkish online shoppers (who represent the economic elite in that country) topped global rankings for credit card usage (91 per cent) for online purchases followed by 86 per cent of Irish online shoppers and 84 per cent of Indian and UAE online shoppers.

The majority of Indian online shoppers are loyal to the sites from which they shop. Fifty-four per cent said that they buy from the same site while making an online purchase.

Forty-eight per cent of the online Indians were influenced by special offers on sites. The survey noted that India is a promotion-oriented country and for an Indian consumer special offers enhance the value of their shopping.

General surfing (40 per cent), personal recommendation (31 per cent), online advertising (26 per cent), search engines and online recommendation and review (all 22 per cent) are some other factors that influence online shoppers in India.

Source: derived from article on Indiantelevision.com website published 2 Feb. 2008. Available at: http://us.indiantelevision.com/mam/headlines/y2k8/feb/febmam2.php

on too much. Despite this, perhaps the biggest drawback with using a questionnaire as part of a survey strategy is, as emphasised in Section 11.2, the capacity to do it badly!

The questionnaire, however, is not the only data collection technique that belongs to the survey strategy. Structured observation, of the type most frequently associated with organisation and methods (O&M) research, and structured interviews, where standardised questions are asked of all interviewees, also often fall into this strategy. Observation techniques are discussed in detail in Section 9.4 and 9.6 and structured interviews in Section 11.5.

Case study

Robson (2002:178) defines **case study** as 'a strategy for doing research which involves an empirical investigation of a particular contemporary phenomenon within its real life context using multiple sources of evidence'. Yin (2003) also highlights the importance of context, adding that, within a case study, the boundaries between the phenomenon being studied and the context within which it is being studied are not clearly evident. This is the complete opposite of the experimental strategy we outlined earlier, where the research is undertaken within a highly controlled context. It also differs from the survey strategy where, although the research is undertaken in context, the ability to explore and understand this context is limited by the number of variables for which data can be collected.

The case study strategy will be of particular interest to you if you wish to gain a rich understanding of the context of the research and the processes being enacted (Morris and Wood 1991). The case study strategy also has considerable ability to generate answers to the question 'why?' as well as the 'what?' and 'how?' questions, although 'what?' and 'how?' questions tend to be more the concern of the survey strategy. For this reason the case study strategy is most often used in explanatory and exploratory research. The data collection techniques employed may be various and are likely to be used in combination. They may include, for example, interviews, observation, documentary analysis and (as if to emphasise the dangers of constructing neat boxes in which to categorise approaches, strategies and techniques) questionnaires. Consequently, if you are using a case study strategy you are likely to need to use and triangulate multiple sources of data. **Triangulation** refers to the use of different data collection techniques within one study in order to ensure that the data are telling you what you think they are telling you. For example, qualitative data collected using semi-structured group interviews may be a valuable way of triangulating quantitative data collected by other means such as a questionnaire.

Yin (2003) distinguishes between four case study strategies based upon two discrete dimensions:

- single case v. multiple case;
- holistic case v. embedded case.

A single case is often used where it represents a critical case or, alternatively, an extreme or unique case. Conversely, a single case may be selected because it is typical or because it provides you with an opportunity to observe and analyse a phenomenon that few have considered before (Section 7.3). Inevitably, an important aspect of using a single case is defining the actual case. For many part-time students this is the organisation for which they work (see Box 5.5). A case study strategy can also incorporate multiple cases, that is, more than one case. The rationale for using multiple cases focuses upon the need to establish whether the findings of the first case occur in other cases and, as a consequence,

Box 5.5
Focus on student research

Using a single organisation as a case study

Simon was interested in discovering how colleagues within his organisation were using a recently introduced financial costing model in their day-to-day work. In discussion with his project tutor, he highlighted how he was interested in finding out how it was actually being used in his organisation as a whole, as well as seeing if the use of the financial costing model differed between senior managers, departmental managers and front-line operatives. Simon's project tutor suggested that he adopt a case study strategy, using his organisation as a single case within which the senior managers', departmental managers' and front-line operatives' groups were embedded cases. He also highlighted that, given the different numbers of people in each of the embedded cases, Simon would be likely to need to use different data collection techniques with each.

the need to generalise from these findings. For this reason Yin (2003) argues that multiple case studies may be preferable to a single case study and that, where you choose to use a single case study, you will need to have a strong justification for this choice.

Yin's second dimension, holistic v. embedded, refers to the unit of analysis. For example, you may well have chosen to use an organisation by which you have been employed or are currently employed as your case. If your research is concerned only with the organisation as a whole then you are treating the organisation as a holistic case study. Conversely, even though you are researching and are concerned with a single organisation as a whole, if you wish to examine also a number of logical sub-units within the organisation, perhaps departments or work groups, then your case will inevitably involve more than one unit of analysis. Whatever way you select these units, this would be called an embedded case study (Box 5.5).

You may be suspicious of using a case study strategy because of the 'unscientific' feel it has. We would argue that a case study strategy can be a very worthwhile way of exploring existing theory. In addition, a well-constructed case study strategy can enable you to challenge an existing theory and also provide a source of new research questions.

Action research

Lewin first used the term **action research** in 1946. It has been interpreted subsequently by management researchers in a variety of ways, but there are four common themes within the literature. The first focuses upon and emphasises the purpose of the research: research in action rather than research about action (Coghlan and Brannick 2005) so that, for example, the research is concerned with the resolution of organisational issues such as the implications of change together with those who experience the issues directly. The second relates to the involvement of practitioners in the research and, in particular, a collaborative democratic partnership between practitioners and researchers, be they academics, other practitioners or internal or external consultants. Eden and Huxham (1996:75) argue that the findings of action research result from 'involvement with members of an organization over a matter which is of genuine concern to them'. Therefore, the researcher is part of the organisation within which the research and the change process are taking place (Coghlan and Brannick 2005) rather than more typical research or consultancy where, for example, employees are subjects or objects of study.

The third theme emphasises the iterative nature of the process of diagnosing, planning, taking action and evaluating (Figure 5.3). The action research spiral commences within a specific context and with a clear purpose. This is likely to be expressed as an objective (Robson 2002). Diagnosis, sometimes referred to as fact finding and analysis, is undertaken to enable action planning and a decision about the actions to be taken. These are then taken and the actions evaluated (cycle 1). Subsequent cycles involve further diagnosis, taking into account previous evaluations, planning further actions, taking these actions and evaluating. The final theme suggests that action research should have implications beyond the immediate project; in other words, it must be clear that the results could inform other contexts. For academics undertaking action research, Eden and Huxham (1996) link this to an explicit concern for the development of theory. However, they emphasise that for consultants this is more likely to focus on the subsequent transfer of knowledge gained from one specific context to another. Such use of knowledge to inform other contexts, we believe, also applies to others undertaking action research, such as students undertaking research in their own organisations. Thus action research differs from other research strategies because of its explicit focus on action, in particular promoting change within the organisation. It is, therefore, particularly useful for 'how' questions. In addition, the person undertaking the research is involved in this action for

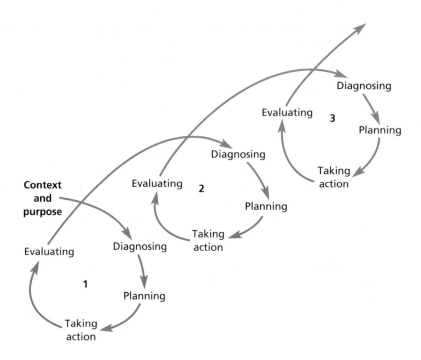

Figure 5.3
The action
research spiral

change and subsequently application of the knowledge gained elsewhere. The strengths of an action research strategy are a focus on change, the recognition that time needs to be devoted to diagnosing, planning, taking action and evaluating, and the involvement of employees (practitioners) throughout the process.

Schein (1999) emphasises the importance of employee involvement throughout the research process, as employees are more likely to implement change they have helped to create. Once employees have identified a need for change and have widely shared this need, it becomes difficult to ignore, and the pressure for change comes from within the organisation. An action research strategy therefore combines both data gathering and facilitation of change.

Action research can have two distinct foci (Schein 1999). The first of these aims to fulfil the agenda of those undertaking the research rather than that of the sponsor. This does not, however, preclude the sponsor from also benefiting from the changes brought about by the research process. The second focus starts with the needs of the sponsor and involves those undertaking the research in the sponsor's issues, rather than the sponsor in their issues. These consultant activities are termed 'process consultation' by Schein (1999). The consultant, he argues, assists the client to perceive, understand and act upon the process events that occur within their environment in order to improve the situation as the client sees it. (Within this definition the term 'client' refers to the persons or person, often senior managers, who sponsor the research.) Using Schein's analogy of a clinician and clinical enquiry, the consultant (researcher) is involved by the sponsor in the diagnosis (action research), which is driven by the sponsor's needs. It therefore follows that subsequent interventions are jointly owned by the consultant and the sponsor, who is involved at all stages. The process consultant therefore helps the sponsor to gain the skills of diagnosis and fixing organisational problems so that the latter can develop autonomy in improving the organisation.

Grounded theory

Classic **grounded theory** (Glaser and Strauss 1967) is often thought of as the best example of the inductive approach, although this conclusion would be too simplistic. It is better to think of it as 'theory building' through a combination of induction and deduction. A grounded theory strategy is, according to Goulding (2002), particularly helpful for research to predict and explain behaviour, the emphasis being upon developing and building theory. As much of business and management is about people's behaviours, for example consumers' or employees', a grounded theory strategy can be used to explore a wide range of business and management issues. Section 13.7 provides a little more detail about grounded theory in relation to analysing data. Here all we shall do is outline briefly what this strategy involves.

In grounded theory, data collection starts without the formation of an initial theoretical framework. Theory is developed from data generated by a series of observations. These data lead to the generation of predictions which are then tested in further observations that may confirm, or otherwise, the predictions. Constant reference to the data to develop and test theory leads Collis and Hussey (2003) to call grounded theory an inductive/ deductive approach, theory being grounded in such continual reference to the data.

Defining grounded theory can lead to over-simplification and so if you are interested in this strategy we strongly recommend that you read Glaser and Strauss (1967). It is more useful to consider what it is not, the approach adopted by Suddaby (2006). He lists six common misconceptions about grounded theory.

Firstly, he argues that grounded theory is not an excuse to ignore the literature, or defer reading existing theory until the data are collected and analysed. Secondly, grounded theory is not presentation of raw data. It is essential that the data collected are considered at a conceptual level in order to draw conclusions which contain theoretical insights. Thirdly, Suddaby asserts that grounded theory is not theory testing, content analysis, or word counts. He accuses some researchers of methodological slurring (Goulding 2002). In most cases these researchers begin with clear sets of positivist assumptions, including hypotheses, and then proceed to report 'tests' of the hypotheses with sets of interviews or counts of words in relevant publications. In other cases such research will start with interpretive premises, such as the social construction of reputation in the popular business press, and then report word counts, with the claim of having performed grounded theory.

Fourthly, Suddaby contends that grounded theory is not simply routine application of formulaic procedures to data. It is not a mechanical involving techniques and procedures such as prescribed amounts of interviews, computer software packages to analyse data or elaborate data sorting into categories. While Suddaby does not criticise the adoption of these processes he warns that the key issue to remember here is that grounded theory is an interpretive process, not a logico-deductive one and researcher should treat it as a highly creative one. Fifthly, Suddaby warns that grounded theory is not perfect. By its nature it is 'messy'. It requires researchers to develop a tacit knowledge of, or feel for, their data. Finally, he cautions against assuming that grounded theory is easy. He argues that 'the seamless craft of a well-executed grounded theory study, however, is the product of considerable experience, hard work, creativity and, occasionally, a healthy dose of good luck' (Suddaby, 2006:640).

Ethnography

Ethnography is rooted firmly in the inductive approach. It emanates from the field of anthropology. The purpose is to describe and explain the social world the research subjects inhabit in the way in which they would describe and explain it. This is obviously a research strategy that is very time consuming and takes place over an extended time period as the researcher needs to immerse herself or himself in the social world being researched as completely as possible. The research process needs to be flexible and responsive to change since the researcher will constantly be developing new patterns of thought about what is being observed.

Most books you read on ethnography emphasise that an ethnographic strategy is **naturalistic**. This means that in adopting an ethnographic strategy, you will be researching the phenomenon within the context in which it occurs and, in addition, not using data collection techniques that oversimplify the complexities of everyday life. Given this, it is not surprising that most ethnographic strategies involve extended participant observation (Section 9.2). However, you need to be mindful that the term naturalism also has a contradictory meaning that is often associated with positivism. Within this context it refers to the use of the principles of scientific method and the use of a scientific model within research.

Although not a dominant research strategy in business, ethnography may be very appropriate if you wish to gain insights about a particular context and better understand and interpret it from the perspective(s) of those involved. However, there are a number of issues that you need to consider. Prior to commencing research using this strategy, you will need to find a setting or group that will enable you to answer your research question and meet your research objectives and then negotiate full access (Sections 6.2 and 6.3). Subsequently you will need to build a high degree of trust with your research participants and, finally, develop strategies to cope with being both a full-time member of the social context in which your research is set as well as undertaking the research.

Archival research

The final strategy we wish to consider, **archival research**, makes use of administrative records and documents as the principal source of data. Although the term archival has historical connotations, it can refer to recent as well as historical documents (Bryman 1989). Whilst the availability of these data is outlined in Section 8.2, it is important that an archival research strategy is not conflated with secondary data analysis discussed in Chapter 8. As we will discuss in Chapter 8, all research that makes use of data contained in administrative records is inevitably secondary data analysis. This is because these data were originally collected for a different purpose, the administration of the organisation. However, when these data are used in an archival research strategy they are analysed because they are a product of day-to-day activities (Hakim 2000). They are, therefore, part of the reality being studied rather than having been collected originally as data for research purposes.

An archival research strategy allows research questions which focus upon the past and changes over time to be answered, be they exploratory, descriptive or explanatory. However, your ability to answer such questions will inevitably be constrained by the nature of the administrative records and documents. Even where these records exist, they may not contain the precise information needed to answer your research question(s) or meet your objectives. Alternatively, data may be missing or you may be refused access or your data censored for confidentiality reasons. Using an archival research strategy therefore necessitates you establishing what data are available and designing your research to make the most of it.

The role of the practitioner-researcher

If you are currently working in an organisation, you may choose to undertake your research project within that organisation, thus adopting the role of the **practitioner-researcher**. As a part-time student, you will be surrounded by exciting opportunities to pursue business and management research. You are unlikely to encounter one of the most difficult hurdles that a researcher has to overcome: that of negotiating research access (Sections 6.2 and 6.3). Indeed, like many people in such a position, you may be asked to research a particular problem by your employer.

Another advantage is your knowledge of the organisation and all this implies about understanding the complexity of what goes on in that organisation. It just is not necessary to spend a good deal of valuable time in 'learning the context' in the same way as the outsider does. However, that advantage carries with it a significant disadvantage. You must be very conscious of the assumptions and preconceptions that you carry around with you. This is an inevitable consequence of knowing the organisation well. It can prevent you from exploring issues that would enrich the research.

Familiarity has other problems. When we were doing case study work in a manufacturing company, we found it very useful to ask 'basic' questions revealing our ignorance about the industry and the organisation. These 'basic' questions are ones that as the practitioner-researcher you would be less likely to ask because you, and your respondents, would feel that you should know the answers already.

There is also the problem of status. If you are a junior employee you may feel that working with more senior colleagues inhibits your interactions as researcher-practitioner. The same may be true if you are more senior than your colleagues.

A more practical problem is that of time. Combining two roles at work is obviously very demanding, particularly as it may involve you in much data recording 'after hours'. This activity is hidden from those who determine your workload. They may not appreciate the demands that your researcher role is making on you. For this reason, Robson (2002) makes much of practitioner-researchers negotiating a proportion of their 'work time' to devote to their research. There are no easy answers to these problems. All you can do is be aware of the threats to the quality of your data by being too close to your research setting.

5.4 Multiple methods choices – combining data collection techniques and analysis procedures

In our earlier discussion we have already referred to quantitative and qualitative data. The terms quantitative and qualitative are used widely in business and management research to differentiate both data collection techniques and data analysis procedures. One way of distinguishing between the two is the focus on numeric (numbers) or non-numeric (words) data. **Quantitative** is predominantly used as a synonym for any data collection technique (such as a questionnaire) or data analysis procedure (such as graphs or statistics) that generates or uses numerical data. In contrast, **qualitative** is used predominantly as a synonym for any data collection technique (such as an interview) or data analysis procedure (such as categorising data) that generates or use non-numerical data. Qualitative therefore can refer to data other than words, such as pictures and video clips.

Within this book we refer to the way in which you choose to combine quantitative and qualitative techniques and procedures as your 'research choice'. However, it is worth noting that some authors, for example Tashakkori and Teddlie (2003), use the more generic term research design when referring to multiple methods. Individual quantitative and qualitative techniques and procedures do not exist in isolation. In choosing your research methods you will therefore either use a single data collection technique and corresponding analysis procedures (**mono method**) or use more than one data collection technique and analysis procedures to answer your research question (**multiple methods**). This choice is increasingly advocated within business and management research (Curran and Blackburn 2001), where a single research study may use quantitative and qualitative techniques and procedures in combination as well as use primary and secondary data.

If you choose to use a mono method you will combine either a single quantitative data collection technique, such as questionnaires, with quantitative data analysis procedures;

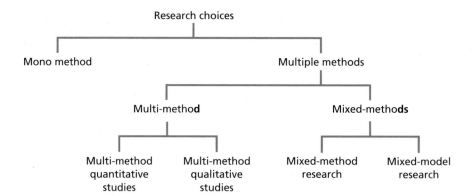

Figure 5.4
Research
choices

or a single qualitative data collection technique, such as in-depth interviews, with qualitative data analysis procedures (Figure 5.4). In contrast, if you choose to combine data collection techniques and procedures using some form of multiple methods design, there are four different possibilities. The term **multi-method** refers to those combinations where more than one data collection technique is used with associated analysis techniques, but this is restricted within either a quantitative or qualitative world view (Tashakkori and Teddlie 2003). Thus you might choose to collect quantitative data using, for example, both questionnaires and structured observation analysing these data using statistical (quantitative) procedures, a **multi-method quantitative study**. Alternatively, you might choose to collect qualitative data using, for example, in-depth interviews and diary accounts and analyse these data using non-numerical (qualitative) procedures, a **multi-method qualitative study** (Box 5.6). Therefore, if you adopted multi-methods you would not mix quantitative and qualitative techniques and procedures.

Mixed methods approach is the general term for when both quantitative and qualitative data collection techniques and analysis procedures are used in a research design (Figure 5.4). It is subdivided into two types. **Mixed method research** uses quantitative and qualitative data collection techniques and analysis procedures either at the same time (parallel) or one after the other (sequential) but does not combine them (Box 5.7). This means that, although mixed method research uses both quantitative and qualitative world views at the research methods stage, quantitative data are analysed quantitatively

Box 5.6
Focus on student research

Multi-method qualitative study

Darren wanted to establish how new supervisors learned to do the job. In order to do this he thought it essential that he should have the clearest possible grasp of what the supervisor's job entailed.

This involved him in:

- shadowing a new supervisor for a week (qualitative data);

- interviewing a day and a night shift supervisor to establish any differences in approach (qualitative data);
- interviewing the managers to whom these two supervisors reported (qualitative data).

This gave Darren a much better grasp of the content of the supervisor's job. It also did much to enhance his credibility in the eyes of the supervisors. He was then able to draw on the valuable data he had collected to complete his main research task: interviewing new supervisors to discover how they learned to do the job. This provided further qualitative data.

Box 5.7
Focus on student research

Mixed-method research

Phil conducted an employee attitude survey in a small insurance company, using mixed method research. Two of his choices were qualitative and one was quantitative. The research consisted of four stages:

1 In-depth interviews with senior managers analysed qualitatively in order to get a picture of the important issues he was likely to encounter in the research. These were essential contextual data.

2 Discussion groups with six to 10 employees representing different grades and occupations in the company, again, analysed qualtiatively. This was to establish the types of issues that were important to staff. This would inform the content of the questionnaire.

3 A questionnaire that was administered to 100 of the 200 head-office employees. This provided quantitative data which when analysed statistically allowed the attitudes of different employee groups to be compared for differences by age, gender, length of service, occupation and grade groupings. This was particularly important to the company.

4 Semi-structured group interviews with further representative employee groups analysed qualitatively to clarify the content of some of the questionnaire results. This was essential to get at the meaning behind some of the data.

and qualitative data are analysed qualitatively. In addition, often either quantitative or qualitative techniques and procedures predominate. In contrast, **mixed-model research** combines quantitative and qualitative data collection techniques and analysis procedures as well as combining quantitative and qualitative approaches at other phases of the research such as research question generation. This means that you may take quantitative data and **qualitise** it, that is, convert it into narrative that can be analysed qualitatively. Alternatively, you may **quantitise** your qualitative data, converting it into to numerical codes so that it can be analysed statistically.

Tashakkori and Teddlie (2003) argue that multiple methods are useful if they provide better opportunities for you to answer your research questions and where they allow you to better evaluate the extent to which your research findings can be trusted and inferences made from them. There are two major advantages to choosing to use multiple methods in the same research project. First, different methods can be used for different purposes in a study. You may wish to employ, for example, interviews at an exploratory stage, in order to get a feel for the key issues before using a questionnaire to collect descriptive or explanatory data. This would give you confidence that you were addressing the most important issues.

Bryman (2006) conducted an examination of over 200 social science articles reporting research in which quantitative and qualitative methods were combined. An examination of the research methods and research designs employed suggests that on the quantitative side structured interview and questionnaire research within a cross-sectional design tends to predominate, while on the qualitative side the semi-structured interview within a cross-sectional design tends to be the prevalent approach. Bryman studied the reasons (see Table 5.1 for some of the main reasons) given for employing a mixed-methods research approach and the ways in which the authors used them in practice. He found that there was often a contradiction between he two.

Bryman argues that his findings suggest that rationales for using multiple methods research may not to be thought through sufficiently. He found that in only 10 articles was there a clear indication that quantitative and qualitative research had each been designed to answer specific and different research questions. The findings also suggested that multiple

Table 5.1 Reasons for using mixed-method designs

Reason	Explanation
Triangulation	Use of two or more independent sources of data or data collection methods to corroborate research findings within a study.
Facilitation	Use of one data collection method or research strategy to aid research using another data collection method or research strategy within a study (e.g. qualitative/quantitative providing hypotheses, aiding measurement, quantitative/qualitative participant or case selection)
Complementarity	Use of two or more research strategies in order that different aspects of an investigation can be dovetailed (e.g. qualitative plus quantitative questionnaire to fill in gaps quantitative plus qualitative questionnaire for issues, interview for meaning)
Generality	Use of independent source of data to contextualise main study or use quantitative analysis to provide sense of relative importance (e.g. qualitative plus quantitative to set case in broader context; qualitative × quantitative analysis is to provide sense of relative importance)
Aid interpretation	Use of qualitative data to help explain relationships between quantitative variables (e.g quantitative/qualitative)
Study different aspects	Quantitative to look at macro aspects and qualitative to look at micro aspects
Solving a puzzle	Use of an alternative data collection method when the initial method reveals unexplainable results or insufficient data

Source: developed from Bryman (2006)

methods research provides such a wealth of data that researchers discover uses of the resultant findings that they had not anticipated. Bryman concluded from the articles research that there is a case for encouraging researchers to be explicit about the grounds on which multiple methods research is conducted and to recognise that, at the same time, the outcomes may not be predictable. Moreover, if both quantitative and qualitative are combined (mixed methods) then the potential – and perhaps the likelihood – of unanticipated outcomes is multiplied.

Quantitative and qualitative data collection techniques and analysis procedures each have their own strengths and weaknesses (Smith 1981). There is inevitably a relationship between the data collection technique you choose and the results you obtain. In short, your results will be affected by the techniques and procedures used. The problem here is that it is impossible to ascertain the nature of that effect. Since all different techniques and procedures will have different effects, it makes sense to use different methods to cancel out the 'method effect'. That will lead to greater confidence being placed in your conclusions.

The question that may occur to you at this stage is: 'How do I know which data collection techniques and analysis procedures to use in which situation?' There is no simple answer. Indeed, Bryman (2007) found that researchers are likely to be influenced by a number or factors; among them, commitments to particular methods, expectations of those likely to form the audience for the findings and methods with which the researcher feels comfortable.

We encourage you to use your imagination and to think of research as a highly creative process. However, above all, it is vital to have clear a clear research question and objectives for your study and ensure that the methods you use will enable you to meet them. It is a great temptation to think about data collection techniques and analysis procedures to be employed before you have clarified the objectives.

5.5 Time horizons

An important question to be asked in planning your research is 'Do I want my research to be a "snapshot" taken at a particular time or do I want it to be more akin to a diary or a series of snapshots and be a representation of events over a given period?' (As always, of course, the answer should be 'It depends on the research question.') The 'snapshot' time horizon is what we call here **cross-sectional** while the 'diary' perspective we call **longitudinal**.

We should emphasise here that these time horizons to research design are independent of which research strategy you are pursuing or your choice of method. So, for example, you may be studying the change in manufacturing processes in one company over a period of a year. This would be a longitudinal case study.

Cross-sectional studies

It is probable that your research will be cross-sectional, the study of a particular phenomenon (or phenomena) at a particular time. We say this because we recognise that most research projects undertaken for academic courses are necessarily time constrained. However, the time horizons on many courses do allow sufficient time for a longitudinal study, provided, of course, that you start it in plenty of time!

Cross-sectional studies often employ the survey strategy (Easterby-Smith *et al.* 2008; Robson 2002). They may be seeking to describe the incidence of a phenomenon (for example, the IT skills possessed by managers in one organisation at a given point in time) or to explain how factors are related in different organisations (e.g. the relationship between expenditure on customer care training for sales assistants and sales revenue). However, they may also use qualitative methods. Many case studies are based on interviews conducted over a short period of time.

Longitudinal studies

The main strength of longitudinal research is the capacity that it has to study change and development. Adams and Schvaneveldt (1991) point out that in observing people or events over time the researcher is able to exercise a measure of control over variables being studied, provided that they are not affected by the research process itself. One of the best-known examples of this type of research comes from outside the world of business. It is the long-running UK television series, 'Seven Up'. This has charted the progress of a cohort of people every seven years of their life. Not only is this fascinating television, it has also provided the social scientist with a rich source of data on which to test and develop theories of human development.

Even with time constraints it is possible to introduce a longitudinal element to your research. As Section 8.2 indicates, there is a massive amount of published data collected over time just waiting to be re-analysed! An example is the Workplace Employee Relations Survey, which was conducted in 1980, 1984, 1990 (Millward *et al.* 1992), 1998 (Cully *et al.* 1999) and 2004 (Kersley *et al.* 2006). From these surveys you would be able to gain valuable data, which would give you a powerful insight into developments in personnel management and employee relations over a period of wide-ranging change. In longitudinal studies the basic question is 'Has there been any change over a period of time?' (Bouma and Atkinson 1995:114).

5.6 The credibility of research findings

Underpinning our earlier discussion on research design has been the issue of the credibility of research findings. This is neatly expressed by Raimond (1993:55) when he subjects findings to the 'how do I know?' test: '. . . will the evidence and my conclusions stand up to the closest scrutiny?' How do you know that the advertising campaign for a new product has resulted in enhanced sales? How do you know that manual employees in an electronics factory have more negative feelings towards their employer than their clerical counterparts? The answer, of course, is that, in the literal sense of the question, you cannot know. All you can do is reduce the possibility of getting the answer wrong. This is why good research design is important. This is aptly summarised by Rogers (1961; cited by Raimond 1993:55): 'scientific methodology needs to be seen for what it truly is, a way of preventing me from deceiving myself in regard to my creatively formed subjective hunches which have developed out of the relationship between me and my material'.

Reducing the possibility of getting the answer wrong means that attention has to be paid to two particular emphases on research design: reliability and validity.

Reliability

Reliability refers to the extent to which your data collection techniques or analysis procedures will yield consistent findings. It can be assessed by posing the following three questions (Easterby-Smith *et al.* 2008:109):

1 Will the measures yield the same results on other occasions?
2 Will similar observations be reached by other observers?
3 Is there transparency in how sense was made from the raw data?

Threats to reliability

Robson (2002) asserts that there may be four threats to reliability. The first of these is **subject or participant error**. If you are studying the degree of enthusiasm employees have for their work and their employer it may be that you will find that a questionnaire completed at different times of the week may generate different results. Friday afternoons may show a different picture from Monday mornings! This should be easy to control. You should choose a more 'neutral' time when employees may be expected to be neither on a 'high', looking forward to the weekend, nor on a 'low' with the working week in front of them.

Similarly, there may be **subject or participant bias**. Interviewees may have been saying what they thought their bosses wanted them to say. This is a particular problem in organisations that are characterised by an authoritarian management style or when there is a threat of employment insecurity. Researchers should be aware of this potential problem when designing research. For example, elaborate steps can be taken to ensure the anonymity of respondents to questionnaires, as Section 11.4 indicates. Care should also be taken when analysing the data to ensure that your data are telling you what you think they are telling you.

Third, there may have been **observer error**. In one piece of research we undertook, there were three of us conducting interviews with potential for at least three different ways of asking questions to elicit answers. Introducing a high degree of structure to the interview schedule (Section 10.2) will lessen this threat to reliability.

Finally, there may have been **observer bias**. Here, of course, there may have been three different ways of interpreting the replies!

There is more detail on how these threats to reliability may be reduced later in the book in the chapters dealing with specific data collection techniques and analysis procedures.

Validity

Validity is concerned with whether the findings are really about what they appear to be about. Is the relationship between two variables a **causal relationship**? For example, in a study of an electronics factory we found that employees' failure to look at new product displays was caused not by employee apathy but by lack of opportunity (the displays were located in a part of the factory that employees rarely visited). This potential lack of validity in the conclusions was minimised by a research design that built in the opportunity for focus groups after the questionnaire results had been analysed.

Robson (2002) has also charted the threats to validity, which provides a useful way of thinking about this important topic.

Threats to validity

History

You may decide to study the opinions that customers have about the quality of a particular product manufactured by a particular organisation. However, if the research is conducted shortly after a major product recall this may well have a dramatic, and quite misleading, effect on the findings (unless, of course, the specific objective of the research was to find out about post-product recall opinions).

Testing

Your research may include measuring how long it takes telesales operators to deal with customer enquiries. If the operators believe that the results of the research may disadvantage them in some way, then this is likely to affect the results.

Instrumentation

In the above example, the telesales operators may have received an instruction that they are to take every opportunity to sell new policies between the times you tested the first and second batches of operators. Consequently, the calls are likely to last longer.

Mortality

This refers to participants dropping out of studies. This was a major problem for one of our students, who was studying the effects on the management styles of managers exposed to a year-long management development programme.

Maturation

In the earlier management development example above, it could be that other events happening during the year have an effect on their management style.

Ambiguity about causal direction

This is a particularly difficult issue. One of our part-time students was studying the effectiveness of performance appraisal in her organisation. One of her findings was that poor performance ratings of employees were associated with a negative attitude about appraisal among those same employees. What she was not clear about was whether the poor performance ratings were causing the negative attitude to appraisal or whether the negative attitude to appraisal was causing the poor performance ratings.

Generalisability

This is sometimes referred to as **external validity**. A concern you may have in the design of your research is the extent to which your research results are **generalisable**: that is, whether your findings may be equally applicable to other research settings, such as other organisations. This may be a particular worry if you are conducting case study research in one organisation, or a small number of organisations. It may also be important if the organisation is markedly 'different' in some way.

In such cases the purpose of your research will not be to produce a theory that is generalisable to all populations. Your task will be simply to try to explain what is going on in your particular research setting. It may be that you want to test the robustness of your conclusions by exposing them to other research settings in a follow-up study. In short, as long as you do not claim that your results, conclusions or theory can be generalised, there is no problem.

Logic leaps and false assumptions

So far in this chapter we have shown that there is a host of research design decisions that need to be made in order that your research project can yield sufficient data of the sort that will result in valid conclusions being drawn. Those decisions necessitate careful thought from you. However, more than just the quantity of thought is involved. It is vital that your thought processes are of high quality. Your research design will be based on a flow of logic and a number of assumptions, all of which must stand up to the closest scrutiny.

These points have been illustrated skilfully by Raimond (1993). Raimond takes the research of Peters and Waterman on 'excellent' US companies and subjects it to just such scrutiny. The ideas of Peters and Waterman (1982) have been enormously influential in the past two decades. Their book is a management 'cookbook' that gives managers eight principles to which they must adhere if their organisations are to be successful. As such, it is fairly typical of a prescriptive type of writing in management books and journals that suggests that 'this is the way it should be done'.

Raimond's (1993) analysis of Peters and Waterman can be categorised into four 'logic steps'.

Identification of the research population

This is similar to the point made about generalisability above. If the intention is to be able to generalise the conclusions across the whole population (in the Peters and Waterman case, all organisations), is the choice of population logical? If your research project is in the National Health Service, for example, it would be fanciful to assume that the findings were valid for software houses or advertising agencies.

Data collection

Is it logical to assume that the way you are collecting your data is going to yield valid data? If you interview top bosses you are likely to encounter the 'good news' syndrome. If you collect press cuttings from newspapers, how can you assume there has been no political bias put on them?

Data interpretation

It is here that there is probably the greatest danger of logic leaps and false assumptions. You will need to move from a position where you have a mountain of data to one where you write a set of conclusions that are presented coherently. This is at the same time an intellectually challenging and highly creative and exciting process.

You are likely to be using a theoretical framework against which you will analyse your data. If you are working deductively (from theory to data), this framework may have given rise to the hypothesis that you are testing in your research. One of our students studied the introduction of pay bonuses assessed by performance appraisal in the police service. Her hypothesis was based on the Meyer *et al.* (1965) hypothesis that the non-pay benefits of appraisal (such as improvement of job performance) will be prejudiced by the introduction of pay considerations to the process, rendering the appraisal interview little more than a salary discussion.

It is less likely that you will be working completely inductively where you collect your data and then analyse it to see what theory emerges.

You may employ a hybrid approach. This could involve using an established theoretical construct to help you to make sense of your findings. For example, you may be studying the way in which different companies within the group in which you work formulate their business strategies. In order to structure your analysis you could use the categorisation of different types of organisational strategy suggested by Mintzberg and Waters (1989). This may lead you to conclude that the dominant strategy employed is a mixture of those suggested by Mintzberg and Waters.

The important point here is that in both the deductive and the hybrid cases you are making assumptions about the appropriateness of the theory that you are using. In both cases it is clear that the theory with which you are working will shape your conclusions. Therefore, it is essential that you choose an appropriate theoretical framework. It is essential that you ask yourself 'Why am I using this theory and not another which may be equally, or more, appropriate?'

We are making the assumption here that you will use a theory to analyse your data. For most undergraduate and postgraduate courses this is likely to be an assessment requirement. Some professional courses may be more concerned with practical management reports that emphasise the importance of the report making viable recommendations, which are the result of clear conclusions based on a set of findings. It is important that you clarify this point with the project tutor prior to commencing the research.

Development of conclusions

The question to ask yourself here is 'Do my conclusions (or does my theory) stand up to the closest scrutiny?' If the declared theory in the police appraisal study is that the introduction of pay to appraisal will lead to the appraisal process being useful for pay purposes only, does this apply to all police appraisals? Will it be true for younger as well as older police and for all grades and locations? In other words, are you asking your readers to make logic leaps?

5.7 The ethics of research design

Sections 6.4 and 6.5 deals in more detail with the subject of research ethics. This has important implications for the negotiation of access to people and organisations and the collection of data. Here we shall address only the ethical issues that you should consider when designing your research.

Your choice of topic will be governed by ethical considerations. You may be particularly interested to study the consumer decision to buy flower bouquets. Although this may provide some interesting data collection challenges (who buys, for whom and why?), there are not the same ethical difficulties as will be involved in studying, say, the funeral purchasing decision. Your research design in this case may have to concentrate on data collection from the undertaker and, possibly, the purchaser at a time as distant from the death as delicacy permits. The ideal population, of course, may be the purchaser at a time as near as possible to the death. It is a matter of judgement as to whether the strategy and data collection method(s) suggested by ethical considerations will yield data that are valid. The general ethical issue here is that the research design should not subject those you are researching (the **research population**) to embarrassment, harm or any other material disadvantage.

Your research design may need to consider the extent to which you should collect data from a research population that is unaware of the fact they are the subject of research and so have not consented. There was a dispute between solicitors and the Consumers' Association (CA). Telephone enquiries were conducted by the CA with a sample of solicitors for the purpose of assessing the accuracy of legal advice given and the cost of specified work. The calls were, allegedly, made without the CA's identity, or the purpose of the research, being disclosed (Gibb 1995). Although it is for you to decide whether a similar research design adopted in your project would be ethical, it is worth noting that many University Research Ethics procedures preclude the use of covert research such as this.

It may be quite a different matter if you are collecting data from individuals, rather than from organisations as in the above example. This may be the case if you are conducting your research while working as an employee in an organisation. It may also be so if you are working on a student placement. In this case you would be researching as a participant observer. If the topic you were researching was one where it might be beneficial for your research that the fact that you were collecting data on individuals was not disclosed, then this would pose a similar ethical dilemma. This will be discussed in more detail when we deal with observation as a data collection method in Chapter 9.

5.8 Summary

- Research projects are undertaken for different purposes. These can be categorised as exploratory, descriptive and explanatory.
- Research design focuses upon turning a research question and objectives into a research project. It considers research strategies, choices and time horizons.
- The main research strategies are experiment, survey, case study, action research, grounded theory, ethnography and archival research. You should not think of these as discrete entities. They may be used in combination in the same research project.
- Using multiple methods can provide better opportunities to answer a research question and to evaluate the extent to which findings may be trusted and inferences made.

- Research projects may be cross-sectional or longitudinal.
- You should take care to ensure that your results are valid and reliable.
- You should always think carefully about the access and ethical issues implied by your research design.

Self-check questions

Help with these questions is available at the end of the chapter.

5.1 You are about to embark on a year-long study of customer service training for sales assistants in two supermarket companies. The purpose of the research is to compare the way in which the training develops and its effectiveness. What measures would you need to take in the research design stage to ensure that the results were valid?

5.2 You are working in an organisation that has branches throughout the country. The managing director is mindful of the fact that managers of the branches need to talk over common problems on a regular basis. That is why there have always been monthly meetings. However, she is becoming increasingly concerned that these meetings are not cost-effective. Too many managers see them as an unwelcome intrusion. They feel that their time would be better spent pursuing their principal job objectives. Other managers see it as a 'day off': an opportunity to recharge the batteries.

She has asked you to carry out some research on the cost-effectiveness of the monthly meetings. You have defined the research question you are seeking to answer as 'What are the managers' opinions of the value of their monthly meetings?'

Your principal data collection method will be a questionnaire to all managers who attend the monthly meetings. However, you are keen to triangulate your findings. How might you do this?

5.3 You have started conducting interviews in a university with the university's hourly paid staff (such as porters, gardeners and caterers). The research objective is to establish the extent to which those employees feel a sense of 'belonging' to the university. You have negotiated access to your interviewees through the head of each of the appropriate departments. In each case you have been presented with a list of interviewees.

It soon becomes apparent to you that you are getting a rather rosier picture than you expected. The interviewees are all very positive about their jobs, their managers and the university. This makes you suspicious. Are all the hourly paid staff as positive as this? Are you being given only the employees who can be relied on to tell the 'good news'? Have they been 'got at' by their manager?

There is a great risk that your results will not be valid. What can you do?

5.4 You wish to study the reasons why car owners join manufacturer-sponsored owners' clubs. Your chosen research design is to have unstructured discussions with some members of these owners' clubs. You are asked by small group of marketing managers to explain why your chosen research design is as valid as a questionnaire-based survey. What would be your answer?

Review and discussion questions

5.5 Use the search facilities of an online database to search for scholarly (peer reviewed) articles which have used firstly a case study, secondly action research and thirdly experiment research strategy in an area of interest to you. Download a copy of each article. What reasons do the articles' authors give for the choice of strategy?

5.6 Agree with a friend to watch the same television documentary.
a To what extent is the purpose of the documentary exploratory, descriptive or explanatory?
b Does the documentary use a mono method, a multiple method or mixed methods? Do not forget to make notes regarding your reasons for your answers to each of these questions and to discuss your answers with your friend.

5.7 Visit the online gateway to the European Union website (http://europa.eu.int/) and click on the link in your own language. Discuss with a friend how you might you use the data available via links from this web page in archival research. In particular, you should concentrate on the research questions you might be able to answer using these data to represent part of the reality you would be researching.

Progressing your research project

Deciding on your research design

- Revisit your research question and objectives. Make notes on the main purpose of your research.
- Decide which of the research strategies is most appropriate for your research question(s) and objectives. Look at studies in the literature that are similar to your own. Which strategies have been used? What explanations do the researchers give for their choice of strategy?
- How may you combine different research methods in your study? Make notes regarding the advantages and disadvantages of using multi-methods.
- Prepare notes on the constraints under which your research is being conducted. Do they, for example, preclude the pursuit of longitudinal research?
- List all the threats to reliability and validity contained in your research design.

References

Adams, G. and Schvaneveldt, J. (1991) *Understanding Research Methods.* (2nd edn). New York: Longman.

Bendoly, E. and Swink, M. (2007) 'Moderating effects of information access on project management behavior, performance and perceptions', *Journal of Operations Management,* Vol. 25, pp. 604–22.

Bouma, G. and Atkinson, G. (1995) *A Handbook of Social Science Research: A Comprehensive and Practical Guide for Students* (2nd edn). Oxford: Oxford University Press.

Bryman, A. (1989) *Research Methods and Organisation Studies.* London: Unwin Hyman.

Bryman, A. (2006) 'Integrating quantitative and qualitative research: how is it done?', *Qualitative Research*, Vol. 6, pp. 97–113.

Bryman, A. (2007) 'The research question in social research: what is its role?', *International Journal of Social Research Methodology*, Vol. 10, No. 1, pp. 5–20.

Coghlan, D. and Brannick, T. (2005) *Doing Action Research in Your Own Organisation* (2nd edn). London: Sage.

Collis, J. and Hussey, R. (2003) *Business Research: A Practical Guide for Undergraduate and Postgraduate Students* (2nd edn). Basingstoke: Macmillan Business.

Cully, M. Woodland, S. O'Reilly, A and Dix, G. (1999) *Britain At Work: As Depicted by the 1998 Workplace Employee Relations Survey.* London: Routledge.

Curran, J. and Blackburn, R.A. (2001) *Researching the Small Enterprise*. London: Sage.

Easterby-Smith, M., Thorpe, R. Jackson, P. and Lowe, A. (2008) *Management Research* (3rd edn). Sage: London.

Eden, C. and Huxham, C. (1996) 'Action research for management research', *British Journal of Management,* Vol. 7, No. 1, pp. 75–86.

Gibb, F. (1995) 'Consumer group accuses lawyers of shoddy service', *The Times*, 5 Oct.

Glaser, B. and Strauss, A. (1967) *The Discovery of Grounded Theory*. Chicago, IL: Aldine.

Goulding, C. (2002) *Grounded Theory: A Practical Guide for Management. Business and Market Researchers*. London: Sage.

Hakim, C. (2000) *Research Design: Successful Designs for Social and Economic Research* (2nd edn). London: Routledge.

Kersley, B., Alpin, C., Forth, J., Bryson, A., Bewley, H., Dix, G. and Oxenbridge, S. (2006) *Inside the Workplace: Findings from the 2004 Workplace Employment Relations Survey*. London: Routledge.

Kuvaas, B. (2008) 'An exploration of how the employee–organization relationship affects the linkage between perception of developmental human resource practices and employee outcomes', *Journal of Management Studies*, Vol. 45, No. 1, pp. 1–25.

Meyer, H., Kay, E. and French, J. (1965) 'Split roles in performance appraisal', *Harvard Business Review,* Vol. 43, No. 1, pp. 123–9.

Millward, N., Stevens, M., Smart, D. and Hawes, W.R. (1992) *Workplace Industrial Relations in Transition*. Aldershot: Dartmouth.

Mintzberg, H. and Waters, J. (1989) 'Of strategies, deliberate and emergent', in D. Asch and C. Bowman (eds) *Readings in Strategic Management*. Basingstoke: Macmillan Education. pp. 4–19.

Morris, T. and Wood, S. (1991) 'Testing the survey method: continuity and change in British industrial relations', *Work Employment and Society,* Vol. 5, No. 2, pp. 259–82.

Naipaul, V.S. (1989) *A Turn in the South*. London: Penguin.

Peters, T. and Waterman, R. (1982) *In Search of Excellence*. New York: Harper & Row.

Raimond, P. (1993) *Management Projects.* London: Chapman & Hall.

Robson, C. (2002) *Real World Research* (2nd edn). Oxford: Blackwell.

Rogers, C.R. (1961) *On Becoming a Person.* London: Constable.

Schein, E. (1999) *Process Consultation Revisited: Building the Helping Relationship.* Reading, MA: Addison-Wesley.

Smith, H. (1981) *Strategies of Social Research: The Methodological Imagination* (2nd edn). Englewood Cliffs, NJ: Prentice-Hall.

Suddaby, R. (2006) 'From the editors: what grounded theory is not', *Academy of Management Journal,* Vol. 49, No. 4, pp. 633–42.

Tashakkori, A. and Teddlie, C. (eds) (2003) *Handbook of Mixed Methods in Social and Behavioural Research*. Thousand Oaks, CA: Sage.

Wright, P. and Boswell, W. (2002) 'Desegregating HRM: A review and synthesis of micro and macro human resource management research', *Journal of Management*, Vol. 28, No. 3, pp. 247–76.

Yin, R.K. (2003) *Case Study Research: Design and Method* (3rd edn). London: Sage.

Further reading

Coghlan, D. and Brannick, T. (2005) *Doing Action Research in Your Own Organisation* (2nd edn). London: Sage. A valuable guide for those wishing to conduct research in their own organisation.

Hakim, C. (2000) *Research Design: Successful Designs for Social and Economic Research* (2nd edn). London: Routledge. This book provides an extremely clear discussion of the issues associated with a range of research designs. It is particularly helpful with regard to how different designs may be combined.

Quinton, S. and Smallbone, T. (2005) 'The troublesome triplets: issues in teaching reliability, validity and generalisation to business students', *Teaching in Higher Education,* Vol. 10, No. 3, pp. 299–311. This article provides a useful discussion of how validity, reliability and generalisability can be considered from positivist and phenomenological viewpoints.

Robson, C. (2002) Real World Research (2nd edn). Oxford: Blackwell. Chapters 4–7 give an excellent readable account of all the topics covered in this chapter. The examples are not drawn principally from management and business. However, do not let that put you off.

Tashakkori, A. and Teddlie, C. (1998) *Mixed Methodology: Combining Quantitative and Qualitative Approaches.* Thousand Oaks, CA: Sage. Chapters 1 to 3 of this book provide a useful introduction to multiple methods.

Case 5
Managing the acquisition from the middle

Source: Paul Repson/Alamy

Kevin found the discussion on insider action research in his part-time Masters research methods module very revealing and stimulating. He had been struggling with the task of finding a project as he found the notion of research as he understood it to be somewhat removed from his concerns as a manager. In this lecture he was exposed to an approach to research that was grounded in the notion of researching *in* action and that he could engage in it as an insider member of his own organisation. He had some challenging issues ahead in his managerial role and the prospect of combining and tackling them with doing his Masters research project appeared to offer him an opportunity to engage his actual experience in his organisation and be of practical use both to himself in completing his Masters qualification and to his organisation.

His organisation had recently been acquired by a larger firm and the acquisition meant that his section would now comprise members of the acquiring organisation as well as his own colleagues in the acquired organisation. Kevin had retained his position as section head and was responsible for the integration of the two groups into the section. The acquiring organisation was moving into Kevin's building. Kevin knew that there was a good deal of anxiety among his staff about the new organisation and the arrival of new colleagues. The talk among his own former staff was that they were anxious about losing the work atmosphere that they valued and that they feared being dominated by the incoming group, who after all, was the acquiring company. His new staff would be arriving in two weeks' time. From his Masters modules on mergers and acquisitions and managing change, Kevin knew that his situation was pretty typical and that unless he managed the process of integration, it could be a disaster. He decided to adopt the management of the integration as his Masters research project.

Kevin began reading the academic literature on mergers and acquisitions and on managing change so that he could understand the broader context in which his project was located. He noted that the root causes of failures of mergers and acquisitions often lie in organisations not attending to issues of organisational culture (Schraeder and Self 2003). When organisations merge or are acquired and if the two cultures are left alone, then typically one culture will dominate the other. An alternative is approach is to work explicitly with employees to identify elements of both cultures in order to create a new one (Schein 2004). Having a reached a degree of clarity on his understanding of the context and the purpose of his project, Kevin planned his first intervention.

He decided to use the weekly team meeting to introduce his sense of the group's anxiety about the acquisition and invited his current staff to discuss it. Hitherto, their reactions had tended to be aired in informal settings, such as at coffee breaks or in the pub on a Friday evening. They were surprised that Kevin brought this up at the team meeting and expressed their appreciation at being given the opportunity to express their views. For most of the meeting, individuals, one after the other, vented their frustration and anger at how senior management appeared to be managing the acquisition, highlighting new imposed information systems and HR systems as examples and a general fear that they would be dominated by the incoming group and would lose their valued way of working. Kevin listened carefully and, after everyone had spoken, invited the group to consider how they could anticipate some of the problems. He suggested that when the new colleagues arrived he would hold a similar meeting and that he would propose that small working groups of two or three staff members from both former organisations would take up particular issues and begin to draw up strategies as to how these issues might be addressed.

After the meeting Kevin reflected on what had taken place and felt good about how he had introduced the issues and how the discussion had led to the working groups. While he knew that he would have to give time and encouragement to the working groups, he felt ill-equipped to deal with the complex interplay of cultural traditions and the organisational and operational processes in his section. He also knew that he had to bring the issues raised to the management team.

The following Monday at the weekly meeting of section heads he raised the topic of integration in terms of the questions his team had posed. He received a mixed reaction. Two of his colleagues dismissed his team's questions as 'They are only trying to avoid hard work'. The Managing Director reiterated his demand for greater efficiencies and the need for the new organisation to be successful and appeared unconcerned that employees were complaining.

Kevin reflected on the meeting and felt that he was on dangerous ground. While he felt confident that he could engage his new section in productive conversation, he also knew that this could not solve problems on its own. He was concerned about the response of the Managing Director and his fellow section heads, some of whom would be from the other company and whom he had not met yet. Unless what he was attempting to do in his section was company-wide, he could find himself in difficulties. He did not have the authority to build integration in the new company; all he could do was make his own section work. He felt isolated. He would have to tread carefully politically because if he was successful and showed up the inaction of the other section heads and the lack of concern of the Managing Director it could damage his career.

References

Schein, E.H. (2004) *Organizational Culture and Leadership* (3rd edn). San Francisco, CA: Jossey-Bass.

Schraeder, M. and Self, D. (2003) 'Enhancing the success of mergers and acquisitions: An organisational culture perspective', *Management Decision*, Vol. 41, No. 5, pp. 511–22.

Further reading

Coghlan, D. and Brannick, T. (2005) *Doing Action Research in Your Own Organization* (2nd edn). London: Sage.

Coghlan, D. and Rashford, N.S. (2006) *Organizational Change and Strategy: An Interlevel Dynamics Approach*. Abingdon: Routledge.

Coghlan, D. and Shani A.B. (Rami) (2008) 'Insider action research: The dynamics of developing new capabilities', in P. Reason and H. Bradbury (eds). *Handbook of Action Research*. (2nd edn). London: Sage, pp. 643–55.

Questions

1 How can Kevin's management project be his research project?

2 How can Kevin contribute to both his company's successful implementation of the acquisition and to understanding mergers and acquisitions?

3 Are Kevin's political concerns a distraction from his research or are they integral to it?

Additional case studies relating to material covered in this chapter are available via the book's Companion Website, **www.pearsoned.co.uk/saunders**. They are:

* The effectiveness of computer-based training at Falcon Insurance Company
* Embedded quality at Zarlink Semi-conductor
* The international marketing management decisions of UK ski tour operators.

Self-check answers

5.1 This would be a longitudinal study. Therefore, the potential of some of the threats to validity explained in Section 5.6 is greater simply because they have longer to develop. You would need to make sure that most of these threats were controlled as much as possible. For example, you would need to:

* account for the possibility of a major event during the period of the research (wide-scale redundancies, which might affect employee attitudes) in one of the companies but not the other;
* ensure that you used the same data collection devices in both companies;
* be aware of the 'mortality' problem. Some of the sales assistants will leave. You would be advised to replace them with assistants with similar characteristics, as far as possible.

5.2 The questionnaire will undoubtedly perform a valuable function in obtaining a comprehensive amount of data that can be compared easily, say, by district or age and gender. However, you would add to the understanding of the problem if you observed managers' meetings. Who does most of the talking? What are the non-verbal behaviour patterns displayed by managers? Who turns up late, or does not turn up at all? You could also consider talking to managers in groups or individually. Your decision here would be whether to talk to them before or after the questionnaire, or both. In addition, you could study the minutes of the meetings to discover who contributed the most. Who initiated the most discussions? What were the attendance patterns?

5.3 There is no easy answer to this question! You have to remember that access to organisations to research is an act of goodwill on the part of managers, and they do like to retain a certain amount of control. Selecting whom researchers may interview is a classic way of managers doing this. If this is the motive of the managers concerned then they are unlikely to let you have free access to their employees.

What you could do is ask to see all the employees in a particular department rather than a sample of employees. Alternatively, you could explain that your research was still uncovering new patterns of information and more interviews were necessary. This way you would penetrate deeper into the core of the employee group and might start seeing those who were rather less positive. All this assumes that you have the time to do this!

You could also be perfectly honest with the managers and confess your concern. If you did a sound job at the start of the research in convincing them that you are purely interested in academic research, and that all data will be anonymous, then you may have less of a problem.

Of course, there is always the possibility that the employees generally are positive and feel as if they really do 'belong'!

5.4 You would need to stress here that your principal interest would be in getting a deep understanding of why car owners join manufacturer-sponsored owners' clubs. You would discover why the owners joined these clubs and what they thought of them. In other words, you would establish what you set out to establish and, no doubt, a good deal besides. You will remember from Section 5.6 that validity is concerned with whether the findings are really about what they appear to be about. There is no reason why your discussions with owners should not be as valid as a questionnaire survey. Your questioning should be skilful enough to elicit rich responses from your interviewees (see Chapter 10). You should be sensitive to the direction in which the discussion is moving. This will mean not being too directive, while still moving the interview in the direction you as the interviewer want. Of course, you may alleviate any fears about validity by administering a questionnaire and conducting interviews so that your findings may be triangulated!

Get ahead using resources on the Companion Website at:
   www.pearsoned.co.uk/saunders

- Improve your SPSS and NVivo research analysis with practice tutorials.
- Save time researching on the Internet with the Smarter Online Searching Guide.
- Test your progress using self-assessment questions.
- Follow live links to useful websites.

Chapter 6

Negotiating access and research ethics

Learning outcomes

By the end of this chapter you should be:

- aware of issues related to gaining access and research ethics;
- able to evaluate a range of strategies to help you to gain access to organisations and to individual participants;
- able to anticipate ethical issues at each stage of your research process and be aware of a range of strategies to help you deal with these;
- able to evaluate the ethical issues associated with a range data collection techniques, so that you can consider these in relation to your proposed research.

6.1 Introduction

Many students want to start their research as soon as they have identified a topic area, forgetting that access and ethics are critical aspects for the success of any research project. Like the sub-contractors used by Procter and Gamble (see vignette), you will need to think about how you are going to gain access to the data you need (hopefully not by sorting through an organisation's rubbish bins!) and how you are going to explain to those from whom you are obtaining data why you need that data. Such considerations are important whether you are using secondary data (Chapter 8), or collecting primary data using Internet-mediated or other methods. Over the past decade, concerns about the ethics of research practice have grown dramatically. Consequently, you need to think carefully about how you will gain access to undertake your research and about possible ethical concerns that could arise in relation to the conduct of your entire research project. Without paying careful attention to how you are going to gain access to the data you require and acting ethically, what seem like good ideas for research may flounder and prove impractical or problematic once you attempt to undertake them. In thinking about these aspects you need to be aware that most universities, as well as an increasing number of organisations, require researchers to obtain formal Research Ethics Committee approval for their proposed research, including their data collection methods, prior to granting access.

In this chapter we start by considering the types and levels of access and the issues associated with these (Section 6.2). Within this we explore issues of feasibility and sufficiency in relation to gaining access and the impact of these on the nature and content of your research question and objectives. In the following section (6.3) we offer a number of proven strategies to help you to gain access to organisations and to your intended participants within these organisations. Section 6.4 is offers an overview of research ethics and outlines why acting ethically is essential. Section 6.5 explores issues that are likely to occur at the various stages of your research project both in relation to the use of particular data collection techniques and in reporting your findings.

6.2 Issues associated with gaining access

Your ability to obtain both primary and secondary data will depend on you gaining **access** to an appropriate source, or sources where there is a choice. The appropriateness of a source will, of course, depend on your research question, related objectives and research design (Chapter 5). The first level of access is **physical access** or entry (Gummesson 2000). Whilst the Internet has undoubtedly made accessing some secondary data easier, for much secondary and primary data gaining physical access can be still be difficult. First, organisations, groups or

Throughout the world companies are involved in research, gathering information about their competitors. Often they sub-contract this research to other organisations, who gather 'competitive intelligence' providing them with a competitive analysis. In 1999 Procter and Gamble (P&G) hired sub-contractors to obtain competitive intelligence about other manufacturers' hair-care products.

According to *Fortune Magazine*, at least one of these sub-contractors, in an attempt to gain information, sorted through rubbish, trespassed at Unilever's hair-care headquarters, and misrepresented himself to Unilever employees (Serwer 2001). P&G confirm that sorting through rubbish took place but deny that misrepresentation took place. The Chief Executive of P&G was, according to *Fortune Magazine*, 'shocked' by the techniques used to obtain data on new product rollouts, selling prices, margins and the like. In what *Fortune Magazine* describe as 'something almost unheard of in corporate America', P&G informed Unilever of what had happened. Subsequently, P&G and Unilever have agreed a settlement that ensures that none of the information obtained will ever be used.

Hair washing in progress.
Source: Getty/Lifestock

Those managers responsible for hiring the sub-contractors have been fired, a company spokeswoman stating that the activities undertaken had violated P&G's strict guidelines regarding business policies.

individuals may not be prepared to engage in additional, voluntary activities because of the time and resources required. Many organisations receive frequent student requests for access and cooperation and would find it impossible to agree to all or even some of these. Second, the request for access and cooperation may fail to interest the person who receives it or to reach the **gatekeeper** or **broker** who controls research access and makes the final decision as to whether or not to allow the researcher to undertake the research. This may be for a number of reasons, related to:

- a lack of perceived value in relation to the work of the organisation, group or the individual;
- the nature of the topic because of its potential sensitivity, or because of concerns about the confidentiality of the information that would be required;
- perceptions about your credibility and doubts about your competence.

Finally, the organisation or group may find itself in a difficult situation owing to external events totally unrelated to any perceptions about the nature of the request or the person making it, so that they have no choice but to refuse access. Even when someone is prepared to offer access this may be overruled at a higher level in the organisation. This may result in a 'false start' and an associated feeling of disappointment (Johnson 1975). Where you are unable to gain this type of access, you will need to find another organisation or group, or even to modify your research question and objectives.

However, even when you are able to negotiate entry there are other levels of access that you will need to consider and plan for if your research strategy is to be realised. Many writers see access as a **continuing** process and not just an initial or single event (Gummesson 2000; Marshall and Rossman 2006; Okumus *et al.* 2007). This may take two forms. First, access may be an iterative process, so that you gain entry to carry out the initial part of your research and then seek further access in order to conduct another part. For example, you may also seek to repeat your collection of data in different parts of the organisation and therefore engage in the negotiation of access in each part (Marshall and Rossman 2006). Second, those from whom you wish to collect data may be a different set of people from those agreed with your gatekeeper in your request for access. **Physical access** to an organisation or group will be formally granted through its management. However, it will also be necessary for you to gain acceptance and consent from intended participants within the organisation or group in order to gain access to the data that they are able to provide (Robson 2002).

Access may impact upon your ability to select a representative sample of participants, or secondary data, in order to attempt to answer your research question and meet your objectives in an unbiased way and to produce reliable and valid data (Sections 7.2 and 5.6 respectively, Box 6.1). This broader meaning of access is referred to as **cognitive access**. Where you achieve this you will have gained access to the precise data that you need your intended participants to share with you in order to be able to address your research question and objectives. Simply obtaining physical access to an organisation is likely to be inadequate unless you are also able to negotiate yourself into a position where you can collect data that reveal the reality of what is occurring in relation to your research question and objectives.

This fundamental point requires you to have established precisely what data you wish to collect and the method or methods you intend to use to collect it. However, there are two specific questions that we shall consider now:

- Have you considered fully the extent and nature of the access that you will require in order to be able to answer your research question and meet your objectives?
- Are you able to gain sufficient access in practice to answer your research question and meet your objectives?

Box 6.1
Focus on student research

Gaining access to a representative sample

Hans wished to discover how component suppliers viewed the just-in-time delivery requirements of large manufacturing organisations which they supplied. Two large manufacturing organisations agreed to introduce him to a sample of their component suppliers which Hans could interview. Whilst undertaking the interviews Hans noted that all of the interviewees' responses were extremely positive about the just-in-time delivery requirements of both large manufacturing organisations. As both manufacturing organisations had selected who would be interviewed, Hans wondered whether these extremely positive responses were typical of all the component suppliers used by these organisations, or whether they were providing an unreliable and untypical picture.

These two questions may be linked in some instances. In particular, your clarity of thought, which should result from sufficiently considering the nature of the access that you require, may be helpful in persuading organisations or groups to grant entry since they are more likely to be convinced about your credibility and competence.

Access is therefore likely to be problematic in terms of gaining permission for physical or (in the case of Internet-mediated research) virtual access, maintaining that access, and being able to create sufficient scope to answer fully the research question and meet the objectives that guide your research. This suggests that the feasibility of your research will be important (Cooper and Schindler 2008; Marshall and Rossman 2006; Sekaran 2003). The issue of feasibility will determine the construction or refinement of your research question and objectives, and may sometimes lead to a clash with these hallmarks of good research. This has been recognised by Buchanan *et al.* (1988:53–4):

> Fieldwork is permeated with the conflict between what is theoretically desirable on the one hand and what is practically possible on the other. It is desirable to ensure representativeness in the sample, uniformity of interview procedures, adequate data collection across the range of topics to be explored, and so on. But the members of organisations block access to information, constrain the time allowed for interviews, lose your questionnaires, go on holiday, and join other organisations in the middle of your unfinished study. In the conflict between the desirable and the possible, the possible always wins.

The extent to which feasibility will affect the nature of your research, or at least the approach that you adopt, is made clear by Johnson (1975). He recognises that the reality of undertaking a research project may be to consider where you are likely to be able to gain access and to develop a topic to fit the nature of that access.

Your request to undertake research may involve you seeking access to a range of participants based on an organisational sample of, for example, customers, clients or employees. In order to select such a sample you will require access to organisational data, either directly or indirectly through a request that outlines precisely how you require the sample to be selected (Chapter 7). Where you wish to undertake a longitudinal study using primary data, you will require access to the organisation and your research participants on more than one occasion. The difficulty of obtaining access in relation to these more **intrusive methods** and approaches has been recognised many times in the literature (e.g.: Buchanan *et al.* 1988; Johnson 1975; Easterby-Smith *et al.* 2008).

With the increased use of the Internet to enable research, issues associated with gaining virtual access have needed to be addressed. Gaining access to online communities requires first identifying those online forums (such as user groups) that are most appropriate to your research question. Kozinets (2002) identifies four types of online community:

- bulletin boards organised around particular products, services or lifestyles;
- independent web pages which provide online community resources for consumer to consumer discussion;
- email lists grouped around specific themes;
- multiuser chat rooms.

The nature of problems of access may also vary in relation to your status as either a full-time or a part-time student. As a full-time student, you are likely to be approaching an organisation or group where you have little or no prior contact, you will be seeking to operate in the role of an **external researcher**. You will need to negotiate access at each level discussed above (physical, continuing and cognitive). Operating as an external researcher is likely to pose problems, although it may have some benefits. Your lack of status in relation to an organisation or group in which you wish to conduct research will mean not only that gaining physical access is a major issue to overcome but also that this concern will remain in relation to negotiating continued and cognitive access (Box 6.2). Goodwill on the part of the organisation or group and its members is something that external researchers have to rely on at each level of access. In this role, you need to remain sensitive to the issue of goodwill and seek to foster it at each level. Your ability to demonstrate clearly your research competence and integrity, and in particular your ability to explain your research project clearly and concisely, will also be critical at each level of access. These are key issues of access faced by all external researchers. Where you are able to demonstrate competence (see Chapters 9 to 11) and integrity, your role as an external researcher may prove to be beneficial. This is because participants are willing to accept you as being objective and without a covert, often organisationally focused, agenda. In doing this your gatekeeper can play an important role, adding credibility and introducing you and your research project to the relevant people and creating an awareness of your research.

Box 6.2
Focus on student research

The impact of the researcher's organisational status

Dave recalls a case of mistaken identity. His research involved gaining access to several employers' and trade union organisations. Having gained access to the regional office of one such organisation, Dave used various types of organisational documentation situated there over a period of a few days. During the first day Dave was located in a large, comfortable room and frequently brought refreshments by the janitor of the building. This appeared to Dave to be very kind treatment. However, Dave did not know that a rumour had spread among some staff that he was from 'head office' and was there to 'monitor' in some way the work of the office. On attending the second day, Dave was met by the janitor and taken to a small, plain room, and no more refreshments appeared for the duration of the research visit. The rumour had been corrected!

Of course, this example of the effect of the researcher's (lack of) organisational status is most unfair on the very considerable proportion of participants who treat very well those who undertake research within their organisation in full knowledge of their status. However, it illustrates the way in which some participants may react to perceptions of status.

As an organisational employee or group member operating in the role of an **internal researcher** or a **participant researcher**, perhaps adopting an action research strategy (Section 5.3), you are still likely to face problems of access to data, although these may vary in relation to those faced by external researchers. As an internal researcher you may still face the problem associated with negotiating physical or continuing access, and may still need to obtain formal approval to undertake research in your organisation or group. In addition, your status in the organisation or group may pose particular problems in relation to cognitive access. This may be related to suspicions about why you are undertaking your research project and the use that will be made of the data, perceptions about the part of the organisation for which you work, and your grade status in relation to those whom you wish to be your research participants. Any such problems may be exacerbated if you are given a project to research, perhaps by your line manager or mentor, where others are aware that this is an issue about which management would like to implement change. This is particularly likely to be the case where resulting change is perceived as being harmful to those whom you would wish to be your research participants. This will not only provide a problem for you in terms of gaining cognitive access but may also suggest ethical concerns as well (which we discuss in Section 6.4). As an internal researcher, you will need to consider these issues and, where appropriate, discuss them with those who wish to provide you with a project to research.

6.3 Strategies to gain access

This section will consider a number of strategies that may help you to obtain physical and cognitive access to appropriate data, in other words where you wish to gain **personal entry** to an organisation. It will be less applicable where you do not need to gain physical access to secondary data such as organisational records or in order to identify participants or an organisation's permission to undertake research, such as when administering a questionnaire to a series of organisations' marketing managers. Even in this case, however, some of the points that follow will still apply to the way in which you construct the pre-survey contact and the written request to complete the questionnaire (Sections 11.4 and 11.5). The applicability of these strategies will also vary in relation to your status as either an internal or an external researcher. Self-check question 6.3 is specifically designed to allow you to explore this aspect, and Box 6.8 summarises the points made as a checklist.

Strategies to help you to gain access, discussed in this section, are:

- ensuring you are familiar with and understand the organisation or group before making contact;
- allowing yourself sufficient time;
- using existing and developing new contacts;
- providing a clear account of purpose and type of access required;
- overcoming organisational concerns;
- highlighting possible benefits to the organisation;
- using suitable language;
- facilitating replies;
- developing access incrementally;
- establishing credibility;
- being open to serendipitous events.

In addition, although not discussed in detail in this book, it is worth noting that many organisations are using specialist research companies to gain access to and obtain the data they require (Box 6.3).

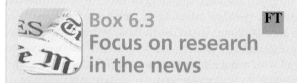

Box 6.3
Focus on research in the news FT

Star performers on back of the Internet

Investors have flocked to Internet-based UK research groups, as evidence from the USA and other markets mounts that companies are increasingly using the Internet for surveys previously conducted by telephone or face-to-face, writes Carlos Grande. Shares in YouGov – adjusted for a five-for-one share split – rose 133 per cent in the year to April 12. Similarly, Research Now and ToLuna, the two other main UK-listed online research groups, saw their shares rise 114.8 per cent and 70.4 per cent, respectively, during the same period.

In a media sector obsessed by concerns over the potential of rising Internet usage to undermine future revenue growth and existing business models, the online research groups have been star performers. This has put the stocks on heady multiples of forecast earnings per share. Despite some similarity between the technical approaches of the companies and a shared interest in growing sales overseas, they have developed different strategies.

YouGov is attempting to become a full-service market research group aiming to compete one day with international players like Taylor Nelson Sofres or Gfk/NOP. This would involve providing regular, syndicated tracking studies as well as one-off pieces of work and recommendations directly to corporate clients. Research Now sees itself as a more complementary data provider to existing players, as research groups pay to gain access to online panels run by the specialists, to then incorporate them in research reports to clients. With UK market research alone valued at $2.4 bn (£1.2 bn) in 2005 there looks to be a big enough opportunity for all the different models to succeed.

Source: article by Grande, Carlos (2007) *Financial Times*, 14 Apr. Copyright © 2007 The Financial Times Ltd.

Ensuring familiarity and understanding

Before attempting to gain physical access it is essential that you familiarise yourself fully with the characteristics of the organisation or group. The knowledge that you gain by doing this will enable you to signal to the gatekeeper that you have thought carefully about your research, as you will be able to provide a convincing argument that is aligned as to why they should grant access to their organisation or group.

Allowing yourself sufficient time

Physical access may take weeks or even months to arrange, and in many cases the time invested will not result in access being granted (Buchanan *et al.* 1988). An approach to an organisation or group will result in either a reply or no response at all. A politely worded but clearly reasoned refusal at least informs you that access will not be granted. The non-reply situation means that if you wish to pursue the possibility of gaining access you will need to allow sufficient time before sending further correspondence, emailing or making a follow-up telephone call. Great care must be taken in relation to this type of activity so that no grounds for offence are given. Seeking access into a large, complex organisations, where you do not have existing contacts, may also necessitate several telephone calls simply to establish who is the best person to ensure that your request for access will be considered by the organisational gatekeeper. As highlighted in Box 6.4 even after the person to contact has been established, access can still take months to achieve. You may also consider using email where you have access to this as a way of obtaining a reply.

If you are able to contact a participant directly, such as a manager, an exchange of correspondence may be sufficient to gain access. Here you should clearly set out what you require from this person and persuade them of the value of your work and your

Box 6.4
Focus on management research

Spending time gaining access

In a paper in the *Annals of Tourism Research*, Okumus *et al.* (2007) reflect on their experiences of gaining access for three distinct research projects. For one of these studies, eight companies were initially approached by letter in which the background, aims and potential benefits to the companies were explained alongside issues of confidentiality and resource and time requirements. Subsequent to this letter, follow up telephone calls were made and further explanations provided. Five of the eight companies responded that they were unable to participate in the research.

After months of negotiation, three companies had shown interest. Access to the first was gained

through a university professor acting as an intermediary between the researchers and the company. In the negotiations it was made clear that the research would need to be of value to the company. The process of gaining access to the first company had taken more than four months from initial contact to starting to collect data.

During data collection, gatekeepers in each of the three companies identified potential informants to approach for interview. These informants then identified others to be interviewed. Okumus and colleagues comment that, although this might be considered to a 'snowball sample', they prefer not to use this term. Initially the three companies selected themselves by agreeing to take part in the research. Subsequently, although the researchers had sought to reach and interview all key informants at different management levels and locations this was in some cases not possible. Potential informants had been identified by the gatekeepers and only those willing to take part could be interviewed.

credibility. Even so, you will still need to allow time for your request to be received and considered and an interview meeting to be arranged at a convenient time for your research participant. This may take a number of weeks, and you may have to wait for longer to schedule the actual interview.

Where you are seeking access to a range of participants to conduct a number of interviews, to undertake a questionnaire, to engage in observation or to use secondary data, your request may be passed 'up' the organisation or group for approval and is likely be considered by a number of people. Where you are able to use a known contact in the organisation or group this may help, especially where they are willing to act as a sponsor for your research. Even so, you will still need to allow for this process to take weeks rather than days. Where the organisation or group is prepared to consider granting access, it is likely that you will be asked to attend a meeting to discuss your research. There may also be a period of delay after this stage while the case that you have made for access is evaluated in terms of its implications for the organisation or group, and it may be necessary to make a number of telephone calls or emails to pursue your request politely.

In the situation where your intended participants are not the same people who grant you physical access, you will need to allow further time to gain their acceptance. This may involve you making **pre-survey contact** by telephoning these intended participants (Section 11.5), or engaging in correspondence or holding an explanatory meeting with them (discussed later). You may well need to allow a couple of weeks or more to establish contact with your intended participants and to secure their cooperation, especially given any operational constraints that restrict their availability.

Once you have gained physical access to the organisation or group and to your participants, you will be concerned with gaining cognitive access. Whichever method you are using to gather data will involve you in a time-consuming process, although some methods will require that more of your time be spent within the organisation or group to understand what is happening. The use of a questionnaire will mean less time spent in the organisation compared with the use of non-standardised interviews, whereas the use of observation techniques may result in even more time being spent to gather data (Bryman 1988). Conversely, the use of Internet-mediated techniques such as netnography, may mean that all of your research can be conducted from your desk! Where you are involved in a situation of continuing access, as outlined in this section, there will also be an issue related to the time that is required to negotiate, or re-negotiate, access at each stage. You will need to consider how careful planning may help to minimise the possibility of any 'stop–go' approach to your research activity.

Using existing and developing new contacts

Most management and organisational researchers suggest that you are more likely to gain access where you are able to use *existing contacts* (Buchanan *et al.* 1988; Easterby-Smith *et al.* 2008; Johnson 1975). Buchanan *et al.* (1988:56) say that 'we have been most successful where we have a friend, relative or student working in the organisation'. We have also found this to be the case. In order to request access we have approached those whom we would consider to be professional colleagues, who may also be present or past students, course advisers, external examiners, or otherwise known to us through local, regional or national networks. Their knowledge of us means that they should be able to trust our stated intentions and the assurances we give about the use that will be made of any data provided. It can also be useful to start a research project by utilising these existing contacts in order to establish a track record that you can refer to in approaches that you make to other organisations or groups where you do not have such contacts. This should help your credibility with these new contacts.

The use of known contacts will depend largely on your choice of research strategy, approach to selecting a sample, research question and objectives. It is likely to be easier to use this approach where you are using a case-study, action research or ethnographic research strategy (Section 5.3). This will certainly be likely where you undertake an in-depth study that focuses on a small, purposively selected sample (Section 7.3). There will clearly be a high level of convenience in terms of gaining access through contacts who are familiar; however, these contacts may also be used as part of a quota sample, or in relation to purposive or snowball sampling (Section 7.3).

Jankowicz (2005) refers to the possibility of using your work placement organisation as a context for your research project, where this applies to your situation as a full-time undergraduate or postgraduate student. Where you have enjoyed a successful work placement, you will undoubtedly have made a number of contacts who may be able to be very helpful in terms of cooperating with you and granting access. You may have become interested in a particular topic because of the time that you spent in your placement organisation. Where this is so, you can spend time reading theoretical work that may be relevant to this topic, then identify a research question and objectives, and plan a research project to pursue your interest within the context of your placement organisation. The combination of genuine interest in the topic and relatively easy access to organisational participants should help towards the production of a good-quality and useful piece of work.

Where you need to develop new contacts, consideration of the points discussed throughout this section will help you to cultivate these. In addition, you will need to be able to identify the most appropriate person to contact for help, either directly or indirectly (Box 6.5). There may be a number of ways to seek to do this, depending on your research topic. You may consider asking the local branch of an appropriate professional association of whom you are a member for the names and business addresses of key employees to contact in organisations where it would be suitable for you to conduct

Box 6.5
Focus on student research

Identifying possible contacts

Andrew identified a number of specific organisations that matched the criteria established for the types of business he wished to include in his research project. Many of these were organisations where he did not have an appropriate contact, or indeed any contact at all. The different types of organisational structure in these organisations added to his difficulties in tracking down the most appropriate employee to contact in order to request access.

Organisations' websites were used to identify the corporate headquarters of each organisation. This part of the organisation was contacted by telephone. When talking to each organisation, Andrew explained that he was a student and gave the title of his course and the name of his university. He also gave a very brief explanation of his research to help the person who answered the telephone. This resulted in him being provided with a telephone number, email address or connected to that part of the organisation that the person who answered the telephone thought was appropriate (see next paragraph). Andrew always ended this initial telephone conversation by thanking the person for the help that had been provided.

At the next stage, Andrew again explained that he was a student and gave the title of his course and the name of his university. The purpose of the research was also explained briefly to the personal assistant who inevitably answered the telephone. Andrew asked for the name and business address of the person whom the personal assistant thought would be the most appropriate person to write to. In most cases the people to whom he spoke at this stage were most helpful and provided some excellent leads.

Sometimes, particularly in relation to complex organisations, Andrew found that he was not talking to someone in the appropriate part of the organisation. He therefore asked the person to help by transferring the telephone call. Sometimes this led to a series of calls to identify the right person. Andrew always remained polite, thanking the person to whom he spoke for their help. He always gave his name and that of his university to reduce the risk of appearing to be threatening in any way. It was most important to create a positive attitude in what could be perceived as a tiresome enquiry.

Andrew chose to ask for the name and business address of a hoped-for organisational 'lead'. Using this he could send a written request to this person, which could be considered when it was convenient, rather than attempt to talk to them at that point in time, when it might well have not been a good time to make such a request. This process resulted in many successes, and Andrew added a number of good contacts to his previous list. However, the key point to note is the great care that was exercised when using this approach.

research. You could also contact your professional association at national level, where this is more appropriate to your research question and objectives. It might also be appropriate to contact either an employers' association for a particular industry, or a trade union, at local or national level. Alternatively, it might be appropriate for you to contact one or more chambers of commerce, learning skills councils or other employers' networks. However, you need to be mindful that such associations and organisations are likely to receive literally hundreds of requests from students every year and so may have insufficient time or resources to respond.

You may also consider making a direct approach to an organisation or group in an attempt to identify the appropriate person to contact in relation to a particular research project. This has the advantage of potentially providing access to organisations or groups that you would like to include in your research project; however, great care needs to be exercised at each stage of the process.

Using the approach outlined in Box 6.5 may result in you obtaining the business email addresses of possible organisational 'leads'. In this case you will need to use the Internet

Box 6.6
Focus on student research

Email requesting access

Annette was undertaking her research project on the use of lean production systems. Having made telephone contact with the production controller's personal assistant, she was asked to send an email requesting access (see below).

Unfortunately, Annette relied on her email software's spell check to proof read her email. This resulted in the production controller receiving an email containing three mistakes:

- the addition of the word 'I' at the end of the first paragraph;
- the phrase 'between 30 minutes and half an hour' instead of 'between 30 minutes and an hour' at the end of the second paragraph;
- two digits being transposed in the mobile telephone number at the end of the last paragraph, resulting in it being incorrect.

Not surprisingly, Annette was denied access.

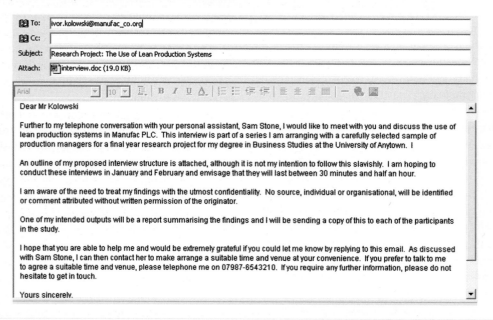

To: ivor.kolowski@manufac_co.org
Cc:
Subject: Research Project: The Use of Lean Production Systems
Attach: interview.doc (19.0 KB)

Arial 10

Dear Mr Kolowski

Further to my telephone conversation with your personal assistant, Sam Stone, I would like to meet with you and discuss the use of lean production systems in Manufac PLC. This interview is part of a series I am arranging with a carefully selected sample of production managers for a final year research project for my degree in Business Studies at the University of Anytown. I

An outline of my proposed interview structure is attached, although it is not my intention to follow this slavishly. I am hoping to conduct these interviews in January and February and envisage that they will last between 30 minutes and half an hour.

I am aware of the need to treat my findings with the utmost confidentiality. No source, individual or organisational, will be identified or comment attributed without written permission of the originator.

One of my intended outputs will be a report summarising the findings and I will be sending a copy of this to each of the participants in the study.

I hope that you are able to help me and would be extremely grateful if you could let me know by replying to this email. As discussed with Sam Stone, I can then contact her to make arrange a suitable time and venue at your convenience. If you prefer to talk to me to agree a suitable time and venue, please telephone me on 07987-6543210. If you require any further information, please do not hesitate to get in touch.

Yours sincerely,

to send an email request to such a person (Box 6.6). Where you consider this to be appropriate you will, of course, still need to follow the standards of care that you should use in drafting and sending a letter. The ease of using email may tempt some to use a lower level of care about the way their written communication is constructed. It may also lead to a temptation to send repeated messages. The use of email is considered later in our discussion about 'netiquette'; however, from a practical point of view it is also a possibility that using this means to make contact may result in a greater danger that the recipient of your request simply deletes the message! Those people who receive large numbers of email every day may cope with these by deleting any that are not essential. It is possible that sending a letter to a potential gatekeeper may result in that person considering your request more carefully!

Making the type of contact outlined in Box 6.5 may result in identifying the person whom you wish to participate in your research. Alternatively, your reason for making contact with this person may be to ask them to grant you access to others in the organisation or group whom you wish to be your participants, or to secondary data. This type of contact may be the functional manager or director of those staff to whom you would like access. Having identified a gatekeeper you will have to persuade that person about your credibility, overcome any issues that exist about the sensitivity of your research project and demonstrate the potential value of this for the organisation.

Providing a clear account of purpose and type of access required

Providing a clear account of your requirements will allow your intended participants to be aware of what will be required from them (Robson 2002). Asking for access and cooperation without being specific about your requirements will probably lead to a cautious attitude on their part since the amount of time that could be required might prove to be disruptive. It is also likely to be considered unethical (Section 6.5). Even where the initial contact or request for access involves a telephone call, it is still probably advisable to send a letter or email that outlines your proposed research and requirements (Box 6.6). Your **introductory letter** requesting access should outline in brief the purpose of your research, how the person being contacted might be able to help, and what is likely to be involved in participating. The success of this letter will be helped by the use of short and clear sentences. Its tone should be polite, and it should seek to generate interest on the part of intended respondents.

Establishing your credibility will be vital in order to gain access. The use of known contacts will mean that you can seek to trade on your existing level of credibility. However, when you are making contact with a potential participant for the first time, the nature of your approach will be highly significant in terms of beginning to establish credibility – or not doing so! Any telephone call, introductory letter or email will need to be well presented, and demonstrate your clarity of thought and purpose. Any lack of preparation at this stage will be apparent and is likely to reduce the possibility of gaining access. These issues are discussed in more detail in Section 10.4.

Overcoming organisational concerns

Organisational concerns may be placed into one of three categories. First, concerns about the amount of time or resources that will be involved in the request for access. Easterby-Smith *et al.* (2008) suggest that your request for access is more likely to be accepted if the amounts of time and resources you ask for are kept to a minimum. As a complementary point to this, Healey (1991) reports earlier work that found that introductory letters containing multiple requests are also less likely to be successful. However, while the achievement of access may be more likely to be realised where your demands are kept to a minimum, there is still a need to maintain honesty. For example, where you wish to conduct an interview you may be more likely to gain access if the time requested is kept within reason. Remember, falsely stating that it will last for only a short time and then deliberately exceeding this is very likely to upset your participant and may prevent your gaining further access.

The second area of concern is related to *sensitivity* about the topic. We have found that organisations are less likely to cooperate where the topic of the research has negative implications. Organisations do not normally wish to present themselves as not performing well in any aspect of their business. If this is likely to be the case you will need to consider carefully the way in which your proposed research topic may be perceived by those whom you ask to grant access. In such cases you may be able to highlight a positive approach to the issue by, for example, emphasising that your work will be designed to identify individual and organisational learning in relation to the topic (a positive inference). You should avoid sending any request that appears to concentrate on aspects associated with non-achievement or failure if you are to gain access. Your request for access is therefore more likely to be favourably considered where you are able to outline a research topic that does not appear to be sensitive to the organisation (Easterby-Smith *et al.* 2008).

The third area of concern is related to the **confidentiality** of the data that would have to be provided and the **anonymity** of the organisation or individual participants. To overcome this concern, you will need to provide clear assurances about these aspects (Box 6.6). When offering these you must be sure that you will be able to keep to your agreement. Strictly, if you have promised confidentiality you should not share your raw data with anyone, not even your project tutor. One advantage of using an introductory letter is to give this guarantee in writing at the time of making the request for access, when this issue may be uppermost in the minds of those who will consider your approach. Once initial access has been granted you will need to repeat any assurances about anonymity and confidentiality to your participants. You will also need to consider how to maintain this when you write up your work in situations where particular participants could be indirectly identified (Bell, 2005) (Section 14.5). Illustrations of how not to do this are provided in Box 6.17!

Possible benefits to the organisation

Apart from any general interest that is generated by the subject of your proposed research, you may find that it will have some level of applicability to the jobs of those whom you approach for access. Practitioners often wrestle with the same subjects as researchers and may therefore welcome the opportunity to discuss their own analysis and course of action related to such an issue, in a non-threatening, non-judgemental environment. A discussion may allow them to think through an issue and to reflect on the action that they have adopted to manage it. In our own interviews with practitioners we are pleased when told that the discussion has been of value to the interviewee, because of this reason.

For those who work in organisations where they are perhaps the only subject practitioner, this may be the first time they have had this type of opportunity. You, therefore, need to consider whether your proposed research topic may provide some advantage to those from whom you wish to gain access, although this does not mean that you should attempt to 'buy' your way in based on some promise about the potential value of your work. Where it is unlikely that your proposed research will suggest any advantage to those whose cooperation you seek, you will need to consider what alternative course of action to take.

It may also help to offer a summary report of your findings to those who grant access. The intention would be to provide each of your participants with something of value and to fulfil any expectations about exchange between the provider and receiver of the research data, thereby prompting some of those whom you approach to grant access (Johnson 1975). We believe it is essential that this summary report is designed specifically to be of use to those who participated rather than, say, a copy of the research report you need to submit to your university. It is also possible that feedback from the organisation about your report may help you further with your research.

Where access is granted in return for supplying a report of your findings it may be important to devise a simple 'contract' to make clear what has been agreed. This should state the broad form of the report and the nature and depth of the analysis that you agree to include in it, and how you intend to deal with issues of confidentiality and anonymity.

This may vary from a summary report of key findings to a much more in-depth analysis. For this reason it will be important to determine what will be realistic to supply to those who grant you access.

Using suitable language

Some researchers advise against referring to certain terms used in relation to research activity when making an approach to an organisation for access, because these may be perceived as threatening or not interesting to the potential participant (e.g. Buchanan *et al.* 1988; Easterby-Smith *et al.* 2008). Buchanan *et al.* (1988:57) suggest using 'learn from your experience' in place of research, 'conversation' instead of interview and 'write an account' rather than publish.

Use of language will depend largely on the nature of the people you are contacting. Your language should be appropriate to the type of person being contacted, without any hint of being patronising, threatening or just boring. Given the vital role of initial telephone conversations, introductory letters or emails, we would suggest allowing adequate time to consider and draft these and using someone to check through your message. You may find Section 11.4, and in particular Box 11.16, helpful in this process. Do not forget that you are intending to engender interest in your research project, and the initial point of contact needs to convey this.

Facilitating replies

We have found that the suggestion of a number of different contact methods (telephone, mobile telephone, fax, email) in our written requests for access helps ensures a reply. These may not be suitable in all cases, and should be selected to fit the data collection technique you intend to use. Inclusion of a stamped or freepost addressed envelope may also facilitate a reply.

Developing access incrementally

We have already referred to the strategy of achieving access by stages, as a means of overcoming organisational concerns about time-consuming, multiple requests. Johnson (1975) provides an example of developing access on an incremental basis. He used a three-stage strategy to achieve his desired depth of access. The first stage involved a request to conduct interviews. This was the minimum requirement in order to commence his research. The next stage involved negotiating access to undertake observation. The final stage was in effect an extension to the second stage and involved gaining permission to tape-record the interactions being observed.

There are potentially a number of advantages related to the use of this strategy. As suggested earlier, a request to an organisation for multiple access may be sufficient to cause them to decline entry. Using an incremental strategy at least gains you access to a certain level of data. This strategy will also allow you the opportunity to develop a positive relationship with those who are prepared to grant initial access of a restricted nature. As you establish your credibility, you can develop the possibility of achieving a fuller level of access. A further advantage may follow from the opportunity that you have to design your request for further access specifically to the situation and in relation to opportunities that may become apparent from your initial level of access. On the other hand, this incremental process will be time consuming, and you need to consider the amount of time that you will have for your research project before embarking on such a strategy. In addition, it can be argued that it is unethical not to explain your access requirements fully.

Establishing your credibility

In Section 6.2 we differentiated between physical and cognitive access. Just because you have been granted entry into an organisation, you will not be able to assume that those whom you wish to interview, survey or observe will be prepared to provide their cooperation. Indeed, assuming that this is going to happen raises an ethical issue that is considered in the next section. Robson (2002) says that gaining cooperation from these intended participants is a matter of developing relationships. This will mean repeating much of the process that you will have used to gain entry into the organisation. You will need to share with them the purpose of your research project, state how you believe that they will be able to help your study, and provide assurances about confidentiality and anonymity. This may involve writing to your intended participants or talking to them individually or in a group. Which of these means you use will depend on the intended data collection technique, your opportunity to make contact with them, the numbers of participants involved, and the nature of the setting. However, your credibility and the probability of individuals' participation is likely to be enhanced if the request for participation is made jointly with a senior person from the organisation (Box 6.7). Where your intended data collection technique may be considered intrusive, you may need to exercise even greater care and take longer to gain acceptance. This might be the case, for example, where you wish to undertake observation (Chapter 9). The extent to which you succeed in gaining cognitive access will depend on this effort.

Box 6.7
Focus on student research

Email request to participate in a focus group

Sara's research project involved her in undertaking a communication audit for an organisation near her university. As part of her research design she had chosen to use mixed method research using focus groups followed by a questionnaire. Those selected to attend the focus groups were invited by individual emails sent jointly from herself and a senior manager within the organisation:

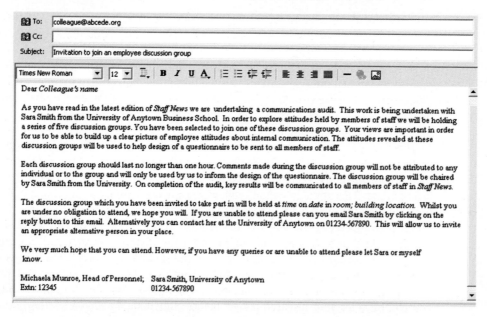

Box 6.8
Checklist

To help to gain access

✔ Have you allowed yourself plenty of time for the entire process?

✔ Are you clear about the purpose of your research project?

✔ Are you clear about your requirements when requesting access (at least your initial requirements)?

✔ Can you use existing contacts, at least at the start of your research project, in order to gain access and gather data?

✔ (If you have been on a work placement) Is your work placement organisation an appropriate setting for your research project?

✔ Have you approached appropriate local and/ or national employer, or employee, professional or trade bodies to see if they can suggest contacts through whom you might gain access?

✔ Have you considered making a direct approach to an organisation to identify the most appropriate person to contact for access?

✔ Have you identified the most appropriate person and been willing to keep on trying to make contact?

✔ Have you drafted a list of the points you wish to make, including your thanks to those to whom you speak?

✔ Have you considered and thought about how you will address likely organisational concerns such as:
  ✔ the amount of time or resources that would be involved on the part of the organisation;
  ✔ the sensitivity of your research topic;
  ✔ the need for confidentiality and/or anonymity?

✔ Have you considered the possible benefits for the organisation should access be granted to you, and the offer of a report summarising your findings to enhance your chance of achieving access?

✔ Are you willing to attend a meeting to present and discuss your request for access?

✔ Where your initial request for access involves a telephone conversation, have you followed this with an introductory letter to confirm your requirements?

✔ Is the construction, tone and presentation of an introductory letter likely to support your gaining access?

✔ Have you ensured that your use of language is appropriate to the person who receives it without any hint of being patronising, threatening or boring?

✔ Have you considered including a range of contact methods for recipients to use to reply?

✔ Are you prepared to work through organisational gatekeepers in order to gain access to intended participants?

✔ Have you allowed sufficient time to contact intended participants and gain their acceptance, once physical access has been granted?

✔ Have you allowed sufficient time within your data collection to gain 'cognitive access' to data?

The strategies that we have outlined to help you to gain access to organisations and to those whom you wish to participate in your research project are summarised as a checklist in Box 6.8.

6.4 Research ethics and why you should act ethically

Defining research ethics

Ethical concerns will emerge as you plan your research, seek access to organisations and to individuals, collect, analyse and report your data. In the context of research, **ethics** refers to the appropriateness of your behaviour in relation to the rights of those who become the subject of your work, or are affected by it. Cooper and Schindler (2008:34) define ethics as the 'norms or standards of behaviour that guide moral choices about our behaviour and our relationships with others'. **Research ethics** therefore relates to questions about how we formulate and clarify our research topic, design our research and gain access, collect data, process and store our data, analyse data and write up our research findings in a moral and responsible way. This means that you will have to ensure that the way you design your research is both methodologically sound and morally defensible to all those who are involved. Inevitably, what is morally defensible behaviour as researchers will be affected by broader social norms of behaviour (Zikmund 2000). A **social norm** indicates the type of behaviour that a person ought to adopt in a particular situation (Robson 2002; Zikmund 2000). However, as Cooper and Schindler (2008) recognise, the norms of behaviour that guide moral choices can in reality allow for a range of ethical positions.

Within business and management research, there are two dominant philosophical standpoints: deontology and teleology. The **deontological view** argues that the ends served by the research can never justify the use of research which is unethical. Consequently, if you adopted this view you would never use, for example, deception to obtain your research data, even if deception was necessary to ensure the data were valid and reliable. In contrast, the **teleological view** argues that the ends served by your research justify the means. Consequently, the benefits of your research findings would be weighed against the costs of acting unethically. This approach has an added complication as you also need to consider whether the benefits of the research are morally just. Unfortunately, it is unlikely that a simple comparison between costs to one group and benefits to another can provide you with a clear answer to such an ethical dilemma! Any deviation from ethical standards therefore needs to be thought through and justified extremely carefully. Not surprisingly, we recommend that you consider ethical issues throughout your research and remain sensitive to the impact (both positive and negative) of your work on those whom you approach to help, those who provide access and cooperation, and those affected by your results.

The conduct of your research is likely to be guided by your university's code of ethics or ethical guidelines. A **code of ethics** will provide you with a statement of principles and procedures for the conduct of your research highlighting what is and what is not considered ethical. This will be helpful and, where followed, should ensure that you do not transgress the behavioural norms established by your university or professional association. However, as pointed out by Bell and Bryman (2007), such codes tend to be written in abstract terms and designed to prevent misconduct. As a member of a university (and where appropriate a professional association) you are likely to be required abide by such ethical codes or adhere to ethical guidelines for research. The Internet can also provide direct links to a number of very useful codes of ethics and ethical guidelines. A selection of these is contained in Table 6.1.

You may also be required to submit your research proposal to a research ethics committee. **Research ethics committees** fulfil a number of objectives. One of these may be a proactive or educational role, which would include constructing an ethical code and disseminating advice about the ethical implications of design aspects of research. An ethics committee may also adopt a reactive role in relation to the consideration of research proposals and calls for advice arising from dilemmas that confront researchers. A research ethics committee is likely to be composed of experienced researchers from a variety of backgrounds, who are able to draw on their range of experience and knowledge of different ethical perspectives to provide advice. A committee may also be used in particular cases to form a judgement about the undertaking of research that appears to contain ethical dilemmas. In some cases you may also have to satisfy the requirements of an

Table 6.1 Internet addresses for ethical codes, guidelines and statements of practice

Name	Internet address
Academy of Management's Code of Ethics	http://www.aomonline.org/aom.asp?id=268
American Psychological Association's Ethical Principles of Psychologists and Code of Conduct	http://www.apa.org/ethics/code.html
British Psychological Society's Code of Conduct and Ethical Guidelines	http://www.bps.org.uk/the-society/code-of-conduct/code-of-conduct_home.cfm
British Sociological Association's Statement of Ethical Practice	http://www.britsoc.co.uk/equality/Statement+Ethical+Practice.htm
Economic and Social Research Council's (ESRC) Research Ethics Framework (REF)	http://www.esrc.ac.uk/ESRCInfoCentre/Images/ESRC_Re_Ethics_Frame_tcm6-11291.pdf
European Commission's (EU) Information Society Technologies (IST) Programme's professional and ethical guidelines for the conduct of socio-economic research (The Respect Project)	http://www.respectproject.org/main/index.php/disciplines.php
Market Research Society's Code of Conduct	http://www.mrs.org.uk/standards/codeconduct.htm
Social Research Association's Ethical Guidelines	http://www.the-sra.org.uk/ethical.htm

ethics committee established in your host organisation as well as your university. This may apply where your research is based in the health service. For example, many of our students undertaking research within the UK's National Health Service (NHS) have had to meet the requirements established by their local NHS Trust's ethics committee (Box 6.9). Such a requirement is often time consuming to meet.

Even where you use a code of ethics in the design of your research and have submitted your proposal to a research ethics committee for approval, this is unlikely to indicate the end of your consideration of ethical issues. We now explore those ethical issues that affect the research generally before looking at those issues that arise at specific stages in the research process, which we discuss in Section 6.5.

General ethical issues

A number of key ethical issues arise across the stages and duration of a research project. These relate to the:

- privacy of possible and actual participants;
- voluntary nature of participation and the right to withdraw partially or completely from the process;
- consent and possible deception of participants;
- maintenance of the confidentiality of data provided by individuals or identifiable participants and their anonymity;
- reactions of participants to the way in which you seek to collect data, including embarrassment, stress, discomfort, pain and harm;

Box 6.9
Focus on student research

Establishing whether research warrants mandated ethical review

Rachel worked for a local hospital. At her first meeting with her project tutor, he had reminded her to check with the hospital and establish if she would need to submit her research project to the hospital's research ethics committee for review. Subsequently, she discussed this with her line manager who suggested she check with the National Health Service's National Research Ethics Service. Using the Google search engine, Rachel found the Service's website and downloaded their two-page leaflet, *Defining Research* (National Patient Safety Agency 2007).

The *Defining Research* leaflet highlighted that, although research always required a Research Ethics Committee review, it was not mandatory for either audit or service evaluation. This did not mean there

were no ethical issues associated with audit or service evaluation, only that there was not a mandatory requirement for a Research Ethics Committee Review. The leaflet also provided clear definitions of what was meant by the terms 'research', 'audit' and 'service evaluation':

Research is 'the attempt to derive generalisable new knowledge including studies that at aim to generate hypotheses, as well as studies that aim to test them'.

Audit is 'designed and conducted to produce information to inform delivery of best care'.

Service evaluation is 'designed and conducted solely to define or judge current care'.

Based on these definitions and the other information in the leaflet, Rachel felt that her research project was 'service evaluation' rather than research. She discussed this with her line manager who agreed, but suggested that she also confirm with the Chair of the Research Ethics Committee that her project was a 'service evaluation'. The Committee Chair agreed with Rachel and her line manager.

- effects on participants of the way in which you use, analyse and report your data, in particular the avoidance of embarrassment, stress, discomfort, pain and harm;
- behaviour and objectivity of you as researcher.

The avoidance of harm (**non-maleficence**) can be seen as the cornerstone of the ethical issues that confront those who undertake research. For example, the way you obtain consent, preserve confidentiality, collect your data from participants and the way in which you use, analyse and report your data all have the capacity to cause harm to participants. Observation, interviews and questionnaires can all be potentially intrusive and provoke anxiety or stress in participants or involve stress. Box 6.10 provides a short checklist for helping reduce the likelihood of your research harming your participants. However, we

Box 6.10
Checklist

Assessing your research in relation to causing harm to participants

✔ Is your research likely to affect negatively the well-being of those participating?

✔ Have any potential risks to particpants that might arise during the course of your research been identified?

✔ Can you justify your research and, in particular, explain why alternatives that involve fewer potential risks cannot be used?

would stress that in order to minimise the likelihood of causing harm, we believe you should use this checklist in conjunction with the others in this and the next sections.

You may also consider using the Internet in relation to your research project. The expression **netiquette** has been developed to provide a heading for a number of 'rules' or guidelines about how to act ethically when using the Internet. As such it allows us to identify a range of potential ethical issues that arise from using the Internet. The Internet may allow you to contact possible **participants** more easily and even to do this repeatedly – a possibility that may be an invasion of their **privacy** in a number of ways. Forms of covert observation that impinge on the rights of 'participants' may also be possible (Cooper and Schindler 2008), as may the monitoring of individuals' use of different websites or collecting data on customers' preferences. In general terms, you should apply the ethical principles that are discussed in this chapter and elsewhere in this book when considering using the Internet as a means to collect data. We return to other aspects of research netiquette later in this section and offer particular advice about Internet-mediated questionnaires in Section 11.5.

6.5 Ethical issues at specific stages of the research process

As can be seen from Figure 6.1, ethical issues are likely to be of importance throughout your research and require ethical integrity from you as researcher, your research sponsor (if any) and the organisation's gatekeeper. In the initial stages of formulating and clarifying your research topic those upon whom your research will impact have the right to expect quality research which takes account of existing knowledge. Where you are undertaking research for an organisation you will need to find the middle ground between the organisation's right for useful research and your right not to be coerced into researching a topic in which you are not at all interested or that does not satisfy the assessment requirements of your university. Dependence on a gatekeeper for access will inevitably lead to a range of ethical issues associated with research design and access. The nature of power relationships in business and management research will raise ethical issues that also need to be considered. Organisational gatekeepers are in a very powerful position in relation to researchers who request organisational access. They will remain in a powerful position in terms of the nature and extent of the access that they allow and in setting expectations regarding output from which they may benefit (Bell and Bryman 2007). However, you need to be sensitive to the way in which the granting of access affects this type of relationship. During data collection face-to-face interviews, even with managers, will place you in a position of some 'power', albeit for a short time, because you will be able to formulate questions, including probing ones, which may cause discomfort or even stress. As a researcher in an organisation you will need to remain sensitive to the fact that your presence is a temporary one, whereas the people from whom you collect data will need to work together after you depart. This will have an impact on the way in which you both analyse your data and report your research findings. In addition, the way in which you process and store data you collect about individuals is likely to be governed by data protection legislation. Such legislation provides protection for individuals in relation to the processing and storing of personal data.

Ethical issues during design and gaining access

Most ethical problems can be anticipated and dealt with during the design stage of any research project. This should be attempted by planning to conduct the research project in

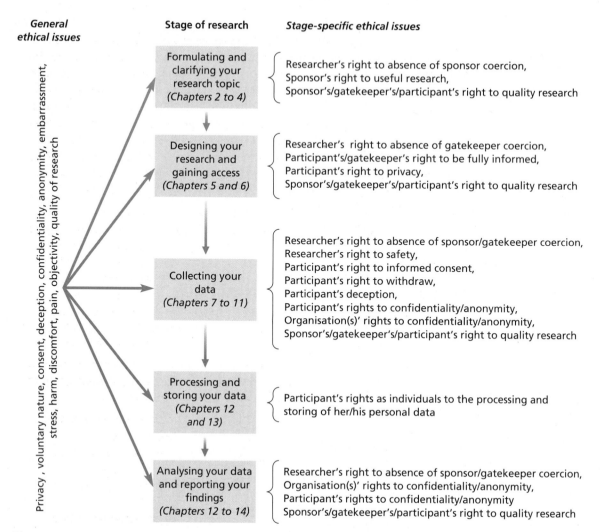

Figure 6.1
Ethical issues at different stages of research

line with the ethical principle of not causing harm (discussed earlier) and by adapting your research strategy or choice of methods where this is appropriate. Evidence that ethical issues have been considered and evaluated at this stage is likely to be one of the criteria against which your research proposal is judged (Cooper and Schindler 2008; Marshall and Rossman 2006).

One of the key stages at which you need to consider the potential for ethical problems to arise is when you seek access (Box 6.11). As referred to earlier, you should not attempt to apply any pressure on intended participants to grant access (Robson 2002; Sekaran 2003). This is unlikely to be the case where you are approaching a member of an organisation's management to request access. However, where you are undertaking a research project as an internal researcher within your employing organisation (Section 6.3), in relation to a part-time qualification, there may be a temptation to apply pressure to others (colleagues or subordinates) to cooperate. Individuals have a right to privacy and should not feel pressurised or coerced into participating. By not respecting this, you may well be causing harm. Consequently, you will have to accept any refusal to take part (Cooper and

Box 6.11
Focus on management research

Reporting confidential interviews

Research by Riach and Wilson (2007) into non-platonic workplace relationships is reported in a recent article in the *British Journal of Management*. This research investigates how workplace romance is discussed and defined within a bar environment and looks at the 'rules of engagement' and the consequences for women. In discussing their research method, Riach and Wilson highlight how taped interviews were conducted with a snowball sample of 48 managers and workers in bars within a group of branded public houses. They also state that all these interviewees were assured that what they said would be treated confidentially.

In writing their paper, Riach and Wilson adopted a number of techniques to ensure that they honoured their commitment to respondent confidentiality. When providing details of the organisational background to their study, they do not mention the branded, public-house group by name. Rather, they provide contextual data including the number of bar outlets in the UK, the number of staff employed and the market segment. These data are referenced to 'internal company documentation', the full reference not appearing in the list references, thereby ensuring the anonymity of the public-house group. Further information about the organisation, such as techniques used to foster close team interaction, is also provided but it is not possible to work out to which organisation this refers.

Within the method section no mention is made of the region or regions within the UK within which the data were collected. Rather, the authors simply refer to interviews being conducted 'in the one-brand region' (Riach and Wilson 2007:83). Individual employees are referred to using letters rather than names or pseudonyms. The letters A to D are used to refer to managers, whilst the letter W followed by a number refers to a worker. For example, when discussing examples of house rules they state:

'One [worker] noted that the bar's "code of conduct" did not allow you to "drink, or smoke or read behind the bar, or talk about politics or pub business, or have romantic relations at work" (WA006). It was clear from the rest of his interview that the majority of employees in his workplace were ignoring this rule. Others were not aware of any rules about relationships with customers (e.g. WC001)'.

(Riach and Wilson 2007:85)

Consequently, whilst actual quotations are included to support the arguments made, the anonymity of those interviewed was ensured by:

* not naming the organisation whilst still providing sufficient contextual information;
* not referencing fully organisational documentation whilst indicating it had been used;
* only naming the geographical location at the country level;
* referring to respondents by codes rather than using their names.

In their penultimate paragraph Riach and Wilson note that their respondents, the participants in workplace romance, were very open. They were prepared to discuss both informal rules and the impact that their relationships had both upon themselves and upon others.

Schindler 2008; Robson 2002). Box 6.12 contains a short checklist to help you ensure you are not putting pressure on individuals to participate. You may also cause harm by the nature and timing of any approach that you make to intended participants – perhaps by telephoning at 'unsociable' times, or, if possible, by 'confronting' those from whom you intend to collect data. Access to secondary data may also raise ethical issues in relation to harm. Where you happen to obtain access to personal data about individuals who have not consented to let you have this (through personnel or client records), you will be obliged to treat this in the strictest confidence and not to use it in any way that might cause harm to these people.

Box 6.12
Checklist

Assessing your research in relation to not pressurising individuals to participate

✔ Have you ensure participants have not been coerced into taking part in the study?

✔ Have you made sure that no inducements (e.g. financial payments), other than reimbursement for travel expenses or in some cases time, are offered?

✔ Have you checked that the risks involved in participation are likely to be acceptable to those participating?

✔ Are participants free to withdraw from your study at any time and have you informed them of this?

Consent to participate in a research project is not a straightforward matter. In general terms, an approach to a potential participant is an attempt to gain consent. However, this raises a question about the scope of any consent given. Where someone agrees to participate in a particular data collection method, this does not necessarily imply consent about the way in which the data provided are subsequently used. Clearly, any assurances that you provide about anonymity or confidentiality will help to develop an understanding of the nature of the consent being entered into, but even this may be inadequate in terms of clarifying the nature of that consent. This suggests a continuum that ranges across a lack of consent, involving some form of deception, a lack of clarity about the nature of consent so that the researcher **implied consent** from taking part, and consent that is fully informed as well as freely given (known as **informed consent**). This is shown in Figure 6.2.

Three points are described in Figure 6.2, although in reality this is likely to operate as a continuum as a multitude of positions are possible around the points described. For example, research that is conducted with those who have agreed to participate can still involve an attempt to deceive them in some way. This **deception** may be related to deceit over the real purpose of the research (Sekaran 2003), or in relation to some undeclared sponsorship (Zikmund 2000), or related to an association with another organisation that will use any data gained for commercial advantage. Where this is the case, it could cause embarrassment or harm to those who promote your request for access within their employing organisation, as well as to yourself.

There are a number of aspects that need to be considered when obtaining consent. These are summarised in Box 6.13 as a checklist, the answers to these questions often being drawn together in a **participant information sheet**. The extent of the detail of informed consent that you will require will depend on the nature of your research project. The nature of establishing informed consent will also vary. If you are intending to collect data using a questionnaire, the return of a completed questionnaire by a respondent is

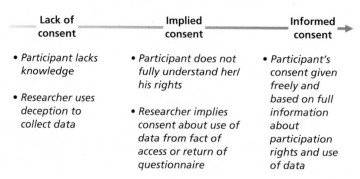

Figure 6.2
The nature of participant consent

Lack of consent	Implied consent	Informed consent
• Participant lacks knowledge	• Participant does not fully understand her/his rights	• Participant's consent given freely and based on full information about participation rights and use of data
• Researcher uses deception to collect data	• Researcher implies consent about use of data from fact of access or return of questionnaire	

Box 6.13
Checklist

Requirements for a participant information sheet

Organisational 'gatekeepers' (discussed earlier in Section 6.3) and intended participants need to be informed about the following aspects of the research. This information can be drawn together in a participant information sheet.

About the nature of the research
✔ What is its purpose?
✔ Who is or will be undertaking it?
✔ Is it being funded or sponsored – if so, by whom and why?
✔ Who is being asked to participate – i.e. broad details about the sampling frame, sample determination and size?
✔ How far has the research project progressed?

About the requirements of taking part
✔ What type of data will be required from those who agree to take part?
✔ How will these data be collected (e.g. interview, observation or questionnaire)?
✔ How much time will be required, and on how many occasions?
✔ What are the target dates to undertake the research and for participation?

About the implications of taking part and participants' rights
✔ Recognition that participation is voluntary.

✔ Recognition that participants have the right to decline to answer a question or set of questions, or to be observed in particular circumstances.
✔ Recognition that participants have control over the right to record any of their responses where a voice recorder is used.
✔ Recognition that participants may withdraw at any time.
✔ What are the consequences of participating – possible risks, depending on the nature of the approach and purpose, and expected benefits?
✔ What assurances will be provided about participant anonymity and data confidentiality?

About the use of the data collected and the way in which it will be reported
✔ Who will have access to the data collected?
✔ How will the results of the research project be disseminated?
✔ How will assurances about anonymity and confidentiality be observed at this stage?
✔ What will happen to the data collected after the project is completed?
✔ Where data are to be preserved, what safeguards will be 'built in' to safeguard the future anonymity and confidentiality of participants?

Whom to contact if there are any questions about the research
✔ Have you established how you will provide the participant with a person to contact about the research, including name, work address, email and contact telephone number?

taken to have implied consent. Alternatively, when interviewing a senior manager, correspondence may be exchanged, such as discussed in Section 6.3, to establish informed consent. When interviewing individuals, informed consent should be supplemented by a more detailed written agreement, such as a **consent form** (Box 6.14), signed by both parties. This will help ensure that data are being obtained consistently (Economic and Social Data Service 2007). Consent when undertaking observation (Chapter 9) relates to whether or not the observation is being undertaken in a public or private area. Embedded within this is an understanding that, if what is being observed takes place in a public area, the public nature of the act means consent is implied. Where this is not the case, consent should be obtained. With regard to online observation, this raises considerable debate as to whether or not Internet sites should be considered private (Kozinets 2002).

Box 6.14
Focus on student research

Consent form

Mats' research involved him in interviewing the employees of a large advertising agency. Prior to commencing each interview, Mats gave each participant an information sheet that summarised his research project, including the benefits and disadvantages of taking part. After carefully explaining his research, the reasons why (with the participant's permission) he wished to audio record the interview and emphasising that individuals were not obliged to participate unless they wished, Mats asked them if they wished to participate. Those who did were asked to complete and sign the following consent form:

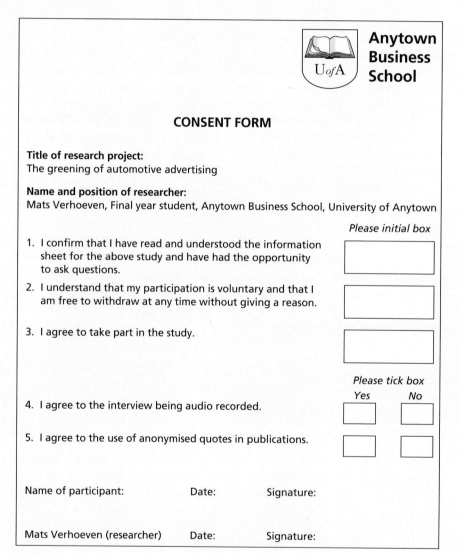

CONSENT FORM

Title of research project:
The greening of automotive advertising

Name and position of researcher:
Mats Verhoeven, Final year student, Anytown Business School, University of Anytown

Please initial box

1. I confirm that I have read and understood the information sheet for the above study and have had the opportunity to ask questions.

2. I understand that my participation is voluntary and that I am free to withdraw at any time without giving a reason.

3. I agree to take part in the study.

Please tick box
Yes   No

4. I agree to the interview being audio recorded.

5. I agree to the use of anonymised quotes in publications.

Name of participant: Date: Signature:

Mats Verhoeven (researcher)   Date: Signature:

Anytown Business School
U*of*A

Although this debate is considered further in Chapter 9, Kozinets' (2002) recommendations for online observation are, we believe, worth following:

- fully disclose your presence, affiliations and intentions to the online community during your research,
- ensure confidentiality and anonymity to informants;
- seek and incorporate feedback from those being researched;
- take a cautious position on the public versus private debate and contact informants to obtain their permission (informed consent) before quoting specific postings.

You will also need to operate on the basis that informed consent is a continuing requirement for your research. This, of course, will be particularly significant where you seek to gain access on an incremental basis (Section 6.3). Although you may have established informed consent through prior written correspondence, it is still worthwhile to reinforce this at the point of collecting data. An example of this is provided in Box 10.9, which contains a worked example about opening a semi-structured interview. You will also need to gain informed consent from those whom you wish to be your intended participants as well as those who act as organisational gatekeepers, granting you access.

Earlier (Section 6.3) we discussed possible strategies to help you to gain access. One of these was related to possible benefits to an organisation of granting you access. You should be realistic about this. Where you are anxious to gain access, you may be tempted to offer more than is feasible. Alternatively, you may offer to supply information arising from your work without intending to do this. Such behaviour would clearly be unethical, and to compound this the effect of such action (or inaction) may result in a refusal to grant access to others who come after you.

Ethical issues during data collection

As highlighted in Figure 6.1, the data collection stage is associated with a range of ethical issues. Some of these are general issues that will apply to whichever technique is being used to collect data. Other issues are more specifically related to a particular data collection technique. Finally, and of equal importance, there are issues associated with ensuring your own safety whilst collecting your data.

Irrespective of data collection technique, there are a number of ethical principles to which you need to adhere. In the previous subsection we referred to the importance of not causing harm or intruding on an intended participant's privacy. This was in relation to the participant's right not to take part. Once participants have consented to take part in your research, they still maintain their rights. This means that they have the right to withdraw as participants, and that they may decline to take part in a particular aspect of your research. You should not ask them to participate in anything that will cause harm or intrude on their privacy, where this goes beyond the scope of the access agreed. We have also referred to rights in relation to deceit. Once access has been granted, you should keep to the aims of your research project that you shared and agreed with your intended participant(s) (Zikmund 2000). To do otherwise, without raising this with your participant(s) and renegotiating access, would be, in effect, another type of deceit. This would be likely to cause upset, and could result in the premature termination of your data collection. There are perhaps some situations where deception may be accepted in relation to 'covert' research, and we shall discuss this later in this subsection.

Another general ethical principle is related to the maintenance of your **objectivity**. During the data collection stage this means making sure that you collect your data accurately and fully – that you avoid exercising subjective selectivity in what you record. The importance of this action also relates to the validity and reliability of your work, which is discussed in Chapters 5 and 7–11. Without objectively collected data, your ability to analyse and report your work accurately will also be impaired. We return to this as an ethical issue in the next subsection. Obviously, fabrication of any data is also a totally unacceptable and unethical course of action.

Confidentiality and anonymity may be important in gaining access to organisations and individuals (Section 6.3). Once such promises have been given, it is of great importance to make sure that these are maintained. Where confidentiality has been promised, then you must ensure the data collected remain confidential. This is particularly important in relation to names, addresses and other personal information (Economic and Social Data Service 2007). Ways of ensuring anonymity are inevitably research method specific. Whilst the main concern is likely to be individuals or organisations being able to be identified, it is worth recognising that respondents may give permission for data to be attributed directly to them. Anonymising quantitative data by aggregating or removing key variables is relatively straight forward. However, where qualitative data are being reported it may be less straightforward. New points of significance will emerge as the research progresses which you will wish to explore with other participants. Your key concern is to ensure that you do not cause harm (Easterby-Smith *et al.* 2008). For example, within interviews respondents can often infer what earlier interviewees might have said from the questions being asked. This may lead to participants indirectly identifying which person was responsible for making the earlier point that you now wish to explore with them and repercussions for the person whose openness allowed you to identify this point for exploration. Where you wish to get others to discuss a potentially sensitive point you may attempt to steer the discussion to see if they will raise it without in any way making clear that one of the other participants has already referred to it.

Use of the Internet and email during data collection will lead to the possibility of serious ethical, or netiquette, issues related to confidentiality and anonymity. For example, it would be technically possible to forward the email (or interview notes) of one research participant to another participant in order to ask this second person to comment on the issues being raised. Such an action would infringe the right to confidentiality and anonymity, perhaps causing harm. It should definitely be avoided. Moreover, it is also likely to lead to a data protection issue related to the use of personal data (discussed later). While the use of the Internet may allow you to correspond with participants in distant locations, this approach may also be seen as intrusive and demanding for any participant where they are expected to supply written answers via this medium. Alternatively, the use of this means to collect data may adversely affect the reliability of the data where participants are not able to devote the time required to supply extensive written answers via their computer. Any consideration of the use of Internet discussion forums or chat rooms to collect data is also likely to suggest ethical and data protection issues related to confidentiality and anonymity, as well as potential issues related to the reliability of any data (Section 10.8).

The ability to explore data or to seek explanations through interview-based techniques means that there will be greater scope for ethical and other issues to arise in relation to this approach to research (Easterby-Smith *et al.* 2008). The resulting personal contact, scope to use non-standardised questions or to observe on a 'face-to-face' basis, and capacity to develop your knowledge on an incremental basis mean that you will be able to exercise a greater level of control (Chapter 10). This contrasts with the use of a quantitative approach based on structured interviews or self-administered questionnaires (Chapter 11).

The relatively greater level of control associated with interview-based techniques should be exercised with care so that your behaviour remains within appropriate and acceptable parameters. In face-to-face interviews, you should avoid over-zealous questioning and pressing your participant for a response. Doing so may make the situation stressful for your participant (Sekaran 2003). You should also make clear to your interview participants that they have the right to decline to respond to any question (Cooper and Schindler 2008). The nature of questions to be asked also requires consideration. Sekaran (2003) states that you should avoid asking questions that are in any way demeaning to your participant (Sections 10.4, 10.5, 10.7 and 10.8 provide a fuller consideration of related issues). In face-to-face interviews it will clearly be necessary to arrange a time that is convenient for your participant; however, where you wish to conduct an interview by telephone (Sections 10.8, 11.2 and 11.5) you should not attempt to do this at an unreasonable time of the day. In the interview situation, whether face to face or using a telephone, it would also be unethical to attempt to prolong the discussion when it is apparent that your participant has other commitments (Zikmund 2000).

The use of *observation* techniques raises its own ethical concerns (Section 9.3). The boundaries of what is permissible to observe need to be drawn clearly. Without this type of agreement the principal participants may find that their actions are being constrained (Bryman 1988). You should also avoid attempting to observe behaviour related to your participant's private life, such as personal telephone calls and so forth. Without this, the relationship between observer and observed will break down, with the latter finding the process to be an intrusion on their right to privacy. There is, however, a second problem related to the use of this method. This is the issue of '"**reactivity**" – the reaction on the part of those being investigated to the investigator and their research instruments' (Bryman 1988:112). This issue applies to a number of strategies and methods (Bryman 1988) but is clearly a particular problem in observation.

A solution to this problem might be to undertake a **covert** study so that those being observed are not aware of this fact. In a situation of likely 'reactivity' to the presence of an observer you might use this approach in a deceitful yet benign way, since to declare your purpose at the outset of your work might lead to non-participation or to problems related to validity and reliability if those being observed altered their behaviour (Bryman 1988; Gummesson 2000; Wells 1994). The rationale for this choice of approach would thus be related to a question of whether 'the ends justify the means', provided that other ethical aspects are considered (Wells 1994:284). However, the ethical concern with deceiving those being observed may prevail over any pragmatic view (Bryman 1988; Cooper and Schindler 2008). Indeed, the problem of reactivity may be a diminishing one where those being observed adapt to your presence as declared observer (Bryman 1988). This adaptation is known as **habituation** (Section 9.6).

Where access is denied after being requested you may decide you have no other choice but to carry out covert observation – where this is practical (Gummesson 2000). However, this course of action may prove to be a considerable source of irritation if revealed, and you will need to evaluate this possibility very carefully. Indeed, many universities' ethical codes prohibit any form of research being carried out if access has been denied. Irrespective of the reason why a deception occurred, it is widely accepted that after the observation has taken place you should inform those affected about what has occurred and why. This process is known as **debriefing**.

One group of students who sometimes consider using a covert approach are internal or practitioner–researchers (see Sections 6.3 and 9.3). There are recognised advantages and disadvantages associated with being an internal researcher (Sections 6.3 and 9.3). One of the possible disadvantages is related to your relationship with those from whom you will need to gain cooperation in order to gain cognitive access to their data. This may be related to the fact that your status is relatively junior to these colleagues, or that you are more senior to them. Any status difference can impact negatively on your intended data collection. One solution would therefore be to adopt a covert approach in order to seek to gain data. You may therefore decide to interview subordinate colleagues, organise focus groups through your managerial status, or observe interactions during meetings without declaring your research interest. The key question to consider is: will this approach be more likely to yield trustworthy data than declaring your real purpose and acting overtly? The answer will depend on a number of factors:

- the existing nature of your relationships with those whom you wish to be your participants;
- the prevailing managerial style within the organisation or that part of it where these people work;
- the time and opportunity that you have to attempt to develop the trust and confidence of these intended participants in order to gain their cooperation.

Absolute assurances about the use of the data collected may also be critical to gain trust, and the time you invest in achieving this may be very worthwhile.

In comparison with the issues discussed in the preceding paragraphs, Dale *et al.* (1988) believe that the ethical problems associated with questionnaires and other research using the survey strategy are fewer. This is due to the nature of structured questions that are clearly not designed to explore responses and the avoidance of the in-depth interview situation, where the ability to use probing questions leads to more revealing information (Dale *et al.* 1988). Zikmund (2000) believes that the ethical issues linked with a survey strategy are those associated with more general issues discussed earlier: privacy, deception, openness, confidentiality and objectivity.

When thinking about avoiding harm, many researchers forget about themselves! The possibility of harm to you as the researcher is an important ethical issue which you should not ignore. This is important with regard to not divulging personal information about yourself such as your home address or telephone number as well as your personal safety such as when alone with your participants. In discussing the latter with our students, we have found the guidance sheets provided by the Suzy Lamplugh Trust (2006) extremely helpful (Box 6.15, opposite). As the Trust's guidance sheets emphasise, you should never allow your working practices (research design) to put your own safety in danger.

Ethical issues associated with data processing and storage

Within the European Union, issues of data protection have assumed an even greater importance with the implementation of Directive 95/46/EC. This provides protection for individuals in relation to the processing, storing and movement of personal data. Within the UK, recent privacy breaches have heightened public awareness of requirement to ensure that personal data are stored securely (Box 6.16). Data protection legislation is likely to exist in countries outside the European Union, and you will need to be familiar with legislative requirements where you undertake your research project.

Article 1 of Directive 95/46/EC requires member states to protect individuals' rights and freedoms, including their right to privacy, with regard to the processing of personal data. Article 2 provides a number of definitions related to the purpose of the Directive.

Box 6.15
Checklist

Personal safety when collecting primary data

In its guidance sheet, 'Personal Safety Alone in the Workplace', the Suzy Lamplugh Trust (2006) highlights how many people find themselves working alone in the workplace, emphasising the corresponding need to make adequate arrangements to ensure they are safe at all times, especially when clients visit. The advice offered by the Trust also applies to you as a researcher if you are intending to collect primary data. In particular, the Trust advises that you should:

✔ let other people know whom you are meeting, when and where so that someone is looking after your welfare;

✔ set up a system where you contact someone every day with a full list of whom you are meeting, where and at what times;

✔ make a telephone call just after a visitor has arrived, telling someone at the other end of the line that you will contact them again at a certain time after the visitor has left;

✔ be careful not to tell anyone that you are alone in a workplace.

As part of this leaflet, the Trust also offer the following general advice for anyone working alone:

Plan your first meeting with a person in a busy public place if at all possible.

Log your visits/meetings with someone and telephone them afterwards to let them know you are safe.

Avoid situations that might be difficult or dangerous.

Never assume it will not happen to you.

However, as emphasised by the Trust, these are suggestions only and should not be regarded as comprehensive sources of advice.

Personal data is defined as any information relating to identified or identifiable persons. Where you process and control this type of data your research will become subject to the provisions of the data protection legislation of the country in which you live. In the context of UK legislation, this refers to the provisions of the Data Protection Act 1998 (Stationery Office 1998). This Act, in following the Articles of the Directive, outlines the principles with which anyone processing personal data must comply. Although the following list provides a summary of these principles, you are strongly advised to familiarise yourself with the definitive legal version and to determine its implications for your research project and the nature of data collection.

Personal data must be:

1 processed fairly and lawfully;

2 obtained for specified, explicit and lawful purposes and not processed further in a manner incompatible with those purposes;

3 adequate, relevant and not excessive in relation to the purpose for which they are processed;

4 accurate and, where necessary, kept up to date;

5 kept (in a form that allows identification of data subjects) for no longer than is necessary;

6 processed in accordance with the rights granted to data subjects by the Act;

7 kept securely;

8 not transferred to a country outside the European Economic Area unless it ensures an adequate level of protection in relation to the rights of data subjects.

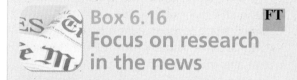

Box 6.16
Focus on research
in the news

FT

Watchdog in call for criminal sanctions

Organisations guilty of privacy breaches such as the data loss at (the UK) HM Revenue and Customs should face criminal sanctions as part of an effort to make 'alarm bells ring in every boardroom', the privacy watchdog said yesterday.

Richard Thomas, information commissioner, called for powers to launch snap privacy audits into companies and public sector bodies in an effort to quell growing public concern that personal information is being widely mishandled and misused. Mr Thomas's comments crystallise wider fears that existing laws and regulatory powers are inadequate to deal with the privacy problems stemming from the rapid growth of personal information databases and data sharing. Mr Thomas said the law must be changed to criminalise security breaches of the magnitude of that at Revenue and Customs, where child benefit details of 25m people were lost in the post. 'Making this a criminal offence would serve as a strong deterrent and would send a very strong signal that it is completely unacceptable to be cavalier with people's personal information', Mr Thomas said. He welcomed Gordon Brown's announcement of a programme of spot checks on data privacy safeguards in government departments, although he would like to go much further. Mr Thomas renewed his calls for sweeping powers to launch unannounced audits of companies and public agencies, to make them take people's privacy much more seriously.

'Alarm bells must ring in every boardroom', he said. 'Data protection safeguards must be technically robust and idiot proof'. The Revenue blunder is merely the highest profile in a growing list of privacy breaches that has provoked alarm from Mr Thomas, privacy campaigners and other information specialists.

A survey released by the information commissioner's office last week said nine out of 10 people were concerned that organisations did not treat their personal information properly.

Richard Archdeacon, a director of Symantec Global Services, the virus and Internet security protection company, said the Revenue case would prove 'a tipping point' for the way companies and government have to deal with data loss. European Union moves to require telecommunications companies formally to disclose data loss to regulators – and tell their customers what they plan to do about it – would have to be extended much more broadly, and to include government, he said. He said a House of Lords committee had recommended that and there was evidence from California, where such requirements were already in place, that company security improved as a result. Surveys suggest data loss is 'hugely costly' to organisations, averaging \$140 (£68) a lost record in notification, legal, recovery and compensation costs.

Beneath the possible technical fixes lies a deeper debate about whether the general 1998 Data Protection Act requirements to take 'appropriate technical and organisational measures' to prevent privacy breaches need to be replaced by more detailed guidance to companies and their employer.

Source: article by Peel, Michael and Timmins, Nicholas (2007) *Financial Times*, 22 Nov. Copyright © 2007 The Financial Times Limited.

These principles have implications for all research projects that involve the processing of personal data. There are certain, limited exemptions to the second, fifth and seventh data principles (and to Section 7 of the 1998 Act) related to the processing and use of personal data for research purposes. These are contained in Section 33 of the Data Protection Act 1998. Where data are not processed to support measures or decisions with respect to particular individuals and are not processed in a way that will cause substantial damage or distress to a data subject:

- personal data may be processed further for a research purpose, although it may be necessary to inform data subjects about this new purpose and who controls these data;

- personal data, where processed only for research purposes, may be kept indefinitely;
- personal data that are processed only for research will be exempt from Section 7, which provides data subjects with rights to request information, where the results of the research including any statistics are not made available in a form that identifies any data subject.

Our brief summary of the legislation should only be treated as providing a general guidance only and not as providing advice. You should instead seek advice that is appropriate to the particular circumstances of your research project where this involves the collection and processing of personal data. In addition, there is a further category of personal data, known as **sensitive personal data**, which covers information held about a data subject's racial or ethnic origin, political opinions, religious or other similar beliefs, trade union membership and the like. This type of data may be processed only if at least one of the conditions in Schedule 3 of the 1998 Act is met. The first of these conditions refers to the data subject providing their explicit consent to the processing of such data. Effective explicit consent is likely to mean clear and unambiguous written consent in this context.

These legally based data protection concerns have hopefully focussed your mind on the question of keeping personal data and also on whether the use of these data allows any participant to be identified. Unless there is a clear reason for processing these types of data, the best course of action is likely to be to ensure your data are completely and genuinely anonymised and that any 'key' to identify data subjects is not retained by those who control these data.

Ethical issues related to analysis and reporting

The maintenance of your objectivity will be vital during the analysis stage to make sure that you do not misrepresent the data collected. This will include not being selective about which data to report or, where appropriate, misrepresenting its statistical accuracy (Zikmund 2000). A great deal of trust is placed in each researcher's integrity, and it would clearly be a major ethical issue were this to be open to question. This duty to represent your data honestly extends to the analysis and reporting stage of your research. Lack of objectivity at this stage will clearly distort your conclusions and any associated recommendations.

The ethical issues of confidentiality and anonymity also come to the fore during the reporting stage of your research. Wells (1994) recognises that it may be difficult to maintain the assurances that have been given. However, allowing a participating organisation to be identified by those who can 'piece together' the characteristics that you reveal may result in embarrassment and also in access being refused to those who seek this after you. Great care therefore needs to be exercised to avoid this situation. You also have the option of requesting permission from the organisation to use their name. To gain this permission you will almost certainly need to let them read your work to understand the context within which they will be named.

This level of care also needs to be exercised in making sure that the anonymity of individuals is maintained (Box 6.17). Embarrassment and even harm could result from reporting data that are clearly attributable to a particular individual (Cooper and Schindler 2008; Robson 2002). Care, therefore, needs to be taken to protect those who participated in your research.

A further ethical concern stems from the use made by others of the conclusions that you reach and any course of action that is explicitly referred to or implicitly suggested, based on your research data. How ethical will it be to use the data collected from a group

Box 6.17
Focus on students' research

Inadvertently revealing participants' identities

Over the years we have been fortunate to read a large number of student research projects. The following examples, drawn from some of these, highlight how easy it is to inadvertently reveal the identities of research participants when presenting your findings:

- reporting a comment made by a female accounts manager when in fact there is only one such person;
- referring to a comment made by a member of the sales team, when only one salesperson would

have had access to the information referred to in the comment;

- reporting data and comments related to a small section of staff, where you state the name or job title of the one person interviewed from that section elsewhere in your research report;
- referring to an 'anonymous' organisation by name on the copy of the questionnaire placed in an appendix;
- attributing comments to named employees;
- thanking those who participated in the research by name;
- using pseudonyms where the initials of the pseudonym – Mike Smith – are the same as those of the actual person interviewed – Mark Saunders;
- including a photograph of the interview site or interviewee in your project report.

of participants effectively to disadvantage them because of the decisions that are then made in the light of your research? On the other hand, there is a view that says that while the identity of your participants should not be revealed, they cannot be exempt from the way in which research conclusions are then used to make decisions (Dale *et al.* 1988). This is clearly a very complicated ethical issue.

Where you are aware that your findings may be used to make a decision that could adversely affect the collective interests of those who were your participants, it may be ethical to refer to this possibility even though it reduces the level of access that you achieve. An alternative position is to construct your research question and objectives to avoid this possibility, or so that decisions taken as a result of your research should have only positive consequences for the collective interests of those who participate. You may find that this alternative is not open to you, perhaps because you are a part-time student in employment and your employing organisation directs your choice of research topic. If so, it will be more honest to concede to your participants that you are in effect acting as an internal consultant rather than in a (dispassionate) researcher's role.

This discussion about the impact of research on the collective interests of those who participate brings us back to the reference made above to the particular ethical issues that arise in relation to the analysis of secondary data derived from questionnaires. Dale *et al.* (1988) point out that where questionnaire data are subsequently used as secondary data the original assurances provided to those who participated in the research may be set aside, with the result that the collective interests of participants may be disadvantaged through this use of data. The use of data for secondary purposes therefore also leads to ethical concerns of potentially significant proportions, and you will need to consider these in the way in which you make use of this type of data.

A final checklist to help you anticipate and deal with ethical issues is given in Box 6.18.

Box 6.18
Checklist

To help anticipate and deal with ethical issues

✓ Attempt to recognise potential ethical issues that will affect your proposed research.

✓ Utilise your university's code on research ethics to guide the design and conduct of your research.

✓ Anticipate ethical issues at the design stage of your research and discuss how you will seek to control these in your research proposal.

✓ Seek informed consent through the use of openness and honesty, rather than using deception.

✓ Do not exaggerate the likely benefits of your research for participating organisations or individuals.

✓ Respect others' rights to privacy at all stages of your research project.

✓ Maintain objectivity and quality in relation to the processes you use to collect data.

✓ Recognise that the nature of an interview-based approach to research will mean that there is greater scope for ethical issues to arise, and seek to avoid the particular problems related to interviews and observation.

✓ Avoid referring to data gained from a particular participant when talking to others, where this would allow the individual to be identified with potentially harmful consequences to that person.

✓ Covert research should be considered only where reactivity is likely to be a significant issue or where access is denied (and a covert presence is practical). However, other ethical aspects of your research should still be respected when using this approach.

✓ Maintain your objectivity during the stages of analysing and reporting your research.

✓ Maintain the assurances that you gave to participating organisations with regard to confidentiality of the data obtained and their organisational anonymity.

✓ Consider the implications of using the Internet and email carefully in relation to the maintenance of confidentiality and anonymity of your research participants and their data, before using this means to collect any data.

✓ Protect individual participants by taking great care to ensure their anonymity in relation to anything that you refer to in your project report unless you have their explicit permission to do otherwise.

✓ Consider how the collective interests of your research participants may be adversely affected by the nature of the data that you are proposing to collect, and alter the nature of your research question and objectives where this possibility is likely. Alternatively, declare this possibility to those whom you wish to participate in your proposed research.

✓ Consider how you will use secondary data in order to protect the identities of those who contributed to its collection or who are named within it.

✓ Unless necessary, base your research on genuinely anonymised data. Where it is necessary to process personal data, comply with all of the data protection legal requirements carefully.

6.6 Summary

- Access and ethics are critical aspects for the conduct of research.
- Physical access refers to gaining entry to an organisation and access to intended participants. Continuing access is necessary to carry out further parts of your research or to be able to repeat the collection of data in another part of the organisation; cognitive access is needed to get sufficiently close to find out valid and reliable data.
- Feasibility is an important determinant of what you choose to research and how you undertake the research.

- There are a range of strategies to help you to gain access to organisations and to intended participants within them.
- Research ethics refer to the appropriateness of your behaviour in relation to the rights of those who become the subject of your work or are affected by the work. They also relate to yourself and ensuring no harm comes to you and other researchers.
- Potential ethical issues should be recognised and considered from the outset of your research and are one of the criteria against which your research is judged.
- Ethical concerns can occur at all stages of your research project: when seeking access, during data collection, as you analyse data and when you report your findings.
- Qualitative research is likely to lead to a greater range of ethical concerns in comparison with quantitative research, although all research methods have specific ethical issues associated with them.
- Ethical concerns are also associated with the 'power relationship' between the researcher and those who grant access, and the researcher's role (as external researcher, internal researcher or internal consultant).
- The use of the Internet and email to collect data also generates specific ethical concerns. Of particular concern is where data are public and where data are private.
- The introduction of data protection legislation has led to this aspect of research assuming a greater importance and to a need for researchers to comply carefully with a set of legal requirements to protect the privacy and interests of their data subjects.

Self-check questions

Help with these questions is available at the end of the chapter.

6.1   How can you differentiate between types of access, and why is it important to do this?

6.2   What do you understand by the use of the terms 'feasibility' and 'sufficiency' when applied to the question of access?

6.3   Which strategies to help to gain access are likely to apply to the following scenarios:
   a   an 'external' researcher seeking direct access to managers who will be the research participants;
   b   an 'external' researcher seeking access through an organisational gatekeeper/broker to their intended participants;
   c   an internal researcher planning to undertake a research project within their employing organisation?

6.4   What are the principal ethical issues you will need to consider irrespective of the particular research methods that you use?

6.5   What problems might you encounter in attempting to protect the interests of participating organisations and individuals despite the assurances that you provide?

Review and discussion questions

6.6   With a friend, discuss how you intend to gain access to the data you need for your research project. In your discussion make a list of possible barriers to your gaining access and how these might be overcome. Make sure that the ways you consider for overcoming these barriers are ethical!

6.7   Agree with a friend to each obtain a copy of your university's or your own professional association's ethical code. Make notes regarding those aspects of the ethical code you

Progressing your research project

Negotiating access and addressing ethical issues

Consider the following aspects:

- Which types of data will you require in order to be able to answer sufficiently your proposed research question and objectives?
- Which research methods will you attempt to use to yield these data (including secondary data as appropriate)?
- What type(s) of access will you require in order to be able to collect data?

- What problems are you likely to encounter in gaining access?
- Which strategies to gain access will be useful to help you to overcome these problems?
- Depending on the type of access envisaged and your research status (i.e. as external researcher or practitioner-researcher), produce appropriate requests for organisational access and/or requests to intended participants for their cooperation.
- Describe the ethical issues that are likely to affect your proposed research project, including your own personal safety. Discuss how you might seek to overcome or control these. This should be undertaken in relation to the various stages of your research project.
- Note down your answers.

have obtained that you feel are relevant to each other's proposed research. Discuss your findings.

6.8 Visit the Suzy Lamplugh Trust website at http://www.suzylamplugh.org and browse their guidance leaflets. Make a list of the actions you should take to help ensure your own personal safety when undertaking your research project. Make sure you actually put these into practice.

References

Bell, E. and Bryman, A. (2007) 'The ethics of management research: an exploratory content analysis', *British Journal of Management,* Vol. 18, No. 1, pp. 63–77.

Bell, J. (2005) *Doing your Research Project* (4th edn). Buckingham, Open University Press.

Cooper, D.R. and Schindler, P.S. (2008) *Business Research Methods* (10th edn). Boston, MA and Burr Ridge, IL: McGraw-Hill.

Bryman, A. (1988) *Quantity and Quality in Social Research.* London, Unwin Hyman.

Buchanan, D., Boddy, D. and McCalman, J. (1988) 'Getting in, getting on, getting out and getting back', in Bryman, A. (ed.) *Doing Research in Organisations.* London, Routledge, pp. 53–67.

Dale, A., Arber, S. and Procter, M. (1988) *Doing Secondary Research.* London: Unwin Hyman.

Easterby-Smith, M., Thorpe, R. and Jackson, P.R. (2008) *Management Research* (3rd edn). London: Sage.

Economic and Social Data Service (2007) A step by step ESDS guide to: archiving and reusing data: consent issues. Available at: http://www.esds.ac.uk/support/E8.asp [Accessed 6 April 2008.]

Gummesson, E. (2000) *Qualitative Methods in Management Research* (2nd edn). Thousand Oaks, CA: Sage.

Healey, M.J. (1991) 'Obtaining information from businesses', in Healey, M.J. (ed.) *Economic Activity and Land Use.* Harlow: Longman, pp. 193–251.

Jankowicz, A.D. (2005) *Business Research Projects* (4th edn). London: Business Press Thomson Learning.

Johnson, J.M. (1975) *Doing Field Research*. New York: Free Press.

Kozinets, R. (2002) 'The field behind the screen: Using netography for market research in online communities', *Journal of Marketing Research*, Vol. 9, No.1, pp. 61–72.

Marshall, C. and Rossman, G.B. (2006) *Designing Qualitative Research* (4th edn). Thousand Oaks, CA: Sage.

National Patient Safety Agency (2007) *Defining Research* Issue 3. London: National Patient Safety Agency.

Okumus, F., Altinay, L. and Roper, A. (2007) 'Gaining access for research: Reflections from experience', *Annals of Tourism Research*, Vol. 34, No. 1, pp. 7–26.

Riach, K. and Wilson, F. (2007) 'Don't screw the crew: Exploring the rules of engagement in organisational romance', *British Journal of Management*, Vol.18, No.1, pp. 79–92.

Robson, C. (2002) *Real World Research* (2nd edn). Oxford: Blackwell.

Sekaran, U. (2003) *Research Methods for Business: A Skill-Building Approach* (4th edn). New York: Wiley.

Serwer, A. (2001) 'P&G's covert operation: an intelligence-gathering campaign against Unilever went way too far', *Fortune Magazine*, 17 Sept. Available at: http://money.cnn.com/magazines/fortune/fortune_archive/2001/09/17/310274/index.htm [Accessed 11 April 2008.]

Stationery Office, The (1998) *Data Protection Act 1998*. London: The Stationery Office.

Suzy Lamplugh Trust, The (2006) 'Personal Safety Alone in the Workplace'. Available at: http://www.suzylamplugh.org/files/pdfs/guidance%20pdfs/aloneinworkplace.pdf [Accessed 4 April 2008.]

Wells, P. (1994) 'Ethics in business and management research', in Wass, V.J. and Wells, P.E. (eds) *Principles and Practice in Business and Management Research*. Aldershot: Dartmouth, pp. 277–97.

Zikmund, W.G. (2000) *Business Research Methods* (6th edn). Fort Worth, TX: Dryden Press.

Further reading

Bell, E. and Bryman, A. (2007) 'The ethics of management research: an exploratory content analysis', *British Journal of Management*, Vol. 18, No. 1, pp. 63–77. This paper questions whether management researchers can rely on codes developed by other disciplines, in the process highlighting the wide range of ethical issues they face.

Buchanan, D., Boddy, D. and McCalman, J. (1988) 'Getting in, getting on, getting out and getting back', in Bryman, A. (ed.) *Doing Research in Organisations*. London: Routledge, pp. 53–67. This provides a highly readable and very useful account of the negotiation of access. Other chapters in Bryman's book also consider issues related to access and research ethics.

Gummesson, E. (2000) *Qualitative Methods in Management Research* (2nd edn). Thousand Oaks, CA: Sage. Chapter 2 provides a very useful examination of access and researcher roles and some highly valuable means of differentiating types of access.

Miles, M.B. and Huberman, A.M. (1994) *Qualitative Data Analysis*. Thousand Oaks, CA: Sage. Chapter 11 provides a very useful examination of a range of ethical issues principally from the perspective of their implications for data analysis.

Suzy Lamplugh Trust, The (2007) 'Personal Safety Tips'. Available at: http://www.suzylamplugh.org/content.asp?PageID=1022&sID=1086 [Accessed 4 April 2008.] This web page provides links to the Trust's guidance sheets. These are designed to give you useful tips and information to help improve your personal safety.

Case 6
Gaining access to business angels networks

Source: Freddie Jones/Alamy

Stephanie had decided to use her Masters project to build upon the research she had undertaken as part of her undergraduate studies. During this she had researched Business Angels, private, wealthy individuals who invested large amounts (between £10 000 and £500 000) of their own money in small, young businesses, with which they have no family connection (Deakins and Freel 2003). For her Masters dissertation she wished to develop this research to answer the research question: 'To what extent and why do Business Angels become involved post investment in the companies in which they have invested?' She had decided to collect data to answer this by administering a questionnaire to Business Angels throughout the United Kingdom (UK).

From her undergraduate studies, Stephanie already knew that Business Angels liked to remain anonymous (Harrison and Mason 1992). As extremely wealthy people, Business Angels knew that, if everyone knew how rich they were, they would be inundated with investment proposals and other requests for money. Consequently, directories or public listings recording names of Business Angels did not exist (Van Osnabrugge and Robinson 2000). She also knew that for both potential investees and researchers interested in Business Angels there were two main ways of gaining access:

- meeting a Business Angel and getting referred to their acquaintances (it is commonly known that Business Angels are well networked with their peers);
- using intermediaries.

Since Stephanie did not know any Business Angels herself, the first option was not open to her. Therefore, the only way to conduct her research was to gain access to intermediaries, whom in turn could provide her with access to the Business Angels. Although a number of different intermediaries exist, Stephanie felt that Business Angel networks were likely to be the most efficient. Such networks are created with the explicit purpose to match angel investors looking for investments with companies looking for funding (Mason and Harrison 1997). There are about 20 Business Angel networks, each of which maintains a list of its members, the Business Angels. These networks distribute newsletters to their members and organise investment events, where entrepreneurs attempt to obtain funding from potentially interested Business Angel investors by pitching their ideas. The Business Angel networks are also part of a national trade association, the British Business Angels Association (BBAA).

Stephanie knew that she had to get access to the Business Angel networks first, before being able to reach the Business Angels. However, she also knew that Business Angel networks receive vast numbers of requests for support in research projects. Consequently, she was concerned that she might not be able to capture their interest, which would result in her research requests being rejected. In order to avoid rejection, she had to make sure that her request was noticed and subsequently gain the respect and confidence of Business Angel network managers. By doing this, she hoped they would be willing to distribute her questionnaire to those Business Angels who were members. During her undergraduate project, Stephanie had established contact with a small number of Business Angel networks, whom she had subsequently updated about her research progress. These she felt would provide starting point for negotiating access to further Business Angel networks.

Stephanie decided to attend a number of investment events, where she would have the opportunity to also discuss her research with the respective Business Angel network managers face to face. During each discussion, Stephanie explained her research intentions and asked the Business Angel network managers for their opinions on her research. The network managers' feedback was, without exception, positive and they were also willing to distribute a questionnaire to their Business Angels. Stephanie also asked each of the Business Angel network managers to provide a short written endorsement regarding her research and for permission to quote it. At one meeting she met the manager of the BBAA, who asked Stephanie to write a short news item for their monthly newsletter, promoting her research to all the member Business Angel networks. She agreed immediately because she knew that this could help establish her credibility as a researcher and encourage other, hitherto unknown, Business Angel networks also to participate at the questionnaire distribution.

Once the newsletter item had been published, Stephanie started by telephoning the Business Angel network managers she had not been in contact with before. She had a vast amount of experience in making telephone calls having worked in a call centre, selling telecommunications platforms to businesses all over Europe during her work placement. Her experiences had taught her that 'cold calls' are often either ignored or rejected. Therefore, she knew that, in order to maximise her chances of obtaining access to the Business Angel networks, she had to appear well prepared, professional and highly interested. Stephanie further knew that she only had one chance with each Business Angel network manager, so that her approach had to be perfect in the first instance. To achieve this, she applied the skills and techniques she had learned whilst working at call centre. These focused on three distinct aspects:

- she developed a document detailing all the information she had to mention in the telephone conversation, so that she could be sure that she would not forget anything;
- prior to each call, she also researched the specific Business Angel network carefully to ensure she addressed the correct person and that she had specific background knowledge of that organisation;
- during each call conversation, she was professional and polite at all times.

Stephanie's work experience in the call centre had taught her an organised and clear way of managing telephone conversations with a wide array of different partners. This she felt would

	A	B	C	D	E	F	G	H	I	J
1					**First Access Negotiation Contacts**					
2	Business Angel Network	Area of Operation	Manager (according to website)	Telephone number	Dates called	Person spoken to	Outcome	Further Action	Interested in Participation	Summary Email Sent
3	NorthEast Business Angel Network	North East England	Mr. Mark Smith	01333333333	14/09/**	Ms Laura Black (Mr. Smith's PA)	Mr. Smith is responsible for this kind of request. He is at a conference.	Call again on Monday, 17/09/**		17/09/**
4					17/09/**	Mr. Mark Smith	He seems very interested in the research and in a collaboration.	Send summary email asap.	Yes.	
5	BA NW	North West England	Mrs. Martha Sample	01222222222	14/09/**	Ms Tomlin (Receptionist)	Mrs. Sample does not work with BA NW anymore. The person I should talk to is Dr. Thomas Smart. He is in a meeting all day. Best is to send him an email.	Call again on Monday, 17/09/** (so that it it not a "cold email")		17/09/**
6					17/09/**	Ms Tomlin (Receptionist)	Dr. Smart is away from his desk at that moment.	Call again half an hour later.		
7					17/09/**	Ms Tomlin (Receptionist), then Dr. Smart	Dr. Smart was not at his desk, but at the moment I wanted to leave a message, he returned and Ms Tomlin put me straight through. He is very busy at the moment and cannot make a decision right away, but he would like an email with a summary.	Send summary email asap.	Potentially, but very busy	
8					19/09/**	Dr. Smart	He likes the project and will participate, but only early November due to time constraints.	Send questionnaire	Yes.	
9	London's Angels	London and South East	Mr. Robert House	01111111111	14/09/**	Mr. Robert House	He got a bit angry because he gets too many calls about research from unknown researchers.	n/a	No.	No.
	Angelic	Scotland	Ms Karen	01555555555	14/09/**	Ms Karen Jones	They are on company holiday	Call again on		

help her cope with the large amount of different telephone conversations, without accidentally confusing people and thereby losing her credibility. She, therefore, recorded detailed notes about each conversation (i.e. person spoken to, date, time, outcome etc.) in a spreadsheet.

At the end of each conversation, Stephanie asked the respective Business Angel network manager if she could send them a brief email summarising the main points of their conversation. All managers agreed to this and Stephanie sent emails the same day. She further ensured that she again remained professional by double-checking each email for even small mistakes, such as the misspelling of the recipient's name. She included her BBAA newsletter entry and the endorsements she had obtained earlier from the initial Business Angel network managers in the email, hoping that they would help further establish her credibility and promote a greater interest from the remaining Business Angel networks. Stephanie spent many hours on the telephone and sending emails, trying to arrange telephone conversations with all 20 Business Angel network managers, clarifying issues, offering to send a copy of her findings and explaining how participation would benefit them.

Due to Stephanie's persistence and professional manner, most Business Angel networks' managers agreed to distribute her questionnaire to their Business Angel members. Unfortunately, her negotiations for access were not yet over as she still had to gain acceptance from the individual Business Angels and ensure their cooperation to fill in the questionnaire, once distributed by the Business Angel network managers. She stuck to the same principles: professionalism, perfectionism and good preparation. Nevertheless, she had less control over this stage of her access negotiations because the actual distribution of the questionnaire was undertaken by the Business Angel network managers. All she could do (and she did) was to ensure the questionnaire was attractive and easy to complete and the covering letter explained the purpose of her research clearly. In addition, she offered each respondent a summary of the findings.

References

Deakins, D. and Freel, M. (2003) *Entrepreneurship and Small Firms*. Maidenhead, Berkshire: McGraw-Hill Education.

Harrison, R.T. and Mason, C.M. (1992) 'International perspectives on the supply of informal venture capital', *Journal of Business Venturing*, Vol. 7, No. 6, pp. 459–75.

Mason, C.M. and Harrison, R.T. (1997) 'Developing the informal venture capital market in the UK: Is there still a role for public sector business angel networks?', *Small Business Economics,* Vol. 9, No. 2, pp. 111–23.

Van Osnabrugge, M. and Robinson, R.J. (2000) *Angel Investing: Matching Start-up Funds with Start-up Companies – The Guide for Entrepreneurs, Individual Investors, and Venture Capitalists*. San Francisco: Jossey-Bass.

Questions

1 Which factors helped Stephanie getting access to these highly sought-after organisations?
2 What problems did Stephanie face in the access negotiation stage of her project? How did she overcome these?
3 What access negotiation techniques has Stephanie applied in her project?
4 What are the downsides of these access negotiation techniques?

Additional case studies relating to material covered in this chapter are available via the book's Companion Website, **www.pearsoned.co.uk/saunders**. They are:

- The effects of a merger in a major UK building society
- The quality of service provided by the accounts department
- Misreading issues related to access and ethics in a small-scale enterprise
- Mystery customer research in restaurant chains.

Self-check answers

6.1 The types of access that we have referred to in this chapter are: physical entry or initial access to an organisational setting; continuing access, which recognises that researchers often need to develop their access on an incremental basis; and cognitive access, where you will be concerned to gain the cooperation of individual participants once you have achieved access to the organisation in which they work. We also referred to personal access, which allows you to consider whether you actually need to meet with participants in order to carry out an aspect of your research as opposed to corresponding with them or sending them a self-administered, postal questionnaire. Access is strategically related to the success of your research project and needs to be carefully planned. In relation to many research designs, it will need to be thought of as a multifaceted aspect and not a single event.

6.2 Gaining access can be problematic for researchers for a number of reasons. The concept of feasibility recognises this and suggests that in order to be able to conduct your research it will be necessary to design it with access clearly in mind. Sufficiency refers to another issue related to access. There are two aspects to the issue of sufficiency. The first of these relates to whether you have sufficiently considered and therefore fully realised the extent and nature of the access that you will require in order to be able to answer your research question and objectives. The second aspect relates to whether you are able to gain sufficient access in practice in order to be able to answer your research question and objectives.

6.3 We may consider the three particular scenarios outlined in the question through Table 6.2.

6.4 The principal ethical issues you will need to consider irrespective of which research methods you use are:

- to respect intended and actual participants' rights to not being harmed and privacy;
- to avoid deceiving participants about why you are undertaking the research, its purpose and how the data collected will be used;
- maintaining your objectivity during the data collection, analysis and reporting stages;
- respecting assurances provided to organisations about the confidentiality of (certain types of) data;
- respecting assurances given to organisations and individuals about their anonymity;
- considering the collective interests of participants in the way you use the data which they provide;
- considering your own personal safety and that of other researchers.

6.5 A number of ethical problems might emerge. These are considered in turn. You may wish to explore a point made by one of your participants but to do so might lead to harmful consequences for this person where the point was attributed to them. It may be possible for some people who read your work to identify a participating organisation, although you do not actually name it. This may cause embarrassment to the organisation. Individual participants may also be identified by the nature of the comments that you report, again leading to harmful consequences for them. Your report may also lead to action being taken within an organisation that adversely affects those who were kind enough to act as participants in your research. Finally, others may seek to reuse any survey data that you collect, and this might be used to disadvantage those who provided the data by responding to your questionnaire.

Get ahead using resources on the Companion Website at:
www.pearsoned.co.uk/saunders
- Improve your SPSS and NVivo research analysis with practice tutorials.
- Save time researching on the Internet with the Smarter Online Searching Guide.
- Test your progress using self-assessment questions.

Table 6.2 Considering access

	Scenario A	Scenario B	Scenario C
Allowing yourself sufficient time to gain access	Universally true in all cases. The practitioner-researcher will be going through a very similar process to those who wish to gain access from the outside in terms of contacting intended participants, meeting with them to explain the research, providing assurances, etc. The only exception will be related to a covert approach, although sufficient time for planning, etc. will of course still be required		
Using any existing contacts	Where possible		Yes
Developing new contacts	Probably necessary		This may still apply within large, complex organisations, depending on the nature of the research
Providing a clear account of the purpose of your research and what type of access you require, with the intention of establishing your credibility	Definitely necessary		Still necessary although easier to achieve (verbally or internal memo) with familiar colleagues. Less easy with unfamiliar colleagues, which suggests just as much care as for external researchers
Overcoming organisational concerns in relation to the granting of access	Definitely necessary	Absolutely necessary. This may be the major problem to overcome since you are asking for access to a range of employees	Should not be a problem unless you propose to undertake a topic that is highly sensitive to the organisation! We know of students whose proposal has been refused within their organisation
Outlining possible benefits of granting access to you and any tangible outcome from doing so	Probably useful		Work-based research projects contain material of value to the organisation although they may largely be theoretically based
Using suitable language	Definitely necessary		Still necessary at the level of participants in the organisation
Facilitating ease of reply when requesting access	Definitely useful		Might be useful to consider in relation to certain internal participants
Developing your access on an incremental basis	Should not be necessary, although you may wish to undertake subsequent work	Definitely worth considering	Might be a useful strategy depending on the nature of the research and the work setting
Establishing your credibility in the eyes of your intended participants	Access is not being sought at 'lower' levels within the organisation: however, there is still a need to achieve credibility in relation to those to whom you are applying directly	Definitely necessary	May still be necessary with unfamiliar participants in the organisation

Chapter 7

Selecting samples

Learning outcomes

By the end of this chapter you should:

- understand the need for sampling in business and management research;
- be aware of a range of probability and non-probability sampling techniques and the possible need to combine techniques within a research project;
- be able to select appropriate sampling techniques for a variety of research scenarios and be able to justify their selection;
- be able to use a range of sampling techniques;
- be able to assess the representativeness of respondents;
- be able to assess the extent to which it is reasonable to generalise from a sample;
- be able to apply the knowledge, skills and understanding gained to your own research project.

7.1 Introduction

Whatever your research question(s) and objectives you will need to consider whether you need to use sampling. Occasionally, it may be possible to collect and analyse data from every possible case or group member; this is termed a **census**. However, for many research questions and objectives, such as those highlighted in the vignette, it will be impossible for you either to collect or to analyse all the data available to you owing to restrictions of time, money and often access. Sampling techniques provide a range of methods that enable you to reduce the amount of data you need to collect by considering only data from a sub-group rather than all possible **cases** or **elements** (Figure 7.1). Some research questions will require sample data to generalise about all the cases from which your **sample** has been selected. For example, if you asked a sample of consumers what they thought of a new chocolate bar and 75 per cent said that they thought it was too expensive, you might infer that 75 per cent of all consumers felt that way. Other research questions may not involve such statistical generalisations. To gain an understanding of how people manage their careers, you may select a sample of company chief

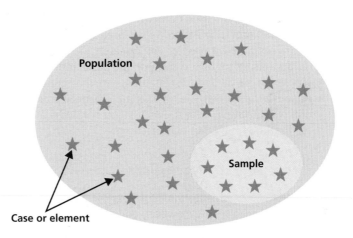

Figure 7.1
Population,
sample and
individual cases

Samples are used all around us. We read a newspaper article and the reporter states that she or he talked to a group of employees; advertisements inform us that, in tests, eight out of ten owners said their pet preferred a particular brand of pet food. Less obviously, television programmes offer us the top 100 best pop songs or the top 100 most scary cinema film moments. Implicit in these is the understanding that, as it is impossible to ask every person these questions, data would have to have been collected from individuals in some form of sample who were willing and able to respond.

Towards the end of 2001 the BBC (British Broadcasting Corporation) invited the British public to nominate their greatest-ever Briton, encouraging nominations through a television campaign and the BBC's website. In the final listing of the top 100, the highest-ranked business person/entrepreneur was Richard Branson at position 85. Whilst it was not possible to discover how representative the sample of tens of thousands of votes cast was, an independent public opinion survey generated an almost identical top ten list (Cooper 2002:6). Subsequently, a series of 10 one-hour television programmes, one for each of the top ten nominations, were broadcast and the public invited to vote by telephone or Internet for the greatest Briton of all time.

Richard Branson – highest-ranking
business person

During and after the voting, numerous questions were raised regarding the extent to which the sample of those voting were representative of the British public as well as there being allegations of vote rigging (Clennell 2002). Overall, 1 622 648 votes were cast, Winston Churchill polling the highest number: 456 498.

executives. For such research your sample selection would be based on the premise that, as these people have reached executive level and have been successful in managing their own careers they are most likely to be able to offer insights from which you can build understanding. Even if you are adopting a case study strategy using one large organisation and collecting your data using unstructured interviews, you will still need to select your case study (sample) organisation and a group (sample) of employees and managers to interview. Consequently, whatever you research question an understanding of techniques for selecting samples is likely to be very important.

The full set of cases from which a sample is taken is called the **population**. In sampling, the term 'population' is not used in its normal sense, as the full set of cases need not necessarily be people. For research to discover relative levels of service at Indian restaurants throughout a country, the population from which you would select your sample would be all Indian restaurants in that country. Alternatively, you might need to establish the normal 'life' of a long-life battery produced over the past month by a particular manufacturer. Here the population would be all the long-life batteries produced over the past month by that manufacturer.

The need to sample

For some research questions it is possible to collect data from an entire population as it is of a manageable size. However, you should not assume that a census would necessarily provide more useful results than collecting data from a sample which represents the entire population. Sampling provides a valid alternative to a census when:

- it would be impracticable for you to survey the entire population;
- your budget constraints prevent you from surveying the entire population;
- your time constraints prevent you from surveying the entire population;
- you have collected all the data but need the results quickly.

For all research questions where it would be impracticable for you to collect data from the entire population, you need to select a sample. This will be equally important whether you are planning to use interviews, questionnaires, observation or some other data collection technique. You might be able to obtain permission to collect data from only two or three organisations. Alternatively, testing an entire population of products to destruction, such as to establish the crash protection provided by cars, would be impractical for any manufacturer.

With other research questions it might be theoretically possible for you to be able to collect data from the entire population but the overall cost would prevent it. It is obviously cheaper for you to collect, enter (if you are analysing the data using a computer) and check data from 250 customers than from 2500, even though the cost per case for your study (in this example, customer) is likely to be higher than with a census. Your costs will be made up of new costs such as sample selection, and the fact that overhead costs such as questionnaire, interview or observation schedule design and setting up computer software for data entry are spread over a smaller number of cases.

Sampling also saves time, an important consideration when you have tight deadlines. The organisation of data collection is more manageable as fewer people are involved. As you have fewer data to enter, the results will be available more quickly. Occasionally, to save time, questionnaires are used to collect data from the entire population but only a sample of the data collected are analysed. Fortunately advances in automated and computer assisted coding software mean that such situations are increasingly rare.

Many researchers, for example Henry (1990), argue that using sampling makes possible a higher overall accuracy than a census. The smaller number of cases for which you need to collect data means that more time can be spent designing and piloting the means of collecting these data. Collecting data from fewer cases also means that you can collect information that is more detailed. In addition, if you are employing people to collect the data (perhaps as interviewers) you can afford higher-quality staff. You also can devote more time to trying to obtain data from more difficult to reach cases. Once your data have been collected, proportionally more time can be devoted to checking and testing the data for accuracy prior to analysis.

An overview of sampling techniques

The sampling techniques available to you can be divided into two types:

- probability or representative sampling;
- non-probability or judgemental sampling.

Those discussed in this chapter are highlighted in Figure 7.2. With **probability samples** the chance, or probability, of each case being selected from the population is known and is usually equal for all cases. This means that it is possible to answer research questions and to achieve objectives that require you to estimate statistically the characteristics of the population from the sample. Consequently, probability sampling is often associated with survey and experimental research strategies (Section 5.3). For **non-probability samples**, the probability of each case being selected from the total population is not known and it is impossible to answer research questions or to address objectives that require you to make statistical inferences about the characteristics of the population. You may still be able to generalise from non-probability samples about the population, but not on statistical grounds. However, with both types of sample you can answer other forms of research questions, such as 'What job attributes attract people to jobs?' or 'How are financial services institutions adapting the services they provide to meet recent legislation?'

Subsequent sections of this chapter outline the most frequently used probability (Section 7.2) and non-probability (Section 7.3) sampling techniques, discuss their advantages and disadvantages, and give examples of how and when you might use them. Although each technique is discussed separately, for many research projects you will

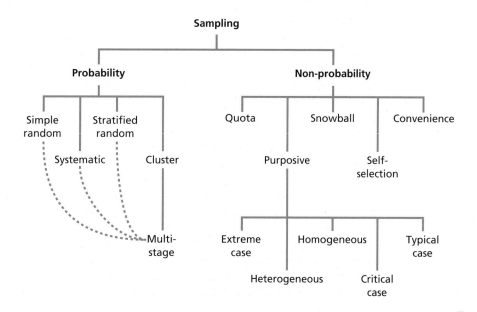

Figure 7.2
Sampling techniques

need to use a variety of sampling techniques at different stages, some projects involving both probability and non-probability sampling techniques.

7.2 Probability sampling

Probability sampling (or **representative sampling**) is most commonly associated with survey-based research strategies where you need to make inferences from your sample about a population to answer your research question(s) or to meet your objectives. The process of probability sampling can be divided into four stages:

1 Identify a suitable sampling frame based on your research question(s) or objectives.
2 Decide on a suitable sample size.
3 Select the most appropriate sampling technique and select the sample.
4 Check that the sample is representative of the population.

Each of these stages will be considered in turn. However, for populations of less than 50 cases Henry (1990) advises against probability sampling. He argues that you should collect data on the entire population as the influence of a single extreme case on subsequent statistical analyses is more pronounced than for larger samples.

Identifying a suitable sampling frame and the implications for generalisability

The **sampling frame** for any probability sample is a complete list of all the cases in the population from which your sample will be drawn. If your research question or objective is concerned with members of a local golf club, your sampling frame will be the complete membership list for that golf club. If your research question or objective is concerned with registered childminders in a local area, your sampling frame will be the directory of all registered childminders in this area. Alternatively if your research question is concerned with organisations in a particular sector, you may be thinking of creating a sampling frame from an existing database of companies' available at your university such as FAME or AMADEUS. For all, you then select your sample from this list.

Obtaining a sampling frame is therefore very important. However, as highlighted by research by Edwards *et al.* (2007), you need to be aware of the possible problems of using existing databases. In their work on multinationals in Britain, they found that:

- individual databases are often incomplete;
- the information held about organisations in databases is sometimes inaccurate;
- the information held in databases soon becomes out of date.

You, therefore, need to ensure your sampling frame is as complete, accurate and up to date as possible. An incomplete or inaccurate list means that some cases will have been excluded and so it will be impossible for every case in the population to have a chance of selection. Consequently, your sample may not be representative of the total population and your research may be criticised for this reason (Box 7.1).

Where no suitable list exists you will have to compile your own sampling frame, perhaps drawing upon existing lists (Box 7.2). It is important to ensure that the sampling frame is valid and reliable. You might decide to use a telephone directory as the sampling frame from which to select a sample of typical UK householders. However, the telephone directory covers only subscribers in one geographical area who rent a telephone landline

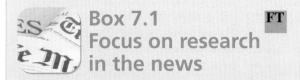

Box 7.1
Focus on research in the news

FT

You don't need to be a mechanical engineer to drive a car

In the 18 years since Fred Davis and Richard Bagozzi published their ground-breaking paper on technology acceptance, the cost of electronics has fallen and functionality improved hugely. Yet, the technology industries still seem reluctant to accept that it is their job to make their products attractive and comprehensible to customers.

Davis and Bagozzi argued essentially that the principal factors at work when an individual is contemplating using a novel technology are 'perceived usefulness' – the degree to which a person believes that using a system would enhance his or her job performance – and 'perceived ease-of-use' – the degree to which a person believes that using a system would be free from effort. They went on to point out, of course, that in a real situation a host of other factors would come into play, including time constraints and the individual's personal, and perhaps unconscious, habits.

Some people are happy using a conventional mouse, for example, while others prefer a tracker ball, joystick or touch pad. Davis and Bagozzi's was an important contribution to a poorly understood area of ergonomics. Some years later the Ease of Use Roundtable was established by companies including Intel, Microsoft, Hewlett-Packard and Dell in recognition of the fact that personal computer sales were being hampered by customers' perception that they were difficult to operate. It continues to tackle a number of outstanding problems. A week or two ago, however, PayPal, the Ebay-owned online payments company, revealed that old attitudes die hard. In one of those self-serving surveys which companies commission from time to time to generate a little publicity – and this time it has succeeded, but for the wrong reasons – it concludes that British consumers are turned off by technology and are in danger of becoming the 'tech illiterates of the world'. A remarkably broad conclusion, considering the sample was just over

1000 UK adults and that no comparative data from overseas were included.

Worse, however, PayPal's technology expert Neil Edwards declared: 'It's a worrying sign for Britain that so many of us are baffled and therefore turned off by technology. There's no hiding from technology, so burying your head in the sand won't make it go away. We must all embrace technology or risk becoming the tech illiterates of the world.' Which is about as sensible as telling people in the early twentieth century that they had better become familiar with mechanical engineering or else give up the idea of becoming a motorist. When was the last time any of us saw a car engine other than when topping up the screen wash?

PayPal compounds its folly by publishing online a quiz through which people can determine their 'technology know-how', a series of questions designed to test an individual's knowledge of industry jargon. This has no significance in terms of public understanding of technology. Is it of any importance, for example, that a lay computer user should know which of JPeg, Gif, Raw and ACC is not a digital photographic format? And some of the answers are borderline: 'bandwidth' is defined as the amount of data that can be transferred to a personal computer from the Internet.

The PayPal survey brings up a selection of the old chestnuts: many people cannot program a video recorder; most only make calls and send text messages from their mobile phones (with the interesting rider that 40 per cent of mobile phone users don't know whether their phone incorporates a camera or not). If there is any value in surveys of this kind, it is actually to flag up a huge failing of the consumer electronics industries. If people cannot program their video recorders, it is because the design and ergonomics of the controls have been poorly thought through and the instruction book badly written. If people use only a few of the functions on their phones, it is because that is all they need and want to use. And if they do not know whether their phone has a camera, at least they will never have had the hassle of trying to move their images to some other medium.

▶ Box 7.1
Focus on research in the news *(continued)*

Curiously, if you talk to the leaders of any segment of the consumer electronics business, they will openly accept that the ergonomics, the fitness for use, of their products leaves much to be desired. But progress is slow. The Apple iPod, essentially a large memory with a clever and intuitive interface is an example of how it should be done. The iPhone, which falls somewhere between an iPod and a BlackBerry, may not quite be as exact a model. What people should be embracing, to use a popular expression, is functionality. The technology itself should be invisible. And if PayPal asks you what 'Tom Tom' brings to mind, tell them it's an Indian drum.

Source: article by Cane, Alan (2007) *Financial Times*, 12 Feb. Copyright © 2007 The Financial Times Ltd.

Box 7.2
Focus on management research

Selecting a suitable sampling frame

In their 2008 *Journal of Management Studies* paper 'Stewardship versus stagnation: an empirical comparison of small family and non family businesses' Miller, Le Breton-Miller and Scholnick outline and justify how they selected their sample of small owner manager businesses in the four western most provinces of Canada. These provinces were selected because they were relatively easy to reach and the most familiar to the researchers.

The researchers used four comprehensive province specific small business databases to create a list of 5000 small businesses from which to select their sample, namely:

- Manitoba: Manitoba Information Service Company Directory;
- Saskatchewan: small business database of the Policy Division of the Saskatchewan Industry and Resources Department;
- Alberta: Alberta Government's Business Attraction Information System Database;
- British Columbia: Info-CANADA database.

The small businesses selected were cross referenced with a range of published directories and organisations' websites to ensure accuracy. Subsequently, a target sample of 1500 small businesses were selected at random. Of these, 30 were rejected due to the businesses having more than 100 employees. This resulted in a actual sample of 1470 businesses. Forty-six per cent of these small businesses fully completed telephone interviews, subsequent analyses revealing there was no significant difference in size and age of those businesses who responded and those who did not.

Source: Miller *et al.* (2008).

from that company. Your survey will therefore be biased towards householders who have a landline telephone. Because the telephone directory is only published biennially, the sampling frame will be out of date ('non-current'). As some householders choose to be ex-directory, or only have mobile telephones, it will not be valid representation as it does not include all those who own telephones. This means that you will be selecting a sample of land-line telephone subscribers at the date the directory was compiled by a particular company who chose not to be ex-directory!

The way you define your sampling frame also has implications regarding the extent to which you can generalise from your sample. As we have already discussed, sampling is used when it is impracticable to collect data from the entire population. Within probability sampling, by defining the sampling frame you are defining the population about which you want to generalise. This means that if your sampling frame is a list of all customers of an organisation, strictly speaking you can only generalise, that is apply the findings based upon your sample, to that population. Similarly, if your sampling frame is all employees of an organisation (the list being the organisation's payroll) you can only generalise to employees of that organisation. This can create problems, as often we hope that our findings have wider applicability than the population from which are sample was selected. However, even if your probability sample has been selected from one large multinational organisation, you should not claim that what you have found will also occur in similar organisations. In other words, you should not generalise beyond your sampling frame. Despite this, researchers often do make such claims, rather than placing clear limits on the generalisability of the findings.

In recent years a number of organisations have been established that specialise in selling lists of names, addresses and email addresses. These lists include a wide range of people such as company directors, chief executives, marketing managers, production managers and human resource managers, for public, private and non-profit-making organisations. They are usually in a format suitable for being read by word-processing and database computer software and can easily be merged into standard letters such as those included with questionnaires (Section 11.4). Because you pay for such lists by the case (individual address), the organisations that provide them usually select your sample. It is therefore important to establish precisely how they will select your sample as well as obtaining an indication of the database's completeness, accracy and currency. For example, when obtaining a list of email addresses you need to be aware that a certain proportion of Internet users change their Internet service provider and also their email address regularly. This means the sampling frame is likely to under-represent this group who, it might be argued, are more likely to be price-sensitive consumers (Bradley 1999). Whilst Internet users do not differ from the total population in terms of sexual orientation, marital status, ethnicity, education and religion, they do in terms of age and gender. In particular, Internet users tend to be younger and have a greater proportion of males (Hewson *et al.* 2003). Box 7.3 provides a checklist against which to check your sampling frame.

Deciding on a suitable sample size

Generalisations about populations from data collected using any probability sample are based on statistical probability. The larger your sample's size the lower the likely error in

Box 7.3
Checklist

Selecting your sampling frame

✔ Are cases listed in the sampling frame relevant to your research topic, in other words will they enable you to answer your research question and meet your objectives?

✔ How recently was the sampling frame compiled, in particular is it up to date?

✔ Does the sampling frame include all cases, in other words is it complete?

✔ Does the sampling frame contain the correct information, in other words is it accurate?

✔ Does the sampling frame exclude irrelevant cases, in other words is it precise?

✔ (For purchased lists) Can you establish and control precisely how the sample will be selected?

generalising to the population. Probability sampling is therefore a compromise between the accuracy of your findings and the amount of time and money you invest in collecting, checking and analysing the data. Your choice of sample size within this compromise is governed by:

- the confidence you need to have in your data – that is, the level of certainty that the characteristics of the data collected will represent the characteristics of the total population;
- the margin of error that you can tolerate – that is, the accuracy you require for any estimates made from your sample;
- the types of analyses you are going to undertake – in particular, the number of categories into which you wish to subdivide your data, as many statistical techniques have a minimum threshold of data cases for each cell (e.g. chi square, Section 12.5); and to a lesser extent:
- the size of the total population from which your sample is being drawn.

Given these competing influences, it is not surprising that the final sample size is almost always a matter of judgement as well as of calculation. For many research questions and objectives, your need to undertake particular statistical analyses (Section 12.5) will determine the threshold sample size for individual categories. In particular, an examination of virtually any statistics textbook (or Sections 12.3 and 12.5 of this book) will highlight that, in order to ensure spurious results do not occur, the data analysed must be normally distributed. Whilst the normal distribution is discussed in Chapter 12, its implications for sample size need to be considered here. Statisticians have proved that the larger the absolute size of a sample, the more closely its distribution will be to the normal distribution and thus the more robust it will be. This relationship, known as the **central limit theorem**, occurs even if the population from which the sample is drawn is not normally distributed. Statisticians have also shown that a sample size of 30 or more will usually result in a sampling distribution for the mean that is very close to a normal distribution. For this reason, Stutely's (2003) advice of a minimum number of 30 for statistical analyses provides a useful rule of thumb for the smallest number in each category within your overall sample. Where the population in the category is less than 30, and you wish to undertake your analysis at this level of detail, you should normally collect data from all cases in that category. Alternatively, you may have access to an expert system such as Ex-Sample™. This software calculates the minimum sample size required for different statistical analyses as well as the maximum possible sample size given resources such as time, money and response rates. In addition, it provides a report justifying the sample size calculated (Idea Works 2008).

It is likely that, if you are undertaking statistical analyses on your sample, you will be drawing conclusions from these analyses about the population from which your sample was selected. This process of coming up with conclusions about a population on the basis of data describing the sample is called **statistical inference** and allows you to calculate how probable it is that your result, given your sample size, could have been obtained by chance. Such probabilities are usually calculated automatically by statistical analysis software. However, it is worth remembering that, providing they are not biased, samples of larger absolute size are more likely to be representative of the population from which they are drawn than smaller samples and, in particular, the mean (average) calculated for the sample is more likely to equal the mean for the population. This is known as the **law of large numbers**.

Researchers normally work to a 95 per cent level of certainty. This means that if your sample was selected 100 times, at least 95 of these samples would be certain to represent the characteristics of the population. The confidence level states the precision of your estimates of the population as the percentage that is within a certain range or margin of

Table 7.1 Sample sizes for different sizes of population at a 95 confidence level
(assuming data are collected from all cases in the sample)

Population	Margin of error			
	5%	3%	2%	1%
50	44	48	49	50
100	79	91	96	99
150	108	132	141	148
200	132	168	185	196
250	151	203	226	244
300	168	234	267	291
400	196	291	343	384
500	217	340	414	475
750	254	440	571	696
1 000	278	516	706	906
2 000	322	696	1091	1655
5 000	357	879	1622	3288
10 000	370	964	1936	4899
100 000	383	1056	2345	8762
1 000 000	384	1066	2395	9513
10 000 000	384	1067	2400	9595

error. Table 7.1 provides a rough guide to the different minimum sample sizes required from different sizes of population given a 95 per cent confidence level for different margins of error. It assumes that data are collected from all cases in the sample (full details of the calculation for minimum sample size and adjusted minimum sample size are given in Appendix 2). For most business and management research, researchers are content to estimate the population's characteristics at 95 per cent certainty to within plus or minus 3 to 5 per cent of its true values. This means that if 45 per cent of your sample are in a certain category then you will be 95 per cent certain that your estimate for the total population within the same category will be 45 per cent plus or minus the margin of error – somewhere between 42 and 48 per cent for a 3 per cent margin of error.

As you can see from Table 7.1, the smaller the absolute size of the sample and, to a far lesser extent, the smaller the relative proportion of the total population sampled, the greater the margin of error. Within this, the impact of absolute sample size on the margin of error decreases for larger sample sizes. deVaus (2002) argues that it is for this reason that many market research companies limit their samples' sizes to approximately 2000. Unfortunately, from many samples, a 100 per cent response rate is unlikely and so your sample will need to be larger to ensure sufficient responses for the margin of error you require.

The importance of a high response rate

The most important aspect of a probability sample is that it represents the population. A perfect **representative sample** is one that exactly represents the population from which it is taken. If 60 per cent of your sample were small service sector companies then, provided that the sample was representative, you would expect 60 per cent of the population to be small service sector companies. You, therefore, need to obtain as high a response rate as possible to ensure that your sample is representative.

In reality, you are likely to have non-responses. Non-respondents are different from the rest of the population because they have refused to be involved in your research for whatever reason. Consequently, your respondents will not be representative of the total population, and the data you collect may be biased. In addition, any non-responses will necessitate extra respondents being found to reach the required sample size, thereby increasing the cost of your data collection.

You should therefore analyse the refusals to respond to both individual questions and entire questionnaires or interview schedules to check for bias (Section 12.2) and report this briefly in your project report. Non-response is due to four interrelated problems:

- refusal to respond;
- ineligibility to respond;
- inability to locate respondent;
- respondent located but unable to make contact.

The most common reason for non-response is that your respondent refuses to answer all the questions or be involved in your research, but does not give a reason. Such non-response can be minimised by paying careful attention to the methods used to collect your data (Chapters 9, 10 and 11). Alternatively, some of your selected respondents may not meet your research requirements and so will be **ineligible** to respond. Non-location and non-contact create further problems; the fact that these respondents are **unreachable** means they will not be represented in the data you collect.

As part of your research report, you will need to include your **response rate**. Neumann (2005) suggests that when you calculate this you should include all eligible respondents:

$$\text{total response rate} = \frac{\text{total number of responses}}{\text{total number in sample} - \text{ineligible}}$$

This he calls the *total response rate*. A more common way of doing this excludes ineligible respondents and those who, despite repeated attempts (Sections 10.3 and 11.5), were unreachable. This is known as the **active response rate**:

$$\text{active response rate} = \frac{\text{total number of responses}}{\text{total number in sample} - (\text{ineligible} + \text{unreachable})}$$

An example of the calculation of both the total response rate and the active response rate is given in Box 7.4.

Even after ineligible and unreachable respondents have been excluded, it is probable that you will still have some non-responses. You therefore need to be able to assess how representative your data are and to allow for the impact of non-response in your calculations of sample size. These issues are explored in subsequent sections.

Estimating response rates and actual sample size required

With all probability samples, it is important that your sample size is large enough to provide you with the necessary confidence in your data. The margin of error must therefore be within acceptable limits, and you must ensure that you will be able to undertake your analysis at the level of detail required. You therefore need to estimate the likely response rate – that is, the proportion of cases from your sample who will respond or from which data will be collected – and increase the sample size accordingly. Once you have

Box 7.4
Focus on student research

Calculation of total and active response rates

Ming had decided to administer a telephone questionnaire to people who had left his company's employment over the past five years. He obtained a list of the 1034 people who had left over this period (the total population) and selected a 50% sample.

Unfortunately, he could obtain current telephone numbers for only 311 of the 517 ex-employees who made up his total sample. Of these 311 people who were potentially reachable, he obtained a response from 147. In addition, his list of people who had left his company was inaccurate, and nine of those he contacted were ineligible to respond, having left the company over five years earlier.

His total response rate $= \dfrac{147}{517 - 9} = \dfrac{147}{508} = 28.9\%$

His active response rate $= \dfrac{147}{311 - 9} = \dfrac{147}{302} = 48.7\%$

an estimate of the likely response rate and the minimum or the adjusted minimum sample size, the *actual sample size* you require can be calculated using the following formula:

$$n^a = \frac{n \times 100}{re\%}$$

where n^a is the actual sample size required,
n is the minimum (or adjusted minimum) sample size (see Table 7.1 or Appendix 2),
$re\%$ is the estimated response rate expressed as a percentage.

This calculation is shown in Box 7.5.

If you are collecting your sample data from a secondary source (Section 8.2) within an organisation that has already granted you access, for example a database recording customer complaints, your response rate should be virtually 100 per cent. Your actual sample size will therefore be the same as your minimum sample size.

In contrast, estimating the likely response rate from a sample to which you will be sending a questionnaire or interviewing is more difficult. One way of obtaining this estimate is to consider the response rates achieved for similar surveys that have already been

Box 7.5
Focus on student research

Calculation of actual sample size

Jan was a part-time student employed by a large manufacturing company. He had decided to send a questionnaire to the company's customers and calculated that an adjusted minimum sample size of 439 was required. Jan estimated the response rate would

be 30 per cent. From this, he could calculate his actual sample size:

$$n^a = \frac{439 \times 100}{30}$$
$$= \frac{43\,900}{30}$$
$$= 1463$$

Jan's actual sample, therefore, needed to be 1463 customers. The likelihood of 70 per cent non-response meant that Jan needed to include a means of checking that his sample was representative when he designed his questionnaire.

undertaken and base your estimate on these. Alternatively, you can err on the side of caution. For most academic studies involving top management or organisations' representatives, a response rate of approximately 35 per cent is reasonable (Baruch 1999).

However, beware: response rates can vary considerably when collecting primary data. Willimack *et al.* (2002) report response rates for North American university-based questionnaire surveys of business ranging from 50 to 65 per cent, with even higher non-response for individual questions. Neuman (2005) suggests response rates of between 10 and 50 per cent for postal questionnaire surveys and up to 90 per cent for face-to-face interviews. The former rate concurs with a questionnaire survey we undertook for a multinational organisation that had an overall response rate of 52 per cent. In our survey, response rates for individual sites varied from 41 to 100 per cent, again emphasising variability. Our examination of response rates to recent business surveys reveals rates as low as 10–20 per cent for postal questionnaires, an implication being that respondents' questionnaire fatigue was a contributory factor! With regard to telephone administered questionnaires, response rates have fallen from 70 to 80 per cent to less than 40 per cent, due principally to people not answering the phone (Dillman 2007). Fortunately a number of different techniques, depending on your data collection method, can be used to enhance your response rate. These are discussed with the data collection method in the appropriate sections (Sections 10.3 and 11.5).

Selecting the most appropriate sampling technique and the sample

Having chosen a suitable sampling frame and established the actual sample size required, you need to select the most appropriate sampling technique to obtain a representative sample. Five main techniques can be used to select a probability sample (Figure 7.3):

- simple random;
- systematic;
- stratified random;
- cluster;
- multi-stage.

Your choice of probability sampling technique depends on your research question(s) and your objectives. Subsequently, your need for face-to-face contact with respondents, the geographical area over which the population is spread, and the nature of your sampling frame will further influence your choice of probability sampling technique (Figure 7.3). The structure of the sampling frame, the size of sample you need and, if you are using support workers, the ease with which the technique may be explained will also influence your decision. The impact of each of these is summarised in Table 7.2.

Simple random sampling

Simple random sampling (sometimes called just **random sampling**) involves you selecting the sample at random from the sampling frame using either random number tables (Appendix 3), a computer or an online random number generator, such as Research Randomizer (2008). To do this you:

1 Number each of the cases in your sampling frame with a unique number. The first case is numbered 0, the second 1 and so on.
2 Select cases using random numbers (Table 7.3, Appendix 3) until your actual sample size is reached.

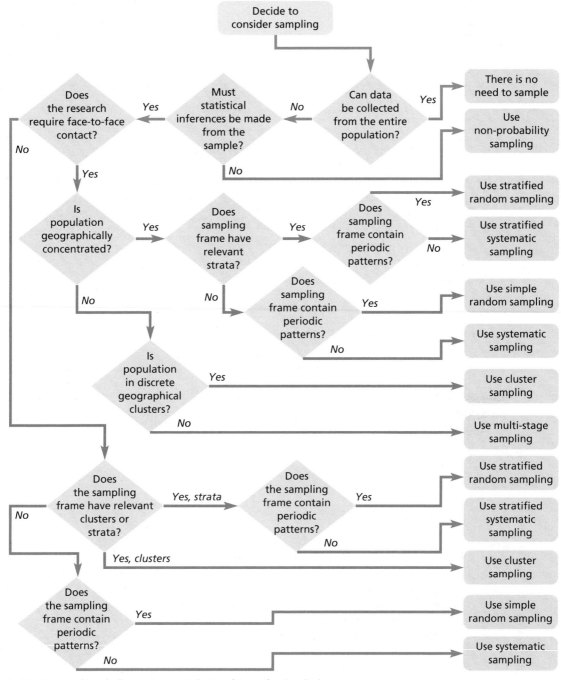

Note: Random sampling ideally requires a sample size of over a few hundred.

Figure 7.3 Selecting a probability sample

It is usual to select your first random number at random (closing your eyes and pointing with your finger is one way!) as this ensures that the set of random numbers obtained for different samples is unlikely to be the same. If you do not, you will obtain sets of numbers that are random but identical.

Table 7.2 Impact of various factors on choice of probability sampling techniques

Sample technique	Sampling frame required	Size of sample needed	Geographical area to which suited	Relative cost	Easy to explain to support workers?	Advantages compared with simple random
Simple random	Accurate and easily accessible	Better with over a few hundred	Concentrated if face-to-face contact required, otherwise does not matter	High if large sample size or sampling frame not computerised	Relatively difficult to explain	–
Systematic	Accurate, easily accessible and not containing periodic patterns. Actual list not always needed	Suitable for all sizes	Concentrated if face-to-face contact required, otherwise does not matter	Low	Relatively easy to explain	Normally no difference
Stratified random	Accurate, easily accessible, divisible into relevant strate (see comments for simple random and systematic as appropriate)	See comments for simple random and systematic as appropriate	Concentrated if face-to-face contact required, otherwise does not matter	Low, provided that lists of relevant strata available	Relatively difficult to explain (once strata decided, see comments for simple random and systematic as appropriate	Better comparison and hence representation across strata. Differential response rates may necessitate re-weighting
Cluster	Accurate, easily accessible, relates to relevant clusters, not individual population members	As large as practicable	Dispersed if face-to-face contact required and geographically based clusters used	Low, provided that lists of relevant clusters available	Relatively difficult to explain until clusters selected	Quick but reduced precision
Multi-stage	Initial stages: geographical. Final stage: needed only for geographical areas selected, see comments for simple random and systematic as appropriate	Initial stages: as large as practicable. Final stage: see comments for simple random and systematic as appropriate	Dispersed if face-to-face contact required, otherwise no need to use this technique!	Low, as sampling frame for actual survey population required only for final stage	Initial stages: relatively difficult to explain. Final stage: see comments for simple random and systematic as appropriate	Difficult to adjust for differential response rates. Substantial errors possible! However, often only practical approach when sampling a large complicated population

Source: © Mark Saunders, Philip Lewis and Adrian Thornhill 2008.

Table 7.3 Extract from random number tables

78	41	11	62	72	18	66	69	58	71	31	90	51	36	78	09	41	00
70	50	58	19	68	26	75	69	04	00	25	29	16	72	35	73	55	85
32	78	14	47	01	**55**	10	91	83	21	13	32	59	53	03	38	79	32
71	60	20	53	86	78	50	57	42	30	73	48	68	09	16	35	21	87
35	30	15	57	99	96	33	25	56	43	65	67	51	45	37	99	54	89
09	08	05	41	66	54	01	49	97	34	38	85	85	23	34	62	60	58
02	59	34	51	98	71	31	54	28	85	23	84	49	07	33	71	17	88
20	13	44	15	22	95												

Source: Appendix 3.

Starting with this number, you read off the random numbers (and select the cases) in a regular and systematic manner until your sample size is reached. If the same number is read off a second time it must be disregarded as you need different cases. This means that you are not putting each case's number back into the sampling frame after it has been selected and is termed 'sampling without replacement'. If a number is selected that is outside the range of those in your sampling frame, you simply ignore it and continue reading off numbers until your sample size is reached (Box 7.6).

If you are using a computer program such as a spreadsheet or a website to generate random numbers, you must ensure that the numbers generated are within your range and that if a number is repeated it is ignored and replaced. If details of your population are stored on the computer it is possible to generate a sample of randomly selected cases. For telephone interviews, many market research companies now use computer-aided telephone interviewing (CATI) software to select and dial telephone numbers at random from an existing database or random digit dialling and to contact each respondent in turn.

Box 7.6
Focus on student research

Simple random sampling

Jemma was undertaking her work placement at a large supermarket, where 5011 of the supermarket's customers used the supermarket's Internet purchase and delivery scheme. She was asked to interview customers and find out why they used this scheme. As there was insufficient time to interview all of them she decided to interview a sample using the telephone. Her calculations revealed that to obtain acceptable levels of confidence and accuracy she needed an actual sample size of approximately 360 customers. She decided to select them using simple random sampling.

Having obtained a list of Internet customers and their telephone numbers, Jemma gave each of the cases (customers) in this sampling frame a unique number. In order that each number was made up in exactly the same way she used 5011 four-digit numbers starting with 0000 through to 5010. So customer 677 was given the number 0676.

The first random number she selected was 55 (shown in bold and italics in Table 7.3). Starting with this number she read off the random numbers in a regular and systematic manner (in this example continuing along the line):

5510 9183 2113 3259 5303 3879 3271 6020

until 360 different cases had been selected. These formed her random sample. Numbers selected that were outside the range of those in her sampling frame (such as 5510, 9183, 5303 and 6020) were simply ignored.

Random numbers allow you to select your sample without bias. The sample selected, therefore, can be said to be representative of the whole population. However, the selection that simple random sampling provides is more evenly dispersed throughout the population for samples of more than a few hundred cases. The first few hundred cases selected using simple random sampling normally consist of bunches of cases whose numbers are close together followed by a gap and then further bunching. For more than a few hundred cases, this pattern occurs far less frequently. Because of the technique's random nature it is, therefore, possible that the chance occurrence of such patterns will result in certain parts of a population being over- or under-represented.

Simple random sampling is best used when you have an accurate and easily accessible sampling frame that lists the entire population, preferably stored on a computer. While you can often obtain these for employees within organisations or members of clubs or societies, adequate lists are often not available for types of organisation. If your population covers a large geographical area, random selection means that selected cases are likely to be dispersed throughout the area. Consequently, this form of sampling is not suitable if you are collecting data over a large geographical area using a method that requires face-to-face contact, owing to the associated high travel costs. Simple random sampling would still be suitable for a geographically dispersed area if you used an alternative technique of collecting data such as online or postal questionnaires or telephone interviewing (Chapter 11).

Sampling frames used for telephone interviewing have been replaced increasingly by random digital dialling. By selecting particular within-country area dialling codes this provides a chance to reach any household within that area represented by that code which has a telephone, regardless of whether or not the number is ex-directory. However, care must be taken as, increasingly, households have more than one telephone number. Consequently there is a higher probability of people in such households being selected as part of the sample. In addition, such a sample would exclude people who use only mobile telephones as their dialling codes are telephone network operator rather than geographical area specific (Tucker and Lepkowski 2008).

Systematic sampling

Systematic sampling involves you selecting the sample at regular intervals from the sampling frame. To do this you:

1 Number each of the cases in your sampling frame with a unique number. The first case is numbered 0, the second 1 and so on.
2 Select the first case using a random number.
3 Calculate the sampling fraction.
4 Select subsequent cases systematically using the sampling fraction to determine the frequency of selection.

To calculate the **sampling fraction** – that is, the proportion of the total population that you need to select – you use the formula

$$\text{sampling fraction} = \frac{\text{actual sample size}}{\text{total population}}$$

If your sampling fraction is $\frac{1}{3}$ you need to select one in every three cases – that is, every third case from the sampling frame. Unfortunately, your calculation will usually result in a more complicated fraction. In these instances it is normally acceptable to round your population down to the nearest 10 (or 100) and to increase your minimum sample size until a simpler sampling fraction can be calculated.

Box 7.7
Focus on student research

Systematic sampling

Stefan worked as a receptionist in a dental surgery with approximately 1500 patients. He wished to find out their attitudes to the new automated appointments scheme. As there was insufficient time and money to collect data from all patients using a questionnaire he decided to send the questionnaire to a sample. The calculation of sample size revealed that to obtain acceptable levels of confidence and accuracy he needed an actual sample size of approximately 300 patients. Using the patient files kept in the filing cabinet as a sampling frame he decided to select his sample systematically.

First he calculated the sampling fraction:

$$\frac{300}{1500} = \frac{1}{5}$$

This meant that he needed to select every fifth patient from the sampling frame.

Next he used a random number to decide where to start on his sampling frame. As the sampling fraction was ⅕, the starting point had to be one of the first five patients. He therefore selected a one-digit random number between 0 and 4.

Once he had selected his first patient at random he continued to select every fifth patient until he had gone right through his sampling frame (the filing cabinet). If the random number Stefan had selected was 2, then he would have selected the following patient numbers:

2   7   12   17   22   27   32   37

and so on until 300 patients had been selected.

On its own, selecting one in every three would not be random as every third case would be bound to be selected, whereas those between would have no chance of selection. To overcome this a random number is used to decide where to start on the sampling frame. If your sampling fraction is ⅓ the starting point must be one of the first three cases. You, therefore, select a random number (in this example a one-digit random number between 0 and 2) as described earlier and use this as the starting point.

Once you have selected your first case at random you then select, in this example, every third case until you have gone right through your sampling frame (Box 7.7). As with simple random sampling, you can use a computer to generate the first random and subsequent numbers that are in the sample.

In some instances it is not necessary to construct a list for your sampling frame. Research Mark undertook for a local authority required data to be collected about every tenth client of a social services department. Although these data were not held on computer they were available from each client's manual record. These were stored in files in alphabetical order and, once the first file (client) was selected at random, it was easy to extract every tenth file (client) thereafter. This process had the additional advantage that it was easy to explain to social services' employees, although Mark still had to explain to inquisitive employees that he needed a representative sample and so their 'interesting' clients might not be selected! For online questionnaires, such as pop-up questionnaires that appear in a window on the computer screen, there is no need to create an actual list if computer software is used to trigger an invitation to participate at random. For systematic sampling, the random selection could be triggered by some mechanism such as every tenth visitor to the site over a specified time period (Bradley 1999).

Despite the advantages, you must be careful when using existing lists as sampling frames. You need to ensure that the lists do not contain periodic patterns.

A high street bank needs you to administer a questionnaire to a sample of individual customers with joint bank accounts. A sampling fraction of ½ means that you will need to select every second customer on the list. The names on the customer lists, which

Table 7.4 The impact of periodic patterns on systematic sampling

Number	Customer	Sample	Number	Customer	Sample
000	Mr L. Baker	✓	006	Mr A. Saunders	✓
001	Mrs B. Baker	*	007	Mrs C. Saunders	*
002	Mr P. Knight	✓	008	Mr J. Smith	✓
003	Ms J. Farnsworth	*	009	Mrs K. Smith	*
004	Mr J. Lewis	✓	010	Ms L. Williams	✓
005	Mrs P. Lewis	*	011	Ms G. Catling	*

✓ Sample selected if you start with 000. * Sample selected if you start with 003.

you intend to use as the sampling frame, are arranged alphabetically by joint account with, predominantly males followed by females (Table 7.4). If you start with a male customer, the majority of those in your sample will be male. Conversely, if you start with a female customer, the majority of those in your sample will be female. Consequently your sample will be biased (Table 7.4). Systematic sampling is therefore not suitable without reordering or stratifying the sampling frame (discussed later).

Unlike simple random sampling, systematic sampling works equally well with a small or large number of cases. However, if your population covers a large geographical area, the random selection means that the sample cases are likely to be dispersed throughout the area. Consequently, systematic sampling is suitable for geographically dispersed cases only if you do not require face-to-face contact when collecting your data.

Stratified random sampling

Stratified random sampling is a modification of random sampling in which you divide the population into two or more relevant and significant strata based on one or a number of attributes. In effect, your sampling frame is divided into a number of subsets. A random sample (simple or systematic) is then drawn from each of the strata. Consequently, stratified sampling shares many of the advantages and disadvantages of simple random or systematic sampling.

Dividing the population into a series of relevant strata means that the sample is more likely to be representative, as you can ensure that each of the strata is represented proportionally within your sample. However, it is only possible to do this if you are aware of, and can easily distinguish, significant strata in your sampling frame. In addition, the extra stage in the sampling procedure means that it is likely to take longer, to be more expensive, and to be more difficult to explain than simple random or systematic sampling.

In some instances, as pointed out by deVaus (2002), your sampling frame will already be divided into strata. A sampling frame of employee names that is in alphabetical order will automatically ensure that, if systematic sampling is used (discussed earlier), employees will be sampled in the correct proportion to the letter with which their name begins. Similarly, membership lists that are ordered by date of joining will automatically result in stratification by length of membership if systematic sampling is used. However, if you are using simple random sampling or your sampling frame contains periodic patterns, you will need to stratify it. To do this you:

1 Choose the stratification variable or variables.
2 Divide the sampling frame into the discrete strata.

3 Number each of the cases within each stratum with a unique number, as discussed earlier.

4 Select your sample using either simple random or systematic sampling, as discussed earlier.

The stratification variable (or variables) chosen should represent the discrete characteristic (or characteristics) for which you want to ensure correct representation within the sample (Box 7.8).

Samples can be stratified using more than one characteristic. You may wish to stratify a sample of an organisation's employees by both department and salary grade. To do this you would:

1 divide the sampling frame into the discrete departments.

2 Within each department divide the sampling frame into discrete salary grades.

3 Number each of the cases within each salary grade within each department with a unique number, as discussed earlier.

4 Select your sample using either simple random or systematic sampling, as discussed earlier.

Box 7.8
Focus on student research

Stratified random sampling

Dilek worked for a major supplier of office supplies to public and private organisations. As part of her research into her organisation's customers, she needed to ensure that both public and private-sector organisations were represented correctly. An important stratum was, therefore, the sector of the organisation. Her sampling frame was thus divided into two discrete strata: public sector and private sector. Within each stratum, the individual cases were then numbered:

Public sector stratum			Private sector stratum		
Number	Customer	Selected	Number	Customer	Selected
000	Anyshire County Council		000	ABC Automotive manufacturer	
001	Anyshire Hospital Trust	✓	001	Anytown printers and bookbinders	
002	Newshire Army Training Barracks		002	Benjamin Toy Company	
003	Newshire Police Force		003	Jane's Internet Flower shop	✓
004	Newshire Housing		004	Multimedia productions	
005	St Peter's Secondary School	✓	005	Roger's Consulting	
006	University of Anytown		006	The Paperless Office	✓
007	West Anyshire Council		007	U-need-us Ltd	

She decided to select a systematic sample. A sampling fraction of ¼ meant that she needed to select every fourth customer on the list. As indicated by the ticks (✓), random numbers were used to select the first case in the public sector (001) and private sector (003) strata. Subsequently, every fourth customer in each stratum was selected.

In some instances the relative sizes of different strata mean that, in order to have sufficient data for analysis, you need to select larger samples from the strata with smaller populations. Here the different sample sizes must be taken into account when aggregating data from each of the strata to obtain an overall picture. The more sophisticated statistical analysis software packages enable you to do this by differentially weighting the responses for each stratum (Section 12.2).

Cluster sampling

Cluster sampling is, on the surface, similar to stratified sampling as you need to divide the population into discrete groups prior to sampling (Henry 1990). The groups are termed *clusters* in this form of sampling and can be based on any naturally occurring grouping. For example, you could group your data by type of manufacturing firm or geographical area (Box 7.9).

For cluster sampling your sampling frame is the complete list of clusters rather than a complete list of individual cases within the population. You then select a few clusters, normally using simple random sampling. Data are then collected from every case within the selected clusters. The technique has three main stages:

1 choose the cluster grouping for your sampling frame.
2 Number each of the clusters with a unique number. The first cluster is numbered 0, the second 1 and so on.
3 Select your sample using some form of random sampling as discussed earlier.

Selecting clusters randomly makes cluster sampling a probability sampling technique. Despite this, the technique normally results in a sample that represents the total population less accurately than stratified random sampling. Restricting the sample to a few relatively compact geographical sub-areas (clusters) maximises the amount of data you can collect using face to face methods within the resources available. However, it may also reduce the representativeness of your sample. For this reason you need to maximise the number of sub-areas to allow for variations in the population within the available resources. Your choice is between a large sample from a few discrete sub-groups and a smaller sample distributed over the whole group. It is a trade-off between the amount of precision lost by using a few sub-groups and the amount gained from a larger sample size.

Box 7.9
Focus on student research

Cluster sampling

Ceri needed to select a sample of firms to undertake an interview-based survey about the use of photocopiers. As she had limited resources with which to pay for travel and other associated data collection costs, she decided to interview firms in four geographical areas selected from a cluster grouping of local administrative areas. A list of all local administrative areas formed her sampling frame. Each of the local administrative areas (clusters) was given a unique number, the first being 0, the second 1 and so on. The four sample clusters were selected from this sampling frame of local administrative areas using simple random sampling.

Ceri's sample was all firms within the selected clusters. She decided that the appropriate telephone directories would probably provide a suitable list of all firms in each cluster.

Multi-stage sampling

Multi-stage sampling, sometimes called *multi-stage cluster sampling*, is a development of cluster sampling. It is normally used to overcome problems associated with a geographically dispersed population when face-to-face contact is needed or where it is expensive and time consuming to construct a sampling frame for a large geographical area. However, like cluster sampling, you can use it for any discrete groups, including those that are not geographically based. The technique involves taking a series of cluster samples, each involving some form of random sampling. This aspect is represented by the dotted lines in Figure 7.1. It can be divided into four phases. These are outlined in Figure 7.4.

Because multi-stage sampling relies on a series of different sampling frames, you need to ensure that they are all appropriate and available. In order to minimise the impact of selecting smaller and smaller sub-groups on the representativeness of your sample, you can apply stratified sampling techniques (discussed earlier). This technique can be further refined to take account of the relative size of the sub-groups by adjusting the sample size for each sub-group. As you have selected your sub-areas using different sampling frames, you only need a sampling frame that lists all the members of the population for those sub-groups you finally select (Box 7.10). This provides considerable savings in time and money.

Phase 1

- Choose sampling frame of relevant discrete groups.
- Number each group with a unique number. The first is numbered 0, the second 2 and so on.
- Select a small sample of relevant discrete groups using some form of random sampling.

Phase 2

- From these relevant discrete groups, select a sampling frame of relevant discrete sub-groups.
- Number each sub-group with a unique number as describe in Phase 1.
- Select a small sample of relevant discrete sub-groups using some form of random sampling.

Phase 3

- *Repeat Phase 2 if necessary.*

Phase 4

- From these relevant discrete sub-groups, choose a sampling frame of relevant discrete sub-sub-groups.
- Number each sub-sub group with a unique number as described in Phase 1.
- Select your sample using some form of random sampling.

Figure 7.4
Phases of multi-stage sampling

Box 7.10
Focus on student research

Multi-stage sampling

Laura worked for a market research organisation who needed her to interview a sample of 400 households in England and Wales. She decided to use the electoral register as a sampling frame. Laura knew that selecting 400 households using either systematic or simple random sampling was likely to result in these 400 households being dispersed throughout England and Wales, resulting in considerable amounts of time spent travelling between interviewees as well as high travel costs. By using multi-stage sampling Laura felt these problems could be overcome.

In her first stage the geographical area (England and Wales) was split into discrete sub-areas (counties).

These formed her sampling frame. After numbering all the counties, Laura selected a small number of counties using simple random sampling. Since each case (household) was located in a county, each had an equal chance of being selected for the final sample.

As the counties selected were still too large, each was subdivided into smaller geographically discrete areas (electoral wards). These formed the next sampling frame (stage 2). Laura selected another simple random sample. This time she selected a larger number of wards to allow for likely important variations in the nature of households between wards.

A sampling frame of the households in each of these wards was then generated using a combination of the electoral register and the UK Royal Mail's postcode address file. Laura finally selected the actual cases (households) that she would interview using systematic sampling.

Checking that the sample is representative

Often it is possible to compare data you collect from your sample with data from another source for the population. For example, you can compare data on the age and socio-economic characteristics of respondents in a marketing survey with these characteristics for the population in that country as recorded by the latest national census of population. If there is no statistically significant difference, then the sample is representative with respect to these characteristics.

When working within an organisation comparisons can also be made. In a questionnaire Mark administered recently to a sample of employees in a large UK organisation he asked closed questions about salary grade, gender, length of service and place of work. Possible responses to each question were designed to provide sufficient detail to compare the characteristics of the sample with the characteristics of the entire population of employees as recorded by the organisation's computerised personnel system. At the same time he kept the categories sufficiently broad to preserve, and to be seen to preserve, the confidentiality of individual respondents. The two questions on length of service and salary grade from a questionnaire he developed illustrate this:

97 How long have you worked for *organisation's name*?

  Up to 1 year Over 1 year to 10 years Over 10 years

98 Which one of the following best describes your job?

  Clerical (grades 1–3)   Management (grades 9–11)

  Supervisory (grades 4–5)   Senior management (grades 12–14)

  Professional (grades 6–8)   Other (please say)

            ....

Using the Kolmogorov test (Section 12.5), Mark found there was no statistically significant difference between the proportions of respondents in each of the length of service groups and the data obtained from the organisation's personnel database for all employees. This meant that the sample of respondents was representative of all employees with respect to length of service. However, those responding were (statistically) significantly more likely to be in professional and managerial grades than in technical, administrative or supervisory grades. He therefore added a note of caution about the representativeness of his findings.

You can also assess the representativeness of samples for longitudinal studies. Obviously, it is still possible to compare respondent characteristics with data from another source. In addition, the characteristics of those who responded can be compared for different data collection periods. For example, you could compare the characteristics of those in your sample who responded to a questionnaire at the start of a research project with those who responded to a questionnaire six months later. We should like to add a note of caution here. Such a comparison will enable you to discuss the extent to which the groups of respondents differed for these characteristics over time. However, depending on your choice of characteristics, these differences might be expected owing to some form of managerial intervention or other change between the data collection periods.

7.3 Non-probability sampling

The techniques for selecting samples discussed earlier have all been based on the assumption that your sample will be chosen statistically at random. Consequently, it is possible to specify the probability that any case will be included in the sample. However, within business research, such as market surveys and case study research, this may either not be possible (as you do not have a sampling frame) or appropriate to answering your research question. This means your sample must be selected some other way. Non-probability sampling (or **non-random sampling**) provides a range of alternative techniques to select samples based on your subjective judgement. In the exploratory stages of some research projects, such as a pilot survey, a non-probability sample may be the most practical, although it will not allow the extent of the problem to be determined. Subsequent to this, probability sampling techniques may be used. For other business and management research projects your research question(s), objectives and choice of research strategy (Sections 2.4, 5.3) may dictate non-probability sampling. To answer your research question(s) and to meet your objectives you may need to undertake an in-depth study that focuses on a small, perhaps one, case selected for a particular purpose. This sample would provide you with an information-rich case study in which you explore your research question and gain theoretical insights. Alternatively, limited resources or the inability to specify a sampling frame may dictate the use of one or a number of non-probability sampling techniques.

Deciding on a suitable sample size

For all non-probability sampling techniques, other than for quota samples (which we discuss later) the issue of sample size is ambiguous and, unlike probability sampling, there are no rules. Rather the logical relationship between your sample selection technique and the purpose and focus of your research is important (Figure 7.5), generalisations being made to theory rather than about a population. Consequently, your sample size is dependent on your research question(s) and objectives – in particular, what you need

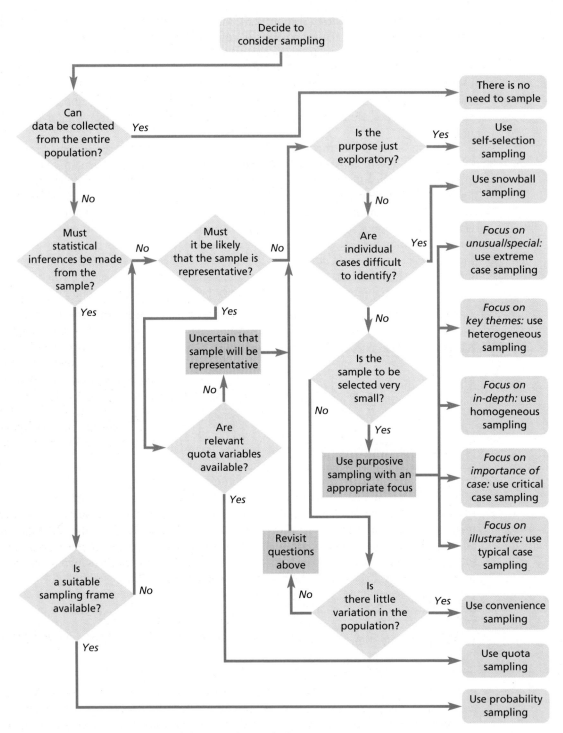

Figure 7.5 Selecting a non-probability sampling technique

to find out, what will be useful, what will have credibility and what can be done within your available resources (Patton 2002). This is particularly so where you are intending to collect qualitative data using interviews. Although the validity, understanding and insights that you will gain from your data will be more to do with your data collection and analysis skills than with the size of your sample (Patton 2002), it is possible to offer guidance as to the sample size to ensure you have conducted sufficient interviews.

In addressing this issue, many research text books simply recommend continuing to collect qualitative data, such as by conducting additional interviews, until **data satura-tion** is reached: in other words until the additional data collected provides few, if any, new insights. However, this does not answer the question, how many respondents are you likely to need in your sample? Fortunately, Guest *et al.* (2006) offers some guidance. For research where your aim is to understand commonalities within a fairly homogenous group, 12 in-depth interviews should suffice. However, they also note that 12 interviews are unlikely to be sufficient where the sample is drawn from a heterogeneous population or the focus of the research question is wide ranging. Given this, we would suggest that, for a general study, you should expect to undertake between 25 and 30 interviews (Creswell 2007).

Selecting the most appropriate sampling technique and the sample

Having decided the likely suitable sample size, you need to select the most appropriate sampling technique to enable you to answer your research question from the range of non-probability sampling techniques available (Figure 7.2). At one end of this range is quota sampling, which, like probability samples, tries to represent the total population. Quota sampling has similar requirements for sample size as probabilistic sampling tech-niques. At the other end of this range are techniques based on the need to obtain a sam-ple as quickly as possible where you have little control over the sample cases and there is no attempt to obtain a representative sample which will allow you to generalise in a sta-tistical sense to a population. These include convenience and self-selection sampling techniques. Purposive sampling and snowball sampling techniques lie between these extremes (Table 7.5).

Quota sampling

Quota sampling is entirely non-random and is normally used for interview surveys. It is based on the premise that your sample will represent the population as the variability in your sample for various quota variables is the same as that in the population. Quota sam-pling is therefore a type of stratified sample in which selection of cases within strata is entirely non-random (Barnett 1991). To select a quota sample you:

1 Divide the population into specific groups.
2 Calculate a quota for each group based on relevant and available data.
3 Give each interviewer an 'assignment', which states the number of cases in each quota from which they must collect data.
4 Combine the data collected by interviewers to provide the full sample.

Quota sampling has a number of advantages over the probabilistic techniques. In par-ticular, it is less costly and can be set up very quickly. If, as with television audience research surveys, your data collection needs to be undertaken very quickly then quota sampling may be the only possibility. In addition, it does not require a sampling frame and, therefore, may be the only technique you can use if one is not available.

Quota sampling is normally used for large populations. For small populations, it is usually possible to obtain a sampling frame. Decisions on sample size are governed by the need to have sufficient responses in each quota to enable subsequent statistical analy-ses to be undertaken. This often necessitates a sample size of between 2000 and 5000.

Table 7.5 Impact of various factors on choice of non-probability sampling techniques

Sample type	Likelihood of sample being representative	Types of research in which useful	Relative costs	Control over sample contents
Quota	Reasonable to high, although dependent on selection of quota variables	Where costs constrained or data needed very quickly so an alternative to probability sampling needed	Moderately high to reasonable	Relatively high
Purposive	Low, although dependent on researcher's choices: extreme case	Where working with very small samples	Reasonable	Reasonable
		focus: unusual or special		
	heterogeneous homogeneous critical case	focus: key themes focus: in-depth focus: importance of case		
	typical case	focus: illustrative		
Snowball	Low, but cases will have characteristics desired	Where difficulties in identifying cases	Reasonable	Quite low
Self-selection	Low, but cases self-selected	Where exploratory research needed	Low	Low
Convenience	Very low	Where very little variation in population	Low	Low

Sources: developed from Kervin (1999); Patton (2002).

Calculations of quotas are based on relevant and available data and are usually relative to the proportions in which they occur in the population (Box 7.11). Without sensible and relevant quotas, data collected may be biased. For many market research projects, quotas are derived from census data. Your choice of quota is dependent on two main factors:

- usefulness as a means of stratifying the data;
- ability to overcome likely variations between groups in their availability for interview.

Where people who are retired are likely to have different opinions from those in work, a quota that does not ensure that these differences are captured may result in the data being biased as it would probably be easier to collect the data from those people who are retired. Quotas used in market research surveys and political opinion polls usually include measures of age, gender and socioeconomic status or social class. These may be supplemented by additional quotas dictated by the research question(s) and objectives (Box 7.12).

Once you have given each interviewer their particular assignment, they decide whom to interview until they have completed their quota. You then combine the data from this assignment with those collected by other interviewers to provide the full sample. Because the interviewer can choose within quota boundaries whom they interview, your quota sample may be subject to bias. Interviewers tend to choose respondents who are easily accessible and who appear willing to answer the questions. Clear controls may therefore be needed. In addition, it has been known for interviewers to fill in quotas incorrectly. This is not to say that your quota sample will not produce good results; they can and often do! However, you cannot measure the level of certainty or margins of error as the sample is not probability based.

Purposive sampling

Purposive or **judgemental sampling** enables you to use your judgement to select cases that will best enable you to answer your research question(s) and to meet your objectives. This form of sample is often used when working with very small samples such as in case study research and when you wish to select cases that are particularly informative

---

Box 7.11
Focus on student research

Devising a quota sample

Mica was undertaking the data collection for his dissertation as part of his full-time employment. For his research he needed to interview a sample of people representing those aged 20–64 who were in work in his country. No sampling frame was available.

Once the data had been collected, he was going to disaggregate his findings into sub-groups dependent on respondents' age and type of employment. Previous research had suggested that gender would also have an impact on responses and so he needed to make sure that those interviewed in each group also reflected the proportions of males and females in the population. Fortunately, his country's national census of population contained a breakdown of the number of people in employment by gender, age and socioeconomic status. These formed the basis of the categories for his quotas:

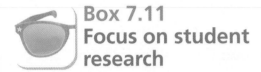

gender	×	age group	×	socioeconomic status
male		20–29		professional
female		30–34		managers/employers
		45–64		intermediate and junior non-manual
				skilled manual
				semi-skilled manual
				unskilled manual

As he was going to analyse the data for individual age and socioeconomic status groups, it was important that each of these categories had sufficient respondents (at least 30) to enable meaningful statistical analyses. Mica calculated that a 0.5 per cent quota for each of the groups would provide sufficient numbers for all groups, provided his analyses were not also disaggregated by gender. This gave him the following quotas:

> ## Box 7.11
> ## Focus on student research (continued)

Gender	Age group	Socioeconomic status	Population (10% sample)	Quota
Male	20–29	Professional	11 210	56
		Managers/employers	7 983	40
		Intermediate and junior non-manual	9 107	43
		Skilled manual	16 116	79
		Semi-skilled manual	12 605	63
		Unskilled manual	5 039	25
	30–44	Professional	21 431	107
		Managers/employers	23 274	116
		Intermediate and junior non-manual	7 997	40
		Skilled manual	21 410	107
		Semi-skilled manual	19 244	96
		Unskilled manual	4 988	25
	45–64	Professional	16 612	83
		Managers/employers	23 970	120
		Intermediate and junior non-manual	9 995	49
		Skilled manual	20 019	100
		Semi-skilled manual	17 616	88
		Unskilled manual	5 763	29
Female	20–29	Professional	8 811	44
		Managers/employers	6 789	34
		Intermediate and junior non-manual	21 585	108
		Skilled manual	1 754	9
		Semi-skilled manual	9 632	48
		Unskilled manual	3 570	18
	30–44	Professional	16 380	82
		Managers/employers	9 765	49
		Intermediate and junior non-manual	28 424	142
		Skilled manual	2 216	11
		Semi-skilled manual	11 801	59
		Unskilled manual	8 797	41
	45–64	Professional	8 823	44
		Managers/employers	7 846	39
		Intermediate and junior non-manual	21 974	110
		Skilled manual	1 578	8
		Semi-skilled manual	9 421	47
		Unskilled manual	8 163	41
Total sample			441 604	2 200

These were then divided into assignments of 50 people for each interviewer.

Box 7.12
Focus on management research

Purposive sampling

Virtual Communities of Interest (VCI) are affiliation groups whose online interactions are based on shared enthusiasm and knowledge for a specific activity or group of activities. They specifically focus upon information exchange and social interaction and are considered to be a sub-group of virtual communities. They are becoming increasingly relevant as they have resulted in a shift of the bargaining power from suppliers to customers, increased web traffic, provided a means of learning from customers and can result in positive word of mouth recommendations.

Research by Valck *et al.* (2007) published in the *British Journal of Management* develops a scale to measure and report on members' satisfaction with VCIs and the effect of this on the frequency of visits to the community. Valck and colleagues selected a single sample VCI which focused on typical teenage interests (school, parents, relationships, money, music, films and television programmes, etc.) as an illustrative case. They justified their sample selection as being 'consistent with other scale development studies in the literature' (Valck *et al.* 2007:247). With the permission and support of the organisation that organised the VCI, emails were sent to all 78 851 community members (the entire population) using the name by which they were known to the organisation. The email outlined the purpose of their research and contained a request to participate and a direct link to an online questionnaire. One week later non-respondents were emailed again. This resulted in 3605 useable responses, a response rate of 4.9 per cent. Valck and colleagues checked for non-response bias in a number of ways. These included comparing the socio-demographic characteristics of the 3605 respondents with those for the entire VCI population. Together these suggested that non-response bias was unlikely to be present in their data.

Source: Valck *et al.* (2007).

(Neuman 2005). Purposive sampling may also be used by researchers adopting the grounded theory strategy. For such research, findings from data collected from your initial sample inform the way you extend your sample into subsequent cases (Section 13.8). Such samples, however, cannot be considered to be statistically representative of the total population. The logic on which you base your strategy for selecting cases for a purposive sample should be dependent on your research question(s) and objectives. Patton (2002) emphasises this point by contrasting the need to select information-rich cases in purposive sampling with the need to be statistically representative in probability sampling. The more common purposive sampling strategies were outlined in Figure 7.2 and are discussed below:

- **Extreme case** or **deviant sampling** focuses on unusual or special cases on the basis that the data collected about these unusual or extreme outcomes will enable you to learn the most and to answer your research question(s) and to meet your objectives most effectively. This is often based on the premise that findings from extreme cases will be relevant in understanding or explaining more typical cases (Patton 2002).

- **Heterogeneous** or **maximum variation sampling** enables you to collect data to describe and explain the key themes that can be observed. Although this might appear a contradiction, as a small sample may contain cases that are completely different, Patton (2002) argues that this is in fact a strength. Any patterns that do emerge are likely to be of particular interest and value and represent the key themes. In addition, the data collected should enable you to document uniqueness. To ensure maximum variation within a sample Patton (2002) suggests you identify your diverse characteristics (sample selection criteria) prior to selecting your sample.

- In direct contrast to heterogeneous sampling, **homogeneous sampling** focuses on one particular sub-group in which all the sample members are similar. This enables you to study the group in great depth.
- **Critical case sampling** selects critical cases on the basis that they can make a point dramatically or because they are important. The focus of data collection is to understand what is happening in each critical case so that logical generalisations can be made (Box 7.12). Patton (2002) outlines a number of clues that suggest critical cases. These can be summarised by the questions such as:
  - If it happens there, will it happen everywhere?
  - If they are having problems, can you be sure that everyone will have problems?
  - If they cannot understand the process, is it likely that no one will be able to understand the process?
- In contrast, **typical case sampling** is usually used as part of a research project to provide an illustrative profile using a representative case. Such a sample enables you to provide an illustration of what is 'typical' to those who will be reading your research report and may be unfamiliar with the subject matter. It is not intended to be definitive.

Snowball sampling

Snowball sampling is commonly used when it is difficult to identify members of the desired population, for example people who are working while claiming unemployment benefit. You, therefore, need to:

1 Make contact with one or two cases in the population.
2 Ask these cases to identify further cases.
3 Ask these new cases to identify further new cases (and so on).
4 Stop when either no new cases are given or the sample is as large as is manageable.

The main problem is making initial contact. Once you have done this, these cases identify further members of the population, who then identify further members, and so the sample snowballs (Box 7.13). For such samples the problems of bias are huge, as respondents are most likely to identify other potential respondents who are similar to themselves, resulting in a homogeneous sample (Lee 1993). The next problem is to find

Box 7.13
Focus on student research

Snowball sampling

Steve was a part-time student. His project was concerned with the career paths of managing directors of large companies. As part of this, Steve needed to interview managing directors. He arranged his first interview with the managing director of his own company. Towards the end of the interview the managing director asked Steve whether he could be of further assistance. Two other managing directors that Steve could interview were suggested. Steve's managing director offered to 'introduce' Steve to them and provided him with contact telephone numbers and the names of their personal assistants. Steve's sample had started to snowball!

these new cases. However, for populations that are difficult to identify, snowball sampling may provide the only possibility.

Self-selection sampling

Self-selection sampling occurs when you allow each case, usually individuals, to identify their desire to take part in the research. You therefore:

1 Publicise your need for cases, either by advertising through appropriate media or by asking them to take part.
2 Collect data from those who respond.

Publicity for convenience samples can take many forms. These include articles and advertisements in magazines that the population are likely to read, postings on appropriate Internet newsgroups and discussion groups, hyperlinks from other websites as well as letters or emails of invitation to colleagues and friends (Box 7.14). Cases that self-select often do so because of their feelings or opinions about the research question(s) or stated objectives. In some instances, as in research undertaken by Adrian, Mark and colleagues on the management of the survivors of downsizing (Thornhill *et al.* 1997), this is exactly what the researcher wants. In this research a letter in the personnel trade press generated a list of self-selected organisations that were interested in the research topic, considered it important and were willing to devote time to being interviewed.

Box 7.14
Focus on student research

Self-selection sampling

Siân's research was concerned with teleworking. She had decided to administer her questionnaire using the Internet. She publicised her research on a range of bulletin boards, asking for volunteers to fill in a questionnaire. Those who volunteered by clicking on a hyperlink were automatically taken to her online questionnaire.

Convenience sampling

Convenience sampling (or **haphazard sampling**) involves selecting haphazardly those cases that are easiest to obtain for your sample, such as the person interviewed at random in a shopping centre for a television programme or the book about entrepreneurship you find at the airport (Box 7.15). The sample selection process is continued until your required sample size has been reached. Although this technique of sampling is used widely, it is prone to bias and influences that are beyond your control, as the cases appear in the sample only because of the ease of obtaining them. Often the sample is intended to represent the total population, for example managers taking an MBA course as a surrogate for all managers! In such instances the selection of individual cases is likely to have introduced bias to the sample, meaning that subsequent generalisations are likely to be at best flawed. These problems are less important where there is little variation in the population, and such samples often serve as pilots to studies using more structured samples.

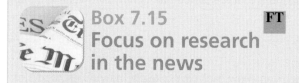

FT

Box 7.15
Focus on research in the news

'How I did it' books give me a sinking feeling

The poolside is twice as pleasurable this year because swimming is so much more enjoyable. The credit goes to pioneers of new methods of swimming instruction, Steven Shaw and Terry Laughlin.

In my experience, most swimming lessons are delivered by charming young Australians, excellent swimmers who have been at home in the water since they were young children. They regard those who flounder in the water with incomprehension. They say 'watch me' as they vanish towards the other end of the pool.

But what bad swimmers need is to be taught to do the things good swimmers do naturally. Bad swimmers must overcome their fear of water and learn to balance and float. The skills of being good at something and being good at teaching others to do it are completely different.

That lesson seems relevant to the pile of bad books by my deckchair. I have been skimming the clutch of recent guides to entrepreneurship. Most are spin-offs from television programmes. The message of all is that anyone can do it, which is indeed the title of two of these books.

I do not know whether skill or luck was the more important contributor to the development of Coffee Republic, the success of mobile phone magnate Peter Jones, or of publisher Felix Dennis or the coups of property speculator Duncan Bannatyne. Nor do these authors know. But whether you are successful because you are skilful, like swimmer Mark Spitz, or successful because you are lucky, like a lottery winner, you can easily, and mistakenly, convince yourself that your own experience shows that anyone can do it. After all, anyone who is Mark Spitz can be an Olympic swimming champion, and anyone can be a lottery winner if they buy the right ticket.

There is nothing to be learnt from memorising the banal tips provided by these books – aim to succeed, show determination, have a good idea, work hard.

John Paul Getty, asked for the secrets of his success, said it all: 'Strike oil'.

If you are looking for common characteristics of these successful entrepreneurs, you learn that none of them can write well and all of them are vain. I am sure you do not need to write well to succeed in business. Perhaps you need to be vain: or perhaps vanity is just a characteristic of the self-selected sample of entrepreneurs who write books about their experiences.

Television finds an even more unrepresentative sample of those who have made it in business. Only a few entrepreneurs aspire to be movie stars. Fewer still commend themselves to producers as having star quality.

The business people whose insights I value mostly think that business is complex, that there are few universal recipes for success, and explain that much of their time is spent gently coaxing the best from people. Such entrepreneurs do not make it onto the small screen. Those who appear on television are, of necessity, people with outsized personalities who exude confidence and possess a talent for one line answers.

That is how Sir Alan Sugar and Donald Trump become the public face of business. It propagates the idea that the main quality required is aggression. This emphasis is misleading for those who want to go into business, and reinforces the prejudices of those who are instinctively hostile to it.

Perhaps I am too hard on these books about entrepreneurship. If you look at the reader reviews on Amazon, you find touching public expressions of gratitude for the inspiration people say they have found in them. This is the role such books can play. No one can seriously imagine that by reading the memoirs of a sporting hero they will learn how to be good at football. But some kids who read these books may be fired with ambition to succeed at football, or in life.

The mistake both authors and publishers of business books make is to confuse a book about 'what I did' with a book about 'how to do it'. The result gives us insight from someone's biography only accidentally and has little to offer in terms of useful advice. The skills of the coach are not the same as the skills of the practitioner. That is true in both the pool and the boardroom.

7.4 Summary

- Your choice of sampling techniques is dependent on the feasibility and sensibility of collecting data to answer your research question(s) and to address your objectives from the entire population. For populations of under 50 it is usually more sensible to collect data from the entire population where you are considering using probability sampling.
- Choice of sampling technique or techniques is dependent on your research question(s) and objectives:
  - Research question(s) and objectives that need you to estimate statistically the characteristics of the population from a sample require probability samples.
  - Research question(s) and objectives that do not require such generalisations can, alternatively, make use of non-probability sampling techniques.
- Factors such as the confidence that is needed in the findings, accuracy required and likely categories for analyses will affect the size of the sample that needs to be collected:
  - Statistical analyses usually require a minimum sample size of 30.
  - Research question(s) and objectives that do not require statistical estimation may need far smaller samples.
- Sample size and the technique used are also influenced by the availability of resources, in particular financial support and time available to select the sample and to collect, enter into a computer and analyse the data.
- Probability sampling techniques all necessitate some form of sampling frame, so they are often more time consuming than non-probability techniques.
- Where it is not possible to construct a sampling frame you will need to use non-probability sampling techniques.
- Non-probability sampling techniques also provide you with the opportunity to select your sample purposively and to reach difficult-to-identify members of the population.
- For many research projects you will need to use a combination of different sampling techniques.
- All your choices will be dependent on your ability to gain access to organisations. The considerations summarised earlier must therefore be tempered with an understanding of what is practically possible.

Self-check questions

Help with these questions is available at the end of the chapter.

7.1 Identify a suitable sampling frame for each of the following research questions.
   a How do company directors of manufacturing firms of over 500 employees think a specified piece of legislation will affect their companies?
   b Which factors are important in accountants' decisions regarding working in mainland Europe?
   c How do employees at Cheltenham Gardens Ltd think the proposed introduction of compulsory Saturday working will affect their working lives?
7.2 Lisa has emailed her tutor with the following query regarding sampling and dealing with non-response. Imagine you are Lisa's tutor. Draft a reply to answer her query.

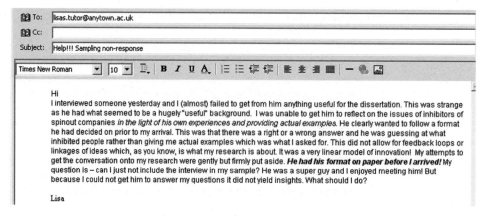

To: lisas.tutor@anytown.ac.uk
Cc:
Subject: Help!!! Sampling non-response

Times New Roman | 10 | B I U A |

Hi
I interviewed someone yesterday and I (almost) failed to get from him anything useful for the dissertation. This was strange as he had what seemed to be a hugely "useful" background. I was unable to get him to reflect on the issues of inhibitors of spinout companies *in the light of his own experiences and providing actual examples.* He clearly wanted to follow a format he had decided on prior to my arrival. This was that there was a right or a wrong answer and he was guessing at what inhibited people rather than giving me actual examples which was what I asked for. This did not allow for feedback loops or linkages of ideas which, as you know, is what my research is about. It was a very linear model of innovation! My attempts to get the conversation onto my research were gently but firmly put aside. *He had his format on paper before I arrived!* My question is – can I just not include the interview in my sample? He was a super guy and I enjoyed meeting him! But because I could not get him to answer my questions it did not yield insights. What should I do?

Lisa

7.3 You have been asked to select a sample of manufacturing firms using the sampling frame below. This also lists the value of their annual output in tens of thousands of pounds over the past year. To help you in selecting your sample the firms have been numbered from 0 to 99.

	Output		Output		Output		Output		Output
0	1163	20	1072	40	1257	60	1300	80	1034
1	10	21	7	41	29	61	39	81	55
2	57	22	92	42	84	62	73	82	66
3	149	23	105	43	97	63	161	83	165
4	205	24	157	44	265	64	275	84	301
5	163	25	214	45	187	65	170	85	161
6	1359	26	1440	46	1872	66	1598	86	1341
7	330	27	390	47	454	67	378	87	431
8	2097	28	1935	48	1822	68	1634	88	1756
9	1059	29	998	49	1091	69	1101	89	907
10	1037	30	1298	50	1251	70	1070	90	1158
11	59	31	10	51	9	71	37	91	27
12	68	32	70	52	93	72	88	92	66
13	166	33	159	53	103	73	102	93	147
14	302	34	276	54	264	74	157	94	203
15	161	35	215	55	189	75	168	95	163
16	1298	36	1450	56	1862	76	1602	96	1339
17	329	37	387	57	449	77	381	97	429
18	2103	38	1934	58	1799	78	1598	98	1760
19	1061	39	1000	59	1089	79	1099	99	898

   a Select two simple random samples, each of 20 firms, and mark those firms selected for each sample on the sampling frame.
   b Describe and compare the pattern on the sampling frame of each of the samples selected.
   c Calculate the average (mean) annual output in tens of thousands of pounds over the past year for each of the samples selected.
   d Given that the true average annual output is £6 608 900, is there any bias in either of the samples selected?

7.4 You have been asked to select a 10 per cent sample of firms from the sampling frame used for self-check question 7.3.
   a Select a 10 per cent systematic sample and mark those firms selected for the sample on the sampling frame.

b Calculate the average (mean) annual output in tens of thousands of pounds over the past year for your sample.

c Given that the true average annual output is £6 608 900, why does systematic sampling provide such a poor estimate of the annual output in this case?

7.5 You need to undertake a face-to-face interview survey of managing directors of small to medium-sized organisations. From the data you collect you need to be able to generalise about the attitude of such managing directors to recent changes in government policy towards these firms. Your generalisations need to be accurate to within plus or minus 5 per cent. Unfortunately, you have limited resources to pay for interviewers, travelling and other associated costs.

a How many managing directors will you need to interview?

b You have been given the choice between cluster and multi-stage sampling. Which technique would you choose for this research? You should give reasons for your choice.

7.6 You have been asked to undertake a survey of residents' opinions regarding the siting of a new supermarket in an inner city suburb (estimated catchment population 111 376 at the last census). The age and gender distribution of the catchment population at the last census is listed below:

Gender	Age group							
	0–4	5–15	16–19	20–29	30–44	45–59/64*	60/65#–74	75+
Males	3498	7106	4884	7656	9812	12 892	4972	2684
Females	3461	6923	6952	9460	8152	9152	9284	4488

*59 females, 64 males; #60 females, 65 males.

a Devise a quota for a quota sample using these data.

b What other data would you like to include to overcome likely variations between groups in their availability for interview and replicate the total population more precisely? Give reasons for your answer.

c What problems might you encounter in using interviewers?

7.7 For each of the following research questions it has not been possible for you to obtain a sampling frame. Suggest the most suitable non-probability sampling technique to obtain the necessary data, giving reasons for your choice.

a What support do people sleeping rough believe they require from social services?

b Which television advertisements do people remember watching last weekend?

c How do employers' opinions vary regarding the impact of European Union legislation on employee recruitment?

d How are manufacturing companies planning to respond to the introduction of road tolls?

e Would users of the squash club be prepared to pay a 10 per cent increase in subscriptions to help fund two extra courts (answer needed by tomorrow morning!)?

Review and discussion questions

7.8 With a friend or colleague choose one of the following research questions (or one of your own) in which you are interested.

– What attributes attract people to jobs?

– How are financial institutions adapting the services they provide to meet recent legislation?

Use the flow charts for both probability sampling (Figure 7.3) and non-probability sampling (Figure 7.5) to decide how you could use each type of sampling independently to answer the research question.

7.9 Agree with a colleague to watch a particular documentary or consumer rights programme on the television. If possible, choose a documentary with a business or management focus. During the documentary, pay special attention to the samples from which the data for the documentary are drawn. Where possible, note down details of the sample such as who were interviewed, or who responded to questionnaires and the reasons why these people were chosen. Where this is not possible, make a note of the information you would have liked to have been given. Discuss your findings with your colleague and come to a conclusion regarding the nature of the sample used, its representativeness and the extent it was possible for the programme maker to generalise from that sample.

7.10 Obtain a copy of a quality daily newspaper and, within the newspaper, find an article which discusses a 'survey' or 'poll'. Share the article with a friend. Make notes of the process used to select the sample for the 'survey' or 'poll'. As you make your notes, note down any areas where you feel there is insufficient information to fully understand the sampling process. Aspects for which information may be lacking include the total population, size of sample, how the sample were selected, representativeness and so on. Discuss your findings with your friend.

Progressing your research project

Using sampling as part of your research

- Consider your research question(s) and objectives. You need to decide whether you will be able to collect data on the entire population or will need to collect data from a sample.
- If you decide that you need to sample, you must establish whether your research question(s) and objectives require probability sampling. If they do, make sure that a suitable sampling frame is available or can be devised, and calculate the actual

sample size required taking into account likely response rates. If your research question(s) and objectives do not require probability sampling, or you are unable to obtain a suitable sampling frame, you will need to use non-probability sampling.

- Select the most appropriate sampling technique or techniques after considering the advantages and disadvantages of all suitable techniques and undertaking further reading as necessary.
- Select your sample or samples following the technique or techniques as outlined in this chapter.
- Remember to note down the reasons for your choices when you make them, as you will need to justify your choices when you write about your research method.

References

Barnett, V. (1991) *Sample Survey Principles and Methods.* London: Edward Arnold.

Baruch, Y. (1999) 'Response rates in academic studies – a comparative analysis', *Human Relations,* Vol. 52, No. 4, pp. 421–38.

Bradley, N. (1999) 'Sampling for Internet surveys: an examination of respondent selection for Internet research', *Journal of the Market Research Society,* Vol. 41, No. 4, pp. 387–95.

Clennell, A. (2002) 'How Brunel lobby came off the rails', *The Guardian*, 25 Nov.

Cooper, J. (2002) *Great Britons, the Great Debate*. London: National Portrait Gallery.

Creswell, J. (2007) *Qualitative Inquiry and Research Design: Choosing among Five Approaches* (2nd edn). Thousand Oaks, CA: Sage.

deVaus, D.A. (2002) *Surveys in Social Research* (5th edn). London: Routledge.

Dillman, D.A. (2007) *Mail and Internet Surveys: The Tailored Design Method* (2nd edn, 2007 update). Hoboken, NJ: Wiley.

Edwards, T., Tregaskis, O., Edwards, P., Ferner, A., Marginson, A. with Arrowsmith, J., Adam, D., Meyer, M. and Budjanovcanin, A. (2007) 'Charting the contours of multinationals in Britain: Methodological challenges arising in survey-based research', Warwick papers in Industrial Relations No. 86. Available at: http://www2.warwick.ac.uk/fac/soc/wbs/research/irru/wpir/ [Accessed 2 February 2008.]

Guest, G., Bunce, A. and Johnson, L. (2006) 'How many interviews are enough? An experiment with data saturation and validity', *Field Methods*, Vol. 18, No. 1, pp. 59–82.

Henry, G.T. (1990) *Practical Sampling.* Newbury Park, CA: Sage.

Hewson, C., Yule, P., Laurent, D. and Vogel, C. (2003) *Internet Research Methods: A Practical Guide for the Social and Behavioural Sciences.* London: Sage.

Idea Works (2008) 'Methodologist's Toolchest Ex-sample'. Available at: http://www.ideaworks.com/mt/exsample.html [Accessed 2 February 2008.]

Kervin, J.B. (1999) *Methods for Business Research* (2nd edn). New York: HarperCollins.

Lee, R.M. (1993) *Doing Research on Sensitive Topic.* London: Sage.

Miller, D., Le Breton-Miller, I. and Scholnick, B. (2008) 'Stewardship versus stagnation: An empirical comparison of small family and non-family businesses', *Journal of Management Studies*, Vol. 45, No.1, pp. 51–78.

Neuman, W.L. (2005) *Social Research Methods* (6th edn). London: Pearson.

Patton, M.Q. (2002) *Qualitative Research and Evaluation Methods* (3rd edn). Thousand Oaks, CA: Sage.

Research Randomizer (2008). Research Randomizer. Available at: http://www.randomizer.org/index.htm [Accessed 20 March 2008.]

Stutely, M. (2003) *Numbers Guide: The Essentials of Business Numeracy*. London: Bloomberg Press.

Thornhill, A., Saunders, M.N.K. and Stead, J. (1997) 'Downsizing, delayering but where's the commitment? The development of a diagnostic tool to help manage survivors', *Personnel Review*, Vol. 26, No. 1/2, pp. 81–98.

Tucker, C. and Lepkowski, J.M. (2008) 'Telephone survey methods: adapting to change', in J.M. Lepkowski, C. Tucker, J.M. Brick, E.D. De Leeuw, L. Japec, P.J. Lavrakas, M.W. Link and R.L. Sangster, *Advances in Telephone Survey Methodology.* Hoboken, NJ: Wiley pp. 3–28.

Valck, K., Langerak, F., Verhoef, P.C. and Verhoef, P.W.J. (2007) 'Satisifaction with virtual communities of interest: Effect of members' visit frequency', *British Journal of Management*, Vol. 18, No. 3, pp. 241–56.

Willimack, D.K., Nichols, E. and Sudman, S. (2002) 'Understanding unit and item nonresponse in business surveys', in D.A. Dillman, J.L. Eltringe, J.L. Groves and R.J.A. Little (eds), *Survey Nonresponse.* New York: Wiley Interscience, pp. 213–27.

Further reading

Barnett, V. (1991) *Sample Survey Principles and Method.* London: Edward Arnold. Chapters 2, 5 and 6 provide an explanation of statistics behind probability sampling and quota sampling as well as the techniques.

Baruch, Y. (1999) 'Response rates in academic studies – a comparative analysis', *Human Relations.* Vol. 52, No. 4, pp. 421–38. This examines 175 different studies in which sampling was used covering approximately 200 000 respondents. The paper suggests likely response rates between studies and highlights a decline in response rates over the period 1975–95.

deVaus, D.A. (2002) *Surveys in Social Research.* (5th edn). London: Routledge. Chapter 6 provides a useful overview of both probability and non-probability sampling techniques.

Diamantopoulos, A. and Schlegelmilch, B.B. (1997) *Taking the Fear Out of Data Analysis.* London: Dryden Press. Chapter 2 contains a clear, humorous discussion of both probability and non-probability sampling.

Dillman, D.A., Eltringe, J.L., Groves, J.L. and Little, R.J.A. (eds) (2002) *Survey Nonresponse.* New York: Wiley Interscience. This book contains a wealth of information on survey non-response. Chapter 1 provides a useful overview in relation to the impact of survey design on non-response. This is discussed in more detail in Chapters 7 to 17, Chapter 14 referring specifically to business surveys and Chapter 15 to Internet-based surveys.

Patton, M.Q. (2002) *Qualitative Research and Evaluation Methods* (3rd edn). Thousand Oaks, CA: Sage. Chapter 5, 'Designing qualitative studies', contains a useful discussion of non-probability sampling techniques, with examples.

Case 7
Implementing strategic change initiatives

Source: Leif Skoogtors/Corbis

'I'm doing really well Mum, you don't have to worry about me. I've lots of friends here. We'll be working hard together. Besides, I have at least three months to complete my research project. No big deal. I will phone again soon. . .'

Mo Cheng put her mobile phone down and walked to the window by her desk. She looked out, scratching her head absentmindedly: 'I know I've told Mum not to fuss, but I am worried myself. My first meeting with my project tutor this morning didn't go as planned. Although Dr Smith agreed that my proposed research topic is interesting and "do-able", he was insistent that I come back to him with a clearer research design and methodology. In particular, he said my sampling section is weak and will need greater attention. I am not sure what he means and I have no idea how to improve things.'

Her concern was well-founded as she did not attend all of the research methods lectures and tutorials. Mo Cheng had struggled to work her way through the numerous module reading lists. A pragmatist at heart, she had arranged with a small number of her friends to take turns attending classes, thus creating time to catch up with the reading for their assignments whose deadlines seemed to be always just around the corner. At the time, she was sure that all she needed was to work her way through her friends' notes and read the module text, *Research Methods for Business Students*.

Now she had doubts as she couldn't quite read her friend's handwriting – no doubt made in haste as the lecturer always spoke quickly as she explained the topic for that session. Sighing, she put the notes down and picked up the module text instead. She turned to the index at the back of the book (something she had learnt from her English tutor) and began looking for the word 'sampling' . . .

Her project tutor also spoke of the need to establish access ahead of firming one's research design and to conduct a pilot study if not using a validated instrument. As her proposed study was to look at problems of implementing strategic change initiatives for mid-ranking officers in the Army, Mo Cheng was positive that access would not be a problem, given her father's position as a senior general. Mo Cheng was pleased that she had already 'piloted' her questionnaire with 20 of her friends straight after the project proposal was submitted, but in view of her project tutor's critique of her proposed methodology chapter, she decided not to say anything yet. She was sure that once she had made the necessary changes to her proposal, Dr Smith would not mind her having gone ahead with her pilot study.

A week in the university library thumbing through numerous research methods texts and journals articles (e.g. Scandura and Williams 2000; Sekaran 2003; Saunders *et al.* 2007) and reading through past research projects produced mixed results for Mo Cheng. She felt she had a greater appreciation of the research process and was certain that her survey-based research strategy was appropriate for her stated objective. She was exploring the factors underlying the apparent reluctance or failure of project personnel to capitalise on the lessons learned from previously completed strategic change projects (Balogun and Hailey 2004).

Mo Cheng was certain from her reading that a 'population' involves all the people or subjects under investigation, while a 'sample' consists of a smaller number of people within the population in question. Importantly, those chosen needed to be 'representative' of the population in their characteristics, attributes or values in order for her study findings and conclusions to be 'generalisable' from the sample to the population. Her population would be the mid-ranking officers in the armed forces. She also understood that sampling techniques refer to how a researcher would select respondents from the population. That is, Mo Cheng knew she could not possibly survey all of the mid-ranking officers and would therefore have to select a sample to approach – but that was the extent of her knowledge. Overwhelmed by the research methods texts' and articles' references to sampling frames, sample size calculations and sampling design, she tried discussing her problem with her friends but found that they were as confused and unsure as she was. She was beginning to fear that she would have to admit her shortfall to her project tutor – something she was really reluctant to do as she would have to own up to the missed lectures.

Later that week, she discovered a past research project in the library. Mo Cheng decided that, as long as she followed faithfully the steps taken in this project all would work out – after all, if it was in the library, it must have been good. She photocopied the entire method chapter and took it back to her room. She checked the sample size formula used in the project against her module text and notes that she had found on the Internet. She was still confused about references to levels of confidence and margins of error but recalled seeing many of the completed projects in the library having sample size estimations at a 95 per cent level of certainty. Most did not even raise the matter of the margin of error. She instinctively knew that a larger sample (although what that would be she still had no idea) would overcome the threat of a large error.

From a conversation with her father, she knew that there were about 200 middle-ranking officers in her city alone. She reasoned, 'As we have pretty standardised processes for recruitment and promotion in the armed forces, officers' attributes from any single geographical location should be representative of the overall population. With my father's help, I will have access to the right category of officers in my locality'. A friend, who is a statistician, advised that she should aim for at least 100 responses. Taking into account the tight lead-time between issuing the questionnaires and getting them back, she decided to be realistic and to assume an actual response rate of 80 per cent. Although tempted to use the formula used in the passed project (which was the same as the one she found on the Internet but differed from that in the textbook), Mo Cheng proceeded to work out the minimum number of study respondents required using the formula:

$$n^a = \frac{n \times 100}{re\%}$$

(*n* represented the 100 minimum responses (as advised by her friend and which represented a 50 per cent sample of the estimated number of officers in the area) and *re*% was the estimated response rate of 80 per cent.)

Mo Cheng whooped for joy when the result showed she needed 125 eligible respondents. She rang her father immediately. Naturally, the General was keen to help his daughter. He instructed Mo Cheng to email him the questionnaire and he would get his adjutant to 'do the rest'. He agreed to collect 'at least 125 responses' and said he would send the completed questionnaires back to her by courier in 10 days.

Putting the phone back on its rest, Mo Cheng smiled to herself, 'What a stroke of luck to have found my friend's completed project and now I can start my data collection without further delay. In the meantime, I will make the necessary changes to my proposal and submit that before seeing my project tutor. If all goes well, I will be finished well before the submission deadline. That should please my parents and I can go home earlier for that long-awaited holiday.'

References

Bolugan, J. and Hailey, V.H. (2004) *Exploring Strategic Change* (2nd edn). Harlow: Prentice Hall.

Scandura, T.A. and Williams, E.A. (2000) 'Research Methods in Management Current Practices, Trends, and Implications for Future Research', *Academy of Management Journal*, Vol. 43, No. 6, pp. 1248–64.

Saunders, M., Lewis, P. and Thornhill, A. (2007) *Research Methods for Business Students* (4th edn). Harlow: FT Prentice Hall.

Sekaran, U. (2003) *Research Methods for Business – A Skill Building Approach* (4th edn). New York: John Wiley & Sons.

Questions

1 Outline the advantages and disadvantages of Mo Cheng's decision to pilot her questionnaire with her friends.

2 Critically review Mo Cheng's approach to sampling and her subsequent data collection strategy. Can Mo Cheng meet her stated objective?

3 What advice would you give as Mo Cheng's project tutor to improve the quality of her study data? Give reasons for your answer.

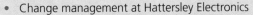

Additional case studies relating to material covered in this chapter are available via the book's Companion Website, **www.pearsoned.co.uk/saunders**. They are:

- Change management at Hattersley Electronics
- Employment networking in the Hollywood film industry
- Auditor independence and integrity in accounting firms.

Self-check answers

7.1 a A complete list of all directors of large manufacturing firms could be purchased from an organisation that specialised in selling such lists to use as the sampling frame. Alternatively, a list that contained only those selected for the sample could be purchased to reduce costs. These data are usually in a format suitable for being read by word-processing and database computer software, and so they could easily be merged into standard letters such as those included with questionnaires.

b A complete list of accountants, or one that contained only those selected for the sample, could be purchased from an organisation that specialised in selling such lists. Care would need to be taken regarding the precise composition of the list to ensure that it included those in private practice as well as those working for organisations. Alternatively, if the research was interested only in qualified accountants then the professional accountancy bodies' yearbooks, which list all their members and their addresses, could be used as the sampling frame.

c The personnel records or payroll of Cheltenham Gardens Ltd could be used. Either would provide an up-to-date list of all employees with their addresses.

7.2 Your draft of Lisa's tutor's reply is unlikely to be worded the same way as the one below. However, it should contain the same key points:

From: "tutor's name" <lisas.tutor@anytown.ac.uk>
To: <lisa@anytown.ac.uk>
Sent: today's date 7:06
Subject: Re: Help!!! Sampling non-response?

Hi Lisa
Many thanks for the email. This is not in the least unusual. I reckon to get about 1 in 20 interviews which go this way and you just have to say 'c'est la vie'. This is not a problem from a methods perspective as, in sampling terms, it can be treated as a non-response due to the person refusing to respond to your questions. This would mean you could not use the material. However, if he answered some other questions then you should treat this respondent as a partial non-response and just not use those answers.

Hope this helps.
'Tutor's name'

7.3 a Your answer will depend on the random numbers you selected. However, the process you follow to select the samples is likely to be similar to that outlined. Starting at randomly selected points, two sets of 20 two-digit random numbers are read from the random number tables (Appendix 3). If a number is selected twice it is disregarded. Two possible sets are:

Sample 1: 38 41 14 59 53 03 52 86 21 88 55 87 85 90 74 18 89 40 84 71
Sample 2: 28 00 06 70 81 76 36 65 30 27 92 73 20 87 58 15 69 22 77 31

These are then marked on the sampling frame (sample 1 is shaded blue, sample 2 is shaded orange) as shown below:

0	1163	20	1072	40	1257	60	1300	80	1034
1	10	21	7	41	29	61	39	81	55
2	57	22	92	42	84	62	73	82	66
3	149	23	105	43	97	63	161	83	165
4	205	24	157	44	265	64	275	84	301
5	163	25	214	45	187	65	170	85	161
6	1359	26	1440	46	1872	66	1598	86	1341
7	330	27	390	47	454	67	378	87	431
8	2097	28	1935	48	1822	68	1634	88	1756
9	1059	29	998	49	1091	69	1101	89	907
10	1037	30	1298	50	1251	70	1070	90	1158
11	59	31	10	51	9	71	37	91	27
12	68	32	70	52	93	72	88	92	66
13	166	33	159	53	103	73	102	93	147
14	302	34	276	54	264	74	157	94	203
15	161	35	215	55	189	75	168	95	163
16	1298	36	1450	56	1862	76	1602	96	1339
17	329	37	387	57	449	77	381	97	429
18	2103	38	1934	58	1799	78	1598	98	1760
19	1061	39	1000	59	1089	79	1099	99	898

b Your samples will probably produce patterns that cluster around certain numbers in the sampling frame, although the amount of clustering may differ, as illustrated by samples 1 and 2 above.

c The average (mean) annual output in tens of thousands of pounds will depend entirely upon your sample. For the two samples selected the averages are:

Sample 1 (blue): £6 752 000
Sample 2 (orange): £7 853 500

d There is no bias in either of the samples, as both have been selected at random. However, the average annual output calculated from sample 1 represents the total population more closely than that calculated from sample 2, although this has occurred entirely at random.

7.4 a Your answer will depend on the random number you select as the starting point for your systematic sample. However, the process you followed to select your sample is likely to be similar to that outlined. As a 10 per cent sample has been requested, the sampling fraction is $\frac{1}{10}$. Your starting point is selected using a random number between 0 and 9, in this case 2. Once the firm numbered 2 has been selected, every tenth firm is selected:

2   12   22   32   42   52   62   72   82   92

These are shaded orange on the sampling frame and will result in a regular pattern whatever the starting point:

0	1163	20	1072	40	1257	60	1300	80	1034
1	10	21	7	41	29	61	39	81	55
2	57	22	92	42	84	62	73	82	66
3	149	23	105	43	97	63	161	83	165
4	205	24	157	44	265	64	275	84	301
5	163	25	214	45	187	65	170	85	161
6	1359	26	1440	46	1872	66	1598	86	1341
7	330	27	390	47	454	67	378	87	431
8	2097	28	1935	48	1822	68	1634	88	1756
9	1059	29	998	49	1091	69	1101	89	907
10	1037	30	1298	50	1251	70	1070	90	1158
11	59	31	10	51	9	71	37	91	27
12	68	32	70	52	93	72	88	92	66
13	166	33	159	53	103	73	102	93	147
14	302	34	276	54	264	74	157	94	203
15	161	35	215	55	189	75	168	95	163
16	1298	36	1450	56	1862	76	1602	96	1339
17	329	37	387	57	449	77	381	97	429
18	2103	38	1934	58	1799	78	1598	98	1760
19	1061	39	1000	59	1089	79	1099	99	898

    b The average (mean) annual output of firms for your sample will depend upon where you started your systematic sample. For the sample selected above it is £757 000.

    c Systematic sampling has provided a poor estimate of the annual output because there is an underlying pattern in the data, which has resulted in firms with similar levels of output being selected.

7.5 **a** If you assume that there are at least 100 000 managing directors of small to medium-sized organisations from which to select your sample, you will need to interview approximately 380 to make generalisations that are accurate to within plus or minus 5 per cent (Table 7.1).

    b Either cluster or multi-stage sampling could be suitable; what is important is the reasoning behind your choice. This choice between cluster and multi-stage sampling is dependent on the amount of limited resources and time you have available. Using multi-stage sampling will take longer than cluster sampling as more sampling stages will need to be undertaken. However, the results are more likely to be representative of the total population owing to the possibility of stratifying the samples from the sub-areas.

7.6 **a** Prior to deciding on your quota you will need to consider the possible inclusion of residents who are aged less than 16 in your quota. Often in such research projects residents aged under 5 (and those aged 5–15) are excluded. You would need a quota of between 2000 and 5000 residents to obtain a reasonable accuracy. These should be divided proportionally between the groupings as illustrated in the possible quota below:

	Age group					
Gender	**16–19**	**20–29**	**30–44**	**45–59/64**	**60/65–74**	**75+**
Males	108	169	217	285	110	59
Females	154	209	180	203	205	99

  b Data on social class, employment status, socioeconomic status or car ownership could also be used as further quotas. These data are available from the Census and are likely to affect shopping habits.

  c Interviewers might choose respondents who were easily accessible or appeared willing to answer the questions. In addition, they might fill in their quota incorrectly or make up the data.

7.7 **a** Either snowball sampling as it would be difficult to identify members of the desired population or, possibly, convenience sampling because of initial difficulties in finding members of the desired population.

  b Quota sampling to ensure that the variability in the population as a whole is represented.

  c Purposive sampling to ensure that the full variety of responses are obtained from a range of respondents from the population.

  d Self-selection sampling as it requires people who are interested in the topic.

  e Convenience sampling owing to the very short timescales available and the need to have at least some idea of members' opinions.

Get ahead using resources on the Companion Website at:
www.pearsoned.co.uk/saunders

- Improve your SPSS and NVivo research analysis with practice tutorials.
- Save time researching on the Internet with the Smarter Online Searching Guide.
- Test your progress using self-assessment questions.
- Follow live links to useful websites.

Chapter 8

Using secondary data

Learning outcomes

By the end of this chapter you should be able to:

- identify the full variety of secondary data that are available;
- appreciate ways in which secondary data can be utilised to help to answer research question(s) and to meet objectives;
- understand the advantages and disadvantages of using secondary data in research projects;
- use a range of techniques, including published guides and the Internet, to locate secondary data;
- evaluate the suitability of secondary data for answering research question(s) and meeting objectives in terms of coverage, validity, reliability and measurement bias;
- apply the knowledge, skills and understanding gained to your own research project.

8.1 Introduction

When first considering how to answer their research question(s) or meet their objectives, few of our students consider initially the possibility of reanalysing data that have already been collected for some other purpose. Such data are known as **secondary data**. Most automatically think in terms of collecting new (**primary**) **data** specifically for that purpose. Yet, despite this, such secondary data can provide a useful source from which to answer, or partially to answer, your research question(s).

Secondary data include both raw data and published summaries. Most organisations collect and store a variety of data to support their operations: for example, payroll details, copies of letters, minutes of meetings and accounts of sales of goods or services. Quality daily newspapers contain a wealth of data, including reports about takeover bids and companies' share prices. Government departments undertake surveys and publish official statistics covering social, demographic and economic topics. Consumer research organisations collect data that are used subsequently by different clients. Trade organisations collect data from their members on topics such as sales that are subsequently aggregated and published.

Some of these data, in particular, documents such as company minutes, are available only from the organisations that produce them, and so access will need to be negotiated (Section 6.3). Others, including government surveys such as a census of population, are widely available in published form as well as via the Internet or on CD-ROM in university libraries. A growing variety have been deposited in, and are available from, data archives. In addition, the vast majority of companies and professional organisations have their own Internet sites from which data may be obtained. Online computer databases containing company information can be accessed via the Internet through information gateways, such as Biz/Ed (Table 3.5).

For certain types of research project, such as those requiring national or international comparisons, secondary data will probably provide the main source to answer your research question(s) and to address your objectives. However, if you are undertaking your research project as part of a course of study, we recommend that you check the assessment regulations before

These days, data about people's whereabouts, purchases, behaviour and personal lives are gathered, stored and shared on a scale that no repressive political dictator would ever have thought possible. Much of the time, there is nothing obviously sinister about this. Governments say they need to gather data to assist the fight against terrorism or protect public safety; commercial organisations argue that they do it to deliver goods and services more effectively. But the widespread use of electronic data-gathering and processing is remarkable compared with the situation even as recently as 10 years ago.

We can all think of examples of how the technology reveals information about what we have been doing. The Oyster payment card used on the London Underground system tells those who want to know where we have travelled and at what time; the mobile phone allows identification of where we are at a particular time and the credit card will show where and when we make purchases; many of our telephone calls to call centres are recorded and the search engine Google stores data on our web searches for 18 months.

Such data are obtained every time we interact directly or indirectly with these organisations' electronic systems. These data are often reused for purposes other than that for which they were originally collected.

Oyster card
Source: © Philip Lewis 2008.

They are aggregated to provide information about, for example, different geographical regions or social groups. They are merged with other data to form new data sets, the creation of these secondary data sets allowing new relationships to be explored. They are also made available or sold to other people and organisations for new purposes as secondary data.

deciding to rely entirely on secondary data. You may be required to collect primary data for your research project. Most research questions are answered using some combination of secondary and primary data. Where limited appropriate secondary data are available, you will have to rely mainly on data you collect yourself.

In this chapter we examine the different types of secondary data that are likely to be available to help you to answer your research question(s) and meet your objectives, how you might use them (Section 8.2), and a range of methods, including published guides, for locating these data (Section 8.3). We then consider the advantages and disadvantages of using secondary data (Section 8.4) and discuss ways of evaluating their validity and reliability (Section 8.5). We do not attempt to provide a comprehensive list of secondary data sources, as this would be an impossible task within the space available.

8.2 Types of secondary data and uses in research

Secondary data include both quantitative and qualitative data (Section 5.4), and they are used principally in both descriptive and explanatory research. The data you use may be **raw data**, where there has been little if any processing, or **compiled data** that have received some form of selection or summarising (Kervin 1999). Within business and management research such data are used most frequently as part of a case study or survey research strategy. However, there is no reason not to include secondary data in other research strategies, including archival research, action research and experimental research.

Different researchers (e.g. Bryman 1989; Dale *et al.* 1988; Hakim 1982, 2000; Robson 2002) have generated a variety of classifications for secondary data. These classifications do not, however, capture the full variety of data. We have therefore built on their ideas to create three main sub-groups of secondary data: documentary data, survey-based data, and those compiled from multiple sources (Figure 8.1).

Documentary secondary data

Documentary secondary data are often used in research projects that also use primary data collection methods. However, you can also use them on their own or with other sources of secondary data, for example for business history research within an archival research strategy. Documentary secondary data include written materials such as notices, correspondence (including emails), minutes of meetings, reports to shareholders, diaries, transcripts of speeches and administrative and public records (Box 8.1). Written documents can also include books, journal and magazine articles and newspapers. These can be important raw data sources in their own right, as well as a storage medium for compiled data. You could use written documents to provide qualitative data such as managers' espoused reasons for decisions. They could also be used to generate statistical measures such as data on absenteeism and profitability derived from company records (Bryman 1989).

Documentary secondary data also include non-written materials (Figure 8.2), such as voice and video recordings, pictures, drawings, films and television programmes (Robson 2002), DVDs and CD-ROMs as well as organisations' databases. These data can be analysed both quantitatively and qualitatively. In addition, they can be used to help to triangulate findings based on other data, such as written documents and primary data collected through observation, interviews or questionnaires (Chapters 9, 10 and 11).

For your research project, the documentary sources you have available will depend on whether you have been granted access to an organisation's records as well as on your

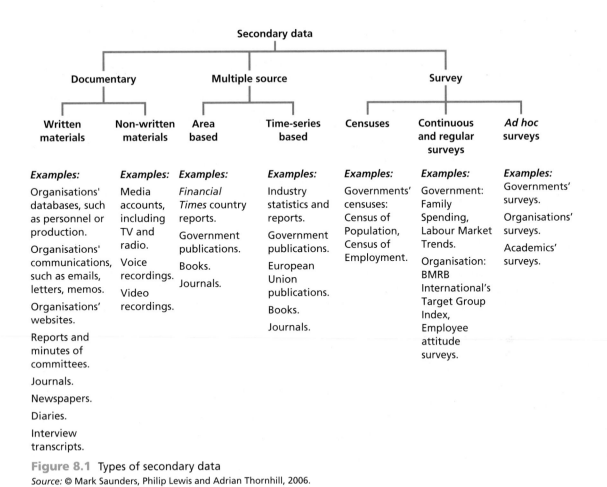

Figure 8.1 Types of secondary data
Source: © Mark Saunders, Philip Lewis and Adrian Thornhill, 2006.

success in locating library, data archive and commercial sources (Section 8.3). Access to an organisation's data will be dependent on gatekeepers within that organisation (Section 6.3). In our experience, those research projects that make use of documentary secondary data often do so as part of a within-company action research project or a case study of a particular organisation.

Survey-based secondary data

Survey-based secondary data refers to data collected using a survey strategy, usually by questionnaires (Chapter 11) that have already been analysed for their original purpose. Such data normally refer to organisations, people or households. They are made available as compiled data tables or, increasingly frequently, as a downloadable matrix of raw data (Section 12.2) for secondary analysis.

Survey-based secondary data will have been collected through one of three distinct sub-types of survey strategy: censuses, continuous/regular surveys or ad hoc surveys (Figure 8.1). Censuses are usually carried out by governments and are unique because, unlike surveys, participation is obligatory (Hakim 2000). Consequently, they provide very good coverage of the population surveyed. They include censuses of population, which have been carried out in many countries since the eighteenth century and in the UK

Box 8.1
Focus on student research

Using documentary secondary data

Sasha was interested in how her work placement organisation dealt with complaints by customers. Her mentor within the organisation arranged for her to have access to the paper-based files containing customers' letters of complaint and the replies sent by the organisation's customer-relations team (written documentary secondary data). Reading through the customer's letters, Sasha soon realised that many of these customers wrote to complain because they had not received a satisfactory response when they had complained earlier by telephone. She, therefore, asked her mentor if records were kept of complaints made by customers by telephone. Her mentor said that summary details of all telephone conversations by the customer-relations team, including complaints, were kept in their database (written documentary secondary data) and offered to find out precisely what data were held. Her mentor was, however, doubtful as to whether these data would be as detailed as the customers' letters.

On receiving details of the data held in the customer-relations database, Sasha realised that the next stage would be to match the complaints data from the paper-based files with telephone complaints data. The latter, she hoped, would enable her to to obtain a complete list of all complaints and set the written complaints in context of all complaints received by the organisation.

since 1801 (Office for National Statistics 2001), and other surveys, such as the UK Annual Survey of Hours and Earnings. Published tabulations are available via the Internet for more recent UK censuses, but it is now also possible to obtain the raw data 100 years after census via the Internet (see Table 8.3). In contrast, the UK Annual Survey of Hours and Earnings, which replaced the New Earnings Survey (1970–2003), provides information on the levels, make-up and distribution of earnings as well as details of hours worked and is only published online (Office for National Statistics 2007a). The data from censuses conducted by many governments are intended to meet the needs of government departments as well as of local government. As a consequence they are usually clearly defined, well documented and of a high quality. Such data are easily accessible in compiled form, and are widely used by other organisations and individual researchers.

Continuous and regular surveys are those surveys, excluding censuses, that are repeated over time (Hakim 1982). They include surveys where data are collected throughout the year, such as the UK's *Social Trends* (Office for National Statistics 2007d), and those repeated at regular intervals. The latter include the Labour Force Survey, which since 1998 has been undertaken quarterly using a core set of questions by Member States throughout the European Union. This means that some comparative data are available for Member States, although access to these data is limited by European and individual countries' legislation (Office for National Statistics 2007a). Non-governmental bodies also carry out regular surveys. These include general-purpose market research surveys such as BMRB International's Target Group Index. Because of the Target Group Index's commercial nature, the data are very expensive. However, BMRB International has provided copies of reports (usually over three years old) to between 20 and 30 UK university libraries. Many large organisations undertake regular surveys, a common example being the employee attitude survey. However, because of the sensitive nature of such information, it is often difficult to gain access to such survey data, especially in its raw form.

Census and continuous and regular survey data provide a useful resource with which to compare or set in context your own research findings. Aggregate data are often available via the Internet, on CD-ROMs or in published form in libraries (Section 8.3), in particular, for government surveys. When using these data you need to check when they were collected, as it often takes at least a year for publication to occur! If you are undertaking research in one UK organisation, you could use these data to place your case-study organisation within the context of its industry group or division using the Census of Employment. Aggregated results of the Census of Employment can be found in *Labour Market Trends* as well as via the UK government's official statistics information gateway *national statistics*. Alternatively, you might explore issues already highlighted by data from an organisation survey through in-depth interviews.

Survey secondary data may be available in sufficient detail to provide the main data set from which to answer your research question(s) and to meet your objectives. Alternatively, they may be the only way in which you can obtain the required data. If your research question is concerned with national variations in consumer spending it is unlikely that you will be able to collect sufficient data. You, therefore, will need to rely on secondary data such as those contained in *Family Spending* (formerly the Family Expenditure Survey; Office for National Statistics 2007b). This reports findings from the Expenditure and Foods Survey. For some research questions and objectives suitable data will be available in published form. For others, you may need more disaggregated data. This may be available via the Internet (Section 3.4), on CD-ROM, or from archives (Section 8.3). We have found that for most business and management research involving secondary data you are unlikely to find all the data you require from one source. Rather, your research project is likely to involve detective work in which you build your own multiple-source data set using different data items from a variety of secondary data sources and perhaps linking these to primary data you have collected yourself (Box 8.2). Like all detective work, finding data that help to answer a research question or meet an objective is immensely satisfying.

Box 8.2
Focus on management research

Comparing eating habits in 1975 and 2000

Since 1975 food preparation and consumption in the UK has seen further and more intense dependence on food being treated as a commercial commodity. Eating and drinking out, the growth of pre-prepared convenience foods and the diffusion of domestic technologies have all impacted on the way in which food is provisioned and consumed. By 2000 eating and drinking out had become a thoroughly established social norm and food preparation a less time consuming activity.

In an article published in the *British Journal of Sociology*, Cheng *et al.* (2007) explore the sociological dimension of food consumption in the UK in the past three decades, the conclusions of which are of great interest and commercial value to all those industries concerned with the food provision.

Cheng *et al.* used two sets of data on individuals' use of time. The first consisted of data on 1274 people

in 1975 and the second, 8522 in 2000. Individuals were asked to keep diaries for seven days in 1975 and for one weekday and one weekend day in 2000. They were asked to record their activities in slots of 30 minutes in 1975 and 10 minutes in 2000. Cheng *et al.* used statistical techniques to take account of over-sampling of specific sub-groups and non-response and corrected for the distributions of sex and age and to bring the sample in line with the national population. Descriptive statistics of mean minutes spent in the components of the practice of eating, and rates of participation, were calculated in order to provide a broad overview of trends in food consumption. Multiple regression analysis was then employed to analyse the socio-demographic basis of the amount of time devoted to the various components of the practice of eating.

Cheng *et al.* found that there has been an overall decline in the amount of time devoted to the consumption of food in the UK. However they found that while time diary data provides strong confirmation of the greater pervasiveness of commercially prepared food provisioning, many aspects of the performance of eating are resilient to change. The researchers saw a substantial increase in the amount of time allocated to eating and drinking

> ## Box 8.2
> ## Focus on management
> ## research *(continued)*

away from home, and also greater variety in the duration of episodes. However, the duration of episodes for eating at home has remained stable since 1975. Cheng *et al.* found that eating out substitutes for eating at home to some extent, but does not cause a radical transformation in patterns of home-based eating and drinking. Thirdly the authors demonstrated that the shifting

temporal organisation of daily life does not appear to transform eating events. They noted an increase in episodes of eating out that are of a short duration, but no apparent decline in longer episodes. Eating remains a sociable and collective practice, despite shifting temporal pressures which make the coordination of eating events within social networks more difficult.

Social differentiation on the basis of employment status, gender, age and household composition persist. Data analysis reveals that some social divisions have eroded; but others persist, with household structure becoming a more important source of differentiation.

Ad hoc surveys are usually one-off surveys and are far more specific in their subject matter. They include data from questionnaires that have been undertaken by independent researchers as well as interviews undertaken by organisations and governments. Because of their *ad hoc* nature, you will probably find it more difficult to discover relevant surveys. However, it may be that an organisation in which you are undertaking research has conducted its own questionnaire, on an issue related to your research. Some organisations will provide you with a report containing aggregated data; others may be willing to let you reanalyse the raw data from this *ad hoc* survey. Alternatively, you may be able to gain access to and use raw data from an *ad hoc* survey that has been deposited in an archive (Section 8.3).

Multiple-source secondary data

Multiple-source secondary data can be based entirely on documentary or on survey secondary data, or can be an amalgam of the two. The key factor is that different data sets have been combined to form another data set prior to your accessing the data. One of the more common types of multiple-source data that you are likely to come across in document form is various compilations of company information such as *Europe's 15,000 Largest Companies* (ELC International 2007). This contains comparable data on the top 15 000 European companies ranked by sales, profits and number of employees as well as alphabetical listings. Other multiple-source secondary data include the various shares price listings for different stock markets in the financial pages of quality newspapers. These are available in most university libraries, including back copies CD-ROM or microfilm. However, you need to beware of relying on CD-ROM copies for tabular data or diagrams as a few still contain only the text of articles.

The way in which a multiple-source data set has been compiled will dictate the sorts of research question(s) or objectives with which you can use it. One method of compilation is to extract and combine selected comparable variables from a number of surveys or from the same survey that has been repeated a number of times to provide a **time series** of data. For many research projects of undergraduate and taught Masters courses, this is one of the few ways in which you will be able to get data over a long period to undertake a longitudinal study. Other ways of obtaining time-series data are to use a series of company documents, such as appointment letters or public and administrative records, to create your own longitudinal secondary data set. Examples include the UK Employment Department's stoppages at work data held by the Data Archive based at the University of Essex and those derived by researchers from nineteenth-century population census returns, which, in the UK, are accessible to the public after 100 years.

Data can also be compiled for the same population over time using a series of 'snapshots' to form **cohort studies**. Such studies are relatively rare, owing to the difficulty of maintaining contact with members of the cohort from year to year. An example is the UK television series, 'Seven Up' (already mentioned in Section 5.5), which has followed a cohort since they were schoolchildren at seven-year intervals for over 50 years.

Secondary data from different sources can also be combined, if they have the same geographical basis, to form area-based data sets (Hakim 2000). Such data sets usually draw together quantifiable information and statistics, and are commonly produced by governments for their country. Area-based multiple-source data sets are usually available in published form for the countries and their component standard economic planning regions. Those more widely used by our students include the UK's *Annual Abstract of Statistics* (Office for National Statistics 2008), *Europe in figures: Eurostat Yearbook 2008* (Eurostat 2008a) and the journal, *Labour Market Trends*. Area-based multiple-source data sets are also available from data archives. These include data such as the Labour Force Survey (Office for National Statistics 2007c) and Eurostat's statistical data collections for member countries (Eurostat 2008b).

8.3 Locating secondary data

Unless you are approaching your research project with the intention of analysing one specific secondary data set that you already know well, your first step will be to ascertain whether the data you need are available. Your research question(s), objectives and the literature you have reviewed will guide this. For many research projects you are likely to be unsure as to whether the data you require are available as secondary data. Fortunately, there are a number of pointers to the sorts of data that are likely to be available.

The breadth of data discussed in the previous sections serves only to emphasise the variety of possible locations in which such data may be found. Finding relevant secondary data requires detective work, which has two interlinked stages:

1 establishing that the sort of data you require are likely to be available as secondary data;
2 locating the precise data you require.

The availability of secondary data

There are a number of clues to whether the secondary data you require are likely to be available. As part of your literature review you will have already read books and journal articles on your chosen topic. Where these have made use of secondary data, they will provide you with an idea of the sort of data that are available. In addition, these books and articles should contain full references to the sources of the data. Where these refer to published secondary data such as multiple-source or survey reports it is usually relatively easy to track down the original source. Quality national newspapers are also often a good source as they often report summary findings of recent government reports. Your tutors have probably already suggested that you read a quality national newspaper on a regular basis, advice we would fully endorse as it is an excellent way of keeping up to date with recent events in the business world. In addition, there are now many online news services, such as BBC News Online (see Box 8.3).

References for unpublished and documentary secondary data are often less specific, referring to 'unpublished survey results' or an 'in-house company survey'. Although these may be insufficient to locate or access the actual secondary data, they still provide useful clues about the sort of data that might be found within organisations and which might prove useful. Subject-specific textbooks such as Curran and Blackburn's (2001) *Researching the Small Enterprise* can provide a clear indication of the secondary sources available in

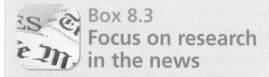

Box 8.3
Focus on research in the news

Britain's favourite fakes: public attitudes to counterfeiting

A 2008 episode of the BBC TV business programme, 'The Money Programme' revealed that counterfeiting cost Britain around £11 bn last year. The programme compared 2008 with the situation 20 years ago when the counterfeiting business was 1 per cent of the its 2008 size. The programme advanced the view that counterfeiting is a serious problem for businesses. A contributor to the programme felt that if businesses had a line in their annual report detailing sales lost due to counterfeits, then more would be done to solve the problem.

The British Video Association believes that nearly 80 million fake DVDs are bought each year in Britain, and it appears to be a growing problem. In 2007, 2.8 million fake DVDs were seized by the authorities, a 74 per cent increase on the previous year. Electrical goods giant Canon has seen its video cameras, and printer cartridges counterfeited. The whole electronics industry is affected. In Europe the printer cartridge market is worth some €30 bn ($44 bn; £22 bn) a year and it's estimated that 7 per cent of it is counterfeit. More worryingly, Canon and other electronics manufacturers are concerned about the rise in counterfeiting of products including batteries and chargers. These fakes have the potential to kill.

A 2007 MORI survey (IPSOS MORI 2007) of 996 adults aged 15+ in the UK shows that perfume/fragrance (67%), watches (64%) and clothing/footwear (63%) are among the most widely known goods to be counterfeited. 40% of respondents said that they would knowingly purchase a counterfeit product if the price and quality of the goods were acceptable. Among these people, the most popular counterfeit goods to purchase were clothing/footwear (76%), watches (43%) and perfume/fragrance (38%).

Around a third of respondents said that they would contact the local trading standards office if they had unknowingly purchased a counterfeit product. However, 29 per cent said that they would not do anything and that they would put it down to experience. Sixty-five per cent agreed that they were against any form of product counterfeiting, and 69 per cent said that the government should do more to tackle the problem of product counterfeiting.

The survey tested the level of the problems that counterfeiting causes: 61 per cent of respondents believed that the government loses millions of pounds in VAT and other taxes because of counterfeiting; 57 per cent thought that counterfeiting can damage the economic well-being of businesses; 56 per cent felt that some fake or counterfeit products can put the purchaser at risk of personal injury or death, and 39 per cent thought that counterfeiting is very often one of the most profitable (and virtually risk-free) illegal activities of organised criminals and terrorists and helps to fund drug dealing.

Source: derived from an article by Harcourt-Webster, Adam (2008) 'BBC Business', 14 Feb. Available at: http://news.bbc.co.uk/1/hi/business/7245040.stm

your research area, in this instance small enterprises. Other textbooks, such as Kingsbury's (1997) *IT Answers to HR Questions*, can provide you with valuable clues about the sort of documentary secondary data that are likely to exist within organisations' management information systems.

Tertiary literature such as indexes and catalogues can also help you to locate secondary data (Sections 3.2–3.4). Data archive catalogues, such as for the UK Data Archive at the University of Essex, may prove a useful source of the sorts of secondary data available.[1] This archive holds the UK's largest collection of qualitative and quantitative digital social science and humanities data sets for use by the research community (UK Data

---

[1]There are numerous other data archives in Europe and the USA. The UK Data Archive can provide access to international data through cooperative agreements and memberships of data archives throughout the world. It also provides a useful gateway to other data archives' websites, such as the Danish Data Archive, DDA and the Dutch Data Archive, Steinmetz (UK Data Archive 2008).

Archive, 2008). These data have been acquired from academic, commercial and government sources, and relate mainly to post-war Britain. The complete catalogue of these can be accessed and searched via the Internet (Section 3.5) through the Archive's home page (see Table 8.2). However, it should be remembered that the supply of data and documentation for all of the UK Data Archive's data sets is charged at cost, and there may be additional administrative and royalty charges.

More recently, online indexes and catalogues have become available with direct linkages to downloadable files, often in spreadsheet format. Government websites such as the UK government's *Directgov* and the European Union's *Europa* provide useful gateways to a wide range of statistical data, reports and legislative documents. However, although data from such government sources are usually of good quality, those from other sources may be neither valid nor reliable. It is important, therefore, that you evaluate the suitability of such secondary data for your research (Section 8.5).

Informal discussions are also often a useful source. Acknowledged experts, colleagues, librarians or your project tutor may well have knowledge of the sorts of data that might be available. In addition, there is a range of published guides to secondary data sources. Those business and management guides that we, and our students, have found most useful are outlined in Table 8.1. However, there are also guides that provide more detail on sources for specific subject areas such as marketing and finance.

Finding secondary data

Once you have ascertained that secondary data are likely to exist, you need to find their precise location. For secondary data published by governments this will be quite easy. Precise references are often given in published guides (Table 8.1) and, where other researchers have made use of them, a full reference should exist. Locating published secondary data that are likely to be held by libraries or secondary data held in archives is relatively

Table 8.1 Published guides to possible secondary data sources

Guide	Coverage
Corris, A., Yin, B. and Ricketts, C. (2000) *Guide to Official Statistics*. London: Office for National Statistics. Available at: http://www.statistics.gov.uk/downloads/theme_compendia/GOS2000_v5.pdf	Official statistics produced by UK government
Mort, D. (2002) *Business Information Handbook*. Headland: Headland Press	Company and market information, online business information and a who's who in business information
Mort, D. and Wilkins, W. (2000) *Sources of Unofficial United Kingdom Statistics* (4th edn). Aldershot: Gower	Unofficial UK statistics collected by major survey organisations; lists of who produces these data
Library Association (2005) *Libraries in the United Kingdom and Republic of Ireland.* London: Library Association	Lists of 3000 libraries in the UK and Eire
Dale, P. (2004) *Guide to Libraries and Information Units in Government Departments and Other Organisations* (34th edn). London: British Library Publishing	Lists libraries and information services in UK government departments and related agencies
McKenzie, E. (2003) *Guide to Libraries in Key UK Companies*. London: British Library	Lists libraries in UK companies that are prepared to accept serious enquiries from outside

Box 8.4
Focus on management research

Using content analysis of the literature to study cross-cultural advertising research

An article in *International Marketing Review* (Okazaki and Mueller 2007) reports a study of the recent history of cross-cultural advertising research and suggests new directions in exploring the role that culture plays in cross-national commercial communications.

To assess the research to date, the authors studied previously conducted content analyses of the literature, and updated these by performing an expanded longitudinal citation analysis of cross-cultural advertising investigations. They used only studies which examined two or more countries in the analysis. Articles were selected from seven journals considered representative in terms of international marketing and advertising research. The publications were analysed by topic areas addressed, research methods employed, and countries examined.

Okazaki and Mueller's analysis revealed that cultural values were the most studied topic area. In terms of methodology, content analysis was the most widely employed approach, followed by surveys. North America and the 'original' EU member countries were most frequently investigated. In contrast, they found that research focusing on newer EU member countries was limited Moreover, there was notable lack of research on Latin America, the Middle East and, in particular, Africa.

Okazaki and Mueller summarised the major cultural theories that have dominated cross-cultural advertising research to date, including Hofstede's (1980) cultural dimensions, albeit they noted that researchers are turning to other disciplines for new insights.

straightforward (Box 8.4). Specialist libraries with specific subject collections such as market research reports can usually be located using the Library Association's (2005) publication or guides by Dale (2004) and McKenzie (2003) (Table 8.1). If you are unsure where to start, confess your ignorance and ask a librarian. This will usually result in a great deal of helpful advice, as well as saving you time. Once the appropriate abstracting tool or catalogue has been located and its use demonstrated, it can be searched using similar techniques to those employed in your literature search (Section 3.5).

Data that are held by organisations are more difficult to locate. For within-organisation data we have found that the information or data manager within the appropriate department is most likely to know the precise secondary data that are held. This is the person who will also help or hinder your eventual access to the data and can be thought of as the gatekeeper to the information (Section 6.3).

Data on the Internet can be located using information gateways such as the University of Michigan's Documents Center (Table 8.2), and search tools where you search for all possible locations that match key words associated with your research question(s) or objectives (Section 3.5). In some cases data will be located at sites hosted by companies and professional organisations and trade associationsu. A good way of finding an organisation's home page is to use a general search engine (Table 3.5) or, in the case of UK-based companies, the links provided by the Yellow Pages UK subject directory (Table 3.5). Additional guidance regarding how to use general search engines such as Google is given in Marketing Insights' *Smarter Internet Searching Guide*, which is available via this book's web page. However, searching for relevant data is often very time consuming. In addition, although the amount of data on the Internet is increasing rapidly, some of it is, in our experience, of dubious quality. The evaluation of secondary data sources, including those available via the Internet, is discussed in Section 8.5.

Once you have located a possible secondary data set, you need to be certain that it will meet your needs. For documentary data or data in a published form the easiest way is to

Table 8.2 Selected information gateways to secondary data on the Internet

Name	Internet address	Comment
Biz/ed	http://www.bized.co.uk/	Gateway for primary and secondary business and management information. UK focus
Directgov	http://www.direct.gov.uk/	UK government information service with links to government departments, official statistics, etc.
Europa	http://europa.eu.int	Information (including press releases, legislation, fact sheets) published by European Union. Links include Eurostat statistics information gateway
RBA Information Services	http://www.rba.co.uk/	Business information gateway with links to business, statistical, government and country sites
SOSIG	http://www.sosig.ac.uk	Evaluates and describes social science sites including those with statistical data. UK focus
UK Data Archive	http://www.data-archive.ac.uk	Collection of UK digital data in the social science and humanities fields. Links to data archives worldwide
University of Michigan	http://www.lib.umich.edu/govdocs/	Although predominantly American in focus, has excellent annotated links to international agencies, non-American governmental websites and their statistical agencies

obtain and evaluate a sample copy of the data and a detailed description of how it was collected. For survey data that are available in computer-readable form, this is likely to involve some cost. One alternative is to obtain and evaluate detailed definitions for the data set variables (which include how they are coded; Section 12.2) and the documentation that describes how the data were collected. This evaluation process is discussed in Section 8.5.

Table 8.3 Selected secondary data sites on the Internet

Name	Internet address	Comment
Economic and Social Data Service (ESDS)	http://www.esds.ac.uk	Access to and support for economic and social data, both quantitative and qualitative for both the UK and other countries
FT Info	http://news.ft.com/	Company information on 11 000 companies, including financial performance
Global Market Information Database	http://www.gmid.euromonitor.com	Produced by Euromonitor. Key business intelligence on countries, companies, markets, and consumers
Hemscott	http://www.hemscott.net	Hemmington Scott's guide to companies and investment trusts, report service and market activity analysis
Hoover's Online	http://www.hoovers.com	Company information on 12 000 US and international companies
MIMAS	http://www.mimas.ac.uk	National data centre for UK higher education institutions providing access to key data such as UK census. NB: for some data sets you will need to register through your university

Table 8.3 *(continued)*

Countries	Internet address	Comment
European Union	http://europa.eu.int/comm/eurostat/	Site of European Union's statistical information service. This site is available in English as well as other languages
France	http://www.insee.fr	Site of France's National Institute for Statistics including both statistics and government publications. Much of this website is available in English
Germany	http://www.destatis.de	Site of Germany's Federal Statistical Office with a number of useful links. Much of this website is available in English
Ireland (Eire)	http://www.cso.ie	Site of the Irish Central Statistical Office (CSO), the government body responsible for compiling Irish official statistics
Netherlands	http://www.cbs.nl	Site of the Netherland's Central Bureau of Statistics (CBS). Much of this website is available in English. Provides access to StatLine, which contains statistical data that can be downloaded free of charge
United Kingdom	http://www.statistics.gov.uk	The official UK statistics site containing official UK statistics and information about statistics, which can be accessed and downloaded free of charge

8.4 Advantages and disadvantages of secondary data

Advantages

May have fewer resource requirements

For many research questions and objectives the main advantage of using secondary data is the enormous saving in resources, in particular your time and money (Ghauri and Grønhaug 2005). In general, it is much less expensive to use secondary data than to collect the data yourself. Consequently, you may be able to analyse far larger data sets such as those collected by government surveys. You will also have more time to think about theoretical aims and substantive issues, as your data will already be collected, and subsequently you will be able to spend more time and effort analysing and interpreting the data.

Unobtrusive

If you need your data quickly, secondary data may be the only viable alternative. In addition, they are likely to be higher-quality data than could be obtained by collecting your own (Stewart and Kamins 1993). Using secondary data within organisations may also have the advantage that, because they have already been collected, they provide an unobtrusive measure. Cowton (1998) refers to this advantage as eavesdropping, emphasising its benefits for sensitive situations.

Longitudinal studies may be feasible

For many research projects time constraints mean that secondary data provide the only possibility of undertaking longitudinal studies. This is possible either by creating your own or by using an existing multiple-source data set (Section 8.2). Comparative research may also be possible if comparable data are available. You may find this to be of particular use for research questions and objectives that require regional or international comparisons. However, you need to ensure that the data you are comparing were collected and recorded using methods that are comparable. Comparisons relying on unpublished data or data that are currently unavailable in that format, such as the creation of new tables from existing census data, are likely to be expensive, as such tabulations will have to be specially prepared. In addition, your research is dependent on access being granted by the owners of the data, principally governments (Dale *et al.* 1988), although this is becoming easier as more data is made available via the Internet. In addition, many countries are enshrining increased rights of access to information held by public authorities through freedom of information legislation such as the UK's Freedom of Information Act 2005. This gives you a general right to access to recorded information held by public authorities, although a charge may be payable (Information Commissioner's Office 2008). However, this is dependent upon your request not being contrary to relevant data protection legislation or agreements (Chapter 6.5).

Can provide comparative and contextual data

Often it can be useful to compare data that you have collected with secondary data. This means that you can place your own findings within a more general context or, alternatively, triangulate your findings (Section 5.3). If you have undertaken a sample survey, perhaps of potential customers, secondary data such as the Census can be used to assess the generalisability of findings, in other words how representative these data are of the total population (Section 7.2).

Can result in unforeseen discoveries

Re-analysing secondary data can also lead to unforeseen or unexpected new discoveries. Dale *et al.* (1988) cite establishing the link between smoking and lung cancer as an example of such a serendipitous discovery. In this example the link was established through secondary analysis of medical records that had not been collected with the intention of exploring any such relationship.

Permanence of data

Unlike data that you collect yourself, secondary data generally provide a source of data that is both permanent and available in a form that may be checked relatively easily by others (Denscombe 2007). This means that the data and your research findings are more open to public scrutiny.

Disadvantages

May be collected for a purpose that does not match your need

Data that you collect yourself will be collected with a specific purpose in mind: to answer your research question(s) and to meet your objectives. Unfortunately, secondary data will

Box 8.5
Focus on management research

The pitfalls of secondary data

Alison Wolf is the Sir Roy Griffiths Professor of public-sector management at King's College, London. In a 2007 article in *The Times Higher Education Supplement* (Wolf 2007), she issues some warnings to students using secondary data in their research, particularly in an era when such data are readily available on the Internet. Her main concern is the lack of questioning that many of us adopt when approaching secondary data. In her view many of us 'have a tendency to assume that quantitative data must be out there waiting to be found: on the web, organised and collated. How the figures get there and who collected the data and analysed them are not questions they seem to ask. Nor do they probe definitions (let alone response rates) – or not unless and until they start trying to locate, manipulate and integrate a variety of data on a specific subject' (Wolf 2007).

According to Wolf, some of the major pitfalls are assuming that samples are representative; and that the people who filled in questionnaires all did so in such a way that we can put faith in the results. They may not have been truthful in their responses, have taken the questions seriously or, indeed, have understood fully the questions. Moreover, Wolf notes that it should not be assumed that whoever coded and entered the data knew what they were doing; and that it was clear what all the observations meant.

Wolf gives the example of one of her recent students who wanted to track how many history graduates from a given university enter teaching over a 20-year period. She points out that 'teaching' as a recorded student destination sometimes includes further education as well as schools, sometimes includes higher education as well, sometimes neither. Also, what counts as a 'history' graduate, may not be clear.

Wolf sounds other warning using the example of official UK government statistics. First, statistics that were routinely calculated can suddenly disappear. She gives the example of the decision, by the Office for National Statistics, suddenly to stop calculating average non-manual earnings. This caused major problems for one of her students. In addition, and more frequently, definitions change constantly in ways that seem to be dictated by changing government priorities which makes it difficult to track changes over time. Wolf cites the example of education, where statistics are reported in terms of performance targets that keep changing. She concludes that this is as serious matter as good statistics are at the heart of governmental accountability, as well as good policymaking.

have been collected for a specific purpose that differs from your research question(s) or objectives (Denscombe 2007). Consequently, the data you are considering may be inappropriate to your research question. If this is the case then you need to find an alternative source, or collect the data yourself! More probably, you will be able to answer your research question or address your objective only partially. Common reasons for this include the data being collected a few years earlier and so not being current, or the methods of collection differing between the original data sources which have been amalgamated subsequently to form the secondary data set you intend to use (Box 8.5). Where the data are non-current and you have access to primary data, such as in a research project that is examining an issue within an organisation, you are likely to have to combine secondary and primary data.

Access may be difficult or costly

Where data have been collected for commercial reasons, gaining access may be difficult or costly. Market research reports, such as those produced by Mintel or KeyNote, may cost a great deal. If the report(s) that you require are not available in your library, they can rarely be accessed free of charge via the Internet or borrowed on inter-library loan and you will need to identify (Section 8.3) and visit the library that holds that collection.

Aggregations and definitions may be unsuitable

The fact that secondary data were collected for a particular purpose may result in other, including ethical (Section 6.4), problems. Much of the secondary data you use is likely to be in published reports. As part of the compilation, process data will have been aggregated in some way. These aggregations, while meeting the requirements of the original research, may not be quite so suitable for your research (Box 8.6). The definitions of data variables may not be the most appropriate for your research question(s) or objectives. In addition, where you are intending to combine data sets, definitions may differ markedly or have been revised over time. Alternatively, the documents you are using may represent the interpretations of those who produced them, rather than offer an objective picture of reality.

Box 8.6
Focus on student research

Changing definitions

As part of his research, Jeremy wished to use longitudinal data on the numbers of males and females disaggregated by some form of social grouping. Using the UK government's national statistics website (Table 8.3),

he quickly found and downloaded data which classified males and females using the National Statistics Socio-economic Classification (NS-SEC). However, this classification appeared to have been used only from 2001. Prior to this date, two separate classifications had been used: social class (SC) and socio-economic group (SEG), for which much longer time series of data were available. Before arranging an appointment with his project tutor to discuss this potential problem, Jeremy made a note of the two classifications:

NS-SEC	SC	
1 Higher managerial and professional occupations	I	Professional
2 Lower managerial and professional occupations	II	Managerial and technical
3 Intermediate occupations	IIIa	Skilled non-manual
4 Small employers and own account workers	IIIb	Skilled manual
5 Lower supervisory and technical occupations	IV	Semi-skilled
6 Semi-routine occupations	V	Unskilled
7 Routine occupations		

During their meeting later that week, Jeremy's tutor referred him to research on the NS-SEC which compared this with the old measures of SC and SEG and made suggestions regarding the continuity of the measures. Jeremy noted down the reference:

Heath, A., Martin, J. and Beerten, R. (2003) 'Old and new social class measures – a comparison', in Rose, D. and Pevalin, D.J. (eds), *A Researcher's Guide to the National Statistics Socio-economic Classification*, London, Sage, pp. 226–42.

No real control over data quality

Although many of the secondary data sets available from governments and data archives are of higher quality than you could ever collect yourself, this is not always the case. For this reason care must be taken and data sources must be evaluated carefully, as outlined in Section 8.5.

Initial purpose may affect how data are presented

When using data that are presented as part of a report you also need to be aware of the purpose of that report and the impact that this will have on the way the data are presented. This is especially so for internal organisational documents and external documents such as published company reports and newspaper reports. Reichman (1962; cited by Stewart and Kamins 1993) emphasises this point referring to newspapers, although the sentiments apply to many documents. He argues that newspapers select what they consider to be the most significant points and emphasise these at the expense of supporting data. This, Reichman states, is not a criticism as the purpose of the reporting is to bring these points to the attention of readers rather than to provide a full and detailed account. However, if we generalise from these ideas, we can see that the culture, predispositions and ideals of those who originally collected and collated the secondary data will have influenced the nature of these data at least to some extent. For these reasons you must evaluate carefully any secondary data you intend to use. Possible ways of doing this are discussed in the next section.

8.5 Evaluating secondary data sources

Secondary data must be viewed with the same caution as any primary data that you collect. You need to be sure that:

- they will enable you to answer your research question(s) and to meet your objectives;
- the benefits associated with their use will be greater than the costs;
- you will be allowed access to the data (Section 6.3).

Secondary sources that appear relevant at first may not on closer examination be appropriate to your research question(s) or objectives. It is therefore important to evaluate the suitability of secondary data sources for your research.

Stewart and Kamins (1993) argue that, if you are using secondary data, you are at an advantage compared with researchers using primary data. Because the data already exist you can evaluate them prior to use. The time you spend evaluating any potential secondary data source is time well spent, as rejecting unsuitable data earlier can save much wasted time later! Such investigations are even more important when you have a number of possible secondary data sources you could use. Most authors suggest a range of validity and reliability (Section 5.6) criteria against which you can evaluate potential secondary data. These, we believe, can be incorporated into a three-stage process (Figure 8.2).

Alongside this process you need also to consider the accessibility of the secondary data. For some secondary data sources, in particular those available via the Internet or in your library, this will not be a problem. It may, however, still necessitate long hours working in the library if the sources are 'for reference only'. For other data sources, such as those within organisations, you need to obtain permission prior to gaining access. This will be necessary even if you are working for the organisation. These issues

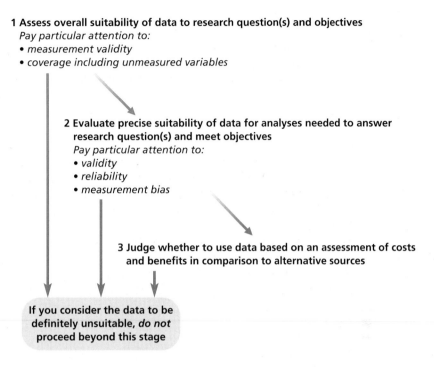

1 Assess overall suitability of data to research question(s) and objectives
Pay particular attention to:
- *measurement validity*
- *coverage including unmeasured variables*

2 Evaluate precise suitability of data for analyses needed to answer research question(s) and meet objectives
Pay particular attention to:
- *validity*
- *reliability*
- *measurement bias*

3 Judge whether to use data based on an assessment of costs and benefits in comparison to alternative sources

If you consider the data to be definitely unsuitable, *do not* proceed beyond this stage

Figure 8.2
Evaluating potential secondary data sources

are discussed in Section 6.3, so we can now consider the evaluation process in more detail.

Overall suitability

Measurement validity

One of the most important criteria for the suitability of any data set is **measurement validity**. Secondary data that fail to provide you with the information that you need to answer your research question(s) or meet your objectives will result in invalid answers (Kervin 1999). Often when you are using secondary survey data you will find that the measures used do not quite match those that you need (Jacob 1994). For example, a manufacturing organisation may record monthly sales whereas you are interested in monthly orders. This may cause you a problem when you undertake your analyses believing that you have found a relationship with sales whereas in fact your relationship is with the number of orders. Alternatively, you may be using minutes of company meetings as a proxy for what actually happened in those meetings. These are likely to reflect a particular interpretation of what happened, the events being recorded from a particular viewpoint, often the chairperson's. You, therefore, need to be cautious before accepting such records at face value (Denscombe 2007).

Unfortunately, there are no clear solutions to problems of measurement invalidity. All you can do is try to evaluate the extent of the data's validity and make your own decision. A common way of doing this is to examine how other researchers have coped with this problem for a similar secondary data set in a similar context. If they found that the measures, while not exact, were suitable, then you can be more certain that they will be suitable for your research question(s) and objectives. If they had problems, then you may be able to incorporate their suggestions as to how to overcome them. Your literature search (Sections 3.4 and 3.5) will probably have identified other such studies already.

Coverage and unmeasured variables

The other important suitability criterion is **coverage**. You need to be sure that the secondary data cover the population about which you need data, for the time period you need, and contain data variables that will enable you to answer your research question(s) and to meet your objectives. For all secondary data sets coverage will be concerned with two issues:

- ensuring that unwanted data are or can be excluded;
- ensuring that sufficient data remain for analyses to be undertaken once unwanted data have been excluded (Hakim 2000).

When analysing secondary survey data, you will need to exclude those data that are not relevant to your research question(s) or objectives. Service companies, for example, need to be excluded if you are concerned only with manufacturing companies. However, in doing this it may be that insufficient data remain for you to undertake the quantitative analyses you require (Sections 12.4 and 12.5). For documentary sources, you will need to ensure that the data contained relate to the population identified in your research. For example, check that the minutes are of board meetings and that they cover the required time period. Where you are intending to undertake a longitudinal study, you also need to ensure that the data are available for the entire period in which you are interested.

Some secondary data sets, in particular those collected using a survey strategy, may not include variables you have identified as necessary for your analysis. These are termed unmeasured variables. Their absence may not be particularly important if you are undertaking descriptive research. However, it could drastically affect the outcome of explanatory research as a potentially important variable has been excluded.

Precise suitability

Reliability and validity

The reliability and validity (Section 5.6) you ascribe to secondary data are functions of the method by which the data were collected and the source. You can make a quick assessment of these by looking at the source of the data. Dochartaigh (2002) and others refer to this as assessing the *authority* or reputation of the source. Survey data from large, well-known organisations such as those found in Mintel and Key Note market research reports are likely to be reliable and trustworthy. The continued existence of such organisations is dependent on the credibility of their data. Consequently, their procedures for collecting and compiling the data are likely to be well thought through and accurate. Survey data from government organisations are also likely to be reliable, although they may not always be perceived as such (Box 8.7). However, you will probably find the validity of documentary data such as organisations' records more difficult to assess. While organisations may argue that their records are reliable, there are often inconsistencies and inaccuracies. You, therefore, need also to examine the method by which the data were collected and try to ascertain the precision needed by the original (primary) user.

Dochartaigh (2002) suggests a number of areas for initial assessment of the authority of documents available via the Internet. These, we believe, can be adapted to assess the authority of all types of secondary data. First, as suggested in the previous paragraph, it is important to discover the person or organisation responsible for the data and to be able to obtain additional information through which you can assess the reliability of the source. For data in printed publications this is usually reasonably straightforward (Section 3.6). However, for secondary data obtained via the Internet it may be more difficult. Although

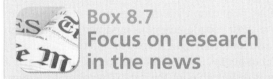

Box 8.7
Focus on research
in the news

The validity of politically sensitive data: binge-drinking in Australia

There has been much publicity in the UK in recent years about the problem of so-called 'binge drinking' – a term usually used to refer to heavy drinking over an evening or similar time span – and often associated with drinking with the intention of becoming intoxicated and, usually, in large groups. But it is not a phenomenon that is to be found in only the UK. A report in the *Sydney Morning Herald* (2008) indicates that it is also a problem in Australia. What this report also indicates is the sensitive political nature of subjects such as this which raise questions about the availability and validity of data on the subject.

The *Sydney Morning Herald* reports that two Sydney pubs named hotels of the year over the past three years have also topped a police list of the 100 most violent pubs and clubs in the state. The Mean Fiddler Hotel at Rouse Hill and The Coogee Bay Hotel are ranked one and two on a list of assaults on licensed premises for 2007. The *Herald* has obtained the figures of assaults in pubs and clubs after a year-long freedom-of-information battle to obtain more comprehensive data held by police that include offences committed on the street after drinkers have left licensed premises. While the battle for this detail continues, the assault data provides the best guide yet to where alcohol-related violence is happening. They rank the Mean Fiddler with 51 assaults at the top, followed by the Coogee Bay with 41.

The list of assaults in the top 100 licensed premises, obtained from the New South Wales (NSW) Bureau of Crime Statistics and Research, is based on police records compiled for the first nine months of last year. The figures only record assaults inside the hotel and were certain to grossly understate the real level of assaults, said the director of the NSW Bureau of Crime Statistics and Research, Don Weatherburn. 'We know from national surveys generally that the vast bulk of assaults are not reported,' he said. 'These would be the most serious assaults and probably the tip of the iceberg.' He said that the Bureau of Statistics carried out a national study on violence in 2005 which found that 33.8 per cent of all assaults for males occurred on licensed premises while the figures for all people were 25 per cent. 'That's why I think the police figures grossly underestimate the number of assaults on licensed premises,' said Dr Weatherburn.

The release of the list of the most violent hotels comes a fortnight after the Prime Minister, Kevin Rudd, said binge drinking among young people had reached epidemic proportions, and that police had told him alcohol abuse 'lies at the core of increasing spates of urban violence around the country'. Just before he made his remarks, the Alcohol Education and Rehabilitation Foundation produced a report on violence and alcohol that found one in 10 Australians were frightened by a drunk during the festive season.

Despite growing pressure for new strategies to curb the level of alcohol-fuelled violence, such as curbing the trading hours of late-opening hotels like the Coogee Bay and the Mean Fiddler, NSW Police and the Australian Hotels Association are fighting to stop the release under freedom-of-information laws of data linking alcohol-related incidents to hotels or clubs, including incidents which take place off the premises. The *Herald* has been trying for more than a year to see the data, which have been gathered by police for nearly a decade. Police have been asking people who were victims or perpetrators of an offence where they were last drinking. As well as assaults, the data include other offences, such as driving and malicious damage.

Police say it would cause 'an unreasonable adverse effect' on the hotels to release the data and would undermine the programme that is designed to reduce the number of alcohol-related incidents by discussing the data with the licensees. But many community groups and local-government officials say the data should be released as they would provide people with evidence about problems associated with hotels. The Mayor of Manly, Dr Peter Macdonald, said that there was not enough information available to consumers about problems linked to alcohol. 'The release of the data would allow patrons and potential patrons to know where a large number of incidents are regularly linked to a particular hotel and to include that information when deciding where to go, especially at night.'

organisation names, such as the 'Center for Research into . . .' or 'Institute for the Study of . . .', may appear initially to be credible, publication via the Internet is not controlled, and such names are sometimes used to suggest pseudo-academic credibility. Dochartaigh (2002) therefore suggests that you look also for a copyright statement and the existence of published documents relating to the data to help validation. The former of these, when it exists, can provide an indication of who is responsible for the data. The latter, he argues, reinforces the data's authority, as printed publications are regarded as more reliable. In addition, Internet sources often contain an email address or other means of contacting the author for comments and questions about the Internet site and its contents (Dees 2000). However, beware of applying these criteria too rigidly as sometimes the most authoritative web pages do not include the information outlined above. Dochartaigh (2002) suggests that this is because those with most authority often feel the least need to proclaim it!

For all secondary data, a detailed assessment of the validity and reliability will involve you in an assessment of the method or methods used to collect the data (Dale *et al.* 1988). These may be provided by hyperlinks for Internet-based data sets. Alternatively, they may be discussed in the methodology section of an associated report. Your assessment will involve looking at who were responsible for collecting or recording the information and examining the context in which the data were collected. From this you should gain some feeling regarding the likelihood of potential errors or biases. In addition, you need to look at the process by which the data were selected and collected or recorded. Where sampling has been used to select cases (usually as part of a survey strategy), the sampling procedure adopted and the associated sampling error and response rates (Section 7.2) will give clues to validity. Secondary data collected through a survey with a high response rate are also likely to be more reliable than from that with a low response rate. However, commercial providers of high-quality, reliable data sets may be unwilling to disclose details about how data were collected. This is particularly the case where these organisations see the methodology as important to their competitive advantage.

For some documentary sources, such as diaries, transcripts of interviews or meetings, it is unlikely that there will be a formal methodology describing how the data were collected. The reliability of these data will therefore be difficult to assess, although you may be able to discover the context in which the data were collected. For example, letters, emails and memos contain no formal obligation for the writer to give a full and accurate portrayal of events. Rather they are written from a personal point of view and expect the recipient to be aware of the context (Denscombe 2007). This means that these data are more likely to be useful as a source of the writer's perceptions and views than as an objective account of reality. The fact that you did not collect and were not present when these data were collected will also affect your analyses. Dale *et al.* (1988) argue that full analyses of in-depth interview data require an understanding derived from participating in social interactions that cannot be fully recorded on tape or by transcript.

The validity and reliability of collection methods for survey data will be easier to assess where you have a clear explanation of the techniques used to collect the data. This needs to include a clear explanation of any sampling techniques used and response rates (discussed earlier) as well as a copy of the survey instrument, which will usually be a questionnaire. By examining the questions by which data were collected, you will gain a further indication of the validity.

Where data have been compiled, as in a report, you need to pay careful attention to how these data were analysed and how the results are reported. Where percentages (or proportions) are used without actually giving the totals on which these figures are based, you need to examine the data very carefully. For example, a 50 per cent increase in the number of clients from two to three for a small company may be of less relevance than the 20 per cent increase in the number of clients from 1000 to 1200 for a larger company in the same market! Similarly, where quotations appear to be used selectively without other supporting evidence you should beware, as the data may be unreliable. Remember, the further away you are from the original data, the more difficult it will be to judge their quality (Patzer 1996).

Measurement bias

Measurement bias can occur for two reasons (Kervin 1999):

- deliberate or intentional distortion of data;
- changes in the way data are collected.

Deliberate distortion occurs when data are recorded inaccurately on purpose, and is most common for secondary data sources such as organisational records. Managers may deliberately fail to record minor accidents to improve safety reports for their departments. Data that have been collected to further a particular cause or the interests of a particular group are more likely to be suspect as the purpose of the study may be to reach a predetermined conclusion (Jacob 1994). Reports of consumer satisfaction surveys may deliberately play down negative comments to make the service appear better to their target audience of senior managers and shareholders, and graphs may deliberately be distorted to show an organisation in a more favourable light.

Other distortions may be deliberate but not intended for any advantage. Employees keeping time diaries might record only the approximate time spent on their main duties rather than accounting precisely for every minute. People responding to a structured interview (questionnaire) might adjust their responses to please the interviewer (Section 11.2).

Unfortunately, measurement bias resulting from deliberate distortion is difficult to detect. While we believe that you should adopt a neutral stance about the possibility of bias, you still need to look for pressures on the original source that might have biased the data. For written documents such as minutes, reports and memos the intended target audience may suggest possible bias, as indicated earlier in this section. Therefore, where possible you will need to triangulate the findings with other independent data sources. This is sometimes referred to as a *cross-check verification* (Patzer 1996). Where data from two or more independent sources suggest similar conclusions, you can have more confidence that the data on which they are based are not distorted. Conversely, where data suggest different conclusions you need to be more wary of the results.

Box 8.8
Focus on student research

Assessing the suitability of data available via the Internet

As part of a research project on changing consumer spending patterns in Europe, Jocelyn wished to establish how the cost of living had altered in the European Union since the accession of the 10 new Member States in 2004. Other research that she had read as part of her literature review had utilised the European Union's Harmonized Index of Consumer Prices (HICPs). She, therefore, decided to see whether this information was available via the Internet from the European Union's

Europa information gateway. On accessing the *Eurostat* home page, she noticed that there was a link to a report on 'Harmonized Indices of Consumer Prices'.

Jocelyn clicked on this link and downloaded the report (Eurostat 2008c), saving it onto her MP3 player. A brief look at the data suggested that it would be suitable in terms of coverage for her research. It also contained a link to the most recent (April 2008) HICPs which she downloaded.

Jocelyn was happy with the data's overall suitability and the credibility of the source, the data having been compiled for the European Union using data collected in each of the Member States. She also discovered that the actual data collected were governed by a series of European Union regulations.

Box 8.8
Focus on student research *(continued)*

Source: © European Communities, 2008. Reproduced with permission.

In order to be certain about the precise suitability of the HICPs, Jocelyn needed to find out exactly how the index had been calculated and how the data on which it was based had been collected. The *Eurostat* publication provided an overview of how the index was calculated, summarising the nature of goods and services that were included. The data for the HICPs were collected in each Member State using a combination of visits to local retailers and service providers and central collection (via mail, telephone, email and the Internet), over 1 million price observations being used each month! One potential problem was also highlighted: there was no uniform basket of goods and services applying to all member states. Rather, the precise nature of some goods and services included in the HICPs varied from country to country, reflecting the reality of expenditure in each of the countries. Jocelyn decided that this would not present too great a problem as she was going to use these data only to contextualise her research.

The Eurostat publication emphasised that the HICP was a price rather than a cost of living index. However, it also emphasised that, despite conceptual differences between price and the cost of living, there were unlikely to be substantial differences in practice. Jocelyn therefore decided to use the HICPs as a surrogate for the cost of living.

Changes in the way in which data were collected can also introduce changes in measurement bias. Provided that the method of collecting data remains constant in terms of the people collecting it and the procedures used, the measurement biases should remain constant. Once the method is altered, perhaps through a new procedure of taking minutes or a new data collection form, then the bias also changes. This is very important for longitudinal data sets such as the UK's Retail Price Index where you are interested in trends rather than actual numbers. Your detection of biases is dependent on discovering that the way data are recorded has changed. Within-company sources are less likely to have documented these changes than government-sponsored sources.

Costs and benefits

Kervin (1999) argues that the final criterion for assessing secondary data is a comparison of the costs of acquiring them with the benefits they will bring. Costs include both time and financial resources that you will need to devote to obtaining the data. Some data will be available in your local library and so will be free, although you will have to pay for any photocopying you need. Other data will require lengthy negotiations before access is granted (Section 6.3). Even then, the granting of access may not be certain (Stewart and Kamins 1993). Data from market research companies or special tabulations from government surveys will have to be ordered specially and will normally be charged for: consequently, these will be relatively costly.

Benefits from data can be assessed in terms of the extent to which they will enable you to answer your research question(s) and meet your objectives. You will be able to form a judgement on the benefits from your assessment of the data set's overall and precise suitability (discussed earlier in this section). This assessment is summarised as a checklist of questions in Box 8.9. An important additional benefit is the form in which you receive the data. If the data are already in computer-readable form this will save you considerable time as you will not need to re-enter the data prior to analysis (Sections 12.2 and 13.3). However, when assessing the costs and benefits you must remember that data that are not completely reliable and contain some bias are better than no data at all, if they enable you to start to answer your research question(s) and achieve your objectives.

Box 8.9
Checklist

Evaluating your secondary data sources

Overall suitability

✔ Does the data set contain the information you require to answer your research question(s) and meet your objectives?

✔ Do the measures used match those you require?

✔ Is the data set a proxy for the data you really need?

✔ Does the data set cover the population that is the subject of your research?

✔ Does the data set cover the geographical area that is the subject of your research?

✔ Can data about the population that is the subject of your research be separated from unwanted data?

✔ Are the data for the right time period or sufficiently up to date?

✔ Are data available for all the variables you require to answer your research question(s) and meet your objectives?

Precise suitability

✔ How reliable is the data set you are thinking of using?

✔ How credible is the data source?

✔ Is it clear what the source of the data is?

✔ Do the credentials of the source of the data (author, institution or organisation sponsoring the data) suggest it is likely to be reliable?

✔ Do the data have an associated copyright statement?

✔ Do associated published documents exist?

✔ Does the source contain contact details for obtaining further information about the data?

✔ Is the method clearly described?

✔ If sampling was used, what was the procedure and what were the associated sampling errors and response rates?

✔ Who was responsible for collecting or recording the data?

✔ (For surveys) Is a copy of the questionnaire or interview checklist included?

✔ (For compiled data) Are you clear how the data were analysed and compiled?

✔ Are the data likely to contain measurement bias?

✔ What was the original purpose for which the data were collected?

✔ Who was the target audience and what was its relationship to the data collector or compiler (were there any vested interests)?

> ## Box 8.9
> ## Checklist *(continued)*
>
> ✔ Have there been any documented changes in the way the data are measured or recorded including definition changes?
> ✔ How consistent are the data obtained from this source when compared with data from other sources?
> ✔ Are you happy that the data have been recorded accurately?
>
> **Costs and benefits**
> ✔ What are the financial and time costs of obtaining these data?
> ✔ Can the data be downloaded into a spread-sheet, statistical analysis software or word processor?
> ✔ Do the overall benefits of using these secondary data sources outweigh the associated costs?
>
> *Source:* authors' experience; Blumberg *et al.* (2008); Dale *et al.* (1988); Dochartaigh (2002); Jacob (1994); Kervin (1999); Stewart and Kamins (1993).

8.6 Summary

- Data that have already been collected for some other purpose, perhaps processed and subsequently stored, are termed secondary data. There are three main types of secondary data: documentary, survey and those from multiple sources.
- Most research projects require some combination of secondary and primary data to answer your research question(s) and to meet your objectives. You can use secondary data in a variety of ways. These include:
  - to provide your main data set;
  - to provide longitudinal (time-series) data;
  - to provide area-based data;
  - to compare with, or set in context, your own research findings.
- Any secondary data you use will have been collected for a specific purpose. This purpose may not match that of your research. In addition, the secondary data are likely to be less current than any data you collect yourself.
- Finding the secondary data you require is a matter of detective work. This will involve you in:
  - establishing whether the sort of data that you require are likely to be available;
  - locating the precise data.
- Once located, you must assess secondary data sources to ensure their overall suitability for your research question(s) and objectives. In particular, you need to pay attention to the measurement validity and coverage of the data.
- You must also evaluate the precise suitability of the secondary data. Your evaluation should include both reliability and any likely measurement bias. You can then make a judgement on the basis of the costs and benefits of using the data in comparison with alternative sources.
- When assessing costs and benefits, you need to be mindful that secondary data that are not completely reliable and contain some bias are better than no data at all if they enable you partially to answer your research question(s) and to meet your objectives.

Self-check questions

Help with these questions is available at the end of the chapter.

8.1 Give three examples of different situations where you might use secondary data as part of your research.

8.2 You are undertaking a research project as part of your course. Your initial research question is 'How has the UK's import and export trade with other countries altered since its entry into the European Union?' List the arguments that you would use to convince someone of the suitability of using secondary data to answer this research question.

8.3 Suggest possible secondary data that would help you answer the following research questions. How would you locate these secondary data?

a To what extent do organisations' employee-relocation policies meet the needs of employees?

b How have consumer-spending patterns in your home country changed in the last 10 years?

c How have governments' attitudes to the public sector altered since 1979?

8.4 As part of case-study research based in a manufacturing company with over 500 customers, you have been given access to an internal market research report. This was undertaken by the company's marketing department. The report presents the results of a recent customer survey as percentages. The section in the report that describes how the data were collected and analysed is reproduced below:

> Data were collected from a sample of current customers selected from our customer database. The data were collected using an Internet-mediated questionnaire designed and administered via the online software tool SurveyMonkey™. Twenty-five customers responded, resulting in a 12.5 per cent response rate. These data were analysed using the SNAP™ computer software. Additional qualitative data based on in-depth interviews with customers were also included.

a Do you consider these data are likely to be reliable?

b Give reasons for your answer.

Review and discussion questions

8.5 With a friend revisit Figure 8.1, types of secondary data, and reread the accompanying text in Section 8.2. Agree to find and, where possible, make copies (either electronic or photocopy) of at least two examples of secondary data for each of the seven sub-headings:

a written materials;

b non-written materials;

c area based;

d time-series based;

e censuses;

f continuous and regular surveys;

g *ad hoc* surveys.

Compare and contrast the different examples of secondary data you have found.

8.6 Choose an appropriate information gateway from Table 8.2 to search the Internet for secondary data on a topic which you are currently studying as part of your course.

a 'Add to favourites' (bookmark) those sites which you think appear most relevant.

b Make notes regarding any secondary data that are likely to prove useful to either seminars for which you have to prepare or coursework you have still to undertake.

8.7 Agree with a friend to each evaluate the same secondary data set obtained via the Internet. This could be one of the data sets you found when undertaking question 8.6. Evaluate independently your secondary data set with regard to its overall and precise suitability using the checklist in Box 8.9. Do not forget to make notes regarding your answers to each of the points raised in the checklist. Discuss your answers with your friend.

Progressing your research project

Assessing the suitability of secondary data for your research

- Consider your research question(s) and objectives. Decide whether you need to use secondary data or a combination of primary and secondary data to answer your research question. (If you decide that you need only use secondary data and you are undertaking this research as part of a course of study, check your course's assessment regulations to ensure that this is permissible.)

- If you decide that you need to use secondary data, make sure that you are clear why and how you intend to use these data.
- Locate the secondary data that you require and make sure that permission for them to be used for your research is likely to be granted. Evaluate the suitability of the data for answering your research question and make your judgement based on assessment of its suitability, other benefits and the associated costs.
- Note down the reasons for your choices, including the possibilities and limitations of the data. You will need to justify your choices when you write about your research methods

References

Blumberg, B., Cooper, D.R. and Schindler, P.S. (2008) *Business Research Methods*. (International student edn). Maidenhead: McGraw-Hill Education.

Bryman, A. (1989) *Research Methods and Organisation Studies*. London: Unwin Hyman.

Cheng Shu-Li, Olsen, W., Southerton, D. and Warde, A. (2007) 'The changing practice of eating: Evidence from UK time diaries: 1975 and 2000', *British Journal of Sociology,* Vol. 58, No. 1, pp. 39–61.

Cowton, C.J. (1998) 'The use of secondary data in business ethics research', *Journal of Business Ethics*, Vol. 17, No. 4, pp. 423–34.

Curran, J. and Blackburn, R.A. (2001) *Researching the Small Enterprise*. London: Sage.

Dale, A., Arber, S. and Proctor, M. (1988) *Doing Secondary Analysis.* London: Unwin Hyman.

Dale, P. (2004) *Guide to Libraries and Information Units in Government Departments and Other Organisations* (4th edn). London: British Library Publishing.

Davies, J. (2001) 'International comparisons of labour disputes in 1999', *Labour Market Trends*, Vol. 109, No. 4, pp. 195–201.

Dees, R. (2000) *Writing the Modern Research Paper*. Boston, MA: Allyn and Bacon.

Denscombe, M. (2007) *The Good Research Guide* (3rd edn). Buckingham: Open University Press.

Dochartaigh, N.O. (2002) *The Internet Research Handbook: A Practical Guide for Students and Researchers in the Social Sciences*. London: Sage.

ELC International (2007) *Europe's 15 000 Largest Companies* (31st edn). Oxford: ELC International.

Eurostat (2008a) *Europe in Figures: Eurostat Yearbook 2008*. Luxembourg: Office for Official Publications of the European Communities.

Eurostat (2008b) Eurostat home page. Available at: http://epp.eurostat.ec.europa.eu/portal/page?_pageid=1090.30070682.1090_33076576&_dad=portal&_schema=PORTAL [Accessed 23 May 2008.]

Eurostat (2008c) 'Harmonized Indices of Consumer Prices'. Available at: http://epp.eurostat.ec.europa.eu/portal/page?_pageid=1073,46587259&_dad=portal&_schema=PORTAL&p_product_code=KS-QA-08-024 [Accessed 29 June 2008.]

Ghauri, P. and Grønhaug, K. (2005) *Research Methods in Business Studies: A Practical Guide* (3rd edn). Harlow: Financial Times Prentice Hall.

Hakim, C. (1982) *Secondary Analysis in Social Research*. London: Allen & Unwin.

Hakim, C. (2000) *Research Design: Successful Designs for Social and Economic Research* (2nd edn). London: Routledge.

Information Commissioners Office (2008) Freedom of Information Act. Available at: http://www.ico.gov.uk/what_we_cover/freedom_of_information.aspx [Accessed 23 May 2008.]

IPSOS MORI (2007) 'What do we really think about counterfeiting?' Available at: http://www.ipsos-mori.com/content/what-do-we-really-think-about-counterfeiting.ashx [Accessed 9 June 2008.]

Jacob, H. (1994) 'Using published data: errors and remedies', in M.S. Lewis-Beck. (ed.) *Research Practice*. London: Sage and Toppan, pp. 339–89.

Kervin, J.B. (1999) *Methods for Business Research* (2nd edn). New York: HarperCollins.

Kingsbury, P. (1997) *IT Answers to HR Questions*. London: Institute of Personnel and Development.

Library Association (2005) *Libraries in the United Kingdom and Republic of Ireland*. London: Library Assocation.

McKenzie, E. (2003) *Guide to Libraries in Key UK Companies*. London: British Library.

Office for National Statistics (2001) '200 years of the Census'. Available at: http://www.statistics.gov.uk/census2001/bicentenary/pdfs/200years.pdf [Accessed 23 May 2008.]

Office for National Statistics (2007a) 'Annual Survey of Hours and Earnings (ASHE) 2007 Results'. Available at: http://www.statistics.gov.uk/statBase/product.asp?vlnk=13101. [Accessed 21 May 2008.]

Office for National Statistics (2007b) 'Family Spending – A Report on the Expenditure and Food Survey'. Available at: http://www.statistics.gov.uk/StatBase/Product.asp?vlnk=361 [Accessed 23 May 2008.]

Office for National Statistics (2007c) 'Labour Force Survey'. Available at: http://www.statistics.gov.uk/StatBase/Source.asp?vlnk=358&More=Y [Accessed 23 May 2008.]

Office for National Statistics (2007d) 'Social Trends'. Available at: http://www.statistics.gov.uk/statbase/Product.asp?vlnk=5748&More=Y [Accessed 21 May 2008.]

Office for National Statistics (2008) 'Annual Abstract of Statistics'. Available at: http://www.statistics.gov.uk/statbase/Product.asp?vlnk=94&More=Y [Accessed 23 May 2008.]

Okazaki, S. and Mueller, B. (2007) 'Cross-cultural advertising research: where we have been and where we need to go', *International Marketing Review,* Vol. 25, No. 5, pp. 499–518.

Patzer, G.L. (1996) *Using Secondary Data in Market Research: United States and World-wide*. Westport, CT: Quorum Books.

Reichman, C.S. (1962) *Use and Abuse of Statistics.* New York: Oxford University Press.

Robson, C. (2002) *Real World Research* (2nd edn). Oxford: Blackwell.

Stewart, D.W. and Kamins, M.A. (1993) *Secondary Research: Information Sources and Methods* (2nd edn). Newbury Park, CA: Sage.

Sydney Morning Herald (2008) 'Revealed: the most violent pubs and clubs', 11 Mar.

UK Data Archive (2008) UK Data Archive. Available at: http://www.data-archive.ac.uk/ [Accessed 23 May 2008.]

Walker, A. (2002) *Living in Britain: Results from the 2000 General Household Survey.* London: Stationery Office.

Wolf, A. (2007) 'People have a tendency to assume that quantitative data must be out there on the web waiting to be found', *The Times Higher Education Supplement*, 12 Oct. Available at: http://www.timeshighereducation.co.uk/story.asp?sectioncode=26&storycode=310797 [Accessed 23 May 2008.]

Further reading

Hakim, C. (2000) *Research Design: Successful Designs for Social and Economic Research* (2nd edn). London: Routledge. Chapter 4 contains a good discussion with a series of examples from the social sciences regarding using administrative records and documents as secondary data.

Levitas, R. and Guy, W. (eds) (1996) *Interpreting Official Statistics.* London: Routledge. Although published more than a decade ago, this book provides a fascinating insight into UK published statistics. Of particular interest are Chapter 1, which outlines the changes in UK statistics since the 1980 Raynor review, Chapter 3, which looks at the measurement of unemployment, the discussion in Chapter 6 of the measurement of industrial injuries and their limitations, and Chapter 7, which examines gender segregation in the labour force, utilising data from the Labour Force Survey.

Stewart, D.W. and Kamins, M.A. (1993) *Secondary Research: Information Sources and Methods* (2nd edn). Newbury Park, CA: Sage. This provides a good discussion on the evaluation of secondary data (Chapter 2). It also provides a wealth of information on American government and non-government data sets and their acquisition.

Case 8
Patent grants and the implications for business

Source: E Streichan/ Zefa/Corbis.

Chris was an MA student in international business and management. After taking a module entitled Intellectual Property (IP) in International Business (IB), he had taken great interest in this subject and had been determined to do a good-quality research project. However, in the first meeting with his supervisor, while feeling motivated, he realised that it was not enough to be determined and he needed to make greater effort on his project. His supervisor pointed out, based on his project proposal, that he needed to be more focused and precise. The supervisor had advised that the proposed focus of his research project – examining how Western corporate managers view the development of IP in the Eastern European countries using primary data – was too wide. He suggested narrowing it to assessing how IP systems differ between Western and Eastern European countries and what these differences imply for cross-border business activities, and only to use secondary data. The supervisor had particularly mentioned that it would be sensible for Chris to use his statistical skills to draw conclusions based on reliable secondary data commenting: 'Western corporate managers' views will involve primary data collection. It would be brilliant to do so, but given that you have only three months to do the project, including writing up, it would be difficult to produce a quality piece of work. There might be difficulties in collecting representative data due to access issues, time constraints and financial support.' At the end of the first meeting, Chris and his supervisor agreed that Chris would undertake a project to assess the differences between Western and Eastern European countries in terms of patent grants and the implications for businesses.

Before the second meeting, Chris conducted a search of the literature regarding IP system development particularly with the empirical focus on the EU countries. To his surprise, there were only three articles that specifically examined the patent grant issues in a comparative manner (Kotabe 1992a, 1992b; Yang 2008). Both authors had used raw data from the World IP Organisation (WIPO) database and conducted regression analyses on which they based their conclusions. When reading the articles referenced in these three papers, Chris found that they were suggesting theoretical reasons as to why France, Germany and the United Kingdom (UK) had higher grant ratios for domestic than for foreign applications to issue patent rights. These, he felt, could provide the justifications for questions for his research project. At this stage, Chris was very eager to see his supervisor to report his achievements. In the meeting, while the supervisor commended Chris's progress on identifying the appropriate literature, she also pointed out: 'The most important work to do at the literature review stage is to be able to critique on the existing work so that you can identify research gaps for your own study.' At the end of the meeting, Chris's supervisor asked him to establish precisely what secondary data he needed to obtain about patent applications and grants for the countries he wanted to focus on.

Following this advice, Chris designed a table to highlight the key information. This indicates the authors, research focus, empirical focus in relation to countries, data source and analytical methods. Upon completion, his findings were clear. The existing literature had not conducted grant ratio (grant lags) analysis with an empirical focus on any Eastern European countries. Meanwhile, although Britain, France and Germany were compared and contrasted with the United States by Kotabe (1992b), the conclusions were dated because they were based on data from the 1980s. A new study would enrich existing empirical findings by not only adding new countries (Eastern Europe) but also revealing the changes in Western Europe over the years in terms of grant ratios. In addition, through the studies, similarities and differences between Eastern and Western Europe could be identified. This, Chris felt, would allow him to make some recommendations relating to policy and business implications. To collect his data, he logged on http:\\www.wipo.org statistics, and downloaded all the annual patent statistics available for all the EU countries.

Author	Focus	Empirical focus	Data and methods
Kotabe (1992a)	Patent grant lags and ratios	US and Japan	WIPO data 1980s Lagged regression
Kotabe (1992b)	The same as above	US, Germany, UK and France	The same as above
Yang (2008)	The same as above	US and China	WIPO data (1985–2002)

With excitement, Chris presented his achievements proudly to his supervisor who was pleased with his enthusiasm and his hard work. In the meantime, the supervisor also pointed out that it was not enough to collect the data only. Chris also needed to justify why the secondary data collected from WIPO were appropriate and what issues arose from the data. Chris was surprised as he thought that data from a United Nations agency source like WIPO would be 'perfect'. The supervisor hinted to Chris that he had to look into the actual source of the WIPO data, the standardisation process to compile the data, and how the data had been categorised. He was advised to discuss possible weaknesses in the data in the 'Methodology' section of his project report. At the end of the meeting, Chris went home with an important task: analyse the data and come to see the supervisor again with some preliminary findings and understanding regarding how it had been collected.

Upon returning home, Chris sat at his computer for half an hour staring at the monitor. There were 27 countries, and each country had at least 90 years' worth of aggregate data. The data for Germany were extremely complex due to it being sub-divided into East and West Germany prior to reunification. He spent another hour trying to understand the data before he picked up the phone to call his supervisor for help. Chris was overwhelmed with the richness of the data and did not know where to start. After discussion, the supervisor suggested that he focus on a few countries instead of all EU countries, for example three countries from Western Europe and three from Eastern Europe, and also only focus on the data for West Germany.

Chris eventually finished his data analysis and submitted his project report. His great effort did not disappoint his supervisor; the project was awarded a distinction. However, the supervisor still commented that the discussion about the weakness of the data could have been more thoroughly presented.

References

Kotabe, M. (1992a) 'A Comparative Study of U.S. and Japanese Patent Systems', *Journal of International Business Studies*, Vol. 23, No. 1, pp. 147–68.

Kotabe, M. (1992b) 'The Impact of Foreign Patents on National Economy: A Case of the US, Japan, Germany and Britain', *Applied Economics*, Vol. 24, pp.1335–43.

Yang, D. (2008) 'Pendency and grant ratios on invention patents: A comparative study of the US and China', *Research Policy*. Available at: http://dx.doi.org/10.1016/j.respol.2008.03.008 [Accessed 14 May 2008.]

Questions

1 Why does the supervisor advise that Chris do a project using secondary data rather than collecting primary data?
2 What sources of information has Chris discovered through his search?
3 Do you find Chris's justification for his research project convincing? Give reasons for your answer?
4 Despite obtaining a distinction for the project, the supervisor commented that Chris should have discussed the limitations of his data sources more thoroughly. Visit the WIPO's website [http://www.wipo.org] and make a note of precisely how the data Chris used were compiled. Based upon this, how would you suggest that Chris present more thorough a discussion?

Additional case studies relating to material covered in this chapter are available via the book's Companion Website, **www.pearsoned.co.uk/saunders**. They are:

- The involvement of auditors in preliminary profit announcements
- Research and development in the UK pharmaceutical industry
- Small firms' internationalisation.

Self-check answers

8.1 Although it would be impossible to list all possible situations, the key features that should appear in your examples are listed below:
- to compare findings from your primary data;
- to place findings from your primary data in a wider context;
- to triangulate findings from other data sources;
- to provide the main data set where you wish to undertake research over a long period, to undertake historical research or to undertake comparative research on a national or international scale with limited resources.

8.2 The arguments you have listed should focus on the following issues:
- The study suggested by the research question requires historical data so that changes that have already happened can be explored. These data will, by definition, have already been collected.

- The timescale of the research (if part of a course) will be relatively short term. One solution for longitudinal studies in a short time frame is to use secondary data.
- The research question suggests an international comparative study. Given your likely limited resources, secondary data will provide the only feasible data sources.

8.3 **a** The secondary data required for this research question relate to organisations' employee relocation policies. The research question assumes that these sorts of data are likely to be available from organisations. Textbooks, research papers and informal discussions would enable you to confirm that these data were likely to be available. Informal discussions with individuals responsible for the personnel function in organisations would also confirm the existence and availability for research of such data.

b The secondary data required for this research question relate to consumer spending patterns in your home country. As these appear to be the sort of data in which the government would be interested, they may well be available via the Internet or in published form. For the UK, examination of various published guides (both governmental and non-governmental sources) would reveal that these data were collected by the annual Family Expenditure Survey, summary results of which are published (e.g. Office for National Statistics 2007). Summary data could then be downloaded via the UK government's statistics information gateway (Table 8.2). In addition, reports could be borrowed either from your university library or by using inter-library loan.

c The secondary data required for this research question are less clear. What you require is some source from which you can infer past and present government attitudes. Transcripts of ministers' speeches and newspaper reports might prove useful. However, to establish suitable secondary sources for this research question you would need to pay careful attention to those used by other researchers. These would be outlined in research papers and textbooks. Informal discussions could also prove useful.

8.4 **a** The data are unlikely to be reliable.

b Your judgement should be based on a combination of the following reasons:

- Initial examination of the report reveals that it is an internally conducted survey. As this has been undertaken by the marketing department of a large manufacturing company, you might assume that those undertaking the research had considerable expertise. Consequently, you might conclude the report contains credible data. However:
- The methodology is not clearly described. In particular:
  - The sampling procedure and associated sampling errors are not given.
  - It does not appear to contain a copy of the questionnaire. This means that it is impossible to check for bias in the way that questions were worded.
  - The methodology for the qualitative in-depth interviews is not described.
- In addition, the information provided in the methodology suggests that the data may be unreliable:
  - The reported response rate of 12.5 per cent is very low for a telephone survey (Section 7.2).
  - Responses from 25 people means that all tables and statistical analyses in the report are based on a maximum of 25 people. This may be too few for reliable results (Sections 7.2 and 12.5).

Get ahead using resources on the Companion Website at:
www.pearsoned.co.uk/saunders
- Improve your SPSS and NVivo research analysis with practice tutorials.
- Save time researching on the Internet with the Smarter Online Searching Guide.
- Test your progress using self-assessment questions.
- Follow live links to useful websites.

Chapter 9

Collecting primary data through observation

Learning outcomes

By the end of this chapter you should be able to:

- understand the role that observation may play as a data collection method in your research design;
- identify two types of observation, participant observation and structured observation, and their differing origins and applications;
- adopt particular approaches to data collection and analysis for both participant observation and structured observation;
- identify threats to validity and reliability faced by the two types of observation.

9.1 Introduction

Observation is a somewhat neglected aspect of research. Yet, it can be rewarding and enlightening to pursue and, what is more, add considerably to the richness of your research data. It can even be fun, as the introductory example illustrates. If your research question(s) and objectives are concerned with what people do, an obvious way in which to discover this is to watch them do it. This is essentially what **observation** involves: the systematic observation, recording, description, analysis and interpretation of people's behaviour.

The two types of observation examined in this chapter are very different. **Participant observation** (Sections 9.2–9.4) is qualitative and derives from the work of social anthropology early in the twentieth century. Its emphasis is on discovering the meanings that people attach to their actions. By contrast, **structured observation** (Sections 9.5–9.6) is quantitative and is more concerned with the frequency of those actions.

A common theme in this book is our effort to discourage you from thinking of the various research methods as the sole means you should employ in your study. This is also true of observation methods. It may meet the demands of your research question(s) and objectives to use both participant and structured observation in your study either as the main methods of data collection or to supplement other methods.

9.2 Participant observation: an introduction

What is participant observation?

If you have studied sociology or anthropology in the past you are certain to be familiar with participant observation. This is where 'the researcher attempts to participate fully in the lives and activities of subjects and thus becomes a member of their group, organisation

Sociologist Roger Penn (2005) has been examining the behaviour of football spectators in England and Italy. His research method makes considerable use of photographs of football matches in both countries. Such a method is both innovative and based upon wider traditions of observation within sociology. The recent advent of digital camera technology has encouraged a burgeoning use of visual data as evidence. Such an approach is particularly appropriate for an understanding of differences between spectators in English and Italian football stadia, since both the game and spectating are central elements within the spectacle of modern football.

The data formed part of a wider comparative approach to football in England and Italy. None of the photographs was staged: all was taken 'in situ' as matches unfolded. Penn presents them both as illustrative of much wider structures and, in the opinion of the author, as typical of patterns of behaviour at major football matches in the two countries.

Penn concluded that behaviour of fans in English and Italian football stadia is radically different. Nowadays the main complaints about English football are the price of tickets and the lack of 'atmosphere' in the new stadia rather than the behaviour of the fans. This represents a major change since the dark days of hooliganism in the 1970s and 1980s. Atmosphere is certainly not lacking in Italian stadia but also there is no shortage of major problems with spectators. Penn's paper attempts to delineate and explain this difference in national forms of spectator behaviour.

Clearly, there are major differences in the organisation of football matches between England and Italy

Crystal Palace fans at 2004 championship play-off final
Source: © Philip Lewis 2004

which have a significant impact upon crowd behaviour. Italian football matches have a strong flavour of carnival and transgression. Games in the English Premier League are more akin to opera or theatre. Each has its own set of assumptions and each produces very different kinds of crowd behaviour. There was considerable irony – and not a little paradox – in the reaction of the Italian sporting press to crowd problems in Italy in the spring of 2005. The English 'model' was held up as an example for Italian football. This reveals the distance that English football has travelled since the dark days of the 1980s.

or community. This enables researchers to share their experiences by not merely observing what is happening but also feeling it' (Gill and Johnson 2002:144). It has been used extensively in these disciplines to attempt to get to the root of 'what is going on' in a wide range of social settings.

Participant observation has its roots in social anthropology, but it was the Chicago school of social research that encouraged its students to study by observation the constantly changing social phenomena of Chicago in the 1920s and 1930s.

Participant observation has been used much less in management and business research. However, this does not mean to say that it has limited value for management and business researchers. Indeed, it can be a very valuable tool, usually as the principal research method, but possibly in combination with other methods.

Delbridge and Kirkpatrick (1994:37) note that participant observation implies 'immersion [by the researcher] in the research setting, with the objective of sharing in peoples' lives while attempting to learn their symbolic world'. It is worth dwelling on this explanation. Whichever role you adopt as the participant observer (the choices open to you will be discussed later), there will be a high level of immersion. This is quite different from data collection by means of questionnaire, where you probably will know little of the context in which the respondents' comments are set or the delicate nuances of meaning with which the respondents garnish their responses. In participant observation the purpose is to discover those delicate nuances of meaning. As Delbridge and Kirkpatrick (1994:39) state: 'in the social sciences we cannot hope to adequately explain the behaviour of social actors unless we at least try to understand their meanings'.

This last comment gives a clue to the point that Delbridge and Kirkpatrick make about 'attempting to learn the [respondents'] symbolic world'. Some understanding of this point is vital if you are to convince yourself and others of the value of using participant observation.

The symbolic frame of reference is located within the school of sociology known as **symbolic interactionism**. In symbolic interactionism the individual derives a sense of identity from interaction and communication with others. Through this process of interaction and communication the individual responds to others and adjusts his or her understandings and behaviour as a shared sense of order and reality is 'negotiated' with others. Central to this process is the notion that people continually change in the light of the social circumstances in which they find themselves. The transition from full-time student to career employee is one example of this. (How often have you heard people say 'she's so different since she's worked at that new place'?) The individual's sense of identity is constantly being constructed and reconstructed as he or she moves through differing social contexts and encounters different situations and different people.

This is a necessarily brief explanation of symbolic interactionism. However, we hope that you can see why Delbridge and Kirkpatrick (1994:37) think that participant observation is about 'attempting to learn the [respondents'] symbolic world'. It is a quest for understanding the identity of the individual, but, more importantly, it is about trying to get to the bottom of the processes by which the individual constantly constructs and reconstructs his or her identity. Examples of such processes which formed the basis of research studies are illustrated in Box 9.1 (opposite) and Box 9.2.

Situations in which participant observation has been used

One of the most famous examples of participant observation is that of Whyte (1955), who lived among a poor American-Italian community in order to understand 'street corner society'. A celebrated business example is the work of Roy (1952). Roy worked in a machine shop for 10 months as an employee. He wanted to understand how and why his

Box 9.1
Focus on student research

Managers and their use of power: a cross-cultural approach

Mong was a young Chinese business graduate who had recently been working in a Chinese/German joint venture in the automobile industry. She was located in the supply chain department. Mong was completing the latter stages of her MBA. As part of the course, she had to submit a research project on a management topic of her choice.

Mong was fascinated by the international management component of her course that dealt with cross-cultural matters. This was particularly significant in her case as she worked at a company site that comprised both Chinese and German managers.

Mong felt that a body of theory that she could profitably link to the issue of cross-cultural integration was that of power. With help from her project tutor she developed a research question that was designed to explore the way in which Chinese and German managers used power to 'negotiate' their relationships in a situation which was unfamiliar to both sets of managers.

Mong was fortunate that one of her duties was to take minutes at the twice-weekly management meetings in the department. She obtained permission to use these meetings as her major data collection vehicle. She developed an observation schedule which related to her research objectives and used this to collect data during each meeting.

Data collection was not easy for Mong as she had to take minutes in addition to noting the type and frequency of responses of managers. However, as time progressed she became very skilled at fulfilling both her minute-taking and data-collection roles. At the end of four months, when she had attended over 30 meetings, she had collected a wealth of data and was in a good position to analyse them and draw some fascinating conclusions.

Mong's observation role raised ethical questions as she did not reveal her researcher role to the meeting delegates. She discussed these questions with her senior manager in the company and project tutor and completed the necessary university ethics committee documentation. It was agreed by all concerned that Mong's research objectives justified the data collection approach chosen and that the university's ethics code had not been breached.

'fellow workers' operated the piecework bonus system. Rather more colourfully, Rosen (1991) worked as a participant observer in a Philadelphia advertising agency. Rosen was working within the theoretical domain of dramaturgy. He wanted to understand how organisations used social drama to create and sustain power relationships and social structures.

These may strike you as rather elaborate examples that suggest little relevance to you as you contemplate your own research project. Yet this would be a disappointing conclusion. Box 9.2 contains an example of participant observation research which you are likely to find a little more familiar.

You may already be a member of an organisation that promises a fertile territory for research. This may be your employing organisation or a social body of which you are a member. One of Phil's students undertook research in his church community. He was a member of the church council and conducted observational research on the way in which decisions were reached in council meetings. A more specific focus was adopted by another of our students. She was a member of a school governing body. Her specific hypothesis was that the focus of decision-making power was the head teacher. Her study confirmed this hypothesis. All the significant decisions were in effect taken prior to governors' meetings as a consequence of the head teacher canvassing the support of those committee members whom he defined as 'influential'.

Box 9.2
Focus on management research

The case for doing research in your own organisation

In an *Organisational Research Methods* article, Brannick and Coghlan (2007) question the established tradition that academic-theory-driven research in organisations is conducted best by outsiders and argue that this can be done acceptably by insider researchers. They define insider researchers as those undertaking research in and on their own organisations while a complete member, which in this context means both having insider pre-understanding and access and wanting the choice to remain a member on a desired career path when the research is completed. Insider research typically is frowned upon because it is perceived not to conform to standards of intellectual rigour, because insider researchers have a personal stake and substantive emotional investment in the setting. It is argued that insider researchers are native to the setting and, therefore, they are perceived to be prone to charges of being too close and thereby not attaining the distance and objectivity necessary for valid research. Brannick and Coghlan challenge this view and show how insider research, in whatever research tradition it is undertaken, is not only valid and useful but also provides important knowledge about what organisations are really like, which traditional approaches may not be able to uncover.

Brannick and Coghlan assemble a number of points to substantiate their argument. They argue that researchers, through a process of reflexive awareness, are able to articulate tacit knowledge that has become deeply segmented because of socialisation in an organisational system and reframe it as theoretical knowledge. Reflexivity is the concept used in the social sciences to explore and deal with the relationship between the researcher and the object of research. Insider researchers are already members of the organisation and so have primary access.

Clearly, any researcher's status in the organisation has an impact on access. Access at one level automatically may lead to limits or access at other levels. The higher the status of the researcher, the more access they have or the more networks they can access, particularly downward through the hierarchy. However, being in a high hierarchical position may exclude access to many informal and grapevine networks.

Insider researchers derive benefits from their experience and preunderstanding. Managers have knowledge of their organisation's everyday life. They know the everyday jargon. They know the legitimate and taboo phenomena of what can be talked about and what cannot. They know what occupies colleagues' minds. They know how the informal organisation works and to whom to turn for information and gossip. They know the critical events and what they mean within the organisation. They are able to see beyond objectives that are merely window dressing. When they are inquiring, they can use the internal jargon, draw on their own experience in asking questions and interviewing, be able to follow up on replies, and so obtain richer data. They are able to participate in discussions or merely observe what is going on without others being necessarily aware of their presence. They can participate freely without drawing attention to themselves and creating suspicion.

There are also some disadvantages to being close to the data. Insider researchers may assume too much and so not probe as much as if they were outsiders or ignorant of the situation. They may think they know the answer and not expose their current thinking to alternative reframing. They may find it difficult to obtain relevant data because, as a member, they have to cross departmental, functional or hierarchical boundaries, or because, as an insider, they may be denied deeper access that might not be denied an outsider.

Insider researchers may have a strong desire to influence and change the organisation. They may feel empathy for their colleagues and so be motivated to keep up the endeavour. These are beneficial in that they may sustain researchers' energy and a drawback in that they may lead to erroneous conclusions. Insider researchers have to deal with the dilemma of writing a report on what they have found. When they are observing colleagues at work and recording their observations, they may be perceived as spying or breaking peer norms. Probably the most important issue for insider researchers, particularly when they want to remain and progress in the organisation, is managing organisational politics.

So, adopting the participant observer role as an existing member of an organisation does present opportunities to you. However, it also has its dangers. We shall deal with these later.

9.3 Participant observation: researcher roles

We have explained what participant observation is, but we have not explained clearly what participant observers do. A number of questions may have occurred to you. For example, should the participant observer keep his or her purpose concealed? Does the participant observer need to be an employee or an organisational member, albeit temporarily? Can the participant observer just observe? The answers here are not straightforward. The role you play as participant observer will be determined by a number of factors. However, before examining those factors, we need to look at the different roles in which the participant observer may be cast.

Gill and Johnson (2002) develop a fourfold categorisation (Figure 9.1) of the role the participant observer can adopt. The roles are:

- complete participant;
- complete observer;
- observer as participant;
- participant as observer.

The first two of these roles, the complete participant and the complete observer, involve you as the researcher in concealing your identity. This has the significant advantage of your not conditioning the behaviour of the research subjects you are studying. The second two, observer as participant and participant as observer, entail you revealing your purpose to those with whom you are mixing in the research setting. Ethically, the latter two roles are less problematic.

Complete participant

The **complete participant** role sees you as the researcher attempting to become a member of the group in which you are performing research. You do not reveal your true purpose to the group members. You may be able to justify this role on pure research grounds

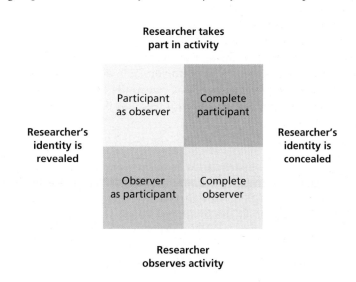

Figure 9.1
Typology of participant observation researcher roles

in the light of your research questions and objectives. For example, you may be interested to know the extent of lunchtime drinking in a particular work setting. You would probably be keen to discover which particular employees drink at lunchtimes, what they drink, how much they drink, and how they explain their drinking. Were you to explain your research objectives to the group you wished to study, it is rather unlikely that they would cooperate since employers would usually discourage lunchtime drinking. In addition, they might see your research activity as prying.

This example raises questions of ethics. You are in a position where you are 'spying' on people who have probably become your friends as well as colleagues. They may have learned to trust you with information that they would not share were they to know your true purpose. On these grounds alone you may agree with us that this is a role that the researcher should not adopt.

There are also objections on pure research grounds. You may work so hard at gaining the trust of your 'colleagues', and value that trust when it is gained, that you lose sight of your research purpose. The objective, detached perspective that all researchers need will be lost.

Complete observer

Here too you would not reveal the purpose of your activity to those you were observing. However, unlike the complete participant role, you do not take part in the activities of the group. For example, the **complete observer** role may be used in studying consumer behaviour in supermarkets. Your research question may concern your wish to observe consumers at the checkout. Which checkouts do they choose? How much interaction is there with fellow shoppers and the cashier? How do they appear to be influenced by the attitude of the cashier? What level of impatience is displayed when delays are experienced? This behaviour may be observed by the researcher being located near the checkout in an unobtrusive way. The patterns of behaviour displayed may be the precursor to research by structured observation (Section 9.5). This would be the exploratory stage of this research.

Observer as participant

You might adopt the role of **observer as participant** in an outward-bound course to assist team building if you were attending to observe without taking part in the activities in the same way as the 'real' candidates. In other words, you would be a 'spectator'. However, your identity as a researcher would be clear to all concerned. They would know your purpose, as would the trainers running the course. This would present the advantage of you being able to focus on your researcher role. For example, you would be able to jot down insights as they occurred to you. You would be able to concentrate on your discussions with the participants. What you would lose, of course, would be the emotional involvement: really knowing what it feels like to be on the receiving end of the experience.

Participant as observer

In the role of **participant as observer** you reveal your purpose as a researcher. Both you and the subjects are aware of the fact that it is a fieldwork relationship (Ackroyd and Hughes 1992). You are particularly interested to gain the trust of the group. This was the role adopted by the sociologist Punch (1993) in his study of police work in Amsterdam. Because of the trust developed by Punch with police officers whom he was researching he was able to gain admission to activities that otherwise would have been 'out of bounds' to him. Because his identity as researcher was clear he could ask questions of his subjects

Box 9.3
Focus on student research

Observer effects on data collection

Rob's research involved observing employees' behaviours in a small business. Having obtained written permission from the organisation's owner manager and explained to those he was observing that he would preserve confidentiality and anonymity, Rob began his observation. For the first few days he wondered if his presence and, in particular, his overt note taking were having an impact on the behaviours of the employees he was observing. Towards the end of the third day of observation one of the employees spoke to Rob as he was leaving the business's premises. 'At first we worried when we came in and you started writing things down; however, now we don't really notice you.' Rob discussed this remark with his friends who felt the remark suggested that, although he was likely to affect the way those he was observing behaved, these effects were lessening as time progressed.

to enhance his understanding. Robson (2002) argues that this leads to another advantage of this role. This is that key informants are likely to adopt a perspective of **analytic reflection** on the processes in which they are involved.

Factors that will determine the choice of participant observer role

The purpose of your research

You should always be guided by the appropriateness of the method for your research question(s) and objectives. A research question about developing an understanding of a phenomenon about which the research subjects would be naturally defensive is one that lends itself to the complete participant role. Discovering what it is like to be a participant on a particular training course is more appropriate to the participant as observer role.

The time you have to devote to your research

Some of the roles covered above may be very time consuming. If you are really to develop a rich and deep understanding of an organisational phenomenon, it will need much careful study. A period of attachment to the organisation will often be necessary. However, many full-time courses have placement opportunities that may be used for this purpose. In addition, most full-time students now have part-time jobs, which provide wonderful opportunities to understand the 'meanings' that their fellow employees, for whom the work is their main occupation, attach to a variety of organisational processes. What is needed is a creative perspective on what constitutes research and research opportunities. The possibilities are endless.

The degree to which you feel suited to participant observation

Delbridge and Kirkpatrick (1994) note that not everybody is suited to this type of research. Much of it relies on the building of relationships with others. A certain amount of personal flexibility is also needed. As the participant observer you have to be 'all things to all people'. Your own personality must be suppressed to a greater extent. This is not something with which you may feel comfortable.

Organisational access

This may present a problem for some researchers. It is obviously a key issue. More is said about gaining access to organisations for research in Sections 6.2. and 6.3.

Ethical considerations

The degree to which you reveal your identity as the researcher will be dictated by ethical considerations. The topic of ethics in research is dealt with in detail in Sections 6.4. and 6.5.

9.4 Participant observation: data collection and analysis

Delbridge and Kirkpatrick (1994) categorise the types of data generated by participant observation as 'primary', 'secondary' and 'experiential'.

Primary observations are those where you would note what happened or what was said at the time. Keeping a diary is a good way of doing this.

Secondary observations are statements by observers of what happened or was said. This necessarily involves those observers' interpretations.

Experiential data are those data on your perceptions and feelings as you experience the process you are researching. Keeping a diary of these perceptions proves a valuable source of data when the time comes to write up your research. This may also include notes on how you feel that your values have intervened, or changed, over the research process.

Finally, you will also collect data on factors material to the research setting: for example, roles played by key participants and how these may have changed; organisational structures and communication patterns.

Data collection

What will be clear from the types of data you will collect as the participant observer is that formal set-piece interviewing is unlikely to take place. Such 'interviewing' as does take place is likely to be informal discussion. It will be part of the overall approach of asking questions that should be adopted in this research method. These questions are of two types (Robson 2002): first, to informants to clarify the situations you have observed and, second, to yourself to clarify the situation and the accounts given of the situation.

Of course, the data that you collect depend on your research question(s) and objectives which have given a particular focus to your observation. Robson (2002:320) suggests that your data may well be classed as '**descriptive observation**' and '**narrative account**'. In descriptive observation you may concentrate on observing the physical setting, the key participants and their activities, particular events and their sequence and the attendant processes and emotions involved. This description may be the basis for your writing of a narrative account, in much the same way as an investigative journalist would write one. However, Robson (2002) makes the point forcefully that the researcher must go much further than the journalist. Your job as the researcher is to go on and develop a framework of theory that will help you to understand, and to explain to others, what is going on in the research setting you are studying.

How you record your data will depend to a great extent on the role you play as the participant observer. The more 'open' you are the more possible it will be for you to make notes at the time the event is being observed or reported. In any event, there is one golden rule: recording must take place on the same day as the fieldwork in order that you do not forget valuable data. The importance placed on this by one complete participant observer, working in a bakery, is evident from the following quotation:

> Right from the start I found it impossible to keep everything I wanted in my head until the end of the day . . . and had to take rough notes as I was going along. But I was 'stuck on the line', and had nowhere to retire to privately to note things down. Eventually, the wheeze of using innocently provided lavatory cubicles occurred to me. Looking back, all my notes for that third summer were on Bronco toilet paper! Apart from the awkward tendency for pencilled notes to be self-erasing from hard toilet paper . . . my frequent requests for 'time out' after interesting happenings or conversations in the bakehouse and the amount of time that I was spending in the lavatory began to get noticed . . .
>
> Ditton (1977), cited in Bryman (1989:145)

Data analysis

We deal with this in more depth in Chapters 12 and 13. However, you should bear in mind that in participant observation research your data collection and analysis activity may be part of the same process. That is, you will be carrying out analysis and collection of data simultaneously. Let us say you were acting as the complete participant observer in attempting to establish 'what is going on' in terms of sex discrimination at the workplace in which you were researching. You would observe informal banter, hear conversations of a discriminatory nature, talk to those who 'approved' and 'disapproved' of the activity. All this would be part of your everyday work. You might mix socially with colleagues in situations where discriminatory attitudes and behaviour might be evident. All these events would yield data that you would record, as far as possible, on the spot, or at least write up soon afterwards. You would turn these rough notes into something rather more systematic along the lines of the procedures suggested in Section 13.5. What would be emerging is what the investigative journalist might call 'promising lines of enquiry' that you might wish to follow up in your continued observation. However, remember that the journalist is interested in the story, while you are interested in generating a theory to help you understand 'what is going on'. This will lead you to adopt the researcher's equivalent of 'promising lines of enquiry'. A common approach to this is what is called analytic induction (Box 9.4).

Threats to reliability and validity

Participant observation is very high on **ecological validity** because it involves studying social phenomena in their natural contexts. Nonetheless, participant observation is subject to the same threats to validity as noted in Section 5.6 (e.g. history and maturation), although the fact that your study is likely to be over an extended time period will overcome most of these.

The greatest threat to the reliability of your research conclusions produced as a result of a participant observation study is that of observer bias. As Delbridge and Kirkpatrick (1994:43) note, 'because we are part of the social world we are studying we cannot detach ourselves from it, or for that matter avoid relying on our common sense knowledge and life experiences when we try to interpret it'.

The propensity that we all have for our own perceptions to colour our interpretation of what we believe to be 'true' is well known. What we advocate here is that we cannot avoid observer bias. All we can do is to be aware of the threat to reliability it poses and seek to control it.

Box 9.4
Focus on student research

Using analytic induction

Parvati had already gained a strong impression from the news media to form an initial hypothesis that the giant supermarkets impose restrictive trading conditions upon their small suppliers. These conditions are such that the suppliers lose effective control of many of their daily operations. Her impression was reinforced by data collected from the the literature, both academic and practitioner.

She spent a period of time working with a small organisation which supplies specialist dairy products to one of the supermarkets. Her research objectives were specifically written in order that her period of time with the supplier would result in data collection which responded to her research objectives.

Parvati's initial findings confirmed the overall hypothesis that the giant supermarkets impose restrictive

trading conditions upon their small suppliers. However, the situation was rather more complex than she imagined. She found that while the supermarket buyers conduct stringent checks on product quality matters, they are less demanding when it comes to such issues as dictating the amount of hours worked by employees.

This led her to redefine the initial hypothesis to one that stated that that the giant supermarkets impose stringent product quality conditions upon their small suppliers but less restrictive conditions in relation to non-product quality issues.

In the next data collection phase, she needed to extend the category of both product quality and non-product quality issues to see if the revised hypothesis required further revision and sophistication.

Note: This Focus on student research is a simplified version of analytic induction. It involves only *one* redefinition of the hypothesis whereas several may be involved. Moreover, an alternative to the redefining of the hypothesis is redefining the phenomenon to be explained so that the particular instance that casts doubt on the hypothesis is excluded (Denzin 1989).

The first way this may be done is to revert to the process of asking yourself questions about your conclusions: Did she really mean that? What other interpretations could I have put on this? The second way is that adopted by one of our students who was researching decision-making power in a school governing body. Her approach was to use **informant verification**. After each of her informal discussions with fellow Parent Teacher Association members she wrote these up, including her own conclusions as to the meanings of the discussions in the light of her research hypothesis. She then presented the written accounts to her informants for them to verify the content. Not only is this a form of triangulation, but it can be a source of new interpretations that have not occurred to the researcher. This method of triangulation is also one that can be used with more formal interview results. The advantages and disadvantages of participant observation are summarised in Table 9.1 (opposite).

Observational data from the perspective of the subject, not the researcher

We are all familiar with the idea of compiling video diaries and, perhaps, sharing these on the Internet through personalised blogs or through social network sites. This method of assembling information opens up a new area of observational research in which advanced miniaturised video recording equipment provides observational data from the perspective of the research subject, not the researcher (i.e. a first-person perspective). These data may then be used as stimuli in an in-depth interview process. As such, this observational method provides an almost perfect example of how technology is able to enhance our ability to do observational research in what could be called a 'traditional'

Table 9.1 Advantages and disadvantages of participant observation

Advantages	Disadvantages
• It is good at explaining 'what is going on' in particular social situations • It heightens the researcher's awareness of significant social processes • It is particularly useful for researchers working within their own organisations • Some participant observation affords the opportunity for the researcher to the experience 'for real' the emotions of those who are being researched • Virtually all data collected are useful	• It can be very time consuming • It can pose difficult ethical dilemmas for the researcher • There can be high levels of role conflict for the researcher (e.g. 'colleague' versus researcher) • The closeness of the researcher to the situation being observed can lead to significant observer bias • The participant observer role is a very demanding one, to which not all researchers will be suited • Access to organisations may be difficult • Data recording is often very difficult for the researcher

sense (Lee and Broderick 2007). As the article in Box 9.5 explains, traditional observation relies on the researcher's interpretation of events and even when using video recording equipment, the researcher is essentially directing how events are recorded. The result is then essentially a partial record (the video) of a partial view of the subject's reality (i.e. the observation by the researcher). Using the video diary method with the data recorded by the subject has the potential to remove this layer of interpretation from observational research, allowing a closer and richer view of how the subject experiences the world.

Box 9.5
Focus on management research

Using 'mindcam' in observational marketing research

In their article in *Qualitative Market Research*, Starr and Fernandez (2007) argue that a film-making approach to consumer marketing research, which they call 'mindcam', is better for understanding the narrative, conveying a rich understanding of a subject, and sheer watchability. They assert that it is better for understanding precise details, exact cognitions, differences between perceptions/recollections and reality, and respondent thoughts and feelings about the processes portrayed.

The mindcam apparatus consists of concealed video equipment, using a small, battery-operated pin-hole video camera and microphone mounted in an unobtrusive, nearly invisible way. The camera moves with the person and requires no attention or effort to operate. The camera is mounted either on the consumer's head by concealing it in a hat or eyeglass frames; or the consumer's body by concealing it in a handbag, or other object such as a button, piece of jewellery or cellular phone housing. The video camera and microphone are connected to other required hardware such as a battery, video recorder or video transmitter. The mindcam technique can be used in wired or wireless form. It can be viewed by the researcher in real time via a wireless transmission, recorded for later analysis, or both. The camera can be placed anywhere on the subject's person, as long as it captures some aspect of the subject's point of view.

Starr and Fernandez explain three distinct stages in a mindcam research project. After the research domain and issues are established, the first stage is recording video data from the informant's point of view. When this is complete, the second stage uses this first-person video as a memory prompt in a detailed and videotaped interview with the informant. The third stage is final analysis, editing and presentation of the findings.

The authors point out that there are serious ethical issues to consider when using this technology. They express concern about the ethics of employing hidden cameras and emphasise the need for good research ethics protocols. They note that the observational research guidelines set out by market research societies are quite suitable to protect the interests of research respondents, non-participants who are inadvertently filmed and researchers, albeit that it should be recognised that filming for mindcam purposes has not yet been specifically considered by market research societies, and there are areas which remain unclear.

Starr and Fernandez note that there are several advantages and disadvantages attending the use of mindcam. Among the former they list: an unobtrusive first-person perspective; an unedited, unfiltered record; a versatile research methodology; a rich record of behaviour; and a verifiable record of behaviour and perceptions. The major disadvantage is a loss of external physical clues (researchers see what the informant sees and hear everything they may say and can watch much of what they do, but do not see what the informant looks like while doing it). The mindcam does not capture informants' facial expressions or body language while they are engaging in the focal activity.

Although they accept that substantial development is necessary, Starr and Fernandez believe the mindcam technique is now ready for use in substantive research, and they encourage other researchers to employ the technology where appropriate.

9.5 Structured observation: an introduction

So far this chapter might have given you the impression that research using observational techniques is unsystematic and unstructured. This need not be the case. A sound research design based on clear research questions and objectives using participant observation should be highly systematic. However, it would be true to say that the degree of predetermined structure in participant observation may not be that high. After all, one of the strengths of this method is its responsiveness.

In contrast, structured observation is systematic and has a high level of predetermined structure (Box 9.6). If you use this method in your data collection strategy you will be adopting a more detached stance. Your concern would be in quantifying behaviour. As such, structured observation may form only a part of your data collection approach because its function is to tell you how often things happen rather than why they happen. Once again, we see that all research methods have their place in an overall research strategy. What is important is choosing the method that meets the research questions and objectives.

Situations in which structured observation may be used

The most powerful image that occurs to many people when they think of structured observation is that of the 'time-and-motion' study expert. This inscrutable figure stalked the factory floor, complete with clipboard and pencil, making notes on what tasks machine operators were performing and how long these tasks took. This may seem to you

Box 9.6
Focus on student research

Observing staff behaviours at Fastfoodchain

Sangeeta worked at Fastdoodchain for her vacation job. She became interested in measuring service quality in her course and decided to do a preliminary study of customer interaction at Fastfoodcahin.

Fastfoodchain has restaurants all over the world. Central to its marketing strategy is that the customer experienece should be the same in every restaurant in every country of the world. An important part of this strategy is ensuring that customer-facing staff observe the same behavioural standards in every restaurant. This is achieved by the defining of standards of behaviour that customers should experience in every transaction undertaken. These standards are used in the training of staff and assessment of their performance. Reproduced below is part of the section of the standards schedule concerned with dealing with the customer. (There are also sections which deal with the behaviours needed to prepare for work, e.g. till readiness, and general issues, e.g. hygiene.)

The standards schedule is as an observation document by trainers in order to evaluate the degree to which their training is effective with individual employees. It is also used by managers in their assessment of the performance of employees. Sangeeta was very impressed with the level of precision contained in this schedule and wondered whether this may form the basis of her research project.

Section 2: Delighting the customer

Behaviour Staff member:	Was the behaviour observed?	Comments
Smiles and makes eye contact with the customer		
Greets the customer in a friendly manner		
Gives the customer undivided attention throughout the transaction		
Suggests extra items that have not been ordered by the customer		
Places items on clean tray with trayliner facing customer		
Ensures that customer is told where all relevant extras (e.g. cream, sugar) are located		
Explains to customer reasons for any delays and indicates likely duration of delay		
Neatly double-folds bags containing items with the Fastfoodchain logo facing the customer		
Price of order is stated and customer thanked for payment		
Lays all money notes across till drawer until change is given and clearly states the appropriate amount of change		
Customer is finally thanked for transaction, hope expressed that the meal will be enjoyed, and an invitation to return to the restaurant issued		

a long way from the definition of 'research' that we have assumed in this book. Is it not simply fact-finding? Yes it is, but establishing straightforward facts may play an important role in answering your research questions and meeting your objectives. This is straight-forward descriptive research, as we noted in Section 5.2. In recent years the call centre has emerged as a focus for structured observation.

One of the best-known examples of managerial research that used structured observa-tion as part of its data collection approach was the study of the work of senior managers by Mintzberg (1973). This led to Mintzberg casting doubt on the long-held theory that managerial work was a rational process of planning, controlling and directing. Mintzberg studied what five chief executives actually did during one of each of the executives' work-ing weeks. He did this by direct observation and the recording of events on three prede-termined coding schedules. This followed a period of 'unstructured' observation in which the categories of activity that formed the basis of the coding schedules he used were developed. So Mintzberg 'grounded' (grounded theory is explained in Section 13.8) his structured observation on data collected in the period of participant observation.

Of course, studying what job-holders of the type not normally 'observed' actually do in their everyday lives lends itself to approaches other than observation. Self-completion of diaries is one approach that is often used. However, involvement of the researcher in the process is one that lends a degree of impartiality and thoroughness. This has benefits for reliability and validity that may not be evident when the job-holder is the 'observer'.

Another well-known setting for structured observation is the fast food retailer, as Box 9.6 illustrates. This is not what we would think of as the sort of research which would neces-sarily be the major focus of a student dissertation. The same could be said of the research reported in Box 9.9. However, the data generated by both studies is useful for the manage-ment of a variety of organisations.

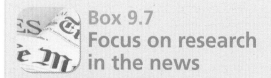

Box 9.7
Focus on research
in the news

Difficulties in monitoring multi-media usage in US households

In the USA, being part of a 'Nielsen household' has long been a point of pride for people whose television habits are monitored by the Nielsen Company. In exchange for token compensation, these viewers know that their per-sonal taste influences what is seen on the screen.

But now Nielsen wants households to let it eaves-drop on many more activities – from web surfing to cell phone use; and they are worried about the extent to which people will grant them access.

In the USA, like the UK, TV watching has lessened as a component of media consumption, so Nielsen has been trying to redesign the way it collects ratings.

This is important as it needs to keep the figures rele-vant to the advertisers and media companies that are its clients. Instead of tracking the TV habits of one set of people, the purchases made by a second set and the Internet use of a third, Nielsen would like to track multiple activities of the same people, allowing it to determine when someone saw an advertisement and then bought the product.

Obviously, this raises potential privacy concerns. 'I'm going to go to a home and say, "I want your TV, I want your Internet, here's a cell phone you're going to use and, by the way, I want to measure your grocery purchases",' said a Nielsen executive. 'That's a lot.'

Nielsen faces growing competition in the ratings business. However, it has a famous brand name, which opens the doors to many American house-holds. The company maintains 17 'panels', or groups, of people who agree to have a certain aspect of their life monitored. Each TV household, for example, can participate for two years and receives a few hundred dollars in cash and gifts; Nielsen promises to keep their identities secret.

In one potential setback to its ambitious modernisation plan, in 2007 Nielsen ran tests to determine the willingness of its TV-monitoring households to allow electronic tracking of Internet usage. Many people refused because of privacy concerns so Nielsen said this month it would scale back the plan and make Internet tracking optional. In 2008 Nielsen announced a second setback: the cancellation of a three-year-old effort, Project Apollo, that has been monitoring the buying and radio and TV habits of 5000 households. The initiative was halted because too few clients wanted to pay for the results. In addition, it transpired that the proportion of households which agreed to have three or four activities tracked was far lower than the percentage that normally agrees to sign up for Nielsen's TV panels, A Nielsen spokesman noted that the more tasks you burden a respondent with, the less likely they are to participate.

Among other projects, Nielsen is working with large retailers to track how much shoppers look at TV screens in malls and stores. The company has given people GPS devices to track where they go. The company is working with Ball State University to observe people in their homes. And in 2008, Nielsen announced an investment in company in California that tracks people's eye movement, brain waves and perspiration while they watch TV.

Nielsen's goal is eventually to persuade all its TV households to agree to web monitoring. At first, the TV households will be asked only for permission to track their viewing of online videos, like You Tube clips or TV shows, not their online financial transactions or web use.

Nielsen understands that tracking multiple activities is more invasive and encounters higher psychological barriers. However, a Nielsen executive is quoted as saying 'the ultimate research dream is to be able to measure everything in the universe. It's not realistic, obviously'.

Source: derived from *New York Times* (2008) 26 Feb.

The proliferation of the Internet has the potential for widening the scope for structured observation. Hewson *et al.* (2003:46) note that at present this may be restricted to what they call 'indirect observation' by which they mean observation of the traces of behaviour. The example which Hewson *et al.* use is observations of the traces of behaviour such as postings to newsgroups (see Box 9.8).

Online retailers similarly use a form of indirect observation of the buying behaviour of their customers and search engines such as Google regularly do research on the search behaviour of their users. Hewson *et al.* (2003) point out that using the Internet

Box 9.8
Focus on management research

Using netnography for marketing research in online communities

In an article in the *Journal of Marketing Research*, Kozinets (2002) notes that consumers making product and brand choices are increasingly turning to computer-mediated communication for information on which to base their decisions. Besides perusing advertising and corporate websites, consumers are using newsgroups, chat rooms, email list servers, personal Internet pages, and other online formats to share ideas, build communities, and contact fellow consumers who are seen as more objective information sources.

Online communities devoted to consumption-related topics are an increasingly important source of

Box 9.8
Focus on management research (*continued*)

data for marketing research. These groups may be construed as individual market segments that are of interest in their own right and may be of noteworthy size. As purchase and consumption decisions are discussed and debated in online communities, it is important that marketing researchers have rigorous and ethical methodological procedures to collect and interpret these data in this novel and challenging context. Kozinets asserts that netnography can be a useful, flexible, ethically sensitive and unobtrusive method adapted to the purpose of studying the language, motivations, consumption linkages and symbols of consumption-oriented online communities.

Kozinets advocates that there are two initial steps that market researchers will find useful as preparation for conducting a netnography. First, researchers must have specific marketing research questions and then identify particular online forums appropriate to the types of questions that are of interest to them. Second, they must learn as much as possible about the forums, the groups and the individual participants they seek to understand.

Among the different types of online communities that Kozinets recommends for study are electronic bulletin boards (also called newsgroups or user groups) which are often organised around particular products, services or lifestyles, each of which may have important uses and implications for marketing researchers who are interested in particular consumer topics, and independent web pages. In general, combining search engines will often provide the bests results for locating specific topics of interest.

The article notes that one of the most important differences between traditional ethnography and netnography may be concerned with research ethics. Marketing researchers desiring to use netnography as a method are obliged to consider and follow ethical guidelines. Ethical concerns about netnography turn on two interrelated questions: first, are online forums to be considered a private or a public site?; and second, what constitutes 'informed consent' in cyberspace? A clear consensus on these issues, and therefore on ethically appropriate procedures for netnography, has not emerged.

Kozinets concludes his article by providing an illuminating example of netnography using contemporary coffee consumption in an online coffee community.

Box 9.9
Focus on management research

Exploring night-time grocery shopping behaviour

Recent legal and societal developments have provided an impetus for rethinking retail opening hours in many European countries. In many of these countries, large supermarket chains are now developing an interest in extending their opening hours to a 24-hour regime.

A paper by Geiger (2007) presents exploratory evidence from a study combining structured and participant observation with a survey of 146 night-time grocery shoppers in a large supermarket in the Republic of Ireland. The results indicate that with a proliferation of 'unconventional' lifestyles among modern consumers, night-time supermarkets offer a service that is highly appreciated by parts of the Irish population. The study also shows that despite the prevalence of functional motivators for night-time grocery shoppers, the hedonic and social aspects of this shopping behaviour should not be overlooked.

Geiger developed an exploratory research design using a combination of quantitative and qualitative data collection methods, namely structured observation, unstructured participant observation and a questionnaire administered to night-time shoppers. The survey consisted of a questionnaire with nine close-ended questions and one open-ended one on shopping motivations, consumers' shopping habits before and after the introduction of 24-hour supermarkets, safety concerns, the influence of shopping location and planned or unplanned patronage behaviour. These questions crystallised from the literature review as the areas of potential importance for night-time shopping patronage.

In addition to the questionnaire, the interviewer filled out a structured observation sheet with the following data for each respondent: amount of people in shopping group, gender, the content of the shopping basket and an approximate amount spent on shopping for each respondent. The interviewer, a graduate student trained in research techniques and part-time employee of the supermarket chain in question, also engaged in casual conversations with supermarket staff and security personnel and observed supermarket shoppers entering the premises during the hours of investigation in an unstructured manner. These unstructured observations, for example, related to the pace in which shoppers browsed the aisles, the trajectories they used and the interactions they engaged in with fellow shoppers or supermarket

staff. Observations and information imparted in conversations with staff were noted down in a research diary and further explored through daily debriefings with Geiger.

Data collection was conducted during one week in 2004 in the local branch of a nationwide chain of supermarkets in the Republic of Ireland, situated in a mixed residential neighbourhood about 2 km from a large hospital. Respondents for the structured observation and questionnaire were chosen on the basis of a systematic sampling procedure, with every fourth person purchasing items in the supermarket being included in the sample between the hours of 11 p.m. and 12 a.m. and again from 6 to 7 a.m., and every shopper purchasing items included between 12 and 6 a.m. In total, 146 complete and usable questionnaires and observation sheets were obtained, with an additional 41 incomplete or unusable questionnaires and 20 questionnaires completed by repeat customers who were excluded from data analysis. Unstructured observational notes filled around 20 pages of a scrapbook. The questionnaires were analysed in the software package *SPSS*; observational data were content categorised and used to complement the questionnaire data. Thus, both data collection methods were combined to provide an exploratory picture of the 24-hour shopper.

for structured observation offers researchers the advantage of non-intrusiveness and the removal of possible observer bias. They also mention the potential for observation of webcam technology, though note that the use of this is very limited at present. The advantages and disadvantages of structured observation are summarised in Table 9.2.

9.6 Structured observation: data collection and analysis

Using coding schedules to collect data

One of the key decisions you will need to make before undertaking structured observation is whether you use an 'off-the-shelf' coding schedule or design your own. You will hardly be surprised to hear us say that this should depend on your research questions and objectives. What follows are two sets of guidelines for assessing the suitability of existing tailor-made coding schedules.

Choosing an 'off-the-shelf' coding schedule

There are a number of questions you should ask yourself when choosing an 'off-the-shelf' coding schedule. These are detailed in Box 9.10.

Table 9.2 Advantages and disadvantages of structured observation

Advantages

- It can be used by anyone after suitable training in the use of the measuring instrument. Therefore, you could delegate this extremely time-consuming task. In addition, structured observation may be carried out simultaneously in different locations. This would present the opportunity of comparison between locations.
- It should yield highly reliable results by virtue of its replicability. We deal with threats to reliability on page 308 but suffice it to say here that the easier the observation instrument to use and understand, the more reliable the results will be.
- Structured observation is capable of more than simply observing the frequency of events. It is also possible to record the relationship between events. For example, is the visit to the retail chemist's counter to present a prescription preceded by an examination of merchandise unrelated to the prescription transaction?
- The method allows the collection of data at the time they occur in their natural setting. Therefore, there is no need to depend on 'second-hand' accounts of phenomena from respondents who put their own interpretation on events.
- Structured observation secures information that most participants would ignore because to them it was too mundane or irrelevant.

Disadvantages

- The observer must be in the research setting when the phenomena under study are taking place.
- Research results are limited to overt action or surface indicators from which the observer must make inferences.
- Data are slow and expensive to collect.

One of the most frequent uses of established coding schedules in management and business is for recording interpersonal interactions in social situations such as meetings or negotiations. This lends itself to structured observation particularly well. Figure 9.2 is an example of just such an 'off-the-shelf' coding schedule that may be used for this purpose.

We would encourage you to use an 'off-the-shelf' coding schedule if you can find one that is suitable. Not only will it save you a lot of time, but it will be tried and tested. Therefore, it is likely to make your results and conclusions more reliable and valid.

Box 9.10
Checklist

Questions to ask when choosing an 'off-the-shelf' coding schedule

✔ For what purpose was the coding schedule developed? Is it consistent with your research question(s) and objectives? (It should be.)

✔ Is there overlap between the behaviours to be observed? (There should not be.)

✔ Are all behaviours in which you are interested covered by the schedule? (They should be.)

✔ Are the behaviours sufficiently clearly specified so that all observers will place behaviours in the same category? (They should be.)

✔ Is any observer interpretation necessary? (It should not be.)

✔ Are codes to be used indicated on the recording form to avoid the necessity for memorisation by the observer? (They should be.)

✔ Will the behaviours to be observed be relevant to the inferences you make? (They should be.)

✔ Have all sources of observer bias been eliminated? (They should have been.)

Source: developed from Walker (1985) *Doing Research: A Handbook for Teachers*, London: Routledge. Reproduced with permission.

	Name of group members (or reference letters)					

Nature of group:
 	
Nature of activity:
 	
Date: Name of observer:
 	
Initial arrangement of group:
 	
       C   D
     B   E
   A F						

	A	B	C	D	E	F
Taking initiative – e.g. attempted leadership, seeking suggestions, offering directions						
Brainstorming – e.g. offering ideas or suggestions, however valid						
Offering positive ideas – e.g. making helpful suggestions, attempting to problem-solve						
Drawing in others – e.g. encouraging contributions, seeking ideas and opinions						
Being responsive to others – e.g. giving encouragement and support, building on ideas						
Harmonising – e.g. acting as peacemaker, calming things down, compromising						
Challenging – e.g. seeking justification, showing disagreement in a constructive way						
Being obstructive – e.g. criticising, putting others down, blocking contributions						
Clarifying/Summarising – e.g. linking ideas, checking progress, clarifying objectives/proposals						
Performing group roles – e.g. spokesperson, recorder, time-keeper, humorist						
Other comments						

Figure 9.2 Recording sheet for observing behaviour in groups

Source: Mullins, L.J. (2002) *Management and Organisational Behaviour* (6th edn). Financial Times Prentice Hall. Copyright © L.J. Mullins 2002. Reprinted with permission of Pearson Education Ltd.

However, you may decide that no 'off-the-shelf' coding schedule is suitable for your purposes. In this case you will need to develop your own schedule. Table 9.3 contains useful guidelines for this activity. The observation categories in your schedule should be devised to be consistent with your research question(s) and objectives. To ensure ease of use and reliability the categories should reflect the attributes shown in Table 9.3.

An alternative to the use of an 'off-the-shelf' coding schedule or the development of your own may be a combination of the two. If this is the option that seems most appropriate in the light of your research question(s) and objectives, we recommend that you

Table 9.3 Guidelines for developing your own coding schedule

Attribute	Comment
Focused	Do not observe and record all that is going on. Concern yourself only with what is strictly relevant
Unambiguous	Therefore requiring the absolute minimum of observer interpretation
Non-context dependent	The observer's job is more difficult if the coding of behaviours is dependent on the context in which the behaviour occurs. It may be essential for your research question(s) and objectives to record contextual data, but this should be kept to a minimum
Explicitly defined	Provide examples for the observer (even if this is you) of behaviours that fall into each category and those that do not
Exhaustive	Ensure that it is always possible to make a coding for those behaviours you wish to observe
Mutually exclusive	Ensure that there is no overlap between behaviour categories
Easy to record	The observer must be able to tick the correct box quickly without having to memorise appropriate categories

Source: developed from Robson (2002) *Real World Research: A Resource for Social Scientists and Practitioner – Researchers* (2nd edn). Oxford: Blackwell. Reproduced with permission.

still use the checklist in Box 9.10 and the guidelines in Table 9.3 to ensure that your schedule is as valid and reliable as possible.

Data analysis

The complexity of your analysis will depend on your research question(s) and objectives. It may be that you are using Figure 9.2 to establish the number of interactions by category in order to relate the result to the output of the meeting. This may enable you to conclude that 'positive' behaviours (e.g. brainstorming) may be more strongly associated with meetings that make clear decisions than 'negative' behaviours (e.g. being obstructive). Simple manual analysis may be sufficient for this purpose.

Alternatively, you may be using Figure 9.2 to see what patterns emerge. It may be that the amount of interactions varies by the nature of the group or its activity, or that seating position is associated with the number of contributions. Patterns reflecting relationships between numbers of interaction categories may become evident (e.g. when 'drawing in others' was high 'clarifying/summarising' was also high). This level of analysis is obviously more complex and will need computer software to calculate the cross-classifications. Section 12.2 contains guidance on preparing data for quantitative analysis by computer.

Threats to validity and reliability

The main threats here are ones to reliability. This section deals with three of these: subject error, time error and observer effects.

Subject error

Subject error may cause your data to be unreliable. You may be concerned with observing the output of sales administrators as measured by the amount of orders they process in a day. Subject error may be evident if you chose administrators in a section that was short-staffed owing to illness. This may mean that they were having to spend more time answering telephones, and less time processing orders, as there were fewer people available to handle telephone calls. The message here is clear: choose subjects who in as many respects as possible are 'normal' examples of the population under study.

Time error

Closely related to the issue of subject error is that of **time error**. It is essential that the time at which you conduct the observation does not provide data that are untypical of the total time period in which you are interested. So the output of the sales administrators may be less in the immediate hour before lunch as their energy levels are lower. If you were interested in the number of customers using a retail store, you would need to conduct observations at different times of the day and week to provide a valid picture of total customer flow.

Observer effect

One of the most powerful threats to the validity and reliability of data collected through observation is that of **observer effect**. This is quite simply that the process of the observer's observation of behaviour changes the nature of that behaviour owing to the fact that the subject is conscious of being observed. The simplest way to overcome this effect is for the observation to take place in secret. However, this is often not possible, even if it were ethically acceptable.

Robson (2002) notes two strategies for overcoming observer effect. The first, **minimal interaction**, means that the observer tries as much as possible to 'melt into the background' – having as little interaction as possible with the subjects of the observation. This may involve sitting in an unobtrusive position in the room and avoiding eye contact with those being observed. The second strategy is **habituation**, where the subjects being observed become familiar with the process of observation so that they take it for granted (Box 9.3). Those of you who use a tape-recorder to record discussions may notice that initially the respondent is very wary of the machine, but after a short period this apprehension wears off and the machine is not noticed.

Adopting a strategy of habituation to reduce observer effect may mean that several observation sessions are necessary in the same research setting with the same subjects. As the observer effect diminishes, so the pattern of interaction will settle down into a predictable pattern.

9.7 Summary

- Participant observation is a method in which the researcher participates in the lives and activities of those whom they are studying. It is used to attempt to get to the root of 'what is going on' in a wide range of social settings.
- You may use the participant observation method in a student placement or you may already be a member of an organisation that will enable you to adopt the role of the practitioner-researcher.

- Participant observation means that you adopt a number of potential roles differentiated by the degree to which your identity is concealed from the subjects of the research and the degree to which you participate in the events you are studying.
- Participant observation must avoid the trap of mere storytelling. The purpose is to develop theory.
- A prevalent form of data analysis used in participant observation is analytic induction. This may lead to an initial hypothesis being redeveloped more than once.
- Structured observation is concerned with the frequency of events. It is characterised by a high level of predetermined structure and quantitative analysis.
- A choice may be made between 'off-the-shelf' and a schedule that you design for your own purpose. Alternatively, you may decide to use a 'hybrid'.
- The main threats to reliability and validity inherent in structured observation are subject error, time error and observer effects.

Self-check questions

Help with these questions is available at the end of the chapter.

9.1 You are a project manager responsible for the overall management of a large project to introduce your company's technology into the development of a new hospital. Most of the members of your team and from UK, France and Germany. However, several of the engineers are from the newest EU member states, principally Poland. You notice at project meetings that the Polish engineers tend to be far more reticent than the other team members in volunteering ideas for solving problems.

This issue has coincided with the arrival on the scene of a management student from the local university who is keen to study a real-life management problem for her final-year undergraduate dissertation. You have asked her to study the assimilation experience of 'new EU member state' engineers into your company with a view to recommending any changes that may be necessary to change the programme designed to effect the assimilation process.

You ask her to start the research by sitting in on the project team meetings and, in particular, observing the behaviour of the 'new EU member state' engineers. What suggestions would you make to your student to help her structure her observation of the meetings?

9.2 You have been asked to give a presentation to a group of managers at the accountancy firm in which you are hoping to negotiate access for research. You wish to pursue the research question, 'What are the informal rules that govern the way in which trainee accountants work, and how do they learn these rules?'

You realise that talk of 'attempting to learn the trainee accountants' symbolic world' would do little to help your cause with this group of non-research-minded business people. However, you wish to point out some of the benefits to the organisation that your research may yield. Outline what you believe these would be.

9.3 You are a building society branch manager. You feel your staff are too reluctant to generate sales 'leads' from ordinary investors and borrowers, which may be passed on to the society's consultants in order that they can attempt to sell life insurance policies, pensions and unit trusts. You would like to understand the reasons for their reluctance. As the participant observer, how would you go about this?

How would you record your observations?

9.4 Look again at Box 9.10. Ask the questions contained in Box 9.10 in relation to the coding schedule in Figure 9.2. How well does it match?

Review and discussion questions

9.5   Compile a behaviour observation sheet similar to that in Box 9.6 in respect of either your job or that of a friend. Use this to compile a record of the behaviours observed.

9.6   Choose an everyday example of social behaviour, such as the way that motorists park their cars in 'open' (not multi-storey) car parks. Observe this behaviour (for example, the distance from the entrance/exit that they park) and draw general conclusions about observed behaviour patterns.

9.7   Video record a current affairs (or similar) discussion on TV. Use the recording sheet in Figure 9.2 to record the interactions and then assess interaction patterns.

Progressing your research project

Deciding on the appropriateness of observation

- Return to your research question(s) and objectives. Decide on how appropriate it would be to use observation as part of your research strategy.
- If you decide that this is appropriate, explain the relationship between your research question(s) and objectives and observation. If you decide that using observation is not appropriate, justify your decision.
- Look again at the previous paragraph and ensure that you have responded for both participant observation and structured observation *separately*.

- If you decide that participant observation is appropriate, what practical problems do you foresee? Are you likely to be faced with any moral dilemmas? How might you overcome both sets of problems?
- If you decide that participant observation is appropriate, what threats to validity and reliability are you likely to encounter? How might you overcome these?
- If you decide that structured observation is appropriate, what practical problems do you foresee? How might you overcome these?
- If you decide that structured observation is appropriate, what threats to validity and reliability are you likely to encounter? How might you overcome these?
- If you decide that structured observation is appropriate, design your own research instrument.

References

Ackroyd, S. and Hughes, J. (1992) *Data Collection in Context* (2nd edn). London: Longman.

Brannick, T. and Coghlan, D. (2007) 'In defense of being native the case for insider academic research', *Organizational Research Methods,* Vol.10, No.1, pp. 59–74.

Bryman, A. (1989) *Research Methods and Organisation Studies*. London: Unwin Hyman.

Delbridge, R. and Kirkpatrick, I. (1994) 'Theory and practice of participant observation', in V. Wass and P. Wells (eds) *Principles and Practice in Business and Management Research*. Aldershot: Dartmouth, pp. 35–62.

Denzin, N. (1989) *The Research Act: A Theoretical Introduction to Sociological Methods* (3rd edn). Englewood Cliffs, NJ: Prentice Hall.

Ditton, J. (1977) *Part-Time Crime: An Ethnography of Fiddling and Pilferage*. London: Macmillan.

Geiger, S. (2007) 'Exploring night-time grocery shopping behaviour', *Journal of Retailing and Consumer Services*, January, pp. 24–34.

Gill, J. and Johnson, P. (2002) *Research Methods for Managers* (3rd edn). London: Sage.

Hewson, C., Yule, P., Laurent, D. and Vogel, C. (2003) *Internet Research Methods*. London: Sage.

Kozinets, R. (2002) 'The field behind the screen: Using netnography for marketing research in online communities', *Journal of Marketing Research*, Vol 39, No. 1, pp. 61–72.

Lee, N. and Broderick, A. (2007) 'The past, present and future of observational research in marketing', *Qualitative Market Research*, Vol. 10, No. 2, pp. 121–9.

Mintzberg, H. (1973) *The Nature of Managerial Work*. New York: Harper & Row.

Mullins, L. (2002) *Management and Organisational Behaviour* (6th edn). Harlow: Financial Times Prentice Hall.

Penn, R. (2005) 'Football spectators in English and Italian stadia'. Available at: http://www.maths. lancs.ac.uk/~penn/papers/roger/FootballSpectators/Football_Spectators_in_English_and_ Italian_Stadia.html [Accessed 24 May 2008.]

Punch, M. (1993) 'Observation and the police: The research experience', in Hammersley. M. *Social Research: Philosophy. Politics and Practice*. London: Sage, pp. 181–99.

Robson, C. (2002) *Real World Research: A Resource for Social Scientists and Practitioner-Researchers* (2nd edn). Oxford: Blackwell.

Rosen, M. (1991) 'Breakfast at Spiros dramaturgy and dominance', in P. Frost, L. Moore, M. Louis, C. Lundberg and J. Martin (eds) *Reframing Organisational Culture*. Newbury Park, CA: Sage, pp. 77–89.

Roy, D. (1952) 'Quota restriction and goldbricking in a machine shop', *American Journal of Sociology*, Vol. 57, pp. 427–42.

Starr, R. and Fernandez, K. (2007) 'The mindcam methodology: Perceiving through the natives eye', *Qualitative Market Research*, Vol. 10, No. 2, pp.168–82.

Walker, R. (1985) *Doing Research: A Handbook for Teachers*. London: Methuen.

Whyte, W. (1955) *Street Corner Society* (2nd edn). Chicago, IL.: University of Chicago Press.

Further reading

Ackroyd, S. and Hughes, J. (1992) *Data Collection in Context* (2nd edn). London: Longman. Chapter 6 contains a helpful analysis of the origins of, and problems with, participant observation. It also has a full analysis of symbolic interactionism.

Hammersley, M. and Atkinson, P. (1995) *Ethnography Principles in Practice* (2nd edn). London: Routledge. Chapters 4 and 8 on field relations and data analysis in participant observation are well worth reading.

Kozinets, R. (2002) 'The field behind the screen: using netnography for marketing research in online communities', *Journal of Marketing Research*, Vol. 39, No. 1, pp. 61–72. A most interesting account of how information technology can be applied in observational research.

Mintzberg, H. (1973) *The Nature of Managerial Work*. New York: Harper & Row. Appendix C has a full account of the methodology that Mintzberg employed. You will be struck by how such a seemingly simple methodology can lead to such important conclusions.

Punch, M. (1993) 'Observation and the police: the research experience', in M. Hammersley. (ed.) *Social Research: Philosophy, Politics and Practice*. London: Sage, pp. 181–99. An absorbing account of fieldwork experience with the Amsterdam police that makes riveting reading; particularly good at the process of negotiating relationships with fellow participants.

Robson, C. (2002) *Real World Research* (2nd edn). Oxford: Blackwell. Chapter 11 is a most thorough and practical guide to observational methods. There is an interesting section at the end of the chapter on inter-observer reliability that you should look at if you intend to use a number of observers.

Taylor, S. and Bogdan, R. (1984) *Introduction to Qualitative Research Methods: A Guidebook and Resource*. New York: Wiley. Chapters 2 and 3 are very practical accounts of how to approach and conduct participant observation.

Case 9
Online images of tourist destinations

The Taj Mahal
Source: © Mridula Dwivedi 2008

Anjali, was in her final year of study for an undergraduate business degree at an Indian university. She was very keen to explore the online image of India as a tourism destination for her research project. Her review of the literature had highlighted that the destination image concept was considered important for the overall success of tourism initiatives (Tasci and Gartner 2007). However, only a few studies were available on the impact of Internet forums on image formation. Anjali was an avid traveller and frequently searched for information on the Internet for her trips. For example, when she was planning a trip to Agra to see the Taj Mahal, she found travel agency websites useful only to a limited extent. They provided a lot of information on the history of the monument along with some stunning pictures of it. However, a very different picture emerged from the consumer-generated content on message boards and blogs. She was surprised to find that even though the tourists were spellbound with the Taj Mahal, many also commented upon the pollution, lack of basic cleanliness and annoyingly aggressive selling at almost all the tourist spots.

An extract from one of the blogs about a trip to Agra stated:

The train arrived right on time at Agra Cant. and deposited the three of us quite clueless on the platform. I had read at Indiamike <http://www.indiamike.com/india/showthread. php?t=24988> about prepaid taxi stand and that was our immediate destination. Our cluelessness must have been quite apparent to the taxi driver who was trying to direct us to the pre-paid booth but skepticism was written all over my face as to his directions. He pointed out the exit to us and we decide to trust him that far because the railway signboard concurred with his directions.

Once we exited, it was easy to spot the prepaid taxi booth. I stood in the line for the ticket. And while the people from other countries before me were asking for taxis to Maurya Sheraton and the like, I could read the signboard at leisure. That is where I came across the phrase 'Shatabdi to Shatabdi' tour first. It was packaged at Rs. 950 (taxi charges only) for a non AC vehicle and Rs. 1400 for AC vehicle. It included a trip to Taj Mahal, Agra Fort and Fatehpur Sikri. Tempting as it sounded, I decided to stick to our original plan to hire a taxi just to the Taj Mahal. The good folks at the prepaid booth charged me Rs. 125 for the service.

The hard sell started in the taxi itself. Our driver for this trip, extended the offer to retain the taxi for the entire day at the charges of an additional Rs. 325. We told him we were not interested. He persisted saying he could take us to the market too and we politely told him we would not do any shopping. He said I will not find any taxi vacant to take us back to the station in the evening and it would not be safe for us at all to roam on our own. I told him it would be really sad if I can't feel safe in our own country in broad daylight. After trying for 15 minutes he gave up.

By that time we were almost at the Taj Mahal car parking. Most types of motorized vehicles are not permitted beyond this point. We decided to walk the remaining one kilometer though one can take a cycle rickshaw or a horse drawn tanga to the entrance. The dual pricing policy remains in place in spite of some news that I read quite sometime back that hinted at some changes. Indian nationals pay Rs. 20 and the foreign nationals Rs. 750.

(Dwivedi 2006)

Anjali knew several threads that discussed the beauty of India and its unique cultural experience that takes one's breath away. But there were also genuine complaints as well. One post that generated more than 100 responses was about the Indian Railways website and the difficulties involved in using it. Then there were the issues regarding the safety of women, poverty and begging, aggressive selling and touting, and lack of infrastructure. Anjali was convinced that if she could use the message board data systematically, it would generate insightful accounts of the destination image of India from a consumer's perspective.

Anjali has been a member of two popular message boards, Thorntree and Indiamike, for two years. Thorntree, (http://www.lonelyplanet.com/thorntree/index.jspa) is a global travel message board managed by the Lonely Planet, with a vibrant India section. Indiamike (www.indiamike.com) emerged from the efforts of just an individual but grew to over 25 000 members. As she followed and participated in many discussions on both the boards, the appeal of online participant observation as a data collection method for her research project grew. It would save her time and money and was comparatively an unobtrusive technique for research. As the data from the message boards were already on the Internet and accessible publicly through various search engines, she foresaw little difficulty in accessing it. An added advantage was that the messages were already in text form and so would not require recording or subsequently transcribing. All she needed to do was observe.

Anjali decided to look further at the research methods literature to better understand the use of Internet data for research. Reading King's (1996) article, she realised that not everyone considered the postings on Internet forums public. Rather, many message board members perceived their interactions to be private and posted their messages exclusively for that particular forum. Members might therefore even resent researcher presence on groups that discussed sensitive issues like illness or personal crisis. Furthermore, a relatively small number of participants in a group might strengthen the notion that the forum was private rather than public. Finally, many sites were only for members who were required to register. In such cases, acquiring informed consent from the participants was likely to be imperative for any researcher. Unlike the print media where the guidelines for quotes, acknowledgements, references, seeking permissions, etc. are clear, in the new medium of the cyberspace the definition of private and public was still blurred, so Anjali decided to explore more recent literature to see how the discussion had evolved.

Anjali found that even a decade later there were still differing opinions regarding whether such Internet message boards were public or private sites. Langer and Beckman (2005) argued that if the message board did not require registration and the membership base was sufficiently large, the information could be considered public. Next, she came across Kozinets's (2006) proposed guidelines for Internet research that were quite comprehensive. He suggested that researchers should, as a first step, try to ascertain whether the site they wanted to use was public or private. If it was private, seeking permission to use it for research was essential. In addition he recommended that, even in public forums, informed consent was required from the members who were being quoted verbatim. After all, search engines, like Google, could identify the sources of any verbatim quotes along with the user profiles on the original site. To complicate the matters further, for sensitive topics many members refused permission to be quoted directly whereas others considered their words a matter of authorship and wanted to be associated with the quote with their screen names or even their real names (Eysenbach and Till 2001).

Anjali realised that both the message boards she wanted to observe had significantly large membership, running into tens of thousands. She was tempted to use this figure to argue that these message boards were public. Further, the messages were there for anyone to see through search engine queries on 'travel India' and such other keywords. But both the message boards required registration and postings could only be made by members. Through her participation she came to know that many members only posted just a few messages and never came back to the board again. This meant it would be difficult, if not impossible, to contact them to seek their permission to quote them. Consequently, the readings, instead of clarifying the way she should approach her research project, in fact, left her further mired in a web of confusion. She was still convinced that the data she had found on the message board was fascinating but she wanted to use it in a way that was both proper and ethical, so she turned to her supervisor to discuss the best course for her research project.

References

Dwivedi, M. (2006) 'Travel Tales from India. Taj Mahal, Agra: Shatabdi to Shatabdi One Day Trip 23 July 2006'. Available at: http://www.gonomad.com/traveltalesfromindia/labels/Agra.html [Accessed 31 January 2008.]

Eysenbach, G. and Till, J.E. (2001) 'Ethical issues in qualitative research on internet communities', *British Medical Journal,* 323:7321, pp. 1103–5.

King, S.A. (1996) 'Researching internet communities: proposed ethical guidelines for the reporting of results', *The Information Society*, Vol. 12, No. 2, pp. 119–27.

Kozinets, R.V. (2006) 'Netnography 2.0', In R.W. Belk (ed.) *Handbook of Qualitative Research Methods in Marketing*. Cheltenham: Edward Elgar Publishing, pp. 129–42.

Langer, R. and Beckman, S.C. (2005) 'Sensitive research topics: netnography revisited', *Qualitative Market Research*, Vol. 8, No. 2, pp. 189–203.

Tasci, A.D.A. and Gartner, W.C. (2007) 'Destination image and its functional relationships', *Journal of Travel Research*, Vol. 45, No. 4, pp. 413–25.

Questions

1 Do you consider the Internet message boards that Anjali wishes to use to be public or private? How would you justify your answer?
2 Do you consider informed consent necessary for Anjali's research project? If informed consent were necessary, how should she go about obtaining it?
3 What do you think should be Anjali's policy regarding the use of direct quotations?
4 What could be the advantages of using online observation for Anjali? Are there any disadvantages that she should be aware of?

Additional case studies relating to material covered in this chapter are available via the book's Companion Website, **www.pearsoned.co.uk/saunders**. They are:

- Manufacturing in a textile company
- Customer satisfaction on a long-haul tour holiday
- Exploring service quality in bank customers' face-to-face experiences.

Self-check answers

9.1 It may be as well to suggest to her that she start her attendance at meetings with an unstructured approach in order to simply get the 'feel' of what is happening. She should make notes of her general impressions of the 'new EU member states' team members' general participation in meetings. She could then analyse these data and develop an observational instrument which could be used in further meetings she attends. This instrument would be based on a coding schedule that allowed her to record, among other things, the amount of contribution by each person at the meeting and the content of that contribution.

  Data collection at the meetings does, of course, raise questions of research ethics. In our view, you, as the project manager, should explain to the team the role that the researcher is playing at the meetings. It would be quite truthful to say that the meeting participation of all team members is being observed with the overall purpose of making the meetings more effective, although it need not be emphasised what gave rise to the project manager's initial concern.

9.2 The research question is very broad. It allows you plenty of scope to discover a host of interesting things about the world of the trainee accountant. Without doubt, one of the things you will emerge with a clear understanding of is what they like about their work and what they do not like. This has practical implications for the sort of people that the firm ought to recruit, how they should be trained and rewarded. You may learn about some of the short cuts practised by all occupations that may not be in the interest of the client. By the same token you will probably discover aspects of good practice that managers can disseminate to other accountants. The list of practical implications is endless.

  All this assumes, of course, that you will supply the managers with some post-research feedback. This does raise issues of confidentiality, which you must have thought through beforehand.

9.3 This is a difficult one. The question of status may be a factor. However, this would depend on your relationship with the staff. If you are, say, of similar age and have an open, friendly, 'one of the team' relationship with them, then it may not be too difficult. The element of threat that would attend a less open relationship would not be present.

  You could set aside a time each day to work on the counter in order really to get to know what life is like for them. Even if you have done their job, you may have forgotten what it is like! It may have changed since your day. Direct conversations about lead generation would probably not feature in your research times. However, you would need to have a period of reflection after each 'research session' to think about the implications for your research question of what you have just experienced.

9.4 Clearly, there are some question marks about the coding schedule in Figure 9.2. There does appear to be some overlap in the behavioural categories covered in the schedule. For example, it could be difficult to distinguish between what is 'offering directions' (taking initiative) and 'offering ideas' (brainstorming). It might be even more difficult to draw a distinction between 'offering suggestions' (brainstorming) and 'making helpful suggestions' (offering positive ideas). Similarly, there does not appear to be much difference between the behaviours in 'drawing in others' and 'being responsive to others'. You may argue that the first is defined by invitation, the second by response. But making the distinction when the interactions are coming thick and fast in the research setting will be much less easy.

The point about all these potential confusions is that different observers may make different estimations. This obviously has potentially harmful implications for the reliability of the coding schedule.

A much smaller point is: How does the observer indicate on the schedule the occurrence of a particular interaction?

Get ahead using resources on the Companion Website at:

www.pearsoned.co.uk/saunders

- Improve your SPSS and NVivo research analysis with practice tutorials.
- Save time researching on the Internet with the Smarter Online Searching Guide.
- Test your progress using self-assessment questions.
- Follow live links to useful websites.

Chapter 10

Collecting primary data using semi-structured, in-depth and group interviews

Learning outcomes

By the end of this chapter you should be:

- able to classify research interviews in order to help you to understand the purpose of each type;
- aware of research situations favouring the use of semi-structured and in-depth interviews, and their limitations;
- able to analyse potential data quality issues and evaluate how to overcome these;
- able to consider the development of your competence to undertake semi-structured and in-depth interviews, and the logistical and resource issues that affect their use;
- aware of the advantages and disadvantages of using one-to-one and group interviews, including focus groups, in particular contexts;
- aware of the issues and advantages of conducting interviews by telephone and via the Internet or intranet.

10.1 Introduction

An interview is a purposeful discussion between two or more people (Kahn and Cannell 1957). The use of interviews can help you to gather valid and reliable data that are relevant to your research question(s) and objectives. Where you have not yet formulated such a research question and objectives, an interview or interviews may help you to achieve this. In reality, the research interview is a general term for several types of interview. This fact is significant since the nature of any interview should be consistent with your research question(s) and objectives, the purpose of your research and the research strategy that you have adopted. We provide an overview of types of interview in the next section of this chapter (Section 10.2) and show how these are related to particular research purposes. However, as indicated by this chapter's title, our main focus is semi-structured, in-depth and group interviews, structured interviews (interviewer administered questionnaires) being discussed in Chapter 11.

Section 10.3 considers situations favouring the use of semi-structured and in-depth interviews. The following three sections examine issues associated with the use of these types of interview. Section 10.4 identifies data quality issues associated with their use and discusses how to overcome them. Section 10.5 considers the areas of competence that you will need to develop. Section 10.6 discusses logistical and resource issues and how to

There is probably not a day that goes by without you reading about, listening to and watching interviews. We read interviews such as those given by business leaders in quality newspapers, listen to interviews such as those with celebrities on radio programmes and watch interviews on television programmes. However, despite the seeming ease with which they are conducted, using the interview to collect research data requires considerable skills.

Interviewer skills are regularly demonstrated by presenters of programmes such as the BBC's *Dragons' Den*. In this programme potential entrepreneurs looking for investment present their business idea to venture captialists (dragons). The dragons use the information they glean from the presentations and the answers to their subsequent questions to make a decision as to whether or not to invest.

When asking questions the dragons inevitable focus on those aspects of the business idea about which they have concerns. Initially they ask more open questions which are followed by more probing questions as the following exchange between a dragon (James Caan) and two entrepreneurs (Ian Forshew and Celia Norowzian) seeking investment in their 'Beach Break Live' event illustrates (Dragons' Den 2007):

> **Caan: Can you just run those numbers by me again?**
> *Forshew: This year we turned over £120 000 . . .*
> *Caan: . . . and you made how much profit?*
> *Forshew: We didn't, we didn't make any profit this year.*
> *Caan: Did you lose money? Break even?*

Source: Eamonn McCormack/Getty.

Eventually, after further questioning and negotiation a different dragon, Peter Jones, agreed to provide them with £50 000 investment in exchange for 25 per cent of their business. This was subject to renegotiation after repayment.

Such interviews between the entrepreneurs and the dragons not only provide attention grabbing television, they also also highlight the importance of asking clear questions and probing to ensure that the information required is obtained.

manage these. Throughout the discussion of issues related to the use of semi-structured and in-depth interviews our focus is on what you will need to think about in order to be able to conduct these interviews. Section 10.7 considers the particular advantages and issues associated with the use of group interviews and focus groups. Finally, Section 10.8 explores the advantages and issues associated with telephone, Internet and intranet-mediated (electronic) interviews.

10.2 Types of interview and their link to the purposes of research and research strategy

Types of interview

Interviews may be highly formalised and structured, using standardised questions for each research participant (often called a **respondent**) (Section 11.2), or they may be informal and unstructured conversations. In between there are intermediate positions. One typology that is commonly used is thus related to the level of formality and structure, whereby interviews may be categorised as one of:

- structured interviews;
- semi-structured interviews;
- unstructured or in-depth interviews.

Another typology (Healey 1991; Healey and Rawlinson 1993, 1994) differentiates between:

- standardised interviews;
- non-standardised interviews.

Robson (2002), based on the work of Powney and Watts (1987), refers to a different typology:

- respondent (participant) interviews;
- informant interviews.

There is overlap between these different typologies, although consideration of each typology adds to our overall understanding of the nature of research interviews.

Structured interviews use questionnaires based on a predetermined and 'standardised' or identical set of questions and we refer to them as interviewer-administered questionnaires (Section 11.2). You read out each question and then record the response on a standardised schedule, usually with pre-coded answers (Sections 11.4 and 12.2). While there is social interaction between you and the participant, such as the preliminary explanations that you will need to provide, you should read out the questions exactly as written and in the same tone of voice so that you do not indicate any bias. As structured interviews are used to collect quantifiable data they are also referred to as 'quantitative research interviews'.

By comparison, semi-structured and in-depth (unstructured) interviews are 'non-standardised'. These are often referred to as 'qualitative research interviews' (King 2004). In **semi-structured interviews** the researcher will have a list of themes and questions to be covered, although these may vary from interview to interview. This means that you may omit some questions in particular interviews, given a specific organisational context that is encountered in relation to the research topic. The order of questions may also be varied depending on the flow of the conversation. On the other hand, additional questions may be required to explore your research question and objectives given the nature of events within particular organisations. The nature of the questions and the ensuing discussion mean that data will be recorded by audio-recording the conversation or perhaps note taking (Section 10.5).

Unstructured interviews are informal. You would use these to explore in depth a general area in which you are interested. We, therefore, refer to these as 'in-depth interviews' in this chapter and elsewhere in this book. There is no predetermined list of questions to work through in this situation, although you need to have a clear idea about the aspect or aspects that you want to explore. The interviewee is given the opportunity to talk freely about events, behaviour and beliefs in relation to the topic area, so that this type of interaction is sometimes called 'non-directive'. It has been labelled as an **informant interview** since it is the interviewee's perceptions that guide the conduct of the interview. In comparison, a **participant** (or respondent) **interview** is one where the interviewer directs the interview and the interviewee responds to the questions of the researcher (Easterby-Smith *et al.* 2008; Ghauri and Grønhaug 2005; Robson 2002).

We can also differentiate between types of interview related to the nature of interaction between the researcher and those who participate in this process. Interviews may be conducted on a one-to-one basis, between you and a single participant. Such interviews are most commonly conducted by meeting your participant 'face to face', but there may be some situations where you conduct an interview by telephone or electronically via the Internet or an organisation's intranet. There may be other situations where you conduct a semi-structured or in-depth interview on a group basis, where you meet with a small number of participants to explore an aspect of your research through a group discussion that you facilitate. These forms of interview are summarised in Figure 10.1. The discussion throughout most of this chapter applies to each of these forms. However, the final two Sections (10.7 and 10.8) include specific consideration of the issues and advantages related to the use of group interviews and focus groups and to the use of a telephone and Internet-mediated interviews as an alternative to a 'face-to-face' meeting, respectively.

Links to the purpose of research and research strategy

Each form of interview outlined above has a distinct purpose. Standardised interviews are normally used to gather data, which will then be the subject of quantitative analysis (Sections 12.3–12.5), for example as part of a survey strategy. Non-standardised (semi-structured and in-depth) interviews are used to gather data, which are normally analysed qualitatively (Sections 13.2–13.7), for example as part of a case study strategy. These data are likely to be used not only to reveal and understand the 'what' and the 'how' but also to place more emphasis on exploring the 'why'.

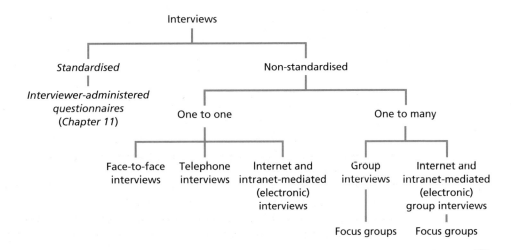

Figure 10.1
Forms of interview

Box 10.1
Focus on management research

The impact of international assignments on career capital

A recent paper by Michael Dickmann and Noleen Doherty in the *British Journal of Management* (2008) explores the perceived impact of international assignments on individuals' career capital. Data were collected from two case study UK-based global organisations, one in the financial services sector and the other in fast moving consumer goods. Both organisations had a long history of international operations and used a large number of international assignees.

Initially three face-to-face interviews were carried out with senior human resource executives in the head offices of each of the organisations. These focused upon general human resource polices and practices and 'were designed to address knowing *how*, *why* and *whom*' with regard to international assignments (Dickmann and Doherty 2008:148). Internal company documents relating to both career management and international assignment policies were also analysed.

Subsequently, a semi-structured interview schedule was designed to collect data from expatriate managers on their perceptions of the impact of international assignments upon their career capital. This included a range of questions with prompts for subsequent discussion such as (2008:159):

Career capital on assignment

- What did you learn from the international experience? Compare now with before your international assignment
- capabilities (*knowing how*, e.g. technical capabilities, international skills)
- networks (*knowing whom*) (e.g. quality of social networks, work and non-work)
- personal motivations (*knowing why*) (clarity in personal and work motivation, sense of purpose, energy and direction of work)

Career capital at repatriation

- What impact has the international assignment had on your career/career prospects?
  - Capabilities
  - Networks
  - Personal motivations
- When was repatriation discussed?
- How was a role identified?
- Where does an international assignment fit in with your career plan?

The schedule was used in interviews with 26 managers conducted over the period 2003 to 2005. Eleven of these interviewees were from the financial services organisation and 15 from the fast moving consumer goods organisation. All interviews were audio-recorded and subsequently transcribed prior to data analysis using NVivo, a computer program for aiding qualitative data analysis.

In Chapter 5 we outlined how the purpose of your research could be classified as exploratory, descriptive and explanatory studies (Section 5.2). By examining these categories we can see how the various types of interview may be used to gather information for, and assist the progress of, each kind of study:

- In an exploratory study, in-depth interviews can be very helpful to 'find out what is happening [and] to seek new insights' (Robson 2002:59). Semi-structured interviews may also be used in relation to an exploratory study (Box 10.1).
- In descriptive studies, structured interviews (Section 11.2) can be used as a means to identify general patterns.
- In an explanatory study, semi-structured interviews may be used in order to understand the relationships between variables, such as those revealed from a descriptive study (Section 5.2). Structured interviews may also be used in relation to an explanatory study, in a statistical sense (Section 12.5).

Table 10.1 Uses of different types of interview in each of the main research categories

	Exploratory	Descriptive	Explanatory
Structured		✓✓	✓
Semi-structured	✓		✓✓
Unstructured	✓✓		

✓✓ = more frequent, ✓ = less frequent.

This is summarised in Table 10.1.

Your research may incorporate more than one type of interview (multiple methods). As part of a survey strategy, for example, you may decide to use in-depth or semi-structured interviews initially to help identify the questions that should be asked in a questionnaire administered as a structured interview. The data that you gather from such exploratory interviews will be used in the design of your structured interview. Alternatively, semi-structured interviews may be used to explore and explain themes that have emerged from the use of a questionnaire (Tashakkori and Teddlie 1998). In addition to the use of multiple methods, different types of interview questions may be used within one interview: 'one section of an interview may ask a common set of factual questions . . . while in another section a semi-structured qualitative approach may be used to explore [responses]' (Healey and Rawlinson 1994:130). Increasingly authors also emphasise how semi-structured or in-depth interviews, may also be used as part of mixed methods research, such as a means to validate findings from questionnaires (Bryman 2006). We can see, therefore, that the various types of interview have a number of potentially valuable uses in terms of undertaking your research project. The key point for you to consider is the consistency between your research question and objectives, the strategy you will employ and the methods of data collection you will use – their fitness for purpose.

10.3 When to use non-standardised (qualitative) interviews

There are many situations in which the use of non-standardised (qualitative) research interviews as a method of data collection may be advantageous. These can be grouped into four aspects related to interview:

- the purpose of the research;
- the significance of establishing personal contact;
- the nature of the data collection questions;
- length of time required and completeness of the process.

We examine each of these in turn.

The purpose of the research

Where you are undertaking an exploratory study, or a study that includes an exploratory element, it is likely that you will include non-standardised (qualitative) research interviews in your design (Cooper and Schindler 2008). Similarly, an explanatory study is also likely to include interviews in order for the researcher to be able to infer causal relationships between variables (Sections 5.2 and 11.4). Where it is necessary for you to understand the reasons for the decisions that your research participants have taken, or to understand the reasons for their attitudes and opinions, you are likely to need to conduct a **qualitative interview**.

Semi-structured and in-depth interviews provide you with the opportunity to 'probe' answers, where you want your interviewees to explain, or build on, their responses. This is important if you are adopting an interpretivist epistemology, where you will be concerned to understand the meanings that participants ascribe to various phenomena (Section 4.2). Interviewees may use words or ideas in a particular way, and the opportunity to probe these meanings will add significance and depth to the data you obtain. They may also lead the discussion into areas that you had not previously considered but which are significant for your understanding, and which help you to address your research question and objectives, or indeed help you formulate such a question. Interviews also afford each interviewee an opportunity to hear themselves 'thinking aloud' about things they may not have previously thought about. The result should be that you are able to collect a rich and detailed set of data. However, you need to be aware that the manner in which you interact with your interviewees and ask questions will impact on the data you collect (Silverman 2007).

The significance of establishing personal contact

We have found that managers are more likely to agree to be interviewed, rather than complete a questionnaire, especially where the interview topic is seen to be interesting and relevant to their current work. An interview provides them with an opportunity to reflect on events without needing to write anything down. Other researchers report similar conclusions, where participants prefer to be interviewed rather than fill in a questionnaire (North *et al.* 1983, cited in Healey 1991). This situation also provides the opportunity for interviewees to receive feedback and personal assurance about the way in which information will be used (Sections 6.2 and 6.5).

Potential research participants who receive a questionnaire via the Internet, the intranet or through the post may be reluctant to complete it for a number of reasons. They may feel that it is not appropriate to provide sensitive and confidential information to someone they have never met. They may also not completely trust the way in which the information they provide is used. They may be reluctant to spend time providing written explanatory answers, where these are requested, especially if the meaning of any question is not entirely clear. The use of personal interviews, where appropriate, may therefore achieve a higher response rate than using questionnaires. Healey (1991:206) also makes the point that 'the interviewer . . . has more control over who answers the questions' in comparison with a questionnaire, which may be passed from one person to another.

The nature of the questions

An interview will undoubtedly be the most advantageous approach to attempt to obtain data in the following circumstances (Easterby-Smith *et al.* 2008; Jankowicz 2005):

- where there are a large number of questions to be answered;
- where the questions are either complex or open-ended;
- where the order and logic of questioning may need to be varied (Box 10.2).

A semi-structured or in-depth interview will be most appropriate for the latter two types of situation.

Box 10.2
Focus on student research

The need to vary the order and logic of questioning

Val undertook a series of semi-structured interviews into the approach used to manage public relations (PR) activities in 30 organisations. It soon became evident that it would not be meaningful to ask exactly the same questions in each organisation. For example, some organisations had centralised PR as part of the marketing function, whereas in other organisations it was devolved to individual business units. Another significant variable was associated with the public relations styles adopted. Some organisations adopted a 'press agency' approach where the main focus was to get the organisation or product mentioned in the media as often as possible, the nature of the mention being of secondary importance. Others adopted a 'public information' approach where the main aim was to get media exposure for the organisation or product.

The impact of these and other variables meant that it was not sensible to ask exactly the same questions at each interview, even though many questions remained applicable in all cases and the underlying intention was to ensure consistency between interviews. It was not until each interview had started that Val was able to learn which of these different variables operated within the particular organisation. Fortunately, the flexibility offered by semi-structured interviews enabled her to do this.

Length of time required and completeness of the process

Apart from the difficulty of trying to design a viable questionnaire schedule to cope with issues that are complex, unclear, or large in number, the time needed for the participant to complete the questionnaire may mean that an interview is in any case the best or only alternative. In our experience, where expectations have been clearly established about the length of time required and participants understand and agree with the objectives of the research interview, they have generally been willing to agree to be interviewed. Some negotiation is, in any case, possible and the interview can be arranged at a time when the interviewee will be under least pressure. We have found that our participants tend to be generous with their time, and sometimes when interviews have been arranged to start at mid-morning they often arrange for lunch, which can allow the discussion and exploration of issues to continue. However, for those of you who fancy a free lunch, we do not want to raise your expectations falsely, and the start time for an interview should not be set with this in mind!

Your aim will be to obtain data to enable you to answer all your research questions, allowing for the right of participants to decline to respond to any question you ask. Where you conduct the event skilfully an interview is more likely to achieve this than the use of a self-administered or interviewer-administered questionnaire. Where your participant does not provide an answer to a particular question or questions in a non-standardised interview, you should be able to form some indication of why a response could not be provided. This may even lead you to modify the question or to compose another where this would be appropriate. Section 6.5 provides a consideration of the ethical issues associated with seeking to obtain answers.

While there are a number of situations favouring the use of non-standardised (qualitative research) interviews, you still need to decide whether or not to use these types of interview to collect your data and, of equal importance, to justify your choice. Silverman emphasises that your choice should depend on what is the best way to answer your

Box 10.3
Checklist

To help you decide whether to use semi-structured or in-depth interviews

✔ Does the purpose of your research suggest using semi-structured and/or in-depth interviews?

✔ Will it help to seek personal contact in terms of gaining access to participants and their data?

✔ Are your data collection questions large in number, complex or open-ended?

✔ Will there be a need to vary the order and logic of questioning?

✔ Will it help to be able to probe interviewees' responses to build on or seek explanation of their answers?

✔ Will the data collection process with each individual involve a relatively lengthy period?

research question referring to a discussion by Speer (2002, cited in Silverman 2007:57) as an illustration '. . . if you are studying gender . . . you should be wary of basing your research on interviews where participants are asked to comment on gender issues . . . You are much more likely to gather reliable data by studying how people actually *do* gender in everyday environments, e.g. in meetings, email messages, etc'. Box 10.3 provides a checklist to help you in your deliberations as to whether or not to use interviews.

10.4 Data quality issues and preparing for the interview

Data quality issues

A number of data quality issues can be identified in relation to the use of semi-structured and in-depth interviews, related to:

- reliability;
- forms of bias;
- validity and generalisability.

These are discussed in turn.

The lack of standardisation in such interviews may lead to concerns about *reliability*. In relation to qualitative research, reliability is concerned with whether alternative researchers would reveal similar information (Easterby-Smith *et al.* 2008; Silverman 2007). The concern about reliability in these types of interview is also related to issues of bias. There are various types of bias to consider. The first of these is related to **interviewer bias**. This is where the comments, tone or non-verbal behaviour of the interviewer creates bias in the way that interviewees respond to the questions being asked. This may be where you attempt to impose your own beliefs and frame of reference through the questions that you ask. It is also possible that you will demonstrate bias in the way you interpret responses (Easterby-Smith *et al.* 2008). Where you are unable to develop the trust of the interviewee, or perhaps where your credibility is seen to be lacking, the value of the information given may also be limited, raising doubts about its validity and reliability.

Related to this is **interviewee** or **response bias**. This type of bias may be caused by perceptions about the interviewer, as referred to above, or in relation to perceived interviewer bias. However, the cause of this type of bias is not necessarily linked to any

perception related to the interviewer. Taking part in an interview is an intrusive process. This is especially true in the case of in-depth or semi-structured interviews, where your aim will be to explore events or to seek explanations. The interviewee may, in principle, be willing to participate but may nevertheless be sensitive to the unstructured exploration of certain themes. Interviewees may therefore choose not to reveal and discuss an aspect of the topic that you wish to explore, because this would lead to probing questions that would intrude on sensitive information that they do not wish, or are not empowered, to discuss with you. The outcome of this may be that the interviewee provides a partial 'picture' of the situation that casts himself or herself in a 'socially desirable' role, or the organisation for which they work in a positive or even negative fashion.

Bias may also result from the nature of the individuals or organisational participants who agree to be interviewed (Box 10.4). The time-consuming requirements of the interview process may result in a reduction in willingness to take part on behalf of some of those to whom you would like to talk. This may bias your sample from whom data are collected (Robson 2002). This is an issue that you will need to consider carefully and attempt to overcome through the approach taken to sampling (Sections 7.2 and 7.3).

There is also likely to be an issue about the generalisability of the findings from qualitatively based interview studies, although the validity of such studies is not raised as an issue. If we consider validity first, this refers to the extent to which the researcher gains access to their participants' knowledge and experience, and is able to infer a meaning that the participant intended from the language that was used by this person. The high level of validity that is possible in relation to non-standardised (qualitative) interviews that are conducted carefully is due to the questions being able to be clarified, meanings of responses probed and topics discussed from a variety of angles.

However, qualitative research using semi-structured or in-depth interviews will not be able to be used to make statistical generalisations about the entire population (whatever this may be in the context of the research topic) where this is based on a small and unrepresentative number of cases. This is often the situation when adopting a case study strategy (Yin 2003).

Overcoming data quality issues

Reliability

One response to the issue of reliability is that the findings derived from using non-standardised research methods are not necessarily intended to be repeatable since they reflect reality at the time they were collected, in a situation which may be subject to change (Marshall and Rossman 1999). The assumption behind this type of research is that the circumstances to be explored are complex and dynamic. The value of using non-standardised interviews is derived from the flexibility that you may use to explore the complexity of the topic. Therefore, an attempt to ensure that qualitative, non-standardised research could be replicated by other researchers would not be realistic or feasible without undermining the strength of this type of research. Marshall and Rossman (1999) suggest that researchers using a qualitative, non-standardised approach need to make this clear – perhaps to transform an aspect perceived to be a weakness by some into a strength based on realistic assumptions about the ability to replicate research findings.

However, they suggest that where you use this approach you should make and retain notes relating to your research design, the reasons underpinning the choice of strategy and methods, and the data obtained. This will be referred to by other researchers in order to understand the processes that you used and your findings and, where appropriate, to enable them to reanalyse the data you collected. The use of non-standardised interviews should not lead to a lack of rigour in relation to the research process – if anything, greater rigour is required to overcome the views of those who may be wedded to the value of quantitative research to the exclusion of any other approach.

Preparation

Like all research methods, the key to a successful interview is careful preparation. When using non-structured interviews the five Ps are a useful mantra: prior planning prevents poor performance. In particular, we believe it is critical that you plan precisely how you are going to demonstrate your credibility and obtain the confidence of the interviewees. Issues associated with this are discussed in the following subsections and summarised in Box 10.12 as a checklist.

Level of knowledge You need to be knowledgeable about the research topic and organisational or situational context in which the interview is to take place. In addition to your literature review, a prior search in your university library (Sections 3.4 and 3.5) may reveal journal articles written by senior employees of the organisation that is participating in your research. There may also be other material about the organisation, and this is particularly likely to be found on the Internet, in the 'trade' press and the quality newspapers. It may also be appropriate to look at company reports and other publications, or financial data relating to the organisation. The ability to draw on this type of information in the interview should help to demonstrate your credibility, assess the accuracy of responses and encourage the interviewee to offer a more detailed account of the topic under discussion. As you undertake a number of interviews, you will also be able to draw on the initial analysis that you make of data previously collected.

Level of information supplied to the interviewee Credibility may also be promoted through the supply of relevant information to participants before the interview. Providing participants with a list of the interview themes before the event, where this is appropriate, should help this. The list of themes (Boxes 10.1 and 10.5) should also promote validity and reliability by enabling the interviewee to consider the information being requested and allowing them the opportunity to assemble supporting organisational documentation from their files. We can testify to this approach and the value of allowing participants to prepare themselves for the discussion in which they are to engage. Access to organisational documentation also allows for triangulation of the data provided (Sections 8.2 and 8.3). Our experience is that participants are generally willing to supply a photocopy of such material, although of course it will be necessary to conceal any confidential or personal details that this contains.

Box 10.5
Focus on student research

Developing interview themes

Karl was interested in understanding why some employees in his organisation used the IT Help Desk whilst others did not. This subject was felt to be significant in relation to the perceptions of service level agreements, service relationships and service quality. He decided to provide his interviewees with a list of themes that he wished to explore during the - interviews. After some deliberation and reading of the academic literature he came up with the

following list (extract):

- what employees understand by the term 'IT Help Desk';
- the extent to which the IT Help Desk is meeting employees' needs;
- the nature of support employees feel they are receiving;
- the extent to which employees feel they know how to use the IT Help Desk;
- the services employees feel the IT Help Desk should be providing;
- knowledge of service level agreements.

He subsequently used these to develop his interview guide (Box 10.6).

Interview themes may be derived from the literature that you read, the theories that you consider, your experience of a particular topic, common sense, discussions with co-workers, fellow students, tutors and research participants, or a combination of these approaches. You will need to have some idea of the theme or themes that you wish to discuss with your participants even if you intend to commence with exploratory, in-depth interviews as part of a grounded theory strategy to your research project (Section 5.3). Without at least some focus, your work will clearly lack a sense of direction and purpose. It will be necessary for you to formulate a focus if your work is to make progress. You should therefore start with a set of themes that reflect the variables being studied, or at least one or more general questions related to your research topic that you could use to start your interview. These can be incorporated into your interview guide (Box 10.6). This lists topics that you intend to cover in the interview along with initial question and probes that may be used to follow up initial responses and obtain greater detail from the participants (King 2004). When creating your guide, you need to try to ensure that the order of questions is likely to be logical to your participants and that the language you use will be comprehensible. Using your guide, you will be able to develop and/or explore research themes through the non-standardised interviews that you conduct to see whether you can identify and test relationships between them (Chapter 13).

Appropriateness of location   It is possible that the place you conduct your interviews may influence the data you collect. As we discussed in Section 6.5, you should choose the location for your interviews with regard to your own personal safety. However, it is also important that you think about the impact that the location will have upon your participants and the responses they are likely to give. In particular, you should choose a location which is convenient for your participants, where they will feel comfortable and where the interview is unlikely to be disturbed (Box 10.7). Finally, you need to choose a place that is quiet so that outside noise will not reduce the quality of your audiorecording of the interview. Mark recalls an interview in a room outside which building work was taking place. Although he was able to hear the participant's responses clearly whilst the

Box 10.6
Focus on student research

Extract from an interview guide

Karl was interested in understanding why some employees in his organisation used the IT Help Desk whilst others did not. Using his interview themes (Box 10.5), he began to develop his guide:

Help Desk Support

1 To what extent does the IT Help Desk meet your needs?

Probe: In what ways? [ask for real-life examples]
Probe: Can you give me an example (if possible) of when you received good support from the IT Help Desk?
Probe: Can you give me an example (if possible) of when you received insufficient support from the IT Help Desk?

2 Do you consider you have enough support from the IT Help Desk?

Probe: How is this support provided (e.g. telephone, face to face)?
Probe: What else (if anything) could usefully be done?

Box 10.7
Focus on student research

Choosing an appropriate location

Anne was pleased that the manufacturing company in which she was undertaking her research had arranged for her to use a room in the Human Resources Department. The room contained a low table and chairs, had an electric plug socket for her audio-recorder and she had been provided with bottled water

and glasses as well. However, after her third interview she was beginning to doubt her own interviewing skills. Her participants, the company's production line workers, seemed unwilling to be open in their responses. She began to wonder if something was wrong with the interview location and decided to ask the next participant about this. At the end of that interview she had her answer. Her participants were unhappy with the interview location. Prior to being interviewed by Anne, the only time they or their colleagues had visited the Human Resources Department was to receive a reprimand. The location was, therefore, inappropriate!

interview was taking place, for much of the audio-recording these responses were unintelligible due to the sound of a very loud pneumatic drill!

Appropriateness of the researcher's appearance at the interview   Your appearance may affect the perception of the interviewee. Where this has an adverse affect on your credibility in the view of interviewees, or results in a failure to gain their confidence, the resulting bias may affect the reliability of the information provided. Robson (2002) advises researchers to adopt a similar style of dress to those to be interviewed. Essentially, you will need to wear clothing that will be generally acceptable for the setting within which the interview is to occur (Box 10.8).

Nature of the opening comments to be made when the interview commences   Where the interviewee has not met you before, the first few minutes of conversation will have a significant impact on the outcome of the interview – again related to the issue of your credibility and the level of the interviewee's confidence. Often such interviews occur in a

Box 10.8
Focus on student research

Checking out the dress code

Mel arranged to visit the administration centre of a large insurance comapny on a Friday to conduct a group interview with staff drawn from one of its telephone sales divisions and two one-to-one interviews with senior managers. He felt that it was appropriate to wear fairly 'formal' clothes to match what he thought would be the dress code of the organisation. Indeed, for four days of the working week this

assumption would have been appropriate. However, the organisation had recently introduced the practice of not wearing such formal work clothes on Fridays. Thus he found himself the only one dressed formally in the organisation on the day of his visit. Taking lunch proved to be a memorable experience, as he intermingled with everyone else dressed in jeans and tee shirts, etc. His 'mistake' proved to be an amusing opening at the start of each interview rather than a barrier to gaining access to participants' data. Indeed, it might not have been appropriate for him to match too closely the 'dress-down' style of participants. Nevertheless, it does provide a useful example of the way in which expectations about appearance are likely to be noticed.

setting that is unfamiliar to you. Despite this, it is your responsibility to shape the start of the discussion. You will need to explain your research to the participant and, hopefully, gain consent (Section 6.5). As part of this you will need to establish your credibility and gain the interviewee's confidence. During these initial discussions we have found that the interviewee often has some uncertainties about sharing information, and about the manner in which these data may be used. Alternatively, she or he may still need clarification about the exact nature of the data that you wish to obtain. We have found that a pre-prepared participant information sheet (Section 6.5, Box 6.13) and consent form (Box 6.14) are both extremely helpful in reducing anxieties. There may also be a degree of curiosity on the part of the interviewee and probably a genuine level of interest in the research, related to the reason why the request to participate was accepted. This curiosity and interest will offer an opening for both parties to start a conversation, probably before the 'intended discussion' commences. You may find it appropriate to follow the initial discussion by demonstrating interest in the interviewee by asking about her or his role within the host organisation (Ghauri and Grønhaug 2005). However, you need to make sure that these opening moves to demonstrate credibility and friendliness, and to relax and develop a positive relationship, are not overstated, so that too much time is used and the interviewee starts to become bored or restive.

The start of the intended discussion therefore needs to be shaped by you. It is your opportunity to allay, wherever possible, the interviewee's uncertainties about providing information, establish the participant's rights and, based upon this, hopefully, obtain informed consent. Box 10.9 provides a structure that you can adapt for starting your interviews.

Healey and Rawlinson (1994) say that an assurance from you that confidential information is not being sought should make interviewees more relaxed and open about the information that they are willing to discuss. Combined with assurances about anonymity, this should increase the level of confidence in your trustworthiness and reduce the possibility of interviewee or response bias. You can also demonstrate your commitment to confidentiality by not naming other organisations that have participated in your research, or by talking about the data you obtained from them.

Approach to questioning   When conducted appropriately, your approach to questioning should reduce the scope for bias during the interview and increase the reliability of the

Box 10.9
Focus on student research

Opening a semi-structured interview

As part of her research project, Bethan undertook a series of semi-structured interviews with freelance consultants working for a range of organisations. She covered the following points at the start of each interview:

- The participant was thanked for considering the request for access and for agreeing to the meeting.
- The purpose of the research and its progress to date were outlined briefly. As part of this, the participant was given an information sheet to keep.
- The previously agreed right to confidentiality and anonymity was reiterated by stating that nothing said by the participant would be attributed to them without first seeking and obtaining permission.
- The participant's right not to answer any question was emphasised and that the interview would be stopped if the participant wished.
- The participant was told about the nature of the outputs to which the research was intended to lead and what would happen to the data collected during and after the project.
- The offer to provide a summary of the research findings to the interviewee was also restated, as was when this would happen.
- The request to record the interview electronically was restated and, where agreed, this was used subsequently.
- Before the substantive discussion started, Bethan again requested permission to undertake the interview, summarised the themes to be covered, confirmed the amount of time available and requested that the participant read and signed the informed consent form.

All of these points were dealt with within five minutes.

information obtained. Your questions need to be phrased clearly, so that the interviewee can understand them, and you should ask them in a neutral tone of voice. Easterby-Smith *et al.* (2008) point out that the use of open questions (Section 10.5) should help to avoid bias. These can then be followed up by the use of appropriately worded probing questions (Section 10.5). The use of these types of question will help you to explore the topic and to produce a fuller account. Conversely, questions that seek to lead the interviewee or which indicate bias on your part should be avoided. Perceived interviewer bias may well lead to interviewee or response bias. Long questions or those that are really made up of two or more questions should also be avoided if you are to obtain a response to each aspect that you are interested to explore (Robson 2002).

Questions should also avoid too many theoretical concepts or jargon since your understanding of such terms may vary from that of your interviewees. Where theoretical concepts or specific terminology need to be used, you will have to ensure that both you and the interviewee have the same understanding (Box 10.10; Easterby-Smith *et al.* 2008; Ghauri and Grønhaug 2005).

When asking questions it is important that wherever possible these are grounded in the real-life experiences of your participants rather than being on an abstract concept. One approach to questioning which makes use of key participant experiences is the **critical incident technique**, in which participants are asked to describe in detail a critical incident or number of incidents that are key to the research question. A **critical incident** is defined as an activity or event where the consequences were so clear that the participant has a definite idea regarding the effects (Keaveney 1995).

Healey and Rawlinson (1994:138) suggest that 'it is usually best to leave sensitive questions until near the end of an interview because this allows a greater time for the

Box 10.10
Focus on student research

(Mis)understanding terminology

Sven was conducting an interview with the European sales manager of a large multinational corporation. Throughout the interview the sales manager referred to the European Division. Sven assumed that the sales manager meant continental Europe. However, by chance, later questions revealed that, for this organisation, Europe extended into parts of Asia, including Turkey, the United Arab Emirates, Saudi Arabia, Kuwait and Israel. Until this point in the interview, Sven had assumed that these countries were the responsibility of another sales manager!

Box 10.11
Focus on student research

Establishing trust and asking sensitive questions

Sam recalls an occasion when her treatment by her participants altered as her group interview progressed. For the first hour of a two-hour interview it appeared to her that the participants were convinced that she was really there to sell them a consultancy service. When they accepted that she was not going to try to sell them something, the mood of the interview changed and they became much more relaxed and responsive to the questions that Sam wished to ask. It was at this point that she was able to ask and pursue more sensitive questions that could have led to the interview being terminated during the period when the participants mistrusted her motives.

participant to build up trust and confidence in the researchers'. They report cases where the first part of an interview is used by participants to assess the level of trust that can be placed in the researcher. Others have witnessed this experience, as Box 10.11 illustrates, affecting the nature of the questions that may be asked during the early part of an interview.

Once this position of trust has been reached and you wish to seek responses to potentially sensitive questions, Ghauri and Grønhaug (2005) point out that the wording of these deserve very particular attention in order to avoid any negative inferences related to, for example, responsibility for failure or error. Care taken over the exploration of sensitive questions should help towards the compilation of a fuller and more reliable account.

Nature and impact of the interviewer's behaviour during the course of the interview

Appropriate behaviour by the researcher should also reduce the scope for bias during the interview. Comments or non-verbal behaviour, such as gestures, which indicate any bias in your thinking should be avoided. A neutral (but not an uninterested) response should be projected in relation to the interviewee's answers in order not to provide any lead that may result in bias. Robson (2002) says that you should enjoy the interview opportunity, or at least appear to do so. An appearance of boredom on your part is hardly likely to encourage your interviewee!

Your posture and tone of voice may also encourage or inhibit the flow of the discussion. You should sit slightly inclined towards the interviewee and adopt an open posture, avoiding folded arms. This should provide a signal of attentiveness to your interviewee

(Torrington 1991). Tone of voice can also provide a signal to the interviewee. You need to project interest and enthusiasm through your voice, avoiding any impression of anxiety, disbelief, astonishment or any other negative signal.

Demonstration of attentive listening skills   The purpose of a semi-structured or in-depth interview will be to understand the participant's explanations and meanings. This type of interaction will not be typical of many of the conversations that you normally engage in, where those involved often compete to speak rather than concentrate on listening. You therefore need to recognise that different skills will be emphasised in this kind of interaction. Torrington (1991:43) says that listening involves people being 'on the look-out for signals and willing to spend the time needed to listen and build understanding, deliberately holding back our own thoughts, which would divert or compete with the other's'.

It will be necessary for you to explore and probe explanations and meanings, but you must also provide the interviewee with reasonable time to develop their responses, and you must avoid projecting your own views (Easterby-Smith *et al.* 2008; Ghauri and Grønhaug 2005; Robson 2002).

Scope to test understanding   You may test your understanding by summarising an explanation provided by the interviewee. This will allow the interviewee to 'evaluate the adequacy of the interpretation and correct where necessary' (Healey and Rawlinson 1994:138). This can be a powerful tool for avoiding a biased or incomplete interpretation. It may also act as a means to explore and probe the interviewee's responses further.

In addition to this opportunity to test understanding at the interview, you may also ask the interviewee to read through the factual account that you produce of the interview. Where the interviewee is prepared to undertake this, it will provide a further opportunity for you to test your understanding and for the interviewee to add any further points of relevance that may not previously have been apparent.

Approach to recording data   As well as audio-recording your interview (discussed in Section 10.5), we believe it is important to also make notes as the interview progresses. In addition to providing a back-up if your audio-recording does not work, this provides another way for you to show that your participant's responses are important to you. If possible, immediately after the interview has taken place you should compile a full record of the interview (Robson 2002), including contextual data. Where you do not do this, the exact nature of explanations provided may be lost as well as general points of value. There is also the possibility that you may mix up data from different interviews, where you carry out several of these within a short period of time and you do not complete a record of each one at the time it takes place (Ghauri and Grønhaug 2005). Either situation will clearly lead to an issue about the trustworthiness of any data. You therefore need to allocate time to write up a full set of notes soon after the event. In addition to your notes from the actual interview, you should also record the following **contextual data**:

- the location of the interview (e.g. the organisation, the place);
- the date and time;
- the setting of the interview (e.g. was the room quiet or noisy, could you be overheard, were you interrupted?);
- background information about the participant (e.g. role, post title, gender);
- your immediate impression of how well (or badly) the interview went (e.g. was the participant reticent, were there aspects about which you felt you did not obtain answers in sufficient depth?).

You are probably wondering how, if you are also recording these data, you can still help ensure confidentiality and anonymity of your participants where this has been promised. As we outlined in Section 6.5, the best course of action is likely to be ensuring that your data are completely and genuinely anonymised. This means that you should store the contextual data separately from your interview transcripts. We suggest that you should be able to link these two sets of data only by using a 'key' such as a code number. We also suggest that if a key to identify participants by name which can link them to these data is absolutely necessary, this should not be retained by those who control these data and should, again, be kept separately. In addition, as pointed out in Section 6.5, you will need to take great care in the way you report your findings to help preserve anonymity and confidentiality.

Cultural differences and bias   As a final note to this particular discussion, we need to recognise that it is often difficult to attempt to control bias in all cases. Other factors may become significant. For example, there may be misinterpretation of responses because of cultural differences between the interviewee and the interviewer (Marshall and Rossman 1999). This issue is not exclusively related to interviews and can be associated with a number of data collection methods. For example, we encountered it in relation to the interpretation of the data produced from a cross-national survey. An in-depth interview at least offers the opportunity to explore meanings, including those that may be culturally specific, but you will need to be aware of cultural differences and their implications (see, for example, Hofstede 2001).

Generalisability

In the first part of this section, which described data quality issues relating to semi-structured and in-depth interviews, we stated that there is likely to be a concern surrounding the generalisability of findings from qualitative research, based on the use of a small and unrepresentative number of cases. However, two arguments have been advanced that seek to clarify and modify the approach often adopted to the generalisability or transferability of qualitative research. The first of these relates to the situation where a single case study is used because of the unstructured nature of the research. Bryman (1988:90) states that 'within a case study a wide range of different people and activities are invariably examined so that the contrast with survey samples is not as acute as it appears at first glance'. The single case may in fact encompass a number of settings, where for example it involves a study in a large organisation with sites across the country, or even around the world. By contrast, Bryman (1988) points out that many research projects adopting a survey strategy use samples restricted to one particular locality. A well-completed and rigorous case study is thus more likely to be useful in other contexts than one that lacks such rigour.

The second argument with the approach that questions the generalisability of qualitative research or a case study is related to the significance of this type of research to theoretical propositions (Bryman 1988; Yin 2003). Where you are able to relate your research project to existing theory you will be in a position to demonstrate that your findings will have a broader theoretical significance than the case or cases that form the basis of your work (Marshall and Rossman 1999). It will clearly be up to you to establish this relationship to existing theory in order to be able to demonstrate the broader significance of your particular case study findings.

This relationship will allow your study to test the applicability of existing theory to the setting(s) that you are examining and where this is found wanting to suggest why. It will also allow theoretical propositions to be advanced that can then be tested in another context. However, as Bryman (1988) points out, this also has implications for the relationship

Box 10.12
Checklist

To help you prepare for your semi-structured or in-depth interview

✔ How might your level of preparation and knowledge (in relation to the research context and your research question) affect the willingness of the interviewee to share data?

✔ What will be the broad focus of your in-depth interview, or what are the themes that you wish to explore or seek explanations for during a semi-structured interview?

✔ What type of information, if any, will it be useful to send to your interviewee prior to the interview?

✔ What did you agree to supply to your interviewee when you arranged the interview? Has this been supplied?

✔ How will your appearance during the interview affect the willingness of the interviewee to share data?

✔ Have you considered the impact that your interview location may have on participants' responses and on your own personal safety?

✔ How will you prepare yourself to be able to commence the interview with confidence and purpose?

✔ What will you tell your interviewee about yourself, the purpose of your research, its funding and your progress?

✔ What concerns, or need for clarification, may your interviewee have?

✔ How will you seek to overcome these concerns or provide this clarification?

✔ In particular, how do you intend to use the data to which you are given access, ensuring, where appropriate, its confidentiality and your interviewee's anonymity?

✔ What will you tell your interviewee about their right not to answer particular questions and to end the interview should they wish?

✔ How would you like to record the data that are revealed to you during the interview? Where this involves using an audio recorder, have you raised this as a request and provided a reason why it would help you to use this technique?

✔ How will you seek to overcome potential issues related to the reliability of the data you collect, including forms of interviewer bias (related to your role and conduct), interviewee bias (the level of access that you gain to the data of those whom you interview) and sampling bias?

between theory and research, since the identification of existing theory and its application will be necessary before the researcher embarks on the collection of data.

10.5 Interviewing competence

There are several areas where you need to develop and demonstrate competence in relation to the conduct of semi-structured and in-depth research interviews. These areas are:

- opening the interview;
- using appropriate language;
- questioning;
- listening;
- testing and summarising understanding;
- recognising and dealing with difficult participants;
- recording data.

Most of these competence areas have already been discussed in relation to overcoming interviewer and interviewee bias in Section 10.4. However, there is still a need to discuss

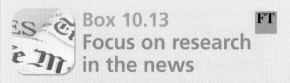

Box 10.13
Focus on research in the news

FT

Sir Adrian's thorn

Delicate times for the British Energy chairman, **Sir Adrian Montague**, and chief executive, **Bill Coley**, as they tried to steer through media and analysts conferences for the annual results while avoiding any mention of talks with European suitors.

At the start of both meetings, Sir Adrian warned there would be no comment on the matter, although the pesky press asked the question in 15 different ways. The analysts didn't even bother, but they did get irritated when their efforts to work out valuations, through capital costs and the cost of developing new nuclear sites, were thwarted.

To a point made by Mr Coley that the 'value proposition of nuclear is that it is the most cost-effective way to reduce carbon emissions', one analyst countered: 'How is it possible to make statements about the value creation of nuclear without having a firm feel for how much the cost of building will be, I just don't understand that.'

At the end, Sir Adrian offered what he probably thought was an olive branch, even though it had thorns, telling the analysts they were 'much better behaved than the wires earlier on'.

Source: article by Mychasuk, Emiliya and Terazono, Emiko (2008) *Financial Times*, 29 May. Copyright © 2008 The Financial Times Ltd.

alternative approaches to asking questions, recognising and dealing with difficult participants (Box 10.13) and recording information in order to be able to develop your competence. These are summarised as a checklist in Box 10.14 (overleaf).

Questioning

Even in an in-depth interview, as well as in a semi-structured one, you will need to consider your approach to asking questions. Allowing the interviewee to talk freely throughout an in-depth interview is unlikely to lead to a clearly focused discussion on issues relevant to the research topic (Easterby-Smith *et al.* 2008; Robson 2002) unless the purpose is simply to discover important concerns relating to the topic at a given time. It will therefore be necessary to devise relevant interview themes (Section 10.4), even though you can adopt a flexible approach about the way these are dealt with during the interview. The use of this approach demands a significant level of competence on your part. Formulating appropriate questions to explore areas in which you are interested will be critical to achieving success in this type of interviewing. We shall now discuss the types of question that you can use during semi-structured and in-depth interviews.

Open questions

The use of **open questions** will allow participants to define and describe a situation or event. An open question is designed to encourage the interviewee to provide an extensive and developmental answer, and may be used to reveal attitudes or obtain facts (Grummitt 1980). It encourages the interviewee to reply as they wish. An open question is likely to start with, or include, one of the following words: 'what', 'how' or 'why'. Examples of open questions include:

'Why did the organisation introduce its marketing strategy?'
'What methods have been used to make employees redundant?'
'How has corporate strategy changed over the past five years?'

Box 10.14
Checklist

To help you think about the questions you are going to ask in your semi-structured or in-depth interview

✔ How long will you have to conduct the interview?

✔ How do you wish to conduct (or structure) the interview?

✔ How will you use appropriate language and tone of voice, and avoid jargon when asking questions or discussing themes?

✔ How will you word open questions appropriately to obtain relevant data?

✔ How will you ask appropriately worded probing questions to build on, clarify or explain your interviewee's responses?

✔ How will you avoid asking leading questions that may introduce forms of bias?

✔ Have you devised an appropriate order for your questions, where the early introduction of sensitive issues may introduce interviewee bias?

✔ How will you avoid over-zealously asking questions and pressing your interviewee for a response where it should be clear that they do not wish to provide one?

✔ How will you listen attentively and demonstrate this to your interviewee?

✔ How will you summarise and test your understanding of the data that are shared with you in order to ensure accuracy in your interpretation?

✔ How will you allow your interviewee to maintain control over the use of a tape recorder, where used, where they may wish to exercise this?

✔ Have you practised to ensure you can carry out a number of tasks at the same time, including listening, note taking and the identifying where you need to probe further?

✔ How might you identify actions and comments made by your interviewee that indicate an aspect of the discussion that should be explored in order to reveal the reason for the response?

✔ How will you avoid projecting your own views or feelings through your actions or comments?

✔ How will you maintain a check on the interview that you intend to cover and to steer the discussion where appropriate to raise and explore these aspects?

✔ How do you plan to draw the interview to a close within the agreed time limit and to thank the interviewee for their time and the data they have shared with you?

Probing questions

Probing questions can be used to explore responses that are of significance to the research topic. They may be worded like open questions but request a particular focus or direction. Examples of this type of question include:

'How would you evaluate the success of this new marketing strategy?'
'Why did you choose a compulsory method to make redundancies?'
'What external factors caused the corporate strategy to change?'

These questions may be prefaced with, for example, 'That's interesting . . .' or 'Tell me more about . . .'.

Probing questions may also be used to seek an explanation where you do not understand the interviewee's meaning or where the response does not reveal the reasoning involved. Examples of this type of question include:

'What do you mean by "bumping" as a means to help to secure volunteers for redundancy?'
'What is the relationship between the new statutory requirements that you referred to and the organisation's decision to set up its corporate affairs department?'

The use of reflection may also help you to probe a theme. This is where you will 'reflect' a statement made by the interviewee by paraphrasing their words. An example of this might be:

'Why don't you think that the employees understand the need for advertising?'

The intention will be to encourage exploration of the point made without offering a view or judgement on your part.

Where an open question does not reveal a relevant response, you may also probe the area of interest by using a supplementary question that finds a way of rephrasing the original question (Torrington 1991).

Specific and closed questions

These types of question are similar to those used in structured interviews. They can be used to obtain specific information or to confirm a fact or opinion (Section 11.4). Examples of these types of question include those designed to obtain a specific piece of data:

'How many people responded to the customer survey?'

and, from our example at the start of this chapter:

'Did you lose money? Break even?'

In phrasing questions, remember that you should avoid using leading or proposing types of question in order to control any bias that may result from their use (Section 11.4).

Recognising and dealing with difficult participants

Inevitably, during the course of your interviews you will meet some participants who are difficult to interview. Although it is impossible for us to highlight all the possible variations, the most common difficulties are summarised in Table 10.2, along with suggestions regarding how to deal with them. However, whilst reading Table 10.2 will give you some ideas of what to do, the best advice we can give is to undertake practice interviews in which a colleague introduces one or more of these 'difficulties' and you have to deal with it!

Recording interview data

The need to create a full record of the interview soon after its occurrence was identified in Section 10.4 as one of the means to control bias and to produce reliable data for analysis. This particular discussion and the accompanying checklist (Box 10.15) look briefly at the use of audio-recorders and the need to develop the skill of making notes during the interview. Most interviewers audio-record their interviews, where permission is given, although, as summarised in Table 10.3, this has both advantages and disadvantages. As an interviewer, you will be interested in both what your participants say and the way in which they say it. By audio-recording your interview, you will be able to concentrate more fully and listen attentively to what is being said and the expressions and other non-verbal cues your interviewee is giving when they are responding. However, as we pointed out earlier, we believe it is also helpful to make brief notes as well in order to maintain your concentration and focus (Ghauri and Grønhaug 2005). This is important because, although audio-recordings can capture the tone of voice and hesitation, they do not record facial expressions and other non-verbal cues. Most people have their own means

Table 10.2 Difficult interview participants and suggestions on how to address them

Recognised difficulty	Suggestion
Participant appears willing only to give monosyllabic answers, these being little more than 'yes' or 'no'	Reasons for this are varied. If it is due to limited time, or worries about anonymity, then this can be minimised by careful opening of the interview (Box 10.9). If the participant gives these answers despite such precautions, try phrasing your questions in as open a way as possible; also use long pauses to signify that you want to hear more.
Participant repeatedly provides long answers which digress from the focus of your interview	Although some digression should be tolerated, as it can lead to aspects about which you are interested, you will need to impose more direction. This must be done subtly so as not to cause offence, such as by referring back to an earlier relevant point and asking them to tell you more, or requesting that they pause so you can note down what they have just said.
Participant starts interviewing you	This can suggest that you have created rapport. However, you need to stress that you are interested in their opinions and that, if they wish, they can ask you questions at the end.
Participant is proud of their status relative to you and wants to show off their knowledge, criticising what you do	This is extremely difficult and at times like this you will have to listen attentively and be respectful. Remember that you are also likely to be knowledgeable about the research topic, so be confident and prepared to justify your research and the research design you have chosen.
Participant becomes noticeably upset during the interview and, perhaps, starts to cry	Another difficult one for you. You need to give your participant time to answer your question and, in particular, do not do anything to suggest that you are feeling impatient. If your participant starts crying or is obviously very distressed, it is probably a good idea to explain that the question does not have to be answered. Do not end the interview straight away as this is likely to make the participant even more upset.

Sources: King (2004); authors' experiences.

Box 10.15
Checklist

Issues to consider regarding your recording of interview data

✔ How do you intend to record the data that are shared with you? What rights will your interviewee have in relation to the use of an audio-recorder where they have agreed in principle to let you use one?

✔ What reference do you need to make about sending your interviewee an output from your data analysis and when this is due to occur?

✔ How will you prepare your approach to note making so that you may recall the interviewee's responses for long enough to make an accurate and more permanent record?

✔ Has your schedule of work been formulated to permit you to find sufficient time in order to write up your notes/transcribe your interview recordings and to analyse them before undertaking further data collection?

✔ How will you organise your material so that you retain a copy of your original notes and interview recordings, an extended version of your notes after writing them up or a transcript of relevant material, and a set of additional notes or memos relating to the interview and your learning from that particular experience? (Section 13.3)

Table 10.3 Advantages and disadvantages of audio-recording the interview

Advantages	Disadvantages
• Allows interviewer to concentrate on questioning and listening	• May adversely affect the relationship between interviewee and interviewer (possibility of 'focusing' on the audio-recorder)
• Allows questions formulated at an interview to be accurately recorded for use in later interviews where appropriate	
• Can re-listen to the interview	• May inhibit some interviewee responses and reduce reliability
• Accurate and unbiased record provided	• Possibility of a technical problem
• Allows direct quotes to be used	• Time required to transcribe the audio-recording (Section 13.3)
• Permanent record for others to use	

Sources: authors' experience; Easterby-Smith *et al.* (2008); Ghauri and Grønhaug (2005); Healey and Rawlinson (1994).

of making notes, which may range from an attempt to create a verbatim account to a diagrammatic style that records key words and phrases, perhaps using mind mapping (Section 2.3). The task of note making in this situation will be a demanding one. As you seek to test your understanding of what your interviewee has told you, this will allow some time to complete your notes concurrently in relation to the particular aspect being discussed. Most interviewees recognise the demands of the task and act accordingly. However, the interview will not be the occasion to perfect your style, and you may be advised to practise in a simulated situation: for example, by watching an interview on television and attempting to produce a set of notes.

Permission should always be sought to audio-record an interview. Healey and Rawlinson (1994) report an earlier study that advises that you should explain why you would prefer to use a recorder rather than simply requesting permission. Where it is likely to have a detrimental effect, it is better not to use a recorder. However, most interviewees adapt quickly to the use of the recorder. It is more ethical to allow your interviewee to maintain control over the recorder so that if you ask a question that they are prepared to respond to, but only if their words are not audio-recorded, they have the option to switch it off (Section 6.5). It will inevitably be necessary to make notes in this situation.

10.6 Managing logistical and resource issues

Logistical and resource issues

Interviewing is a time-consuming process. Where the purpose of the interview is to explore themes or to explain findings, the process may call for a fairly lengthy discussion. In such cases the time required to obtain data is unlikely to be less than one hour and could easily exceed this, perhaps taking two hours or longer. This may have an adverse impact on the number and representativeness of those who are willing to be interview participants, as we discussed earlier. Where managers or other potential participants receive frequent requests to participate in research projects, they will clearly need to consider how much of their time they may be willing to devote to such activities. This issue may arise in relation to either the completion of a questionnaire or participation in an interview. However, there will be more flexibility about when and where to fill in a questionnaire. It is therefore important you establish credibility with, and to engender the interest of, potential interviewees.

Your choice of an approach that involves data collection through interviewing will have particular resource issues. Conducting interviews may become a costly process where it is necessary to travel to the location of participants, although this can be kept to a minimum by cluster sampling (Section 7.2) or using the Internet (Section 10.8). Interviews are almost certainly likely to be more expensive than using self-administered or telephone questionnaires to collect data. Choice of method should be determined primarily by the nature of the research question and objectives rather than by cost considerations. This highlights the need to examine the feasibility of the proposed question and research strategy in relation to resource constraints, including time available and expense, before proceeding to the collection of data. Where your research question and objectives require you to undertake semi-structured or in-depth interviews, you need to consider the logistics of scheduling interviews. Thought needs to be given to the number of interviews to be arranged within a given period, and to the time required to compose notes and/or transcribe audio-recordings of each one, and undertake an initial analysis of the data collected (Section 13.3).

Managing logistical and resource issues

In the preceding subsection, the issue of time required to collect data through interviewing was raised. You need to consider very carefully the amount of time that will be required to conduct an interview. In our experience, the time required to undertake qualitative research interviews is usually underestimated. The likely time required should be clearly referred to in any initial contact, and it may be better to suggest that interviews are envisaged to last up to, say, one, one and a half, or two hours, so that a willing participant sets aside sufficient time. They may then be in a position to recoup time not required from a shorter interview should this be the case. Some negotiation is in any case possible with an interested participant who feels unable to agree to a request for, say, two hours but who is prepared to agree to a briefer meeting. The interview can also be arranged at a time when the interviewee will be under least pressure.

Another possible strategy is to arrange two or more shorter interviews in order to explore a topic thoroughly. This might have the added advantage of allowing participants to reflect on the themes raised and questions being asked, and therefore to provide a fuller account and more accurate set of data. In order to establish this option, it may be beneficial to arrange an initial meeting with a potential participant to discuss this request,

Box 10.16
Focus on student research

Calculating the number of non-standardised (qualitative) interviews to be undertaken in one day

Feroz arranged two interviews in a capital city during the course of a day, which involved travelling some miles across the city during the lunch hour. Two interviews appeared to be a reasonable target. However, a number of logistical issues were experienced even in relation to the plan to undertake two such interviews in one day. These issues included the following: the total travelling time to and from the city; the time to find the appropriate buildings; the transfer time during a busy period; the time to conduct the interviews; the need to maintain concentration, to probe responses, to make initial notes and then to write these up without too much time elapsing. Because of his experience, Feroz took a decision not to conduct more than one interview per day where significant travel was involved, even though this necessitated more journeys and greater expense.

where you will be able to establish your credibility. A series of exploratory interviews may then be agreed. Consideration also needs to be given to the number of interviews that may be undertaken in a given period. It is easy to overestimate what is practically possible, as Box 10.16 highlights.

These are all factors that need to be considered in the scheduling of semi-structured and in-depth interviews. Where you are involved in a study at one establishment, it may be more practical to undertake a number of interviews in one day, although there is still a need to maintain concentration, to make notes and write up information and to conduct your initial analysis. Phil found that undertaking three interviews per day in this type of study was enough.

The nature of semi-structured or in-depth interviews also has implications for the management of the time available during the meeting. The use of open-ended questions and reliance on informant responses means that, while you must remain responsive to the objectives of the interview and the time constraint, interviewees need the opportunity to provide developmental answers. You should avoid making frequent interruptions but will need to cover the themes and questions indicated and probe responses in the time available (Ghauri and Grønhaug 2005). The intensive nature of the discussion and the need to optimise one's understanding of what has been revealed means that time must be found to write up notes as soon as possible after an interview. Where an audio-recorder has been used, time will be required to produce a transcription, and Robson (2002) states that a one-hour recording may take up to 10 hours to transcribe.

10.7 Group interviews and focus groups

Non-standardised interviews may also be conducted on a group basis, where the interviewer asks questions to a group of participants. Figure 10.1 summarised these variations earlier in this chapter. Currently there are a variety of terms that are used interchangeably to describe group interviews and which are often assumed to have equivalent meanings (Boddy 2005). These include focus group, group interview, group discussion and various combinations of these words! In this section we use **group interview** as a general term to describe all non-standardised interviews conducted with two or more people. In contrast, and as suggested by Figure 10.1, the term **focus group** is used to refer to those group interviews where the topic is defined clearly and precisely and there is a focus on enabling and recording interactive discussion between participants (Carson *et al.* 2001).

Typically group interviews (and focus groups) involve between four and eight participants, or perhaps even 12, the precise number depending upon the nature of the participants, the topic matter and the skill of the interviewer. Inevitably, the more complex the subject matter the smaller the number of interviewees. Participants are normally chosen using non-probability sampling, often with a specific purpose in mind (Section 7.3). For many group interviews this purpose is because you feel that you can learn a great deal from these individuals. Krueger and Casey (2000:25) refer to such participants as being 'information rich'.

If you are thinking about using group interviews, or specifically focus groups, consideration of the following issues may help.

- Where your research project (or part of it) occurs within an organisation the request to participate in a group interview may be received by individuals as an instruction rather than allowing them a choice about whether to take part. This may be the case where an organisation is acting as a host for your research and the request is sent out on official notepaper or in the name of a manager, or because of your own position in the organisation. Where this is the case it is likely to lead to some level of non-attendance, or to unreliable data. In our experience, participants often welcome the chance to 'have their say'. However, where any request may be perceived as indicating lack of choice, to gain their confidence and participation you will need to exercise care over the wording to be used in the request that is sent to them to take part. You will also need to exercise similar care in your introduction to the group when the interview occurs in order to provide a clear assurance about confidentiality.

- Once your sample have been selected, participants should be grouped so as not to inhibit individuals' possible contributions. Inhibitions may be related to lack of trust, to perceptions about status differences, or because of the dominance of certain individuals. The nature and selection of each group will affect the first two elements. We would advise using a series of horizontal slices through an organisation so that, within each group, participants have a similar status and similar work experiences. (Using a vertical slice would introduce perceptions about status differences and variations in work experience.) In this way, group interviews can be conducted at a number of levels within an organisation. A reference may be made about the nature of the group to provide reassurance, and you may consider asking people to introduce themselves by their first name only without referring to their exact job.

- Where one or two people dominate the discussion, you should seek to reduce their contributions carefully and to bring others in. Torrington (1991) suggests that this may be attempted in a general way:

  'What do you think, Yuksel?'
  'What do other people think about this?'

  Alternatively, more specifically:

  'How does Sandra's point relate to the one that you raised, Sharon?'

  A question posed to other group members should also have the effect of inhibiting the contribution of a dominant member:

  'What do you think about Johan's suggestion?'

- You will need to ensure that participants understand each other's contributions and that you develop an accurate understanding of the points being made. Asking a participant to clarify the meaning of a particular contribution, where it has not been understood, and testing understanding through summarising should help to ensure this.

- You will need to consider the location and setting for a group interview. It is advisable to conduct the interview in a neutral setting rather than, say, in a manager's office, where participants may not feel relaxed. There should be no likelihood of interruption or being overheard. You should consider the layout of the seating in the room where the interview is to be held. Where possible, arrange the seating in a circular fashion so that everyone will be facing inward and so that they will be an equal distance from the central point of this circle.

- Finally, students often ask, 'When will I know that I have undertaken sufficient group interviews or focus groups?' Writing about focus groups, Krueger and Casey (2000) suggest that you should plan to undertake three or four group interviews with any one type of participant. If after the third or fourth group interview you are no longer receiving new information, this means that you have heard the full range of ideas and reached saturation.

The demands of conducting all types of group interview, including focus groups, and the potential wealth of ideas that may flow from them mean that it is likely to be difficult to manage the process and note key points at the same time. We have managed to overcome this in two ways: by audio-recording the group interviews or using two interviewers. Where two interviewers are used, one person facilitates the discussion and the other person makes notes. We would recommend that you use two interviewers even if you are audio-recording the group interview as it will allow one interviewer to concentrate fully on managing the process whilst the other ensures the data are recorded. Where you cannot audio-record the group interview, you will need to write up any notes immediately afterwards so as not to lose data. As with one-to-one interviews, your research will benefit from the making of notes about the nature of the interactions that occur in the group interviews that you conduct. We would not advise you to undertake more than one group interview in a day on your own because of the danger of losing or confusing data.

Group interviews

In a group interview your role will be to ensure that all participants have the opportunity to state their points of view and answer your question and that these data are captured. This type of interview can range from being highly structured to unstructured, although it tends to be relatively unstructured and fairly free-flowing (Zikmund 2000) in terms of both breadth and depth of topics. The onus will be placed firmly on you to explain its purpose, to encourage participants to relax, and to initiate their comments and, with focus groups, detailed discussion. The use of this method is likely to necessitate a balance between encouraging participants to provide answers to a particular question or questions that you introduce and allowing them to range more freely in discussion where this may reveal data that provide you with important insights. Thus once you have opened the interview (Box 10.9) and the discussion is established, it will need to be managed carefully. Group interactions may lead to a highly productive discussion as interviewees respond to your questions and evaluate points made by the group. However, as your opportunity to develop an individual level of rapport with each participant will not be present (compared with a one-to-one interview), there may also emerge a group effect where certain participants effectively try to dominate the interview whilst others may feel inhibited. This may result in some participants publically agreeing with the views of others, whilst privately disagreeing. As a consequence a reported consensus may, in reality, be a view that nobody wholly endorses and nobody disagrees with (Stokes and Bergin 2006). At the same time the task of trying to encourage involvement by all group members and of maintaining the interview's exploratory purpose. A high level of skill, therefore, will be required in order for you to be able to conduct this type of discussion successfully, as well as to try to record its outcomes.

Despite this reference to the potential difficulties of using group interviews, there are distinct advantages arising from their use. Because of the presence of several participants, this type of situation allows a breadth of points of view to emerge and for the group to respond to these views. A dynamic group can generate or respond to a number of ideas and evaluate them, thus helping you to explain or explore concepts. You are also likely to benefit from the opportunity that this method provides in terms of allowing your participants to consider points raised by other group members and to challenge one another's views. In one-to-one interviews, discussion is of course limited to the interviewer and interviewee. Stokes and Bergin (2006) highlight that whilst group interviews, and in particular focus groups, are able to identify accurately principal issues, they are not able to provide the depth and detail in relation to specific issues that can be obtained from individual interviews.

The use of group interviews may also provide an efficient way for you to interview a larger number of individuals than would be possible through the use of one-to-one interviews (Box 10.17). Linked to this point, their use may allow you to adopt an interview-based strategy that can more easily be related to a representative sample, particularly where the research project is being conducted within a specific organisation or in relation to a clearly defined population. This may help to establish the credibility of this research where an attempt is made to overcome issues of bias associated with interviews in general and this type in particular.

Group interviews can also be used to identify key themes that will be used to develop items that are included in a survey questionnaire. This particular use of group interviews may inform subsequent parts of your data collection, providing a clearer focus. For example, in an attitude survey the initial use of group interviews can lead to a 'bottom-up' generation of concerns and issues, which helps to establish the survey.

Box 10.17
Focus on management research

The impact of international air travel on global climate and potential climate change policies

Research by Susanne Becken (2007) explored tourists' knowledge and awareness of the impact or air travel on climate, their sense of personal responsibility and their reactions to specified climate change policies. Initially in-depth interviews with tourists leaving New Zealand were used to inform the development of focus groups.

Five focus groups were conducted with groups of between four and eight participants, each meeting lasting between 1.5 and 2.5 hours. Within each group's meeting the moderator provided participants with a brief introduction to climate change and its relationship to tourism, taking care not to influence their thinking. Subsequently, the meeting was structured into three sections:

1 quiz on climate and travel to stimulate discussion between participants;
2 role-play exercise in which participants were invited to discuss the implementation of different climate change scenarios;
3 general discussion relating to the previous sections.

Each focus group was moderated by one researcher and observed by a second. The focus groups were also video- and audio-recorded.

Focus groups

Focus groups are well known because of the way they have been used by political parties to test voter reactions to particular policies and election strategies, and through their use in market research to test reactions to products. A **focus group**, sometimes called a 'focus group interview', is a group interview that focuses clearly upon a particular issue, product, service or topic and encompasses the need for interactive discussion amongst participants (Carson *et al.* 2001). This means that, in comparison with other forms of group interview, individual group members' interactions and responses are both encouraged and more closely controlled to maintain the focus. Participants are selected because they have certain characteristics in common that relate to the topic being discussed and they are encouraged to discuss and share their points of view without any pressure to reach a consensus (Krueger and Casey 2000). These discussions are conducted several times, with similar participants, to enable trends and patterns to be identified when the data collected are analysed.

If you are running a focus group, you will probably be referred to as the **moderator** or 'facilitator'. These labels emphasise the dual role of the person running the focus group, namely to:

- keep the group within the boundaries of the topic being discussed;
- generate interest in the topic and encourage discussion, whilst at the same time not leading the group towards certain opinions.

Where focus groups are being used this is likely to be associated with a higher level of interviewer-led structure and intervention to facilitate discussion than where group interviews are being used. The size of groups may also be related to topic. Thus a focus group designed to obtain views about a product range (Box 10.18) is likely to be larger than a group interview that explores a topic related to a more emotionally involved construct, such as attitudes to performance-related pay or the way in which employees rate their treatment by management. You may also choose to design smaller groups as you seek to develop your competence in relation to the use of this interviewing technique to collect qualitative data.

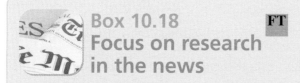

Box 10.18
Focus on research in the news
FT

BT keeps an eye on surfing habits in quest for better advert targeting

BT will shortly begin trials of an advertising technology that could have profound implications for the Internet economy and online privacy. The telecoms group will use technology from an Aim-listed company, Phorm, to track the web-surfing habits of its Internet users to enable it to target advertising more tightly. Carphone Warehouse's Talk Talk and Virgin Media have also signed up for the technology. If trials go well, Phorm is expected to sign deals with other Internet service providers around the world. Improving targeting is the perennial obsession of the advertising sector, in line with the often-quoted saw: 'I know half my advertising budget is wasted, I just don't know which half.'

The Internet, where it is possible to count how many people see or click on an advert, has allowed marketeers to cut down on some wastage but getting the right advert in front of the right consumer remains a problem. Targeted ads are estimated to generate about 35 per cent more 'clicks' than non-targeted ones.

Box 10.18
Focus on research in
the news *(continued)*

Phorm's software will monitor all the web pages that a BT broadband customer visits, creating a profile of their interests – for example, noting if they visit sites related to luxury cars. A carmaker, such as Jaguar, would then be able to ensure that these individuals would be shown adverts for its range, wherever they surfed on the web.

'This kind of behavioural targeting isn't a new thing. It already exists within certain websites or portals such as Yahoo. But it will be the first time it will be done at an Internet service provider level, observing behaviour across all pages', said Jason Carter, head of digital advertising at Universal McCann.

The technology could also help websites make more money. Currently, just 30 per cent of web pages are estimated to have any advertising, and only the most popular generate significant revenues.

The effectiveness of online advertising depends not on the content of a web page but who is visiting it. Even an obscure site about knitting or model railways could make money from showing expensive Jaguar ads, if people identified as potential Jaguar-buyers visited their pages. Sites such as FT.com and iVillage have already signed up to be part of the early Phorm trials.

The technology will give Internet service providers, such as BT, a cut from online advertising. Advertising money has previously gone to website owners and advertising services companies such as Google. Content owners are expected to get about 75 per cent of the ad revenues with Phorm and internet companies sharing the remainder. Analysts at Charles Stanley estimate that if the Phorm technology takes off, it could generate $1.5 bn in 2012. This compares with $16.6 bn of revenues reported by Google for 2007. The big question, however, is whether consumers will be happy to be monitored in this way. Phorm has sparked controversy among Internet bloggers and privacy activists who have branded the technology 'spyware'. Websites such as www.guardian.co.uk are holding off from signing up to the scheme and advertising companies say big clients such as Microsoft are wary of getting involved, because they are worried about bad publicity. Phorm promises that it will not link the profiles it compiles to any personally identifiable information about Internet users, such as name, address or even the IP address of their computer. Users will simply be a random number on the system.

The Information Commissioner's Office and Home Office have indicated that the technology does not breach data laws. The system claims to be less invasive than search engines such as Google. 'I don't understand how this has become a big issue for Phorm, when someone like Google collects far more personal data and has been doing it for years', said Katie Eyton, head of online advertising at Manning Gottlieb OMD.

BT says its own focus group research has shown a favourable response among the public.

The telecoms group will invite selected subscribers to take part in the trials and promises that if it extends them it will ask for consent before starting monitoring.

Source: article by Maija Palmer, *Financial Times*, 24 May 2008. Copyright © 2008 The Financial Times Ltd.

10.8 Telephone, Internet- and intranet-mediated interviews

Most non-standardised interviews occur on a face-to-face basis. However, such qualitative interviews may also be conducted by telephone or electronically via the Internet or intranet. These pose particular problems as well as providing advantages in certain circumstances that we discuss in this section.

Telephone interviews

Attempting to conduct non-standardised interviews by telephone may offer potential advantages associated with access, speed and lower cost. This method may allow you to make contact with participants with whom it would be impractical to conduct an interview on a face-to-face basis because of the distance and prohibitive costs involved and time required. Even where 'long-distance' access is not an issue, conducting interviews by telephone may still offer advantages associated with speed of data collection and lower cost. In other words, this approach may be seen as more convenient.

However, there are a number of significant issues that militate against attempting to collect qualitative data by telephone contact. We have already discussed the importance of establishing personal contact in this type of interviewing. The intention of non-standardised interviewing is to be able to explore the participant's responses. This is likely to become more feasible once a position of trust has been established, as discussed earlier. This situation, of establishing trust, will become particularly important where you wish to ask sensitive questions. For these reasons, seeking to conduct qualitative interviews by telephone may lead to issues of (reduced) reliability, where your participants are less willing to engage in an exploratory discussion, or even a refusal to take part.

There are also some other practical issues that would need to be managed. These relate to your ability to control the pace of a telephone interview and to record any data that were forthcoming. Conducting an interview by telephone and taking notes is an extremely difficult process and so we would recommend using audio-recording. In addition, the normal visual cues that allow your participant to control the flow of the data that they share with you would be absent. With telephone interviews you lose the opportunity to witness the non-verbal behaviour of your participant, which may adversely affect your interpretation of how far to pursue a particular line of questioning. Your participant may be less willing to provide you with as much time to talk to them in comparison with a face-to-face interview. You may also encounter difficulties in developing more complex questions in comparison with a face-to-face interview situation. Finally, attempting to gain access through a telephone call may lead to ethical issues, as we discussed in Section 6.5.

For these reasons, we believe that non-standardised interviewing by telephone is likely to be appropriate only in particular circumstances. It may be appropriate to conduct a short, follow-up telephone interview to clarify the meaning of some data, where you have already undertaken a face-to-face interview with a participant with whom you have been able to establish your integrity and to demonstrate your competence. It may also be appropriate where access would otherwise be prohibited because of long distance, where you have already been able to establish your credibility through prior contact, perhaps through correspondence, and have made clear that your requirements are reasonable and guided by ethical principles. Where this situation involves a request to undertake a telephone interview with a participant from another country, you will need to be aware of any cultural norms related to the conduct and duration of telephone conversations.

Internet- and intranet-mediated interviewing

Morgan and Symon (2004) use the term **electronic interviews** to refer to interviews held both in real time using the Internet and organisations' intranets as well as those that are, in effect, undertaken off-line. This sub-division into asynchronous and synchronous (Figure 10.2) offers a useful way of categorising electronic interviews as there are significant differences in electronic interviews dependent upon whether the interview is undertaken in real time (**synchronous**) or offline (**asynchronous**).

```
                          Electronic interviews
                                   |
              +--------------------+--------------------+
              |                                         |
        Asynchronous                              Synchronous
              |                                         |
      +-------+-------+                                 |
      |               |                                 |
    Email        Internet                            Chat
                  forums                             rooms
```

Figure 10.2 Forms of electronic interviews

Using the Internet or an organisation's intranet has significant advantages where the population you wish to interview are geographically dispersed. In addition, with all forms of electronic interview the software automatically records as they are typed in, thereby removing problems associated with audio-recording and transcription such as cost, accuracy and participants' apprehension. However, as you will remember from Section 6.5, electronic interviews have their own set of ethical issues that you will need to consider.

Web conferencing software can be used for both synchronous (real time) and asynchronous one-to-one and group interviews. Where this requires participants to have the software loaded onto their computers this can cause problems, especially where they are unfamiliar with the software or there is incompatibility with hardware or operating systems. Internet forums and emails can be used for asynchronous interviews. In contrast, a **chat room** is an online forum operating in synchronous mode.

By far the most common form of chat room is instant messaging such as MSN Messenger™. Although some would argue that this is not a true chat room as conversations are restricted to those named in a user's list, such instant messaging can be used to undertake real-time one-to-one and group interviews, providing netiquette is observed. The considerable debate regarding the suitability of Internet- and intranet-mediated communication for synchronous interviewing has been reviewed by Mann and Stewart (2000). Some researchers argue that interviewing participants online such as through web conferencing or chat rooms is unlikely to achieve the same high levels of interactivity and rich and spontaneous communication that can be obtained with face-to-face interviewing. This is often explained by the relatively narrow bandwidth of these electronic media when compared with face-to-face communication, it being argued that electronic media transmit fewer social cues. Others argue that this is not the case and that, after the initial invitation to participate, it is possible to build up considerable rapport between the interviewer and the interviewee during an online interview. It has also been suggested that the relative anonymity of online interviews facilitates more open and honest responses, in particular with regard to sensitive issues where participants have adopted pseudonyms (Sweet 2001). Where group interviews or focus groups are being conducted, participants are less likely to be influenced by characteristics such as age, ethnicity or appearance. Overbearing participants are less likely to predominate, although variations in keyboard skills are likely to impact on participation levels.

For asynchronous interviewing, email and **Internet forums** or discussion groups mean that interviews are normally conducted over an extended time period of weeks. A **forum** usually deals only with one topic and personal exchanges are discouraged. Forums are commonly referred to as web forums, message boards, discussion boards, discussion forums, discussion groups and bulletin boards. Although forums do not allow people to edit each other's messages, there is usually a moderator or forum administrator who typically is responsible for netiquette being observed (Sections 6.4 and 11.5) and has the ability to edit, delete or modify any content.

An **email interview** consist of a series of emails each containing a small number of questions rather than one email containing a series of questions (Morgan and Symon 2004). Although you can send one email containing a series of questions, this is really an Internet- or intranet-mediated questionnaire (Sections 11.2 and 11.5). After making contact and obtaining agreement to participate, you initially email a small number of questions or introduce a topic to which the participant will (hopefully) reply. You then need to respond to these ideas, specifically asking further questions, raising points of clarification and pursuing ideas that are of further interest. Morgan and Symon (2004) emphasise that, because of the nature of email communications, such interviews may last for some weeks, there being a time delay between a question being asked and its being answered. This, they argue, can be advantageous as it allows both the interviewer and the interviewee to reflect on the questions and responses prior to providing a considered response.

10.9 Summary

- The use of non-standardised (qualitative) research interviews should allow you to collect a rich and detailed set of data, although you will need to develop a sufficient level of competence to conduct these and to be able to gain access to the type of data associated with their use.
- Interviews can be differentiated according to the level of structure and standardisation adopted. Different types of interviews are useful for different research purposes.
- Non-standardised (qualitative) research interviews include two broad types that are generally referred to as in-depth or unstructured interviews and semi-structured interviews. You can use non-standardised interviews to explore topics and explain other findings.
- Your research design may incorporate more than one type of interview.
- In-depth and semi-structured interviews can be used in quantitative as well as qualitative research.
- There are situations favouring non-standardised (qualitative) interviews that will lead you to use this method to collect data. Apart from the nature of your research strategy, these are related to the significance of establishing personal contact, the nature of your data collection questions, and the length of time required from those who provide data.
- Data quality issues, your level of competence and logistical and resource matters will all need to be considered when you use in-depth and semi-structured interviews.
- Apart from one-to-one interviews conducted on a face-to-face basis, you may consider conducting such an interview by telephone or electronically in particular circumstances. In addition, you may consider using group interviews such as focus groups. There may be particular advantages associated with group interviews, but these are considerably more difficult to manage than one-to-one interviews.

Self-check questions

Help with these questions is available at the end of the chapter.

10.1 What type of interview would you use in each of the following situations:
    a a market research project?
    b a research project seeking to understand whether trade union attitudes have changed?
    c following the analysis of a questionnaire?

10.2 What are the advantages of using semi-structured and in-depth interviews?

10.3 During a presentation of your proposal to undertake a research project, which will be based on semi-structured or in-depth interviews, you feel that you have dealt well with the relationship between the purpose of the research and the proposed methodology when one of the panel leans forward and asks you to discuss the trustworthiness and usefulness of your work for other researchers. This is clearly a challenge to see whether you can defend such an approach. How do you respond?

10.4 Having quizzed you about the trustworthiness and usefulness of your work for other researchers, the panel member decides that one more testing question is in order. He explains that qualitatively based work isn't an easy option. 'It is not an easier alternative for those who want to avoid statistics', he says. 'How can we be sure that you're competent to get involved in interview work, especially where the external credibility of this organisation may be affected by the impression that you create in the field?' How will you respond to this concern?

10.5 What are the key issues to consider when planning to use semi-structured or in-depth interviews?

10.6 What are the key areas of competence that you need to develop in order to conduct an interview successfully?

Review and discussion questions

10.7 Watch and, if possible, video-record a television interview such as one that is part of a chat show or a documentary. It does not matter if you only record an interview of 10 to 15 minutes' duration.

   a As you watch the interview, make notes about what the participant is telling the interviewer. After the interview review your notes. How much of what was being said did you manage to record?

   b If you were able to video-record the television interview, watch the interview again and compare your notes with what was actually said. What other information would you like to add to your notes?

   c Either watch the interview again or another television interview that is part of a chat show or a documentary. This time pay careful attention to the questioning techniques used by the interviewer. How many of the different types of question discussed in Section 10.5 can you identify?

   d How important do you think the non-verbal cues given by the interviewer and the interviewee are in understanding the meaning of what is being said?

10.8 With a friend, each decide on a topic about which you think it would be interesting to interview the other person. Separately develop your interview themes and prepare an interview guide for a semi-structured interview. At the same time, decide which one of the 'difficult' participants in Table 10.2 you would like to role-play when being interviewed.

   a Conduct both interviews and, if possible, make an audio-recording. If this is not possible the interviewer should take notes.

   b Listen to each of the audio-recordings – what aspects of your interviewing technique do you each need to improve?

   c If you were not able to audio-record the interview, how good a record of each interview do you consider the notes to be? How could you improve your interviewing technique further?

10.9 Obtain a transcript of an interview that has already been undertaken. If your university subscribes to online newspapers such as ft.com, these are a good source of business-related transcripts. Alternatively, typing 'interview transcript' into a search engine such as Google will generate numerous possibilities on a vast range of topics!

a Examine the transcript, paying careful attention to the questioning techniques used by the interviewer. To what extent do you think that certain questions have led the interviewee to certain answers?

b Now look at the responses given by the interviewer. To what extent do you think these are the actual verbatim responses given by the interviewee? Why do you think this?

Progressing your research project

Using semi-structured or in-depth interviews in your research

- Review your research question(s) and objectives. How appropriate would it be to use non-standardised (qualitative) interviews to collect data? Where it is appropriate, explain the relationship between your research question(s) and objectives, and the use of such interviews. Where this type of interviewing is not appropriate, justify your decision.

- If you decide that semi-structured or in-depth interviews are appropriate, what practical problems do you foresee? How might you attempt to overcome these practical problems?

- What threats to the trustworthiness of the data collected are you likely to encounter? How might you overcome these?

- Draft a list of interview themes to be explored and compare these thoroughly with your research question(s) and objectives.

- Ask your project tutor to comment on your judgement about the use of non-standardised (qualitative) interviews, the issues and threats that you have identified, your suggestions to overcome these, and the fit between your interview themes and your research question(s) and objectives.

References

Becken, S. (2007) 'Tourist perception of international air travel's impact on global climate and potential climate change policies', *Journal of Sustainable Tourism*, Vol. 15, No. 4, pp. 351–60.

Boddy, C. (2005) 'A rose by any other name may smell as sweet but "group discussion" is not another name for "focus group" nor should it be', *Qualitative Market Research*, Vol. 8, No. 3, pp. 248–55.

Bryman, A. (1988) *Quantity and Quality in Social Research*. London: Unwin Hyman.

Bryman, A. (2006) 'Editor's introduction: Mixed methods research', in A. Bryman (ed.) *Mixed Methods: Volume 1*. London: Sage, pp. XXV– LII.

Carson, D., Gilmore, A., Perry, C. and Grønhaug, K. (2001) *Qualitative Marketing Research*. London: Sage.

Cooper, D.R. and Schindler, P.S. (2008) *Business Research Methods* (10th edn). London: McGraw-Hill.

Dickmann M. and Doherty, N. (2008) 'Exploring the Career Capital Impact of International Assignments within Distinct Organizational Contexts', *British Journal of Management*, Vol. 19, No. 2, pp. 145–61.

Dragons' Den (2007) Series 5, Episode 1. Beach Break Live. British Broadcasting Corporation Television broadcast, 15 Oct. Available at: http://www.bbc.co.uk/dragonsden/series5/episode1.shtml [Accessed 8 June 2008.]

Easterby-Smith, M., Thorpe, R. and Jackson, P.R. (2008) *Management Research* (3rd edn). London: Sage.

Ghauri, P. and Grønhaug, K. (2005) *Research Methods in Business Studies: A Practical Guide* (3rd edn). Harlow: Financial Times Prentice Hall.

Grummitt, J. (1980) *Interviewing Skills.* London: Industrial Society.

Healey, M.J. (1991) 'Obtaining information from businesses', in M.J. Healey (ed.) *Economic Activity and Land Use.* Harlow: Longman, pp. 193–251.

Healey, M.J. and Rawlinson, M.B. (1993) 'Interviewing business owners and managers: a review of methods and techniques', *Geoforum,* Vol. 24, No. 3, pp. 339–55.

Healey, M.J. and Rawlinson, M.B. (1994) 'Interviewing techniques in business and management research', in V.J. Wass, V.J. and P.E. Wells (eds) *Principles and Practice in Business and Management Research.* Aldershot: Dartmouth, pp. 123–46.

Hofstede, G. (2001) *Culture's Consequences: Comparing Values, Behaviours, Institutions and Organisations Across Nations* (2nd edn). London: Sage.

Jankowicz, A.D. (2005) *Business Research Projects* (4th edn). London: Business Press Thomson Learning.

Kahn, R. and Cannell, C. (1957) *The Dynamics of Interviewing.* New York and Chichester: Wiley.

Keaveney, S.M. (1995) 'Customer switching behaviour in service industries: an exploratory study', *Journal of Marketing,* Vol. 59, No. 2, pp. 71–82.

King, N. (2004) 'Using interviews in qualitative research', in C. Cassell and G. Symon (eds) *Essential Guide to Qualitative Methods in Organizational Research.* London: Sage. pp. 11–22.

Krueger, R.A. and Casey, M.A. (2000) *Focus Groups: A Practical Guide for Applied Research* (3rd edn). Thousand Oaks, CA: Sage.

Mann, C. and Stewart, F. (2000) *Internet Communication and Qualitative Research: A Handbook for Researching Online.* London: Sage.

Marshall, C. and Rossman, G.B. (1999) *Designing Qualitative Research* (3rd edn). Thousand Oaks, CA: Sage.

Morgan, S.J. and Symon, G. (2004) 'Electronic interviews in organizational research' in C. Cassell and G. Symon (eds) *Essential Guide to Qualitative Methods in Organizational Research.* London: Sage. pp. 3–33.

North, D.J., Leigh, R. and Gough, J. (1983) 'Monitoring industrial change at the local level: some comments on methods and data sources', in M.J. Healey (ed.) *Urban and Regional Industrial Research: The Changing UK Data Base.* Norwich: Geo Books, pp. 111–29.

Powney, J. and Watts, M. (1987) *Interviewing in Educational Research.* London: Routledge and Kegan Paul.

Robson, C. (2002) *Real World Research* (2nd edn). Oxford: Blackwell.

Silverman, D. (2007) *A Very Short, Fairly Interesting and Reasonably Cheap Book about Qualitative Research.* London: Sage.

Speer, S. (2002) 'Natural' and "contrived" data: A sustainable distinction?', *Discourse Studies,* Vol. 4, No. 4, pp. 511–25.

Stokes, D. and Bergin, R. (2006) 'Methodology or "methodolatry"? An evaluation of focus groups and depth interviews', *Qualitative Market Research,* Vol. 9, No. 1, pp. 26–37.

Sweet, C. (2001) 'Designing and conducting virtual focus groups', *Qualitative Market Research,* Vol. 4, No. 3, pp. 130–5.

Tashakkori, A. and Teddlie, C. (1998) *Mixed Methodology: Combining Qualitative and Quantitative Approaches.* Thousand Oaks, CA: Sage.

Torrington, D. (1991) *Management Face to Face.* London: Prentice Hall.

Yin, R.K. (2003) *Case Study Research: Design and Methods* (3rd edn). Beverly Hills, CA: Sage.

Zikmund, W.G. (2000) *Business Research Methods* (6th edn). Fort Worth, TX: Dryden Press.

Further reading

Cassell, C. and Symon, G. (2004) (eds) *Essential Guide to Qualitative Methods in Organizational Research*. London: Sage. Chapter 2 by Nigel King and Chapter 3 by Stephanie Morgan and Gillian Symon are readable accounts of interviews and electronic interviews, respectively, both with extremely useful detailed case studies.

Krueger, R.A. and Casey, M.A. (2000) *Focus Groups: A Practical Guide for Applied Research* (3rd edn). Thousand Oaks, CA: Sage. A very useful work for those considering the use of this method of group interviewing.

Mann, C. and Stewart, F. (2000) *Internet Communication and Qualitative Research: A Handbook for Researching Online*. London: Sage. Although written in 2000, Chapter 6 still provides a useful guide to using online interviews and Chapter 5 to online focus groups.

Case 10
Students' and former students' debt problems

Source: Gregor Schuster/Corbis.

Michelle had been a student union welfare officer on a year's sabbatical from her undergraduate accounting and financial management degree. During that time, she had encountered many students who had suffered hardship while at university as a consequence of limited financial support. Prior to her sabbatical year, in the second year of her studies, she had encountered social accounting, the idea that accounting could capture alternative goals and outcomes to economic performance, such as community, social values and fairness in the distribution of social resources (Ball and Seal 2005; Owen 2008). She was particularly impressed by a paper by Cooper *et al.* (2005) suggesting that social accounting could have a real impact in the struggle for change if it was linked to the aspirations of social movements.

When she returned for the final year of her studies she had to conduct a final year research project. She thought that it would be a good idea to explore whether students who had experienced financial hardship thought that social accounts could be a good way of highlighting the weaknesses of the funding regime that charged students tuition fees and provided loans of limited value. She reasoned that not only would such an exploration provide a viable academic project, but it would also satisfy the social accounting concerns of promoting fairness and community. Furthermore, by linking the project to her student union work, she might provide some help to any campaign that the National Union of Students might run to highlight the problems that loans and tuition fees brought to students.

Michelle conducted a review of the literature on social accounting as well as reading debates about the different methods of funding higher education. She prepared her focus group interview schedule. In the schedule, Michelle included topics such as:

- participants' views about whether the government should seek to identify hidden costs in its assessment of the viability of different systems of funding higher education;
- participants' views of the hidden costs associated with the systems of tuition fees and loans employed by government;
- the potential impact of students having large debts on the participants, their families and society more widely;
- how the participants had dealt with large amounts of debt;
- whether participants believed that it was possible for anyone to organise a successful campaign to convince the government to rethink its funding policy;
- participants' views on who they thought should organise that campaign and the types of actions that they could include in that campaign;
- the role participants felt that social accounting could play in helping to articulate messages for that campaign.

Michelle showed her ideas to her project tutor who said that he thought that they were good. Michelle informed her project tutor that she intended to use focus group interviews. She explained that the reason for her choice of method was that she wanted to see whether participants thought that the funding regime was unfair. In addition she wanted to assess whether there was any capacity for the construction of a movement for change through their sharing of experiences. Michelle's project tutor thought that the idea could work, but said that they should meet again to discuss how best to implement her plan. Unfortunately, the tutor was about to go away on a research visit and Michelle did not anticipate seeing him again before the new year vacation. Michelle wanted to conduct the interviews very early in the new year. This she hoped would give her plenty of time to analyse her data in preparation for writing a draft of her project over the spring vacation so that she would be ready to submit the dissertation in advance of the deadline date. She, therefore, decided to organise the focus group interviews as soon as possible.

At home that night Michelle went through her copy of the file she had kept about all of the students who had come to see her about money problems during her sabbatical year. In total, there were 400 students, divided roughly equally between students in each of the first, second and final years of their respective degrees. Michelle decided to organise five focus groups of students from the time of her sabbatical:

- students who were in their first year;
- students who were in their second year;
- students who were in their final year;
- equal numbers of students who were in the first, second and final years;
- equal numbers of students who were in their first, second and final years.

Michelle had read that the optimal number of people to include in a focus group interview was between eight to 12 people and she decided to go for the maximum within this range.

Michelle had kept mobile telephone numbers of a lot of people as well as their university addresses as part of her student union welfare officer records. She used these to help her contact her prospective participants. Michelle telephoned people to invite them to participate in research about student debt. In making the initial telephone calls, Michelle thought that to explain her exact method of data collection would extend the length of the phone calls unnecessarily, so she simply told the prospective participants that the research would require them to visit the university for around one hour. Michelle promised to write to those who agreed to participate with details of the exact venue, once she had identified and organised an appropriate room. Michelle had contacted around 100 people before she got the 60 participants that she needed for her five focus groups.

Michelle decided to hold the focus groups in the evenings. She wrote to the 60 people that had agreed to help, at the addresses that she had obtained last year from the student union records. Michelle provided details of the venue, but no further details of the research in the letter. Michelle's plan was to explain the logic of using focus groups at the same time as she explained her research questions to the participants. She thought that this would mean that she would only have to answer any questions once, rather than dealing with similar queries for each participant individually. All of the participants who were either in the first year and second year of their studies during Michelle's sabbatical year turned up to the focus group to which they were invited, but none of the people who had been in the final year of their studies when Michelle was the students union's welfare officer attended any focus groups. So Michelle only conducted four, rather than five focus group interviews.

Michelle decided to have minimum input in her role as moderator of the focus groups. Instead, she simply prepared a schedule showing a list of headings that she wanted to cover. At the start of each focus group, Michelle explained the purpose of the research to the attendees, she distributed a copy of the schedule to each person and asked them to conduct a discussion involving the whole group to cover the issues on the schedule and to take shared responsibility for ensuring that at the end of the discussion everyone felt that they had said all that they wanted to say about the issues. Michelle explained that she wanted to audio-record the discussion and asked everybody present at each focus group if that was OK. Michelle was pleased that no one objected. The final thing that Michelle did was ask that each of the participants state their first names as soon as the recorder was turned on to help the person who transcribed the recording to attribute opinions correctly. Michelle then sat back and kept notes on her observations of patterns of interaction. Michelle was pleased that all of the issues enthused all of the focus groups of participants and all of the issues were covered thoroughly by all participants.

References

Ball, A. and Seal, W. (2005) 'Social justice in a cold climate: could social accounting make a difference?', *Accounting Forum*, Vol. 29, No. 4, pp. 455–73.

Cooper, C., Taylor, P, Smith, N. and Catchpowle, L. (2005) 'A discussion of the political potential of Social Accounting', *Critical Perspectives on Accounting*, Vol. 16, No. 7, pp. 951–74.

Owen, D. (2008) 'Adventures in social and environmental accounting and auditing research: A personal reflection', in C. Humphrey and B. Lee (eds) *The Real Life Guide to Accounting Research*. Oxford: Elsevier/CIMA.

Questions

1 What advice would you give Michelle about the ethical issues involved in her project?
2 What advice would you give to Michelle about her selection of participants for her focus groups?
3 What advice would you give Michelle about whether she should attempt to organise another focus group of students who were in the final year of their studies last year to make her research more representative?

Additional case studies relating to material covered in this chapter are available via the book's Companion Website, **www.pearsoned.co.uk/saunders**. They are:

- Equal opportunities in the publishing industry
- The practices and styles of public relations practitioners
- Students' use of work-based learning in their studies.

Self-check answers

10.1 The type of interview that is likely to be used in each of these situations is as follows:

   a A standardised and structured interview where the aim is to develop response patterns from the views of people. The interview schedule might be designed to combine styles so that comments made by interviewees in relation to specific questions could also be recorded.

   b The situation outlined suggests an exploratory approach to research, and therefore an in-depth interview would be most appropriate.

   c The situation outlined here suggests that an explanatory approach is required in relation to the data collected, and in this case a semi-structured interview is likely to be appropriate.

10.2 Reasons that suggest the use of interviews include:

- the exploratory or explanatory nature of your research;
- situations where it will be significant to establish personal contact, in relation to interviewee sensitivity about the nature of the information to be provided and the use to be made of this;
- situations where the researcher needs to exercise control over the nature of those who will supply data;
- situations where there are a large number of questions to be answered;
- situations where questions are complex or open ended;
- situations where the order and logic of questioning may need to be varied.

10.3 Certainly politely! Your response needs to show that you are aware of the issues relating to reliability, bias and generalisability that might arise. It would be useful to discuss how these might be overcome through the following: the design of the research; the keeping of records or a diary in relation to the processes and key incidents of the research project as well as the recording of data collected; attempts to control bias through the process of collecting data; the relationship of the research to theory.

10.4 Perhaps it will be wise to say that you understand his position. You realise that any approach to research calls for particular types of competence. Your previous answer touching on interviewee bias has highlighted the need to establish credibility and to gain the interviewee's confidence. While competence will need to be developed over a period of time, allowing for any classroom simulations and dry runs with colleagues, probably the best approach will be your level of preparation before embarking on interview work. This relates first to the nature of the approach made to those whom you would like to participate in the research project and the information supplied to them, second to your intellectual preparation related to the topic to be explored and the particular context of the organisations participating in the research, and third to your ability to conduct an interview. You also recognise that piloting the interview themes will be a crucial element in building your competence.

10.5 Key issues to consider include the following:

- planning to minimise the occurrence of forms of bias where these are within your control, related to interviewer bias, interviewee bias and sampling bias;
- considering your aim in requesting the research interview and how you can seek to prepare yourself in order to gain access to the data that you hope your participants will be able to share with you;
- devising interview themes that you wish to explore or seek explanations for during the interview;
- sending a list of your interview themes to your interviewee prior to the interview, where this is considered appropriate;

- requesting permission and providing a reason where you would like to use a tape recorder during the interview;
- making sure that your level of preparation and knowledge (in relation to the research context and your research question and objectives) is satisfactory in order to establish your credibility when you meet your interviewee;
- considering how your intended appearance during the interview will affect the willingness of the interviewee to share data.

10.6 There are several areas where you need to develop and demonstrate competence in relation to the conduct of semi-structured and in-depth research interviews. These areas are:

- opening the interview;
- using appropriate language;
- questioning;
- listening;
- testing and summarising understanding;
- behavioural cues;
- recording data.

Get ahead using resources on the Companion Website at:
www.pearsoned.co.uk/saunders

- Improve your SPSS and NVivo research analysis with practice tutorials.
- Save time researching on the Internet with the Smarter Online Searching Guide.
- Test your progress using self-assessment questions.
- Follow live links to useful websites.

Chapter 11

Collecting primary data using questionnaires

> ## Learning outcomes
>
> By the end of this chapter you should:
>
> - understand the advantages and disadvantages of questionnaires as a data collection method;
> - be aware of a range of self-administered and interviewer-administered questionnaires;
> - be aware of the possible need to combine techniques within a research project;
> - be able to select and justify the use of appropriate questionnaire techniques for a variety of research scenarios;
> - be able to design, pilot and administer a questionnaire to answer research questions and to meet objectives;
> - be able to take appropriate action to enhance response rates and to ensure the validity and reliability of the data collected;
> - be able to apply the knowledge, skills and understanding gained to your own research project.

11.1 Introduction

Within business and management research, the greatest use of questionnaires is made within the survey strategy (Section 5.3). However, both experiment and case study research strategies can make use of these techniques. Although you probably have your own understanding of the term 'questionnaire', it is worth noting that there are a variety of definitions in common usage (Oppenheim 2000). Some people reserve it exclusively for questionnaires where the person answering the question actually records their own answers. Others use it as a more general term to also include interviews that are administered either face to face or by telephone.

In this book we use **questionnaire** as a general term to include all techniques of data collection in which each person is asked to respond to the same set of questions in a predetermined order (deVaus 2002). It, therefore, includes both structured interviews and telephone questionnaires as well as those in which the questions are answered without an interviewer being present, such as the Nando's online questionnaire. The range of techniques that fall under this broad heading are outlined in the next Section (11.2), along with their relative advantages and disadvantages.

The use of questionnaires is discussed in many research methods texts. These range from those that devote a few pages to it to those that specify precisely how you should construct and use them, such as Dillman's (2007) **tailored design method**. Perhaps not surprisingly, the questionnaire is one of the most widely used data collection techniques within the survey strategy. Because each person (respondent) is asked to respond to the same set of questions, it provides an efficient way of collecting responses from a large sample prior to quantitative analysis (Chapter 12). However, before you decide to use a questionnaire we should like to include a note of caution. Many authors (for example, Bell 2005; Oppenheim 2000) argue that it is far harder to produce a good questionnaire than you might think. You need to ensure that it will collect the precise data that you require to answer your research question(s) and achieve your objectives. This is of paramount importance because, like Nando's, you are unlikely to have more than one opportunity to collect the data. In particular, you will be unable to go back to

Questionnaires are a part of our everyday lives. For modules in your course, your lecturers have probably asked you and your fellow students to complete module-evaluation questionnaires, thereby collecting data on students' views. Similarly, when we visit a tourist attraction or have a meal in a restaurant, there is often the opportunity to complete a comment card. Some restaurants, such as Nando's, also use online questionnaires administered via their website as a way of collecting data from, and keeping in contact with, customers. As can be seen from the illustration, Nando's online questionnaire begins by emphasising the importance of feedback to them. A drop-down menu of choices is used to establish the category of feedback and details about the respondents including their name and contact details. The Nando's questionnaire provides space for general comments. David Manly from Nando's Marketing says, 'By asking the user to select the reason for their comment Nando's are able to respond to them as quickly as possible. The "category" acts as a filter for the messages to be distributed into the appropriate inboxes of the Customer Care team at Nando's.' These data help Nando's to maintain high levels of customer satisfaction.

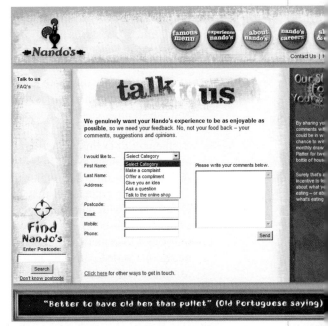

Extract from Nando's online questionnaire
Source: Nando's (2008), reproduced with permission.

those individuals who choose to remain anonymous and collect additional data using another questionnaire. These issues are discussed in Section 11.3.

The design of your questionnaire will affect the response rate and the reliability and validity of the data you collect. Response rates, validity and reliability can be maximised by:

- careful design of individual questions;
- clear and pleasing layout of the questionnaire;
- lucid explanation of the purpose of the questionnaire;
- pilot testing;
- carefully planned and executed administration.

Together these form Sections 11.4 and 11.5. In Section 11.4 we discuss designing your questionnaire. Administering the actual questionnaire is considered in Section 11.5 along with actions to help ensure high response rates.

11.2 An overview of questionnaire techniques

When to use questionnaires

We have found that many people use a questionnaire to collect data without considering other methods such as examination of secondary sources (Chapter 8), observation (Chapter 9), and semi-structured or unstructured interviews (Chapter 10). Our advice is to evaluate all possible data collection methods and to choose those most appropriate to your research question(s) and objectives. Questionnaires are usually not particularly good for exploratory or other research that requires large numbers of open-ended questions (Sections 10.2 and 10.3). They work best with standardised questions that you can be confident will be interpreted the same way by all respondents (Robson 2002).

Questionnaires therefore tend to be used for descriptive or explanatory research. Descriptive research, such as that undertaken using attitude and opinion questionnaires and questionnaires of organisational practices, will enable you to identify and describe the variability in different phenomena. In contrast, explanatory or analytical research will enable you to examine and explain relationships between variables, in particular cause-and-effect relationships. These two purposes have different research design requirements (Gill and Johnson 2002), which we shall discuss later (Section 11.3).

Although questionnaires may be used as the only data collection method, it may be better to link them with other methods in a multiple-methods research design (Section 5.4). For example, a questionnaire to discover customers' attitudes can be complemented by in-depth interviews to explore and understand these attitudes (Section 10.3). In addition, questionnaires, if worded correctly, normally require less skill and sensitivity to administer than semi-structured or in-depth interviews (Jankowicz 2005).

Types of questionnaire

The design of a questionnaire differs according to how it is administered and, in particular, the amount of contact you have with the respondents (Figure 11.1). **Self-administered questionnaires** are usually completed by the respondents. Such questionnaires are administered electronically using the Internet (**Internet-mediated questionnaires**) or intranet (**intranet-mediated questionnaires**), posted to respondents who return them by post after completion (**postal** or **mail questionnaires**), or delivered by hand to each

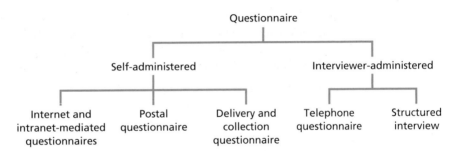

Figure 11.1
Types of
questionnaire

respondent and collected later (**delivery and collection questionnaires**). Responses to **interviewer-administered questionnaires** are recorded by the interviewer on the basis of each respondent's answers. Questionnaires administered using the telephone are known as **telephone questionnaires**. The final category, **structured interviews** (sometimes known as **interview schedules**), refers to those questionnaires where interviewers physically meet respondents and ask the questions face to face. These differ from semi-structured and unstructured (in-depth) interviews (Section 10.2), as there is a defined schedule of questions, from which interviewers should not deviate.

The choice of questionnaire

Your choice of questionnaire will be influenced by a variety of factors related to your research question(s) and objectives (Table 11.1), and in particular the:

- characteristics of the respondents from whom you wish to collect data;
- importance of reaching a particular person as respondent;
- importance of respondents' answers not being contaminated or distorted;
- size of sample you require for your analysis, taking into account the likely response rate;
- types of question you need to ask to collect your data;
- number of questions you need to ask to collect your data.

These factors will not apply equally to your choice of questionnaire, and for some research questions or objectives may not apply at all. The type of questionnaire you choose will dictate how sure you can be that the respondent is the person whom you wish to answer the questions and thus the reliability of responses (Table 11.1). Even if you address a postal questionnaire to a company manager by name, you have no way of ensuring that the manager will be the respondent. The manager's assistant or someone else could complete it! Internet- and intranet-mediated questionnaires, and in particular those administered in conjunction with email, offer greater control because most users read and respond to their own mail at their personal computer (Witmer *et al.* 1999). With delivery and collection questionnaires, you can sometimes check who has answered the questions at collection. By contrast, interviewer-administered questionnaires enable you to ensure that the respondent is whom you want. This improves the reliability of your data. In addition, you can record who were non-respondents, allowing you to give some assessment of the impact of bias caused by refusals.

Any contamination of respondents' answers will reduce your data's reliability (Table 11.1). Sometimes, if they have insufficient knowledge or experience they may deliberately guess at the answer, a tendency known as **uninformed response.** This is particularly likely when the questionnaire has been incentivised (Section 11.5). Respondents to self-administered questionnaires are relatively unlikely to answer to please you

Table 11.1 Main attributes of questionnaires

Attribute	Internet- and intranet-mediated	Postal	Delivery and collection	Telephone	Structured interview
Population's characteristics for which suitable	Computer-literate individuals who can be contacted by email, Internet or intranet	Literate individuals who can be contacted by post; selected by name, household, organisation, etc.		Individuals who can be telephoned; selected by name, household, organisation, etc.	Any; selected by name, household, organisation, in the street etc.
Confidence that right person has responded	High if using email	Low	Low but can be checked at collection	High	
Likelihood of contamination or distortion of respondent's answer	Low	May be contaminated by consultation with others		Occasionally distorted or invented by interviewer	Occasionally contaminated by consultation or distorted/invented by interviewer
Size of sample	Large, can be geographically dispersed	Large, can be geographically dispersed	Dependent on number of field workers	Dependent on number of interviewers	
Likely response rate[a]	Variable, 30% reasonable within organisations/via intranet, 11% or lower using Internet	Variable, 30% reasonable		High, 50–70% reasonable	
Feasible length of questionnaire	Conflicting advice; however, fewer 'screens' probably better	6–8 A4 pages		Up to half an hour	Variable depending on location
Suitable types of question	Closed questions but not too complex, complicated sequencing fine if uses IT, must be of interest to respondent	Closed questions but not too complex, simple sequencing only, must be of interest to respondent		Open and closed questions, complicated sequencing fine	Open and closed questions, including complicated questions, complicated sequencing fine
Time taken to complete collection	2–6 weeks from distribution (dependent on number of follow-ups)	4–8 weeks from posting (dependent on number of follow-ups)	Dependent on sample size, number of field workers, etc.	Dependent on sample size, number of interviewers, etc., but slower than self-administered for same sample size	
Main financial resource implications	Web page design, although automated expert systems providers are reducing this dramatically	Outward and return postage, photocopying, clerical support, data entry	Field workers, travel, photocopying, clerical support, data entry	Interviewers, telephone calls, clerical support. Photocopying and data entry if not using CATI.[c] Programming, software and computers if using CATI	Interviewers, travel, clerical support. Photocopying and data entry if not using CAPI.[d] Programming, software and computers if using CAPI
Role of the interviewer/ field worker	None		Delivery and collection of questionnaires, enhancing respondent participation	Enhancing respondent participation, guiding the respondent through the questionnaire, answering respondents' questions	
Data input[b]	Usually automated	Closed questions can be designed so that responses may be entered using optical mark readers after questionnaire has been returned		Response to all questions entered at time of collection using CATI[c]	Response to all questions can be entered at time of collection using CAPI[d]

[a]Discussed in Chapter 7. [b]Discussed in Section 12.2. [c]Computer-aided telephone interviewing. [d]Computer-aided personal interviewing.

Sources: authors' experience; Dillman (2007); Hewson *et al.* (2003); Oppenheim (2000); deVaus (2002); Witmer *et al.* (1999).

or because they believe certain responses are more **socially desirable** (Dillman 2007). They may, however, discuss their answers with others, thereby contaminating their response. Respondents to telephone questionnaires and structured interviews are more likely to answer to please due to their contact with you, although the impact of this can be minimised by good interviewing technique (Section 10.5). Responses can also be contaminated or distorted when recorded. In extreme instances, interviewers may invent responses. For this reason, random checks of interviewers are often made by survey organisations. When writing your project report you will be expected to state your response rate. When doing this you need to be careful not to make unsubstantiated claims if comparing with other surveys' response rates. Whilst such comparisons place your survey's response rate in context, a higher than normal response rate does not prove that your findings are unbiased (Rogelberg and Stanton 2007). Similarly, a lower than normal response rate does not necessarily mean that responses are biased.

The type of questionnaire you choose will affect the number of people who respond (Section 7.2). Interviewer-administered questionnaires will usually have a higher response rate than self-administered questionnaires (Table 11.1). The size of your sample and the way in which it is selected will have implications for the confidence you can have in your data and the extent to which you can generalise (Section 7.2).

Longer questionnaires are best presented as a structured interview. In addition, they can include more complicated questions than telephone questionnaires or self-administered questionnaires (Oppenheim 2000). The presence of an interviewer (or the use of questionnaire software) means that it is also easier to route different subgroups of respondents to answer different questions using a filter question (Section 11.4). The suitability of different types of question also differs between techniques.

Your choice of questionnaire will also be affected by the resources you have available (Table 11.1), and in particular the:

- time available to complete the data collection;
- financial implications of data collection and entry;
- availability of interviewers and field workers to assist;
- ease of automating data entry.

The time needed for data collection increases markedly for delivery and collection questionnaires and structured interviews where the samples are geographically dispersed (Table 11.1). One way you can overcome this constraint is to select your sample using cluster sampling (Section 7.2). Unless your questionnaire is Internet or intranet-mediated, or **computer-aided personal interviewing (CAPI)** or **computer-aided telephone interviewing (CATI)** is used, you will need to consider the costs of reproducing the questionnaire, clerical support and entering the data for computer analysis. For postal and telephone questionnaires, cost estimates for postage and telephone calls will need to be included. If you are working for an organisation, postage costs may be reduced by using *Freepost* for questionnaire return. This means that you pay only postage and a small handling charge for those questionnaires that are returned by post. However, the use of Freepost rather than a stamp may adversely affect your response rates (see Table 11.4).

Virtually all data collected by questionnaires will be analysed by computer. Some packages (e.g. Snap Surveys™, Sphinx Development™ and SurveyMonkey.com™) allow you both to design your questionnaire, collect, enter and analyse the data within the same software. Once your data have been coded and entered into the computer you will be able to explore and analyse them far more quickly and thoroughly than by hand (Section 12.2). As a rough rule, you should analyse questionnaire data by computer if they have been collected from 30 or more respondents. For larger surveys, you may wish to automate the capture and input of data. For Internet- and intranet-mediated questionnaires (electronic

Box 11.1
Focus on student research

Closed question designed for an optical mark reader

Ben's research project involved sending out a questionnaire to a large number of people. Because of this he obtained permission to use his university's optical mark reader to input the data from his questionnaire. In his questionnaire, respondents are given clear instructions on how to mark their responses:

Please use a pencil to mark your answer as a solid box like this: [—]

If you make a mistake use an eraser to rub out your answer.

1 Please mark all the types of music that you regularly listen to:		
	Rock and Pop	[ ]
	Dance and Urban	[ ]
	Soundtracks	[ ]
	Jazz and Blues	[ ]
	Country	[ ]
	Easy listening	[ ]
	Folk	[ ]
	World	[ ]
	Classical	[ ]
	Other	[ ]
	(please describe):	
	....	

questionnaires), this is normally undertaken at the questionnaire design stage and, where the software is automated, costs are minimal. For example, SurveyMonkey.com™, an online software tool for creating and administering web-based questionnaires, at the time of writing charged $19.95 for up to 1000 responses a month, whilst a survey of 10 or fewer questionnaires and with 100 or fewer responses is free (SurveyMonkey.com 2008). For self-administered questionnaires, data capture and input is most straightforward for closed questions where respondents select and mark their answer from a prescribed list (Box 11.1).

The mark is read using an **optical mark reader**, which recognises and converts marks into data at rates often exceeding 200 pages a minute. Data for interviewer-administered questionnaires can be entered directly into the computer at the time of interview using CATI or CAPI software. With both types of software you read the questions to the respondent from the screen and enter their answers directly into the computer. Because of the costs of high-speed and high-capacity scanning equipment, software and pre-survey programming, CATI and CAPI are financially viable only for very large surveys or where repeated use of the hardware and software will be made.

In reality, you are almost certain to have to make compromises in your choice of questionnaire. These will be unique to your research as the decision about which questionnaire is most suitable cannot be answered in isolation from your research question(s) and objectives and the population or sample from whom you are collecting data.

11.3 Deciding what data need to be collected

Research design requirements

Unlike in-depth and semi-structured interviews (Chapter 10), the questions you ask in questionnaires need to be defined precisely prior to data collection. Whereas you can prompt and explore issues further with in-depth and semi-structured interviews, this will not be possible for questionnaires. In addition, the questionnaire offers only one chance to collect the data, as it is often difficult to identify respondents or to return to collect additional information. This means that the time you spend planning precisely what data you need to collect, how you intend to analyse them (Chapter 12) and designing your questionnaire to meet these requirements is crucial if you are to answer your research question(s) and meet your objectives.

For most management and business research the data you collect using questionnaires will be used for either descriptive or explanatory purposes. For questions where the main purpose is to describe the population's characteristics either at a fixed time or at a series of points over time to enable comparisons, you will normally need to administer your questionnaire to a sample. The sample needs to be as representative and accurate as possible where it will be used to generalise about the total population (Sections 7.1–7.3). You will also probably need to relate your findings to earlier research. It is therefore important that you select the appropriate characteristics to answer your research question(s) and to address your objectives. You, therefore, will need to have:

- reviewed the literature carefully;
- discussed your ideas with colleagues, your project tutor and other interested parties.

For research involving organisations, we have found it essential to understand the organisations in which we are undertaking the research. Similarly, for international or cross-cultural research it is important to have an understanding of the countries or cultures in which you are undertaking the research. Without this it is easy to make mistakes, such as using the wrong terminology or language, and to collect useless data. For many research projects an understanding of relevant organisations can be achieved through browsing company publications or their Internet sites (Section 8.3), observation (Chapter 9) and in-depth and semi-structured interviews (Chapter 10).

Explanatory research requires data to test a theory or theories. This means that, in addition to those issues raised for descriptive research, you need to define the theories you wish to test as relationships between variables prior to designing your questionnaire. You, therefore, will need to have reviewed the literature carefully, discussed your ideas widely, and conceptualised your own research clearly prior to designing your questionnaire (Ghauri and Grønhaug 2005). In particular, you need to be clear about which relationships you think are likely to exist between variables:

- a **dependent variable** changes in response to changes in other variables;
- an **independent variable** causes changes in a dependent variable;
- an **extraneous variable** might also cause changes in a dependent variable, thereby providing an alternative explanation to your independent variable or variables (Box 11.2).

Box 11.2
Focus on student research

Defining theories in terms of relationships between variables

As part of her research, Marie-Claude wished to test the theory that the incidence of repetitive strain injury (RSI) was linked to the number of rest periods that keyboard operators took each working day.

The relationship that was thought to exist between the variables was that the incidence of RSI was higher when fewer or no rest periods were taken each day. The dependent variable was the incidence of RSI and the independent variable was the number of rest periods taken each day. Marie-Claude thought that extraneous variables, such as the use of proper seating and wrist rests, might also influence the incidence of RSI. Data were collected, therefore, on these variables as well.

As these relationships are likely to be tested through statistical analysis (Section 12.5) of the data collected by your questionnaire, you need to be clear about the detail in which they will be measured at the design stage. Where possible, you should ensure that measures are compatible with those used in other relevant research so that comparisons can be made (Section 12.2).

Types of variable

Dillman (2007) distinguishes between three types of data variable that can be collected through questionnaires:

- opinion;
- behaviour;
- attribute.

These distinctions are important, as they will influence the way your questions are worded (Box 11.3). **Opinion variables** record how respondents feel about something or what they think or believe is true or false. In contrast, data on behaviours and attributes record what respondents do and are. When recording what respondents do, you are recording their behaviour. This differs from respondents' opinions because you are recording a concrete experience. **Behavioural variables** contain data on what people (or their organisations) did in the past, do now or will do in the future. By contrast, **attribute variables** contain data about the respondents' characteristics. Attributes are best thought of as things a respondent possesses, rather than things a respondent does (Dillman 2007). They are used to explore how opinions and behaviour differ between respondents as well as to check that the data collected are representative of the total population (Section 7.2). Attributes include characteristics such as age, gender, marital status, education, occupation and income.

Ensuring that essential data are collected

A problem experienced by many students and organisations we work with is how to ensure that the data collected will enable the research question(s) to be answered and the objectives achieved. Although no method is infallible, one way is to create a **data requirements table** (Table 11.2). This summarises the outcome of a six-step process:

1 Decide whether the main outcome of your research is descriptive or explanatory.
2 Sub-divide each research question or objective into more specific investigative questions about which you need to gather data.
3 Repeat the second stage if you feel that the investigative questions are not sufficiently precise.
4 Identify the variables about which you will need to collect data to answer each investigative question.
5 Establish the level of detail required from the data for each variable.
6 Develop measurement questions to capture the data at the level of data required for each variable.

Table 11.2 Data requirements table

Research question/objective:

Type of research:

Investigative questions	Variable(s) required	Detail in which data measured	Check measurement question included in questionnaire ✓

Box 11.3
Focus on student research

Opinion, behaviour and attribute questions

Sally was asked by her employer to undertake an anonymous survey of financial advisers' ethical values. In particular, her employer was interested in the advice given to clients. After some deliberation she came up with three questions that addressed the issue of putting clients' interests before their own:

2 How do you feel about the following statement? 'Financial advisers should place their clients' interest before their own'.

(Please tick the appropriate box)

Strongly agree	❑
Mildly agree	❑
Neither agree or disagree	❑
Mildly disagree	❑
Strongly disagree	❑

3 In general, do financial advisers place their clients' interests before their own?

(Please tick the appropriate box)

Always yes	❑
Usually yes	❑
Sometimes yes	❑
Seldom yes	❑
Never yes	❑

4 How often do you place your clients' interests before your own?

(Please tick the appropriate box)

81–100% of my time	❑
61–80% of my time	❑
41–60% of my time	❑
21–40% of my time	❑
0–20% of my time	❑

Sally's choice of question or questions to include in her questionnaire was dependent on whether she needed to collect data on financial advisers' opinions or behaviours. She designed question 2 to collect data on respondents' opinions about financial advisers placing their clients' interest before their own. This question asks respondents how they feel. In contrast, question 3 asks respondents whether financial advisers in general place their clients' interests before their own. It is, therefore, concerned with their opinions in terms of their individual beliefs regarding how financial advisers act.

Question 4 focuses on how often the respondents actually place their clients' interests before their own. Unlike the previous questions, it is concerned with their actual behaviour rather than their opinion.

To answer her research questions and to meet her objectives, Sally also needed to collect data to explore how ethical values differed between sub-groupings of financial advisors. One theory she had was that ethical values were related to age. To test this she needed to collect data on the attribute age. After some deliberation she come up with question 5:

5 How old are you?

(Please tick the appropriate box)

Less than 30 years	❑
30 to less than 40 years	❑
40 to less than 50 years	❑
50 to less than 60 years	❑
60 years or over	❑

Investigative questions are the questions that you need to answer in order to address satisfactorily each research question and to meet each objective (Cooper and Schindler 2008). They need to be generated with regard to your research question(s) and objectives. For some investigative questions you will need to subdivide your first attempt into more detailed investigative questions. For each you need to be clear whether you are interested in respondents' opinions, behaviours or attributes (discussed earlier), as what appears to be a need to collect one sort of variable frequently turns out to be a need for another. We have found the literature review, discussions with interested parties and pilot studies to be of help here.

You then need to identify the variables about which you need to collect data to answer each investigative question and to decide the level of detail at which these are measured. Again, the review of the literature and associated research can suggest possibilities. However, if you are unsure about the detail needed you should measure at the more precise level. Although this is more time consuming, it will give you flexibility in your analyses. In these you will be able to use computer software to group or combine data (Section 12.2).

Once your table is complete (Box 11.4), it must be checked to make sure that all data necessary to answer your investigative questions are included. When checking, you need to be disciplined and to ensure that only data that are essential to answering your research question(s) and meeting your objectives are included. The final column is to remind you to check that your questionnaire actually includes a measurement question that collects the precise data required!

Box 11.4
Focus on student research

Data requirements table

As part of his work placement, Greg was asked to discover customer attitudes to the outside smoking area at restaurants and bars. Discussion with senior management and colleagues and reading relevant literature helped him to firm up his objective and investigative questions. A selection of these is included in the extract from his table of data requirements:

Research question/objective: To establish customers' attitudes to the outside smoking area at restaurants and bars			
Type of research: Predominantly descriptive, although wish to examine differences between restaurants and bars, and between different groups of customers			
Investigative questions	**Variable(s) required**	**Detail in which data measured**	**Check included in questionnaire ✓**
Do customers feel that they should have an outside smoking area at restaurants and bars as a right? (opinion)	*Opinion of customer on restaurants and bars providing an outside smoking area as a right*	*Feel . . . should be a right, should not be a right, no strong feelings [N.B. will need separate questions for restaurants and for bars]*	

Investigative questions	Variable(s) required	Detail in which data measured	Check included in questionnaire ✓
Do customers feel that restaurants and bars should provide an outside smoking area for smokers? (opinion)	Opinion of customer to the provision of an outside smoking area for smokers	Feel . . . very strongly that it should, quite strongly that it should, no strong opinions, quite strongly that it should not, very strongly that it should not [N.B. will need separate questions for restaurants and for bars]	
Do customers' opinions differ depending on	(Opinion of employee – outlined above)	(Included above)	
Age? (attribute)	Age of employee	To nearest 5-year band (youngest 16, oldest 65+)	
Whether or not a smoker? (behaviour)	Smoker	Non-smoker, smokes but not in own home, smokes in own home	
How representative are the responses of customers? (attributes)	Age of customer Gender of customer Job [Note: must be able to compare with National Statistics Socio-Economic Classification (Rose and Pevalin 2003)]	(Included above) Male, female Higher managerial and professional occupations, Lower managerial and professional occupations, Intermediate occupations, Small employers and own-account workers, Lower supervisory and technical occupations, Semi-routine occupations, Routine occupations, Never worked and long-term unemployed	

11.4 Designing the questionnaire

The internal validity and reliability of the data you collect and the response rate you achieve depend, to a large extent, on the design of your questions, the structure of your questionnaire, and the rigour of your pilot testing (all discussed in this section). A valid questionnaire will enable accurate data to be collected, and one that is reliable will mean that these data are collected consistently. Foddy (1994:17) discusses validity and reliability in terms of the questions and answers making sense. In particular, he emphasises that 'the question must be understood by the respondent in the way intended by the researcher and the answer given by the respondent must be understood by the researcher in the way intended by the respondent'. This means that there are at least four stages that must occur if the question is to be valid and reliable (Figure 11.2, Box 11.5). It also means that the

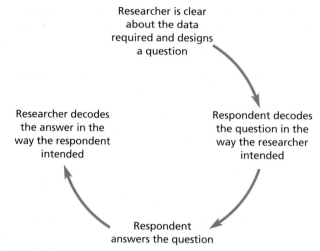

Figure 11.2 Stages that must occur if a question is to be valid and reliable

Source: developed from Foddy (1994) *Constructing Questions for Interviews and Questionnaires*. Reproduced with permission of Cambridge University Press.

design stage is likely to involve you in substantial rewriting in order to ensure that the respondent decodes the question in the way you intended. We, therefore, recommend that you use a word processor or survey design software such as SurveyMonkey.com™, Snap Surveys™ or Sphinx Development™.

Assessing validity

Internal validity in relation to questionnaires refers to the ability of your questionnaire to measure what you intend it to measure. This means you are concerned that what you find with your questionnaire actually represents the reality of what you are measuring. This presents you with a problem as, if you actually knew the reality of what you were measuring,

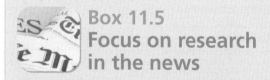

Box 11.5
Focus on research in the news

More poll questions than answers

A series of opinon polls conducted by different polling organisations to coincide with the 300th anniversary of Scotland's union with England produced very different results (Taylor 2007).

The poll conducted by Opinion Research Business on behalf of the BBC included the question:

'Would you like the Union to continue as it is or would you like to see it come to an end? If it were to end this would mean that Scotland became an independent country.'

In answering this question, 56 per cent of Scottish respondents said they would prefer the Union to continue as it is; 32 per cent responding they would prefer the Union to end.

In contrast, an earlier poll conducted by YouGov and reported in the *Sunday Times* asked:

'If there was a referendum tomorrow on whether Scotland should become independent, how would you vote?' When answering this question, 42 per cent of Scottish respondents voted against independence and 44 per cent of Scottish respondents voted for independence.

A separate poll conducted by ICM for the *Sunday Telegraph* found that 28 per cent of Scottish respondents did not approve of 'Scotland becoming an independent country', whilst 59 per cent did approve.

there would be no point in designing your questionnaire and using it to collect data! Researchers get round this problem by looking for other relevant evidence that supports the answers found using the questionnaire, relevance being determined by the nature of their research question and their own judgement.

Often, when discussing the validity of a questionnaire, researchers refer to content validity, criterion-related validity and construct validity (Cooper and Schindler 2008). **Content validity** refers to the extent to which the measurement device, in our case the measurement questions in the questionnaire, provides adequate coverage of the investigative questions. Judgement of what is 'adequate coverage' can be made in a number of ways. One is through careful definition of the research through the literature reviewed and, where appropriate, prior discussion with others. Another is to use a panel of individuals to assess whether each measurement question in the questionnaire is 'essential', 'useful but not essential', or 'not necessary'.

Criterion-related validity, sometimes known as **predictive validity**, is concerned with the ability of the measures (questions) to make accurate predictions. This means that if you are using the measurement questions within your questionnaire to predict customers' future buying behaviours, then a test of these measurement questions' criterion-related validity will be the extent to which they actually predict these customers' buying behaviours. In assessing criterion-related validity, you will be comparing the data from your questionnaire with that specified in the criterion in some way. Often this is undertaken using statistical analysis such as correlation (Section 12.5).

Construct validity refers to the extent to which your measurement questions actually measure the presence of those constructs you intended them to measure. This term is normally used when referring to constructs such as attitude scales, aptitude and personality tests and the like (Section 11.4) and can be thought of as answering the question: 'How well can you generalise from you measurement questions to your construct?' Because validation of such constructs against existing data is difficult, other methods are used. These are discussed in more detail in a range of texts, including Cooper and Schindler (2008).

Testing for reliability

As we outlined earlier, reliability refers to consistency. Although for a questionnaire to be valid it must be reliable, this is not sufficient on its own. Respondents may consistently interpret a question in your questionnaire in one way, when you mean something else! As a consequence, although the question is reliable, it does not really matter as it has no internal validity and so will not enable your research question to be answered. Reliability is therefore concerned with the robustness of your questionnaire and, in particular, whether or not it will produce consistent findings at different times and under different conditions, such as with different samples or, in the case of an interviewer-administered questionnaire, with different interviewers.

Mitchell (1996) outlines three common approaches to assessing reliability, in addition to comparing the data collected with other data from a variety of sources. Although the analysis for each of these is undertaken after data collection, they need to be considered at the questionnaire design stage. They are:

- test re-test;
- internal consistency;
- alternative form.

Test re-test estimates of reliability are obtained by correlating data collected with those from the same questionnaire collected under as near equivalent conditions as possible. The questionnaire therefore needs to be administered twice to respondents. This may create difficulties, as it is often difficult to persuade respondents to answer the same questionnaire twice. In addition, the longer the time interval between the two questionnaires, the lower the likelihood that respondents will answer the same way. We, therefore, recommend that you use this method only as a supplement to other methods.

Internal consistency involves correlating the responses to each question in the questionnaire with those to other questions in the questionnaire. It therefore measures the consistency of responses across either all the questions or a sub-group of the questions from your questionnaire. There are a variety of methods for calculating internal consistency, of which one of the most frequently used is Cronbach's alpha. Further details of this and other approaches can be found in Mitchell (1996) and in books discussing more advanced statistical analysis software such as Field (2005).

The final approach to testing for reliability outlined by Mitchell (1996) is 'alternative form'. This offers some sense of the reliability within your questionnaire through comparing responses to alternative forms of the same question or groups of questions. Where questions are included for this purpose, usually in longer questionnaires, they are often called 'check questions'. However, it is often difficult to ensure that these questions are substantially equivalent. Respondents may suffer from fatigue owing to the need to increase the length of the questionnaire, and they may spot the similar question and just refer back to their previous answer! It is therefore advisable to use check questions sparingly.

Designing individual questions

The design of each question should be determined by the data you need to collect (Section 11.3). When designing individual questions researchers do one of three things (Bourque and Clark 1994):

- adopt questions used in other questionnaires;
- adapt questions used in other questionnaires;
- develop their own questions.

Adopting or adapting questions may be necessary if you wish to replicate, or to compare your findings with, another study. This can allow reliability to be assessed. It is also more efficient than developing your own questions, provided that you can still collect the data you need to answer your research question(s) and to meet your objectives. Some survey design software includes questions that you may use. Alternatively, you may find questions and coding schemes that you feel will meet your needs in existing questionnaires, journal articles or in Internet-based question banks, such as the ESRC Question Bank. This consists of a database of questions and question methodology of UK social surveys going back to 1991 and is available from http://qb.soc.surrey.ac.uk.

However, before you adopt questions, beware! There are a vast number of poor questions in circulation, so always assess each question carefully. In addition, you need to check whether they are under copyright. If they are, you need to obtain the author's permission to use them. Even where there is no formal copyright you should, where possible, contact the author and obtain permission. In your project report you should state where you obtained the questions and give credit to their author.

Initially, you need only consider the type and wording of individual questions rather than the order in which they will appear on the form. Clear wording of questions using terms that are likely to be familiar to, and understood by, respondents can improve the validity of the questionnaire. Most types of questionnaire include a combination of open and closed questions. **Open questions**, sometimes referred to as open-ended questions (Dillman 2007), allow respondents to give answers in their own way (Fink 2003a). **Closed questions**, sometimes referred to as closed-ended questions (Dillman 2007) or **forced-choice questions** (deVaus 2002), provide a number of alternative answers from which the respondent is instructed to choose. The latter type of question is usually quicker and easier to answer, as they require minimal writing. Responses are also easier to compare as they have been predetermined. However, if these responses cannot be easily interpreted then these benefits are, to say the least, marginal (Foddy 1994). Within this chapter we highlight six types of closed question that we discuss later:

- list, where the respondent is offered a list of items, any of which may be selected;
- category, where only one response can be selected from a given set of categories;
- ranking, where the respondent is asked to place something in order;
- rating, in which a rating device is used to record responses;
- quantity, to which the response is a number giving the amount;
- matrix, where responses to two or more questions can be recorded using the same grid.

Prior to data analysis, you will need to group and code responses to each question. Detailed coding guidance is given in Section 12.2. You are strongly advised also to read this chapter prior to designing your questions.

Open questions

Open questions are used widely in in-depth and semi-structured interviews (Section 10.5). In questionnaires they are useful if you are unsure of the response, such as in exploratory research, when you require a detailed answer or when you want to find out what is uppermost in the respondent's mind. An example of an open question (from a self-administered questionnaire) is:

6 Please list up to three things you like about your job:

    1 ....

    2 ....

    3 ....

With open questions, the precise wording of the question and the amount of space partially determine the length and fullness of response. However, if you leave too much space the question becomes off-putting. Question 6 collects data about what each respondent believes they like about their job. Thus if salary had been the reason uppermost in their mind this would probably have been recorded first. Unfortunately, when questionnaires are administered to large numbers of respondents, responses to open questions are extremely time consuming to code (Section 12.2). For this reason, it is usually advisable keep their use to a minimum.

List questions

List questions offer the respondent a list of responses, any of which they can choose. Such questions are useful when you need to be sure that the respondent has considered all possible responses. However, the list of responses must be defined clearly and meaningfully to the respondent. For structured interviews, it is often helpful to present the respondent with a prompt card listing all responses. The response categories you can use vary widely and include 'yes/no', 'agree/disagree' and 'applies/does not apply' along with 'don't know' or 'not sure'. If you intend to use what you hope is a complete list, you may wish to add a catch-all category of 'other'. This has been included in question 7, which collects data on respondents' religion. However, as you can read in Box 11.6, the use of 'other' can result in unforeseen responses!

Box 11.6
Research
in the news

FT

George Lucas is a god in Britain. Literally

According to official census figures, 390 000 Brits said their religious faith was 'Jedi'. Had this been an official category, it would have been the fourth largest religion in the UK, ahead of Sikhism.

Instead, the *Star Wars* fans were registered as atheists. 'We have put them among the 7.7 m people who said they had no religion,' a census official said.

'I suspect this was a decision which will not be challenged greatly.'

Evidently, aspirant Jedi masters were inspired by an email that asked them to record the unrecognised faith in the hope that their support would force the government to put Lucas on the same level as Moses, Christ and Mohammed.

'Imagine the official statistics of your country claiming a percentage of the population as practising "Jedi Knights"!!!' says the website *jedicensus.com*. Yes, imagine that.

Source: Financial Times (2003) 14 Feb. Copyright © 2003 The Financial Times Ltd.

---

7 What is your religion?

Please tick ✓ the appropriate box.

Buddhist ❑	None ❑
Christian ❑	Other ❑
Hindu ❑	
Jewish ❑	(Please say:)................................
Muslim ❑	
Sikh ❑	

Question 7 collects data on the religion of the respondent. In this list question, the common practice of omitting negative response boxes has been adopted. Consequently, negative responses in this question not being, for example, a Christian, are inferred from each unmarked response. If you choose to do this, beware: non-response could also indicate uncertainty or, for some questions, that an item does not apply!

Category questions

In contrast, **category questions** are designed so that each respondent's answer can fit only one category. Such questions are particularly useful if you need to collect data about behaviour or attributes. The number of categories that you can include without affecting the accuracy of responses is dependent on the type of questionnaire. Self-administered questionnaires and telephone questionnaires should usually have no more than five response categories (Fink 2003a). Structured interviews can have more categories provided that a *prompt card* is used (Box 11.7) or, as in question 8, the interviewer categorises the responses.

8 How often do you visit this shopping centre?

Interviewer: listen to the respondent's answer and tick ✓ as appropriate.

❑ First visit	2 or more times a week ❑
❑ Once a week	Less than once a week to fortnightly ❑
❑ Less than fortnightly to once a month	Less often ❑

Box 11.7
Focus on student research

Use of a prompt card as part of a structured interview

As part of his interview schedule, Peter asked the following question:

Which of the following daily newspapers have you read during the past month?

Show respondent card 3 with the names of the newspapers. Read out names of the newspapers one at a time. Record their response with a ✓ in the appropriate box.

	Read	Not read	Don't know
The Daily Express	❑	❑	❑
Daily Mail	❑	❑	❑
The Daily Mirror	❑	❑	❑
Daily Star	❑	❑	❑
Financial Times	❑	❑	❑
The Guardian	❑	❑	❑
The Daily Telegraph	❑	❑	❑
The Independent	❑	❑	❑
The Sun	❑	❑	❑
The Times	❑	❑	❑

Peter gave card 3 to each respondent prior to reading out newspaper names and collected the card after the question had been completed.

3

THE DAILY EXPRESS

Daily Mail

The Daily Mirror

Daily Star

FINANCIAL TIMES

The **Guardian**

The Daily Telegraph

THE INDEPENDENT

The Sun

THE TIMES

You should arrange responses in a logical order so that it is easy to locate the response category that corresponds to each respondent's answer. Your categories should be mutually exclusive (should not overlap), and should cover all possible responses. The layout of your questionnaire should make it clear which boxes refer to which response category by placing them close to the appropriate text.

Ranking questions

A **ranking question** asks the respondent to place things in rank order. This means that you can discover their relative importance to the respondent. In question 9, taken from a postal questionnaire, the respondents are asked their beliefs about the relative importance of a series of features when choosing a new car. The catch-all feature of 'other' is included to allow respondents to add one other feature.

9 Please number each of the factors listed below in order of importance to you in your choice of a new car. Number the most important 1, the next 2 and so on. If a factor has no importance at all, please leave blank.

Factor	Importance
Carbon dioxide emissions	[ ]
Boot size	[ ]
Depreciation	[ ]
Safety features	[ ]
Fuel economy	[ ]
Price	[ ]
Driving enjoyment	[ ]
Other	[ ]
....	(⇐ Please describe)

With such questions, you need to ensure that the instructions are clear and will be understood by the respondent. In general, respondents find that ranking more than seven items takes too much effort reducing their motivation to complete the questionnaire, so you should keep your list to this length or shorter (Cooper and Schindler 2008). Respondents can rank accurately only when they can see or remember all items. This can be overcome with face-to-face questionnaires by using prompt cards on which you list all of the features to be ranked. However, telephone questionnaires should ask respondents to rank fewer items, as the respondent will need to rely on their memory.

Rating questions

Rating questions are often used to collect opinion data. They should not be confused with **scales** (discussed later in this section), which are a coherent set of questions or items that are regarded as indicators of a construct or concept (Corbetta 2003). Rating questions most frequently use the **Likert-style rating scale** in which the respondent is asked how strongly she or he agrees or disagrees with a statement or series of statements, usually on a four-, five-, six- or seven-point rating scale. Possible responses to rating questions should be presented in a straight line (such as in question 10) rather than in multiple lines or columns as this is how respondents are most likely to process the data (Dillman 2007). If you intend to use a series of statements, you should keep the same order of response categories to avoid confusing respondents (Dillman 2007). You should include, however, both positive and negative statements so as to ensure that the respondent reads each one carefully and thinks about which box to tick.

10 For the following statement please tick ✓ the box that matches your view most closely.

	Agree	Tend to agree	Tend to agree	Disagree
I feel employees' views have influenced the decisions taken by management.	❏	❏	❏	❏

Question 10 has been taken from a delivery and collection questionnaire to employees in an organisation and is designed to collect opinion data. In this rating question, an even number of points (four) has been used to force the respondent to express their feelings towards an implicitly positive statement. By contrast, question 11, also from a delivery and collection questionnaire, contains an odd number (five) of points on the rating scale. This rating scale allows the respondent to 'sit on the fence' by ticking the middle 'not sure' category when considering an implicitly negative statement. The phrase 'not sure' is used here as it is less threatening to the respondent than admitting they do not know. This rating question is designed to collect data on employees' opinions of the situation now.

11 For the following statement please tick ✓ the box that matches your view most closely.

	Agree	Tend to agree	Not sure	Tend to disagree	Disagree
I believe there are 'them and us' barriers to communication in the company now.	❏	❏	❏	❏	❏

You can expand this form of rating question further to record finer shades of opinion, a variety of which are outlined in Table 11.3. However, respondents to telephone questionnaires find it difficult to distinguish between values on rating scales of more than five points plus 'don't know'. In addition, there is little point in collecting data for seven or nine response categories, if these are subsequently combined in your analysis (Chapter 12). Colleagues and students often ask us how many points they should have on their rating scale. This is related to the likely measurement error. If you know that your respondents can only respond accurately to a three-point rating, then it is pointless to have a finer rating scale with more points!

In question 12 the respondent's attitude is captured on a 10-point **numeric rating scale**. In such rating questions it is important that the numbers reflect the feeling of the respondent. Thus, 1 reflects poor value for money, and 10 good value for money. Only these end categories (and sometimes the middle) are labelled and are known as self-anchoring rating scales. As in this question, graphics may also be used to reflect the rating scale visually, thereby aiding the respondent's interpretation. An additional category of 'not sure' or 'don't know' can be added and should be separated slightly from the rating scale.

Table 11.3 Response categories for different types of rating questions

Type of rating	Five categories	Seven categories
Agreement	Strongly agree	Strongly agree
	Agree	Agree/moderately agree/mostly agree*
	Neither agree nor disagree/not sure/uncertain*	Slightly agree
	Disagree	Neither agree nor disagree/not sure/uncertain*
	Strongly disagree	Slightly disagree
		Disagree/moderately disagree/mostly disagree*
		Strongly disagree
Amount	Far too much/nearly all/very large*	Far too much/nearly all/very large*
	Too much/more than half/large*	Too much/more than half/large*
	About right/about half/some*	Slightly too much/quite large*
	Too little/less than half/small*	About right/about half/some*
	Far too little/almost none/not at all*	Slightly too little/quite small*
		Too little/less than half/small*
		Far too little/almost none/not at all*
Frequency	All the time/always*	All the time/always*
	Frequently/very often/most of the time*	Almost all the time/almost always*
	Sometimes/about as often as not/about half the time*	Frequently/very often/most of the time*
	Rarely/seldom/less than half the time*	Sometimes/about as often as not/about half the time*
	Never/practically never*	Seldom
		Almost never/practically never*
		Never/not at all*
Likelihood	Very	Extremely
	Good	Very
	Reasonable	Moderately
	Slight/bit*	Quite/reasonable*
	None/not at all*	Somewhat
		Slight/bit*
		None/not at all*

*Response dependent on investigative question.
Source: developed from Tharenou *et al.* (2007) and authors' experience.

12 For the following statement please circle **O** the number that matches your view most closely.

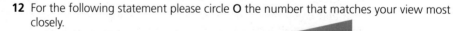
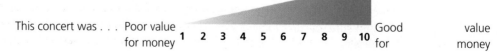

This concert was . . . Poor value for money **1 2 3 4 5 6 7 8 9 10** Good value for money

Box 11.8
Focus on management research

Semantic differential rating scales

In their study of the perception of messages conveyed by review and audit reports published in the *Accounting, Auditing and Accountability Journal*, Gay *et al.* (1998) reviewed the academic literature to identify the messages that these two types of report were intended to convey. Based upon this they developed a semantic differential scale consisting of 35 bipolar adjectival statements separated by a seven-point scale.

These adjectival statements were worded as polar opposites and included the following (Gay *et al.* 1998: 480):

| The financial statements give a true and fair view | 1 2 3 4 5 6 7 | The financial statements do not give a true and fair view |
| The entity is free from fraud | 1 2 3 4 5 6 7 | The entity is not free from fraud |

By using the semantic differential scale, Gay *et al.* (1998) were able to measure perceived messages in relation to the reliability of financial statements, auditor/management responsibility and the usefulness of such financial statements for decision making.

Another variation is the **semantic differential rating scale**. These are often used in consumer research to determine underlying attitudes. The respondent is asked to rate a single object or idea on a series of bipolar rating scales (Box 11.8). Each bipolar scale is described by a pair of opposite adjectives (question 13) designed to anchor respondents' attitudes towards service. For these rating scales, you should vary the position of positive and negative adjectives from left to right to reduce the tendency to read only the adjective on the left (Cooper and Schindler 2008).

13 On each of the lines below, place a x to show how you feel about the service you received at our restaurant.

Fast	_|_|_|_|_|_|_|_|_	Slow
Unfriendly	_|_|_|_|_|_|_|_|_	Friendly
Value for money	_|_|_|_|_|_|_|_|_	Over-priced

Rating questions have been combined to measure a wide variety of concepts such as customer loyalty, service quality and job satisfaction. For each concept the resultant measure or **scale** is represented by a scale score created by combining the scores for each of the rating questions. Each question is often referred to as a **scale item**. In the case of a simple Likert scale, for example, the scale score for each case would be calculated by adding together the scores of each of the questions (items) selected (deVaus 2002). A detailed discussion of creating scales, including those by Likert and Guttman, can be found in Corbetta (2003). However, rather than developing your own scales, it often makes sense to use or adapt existing scales (Schrauf and Navarro 2005). Since scaling techniques were first used in the 1930s, literally thousands of scales have been developed to measure attitudes and personality dimensions and to assess skills and abilities. Details

Box 11.9
Focus on student research

Using existing scales from the literature

When planning his questionnaire David, like most students, presumed he would need to design and develop his own measurement scale. However, after reading Schrauf and Navarro's (2005) paper on using existing scales, he realised that it would probably be possible to adopt an existing scale which had been reported in the academic literature. As he pointed out

to his project tutor, this was particularly fortunate because the process of scale development was hugely time-consuming and could detract his attention from answering the actual research question.

In looking for a suitable published scale David asked himself a number of questions:

- Does the scale measure what I am interested in?
- Has the scale been empirically tested and validated?
- Was the scale designed for a similar group of respondents as my target population?

Fortunately, the answer to all these questions was 'yes'. David, therefore, emailed the scale's author to ask for formal permission.

of an individual scale can often be found by following up references in an article reporting research that uses that scale. In addition, there are a wide variety of handbooks that list these scales (e.g. Miller and Salkind 2002). These scales can, as highlighted in Box 11.9, be used in your own research providing they:

- measure what you interested in;
- have been empirically tested and validated;
- were designed for a reasonably similar group of respondents.

It is worth remembering that you should only make amendments to the scale where absolutely necessary as significant changes could impact upon both the validity of the scale and, subsequently, your results! You also need to beware that existing scales may be subject to copyright constraints. Even where there is no formal copyright, you should, where possible, contact the author and ask for permission. In your project report you should note where you obtained the scale and give credit to the author.

Quantity questions

The response to a **quantity question** is a number, which gives the amount of a characteristic. For this reason, such questions tend to be used to collect behaviour or attribute data. A common quantity question, which collects attribute data, is:

14 What is your year of birth?

(For example, for 1988 write:)

| 1 | 9 | | |

| 1 | 9 | 8 | 8 |

Because the data collected by this question could be entered into the computer without coding, the question can also be termed a **self-coded** question, that is one which each respondent codes her or himself.

Matrix questions

A **matrix** or grid of questions enables you to record the responses to two or more similar questions at the same time. As can be seen from question 15, created in SurveyMonkey.com™, questions are listed down the left-hand side of the page, and responses listed across the top.

The appropriate response to each question is then recorded in the cell where the row and column met. Although using a matrix saves space, Dillman (2007) suggests that respondents may have difficulties comprehending these designs and that they are a barrier to response.

15. The following items refer to your treatment by managers in general, who are responsible for making decisions in Anytown Manufacturing Company that affects your work. To what extent:

	to a large extent	to a quite large extent	to some extent	to a quite small extent	to a small extent	not at all
a. do they treat you with dignity?	○	○	○	○	○	○
b. do they treat you with respect?	○	○	○	○	○	○
c. are they at least as honest with bad news as good news in their communications with you?	○	○	○	○	○	○

Source: question layout created by SurveyMonkey.com (2008), Portland, Oregon, USA; author/owner: Ryan Finley. Reproduced with permission.

Question wording

The wording of each question will need careful consideration to ensure that the responses are valid – that is, measure what you think they do. Your questions will need to be checked within the context for which they were written rather than in abstract to ensure they are not misread (Box 11.10). Given this, the checklist in Box 11.11 should help you to avoid the most obvious problems associated with wording that threaten the validity of responses.

Box 11.10
Focus on student research

Misreading questions

Before becoming a student, Tracey worked for a UK-based market research agency and was responsible for much of their questionnaire design and analysis work. During her time at the agency she noted that certain words in questions were likely to be misread by respondents. The question 'In which county do you live?' was often answered as if the question had been 'In which country do you live?' This meant that rather than answering 'Worcestershire', the respondent would answer either 'England' or 'UK'. Later questionnaires for which Tracey was responsible used the question 'In which town do you live?', the response being used to establish and code the county in which the respondent lived.

Translating questions into other languages

Translating questions and associated instructions into another language requires care if your translated or target questionnaire is to be decoded and answered by respondents in the way you intended. For international research this is extremely important if the questions are to have the same meaning to all respondents. For this reason Usunier (1998) suggests that when translating the source questionnaire attention should be paid to:

- **lexical meaning** – the precise meaning of individual words (e.g. the French word *chaud* can be translated into two concepts in English and German, 'warm' and 'hot');
- **idiomatic meaning** – the meanings of a group of words that are natural to a native speaker and not deducible from those of the individual words (e.g. the English expression for informal communication, 'grapevine', has a similar idiomatic meaning as the

Box 11.11
Checklist

Your question wording

✔ Does your question collect data at the right level of detail to answer your investigative question as specified in your data requirements table?

✔ Will respondents have the necessary knowledge to answer your question? A question on the implications of a piece of European Union legislation would yield meaningless answers from those who were unaware of that legislation.

✔ Does your question talk down to respondents? It should not!

✔ Are the words used in your question familiar, and will all respondents understand them in the same way? In particular, you should use simple words and avoid jargon, abbreviations and colloquialisms.

✔ Are there any words that sound similar and might be confused with those used in your question? This is a particular problem with interviewer-administered questionnaires.

✔ Are there any words that look similar and might be confused if your question is read quickly? This is particularly important for self-administered questionnaires.

✔ Are there any words in your question that might cause offence? These might result in biased responses or a lower response rate.

✔ Can your question be shortened? Long questions are often difficult to understand, especially in interviewer-administered questionnaires, as the respondent needs to remember the whole question. Consequently, they often result in no response at all.

✔ Are you asking more than one question at the same time? The question 'How often do you visit your mother and father?' contains two separate questions, one about each parent, so responses would probably be impossible to interpret.

✔ Does your question include a negative or double negative? Questions that include the word 'not' are sometimes difficult to understand. The question 'Would you rather not use a non-medicated shampoo?' is far easier to understand when rephrased as: 'Would you rather use a medicated shampoo?'

✔ Is your question unambiguous? This can arise from poor sentence structure, using words with several different meanings or having an unclear investigative question. If you ask 'When did you leave school?' some respondents might state the year, others might give their age, while those still in education might give the time of day! Ambiguity can also occur in category questions. If you ask employers how many employees they have on their payroll and categorise their answers into three groups (up to 100, 100–250, 250 plus), they will not be clear which group to choose if they have 100 or 250 employees.

✔ Does your question imply that a certain answer is correct? If it does, the question is biased and will need to be reworded, such as with the question 'Many people believe that too little money is spent on our public Health Service. Do you believe this to be the case?' For this question, respondents are more likely to answer 'yes' to agree with and please the interviewer.

✔ Does your question prevent certain answers from being given? If it does, the question is biased and will need to be reworded. The question 'Is this the first time you have pretended to be sick?' implies that the respondent has pretended to be sick whether they answer yes or no!

✔ Is your question likely to embarrass the respondent? If it is, then you need either to reword it or to place it towards the end of the survey when you will, it is to be hoped, have gained the respondent's confidence. Questions on income can be asked as either precise amounts (more embarrassing), using a quantity question, or income bands (less embarrassing), using a category question.

✔ Have you incorporated advice appropriate for your type of questionnaire (such as the maximum number of categories) outlined in the earlier discussion of question types?

✔ Are answers to closed questions written so that at least one will apply to every respondent and so each of the list of responses is mutually exclusive ?

✔ Are the instructions on how to record each answer clear?

French expression *téléphone arabe,* meaning literally 'arab telephone' and the German expression *Mundpropaganda,* meaning literally 'mouth propaganda');

- **experiential meaning** – the equivalence of meanings of words and sentences for people in their everyday experiences (e.g. terms that are familiar in the source questionnaire's context such as 'dual career household' may be unfamiliar in the target questionnaire's context);
- grammar and syntax – the correct use of language, including the ordering of words and phrases to create well-formed sentences (e.g. in Japanese the ordering is quite different from English or Dutch, as verbs are at the end of sentences).

Usunier (1998) outlines a number of techniques for translating your source questionnaire. These, along with their advantages and disadvantages, are summarised in Table 11.4. In this table, the **source questionnaire** is the questionnaire that is to be translated, and the **target questionnaire** is the translated questionnaire. When writing your final project report, remember to include a copy of both the source and the target questionnaire as appendices. This will allow readers familiar with both languages to check that equivalent questions in both questionnaires have the same meaning.

Table 11.4 Translation techniques for questionnaires

	Direct translation	**Back-translation**	**Parallel translation**	**Mixed techniques**
Approach	Source questionnaire to target questionnaire	Source questionnaire to target questionnaire to source questionnaire; comparison of two new source questionnaires; creation of final version	Source questionnaire to target questionnaire by two or more independent translators; comparison of two target questionnaires; creation of final version	Back-translation undertaken by two or more independent translators; comparison of two new source questionnaires; creation of final version
Advantages	Easy to implement, relatively inexpensive	Likely to discover most problems	Leads to good wording of target questionnaire	Ensures best match between source and target questionnaires
Disadvantages	Can lead to many discrepancies (including those relating to meaning) between source and target questionnaire	Requires two translators, one a native speaker of the source language, the other a native speaker of the target language	Cannot ensure that lexical, idiomatic and experiential meanings are kept in target questionnaire	Costly, requires two or more independent translators. Implies that the source questionnaire can also be changed.

Source: developed from Usunier (1998) 'Translation techniques for questionnaires' in *International and Cross-Cultural Management Research.* Copyright © 1998 Sage Publications, reprinted with permission.

Question coding

If you are planning to analyse your data by computer, they will need to be coded prior to entry. For quantity questions, actual numbers can be used as codes. For other questions, you will need to design a coding scheme. Whenever possible, you should establish the coding scheme prior to collecting data and incorporate it into your questionnaire. This should take account of relevant existing coding schemes to enable comparisons with other data sets (Section 12.2).

For most closed questions you should be able to add codes to response categories. These can be printed on the questionnaire, thereby **pre-coding** the question and removing the need to code after data collection. Two ways of doing this are illustrated by questions 16 and 17, which collect data on the respondents' opinions.

16 Is the service you receive? (Please circle O the number)	Excellent	Good	Reasonable	Poor	Awful
	5	4	3	2	1

17 Is the service you receive? (Please tick ✓ the box)	Excellent	Good	Reasonable	Poor	Awful
	❑$_5$	❑$_1$	❑$_3$	❑$_2$	❑$_4$

The codes allocated to response categories will affect your analyses. In question 16 an ordered scale of numbers has been allocated to adjacent responses. This will make it far easier to aggregate responses using a computer (Section 12.2) to 'satisfactory' (5, 4 or 3) and 'unsatisfactory' (2 or 1) compared with the codes in question 17. We therefore recommend that you do not allocate codes as in question 17.

In contrast, if you are considering using an Internet- or intranet-mediated questionnaire you can create an **online form (questionnaire)** containing text boxes where the respondent enters information, check boxes that list the choices available to the respondent allowing them to 'check' or 'tick' one or more of them, and drop-down list boxes that restrict the respondent to selecting only one of the answers you specify (as in the Nando's questionnaire). Online forms are often included as part of word-processing software such as Microsoft Word™. Alternatively, as for question 18, you can use online software tools such as SurveyMonkey.com™ to create your online form. Both allow you to create a professional questionnaire and the respondent to complete the questionnaire online and return the data electronically in a variety of formats such as Excel™, SPSS™ compatible or a comma-delimited file.

Source: question layout created by SurveyMonkey.com (2008), Portland, Oregon, USA; author/owner: Ryan Finley. Reproduced with permission.

For open questions you will need to reserve space on your data collection form to code responses after data collection. Question 19 has been designed to collect attribute data in a sample survey of 5000 people. Theoretically there could be hundreds of possible responses, and so sufficient spaces are left in the 'For office use only' box.

19 What is your full job title?	For Office use only
....	❑ ❑ ❑

Open questions, which generate lists of responses, are likely to require more complex coding using either the multiple-response or the multiple-dichotomy method. These are discussed in Section 12.2, and we recommend that you read this prior to designing your questions.

Constructing the questionnaire

The order and flow of questions

When constructing your questionnaire it is a good idea to spend time considering the order and flow of your questions. These should be logical to the respondent (and interviewer) rather than follow the order in your data requirements table (Table 11.2). To assist the flow of the survey it may be necessary to include **filter questions**. These identify those respondents for whom the following question or questions are not applicable, so they can skip those questions. You should beware of using more than two or three filter questions in self-administered questionnaires, as respondents tend to find having to skip questions annoying. More complex filter questions can be programmed using Internet- and intranet-mediated questionnaires and CAPI and CATI software so that skipped questions are never displayed on the screen and as a consequence never asked (Dillman 2007). In such situations the respondent is unlikely to be aware of the questions that have been skipped. The following example uses the answer to question 20 to determine whether questions 21 to 24 will be answered. (Questions 20 and 21 both collect data on attributes.)

20 Are you currently registered as unemployed? Yes $\square_1$

    If 'no' go to question 25 No $\square_2$

21 How long have you been registered as unemployed? ☐ years ☐ months

    (For example, for no years and six months write: $\boxed{0}$ years $\boxed{6}$ months)

Where you need to introduce new topics, phrases such as 'the following questions refer to . . .' or 'I am now going to ask you about . . .' are useful. And when wording your questions, you should remember the particular population for whom your questionnaire is designed. For interviewer-administered questionnaires, you will have to include instructions for the interviewer (Box 11.12). The checklist in Box 11.13 should help you to avoid the most obvious problems associated with question order and flow. For some questionnaires the advice contained may be contradictory. Where this is the case, you need to decide what is most important for your particular population.

The layout of the questionnaire

Layout is important for both self-administered and interviewer-administered questionnaires. Interviewer-administered questionnaires should be designed to make reading questions and filling in responses easy. The layout of self-administered questionnaires should, in addition, be attractive to encourage the respondent to fill it in and to return it, while not appearing too long. However, where the choice is between an extra page and a cramped questionnaire the former is likely to be more acceptable to respondents (Dillman 2007). Survey design and analysis software such as Snap™, Sphinx Development™ andSurveyMonkey.com™ contain a series of style templates for typefaces, colours and page layout, which are helpful in producing a professional-looking questionnaire more quickly (Snap Surveys 2008; Sphinx Development 2008; SurveyMonkey.com 2008). For paper-based surveys, the use of colour will increase the printing costs. However, it is worth noting that the best way of obtaining valid responses to questions is to keep both the visual appearance of the questionnaire and the wording of each question simple (Dillman 2007).

Box 11.12
Focus on student research

Introducing a series of rating questions in a telephone questionnaire

As part of a telephone questionnaire, Stefan needed to collect data on respondents' attitudes to motorway service stations. To do this he asked respondents to rate a series of statements using a Likert-type rating scale. These were recorded as a matrix. Because his survey was conducted by telephone the rating scale was restricted to four categories: strongly agree, agree, disagree, strongly disagree.

In order to make the questionnaire easy for the interviewer to follow, Stefan used italic script to highlight the interviewer's instructions and the words that the interviewer needed to read in bold. An extract is given below:

Now I'm going to read you several statements. Please tell me whether you strongly agree, agree, disagree or strongly disagree with each.

Interviewer: read out statements 22 to 30 one at a time and after each ask …

Do you strongly agree, agree, disagree or strongly disagree?

Record respondent's response with a tick ✓

---

	strongly agree	agree	disagree	strongly disagree
22 I wish there were a greater number of service stations on motorways	☐4	☐3	☐2	☐1

Box 11.13
Checklist

Your question order

✔ Are questions at the beginning of your questionnaire more straightforward and ones the respondent will enjoy answering? Questions about attributes and behaviours are usually more straightforward to answer than those collecting data on opinions.

✔ Are questions at the beginning of your questionnaire obviously relevant to the stated purpose of your questionnaire? For example, questions requesting contextual information may appear irrelevant.

✔ Are questions and topics that are more complex placed towards the middle of your questionnaire? By this stage most respondents should be completing the survey with confidence but should not yet be bored or tired.

✔ Are personal and sensitive questions towards the end of your questionnaire, and is their purpose clearly explained? On being asked these a respondent may refuse to answer; however, if they are at the end of an interviewer-administered questionnaire you will still have the rest of the data!

✔ Are filter questions and routing instructions easy to follow so that there is a clear route through the questionnaire?

✔ (For interviewer-administered questionnaires) Are instructions to the interviewer easy to follow?

✔ Are questions grouped into obvious sections that will make sense to the respondent?

✔ Have you re-examined the wording of each question and ensured it is consistent with its position in the questionnaire as well as with the data you require?

Research findings on the extent to which the length of your questionnaire will affect your response rate are mixed (deVaus 2002). There is a widespread view that longer questionnaires will reduce response rates relative to shorter questionnaires (Edwards *et al.* 2002). However, a very short questionnaire may suggest that your research is insignificant and hence not worth bothering with. Conversely, a questionnaire that takes over two hours to complete might just be thrown away by the intended respondent. In general, we have found that a length of between four and eight A4 pages has been acceptable for within-organisation self-administered questionnaires. Telephone questionnaires of up to half an hour have caused few problems, whereas the acceptable length for structured interviews can vary from only a few minutes in the street to over two hours in a more comfortable environment (Section 10.6). Based on these experiences, we recommend you follow deVaus' (2002) advice:

- Do not make the questionnaire longer than is really necessary to meet your research questions and objectives.
- Do not be too obsessed with the length of your questionnaire.

Remember you can reduce apparent length without reducing legibility by using matrix questions (discussed earlier). Box 11.14 (overleaf)discusses the impact of administering a questionnaire online on response rates and Box 11.15 summarises the most important layout issues as a checklist.

Explaining the purpose of the questionnaire

The covering letter

Most self-administered questionnaires are accompanied by a **covering letter** or email, which explains the purpose of the survey. This is the first part of the questionnaire that a respondent should look at. Unfortunately, some of your sample will ignore it, while others use it to decide whether to answer the accompanying questionnaire.

Research by Dillman (2007) and others has shown that the messages contained in a self-administered questionnaire's covering letter will affect the response rate. The results of this research are summarised in the annotated letter (Figure 11.3).

For some research projects you may also send a letter prior to administering your questionnaire. This will be used by the respondent to decide whether to grant you access. Consequently, it is often the only opportunity you have to convince the respondent to participate in your research. Ways of ensuring this are discussed in Section 6.3.

Introducing the questionnaire

At the start of your questionnaire you need to explain clearly and concisely why you want the respondent to complete the survey. Dillman (2007) argues that, to achieve as high a response rate as possible, this should be done on the first page of the questionnaire in addition to the covering letter. He suggests that in addition to a summary of the main messages in the covering letter (Figure 11.3 on page 392) you include:

- a clear unbiased banner or title, which conveys the topic of the questionnaire and makes it sound interesting;
- a subtitle, which conveys the research nature of the topic (optional);
- a neutral graphic illustration or logo to add interest and to set the questionnaire apart (self-administered questionnaires).

This advice also applies to Internet and intranet-mediated questionnaires and is discussed later in this section.

Box 11.14
Focus on management research

Non-response and Internet- and intranet-mediated questionnaires

Thompson and Surface's (2007) paper, 'Employee Surveys Adminstered Online – Attitudes to the medium, non-response, and data representativeness' in the journal, *Organizational Research Methods*, notes a negative trend in response to web-based questionnaires and addresses research questions associated with how employees feel about completing questionnaires online. In addition, it asks whether web-based questionnaire media discourage response.

Data were collected from employees working at the headquarters of a military organisation using a combination of two web based questionnaires and focus groups. Their first research question 'To what degree do people dislike taking employee surveys online?' (Thompson and Surface 2007:242) was addressed, in part using data collected as responses to questions in the organisation's 'staff climate survey' and a paper based questionnaire administered as part of a focus group. This included questions such as (Thompson and Surface 2007:250):

	Strongly disagree	Disagree	Neutral	Agree	Strongly agree
I like taking the Command Climate Survey via the Web	❏	❏	❏	❏	❏

Their second research question 'Do reactions to the online medium deter survey participation?' (Thompson and Surface 2007:244) was addressed by a brief online follow-up questionnaire and focus groups within the organisation. Within the online questionnaire, participants were asked whether or not they had worked for the organisation at the time the first questionnaire had been administered and whether they had completed the staff climate survey. Those who worked for the organisation at the time of the first questionnaire and had not completed the staff climate survey were asked to select all the reasons that applied from the following list (Thompson and Surface 2007:246):

- *Waste of time because nothing is done with the results.*
- *Was concerned the response would be traced back to me.*
- *The survey didn't ask the right questions.*
- *Satisfied with the way things are and therefore didn't see the need to respond.*
- *Too busy to complete.*
- *Travelling for work/off sick/on leave/away from office.*

- *Not aware/never received it.*
- *Probably thought it was organisational spam and deleted it.*
- *Accidentally forgot to finish it.*
- *Computer problems.*

With regard to their first research question, Thompson and Surface found that whilst only 8 per cent of respondents to the online questionnaire disapproved of the web based format, 37 per cent of those responding to the same question in the paper based questionnaire disapproved. Based on this and other evidence they argued that web based questionnaires attract respondents whose attitudes to web based questionnaires are not representative of the broader population.

In considering their second research question, Thompson and Surface were particularly concerned as to whether administering a questionnaire using the web discouraged participation. They found that three adverse reactions to the medium had negative implications for web-based questionnaire response rates. These related to concerns about anonymity, computer problems and a failure to distinguish the email relating to the questionnaire from organisational spam.

Box 11.15
Checklist

Your questionnaire layout

✔ (For self-administered questionnaires) Do questions appear squashed on the page or screen? This will put the respondent off reading it and reduce the response rate. Unfortunately, a thick questionnaire is equally off-putting!

✔ (For paper based self-administered questionnaires) Is the questionnaire going to be printed on good-quality paper? This will imply that the survey is important.

✔ (For self-administered questionnaires) Is the questionnaire going to be printed or displayed on a warm-pastel colour? Warm pastel shades, such as yellow and pink, generate slightly more responses than white (Edwards *et al*. 2002) or cool colours, such as green or blue. White is a good neutral colour but bright or fluorescent colours should be avoided.

✔ (For structured interviews) Will the questions and instructions be printed on one side of the paper only? You will find it difficult to read the questions on back pages if you are using a questionnaire attached to a clipboard!

✔ Is your questionnaire easy to read? Questionnaires should be typed in 12 point or 10 point using a plain font. Excessively long and excessively short lines reduce legibility. Similarly, respondents find CAPITALS, *italics* and shaded backgrounds more difficult to read. However, if used consistently, they can make completing the questionnaire easier.

✔ Have you ensured that the use of shading, colour, font sizes, spacing and the formatting of questions is consistent throughout the questionnaire?

✔ Is your questionnaire laid out in a format that respondents are accustomed to reading? Research has shown that many people skim-read questionnaires (Dillman 2007). Instructions that can be read one line at a time from left to right moving down the page are, therefore, more likely to be followed correctly.

Interviewer-administered questionnaires will require this information to be phrased as a short introduction, which the interviewer can read to each respondent. A template for this (developed from deVaus 2002) is given in the next paragraph, while Box 11.16 on page 393 provides an example from a self-administered questionnaire.

> Good morning / afternoon / evening. My name is (your name) from (your organisation). I am doing a research project to find out (brief description of purpose of the research). Your telephone number was drawn from a random sample of (brief description of the total population). The questions I should like to ask will take about (number) minutes. If you have any queries, I shall be happy to answer them. (Pause). Before I continue please can you confirm that this is (read out the telephone number) and that I am talking to (read out name/occupation/position in organisation to check that you have the right person). Please can I ask you the questions now?

You will also need to have prepared answers to the more obvious questions that the respondent might ask you. These include the purpose of the survey, how you obtained the respondent's telephone number, who is conducting or sponsoring the survey, and why someone else cannot answer the questions instead (Lavrakas 1993).

Closing the questionnaire

At the end of your questionnaire you need to explain clearly what you want the respondent to do with their completed questionnaire. It is usual to start this section by thanking the respondent for completing the questionnaire, and by providing a contact name and telephone number for any queries they may have (Figure 11.3). You should then give

Banner: explains purpose clearly

Paper: good quality, warm pastel colour or white

Letterhead: official; includes logo, address, telephone number and (if possible) email

Recipient's name: title, initial/forename (absence suggests impersonality)

Recipient's address: (absence suggests impersonality)

Date: in full

Salutation: title and name if possible

1st set of messages: what research is about, why it is useful

2nd set of messages: recipient's response valued, time needed

3rd set of messages: confidentiality and/or anonymity

4th set of messages: how results will be used, token reward for participation (if any)

Final set of messages: contact for queries, who to return to, date for return

Signature: by hand, in ink

Name: title, forename and surname

Closing remarks: thank recipient

Font size: 12 or 11 point

Length: one side maximum

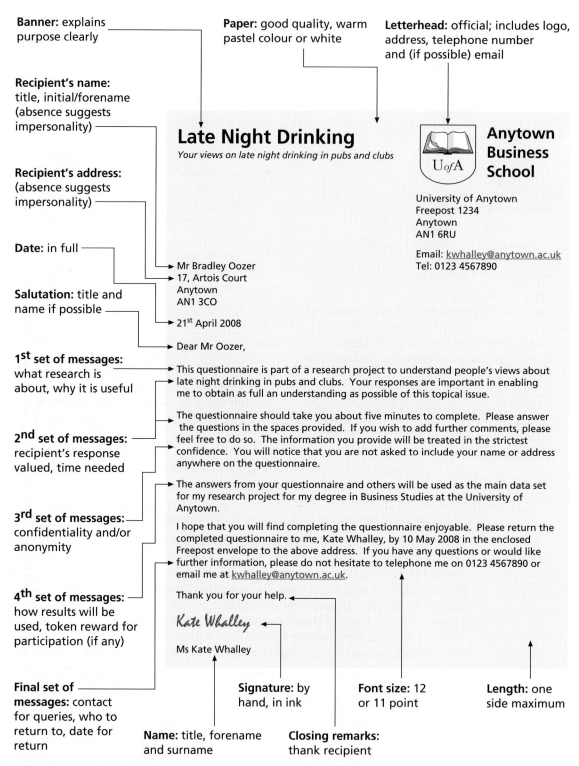

Late Night Drinking
Your views on late night drinking in pubs and clubs

Anytown Business School

U*of*A

University of Anytown
Freepost 1234
Anytown
AN1 6RU

Email: kwhalley@anytown.ac.uk
Tel: 0123 4567890

Mr Bradley Oozer
17, Artois Court
Anytown
AN1 3CO

21st April 2008

Dear Mr Oozer,

This questionnaire is part of a research project to understand people's views about late night drinking in pubs and clubs. Your responses are important in enabling me to obtain as full an understanding as possible of this topical issue.

The questionnaire should take you about five minutes to complete. Please answer the questions in the spaces provided. If you wish to add further comments, please feel free to do so. The information you provide will be treated in the strictest confidence. You will notice that you are not asked to include your name or address anywhere on the questionnaire.

The answers from your questionnaire and others will be used as the main data set for my research project for my degree in Business Studies at the University of Anytown.

I hope that you will find completing the questionnaire enjoyable. Please return the completed questionnaire to me, Kate Whalley, by 10 May 2008 in the enclosed Freepost envelope to the above address. If you have any questions or would like further information, please do not hesitate to telephone me on 0123 4567890 or email me at kwhalley@anytown.ac.uk.

Thank you for your help.

Kate Whalley

Ms Kate Whalley

Figure 11.3 Structure of a covering letter

Box 11.16
Focus on student research
Introducing a self-administered questionnaire

Liz asked her project tutor to comment on what she hoped was the final draft of her questionnaire. This included the following introduction:

ANYTOWN PRIVATE HOSPITAL STAFF SURVEY

All your responses will be treated in the strictest of confidence and only aggregated data will be available to the Hospital. All questionnaires will be shredded once the data have been extracted. The Hospital will publish a summary of the results.

Not surprisingly, her project tutor suggested that she redraft her introduction. Her revised introduction follows:

Anytown Private Hospital

Staff Survey 2009

This survey is being carried out to find out how you feel about the Hospital's policies to support colleagues like you in your work. Please answer the questions freely. You cannot be identified from the information you provide, and no information about individuals will be given to the Hospital.

Caring for All

ALL THE INFORMATION YOU PROVIDE WILL BE TREATED IN THE STRICTEST CONFIDENCE

The questionnaire should take you about five minutes to complete. Please answer the questions in the space provided. Try to complete the questions at a time when you are unlikely to be disturbed. Also, do not spend too long on any one question. Your first thoughts are usually your best! Even if you feel the items covered may not apply directly to your working life, please do not ignore them. Your answers are essential in building an accurate picture of the issues that are important to improving our support for people working for this Hospital.

WHEN YOU HAVE COMPLETED THE QUESTIONNAIRE, PLEASE RETURN IT TO US IN THE ENCLOSED FREEPOST ENVELOPE NO LATER THAN 6 APRIL.

I hope you find completing the questionnaire enjoyable, and thank you for taking the time to help us. A summary of the findings will be published on the Hospital intranet. If you have any queries or would like further information about this project, please telephone me on 01234-5678910 or email me on epetrie@anytownhealthcare.com.

Thank you for your help.

Elizabeth Petrie

Elizabeth Petrie
Human Resources Department
Anytown Private Hospital
Anytown AN99 9HS

details of the date by which you would like the questionnaire returned and how and where to return it. A template for this is given in the next paragraph:

Thank you for taking the time to complete this questionnaire. If you have any queries please do not hesitate to contact (your name) by telephoning (contact telephone number with answer machine/voice mail) or emailing (email address).

Please return the completed questionnaire by (date) in the envelope provided to:

(your name)

(your address)

Pilot testing and assessing validity

Prior to using your questionnaire to collect data it should be pilot tested. The purpose of the **pilot test** is to refine the questionnaire so that respondents will have no problems in answering the questions and there will be no problems in recording the data. In addition, it will enable you to obtain some assessment of the questions' validity and the likely reliability of the data that will be collected. Preliminary analysis using the pilot test data can be undertaken to ensure that the data collected will enable your investigative questions to be answered.

Initially you should ask an expert or group of experts to comment on the representativeness and suitability of your questions. As well as allowing suggestions to be made on the structure of your questionnaire, this will help establish content validity and enable you to make necessary amendments prior to pilot testing with a group as similar as possible to the final population in your sample. For any research project there is a temptation to skip the pilot testing. We would endorse Bell's (2005:147) advice, 'however pressed for time you are, do your best to give the questionnaire a trial run', as, without a trial run, you have no way of knowing whether your questionnaire will succeed.

The number of people with whom you pilot your questionnaire and the number of pilot tests you conduct are dependent on your research question(s), your objectives, the size of your research project, the time and money resources you have available, and how well you have initially designed your questionnaire. Very large questionnaire surveys such as national censuses will have numerous field trials, starting with individual questions and working up to larger and more rigorous pilots of later drafts.

For smaller-scale questionnaires you are unlikely to have sufficient financial or time resources for large-scale field trials. However, it is still important that you pilot test your questionnaire. The number of people you choose should be sufficient to include any major variations in your population that you feel are likely to affect responses. For most student questionnaires this means that the minimum number for a pilot is 10 (Fink 2003b), although for large surveys between 100 and 200 responses is usual (Dillman 2007). Occasionally you may be extremely pushed for time. In such instances it is better to pilot test the questionnaire using friends or family than not at all! This will provide you with at least some idea of your questionnaire's **face validity**: that is, whether the questionnaire appears to make sense.

As part of your pilot you should check each completed pilot questionnaire to ensure that respondents have had no problems understanding or answering questions and have followed all instructions correctly (Fink 2003b). Their responses will provide you with an idea of the reliability and suitability of the questions. For self-administered questionnaires additional information about problems can be obtained by giving respondents a further short questionnaire. Bell (2005) suggests you should use this to find out:

- how long the questionnaire took to complete;
- the clarity of instructions;
- which, if any, questions were unclear or ambiguous;
- which, if any, questions the respondent felt uneasy about answering;
- whether in their opinion there were any major topic omissions;
- whether the layout was clear and attractive;
- any other comments.

Interviewer-administered questionnaires need to be tested with the respondents for all these points other than layout. One way of doing this is to form an assessment as each questionnaire progresses. Another is to interview any interviewers you are employing. However, you can also check by asking the respondent additional questions at the end of their interview. In addition, you will need to pilot test the questionnaire with interviewers to discover whether:

- there are any questions for which visual aids should have been provided;
- they have difficulty in finding their way through the questionnaire;
- they are recording answers correctly.

Once you have completed pilot testing you should write to your respondents thanking them for their help.

11.5 Administering the questionnaire

Once your questionnaire is designed, pilot tested and amended and your sample selected, the questionnaire can be used to collect data. This final stage is called administering the questionnaire. In administering your questionnaire it is important that you abide by your university's or professional body's code of ethics (Sections 6.4 and 6.5). When a respondent ticks a box they are giving their implied consent and have rights just like all research participants.

Inevitably you will need to gain access to your sample (Sections 6.2 and 6.3) and attempt to maximise the response rate. Edwards *et al.* (2002) identify 292 studies that have assessed between them the impact of 75 different strategies for increasing the response to postal questionnaires. These trials were published predominantly in marketing, business and statistical journals (42 per cent), medical and health-related journals (32 per cent) and psychological, educational and sociological journals (23 per cent). The findings of those studies that had more than 1000 participants are summarised in Table 11.5. Such increases in response rates are dependent upon your questionnaire being clearly worded and well laid out. In addition, it must be remembered that organisations and individuals are increasingly being bombarded with requests to respond to questionnaires and so may be unwilling to answer your questionnaire.

Which of these techniques you use to help to maximise responses will inevitably be dependent on the way in which your questionnaire is administered. It is the processes associated with administering each of the five types of questionnaire that we now consider.

Internet- and intranet-mediated questionnaires

For Internet- and intranet-mediated questionnaires, it is important to have a clear timetable that identifies the tasks that need to be done and the resources that will be needed. A good response is dependent on the recipient being motivated to answer the questionnaire and to send it back. Although the covering email (Section 11.4) and good design will help to ensure a high level of response, it must be remembered that, unlike paper questionnaires, the designer and respondent may see different images displayed on their monitors. Alternative computer operating systems, Internet browsers and display screens can all result in the image being displayed differently, emphasising the need to ensure the questionnaire design is clear (Dillman 2007).

Internet- and intranet-mediated questionnaires are usually administered in one of two ways: via email or via a website (Hewson *et al.* 2003). The first of these uses email to 'post' and receive questionnaires or the web link to the questionnaire and is dependent on having a list of addresses. Although it is possible to obtain such lists from an Internet-based employment directory or via a search engine (Section 3.5), we would not recommend you

Table 11.5 Relative impact of strategies for raising postal questionnaire response rates

Strategy	Relative impact
Incentives	
Monetary incentive v. no incentive	Very high
Incentive sent with questionnaire v. incentive on questionnaire return	High
Non-monetary incentive v. no incentive	Low
Length	
Shorter questionnaire v. longer questionnaire	Very high
Appearance	
Brown envelope v. white envelope	High but variable
Coloured ink v. standard	Medium
*Folder or booklet.*v. stapled pages	Low
More personalised v. less personalised	Low
Coloured *questionnaire* v. white questionnaire	Very low
Identifying feature on the return v. none	Very low but variable
Delivery	
Recorded delivery v. standard delivery	Very high
Stamped return envelope v. business reply or franked	Medium
First class post outwards v. other class	Low
Sent to work address v. sent to home address	Low but variable
Pre-paid return v. not pre-paid	Low but variable
Commemorative stamp v. *ordinary stamp*	Low but variable
Stamped outward envelope v. franked	Negligible
Contact	
Pre-contact v. no pre-contact	Medium
Follow-up v. no follow-up	Medium
Postal follow-up including questionnaire v. postal follow-up excluding questionnaire	Medium
Pre-contact by telephone v. *pre-contact by post*	Low
Mention of follow-up contact v. none	Negligible
Content	
More interesting v. less interesting questionnaire	Very high
User friendly questionnaire v. standard	Medium
Attribute and behaviour questions only v. attribute, behaviour and attitude questions	Medium
More relevant questions first v. other questions first	Low
Most general question first v. last	Low
Sensitive questions included v. *sensitive questions not included*	Very low
Demographic questions first v. other questions first	Negligible
'Don't know' boxes included v. not included	Negligible
Origin	
University sponsorship as a source v. *other organisation*	Medium
Sent by more senior or well-known person v. less senior or less well-known	Low but variable
Ethnically unidentifiable/white name v. other name	Low but variable
Communication	
Explanation for not participating requested v. not requested	Medium
Choice to opt out from study offered v. not given	Low
Instructions given v. *not given*	Low but variable
Benefits to respondent stressed v. other benefits	Very low
Benefits to sponsor stressed v. other benefits	Negligible
Benefits to society stressed v. other benefits	Negligible
Response deadline given v. no deadline	Negligible

Note: strategies in italics increase response rates relative to those in normal font.
Source: developed from Edwards *et al.* 2002.

obtain them this way. If you are considering using the Internet for research, you should abide by the general operating guidelines or **netiquette**. This includes (Hewson *et al.* 2003):

- ensuring emails and postings to user groups are relevant and that you do not send junk emails (spam);
- remembering that invitations to participate sent to over 20 user groups at once are deemed as unacceptable by many net vigilantes and so you should not exceed this threshold;
- avoiding sending your email to multiple mailing lists as this is likely to result in individuals receiving multiple copies of your email (this is known as **cross-posting**);
- avoiding the use of email attachments as these can contain viruses.

Failure to do this is likely to result in 'few responses and a barrage of emails informing the researcher of their non-compliance' (Coomber 1997:10). Despite this, questionnaires can be successfully administered by email within organisations provided that all of the sample have access to it and use it (Box 11.17). However, unless an anonymous server or mailbox that removes email addresses is used for returning questionnaires, respondents will be identifiable by their email addresses (Witmer *et al.* 1999). If you choose to use email, we suggest that you:

1 contact recipients by email and advise them to expect a questionnaire – a **pre-survey contact** (Section 6.3);
2 email the questionnaire or a direct web link (hyperlink) with a covering email. Where possible, the letter and questionnaire or hyperlink should be part of the email message rather than an attached file to avoid viruses. You should make sure that this will arrive when recipients are likely to be receptive. For most organisations Fridays and days surrounding major public holidays have been shown to be a poor time;

Box 11.17
Research in
the news

TNS warns over reliability of data collected online

Businesses are challenging the reliability of some data collected online – the fastest-growing method in the market research industry.

Taylor Nelson Sofres, the global market research group, said companies were concerned that the emergence of 'professional' web respondents simultaneously signed up to several online research panels could skew results from the web.

Over-questioning of panellists, who can be interviewed quicker and cheaper online than by telephone or in person, is also seen as a danger, while maintaining the credibility of web data will be vital if the medium is to continue its recent growth as a research tool, according to TNS.

David Lowden, Chief Executive of TNS, said: 'We have strict rules on how we use online respondents. That is not the case with all suppliers. Our response rates to online questionnaires tend to be 40–50 per cent. But there are companies where it is less than 5 per cent, because they simply send too many questions'.

The amount of TNS business based on data from its Internet panels rose 22 per cent during the first half of 2007, compared with a forecast 5.9 per cent rise in underlying group revenues. Overall, in the six months to June 30, pre-tax profits rose 13 per cent from £30 m to £33.9 m on revenues of £497.4 m (£480.5 m). Earnings per share increased 33 per cent to 5.9p (3.9p) and the interim dividend is 1.6p (1.4p). The shares fell ½p to 228p.

Source: article by Grande, Carlos (2007) *Financial Times*, 4 Sept. Copyright © The Financial Times Ltd.

3 email the first **follow-up** one week after emailing out the questionnaire to all recipients. This should thank early respondents and remind non-respondents to answer (a copy of the questionnaire or hyperlink should be included);

4 email the second follow-up to people who have not responded after three weeks. This should include another covering letter and a copy of the questionnaire or hyperlink. The covering letter should be reworded to further emphasise the importance of completing the questionnaire;

5 also use a third follow-up if time allows or your response rate is low.

Alternatively, the questionnaire can be advertised on the Internet or on the intranet and respondents invited to access the questionnaire via a hyperlink and to fill it in. Adopting this web-based approach observes netiquette and means that respondents can remain anonymous and, of equal importance, are unable to modify the questionnaire (Witmer *et al*. 1999). The stages involved are:

1 Ensure that a website has been set up that explains the purpose of the research and how to complete the questionnaire (this takes the place of the covering letter).

2 Ensure that the questionnaire has been set up on the web and has a hyperlink from the website.

3 Advertise the website widely using a range of media (for example, an email pre-survey contact or a banner advertisement on a page that is likely to be looked at by the target population), using a hyperlink to the questionnaire and highlighting the closing date.

4 When the respondent completes the questionnaire, ensure that the data file is generated and saved automatically and that the web-based software prevents multiple responses from one respondent.

5 For web-based questionnaires advertised using an email pre-survey contact, email all recipients one week after the initial email thanking early respondents and reminding others to respond. The hyperlink should be embedded in the email.

6 For web-based questionnaires advertised using an email pre-survey contact, email a second follow-up to people who have not responded after three weeks. The email should be reworded to emphasise further the importance of completing the questionnaire. For anonymous questionnaires, a second follow-up will not be possible, as you should not be able to tell who has responded!

Response rates from web advertisements are likely to be very low, and there are considerable problems of non-response bias as the respondent has to take extra steps to locate and complete the questionnaire (Coomber 1997). Consequently, it is likely to be very difficult to obtain a representative sample from which you might generalise. This is not to say that this approach should not be used as it can, for example, enable you to contact difficult-to-access groups. It all depends, as you would expect us to say, on your research question and objectives!

Postal questionnaires

For postal questionnaires, it is also important to have a well-written covering letter and good design to help to ensure a high level of response. As with online questionnaires, a clear timetable and well-executed administration process are important (Box 11.18).

Our advice for postal questionnaires (developed from deVaus 2002) can be split into six stages:

1 Ensure that questionnaires and letters are printed, and envelopes addressed.

2 Contact recipients by post, telephone or email and advise them to expect a questionnaire – a pre-survey contact (Section 6.3). This stage is often omitted for cost reasons.

Box 11.18
Focus on management research

Questionnaire administration

Mark and Adrian undertook an attitude survey of parents of pupils at a school using a questionnaire. Prior to the survey, a pre-survey contact letter was sent to all parents, using their children to deliver the letter. The questionnaire, covering letter and postage-paid reply envelope were delivered in the same manner a week later. By the end of the first week after the questionnaire had been delivered, 52 questionnaires had been returned. This represented 16 per cent of families whose children attended the school. At the start of the next week a follow-up letter was delivered by hand to all parents. This thanked those who had already responded and encouraged those parents who had yet to return their completed questionnaire to do so. After this, the rate at which questionnaires were returned increased. By the end of the second week 126 questionnaires had been returned, representing a 38 per cent response rate. By the last day for receipt of questionnaires specified in the covering letter, 161 had been returned, increasing the response rate to 48 per cent. However, an additional 41 questionnaires were received after this deadline, resulting in an overall response rate of 60 per cent. The administration of the questionnaire had taken over four weeks from the pre-survey contact letter to the receipt of the last completed questionnaire.

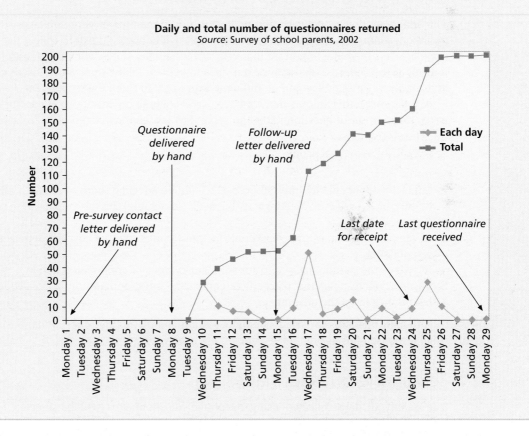

Daily and total number of questionnaires returned
Source: Survey of school parents, 2002

3 Post the survey with a covering letter and a return envelope (and fax cover sheet). You should make sure that this will arrive when recipients are likely to be receptive. For most organisations Fridays and days surrounding major public holidays have been shown to be a poor time.

4 Post (or email) the first follow-up one week after posting out the survey to all recipients. For posted questionnaires this should take the form of a postcard designed to thank early respondents and to remind rather than to persuade non-respondents.

5 Post the second follow-up to people who have not responded after three weeks. This should contain another copy of the questionnaire, a new return envelope and a new covering letter. The covering letter should be reworded to emphasise further the importance of completing the questionnaire. For anonymous questionnaires a second follow-up will not be possible, as you should not be able to tell who has responded!

6 Also use a third follow-up if time allows or your response rate is low. For this it may be possible to use recorded delivery (post), telephone calls or even call in person to emphasise the importance of responding.

Additionally, deVaus (2002) advises placing a unique identification number on each questionnaire, which is recorded on your list of recipients. This makes it easy to check and follow up non-respondents and, according to Dillman (2007) and Edwards *et al.* (2002), has little, if any, effect on response rates. However, identification numbers should not be used if you have assured respondents that their replies will be anonymous!

Delivery and collection questionnaires

The administration of delivery and collection questionnaires is very similar to that of postal questionnaires. However, you or field staff will deliver and call to collect the questionnaire. It is therefore important that your covering letter states when the questionnaire is likely to be collected. As with postal questionnaires, follow-ups can be used, calling at a variety of times of day and on different days to try to catch the respondent.

A variation on this process that we have used widely in organisations allows for delivery and collection of questionnaires the same day and eliminates the need for a follow-up. The stages are:

1 Ensure that all questionnaires and covering letters are printed and a collection box is ready.

2 Contact respondents by internal post or telephone advising them to attend a meeting or one of a series of meetings to be held (preferably) in the organisation's time (Section 6.3).

3 At the meeting or meetings, hand out the questionnaire with a covering letter to each respondent.

4 Introduce the questionnaire and stress its anonymous or confidential nature.

5 Ensure that respondents place their completed questionnaires in a collection box before they leave the meeting.

Although this adds to costs, as employees are completing the questionnaire in work time, response rates as high as 98 per cent are achievable!

Telephone questionnaires

The quality of data collected using telephone questionnaires will be affected by the researcher's competence to conduct interviews. This is discussed in Section 10.5. Once your sample has been selected, you need to:

1 ensure that all questionnaires are printed or, for CATI, that the software has been programmed and tested;

2 where possible and resources allow, contact respondents by post, email or telephone advising them to expect a telephone call (Section 6.3);

3 telephone each respondent, recording the date and time of call and whether or not the questionnaire was completed. You should note any specific times that have been arranged for call-backs. For calls that were not successful you should note the reason, such as no reply or telephone disconnected;

4 for unsuccessful calls where there was no reply, try three more times, each at a different time and on a different day, and note the same information;

5 make call-back calls at the time arranged.

Structured interviews

Conducting structured interviews uses many of the skills required for in-depth and semi-structured interviews (Section 10.5). Issues such as interviewer appearance and preparedness are important and will affect the response rate (Section 10.4). However, once your sample has been selected you need to:

1 ensure that all questionnaires are printed or, for CAPI, that the software has been programmed and tested;

2 contact respondents by post, email or telephone advising them to expect an interviewer to call within the next week. This stage is often omitted for cost reasons;

3 (for large-scale surveys) divide the sample into assignments that are of a manageable size (50–100) for one interviewer;

4 contact each respondent or potential respondent in person, recording the date and time of contact and whether or not the interview was completed. You should note down any specific times that have been arranged for return visits. For contacts that were not successful, you should note down the reason;

5 try unsuccessful contacts at least twice more, each at a different time and on a different day, and note down the same information;

6 visit respondents at the times arranged for return visits.

11.6 Summary

- Questionnaires collect data by asking people to respond to exactly the same set of questions. They are often used as part of a survey strategy to collect descriptive and explanatory data about opinions, behaviours and attributes. Data collected are normally analysed by computer.

- Your choice of questionnaire will be influenced by your research question(s) and objectives and the resources that you have available. The five main types are Internet- or intranet-mediated, postal, delivery and collection, telephone and interview schedule.

- Prior to designing a questionnaire, you must know precisely what data you need to collect to answer your research question(s) and to meet your objectives. One way of helping to ensure that you collect these data is to use a data requirements table.

- The validity and reliability of the data you collect and the response rate you achieve depend largely on the design of your questions, the structure of your questionnaire, and the rigour of your pilot testing.

- When designing your questionnaire you should consider the wording of individual questions prior to the order in which they appear. Questions can be divided into open and closed. The six types of closed questions are list, category, ranking, rating, quantity and matrix.

- Wherever possible, closed questions should be pre-coded on your questionnaire to facilitate data input and subsequent analyses.

- The order and flow of questions in the questionnaire should be logical to the respondent. This can be assisted by filter questions and linking phrases.

- The questionnaire should be laid out so that it is easy to read and the responses are easy to fill in.
- Questionnaires must be introduced carefully to the respondent to ensure a high response rate. For self-administered questionnaires this should take the form of a covering letter; for interviewer-administered questions it will be done by the interviewer.
- All questionnaires should be pilot tested prior to their administration to assess the validity and likely reliability of the questions.
- Administration of questionnaires needs to be appropriate to the type of questionnaire.

Self-check questions

Help with these questions is available at the end of the chapter.

11.1 In what circumstances would you choose to use a delivery and collection questionnaire rather than a postal questionnaire? Give reasons for your answer.

11.2 The following questions have been taken from a questionnaire about flexibility of labour.

    i Do you agree or disagree with the use of nil hours contracts by employers?

             Strongly agree ❏$_4$

    (Please tick appropriate box)   Agree ❏$_3$

             Disagree ❏$_2$

           Strongly disagree ❏$_1$

    ii Have you ever been employed on a nil hours contract?   Yes ❏$_1$

    (Please tick appropriate box)   No ❏$_2$

           Not sure ❏$_3$

    iii What is your marital status?   Single ❏$_1$

    (Please tick appropriate box)   Married or living in long-term relationship ❏$_2$

           Widowed ❏$_3$

           Divorced ❏$_4$

           Other ❏$_5$
    .... (⇐ Please describe)

    iv Please describe what you think would be the main impact on employees of a nil hours contract.

    For each question identify:
    a the type of data variable for which data are being collected;
    b the type of question.
    You should give reasons for your answers.

11.3 You are undertaking research on the use of children's book clubs by householders within mainland Europe. As part of this, you have already undertaken in-depth interviews with households who belong and do not belong to children's book clubs. This, along with a literature review, has suggested a number of investigative questions from which you start to construct a table of data requirements.

    a For each investigative question listed, decide whether you will need to collect data on opinions, behaviours or attributes.

Research question/objective: *To establish mainland Europe's householders' opinions about children's book clubs*			
Type of research: *Predominantly descriptive, although wish to explain differences between householders*			
Investigative questions	**Variable(s) required**	**Detail in which data measured**	**Check measurement question included in questionnaire ✓**
a *Do householders think that children's book clubs are a good or a bad idea?*			
b *What things do householders like most about children's book clubs?*			
c *Would householders be interested in an all-ages book club?*			
d *How much per year do households spend on children's books?*			
e *Do households' responses differ depending on: (i) number of children? (ii) whether already members of a children's book club?*			

   b Complete the table of data requirements for each of the investigative questions already listed. (You may embellish the scenario to help in your choice of variables required and how the data will be measured as you feel necessary.)

11.4 Design pre-coded or self-coded questions to collect data for each of the investigative questions in self-check question 11.3. Note that you will need to answer self-check question 11.3 first (or use the answer at the end of this chapter).

11.5 What issues will you need to consider when translating your questionnaire?

11.6 You work for a major consumer research bureau that has been commissioned by 11 major UK companies to design and administer a telephone questionnaire. The purpose of this questionnaire is to describe and explain relationships between adult consumers' lifestyles, opinions and purchasing intentions. Write the introduction to this telephone questionnaire, to be read by an interviewer to each respondent. You may embellish the scenario and include any other relevant information you wish.

11.7 You have been asked by a well-known national charity 'Work for All' to carry out research into the effects of long-term unemployment throughout the UK. The charity intends to use the findings of this research as part of a major campaign to highlight public awareness about the effects of long-term unemployment. The charity has drawn up a list of names and addresses of people who are or were long-term unemployed with whom they have had contact over the past six months. Write a covering letter to accompany the postal questionnaire. You may embellish the scenario and include any other relevant information you wish.

11.8 You have been asked to give a presentation to a group of managers at an oil exploration company to gain access to undertake your research. As part of the presentation you outline your methodology, which includes piloting the questionnaire. In the ensuing question and answer session one of the managers asks you to justify the need for a pilot study, arguing that 'given the time constraints the pilot can be left out'. List the arguments that you would use to convince him that pilot testing is essential to your methodology'.

Review and discussion questions

11.9 If you wish for more help with designing questionnaires, visit the website http:www.statpac.com/surveys/ and download and work through the tutorial 'Designing Surveys and Questionnaires'.

11.10 Obtain a copy of a 'customer questionnaire' from a department store or restaurant. For each question on the questionnaire establish whether it is collecting data about opinions, behaviours or attributes. Do you consider any of the questions are potentially misleading? If yes, how do you think the question could be improved? Discuss the answer to these questions in relation to your questionnaire with a friend.

11.11 Visit the website of an online questionnaire provider. A selection of possible providers can be found by typing 'online questionnaire provider' or 'online survey provider' into the Google search engine. Use the online software to design a simple questionnaire. To what extent does the questionnaire you have designed meet the requirements of the checklists in Boxes 11.11, 11.13 and 11.15?

11.12 Visit your university library or use the Internet to view a copy of a report for a recent national government survey in which you are interested. If you are using the Internet, the national government websites listed in Table 8.3 are a good place to start. Check the appendices in the report to see if a copy of the questionnaire used to collect the data is included. Of the types of question – open, list, category, ranking, rating, quantity and grid – which is most used and which is least frequently used? Note down any that may be of use to you in your research project.

Progressing your research project

Using questionnaires in your research

- Return to your research question(s) and objectives. Decide on how appropriate it would be to use questionnaires as part of your research strategy. If you do decide that this is appropriate, note down the reasons why you think it will be sensible to collect at least some of your data in this way. If you decide that using a questionnaire is not appropriate, justify your decision.

- If you decide that using a questionnaire is appropriate, re-read Chapter 7 on sampling and, in conjunction with this chapter, decide which of the five types of questionnaire will be most appropriate. Note down your choice of questionnaire and the reasons for this choice.

- Construct a data requirements table and work out precisely what data you need to answer your investigative questions. Remember that you will need to relate your investigative questions and data requirements back to the literature you have reviewed and any preliminary research you have already undertaken.

- Design the separate questions to collect the data specified in your data requirements table. Wherever possible, try to use closed questions and to adhere to the suggestions in the question wording checklist. If you are intending to analyse your questionnaire by computer, read Section 12.2 and pre-code questions on the questionnaire whenever possible.
- Order your questions to make reading the questions and filling in the responses as logical as possible to the respondent. Wherever possible, try to adhere to the checklist for layout. Remember that interviewer-administered questionnaires will need instructions for the interviewer.
- Write the introduction to your questionnaire and, where appropriate, a covering letter.
- Pilot test your questionnaire with as similar a group as possible to the final group in your sample. Pay special attention to issues of validity and reliability.
- Administer your questionnaire and remember to send out a follow-up survey to non-respondents whenever possible.

References

Bell, J. (2005) *Doing Your Research Project* (4th edn). Buckingham: Open University Press.

Bourque, L.B. and Clark, V.A. (1994) 'Processing data: the survey example', in M.S. Lewis-Beck *Research Practice*. London: Sage, pp. 1–88.

Coomber, R. (1997) 'Using the Internet for survey research', *Sociological Research Online*, Vol. 2, No. 2. Available at: http://www.socresonline.org.uk/socresonline/2/2/2.html [Accessed 20 April 2008.]

Cooper, D.R. and Schindler, P.S. (2008) *Business Research Methods*, (10th edn). Boston, MA and Burr Ridge, IL: McGraw-Hill.

Corbetta, P. (2003) *Social Research: Theory, Methods and Techniques.* London: Sage.

deVaus, D.A. (2002) *Surveys in Social Research.* (5th edn). London: Routledge.

Dillman, D.A. (2007) *Mail and Internet Surveys: The Tailored Design Method* (2nd edn). Hoboken, NJ: Wiley.

Edwards, P., Roberts, I., Clarke, M., Di Giuseppe, C., Pratap, S., Wentz, R., and Kwan, I. (2002) 'Increasing response rates to postal questionnaires: systematic review', *British Medical Journal,* No. 324, May, pp. 1183–91.

Field, A. (2005) *Discovering Statistics Using SPSS* (2nd edn). London: Sage.

Fink, A. (2003a) *How to Ask Survey Questions.* (2nd edn). Thousand Oaks, CA: Sage.

Fink, A. (2003b) *The Survey Handbook.* (2nd edn). Thousand Oaks, CA: Sage.

Foddy, W. (1994) *Constructing Questions for Interviews and Questionnaires.* Cambridge: Cambridge University Press.

Gay, G., Schelluch, P. and Baines, A. (1998) 'Perceptions of messages conveyed by review and audit reports', *Accounting, Auditing and Accountability Journal,* Vol. 11, No. 4, pp. 472–94.

Ghauri, P. and Grønhaug, K. (2005) *Research Methods in Business Studies: A Practical Guide* (3rd edn). Harlow: Financial Times Prentice Hall.

Gill, J. and Johnson, P. (2002) *Research Methods for Managers* (3rd edn). London: Paul Chapman.

Hewson, C., Yule, P., Laurent, D. and Vogel, C. (2003) *Internet Research Methods: A Practical Guide for the Social and Behavioural Sciences.* London: Sage.

Jankowicz, A.D. (2005) *Business Research Projects* (4th edn). London: Thomson Learning.

Lavrakas, P.J. (1993) *Telephone Survey Methods: Sampling, Selection and Supervision.* Newbury Park, CA: Sage.

Miller, D.C. and Salkind, N.J. (eds) (2002) *Handbook of Research Design and Social Measurement* (6th edn). Thousand Oaks, CA: Sage.

Mitchell, V. (1996) 'Assessing the reliability and validity of questionnaires: an empirical example', *Journal of Applied Management Studies,* Vol. 5, No. 2, pp. 199–207.

Nando's (2008) 'Talk to us'. Available at: http://www.nandos.co.uk/faq/CU/Contact_Us.html# [Accessed 27 April 2008.]

Oppenheim, A.N. (2000) *Questionnaire Design, Interviewing and Attitude Measurement* (new edn). London: Continuum International.

Robson, C. (2002) *Real World Research* (2nd edn). Oxford: Blackwell.

Rogelberg, S.G. and Stanton, J.M. (2007) 'Understanding and dealing with organizational survey nonresponse', *Organizational Research Methods*, Vol. 10. pp. 195–208.

Rose, D. and Pevalin, D.J. (2003) 'The NS-SEC explained', in D. Rose and D.J. Pevalin (eds) *A Researcher's Guide to the National Statistics Socio-economic Classification*. London: Sage, pp. 28–43.

Schrauf, R.W. and Navarro, E. (2005) 'Using existing tests and scales in the field', *Field Methods,* Vol. 17, No. 4, pp. 373–93.

Snap Surveys (2008) 'Snap Surveys: The complete survey solution'. Available at: http://www.snapsurveys.com [Accessed 20 April 2008.]

Sphinx Development (2008) 'Sphinx Development'. Available at: http://www.sphinxdevelopment.co.uk/ [Accessed 20 April 2008.]

SurveyMonkey.com (2008) SurveyMonkey.com. Available at: http://www.surveymonkey.com [Accessed 20 April 2008.]

Taylor, B. (2007) 'More poll questions than answers'. Available at: http://news.bbc.co.uk/1/hi/scotland/6264483.stm [Accessed 14 April 2008.]

Tharenou, P., Donohue, R. and Cooper, B. (2007) *Management Research Methods.* Melbourne: Cambridge University Press.

Thompson and Surface (2007) 'Employee surveys administered online – attitudes to the medium, non-response, and data representativeness', *Organizational Research Methods*, Vol. 10, No. 2, pp. 241–61.

Usunier, J.-C. (1998) *International and Cross-Cultural Management Research*. London: Sage.

Witmer, D.F., Colman, R.W. and Katzman, S.L. (1999) 'From paper and pen to screen and keyboard: Towards a methodology for survey research on the Internet', in S. Jones (ed.) *Doing Internet Research*. Thousand Oaks, CA: Sage, pp. 145–62.

Further reading

deVaus, D.A. (2002) *Surveys in Social Research* (5th edn). London: Routledge. Chapters 7 and 8 provide a detailed guide to constructing and administering questionnaires, respectively.

Dillman, D.A. (2007) *Mail and Internet Surveys: The Tailored Design Method* (2nd edn). Hoboken, NJ: Wiley. The updated second edition of this classic text contains an extremely detailed and well-researched discussion of how to design postal and Internet-based questionnaires to maximise response rates. The new appendix is particularly helpful regarding recent developments.

Foddy, W. (1994) *Constructing Questions for Interviews and Questionnaires*. Cambridge: Cambridge University Press. This contains a wealth of information on framing questions, including the use of scaling techniques.

Hewson, C., Yule, P., Laurent, D. and Vogel, C. (2003) *Internet Research Methods: A Practical Guide for the Social and Behavioural Sciences.* London: Sage. Chapter 3 offers a useful overview of Internet-mediated research, including a discussion of questionnaires, whilst Chapter 5 discusses design issues concerned with Internet-mediated questionnaires.

Case 11
Downsizing in the Middle East

Amman, Jordan
Source: ©2008 Mohammad Al Kilani

As an overseas student, Zaid Kilani chose to research downsizing in his home country in the Middle East. He was encouraged by his tutor to research downsizing in a non-Western context. Zaid decided to investigate how employees perceive the downsizing process. To delimit his research project, he decided to focus on one downsizing method that is used in downsizing the civil service in his home country. Further, he focused on one aspect of employees' perception, which was fairness of the downsizing process.

Zaid undertook his research from a positivistic philosophical stance. He conducted a thorough review of the literature, stated his research aims, and formed hypotheses that could be tested statistically. The required data were to be collected via self-administered postal questionnaire, which he wished to send to a sample of the total population of the of 2800 ex-civil servants.

A list of these ex-civil servants that included their names, ex-employers, and other details were provided by the Civil Service Bureau in his home country. Unfortunately, no contact details were available. One possible way to overcome this obstacle could have been to contact their previous employers and ask them for the contact details. However, this was deemed unethical as he would be requesting personal details. The alternative, which Zaid adopted, was to search for the ex-employees' names in the general telephone book, contact them by telephone, ask for their informed consent to participate, and, if they accepted, ask for their convenient postal address. Zaid realised that a further obstacle was that as an unknown male, even though he was a researcher, it would not be tolerable for him to contact female respondents and ask for such information. He, therefore, assigned a female assistant to contact female respondents. To facilitate the process of searching for telephone numbers, Zaid purchased an electronic copy of the general telephone book, enabling him to search using a computer.

As Arabic is the first language in Zaid's home country, it was prudent to translate the questionnaire into Arabic to minimise the possibility of non-response due to language difficulties. To fulfil this object, he decided to follow Usunier's (1998) suggestion and used parallel translation. This involved having several independent translations from English to Arabic, comparing the translated versions, and subsequently arriving at a final version in Arabic. As Zaid is an Arabic native, he felt this would help to ensure that the specific meanings included in his questionnaire were fully rendered in the Arabic version.

To translate the questionnaire by using the parallel-translation technique, two Arabic native translators were appointed. One of the translators had an MBA degree while the other had a Bachelor degree in business administration. Each of them had experience in translation from English to Arabic and back while working with his home country's civil service. Zaid provided each of the translators with a copy of the English version of the questionnaire and its covering letter to translate independently into Arabic. Subsequently, the translators and Zaid had a meeting to discuss the translated versions question by question. The Arabic version was prepared after minor differences between the two translated questionnaires were found and then reconciled. The differences pertained to the expressions 'job' and 'civil servant'. The word 'job' has several equivalents, so the translators and the author agreed on the most appropriate word. In addition, the expression 'civil servant' may imply inferiority in Arabic. For this reason, the term 'civil employee' was used. For language-gender considerations, two versions of the covering letters were prepared: one to address female respondents and the other to address male respondents. Afterwards, the Arabic version of the questionnaire and its covering letter were piloted.

Date

Title and name of respondent

Address of respondent

Dear respondent name,

Participating in a survey

I am a student in the UK. The topic I am researching is the attitudes of civil servants who were downsized. I enclose a questionnaire, which asks for your views about the topic.

You are one of a sample of 843 civil servants who were downsized. You were selected randomly from a list of all the civil servants' names who were downsized. This list was obtained from the Civil Service Bureau.

The questionnaire forms a major part of my research, and I would value it highly if you would agree to participate by filling it in. In giving your views, you will also help to further my understanding about the downsizing process.

I must emphasise that your participation is entirely voluntary, and it is up to you to decide whether or not you wish to take part.

Let me assure you that all the information that you provide will be dealt with anonymously and confidentially, and will only be used for purpose of this study. I will ensure that the data collected from you and others are stored electronically at the University and are password protected. It will be kept for a minimum of five years.

Please complete the questionnaire and return it in the enclosed stamped, addressed envelope by [a date, give them about a week or 10 days].

Should you have any query, please contact me on my mobile 0712 345 678 910, or the daytime landline 0987 654 321 000.

This research has been reviewed by the University Research Ethics Committee at the University of Anytown. If you have any concerns about the conduct of this research, please contact the Chair of the committee on ethics@anytown.ac.uk or telephone the Secretary to the committee on 012345555555.

I am grateful for your kindness, and thank you for your generous help in completing this questionnaire to help me with my postgraduate research.

Yours faithfully

Zaid

Student at the University of Anytown

Questions

1 What are the possible disadvantages of the way that Zaid used to contact respondent?
2 Outline the possible disadvantages of using a parallel translation technique?
3 You have been asked to comment on the covering letter that Zaid prepared. What are your suggestions to improve this covering letter?

Additional case studies relating to material covered in this chapter are available via the book's Companion Website, **www.pearsoned.co.uk/saunders**. They are:

- The provision of leisure activities for younger people in rural areas
- Job satisfaction in an Australian organisation
- Service quality in health-care supply chains.

Self-check answers

11.1 When you:
- wanted to check that the person whom you wished to answer the questions had actually answered the questions;
- have sufficient resources to devote to delivery and collection and the geographical area over which the questionnaire is administered is small;
- can use field workers to enhance response rates. Delivery and collection questionnaires have a moderately high response rate of between 30 and 50 per cent compared with 30 per cent offered on average by a postal questionnaire;
- are administering a questionnaire to an organisation's employees and require a very high response rate. By administering the questionnaire to groups of employees in work time and collecting it on completion, response rates of up to 98 per cent can be achieved.

11.2 **a i** Opinion data: the question is asking how the respondent *feels* about the use of nil hours contracts by employees.
  ii Behaviour data: the question is asking about the *concrete experience* of being employed on a nil hours contract.
  iii Attribute data: the question is asking about the respondent's *characteristics*.
  iv Opinion data: the question is asking the respondent what they *think* or *believe* would be the impact on employees.
  b i Rating question using a Likert-type scale in which the respondent is asked how strongly they agree or disagree with the statement.
  ii Category question in which the respondent's answer can fit only one answer.
  iii Category question as before.
  iv Open question in which the respondent can answer in their own way.

11.3 Although your answer is unlikely to be precisely the same, the completed table of data requirements below should enable you to check you are on the right lines.

Research question/objective: To establish householders' opinions about children's book clubs			
Type of research: Predominantly descriptive, although wish to explain differences between householders			
Investigative questions	**Variable(s) required**	**Detail in which data measured**	**Check measurement question included in questionnaire ✓**
Do householders think that children's book clubs are a good or a bad idea? (opinion – this is because you are really asking how householders feel)	Opinion about children's book clubs	Very good idea, good idea, neither a good nor a bad idea, bad idea, very bad idea	
What things do householders like most about children's book clubs? (opinion)	What householders like about children's book clubs	Get them to rank the following things (generated from earlier in-depth interviews): monthly magazine, lower prices, credit, choice, special offers, shopping at home	
Would householders be interested in an all-ages book club? (behaviour)	Interest in a book club which was for both adults and children	Interested, not interested, may be interested	
How much per year do households spend on children's books? (behaviour)	Amount spent on children's books by adults and children per year by household	(Answers to the nearest €) €0 to €10, €11 to €20, €21 to €30, €31 to €50, €51 to €100, over €100	
Do households' responses differ depending on: • *Number of children?* (attribute) • *Whether already members of a children's book club?* (behaviour)	Number of children aged under 16 Children's book club member	Actual number Yes, no	

11.4 a Please complete the following statement by ticking the phrase that matches your feelings most closely . . .

I feel children's book clubs are . . . . . . a very good idea $\square_5$

. . . a good idea $\square_4$

. . . neither a good nor a bad idea $\square_3$

. . . a bad idea $\square_2$

. . . a very bad idea $\square_1$

b Please number each of the features of children's book clubs listed below in order of how much you like them. Number the most important 1, the next 2 and so on. The feature you like the least should be given the highest number.

Feature	How much liked
Monthly magazine	⊔
Lower prices	⊔
Credit	⊔
Choice	⊔
Special offers	⊔
Shopping at home	⊔

c Would you be interested in a book club that was for both adults and children?
(Please tick the appropriate box)   Yes $\square_1$

No $\square_2$

Not sure $\square_3$

d How much money is spent in total each year on children's books by all the adults and children living in your household?
(Please tick the appropriate box)   €0 to €10 $\square_1$

€11 to €20 $\square_2$

€21 to €30 $\square_3$

€31 to €50 $\square_4$

€51 to €100 $\square_5$

Over €100 $\square_6$

e i. How many children aged under 16 are living in your household?
☐ children
(For example, for 3 write:)   3 children

ii. Is any person living in your household a member of a children's book club?
(Please tick the appropriate box)   Yes $\square_1$

No $\square_2$

11.5 When translating your questionnaire you will need to ensure that:
- the precise meaning of individual words is kept (lexical equivalence);
- the meanings of groups of words and phrases that are natural to a native speaker but cannot be translated literally are kept (idiomatic equivalence);
- the correct grammar and syntax are used.

In addition, you should, if possible, use back translation, parallel translation or mixed translation techniques to ensure that there are no differences between the source and the target questionnaire.

11.6 Although the precise wording of your answer is likely to differ, it would probably be something like this:

Good morning/afternoon/evening. My name is ____ from JJ Consumer Research. We are doing an important national survey covering lifestyles, opinions and likely future purchases of adult consumers. Your telephone number has been selected at random. The questions I need to ask you will take about 15 minutes. If you have any queries I shall be happy to answer them (*pause*). Before I continue please can you confirm that this is (*read out telephone number including dialling code*) and that I am talking to a person aged 18 or over. Please can I ask you the first question now?

11.7 Although the precise wording of your answer is likely to differ, it would probably be something like the letter below.

Work for All

Registered charity No: 123456789

B&J Market Research Ltd
St Richard's House
Malvern
Worcestershire WR14 12Z
Phone 01684–56789101
Fax 01684–56789102

Respondent's name

Respondent's address

Email andy@b&jmarketresearch.co.uk

Today's date

Dear *title name*

Work for All is conducting research into the effects of long-term unemployment. This is an issue of great importance within the UK and yet little is currently known about the consequences.

You are one of a small number of people who are being asked to give your opinion on this issue. You were selected at random from Work for All's list of contacts. In order that the results will truly represent people who have experienced long-term unemployment, it is important that your questionnaire is completed and returned.

All the information you give us will be totally confidential. You will notice that your name and address do not appear on the questionnaire and that there is no identification number. The results of this research will be passed to Work for All, who will be mounting a major campaign in the New Year to highlight public awareness about the effects of long-term unemployment.

If you have any questions you wish to ask or there is anything you wish to discuss please do not hesitate to telephone me, or my assistant Benjamin Marks, on 01684–56789101 during the day. You can call me at home on 01234–123456789 evenings and weekends. Thank you for your help.

Yours sincerely

Andy Nother

Mr Andy Nother

Project Manager

11.8 Despite the time constraints, pilot testing is essential to your methodology for the following reasons:
- to find out how long the questionnaire takes to complete;
- to check that respondents understand and can follow the instructions on the questionnaire (including filter questions);
- to ensure that all respondents understand the wording of individual questions in the same way and that there are no unclear or ambiguous questions;
- to ensure that you have the same understanding of the wording of individual questions as the respondents;
- to check that respondents have no problems in answering questions; for example:
  - all possible answers are covered in list questions;
  - whether there are any questions that respondents feel uneasy about answering;
- to discover whether there are any major topic omissions;
- to provide an idea of the validity of the questions that are being asked;

- to provide an idea of the reliability of the questions by checking responses from individual respondents to similar questions;
- to check that the layout appears clear and attractive;
- to provide limited test data so you can check that the proposed analyses will work.

Get ahead using resources on the Companion Website at:
www.pearsoned.co.uk/saunders

- Improve your SPSS and NVivo research analysis with practice tutorials.
- Save time researching on the Internet with the Smarter Online Searching Guide.
- Test your progress using self-assessment questions.
- Follow live links to useful websites.

Chapter 12

Analysing quantitative data

12.1 Introduction

Quantitative data in a raw form, that is, before these data have been processed and analysed, convey very little meaning to most people. These data, therefore, need to be processed to make them useful, that is, to turn them into information. Quantitative analysis techniques such as graphs, charts and statistics allow us to do this; helping us to explore, present, describe and examine relationships and trends within our data.

Virtually any business and management research you undertake is likely to involve some numerical data or contain data that could usefully be quantified to help you answer your research question(s) and to meet your objectives. **Quantitative data** refer to all such data and can be a product of all research strategies (Section 5.3). It can range from simple counts such as the frequency of occurrences to more complex data such as test scores, prices or rental costs. To be useful these data need to be analysed and interpreted. Quantitative analysis techniques assist you in this process. They range from creating simple tables or diagrams that show the frequency of occurrence and using statistics such as indices to enable comparisons, through establishing statistical relationships between variables to complex statistical modelling.

Until the advent of powerful personal computers, data were analysed either by hand or by using mainframe computers. The former of these was extremely time consuming and prone to error, the latter expensive. Fortunately, the by-hand or calculator 'number-crunching' and 'charting' elements of quantitative analysis have been incorporated into relatively inexpensive personal-computer-based analysis software. These range from spreadsheets such as Excel™ to more advanced data management and statistical analysis software packages such as Minitab™, SAS™, SPSS for Windows™ and Statview™. They also include more specialised survey design and analysis packages such as SNAP™ and SphinxSurvey™. Consequently, it is no longer necessary for you to be able to draw presentation-quality diagrams or to calculate statistics by hand as these can be done using a computer. However, if your analyses are to be straightforward and of any value you need to:

- have prepared your data with quantitative analyses in mind;
- be aware of and know when to use different charting and statistical techniques.

For prospective students, the cost of living is an important aspect in their choice of where to study, these costs varying markedly between different university towns and cities. Quantitative analysis techniques can help make sense of the thousands of pieces of data needed to work out a typical student's living costs. One such analysis conducted by the organisation Push (2007) in conjunction with Costcutter is the student living costs index. This uses data relating to 136 UK universities and colleges about student housing costs (collected by questionnaires and 'visits'), grocery costs (collected for a specified basket of goods as purchased from the branch of Costcutter nearest to the university's main address) and drink costs (collected by 'visits' to the student bar and a local public house). The index gave the average weekly student living cost at each of the UK's universities and colleges (£119.52 in 2007) the value of 100. Those universities and colleges with a weekly student living cost closest to this average in 2007 were the University of Chester (index = 99.6) and the University College for the Creative Arts (index = 100.4). The university with the lowest student living

Student accommodation in Birmingham
Source: © Mark Saunders 2008

cost index was Bradford (index = 73.0), where costs were 73 per cent of the average. In contrast, the index for the Royal Academy of Music, which had the highest weekly student living cost was 168.2, 68 per cent higher than the average. Push's index allows easy comparisons between the UK's universities and colleges.

Robson (2002:393) summarises this, arguing that quantitative data analysis is:

> . . . a field where it is not at all difficult to carry out an analysis which is simply wrong, or inappropriate for your purposes. And the negative side of readily available analysis software is that it becomes that much easier to generate elegantly presented rubbish.

He also emphasises the need to seek advice regarding statistical analyses, a sentiment that we support strongly.

This chapter builds on the ideas outlined in earlier chapters about data collection. It assumes that you will use a personal computer (with at least a spreadsheet) to undertake all but the most simple quantitative analyses. Although it does not focus on one particular piece of analysis software, you will notice in the Focus on Student Research boxes that many of the analyses were undertaken using widely available software such as Excel and SPSS. If you wish to develop your skills in either of these software packages, self-teach packages are available via our companion website. In addition, there are numerous statistics books already published that concentrate on specific software packages. These include Dancey and Reidy (2008), Field (2005) or Kinnear and Gray (2007) on SPSS, and Morris (2003) or Curwin and Slater (2007) on Excel. Likewise, this chapter does not attempt to provide an in-depth discussion of the wide range of graphical and statistical techniques available or to cover more complex statistical modelling, as these are already covered elsewhere (e.g. Dancey and Reidy 2008; Hair *et al.* 2006; Everitt and Dunn 2001; Hays 1994; Henry 1995). Rather it discusses issues that need to be considered at the planning and analysis stages of your research project, and outlines analytical techniques that our students have found to be of most use. In particular, the chapter is concerned with:

- preparing, inputting into a computer and checking your data (Section 12.2);
- choosing the most appropriate tables and diagrams to explore and present your data (Section 12.3);
- choosing the most appropriate statistics to describe your data (Section 12.4);
- choosing the most appropriate statistics to examine relationships and trends in your data (Section 12.5).

12.2 Preparing, inputting and checking data

If you intend to undertake quantitative analysis we recommend that you consider the:

- type of data (scale of measurement);
- format in which your data will be input to the analysis software;
- impact of data coding on subsequent analyses (for different data types);
- need to weight cases;
- methods you intend to use to check data for errors.

Ideally, all of these should be considered before obtaining your data. This is equally important for both primary and secondary data analysis, although you obviously have far greater control over the type, format and coding of primary data. We shall now consider each of these.

Data types

Many business statistics textbooks classify quantitative data into *data types* using a hierarchy of measurement, often in ascending order of numerical precision (Berman Brown and

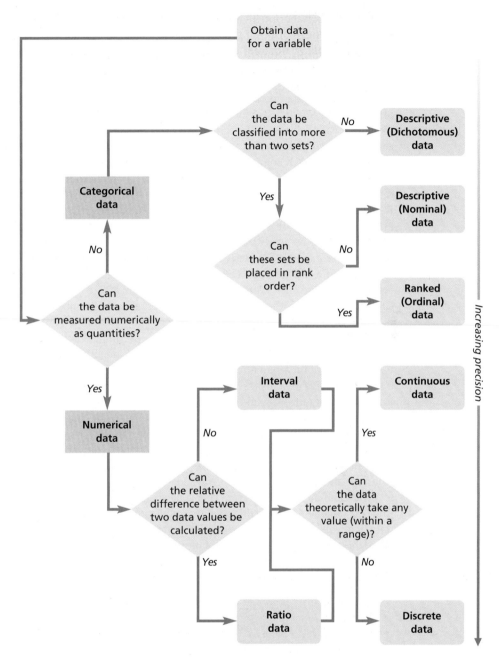

Figure 12.1 Defining the data type

Saunders 2008; Dancey and Reidy 2008). These different levels of numerical measurement dictate the range of techniques available to you for the presentation, summary and analysis of your data. They are discussed in more detail in subsequent sections of this chapter.

Quantitative data can be divided into two distinct groups: categorical and numerical (Figure 12.1). **Categorical data** refer to data whose values cannot be measured numerically but can be either classified into sets (categories) according to the characteristics that identify or describe the variable or placed in rank order (Berman Brown and Saunders 2008).

They can be further sub-divided into descriptive and ranked. A car manufacturer might categorise the types of cars it produces as hatchback, saloon and estate. These are known as **descriptive data** or **nominal data** as it is impossible to define the category numerically or to rank it. Rather these data simply count the number of occurrences in each category of a variable. For virtually all analyses the categories should be unambiguous and discrete; in other words, having one particular feature, such as a car being a hatchback, excludes all other features for that variable. This prevents questions arising as to which category an individual case belongs. Although these data are purely descriptive, you can count them to establish which category has the most and whether cases are spread evenly between categories (Morris 2003). Some statisticians (and statistics) also separate descriptive data where there are only two categories. These are known as **dichotomous data**, as the variable is divided into two categories, such as the variable gender being divided into female and male. **Ranked** (or **ordinal**) **data** are a more precise form of categorical data. In such instances you know the relative position of each case within your data set, although the actual numerical measures (such as scores) on which the position is based are not recorded (Box 12.1). Rating or scale questions, such as where a respondent is asked to rate how strongly she or he agrees with a statement, collect ranked (ordinal) data. Despite this, some researchers argue that, where such data are likely to have similar size gaps between data values, they can be analysed as if they were numerical interval data (Blumberg *et al.* 2008).

Numerical data, which are sometimes termed 'quantifiable', are those whose values are measured or counted numerically as quantities (Berman Brown and Saunders 2008). This means that numerical data are more precise than categorical as you can assign each data value a position on a numerical scale. It also means that you can analyse these data using a far wider range of statistics. There are two possible ways of sub-dividing numerical data: into interval or ratio data and, alternatively, into continuous or discrete data (Figure 12.1). If you have **interval data** you can state the difference or 'interval' between any two data values for a particular variable, but you cannot state the relative difference. This means that values on an interval scale can meaningfully be added and subtracted, but not multiplied and divided. The Celsius temperature scale is a good example of an interval scale. Although the difference between, say, 20°C and 30°C is 10°C it does not mean that 30°C is one and a half times as warm. This is because 0°C does not represent a true zero. When it is 0°C outside, there is still some warmth, rather than none at all! In contrast, for **ratio data**, you can also calculate the relative difference or ratio between any two data values for a variable. Consequently, if a multinational company makes a profit of $300 000 000 in one year and $600 000 000 the following year, we can say that profits have doubled.

Box 12.1
Focus on student research

Scales of measurement

As part of a marketing questionnaire, Rashid asked individual customers to rank up to five features of a new product in order of importance to them. Data collected were, therefore, categorical and ranked (ordinal).

Initial analyses made use of these ranked data. Unfortunately, a substantial minority of customers had ticked, rather than ranked, those features of importance to them.

All responses that had been ranked originally were therefore recoded to 'of some importance'. This reduced the precision of measurement from ranked (ordinal) to descriptive (nominal) but enabled Rashid to use all responses in the subsequent analyses.

Continuous data are those whose values can theoretically take any value (sometimes within a restricted range) provided that you can measure them accurately enough (Dancey and Reidy 2008). Data such as furnace temperature, delivery distance and length of service are therefore continuous data. **Discrete data** can, by contrast, be measured precisely. Each case takes one of a finite number of values from a scale that measures changes in discrete units. These data are often whole numbers (**integers**) such as the number of mobile telephones manufactured or customers served. However, in some instances (e.g. UK shoe size) discrete data will include non-integer values. Definitions of discrete and continuous data are, in reality, dependent on how your data values are measured. The number of customers served by a large organisation is strictly a discrete datum as you are unlikely to get a part customer! However, for a large organisation with many customers you might treat this as a continuous datum, as the discrete measuring units are exceedingly small compared with the total number being measured.

Understanding differences between types of data is extremely important when analysing your data quantitatively, for two reasons. Firstly, it is extremely easy with analysis software to generate statistics from your data that are inappropriate for the data type and are consequently of little value (Box 12.2, overleaf). Secondly, the more precise the scale of measurement, the greater the range of analytical techniques available to you. Data that have been collected and coded using a precise numerical scale of measurement can also be regrouped to a less precise level where they can also be analysed (Box 12.1). For example, a student's score in a test could be recorded as the actual mark (discrete data) or as the position in their class (ranked data). By contrast, less precise data cannot be made more precise. Therefore, if you are not sure about the scale of measurement you require, it is usually better to collect data at the highest level of precision possible and to regroup them if necessary.

Data layout

Some primary data collection methods, such as computer-aided personal interviewing (CAPI), computer-aided telephone interviewing (CATI) and online questionnaires automatically enter and save data to a computer file at the time of collection, often using predefined codes. These data can subsequently be exported in a range of formats to ensure they are compatible with different analysis software. Survey design and analysis software such as SNAP and SphinxSurvey goes one stage further and integrates the analysis software in the same package as the questionnaire design/data input software (Snap Surveys, 2008; Sphinx, 2008). Alternatively, secondary data (Section 8.3) accessed from CD-ROMs or via the Internet can be saved to a file, removing the need for re-entering. For such data, it is often possible to specify a data layout compatible with your analysis software. For other data collection methods, you will have to prepare and enter your data for computer analysis. You therefore need to be clear about the precise data layout requirements of your analysis software.

Virtually all analysis software will accept your data if they are entered in table format. This table is called a **data matrix** (Table 12.1). Once data have been entered into your

Table 12.1 A simple data matrix

	Id	Variable 1	Variable 2	Variable 3	Variable 4
Case 1	1	27	1	2	1
Case 2	2	19	2	1	2
Case 3	3	24	2	3	1

Box 12.2
Focus on management research

Ownership structure and operating performance of acquiring firms

The relationship between ownership structures and the long-term operating profit of acquiring firms has been the subject of much work on mergers and acquisitions. Research by Yen and André (2007) published in the *Journal of Economics and Business* explores the role of governance mechanisms and deal characteristics on value creation subsequent to such mergers and acquisitions revealing that, once such factors are taken into account, the relationship between ownership and value creation is non-linear. Higher levels of ownership are associated with positive post-acquisition performance; companies with large shareholders but only between 10 per cent and 20 per cent of the voting shares, significantly under-performing compared to their peers. Based upon data relating to 287 takeovers in English origin countries excluding the United States they reveal a number of insights as to why this might be the case.

In their paper, Yen and André outline clearly the variables used in their analysis, and the level of numerical measurement recorded. The variables include:

Variable	Numerical measurement recorded
Concentration of ownership	Ranked data – more than 10% to 20%, more than 20% to 50%, more than 50%
Percentage of voting shares	Continuous data – actual percentage held by largest shareholder
Separation of ownership and cash flow rights in acquiring firm	Dichotomous data – separated, not separated
Relationship of chief executive officer to largest shareholder	Dichotomous data – related, not related
Number of directors on the board	Discrete data – actual number on the board
Legal origin of the target firm	Dichotomous data – English, not English
Initial opposition of management or the board of target firm to the deal	Dichotomous data – opposed, not opposed

analysis software, it is usually possible to save them in a format that can be read by other software. Within a data matrix, each column usually represents a separate **variable** for which you have obtained data. Each matrix row contains the variables for an individual **case**, that is, an individual unit for which data have been obtained. If your data have been collected using a survey, each row will contain the data from one survey form. Alternatively, for longitudinal data such as a company's share price over time, each row (case) might be a different time period. Secondary data that have already been stored in computer-readable form will almost always be held as a large data matrix. For such data sets you usually select the subset of variables and cases you require and save these as a separate matrix. If you are entering your own data, they are typed directly into your chosen analysis software one case (row) at a time using codes to record the data (Box 12.4). Larger data sets with more data variables and cases are recorded using larger data matrices. Although data matrices store data using one column for each variable, this may not be the same as one column for each question for data collected using surveys.

Box 12.3
Focus on student research

The implications of data types for analysis

Pierre's research was concerned with customers' satisfaction for a small hotel group of six hotels. In collecting the data he had asked 1044 customers to indicate the hotel at which they were staying when they completed their questionnaires. Each hotel was subsequently allocated a numerical code and this data entered into the computer in the variable 'Hotel':

Hotel	Code
Amsterdam	1
Antwerp	2
Eindhoven	3
Nijmegen	4
Rotterdam	5
Tilburg	6

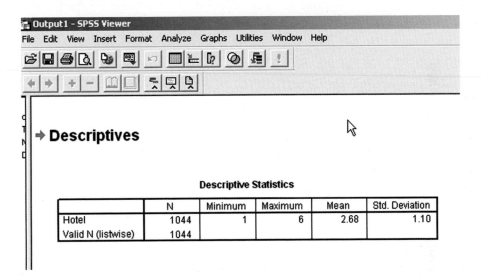

Descriptives

Descriptive Statistics

	N	Minimum	Maximum	Mean	Std. Deviation
Hotel	1044	1	6	2.68	1.10
Valid N (listwise)	1044				

In his initial analysis, Pierre used the computer to calculate descriptive statistics for every data variable including the variable 'Hotel'. These included the minimum value (the code for Amsterdam), the maximum value (the code for Tilburg), the mean and the standard deviation. Looking at his computer screen, Pierre noted that the mean (average) was 2.68 and the standard deviation was 1.10. He had forgotten that the data for this variable were categorical and, consequently, the descriptive statistics he had chosen were inappropriate.

We strongly recommend that you save your data regularly as you are entering it, to minimise the chances of deleting it all by accident! In addition, you should save a back-up or security copy on your MP3 player or other mass storage device, or burn it onto a CD.

If you intend to enter data into a spreadsheet, the first variable is in column A, the second in column B and so on. Each cell in the first row (1) should contain a short variable name to enable you to identify each variable. Subsequent rows (2 onwards) will each contain the data for one case (Box 12.4). Statistical analysis software follows the same logic, although the variable names are usually displayed 'above' the first row (Box 12.5).

Box 12.4
Focus on student research

An Excel data matrix

Lucy's data related to employees who were working or had worked for a large public sector organisation. In her Excel spreadsheet, the first variable (id) was the *survey form identifier*. This meant that she could link data for each case (row) in her matrix to the survey form when checking for errors (discussed later). The second variable (age) contained numerical data, the age of each respondent (case) at the time her questionnaire was administered. Subsequent variables contained the remaining data: the third (gender) recorded this dichotomous data using code 1 for male and 2 for female; the fourth (service) recorded numerical data about each case's length of service to the nearest year in the organisation. The final dichotomous variable (employed) recorded whether each respondent was (code 1) or was not (code 2) employed by the organisation at the time the data were collected. The codes used by Lucy, therefore, had different meanings for different variables.

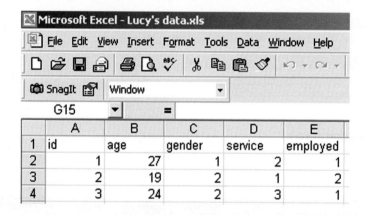

The **multiple-response method** of coding uses the same number of variables as the maximum number of different responses from any one case. For question 2 these were named 'like1', 'like2', 'like3', 'like4' and 'like5' (Box 12.5). Each of these variables would use the same codes and could include any of the responses as a category. Statistical analysis software often contains special multiple-response procedures to analyse such data. The alternative, the **multiple-dichotomy method** of coding, uses a separate variable for each different answer (Box 12.5). For question 2 (Box 12.5) a separate variable could have been used for each 'thing' listed: for example, salary, location, colleagues, hours, holidays, car and so on. You subsequently would code each variable as 'listed' or 'not listed' for each case. This makes it easy to calculate the number of responses for each 'thing' (deVaus 2002).

Coding

All data types should, with few exceptions, be recorded using numerical codes. This enables you to enter the data quickly using the numeric keypad on your keyboard and with fewer errors. It also makes subsequent analyses, in particular those that require re-coding of data to create new variables, more straightforward. Unfortunately, analyses of limited meaning are also easier, such as calculating a mean (average) gender from codes 1 and 2, or the average hotel location (Box 12.3)! A common exception to using a numerical

Box 12.5
Focus on student research

Data coding

As part of a market-research interview survey, Zack needed to discover which of four products (tomato ketchup, brown sauce, soy sauce, vinegar) had been purchased within the last month by consumers. He, therefore, needed to collect four data items from each respondent:

- Tomato ketchup purchased within the last month? Yes/No
- Brown sauce purchased within the last month? Yes/No
- Soy sauce purchased within the last month? Yes/No
- Salad dressing purchased within the last month? Yes/No

Each of these data items is a separate variable. However, the data were collected using one question:

1 Which of the following items have you purchased within the last month?

Item	Purchased	Not purchased	Not sure
Tomato ketchup	☐1	☐2	☐3
Brown sauce	☐1	☐2	☐3
Soy sauce	☐1	☐2	☐3
Salad dressing	☐1	☐2	☐3

The data Zack collected from each respondent formed four separate variables in the data matrix using numerical codes (1 = purchased, 2 = not purchased, 3 = not sure). This is known as multiple-dichotomy coding:

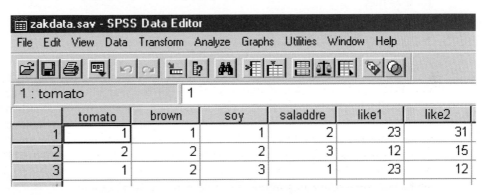

Zack also included a question (Question 2 below) that could theoretically have millions of possible responses for each of the 'things'. For such questions, the number that each respondent mentions may also vary. Our experience suggests that virtually all respondents will select five or fewer. Zack, therefore, left space to code up to five responses after data had been collected.

For office use only

2 List up to five things you like about tomato ketchup
. . . . ☐ ☐ ☐ ☐
. . . . ☐ ☐ ☐ ☐
. . . . ☐ ☐ ☐ ☐
. . . . ☐ ☐ ☐ ☐
. . . . /. . . . . ☐ ☐ ☐ ☐

code for categorical data is where a postcode is used as the code for a geographical refer-ence. If you are using a spreadsheet, you will need to keep a list of codes for each variable. Statistical analysis software can store these so that each code is automatically labelled.

Coding numerical data

Actual numbers are often used as codes for numerical data, even though this level of pre-cision may not be required. Once you have entered your data as a matrix, you can use analysis software to group or combine data to form additional variables with less detailed categories. This process is referred to as **re-coding**. For example, a Republic of Ireland's employee's salary could be coded to the nearest euro and entered into the matrix as 43543 (numerical discrete data). Later, re-coding could be used to place it in a group of similar salaries, from €40 000 to €49 999 (categorical ranked data).

Coding categorical data

Codes are often applied to categorical data with little thought, although you can design a coding scheme that will make subsequent analyses far simpler. For many secondary data sources (such as government surveys), a suitable coding scheme will have already been devised when the data were first collected. However, for some secondary and all primary data you will need to decide on a coding scheme. Prior to this, you need to establish the highest level of precision required by your analyses (Box 12.2).

Existing coding schemes can be used for many variables. These include industrial clas-sification (Great Britain Office for National Statistics 2002), occupation (Great Britain Office for National Statistics 2000a, 2000b), social class (Heath *et al.* 2003), socioeco-nomic classification (Rose and Pevalin 2003) and ethnic group (Smith 2002) as well as social attitude variables (Park *et al.* 2007). Wherever possible, we recommend you use these as they:

- save time;
- are normally well tested;
- allow comparisons of your results with other (often larger) surveys.

These codes should be included on your data collection form as **pre-set codes** provided that there are a limited number of categories (Section 11.4), and they will be understood by the person filling in the form. Even if you decide not to use an existing coding scheme, per-haps because of a lack of detail, you should ensure that your codes are still compatible. This means that you will be able to compare your data with those already collected.

Coding at data collection occurs when there is a limited range of well-established cat-egories into which the data can be placed. These are included on your data collection form, and the person filling in the form selects the correct category.

Coding after data collection is necessary when you are unclear of the likely responses or there are a large number of possible responses in the coding scheme. To ensure that the cod-ing scheme captures the variety in responses (and will work!) it is better to wait until data from the first 50 to 100 cases are available and then develop the coding scheme. This is called the **codebook** (Box 12.6). As when designing your data collection method(s) (Chapters 8, 9, 10, and 11), it is essential to be clear about the intended analyses, in particular:

- the level of precision required;
- the coding schemes used by surveys with which comparisons are to be made.

To create your codebook for each variable you:

1 examine the data and establish broad groupings;
2 sub-divide the broad groupings into increasingly specific sub-groups dependent on your intended analyses;

3 allocate codes to all categories at the most precise level of detail required;
4 note the actual responses that are allocated to each category and produce a codebook;
5 ensure that those categories that may need to be aggregated are given adjacent codes to facilitate re-coding.

Coding missing data

Each variable for each case in your data set should have a code, even if no data have been collected. The choice of code is up to you, although some statistical analysis software have a code that is used by default. A missing data code is used to indicate why data are missing. Four main reasons for missing data are identified by deVaus (2002):

- The data were not required from the respondent, perhaps because of a skip generated by a filter question in a survey.
- The respondent refused to answer the question (a **non-response**).
- The respondent did not know the answer or did not have an opinion. Sometimes this is treated as implying an answer; on other occasions it is treated as missing data.
- The respondent may have missed a question by mistake, or the respondent's answer may be unclear.

In addition, it may be that:

- leaving part of a question in a survey blank implies an answer; in such cases the data are not classified as missing (Section 11.4).

Statistical analysis software often reserves a special code for missing data. Cases with missing data can then be excluded from subsequent analyses when necessary (Box 12.6, overleaf). For some analyses it may be necessary to distinguish between reasons for missing data using different codes.

Entering data

Once your data have been coded, you can enter them into the computer. Increasingly, data analysis software contains algorithms that check the data for obvious errors as it is entered. Despite this, it is essential that you take considerable care to ensure that your data are entered correctly. When entering data the well-known maxim 'rubbish in, rubbish out' certainly applies! More sophisticated analysis software allows you to attach individual labels to each variable and the codes associated with each of them. If this is feasible, we strongly recommend that you do this. By ensuring the labels replicate the exact words used in the data collection, you will reduce the number of opportunities for misinterpretation when analysing your data. Taking this advice for the variable 'like1' in Box 12.6 would result in the variable label 'List up to three things you like about this restaurant', each value being labelled with the actual response in the coding scheme.

Checking for errors

No matter how carefully you code and subsequently enter data there will always be some errors. The main methods to check data for errors are as follows:

- Look for illegitimate codes. In any coding scheme, only certain numbers are allocated. Other numbers are, therefore, errors. Common errors are the inclusion of letters O and o instead of zero, letters l or I instead of 1, and number 7 instead of 1.

Box 12.6
Focus on student research

Creating a codebook, coding multiple responses and entering data

As part of his research project, Amil used a questionnaire to collect data from the customers of a local themed restaurant. The questionnaire included an open question which asked 'List up to three things you like about this restaurant.' The data included over 50 different 'things' that the 186 customers responding liked about the restaurant, although the maximum number mentioned by any one customer was three.

Once data had been collected, Amil devised a hierarchical coding scheme based on what the customers liked about the restaurant. Codes were allocated to each 'thing' a customer liked, as shown in the extract below.

Codes were entered into three (the maximum number customers were asked to list) variables, like1, like2 and like3 in the data matrix using the multiple-response method for coding. This meant that any response could appear in any of the three variables. When there were fewer than three responses given, the code '.' was entered in the remaining outlet variables, signifying missing data. The first customer in the extract below listed 'things' coded 11, 21 and 42, the next 3 and 21 and so on. No significance was attached to the order of variables to which responses were coded.

```
▦ Restaurant data.sav - SPSS Data Editor
File  Edit  View  Data  Transform  Analyze  Graphs  Utilities  Window  Help
```

	numvisit	reason	like1	like2	like3	offer
5 : numvisit	3					
1	3	14	11	21	42	.
2	5	12	3	21	.	2
3	6	22	32	11	38	1

Extract from coding scheme used to classify responses

Grouping	Sub-grouping	Response	Code
Physical surroundings			1–9
		Decoration	1
		Use of colour	2
		Comfort of seating	3
Dining experience	*Menu*		10–19
		Choice	11
		Regularly changed	12
	Food		20–29
		Freshly prepared	21
		Organic	22
		Served at correct temperature	23

Grouping	Sub-grouping	Response	Code
	Staff attitude		30–39
		Knowledgeable	31
		Greet by name	32
		Know what diners prefer	33
		Discreet	34
		Do not hassle	35
		Good service	36
		Friendly	37
		Have a sense of humour	38
	Drinks		40–49
		Value for money	41
		Good selection of wines	42
		Good selection of beers	43
		Served at correct temperature	44

The hierarchical coding scheme meant that individual responses could subsequently be re-coded into sub-groupings and groupings such as those indicated earlier to facilitate a range of different analyses. These were undertaken using statistical analysis software.

- Look for illogical relationships. For example, if a person is coded to the 'higher managerial occupations' socioeconomic classification category and she describes her work as 'manual' it is likely an error has occurred.
- Check that rules in filter questions are followed. Certain responses to filter questions (Section 11.4) mean that other variables should be coded as missing values. If this has not happened there has been an error.

For each possible error, you need to discover whether it occurred at coding or data entry and then correct it. By giving each case a unique identifier (normally a number), it is possible to link the matrix to the original data. You must remember to write the identifier on the data collection form and enter it along with the other data into the matrix.

Data checking is very time consuming and so is often not undertaken. Beware: not doing it is very dangerous and can result in incorrect results from which false conclusions are drawn!

Weighting cases

Most data you use will be a sample. For some forms of probability sampling, such as stratified random sampling (Section 7.2), you may have used a different sampling fraction for each stratum. Alternatively, you may have obtained a different response rate for each of the strata. To obtain an accurate overall picture you will need to take account of these differences in response rates between strata. A common method of achieving this is to use cases from those strata that have lower proportions of responses to represent more

Box 12.7
Focus on student research

Weighting cases

Doris had used stratified random sampling to select her sample. The percentage of each stratum's population that responded is given below:

- Upper stratum: 90%
- Lower stratum: 65%

To account for the differences in the response rates between strata she decided to weight the cases prior to analysis.

The weight for the upper stratum was: $\frac{90}{90} = 1$

This meant that each case in the upper stratum counted as 1 case in her analysis.

The weight for the lower stratum was: $\frac{90}{65} = 1.38$

This meant that each case in the lower stratum counted for 1.38 cases in her analysis.

Doris entered these as a separate variable in her data set and used the statistical analysis software to apply the weights.

than one case in your analysis (Box 12.7). Most statistical analysis software allows you to do this by **weighting** cases. To weight the cases you:

1 Calculate the percentage of the population responding for each stratum.
2 Establish which stratum had the highest percentage of the population responding.
3 Calculate the weight for each stratum using the following formula:

$$\text{weight} = \frac{\text{highest proportion of population responding for any stratum}}{\text{proportion of population responding in stratum for which calculating weight}}$$

(Note: if your calculations are correct this will always result in the weight for the stratum with the highest proportion of the population responding being 1.)

4 Apply the appropriate weight to each case.

Beware: many authors (for example, Hays 1994) question the validity of using statistics to make inferences from your sample if you have weighted cases.

12.3 Exploring and presenting data

Once your data have been entered and checked for errors, you are ready to start your analysis. We have found Tukey's (1977) **exploratory data analysis (EDA)** approach useful in these initial stages. This approach emphasises the use of diagrams to explore and understand your data, emphasising the importance of using your data to guide your choices of analysis techniques. As you would expect, we believe that it is important to keep your research question(s) and objectives in mind when exploring your data. However, the exploratory data analysis approach allows you flexibility to introduce previously unplanned analyses to respond to new findings. It therefore formalises the common practice of looking for other relationships in data, which your research was not initially designed to test. This should not be discounted, as it may suggest other fruitful avenues for analysis. In addition, computers make this relatively easy and quick.

Even at this stage it is important that you structure and label clearly each diagram and table to avoid possible misinterpretation. Box 12.8 provides a summary checklist of the points to remember when designing a diagram or table.

Box 12.8
Checklist

Designing your diagrams and tables

For both diagrams and tables
✔ Does it have a brief but clear and descriptive title?
✔ Are the units of measurement used stated clearly?
✔ Are the sources of data used stated clearly?
✔ Are there notes to explain abbreviations and unusual terminology?
✔ Does it state the size of the sample on which the values in the table are based?

For diagrams
✔ Does it have clear axis labels?
✔ Are bars and their components in the same logical sequence?
✔ Is more dense shading used for smaller areas?
✔ Have you avoided misrepresenting or distorting the data
✔ Is a key or legend included (where necessary)?

For tables
✔ Does it have clear column and row headings?
✔ Are columns and rows in a logical sequence?

We have found it best to begin exploratory analysis by looking at individual variables and their components. The key aspects you may need to consider will be guided by your research question(s) and objectives, and are likely to include (Sparrow 1989):

- specific values;
- highest and lowest values;
- trends over time;
- proportions;
- distributions.

Once you have explored these, you can then begin to compare and look for relationships between variables, considering in addition (Sparrow 1989):

- conjunctions (the point where values for two or more variables intersect);
- totals;
- interdependence and relationships.

These are summarised in Table 12.2. Most analysis software contains procedures to create tables and diagrams. Your choice will depend on those aspects of the data that you wish to emphasise and the scale of measurement at which the data were recorded. This section is concerned only with tables and two-dimensional diagrams, including pictograms, available on most spreadsheets (Table 12.2). Three-dimensional diagrams are not discussed, as these often can hinder interpretation. Those tables and diagrams most pertinent to your research question(s) and objectives will eventually appear in your research report to support your arguments. You, therefore, should save an electronic copy of all tables and diagrams which you create.

Exploring and presenting individual variables

To show specific values

The simplest way of summarising data for individual variables so that specific values can be read is to use a **table** (**frequency distribution**). For categorical data, the table summarises the number of cases (frequency) in each category. For variables where there are likely to be a large number of categories (or values for numerical data), you will need to group the data into categories that reflect your research question(s) and objectives.

Table 12.2 Data presentation by data type: a summary

	Categorical		Numerical	
	Descriptive	**Ranked**	**Continuous**	**Discrete**
To show one variable so that any specific value can be read easily	Table/frequency distribution (data often grouped)			
To show the frequency of occurrences of categories or values for one variable so that highest and lowest are clear	Bar chart or pictogram (data may need grouping)		Histogram or frequency polygon (data must be grouped)	Bar chart or pictogram (data may need grouping)
To show the trend for a variable		Line graph or bar chart	Line graph or histogram	Line graph or bar chart
To show the proportion of occurrences of categories or values for one variable	Pie chart or bar chart (data may need grouping)		Histogram or pie chart (data must be grouped)	Pie chart or bar chart (data may need grouping)
To show the distribution of values for one variable			Frequency polygon, histogram (data must be grouped) or box plot	Frequency polygon, bar chart (data may need grouping) or box plot
To show the *interdependence* between two or more variables so that any *specific* value can be read easily	Contingency table/cross-tabulation (data often grouped)			
To compare the frequency of occurrences of categories or values for two or more variables so that *highest* and *lowest* are clear	Multiple bar chart (continuous data must be grouped, other data may need grouping)			
To compare the *trends* for two or more variables so that *conjunctions* are clear		Multiple line graph or multiple bar chart		
To compare the *proportions* of occurrences of categories or values for two or more variables	Comparative pie charts or percentage component bar chart (continuous data must be grouped, other data may need grouping)			
To compare the *distribution* of values for two or more variables			Multiple box plot	
To compare the frequency of occurrences of categories or values for two or more variables so that *totals* are clear	Stacked bar chart (continuous data must be grouped, other data may need grouping)			
To compare the *proportions* and *totals* of occurrences of categories or values for two or more variables	Comparative proportional pie charts (continuous data must be grouped, other data may need grouping)			
To show the *relationship* between cases for two variables		Scatter graph/scatter plot		

Source: © Mark Saunders, Philip Lewis and Adrian Thornhill 2008.

To show highest and lowest values

Tables attach no visual significance to highest or lowest values unless emphasised by alternative fonts. Diagrams can provide visual clues, although both categorical and numerical data may need grouping. For categorical and discrete data, bar charts and pictograms are both suitable. Generally, bar charts provide a more accurate representation and should be used for research reports, whereas pictograms convey a general impression and can be used to gain an audience's attention. In a **bar chart**, the height or length of each bar represents the frequency of occurrence. Bars are separated by gaps, usually half the width of the bars. Bar charts where the bars are vertical (as in Figure 12.2) are sometimes called column charts. This bar chart emphasises that the European Union Member State with the highest total carbon dioxide emissions in 2005 was Germany, whilst Malta had the lowest total carbon dioxide emissions.

To emphasise the relative values represented by each of the bars in a bar chart, the bars may be reordered in either descending or ascending order of the frequency of occurrence represented by each bar (Figure 12.3).

Most researchers use a histogram to show highest and lowest values for continuous data. Prior to being drawn, data will often need to be grouped into class intervals. In a **histogram**, the area of each bar represents the frequency of occurrence and the continuous nature of the data is emphasised by the absence of gaps between the bars. For equal width class intervals, the height of your bar still represents the frequency of occurrences (Figures 12.4 and 12.5) and so the highest and lowest values are easy to distinguish. For histograms with unequal class interval widths, this is not the case. In Figure 12.4 the

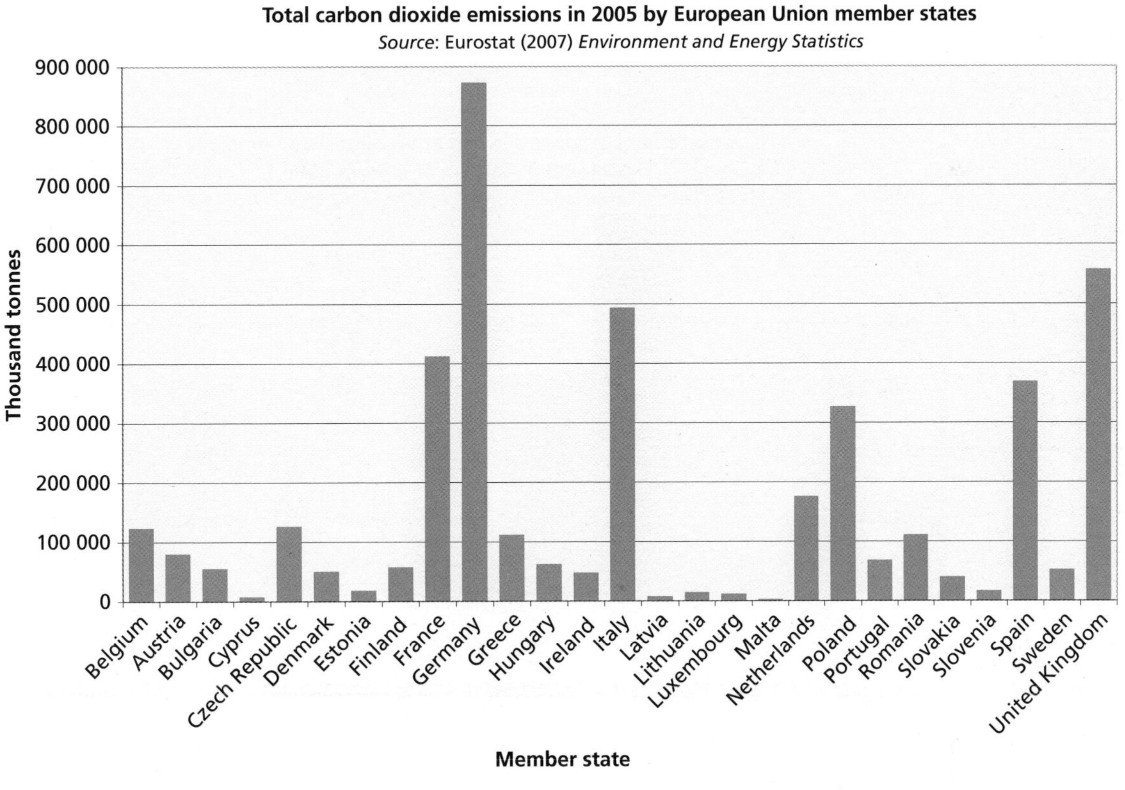

Total carbon dioxide emissions in 2005 by European Union member states
Source: Eurostat (2007) *Environment and Energy Statistics*

Figure 12.2 Bar chart
Source: adapted from Eurostat (2007) © European Communities, 2007. Reproduced with permission.

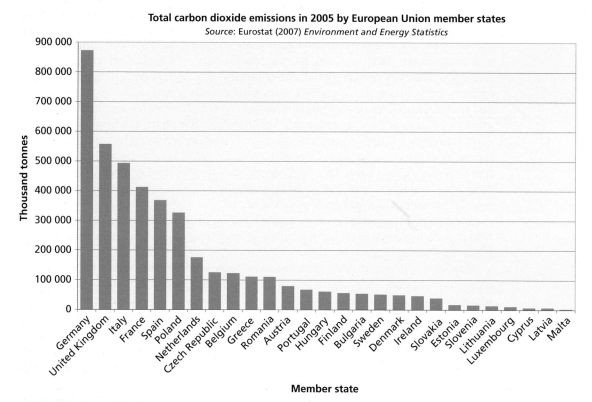

Figure 12.3 Bar chart (data reordered)
Source: adapted from Eurostat (2007) © European Communities, 2007. Reproduced with permission.

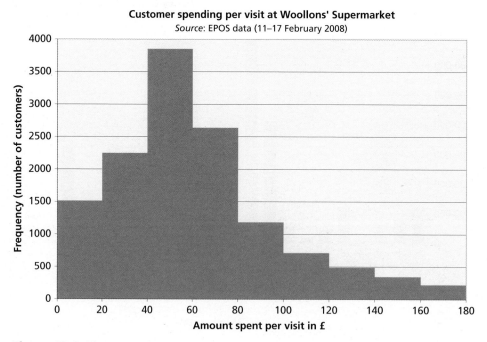

Figure 12.4 Histogram

histogram emphasises that the most frequent amount spent is £40 to £60, whilst the least frequent amount spent is £160 to £180. In Figure 12.5 the histogram emphasises that the highest number of Harley-Davidson motorcycles shipped worldwide was in 2006, and the lowest number in 1996.

Analysis software treats histograms for data of equal width class intervals as a variation of a bar chart. Unfortunately, few spreadsheets will cope automatically with the calculations required to draw histograms for unequal class intervals. Consequently, you may have to use a bar chart owing to the limitations of your analysis software.

In a **pictogram**, each bar is replaced by a picture or series of pictures chosen to represent the data. To illustrate the impact of doing this, we have used data of worldwide Harley-Davidson motorcycle shipments to generate both a histogram (Figure 12.5) and a pictogram (Figure 12.6). In the pictogram each picture represents 20 000 motorcycles. Pictures in pictograms can, like bars in bar charts and histograms, be shown in columns or horizontally. The height of the column or length of the bar made up by the pictures represents the frequency of occurrence. In this case we felt it was more logical to group the pictures as a horizontal bar rather than vertically on top of each other. You will have probably also noticed that, in the pictogram, there are gaps between the bars. Whilst this normally signifies discrete categories of data, it is also acceptable to do this for continuous data (such as years) when drawing a pictogram to aid clarity. Although analysis software allows you to convert a bar chart or histogram to a pictogram both easily and accurately, it is more difficult to establish the actual data values from a pictogram. This is because the number of units part of a picture represents is not immediately clear. For example, in Figure 12.6, how many motorcycles shipped would a rear wheel represent?

Pictograms have a further drawback, namely that it is very easy to misrepresent the data. Both Figure 12.5 and Figure 12.6 show that shipments of Harley-Davidson

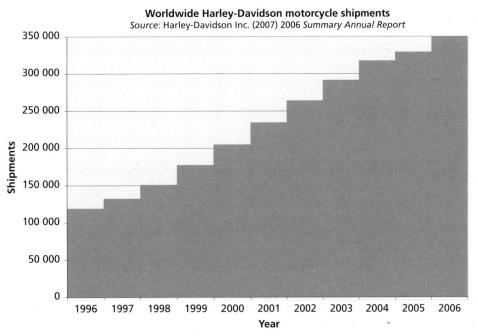

Figure 12.5 Histogram

Source: Harley-Davidson Inc. (2007) 2006 Summary Annual Report. Reproduced with permission.

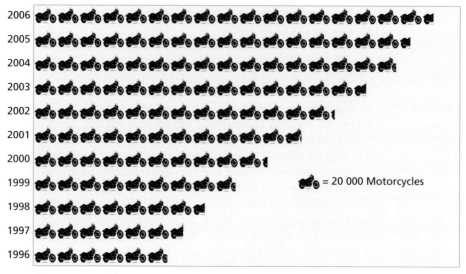

Worldwide Harley-Davidson motorcycle shipments
Source: Harley-Davidson Inc. (2007) 2006 *Summary Annual Report*

= 20 000 Motorcycles

Figure 12.6 Pictogram
Source: Harley-Davidson Inc. (2007) 2006 Summary Annual Report. Reproduced with permission.

motorcycles doubled between 1999 and 2006. Using our analysis software, this could have been represented using a picture of a motorcycle in 2006 that was nearly twice as long as the picture in 1999. However, in order to keep the proportions of the motorcycle accurate, the picture would have needed to be nearly twice as tall. Consequently, the actual area of the picture would have been nearly four times as great and would have been interpreted as motorcycle shipments almost quadrupling. Because of this we would recommend that, if you are using a pictogram, you decide on a standard value for each picture and do not alter its size. In addition, you should include a key or note to indicate the value each picture represents.

Frequency polygons are used less often to illustrate limits. Most analysis software treats them as a version of a line graph (Figure 12.7) in which the lines are extended to meet the horizontal axis, provided that class widths are equal.

To show a trend

Trends can only be presented for variables containing numerical (and occasionally ranked) longitudinal data. The most suitable diagram for exploring the trend is a **line graph** (Anderson *et al.* 1999) in which your data values for each time period are joined with a line to represent the trend (Figure 12.7). In Figure 12.7 the line graph emphasises the upward trend in the number of Harley-Davidson motorcycles shipped worldwide between 1996 and 2006. You can also use histograms (Figure 12.5) to show trends over continuous time periods and bar charts (Figure 12.2) to show trends between discrete time periods. The trend can also be calculated using time series-analysis (Section 12.5).

To show proportions

Research has shown that the most frequently used diagram to emphasise the proportion or share of occurrences is the pie chart, although bar charts have been shown to give

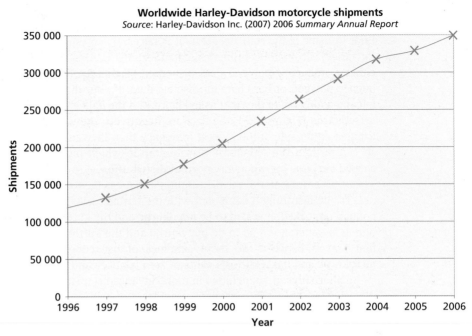

Figure 12.7 Line graph

Source: Harley-Davidson Inc. (2007) 2006 Summary Annual Report. Reproduced with permission.

equally good results (Anderson *et al.* 1999). A **pie chart** is divided into proportional segments according to the share each has of the total value (Figure 12.8). For numerical and some categorical data you will need to group data prior to drawing the pie chart, as it is difficult to interpret pie charts with more than six segments (Morris 2003).

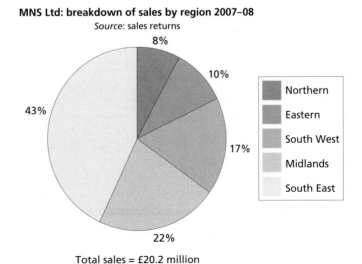

Figure 12.8 Pie chart

To show the distribution of values

Prior to using many statistical tests it is necessary to establish the distribution of values for variables containing numerical data (Sections 12.4, 12.5). This can be seen by plotting either a frequency polygon or a histogram (Figure 12.4) for continuous data or a frequency polygon or bar chart for discrete data. If your diagram shows a bunching to the left and a long tail to the right as in Figure 12.4 the data are **positively skewed**. If the converse is true (Figure 12.5), the data are **negatively skewed**. If your data are equally distributed either side of the highest frequency then they are **symmetrically distributed**. A special form of the symmetric distribution, in which the data can be plotted as a bell-shaped curve, is known as the **normal distribution**.

The other indicator of the distribution's shape is the **kurtosis** – the pointedness or flatness of the distribution compared with the normal distribution. If a distribution is more pointed or peaked, it is said to be leptokurtic and the kurtosis value is positive. If a distribution is flatter, it is said to be platykurtic and the kurtosis value is negative. A distribution that is between the more extremes of peakedness and flatness is said to be mesokurtic and has a kurtosis value of zero (Dancey and Reidy 2008).

An alternative often included in more advanced statistical analysis software is the **box plot** (Figure 12.9). This diagram provides you with a pictorial representation of the distribution of the data for a variable. The plot shows where the middle value or median is, how this relates to the middle 50 per cent of the data or inter-quartile range, and highest and lowest values or *extremes* (Section 12.4). It also highlights outliers, those values that are very different from the data. In Figure 12.9 the two outliers might be due to mistakes in data entry. Alternatively, they may be correct and emphasise that sales for these two cases (93 and 88) are far higher. In this example we can see that the data values for the variable are positively skewed as there is a long tail to the right.

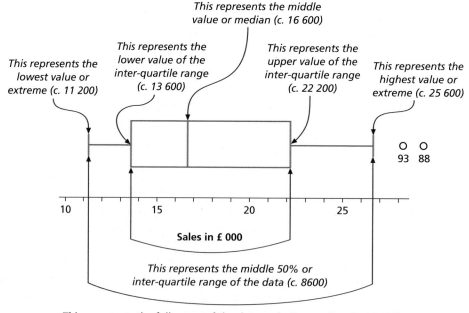

Figure 12.9
Annotated box plot

Box 12.9
Focus on student research

Exploring and presenting data for individual variables

As part of audience research for his dissertation, Valentin asked people attending a play at a provincial theatre to complete a short questionnaire. This collected responses to 25 questions including:

3 How many plays (including this one) have you seen at this theatre in the past year?

___ ___

11 This play is good value for money
strongly disagree ❑₁   disagree ❑₂
agree ❑₃   strongly agree ❑₄

24 How old are you?
Under 18 ❑₁   18 to 34 ❑₂
35 to 64 ❑₃   65 and over ❑₄

Exploratory analyses were undertaken using analysis software and diagrams and tables generated. For question 3, which collected discrete data, the aspects that were most important were the distribution of values and the highest and lowest numbers of plays seen. A bar chart, therefore, was drawn:

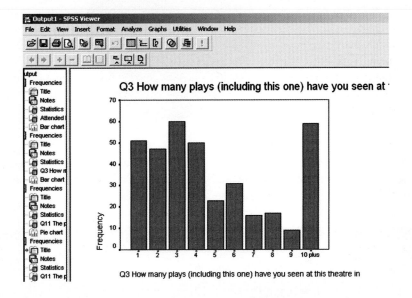

This emphasised that the most frequent number of plays seen by respondents was three and the least frequent number of plays seen by the respondents was either nine or probably some larger number. It also suggested that the distribution was positively skewed towards lower numbers of plays seen.

For question 11 (categorical data), the most important aspect was the proportions of people agreeing and disagreeing with the statement. A pie chart (see overleaf) was therefore drawn using similar shadings for the two agree categories and for the two disagree categories.

This emphasised that the vast majority of respondents (95 per cent) agreed that the play was good value for money.

▶ Box 12.9
Focus on student
research (continued)

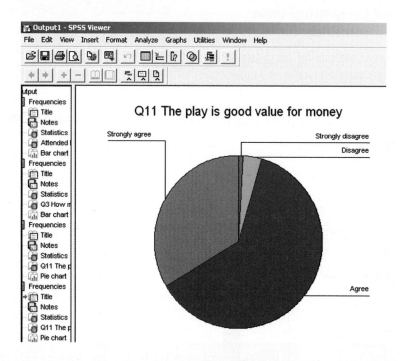

Question 24 collected data on each respondent's age. This question had grouped continuous data into four unequal-width age groups. For this analysis, the most important aspects were the specific number and percentage of respondents in each age category and so a table was constructed.

Q24 How old are you?

		Frequency	Percent	Valid Percent	Cumulative Percent
Valid	Under 18	30	4.4	4.4	4.4
	18 to 34	144	20.9	21.0	25.4
	35 to 64	366	53.2	53.4	78.8
	65 plus	145	21.1	21.2	100.0
	Total	685	99.6	100.0	
Missing	System	3	.4		
Total		688	100.0		

Comparing variables

To show specific values and interdependence

As with individual variables the best method of finding specific data values is a table. This is known as a **contingency table** or **cross-tabulation** (Table 12.3), and it also enables you to examine interdependence between the variables. For variables where there are likely to be a large number of categories (or values for numerical data), you may need to group the data to prevent the table from becoming too large.

Most statistical analysis software allows you to add totals, and row and column percentages when designing your table. Statistical analyses such as chi square can also be undertaken at the same time (Section 12.5).

Table 12.3 Contingency table: number of insurance claims by gender, 2008

Number of claims*	Male	Female	Total
0	10032	13478	23510
1	2156	1430	3586
2	120	25	145
3	13	4	17
Total	12321	14937	27258

*No clients had more than three claims.
Source: PJ Insurance Services.

To compare highest and lowest values

Comparisons of variables that emphasise the highest and lowest rather than precise values are best explored using a **multiple bar chart** (Anderson *et al.* 1999), also known as a *compound bar chart*. As for a bar chart, continuous data – or data where there are many values or categories – need to be grouped. Within any multiple bar chart you are likely to find it easiest to compare between adjacent bars. The multiple bar chart (Box 12.10, overleaf) has therefore been drawn to emphasise comparisons between new fund launches, mergers and closures and the net increase in funds rather than between years.

To compare proportions

Comparison of proportions between variables uses either a **percentage component bar chart** or two or more pie charts. Either type of diagram can be used for all data types, provided that continuous data, and data where there are more than six values or categories, are grouped. Percentage component bar charts are more straightforward to draw than comparative pie charts when using most spreadsheets. Within your percentage component bar chart, comparisons will be easiest between adjacent bars. The chart in Figure 12.10 (see overleaf) has been drawn to compare proportions of each type of response between products. Consumers' responses for each product, therefore, form a single bar.

To compare trends and conjunctions

The most suitable diagram to compare trends for two or more numerical (or occasionally ranked) variables is a **multiple line graph** where one line represents each variable

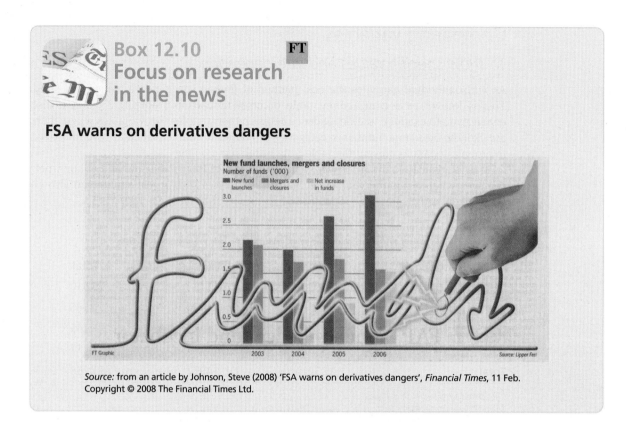

Figure 12.10
Percentage component bar chart

(Henry 1995). You can also use multiple bar charts (Box 12.10) in which bars for the same time period are placed adjacent.

If you need to look for conjunctions in the trends – that is, where values for two or more variables intersect – this is where the lines on a multiple line graph cross.

To compare totals

Comparison of totals between variables uses a variation of the bar chart. A **stacked bar chart** can be used for all data types provided that continuous data and data where there are more than six possible values or categories are grouped. As with percentage component bar charts, the design of the stacked bar chart is dictated by the totals you want to compare. For this reason, in Figure 12.11 sales for each quarter have been stacked to give totals which can be compared between companies.

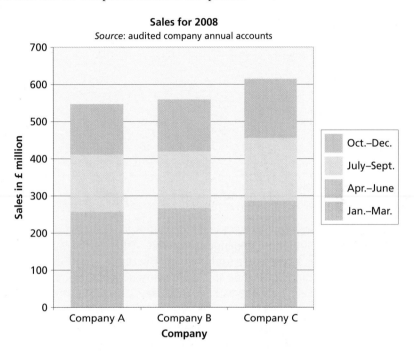

Figure 12.11
Stacked bar chart

To compare proportions and totals

To compare both proportions of each category or value and the totals for two or more variables it is best to use **comparative proportional pie charts** for all data types. For each comparative proportional pie chart the total area of the pie chart represents the total for that variable. By contrast, the angle of each segment represents the relative proportion of a category within the variable (Figure 12.8). Because of the complexity of drawing comparative proportional pie charts, they are rarely used for exploratory data analysis, although they can be used to good effect in research reports.

To compare the distribution of values

Often it is useful to compare the distribution of values for two or more variables. Plotting multiple frequency polygons or bar charts (Box 12.10) will enable you to compare distributions for up to three or four variables. After this your diagram is likely just to look a mess! An alternative is to use a diagram of multiple box plots, similar to the one in Figure 12.9. This provides a pictorial representation of the distribution of the data for the variables in which you are interested. These plots can be compared and are interpreted in the same way as the single box plot.

To show the relationship between cases for variables

You can explore possible relationships between ranked and numerical data variables by plotting one variable against another. This is called a **scatter graph** or **scatter plot**, and

Figure 12.12
Scatter graph

each cross (point) represents the values for one case (Figure 12.12). Convention dictates that you plot the **dependent variable** – that is, the variable that changes in response to changes in the other **(independent) variable** – against the vertical axis. The strength of the relationship is indicated by the closeness of the points to an imaginary straight line. If, as the values for one variable increase, so do those for the other, you have a positive relationship. If, as the values for one variable decrease, those for the other variable increase, you have a negative relationship. Thus in Figure 12.12 there is a negative relationship between the two variables. The strength of this relationship can be assessed statistically using techniques such as correlation or regression (Section 12.5).

Box 12.11
Focus on student research

Comparing variables

Francis was asked by his uncle, an independent ice cream manufacturer, to examine the records of monthly sales of ice cream for 2007 and 2008. In addition, his uncle had obtained longitudinal data on average (mean) daily hours of sunshine for each month for the same time period from their local weather station. Francis decided to explore data on sales of the three best-selling flavours (vanilla, strawberry and chocolate), paying particular attention to:

- comparative trends in sales;
- the relationship between sales and amount of sunshine.

To compare trends in sales between the three flavours he plotted a multiple line graph using a spreadsheet.

This indicated that sales for all flavours of ice cream were following a seasonal pattern but with an overall upward trend. It also showed that sales of vanilla ice cream were highest, and that those of chocolate had overtaken strawberry. The multiple line graph highlighted the conjunction when sales of chocolate first exceeded strawberry, September 2008.

To show relationships between sales and amount of sunshine Francis plotted scatter graphs for sales

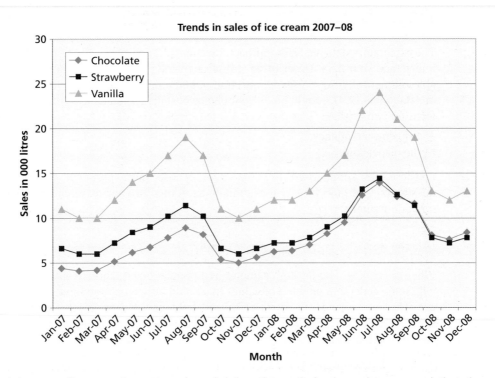

Trends in sales of ice cream 2007–08

of each ice cream flavour against average (mean) daily hours of sunshine for each month. He plotted sales on the vertical axis, as he presumed that these were dependent on the amount of sunshine, for example:

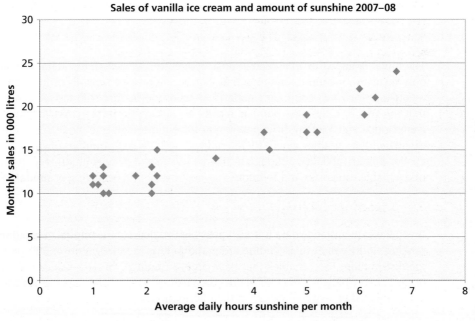

Sales of vanilla ice cream and amount of sunshine 2007–08

The scatter graph showed that there was a positive relationship between the amount of sunshine and sales of vanilla flavour ice cream. Subsequent scatter plots revealed similar relationships for strawberry and chocolate flavours.

12.4 Describing data using statistics

The exploratory data analysis approach (Section 12.3) emphasised the use of diagrams to understand your data. **Descriptive statistics** enable you to describe (and compare) variables numerically. Your research question(s) and objectives, although limited by the type of data (Table 12.4), should guide your choice of statistics. Statistics to describe a variable focus on two aspects:

- the central tendency;
- the dispersion.

These are summarised in Table 12.4. Those most pertinent to your research question(s) and objectives will eventually be quoted in your research report as support for your arguments.

Describing the central tendency

When describing data for both samples and populations quantitatively it is usual to provide some general impression of values that could be seen as common, middling or average. These are termed measures of **central tendency** and are discussed in virtually all statistics textbooks. The three ways of measuring the central tendency most used in business research are the:

- value that occurs most frequently (mode);
- middle value or mid-point after the data have been ranked (median);
- value, often known as the average, that includes all data values in its calculation (mean).

However, as we saw in Box 12.3, beware: if you have used numerical codes, most analysis software can calculate all three measures whether or not they are appropriate!

To represent the value that occurs most frequently

The **mode** is the value that occurs most frequently. For descriptive data, the mode is the only measure of central tendency that can be interpreted sensibly. You might read in a report that the most common (modal) colour of motor cars sold last year was silver, or that the two equally most popular makes of motorcycle in response to a questionnaire were Honda and Yamaha (it is possible to have more than one mode). The mode can be calculated for variables where there are likely to be a large number of categories (or values for numerical data), although it may be less useful. One solution is to group the data into suitable categories and to quote the most frequently occurring or **modal group**.

To represent the middle value

If you have quantitative data it is also possible to calculate the middle or **median** value by ranking all the values in ascending order and finding the mid-point (or **50th percentile**) in the distribution. For variables that have an even number of data values the median will occur halfway between the two middle data values. The median has the advantage that it is not affected by extreme values in the distribution.

To include all data values

The most frequently used measure of central tendency is the **mean** (average in everyday language), which includes all data values in its calculation. However, it is usually only possible to calculate a meaningful mean using numerical data.

Table 12.4 Descriptive statistics by data type: a summary

To calculate a measure of:		Categorical		Numerical	
		Descriptive	**Ranked**	**Continuous**	**Discrete**
Central tendency that . . .	. . . represents the value that occurs most frequently	Mode			
	. . . represents the middle value			Median	
	. . . includes all data values (average)			Mean	
Dispersion that . . .	. . . states the difference between the highest and lowest values			Range (data need not be normally distributed but must be placed in rank order)	
	. . . states the difference within the middle 50% of values			Inter-quartile range (data need not be normally distributed but must be placed in rank order)	
	. . . states the difference within another fraction of the values			Deciles or percentiles (data need not be normally distributed but must be placed in rank order)	
	. . . describes the extent to which data values differ from the mean			Variance, or more usually, the standard deviation (data should be normally distributed)	
	. . . compares the extent to which data values differ from the mean between variables			Coefficient of variation (data should be normally distributed)	
	. . . allows the relative extent that different data values differ to be compared			Index numbers	

Source: © Mark Saunders, Philip Lewis and Adrian Thornhill 2008.

Box 12.12
Focus on student research

Measuring the central tendency

As part of her research project, Kylie had obtained secondary data from the service department of her organisation on the length of time for which their customers had held service contracts:

Length of time held contract	Number of customers
<3 months	50
3 to <6 months	44
6 months to <1 year	71
1 to <2 years	105
2 to <3 years	74
3 to <4 years	35
4 to <5 years	27
5+ years	11

Her exploratory analysis revealed a positively skewed distribution (long tail to the right).

From the table, the largest single group of customers were those who had contracts for 1 to 2 years. This was the modal time period (most commonly occurring). However, the usefulness of this statistic is limited owing to the variety of class widths. By definition, half of the organisation's customers will have held contracts below the median time period (approximately 1 year 5 months) and half above it. As there are 11 customers who have held service contracts for over 5 years, the mean time period (approximately 1 year 9 months) is pulled towards longer times. This is represented by the skewed shape of the distribution.

Kylie needed to decide which of these measures of central tendency to include in her research report. As the mode made little sense she quoted the median and mean when interpreting her data:

> The length of time for which customers have held service contracts is positively skewed. Although mean length of time is approximately 1 year 9 months, half of customers have held service contracts for less than 1 year 5 months (median). Grouping of these data means that it is not possible to calculate a meaningful mode.

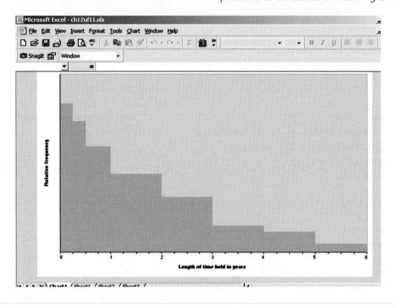

The value of your mean is unduly influenced by extreme data values in skewed distributions (Section 12.3). In such distributions the mean tends to get drawn towards the long tail of extreme data values and may be less representative of the central tendency. For this and other reasons Anderson *et al.* (1999) suggests that the median may be a more useful descriptive statistic. However, because the mean is the building block for many of the statistical tests used to explore relationships (Section 12.5), it is usual to include it as at least one of the measures of central tendency for numerical data in your report. This is, of course, provided that it makes sense!

Describing the dispersion

As well as describing the central tendency for a variable, it is important to describe how the data values are dispersed around the central tendency. As you can see from Table 12.4, this is only possible for numerical data. Two of the most frequently used ways of describing the dispersion are the:

- difference within the middle 50 per cent of values (inter-quartile range);
- extent to which values differ from the mean (standard deviation).

Although these **dispersion measures** are suitable only for numerical data, most statistical analysis software will also calculate them for categorical data if you have used numerical codes!

To state the difference between values

In order to get a quick impression of the distribution of data values for a variable you could simply calculate the difference between the lowest and the highest values – that is, the **range**. However, this statistic is rarely used in research reports as it represents only the extreme values.

A more frequently used statistic is the **inter-quartile range**. As we discussed earlier, the median divides the range into two. The range can be further divided into four equal sections called **quartiles**. The **lower quartile** is the value below which a quarter of your data values will fall; the **upper quartile** is the value above which a quarter of your data values will fall. As you would expect, the remaining half of your data values will fall between the lower and upper quartiles. The difference between the upper and lower quartiles is the inter-quartile range (Morris 2003). As a consequence, it is concerned only with the middle 50 per cent of data values and ignores extreme values.

You can also calculate the range for other fractions of a variable's distribution. One alternative is to divide your distribution using **percentiles**. These split your distribution into 100 equal parts. Obviously the lower quartile is the 25th percentile and the upper quartile the 75th percentile. However, you could calculate a range between the 10th and 90th percentiles so as to include 80 per cent of your data values. Another alternative is to divide the range into 10 equal parts called **deciles**.

To describe and compare the extent by which values differ from the mean

Conceptually and statistically in research it is important to look at the extent to which the data values for a variable are spread around their mean, as this is what you need to know to assess its usefulness as a typical value for the distribution. If your data values are all close to the mean, then the mean is more typical than if they vary widely. To describe the extent of spread of numerical data you use the **standard deviation**. If your data are a sample (Section 7.1) this is calculated using a slightly different formula than if your data are a population, although if your sample is larger than about 30 cases there is little difference in the two statistics (Morris 2003).

You may need to compare the relative spread of data between distributions of different magnitudes (e.g. one may be measured in hundreds of tonnes, the other in billions of tonnes). To make a meaningful comparison you will need to take account of these different magnitudes. A common way of doing this is:

1 to divide the standard deviation by the mean;
2 then to multiply your answer by 100.

This results in a statistic called the **coefficient of variation** (Diamantopoulos and Schlegelmilch 1997). The values of this statistic can then be compared. The distribution with the largest coefficient of variation has the largest relative spread of data (Box 12.13).

Alternatively, as discussed in the introduction in relation to the cost of living at different universities and colleges, you may wish to compare the relative extent to which data values differ. One way of doing this is to use **index numbers** and consider the relative differences rather than actual data values. Such indices compare each data value against a base value that is normally given the value of 100, differences being calculated relative to this value. An index number greater than 100 would represent a larger or higher data value relative to the base value and an index less than 100, a smaller or lower data value.

Box 12.13
Focus on student research

Describing variables and comparing their dispersion

Cathy was interested in the total value of transactions at the main and sub-branches of a major bank. The mean value of total transactions at the main branches was approximately five times as high as that for the sub-branches. This made it difficult to compare the relative spread in total value of transactions between the two types of branches. By calculating the coefficients of variation Cathy found that there was relatively more variation in the total value of transactions at the main branches than at the sub-branches. This is because the coefficient of variation for the main branches was larger (23.62) than the coefficient for the sub-branches (18.08).

Microsoft Excel - ch12uf12.xls

File Edit View Insert Format Tools Data Window Help

138   =

	A	B	C	D
23	**Branch type**	**Mean total transaction value**	**Standard deviation**	**Coefficient of variation**
24	Main	£ 6,000,000	£1,417,000	23.62
25	Sub	£ 1,200,000	£ 217,000	18.08

To calculate an index number for each case for a data variable you use the following formula:

$$\text{index number for case} = \frac{\text{data value for case}}{\text{base data value}} \times 100$$

For our introductory example, the data value for each case (university or college) was calculated by creating a weighted total cost of three different indicators: the weighted mean cost of a range of accommodation options, the weighted mean cost of a tray of drinks (beer, wine and orange juice) and the cost of the student 'basket of goods' of specified foodstuffs and drinks (Push 2007). The base data value was the mean weighted total cost for all the universities and colleges in the UK.

12.5 Examining relationships, differences and trends using statistics

One of the questions you are most likely to ask in your analysis is: 'How does a variable relate to another variable?' In statistical analysis you answer this question by testing the likelihood of the relationship (or one more extreme) occurring by chance alone, if there really was no difference in the population from which the sample was drawn (Robson 2002). This process is known as significance or hypothesis testing as, in effect, you are comparing the data you have collected with what you would theoretically expect to happen. Significance testing can therefore be thought of as helping to rule out the possibility that your result could be due to random variation in your sample.

There are two main groups of statistical significance tests: non-parametric and parametric. **Non-parametric statistics** are designed to be used when your data are not normally distributed. Not surprisingly, this most often means they are used with categorical data. In contrast, **parametric statistics** are used with numerical data. Although parametric statistics are considered more powerful because they use numerical data, a number of assumptions about the actual data being used need to be satisfied if they are not to produce spurious results (Blumberg *et al*. 2008). These include:

- the data cases selected for the sample should be independent, in other words the selection of any one case for your sample should not affect the probability of any other case being included in the same sample;
- the data cases should be drawn from normally distributed populations (Section 12.3);
- the populations from which the data cases are drawn should have equal variances (don't worry, the term variance is explained later in Section 12.5);
- the data used should be numerical.

If these assumptions are not satisfied, it is often still possible to use non-parametric statistics.

The way in which this significance is tested using both non-parametric and parametric statistics can be thought of as answering one from a series of questions, dependent on the data type:

- Is the association statistically significant?
- Are the differences statistically significant?

- What is the strength of the relationship, and is it statistically significant?
- Are the predicted values statistically significant?

These are summarised in Table 12.5 along with statistics used to help examine trends.

Testing for significant relationships and differences

Testing the probability of a pattern such as a relationship between variables occurring by chance alone is known as **significance testing** (Berman Brown and Saunders 2008). As part of your research project, you might have collected sample data to examine the relationship between two variables. Once you have entered data into the analysis software, chosen the statistic and clicked on the appropriate icon, an answer will appear as if by magic! With most statistical analysis software this will consist of a test statistic, the degrees of freedom (df) and, based on these, the probability (p-$value$) of your test result or one more extreme occurring by chance alone. If the probability of your test statistic or one more extreme having occurred by chance alone is very low (usually $p < 0.05$ or lower[1]), then you have a statistically significant relationship. Statisticians refer to this as rejecting the null hypothesis and accepting the hypothesis, often abbreviating the terms null hypothesis to H_0 and hypothesis to H_1. Consequently, rejecting a null hypothesis will mean rejecting a testable statement something like 'there is no significant difference between . . .' and accepting a testable statement something like 'there is a significant difference between . . .'. If the probability of obtaining the test statistic or one more extreme by chance alone is higher than 0.05, then you conclude that the relationship is not statistically significant. Statisticians refer to this as accepting the **null hypothesis**. There may still be a relationship between the variables under such circumstances, but you cannot make the conclusion with any certainty.

Despite our discussion of hypothesis testing, albeit briefly, it is worth mentioning that a great deal of quantitative analysis, when written up, does not specify actual hypotheses. Rather, the theoretical underpinnings of the research and the research questions provide the context within which the probability of relationships between variables occurring by chance alone is tested. Thus although hypothesis testing has taken place, it is often only discussed in terms of statistical significance.

The statistical significance of the relationship indicated by a test statistic is determined in part by your sample size (Section 7.2). One consequence of this is that it is very difficult to obtain a significant test statistic with a small sample. Conversely, by increasing your sample size, less obvious relationships and differences will be found to be statistically significant until, with extremely large samples, almost any relationship or difference will be significant (Anderson 2003). This is inevitable as your sample is becoming closer in size to the population from which it was selected. You, therefore, need to remember that small populations can make statistical tests insensitive, while very large samples can make statistical tests overly sensitive. One consequence of this is that, if you expect a difference or relationship will be small, you need to have a larger sample size.

---

[1]A probability of 0.05 means that the probability of your test result or one more extreme occurring by chance alone, if there really was no difference in the population from which the sample was drawn, is 5 in 100, that is 1 in 20.

Table 12.5 Statistics to examine relationships, differences and trends by data type: a summary

	Categorical		Numerical	
	Descriptive	**Ranked**	**Continuous**	**Discrete**
To test whether two variables are associated	Chi square (data may need grouping)		Chi square if variable grouped into discrete classes	
	Cramer's V Phi (both variables must be dichotomous)			
To test whether two groups (categories) are different		Kolmogorov-Smirnov (data may need grouping) or Mann-Whitney U test	Independent t-test or paired t-test (often used to test for changes over time) or Mann-Whitney U test (where data skewed or a small sample)	
To test whether three or more groups (categories) are different			Analysis of variance (ANOVA)	
To assess the strength of relationship between two variables		Spearman's rank correlation coefficient (Spearman's rho) or Kendall's rank order correlation coefficient (Kendall's tau)	Pearson's product moment correlation coefficient (PMCC)	
To assess the strength of a relationship between one dependent and one independent variable			Coefficient of determination (regression coefficient)	
To assess the strength of a relationship between one dependent and two or more independent variables			Coefficient of multiple determination (multiple regression coefficient)	
To predict the value of a dependent variable from one or more independent variables			Regression equation (regression analysis)	
To examine relative change (trend) over time			Index numbers	
To compare relative changes (trends) over time			Index numbers	
To determine the trend over time of a series of data			Time series: moving averages or Regression equation (regression analysis)	

Source: © Mark Saunders, Philip Lewis and Adrian Thornhill 2008.

Type I and Type II errors

Inevitably, errors can occur when making inferences from samples. Statisticians refer to these as Type I and Type II errors. Blumberg *et al.* (2008) use the analogy of legal decisions to explain Type I and Type II errors. In their analogy they equate a Type I error to a person who is innocent being unjustly convicted and a Type II error to a person who is guilty of a crime being unjustly acquitted. In business and management research we would say that an error made by wrongly coming to a decision that something is true when in reality it is not is a **Type I error**. Type I errors might involve your concluding that two variables are related when they are not, or incorrectly concluding that a sample statistic exceeds the value that would be expected by chance alone. This means you are rejecting your null hypothesis when you should not. The term '**statistical significance**' discussed earlier therefore refers to the probability of making a Type I error. A **Type II error** involves the opposite occurring. In other words, you conclude that something is not true, when in reality it is, and accept your null hypothesis. This means that Type II errors might involve you in concluding that two variables are not related when they are, or that a sample statistic does not exceed the value that would be expected by chance alone.

Given that a Type II error is the inverse of a Type I error, it follows that if we reduce our chances of making a Type I error by setting the significance level to 0.01 rather than 0.05, we increase our chances of making a Type II error by a corresponding amount. This is not an insurmountable problem, as researchers usually consider Type I errors more serious and prefer to take a small chance of saying something is true when it is not (Figure 12.13). It is, therefore, generally more important to minimise Type I than Type II errors.

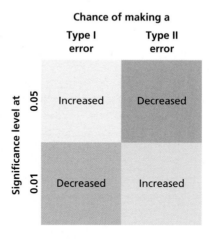

Figure 12.13
Type I and
Type II errors

To test whether two variables are associated

Often descriptive or numerical data will be summarised as a two-way contingency table (such as Table 12.3). The **chi square test** enables you to find out how likely it is that the two variables are associated. It is based on a comparison of the observed values in the table with what might be expected if the two distributions were entirely independent. Therefore you are assessing the likelihood of the data in your table, or data more extreme, occurring by chance alone by comparing it with what you would expect if the two variables were independent of each other. This could be phrased as the null hypothesis: 'there is no significant difference . . .'.

The test relies on:

- the categories used in the contingency table being mutually exclusive, so that each observation falls into only one category or class interval;
- no more than 25 per cent of the cells in the table having expected values of less than 5. For contingency tables of two rows and two columns, no expected values of less than 10 are preferable (Dancey and Reidy 2008).

If the latter assumption is not met, the accepted solution is to combine rows and columns where this produces meaningful data.

The chi square (χ^2) test calculates the probability that the data in your table, or data more extreme, could occur by chance alone. Most statistical analysis software does this automatically. However, if you are using a spreadsheet you will usually need to look up the probability in a 'critical values of chi square' table using your calculated chi square value and the degrees of freedom.[2] This table is included in most statistics textbooks. A probability of 0.05 means that there is only a 5 per cent chance of the data in your table occurring by chance alone, and is termed statistically significant. Therefore, a probability of 0.05 or smaller means you can be at least 95 per cent certain that the relationship between your two variables could not have occurred by chance factors alone. When interpreting probabilities from software packages, beware: owing to statistical rounding of numbers a probability of 0.000 does not mean zero, but that it is less than 0.001 (Box 12.14).

Some software packages, such as SPSS, calculate the statistic **Cramer's V** alongside the chi square statistic (Box 12.14). If you include the value of Cramer's V in your research report, it is usual to do so in addition to the chi square statistic. Whereas the chi square statistic gives the probability that data in a table, or data more extreme, could occur by chance alone; Cramer's V measures the association between the two variables within the table on a scale where 0 represents no association and 1 represents perfect association. Because the value of Cramer's V is always between 0 and 1, the relative strengths of significant associations between different pairs of variables can be compared.

An alternative statistic used to measure the association between two variables is **Phi**. This statistic measures the association on a scale between –1 (perfect negative association), through 0 (no association) to 1 (perfect association). However, unlike Cramer's V, using Phi to compare the relative strengths of significant associations between pairs of variables can be problematic. This is because, although values of Phi will only range between –1 and 1 when measuring the association between two dichotomous variables, they may exceed these extremes when measuring the association for categorical variables where at least one of these variables has more than two categories. For this reason, we recommend that you use Phi only when comparing pairs of dichotomous variables.

To test whether two groups are different

Ranked data Sometimes it is necessary to see whether the distribution of an observed set of values for each category of a variable differs from a specified distribution, for example whether your sample differs from the population from which it was selected. The **Kolmogorov–Smirnov test** enables you to establish this for ranked data (Kanji 2006). It is based on a comparison of the cumulative proportions of the observed values in each category with the cumulative proportions in the same categories for the specified population. Therefore you are testing the likelihood of the distribution of your observed data differing from that of the specified population by chance alone.

---

[2]Degrees of freedom are the number of values free to vary when computing a statistic. The number of degrees of freedom for a contingency table of at least 2 rows and 2 columns of data is calculated from (number of rows in the table -1) $\times$ (number of columns in the table -1).

Box 12.14
Focus on student research

Testing whether two variables are associated

As part of his research project, John wanted to find out whether there was a significant association between grade of respondent and gender. Earlier analysis using SPSS had indicated that there were 385 respondents in his sample with no missing data for either variable. However, it had also highlighted the small numbers of respondents in the highest grade (GC01 to GC05) categories:

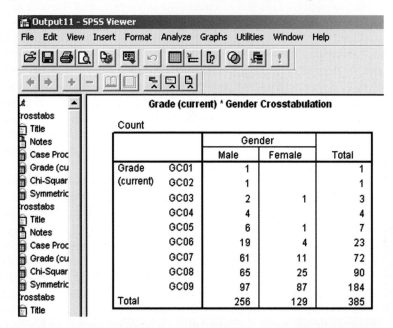

Bearing in mind the assumptions of the chi square test, John decided to combine categories GC01 through GC05 to create a new grade GC01-5 using SPSS:

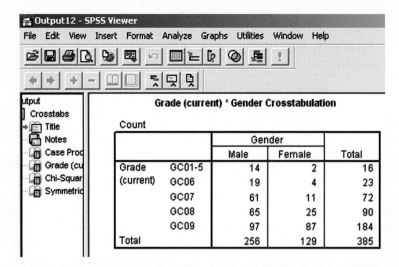

He then used his analysis software to undertake a chi square test and calculate Cramer's V:

As can be seen, this resulted in an overall chi square value of 33.59 with 4 degrees of freedom (df).

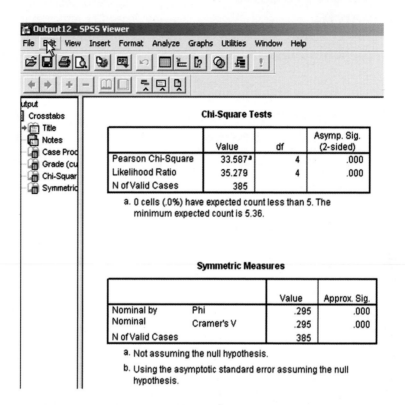

The significance of .000 (Asymp. Sig.) meant that the probability of the values in his table occurring by chance alone was less than 0.001. He therefore concluded that the relationship between gender and grade was extremely unlikely to be explained by chance factors alone and quoted the statistic in his project report:

$$[\chi^2 = 33.59, df = 4, p < 0.001]*$$

The Cramer's V value of .295, significant at the .000 level (Approx. Sig.), showed that the association between gender and grade, although weak, was positive. This meant that men (coded 1 whereas females were coded 2) were more likely to be employed at higher grades GC01–5 (coded using lower numbers). John also quoted this statistic in his project report:

$$[V_c = 0.295, p < 0.001]$$

To explore this association further, John examined the cell values in relation to the row and column totals. Of males, 5 per cent were in higher grades (GC01–5) compared to less than 2 per cent of females. In contrast, only 38 per cent of males were in the lowest grade (GC09) compared with 67 per cent of females.

---

*You will have noticed that the computer printout in this box does not have a zero before the decimal point. This is because most software packages follow the North American convention, in contrast to the UK convention of placing a zero before the decimal point.

Box 12.15
Focus on student research

Testing the representativeness of a sample

Benson's research question was, 'To what extent do the espoused values of an organisation match the underlying cultural assumptions?' As part of his research, he sent a questionnaire to the 150 employees in the organisation where he worked and 97 of these responded. The responses from each category of employee in terms of their seniority within the organisation's hierarchy were as shown in the spreadsheet:

		Shop floor workers	Technicians	Supervisors	Quality managers	Management team	Total
1							
2 Respondents	Number	49	15	21	8	4	97
3	Cumulative proportion	0.505	0.660	0.876	0.959	1.000	
4 Total Employees	Number	73	31	24	17	5	150
5	Cumulative proportion	0.487	0.693	0.853	0.967	1.000	
6 *Difference*		0.018	0.034	0.023	0.008	0.000	

The maximum difference between his observed cumulative proportion (that for respondents) and his specified cumulative proportion (that for total employees) was 0.034. This was the value of his *D* statistic. Consulting a 'critical values of *D* for the Kolmogorov–Smirnov test' table for a sample size of 97 revealed the probability that the two distributions differed by chance alone was less than 0.01, in other words, less than 1 per cent. He concluded that those employees who responded did not differ significantly from the total population in terms of their seniority with the organisation's hierarchy. This was stated in his research report:

Statistical analysis showed the sample selected did not differ significantly from all employees in terms of their seniority within the organisation's hierarchy $[D = .034, p < .01]$.

The Kolmogorov–Smirnov test calculates a *D* statistic that is then used to work out the probability of the two distributions differing by chance alone. Although the test and statistic are not often found in analysis software, they are relatively straightforward to calculate using a spreadsheet (Box 12.15). A reasonably clear description of this can be found in Cohen and Holliday (1996). Once calculated, you will need to look up the significance of your *D* value in a 'critical values of *D* for the Kolmogorov–Smirnov test' table. A probability of 0.05 means that there is only a 5 per cent chance that the two distributions differ by chance alone, and is termed statistically significant. Therefore a probability of 0.05 or smaller means you can be at least 95 per cent certain that the difference between your two distributions cannot be explained by chance factors alone.

Numerical data If a numerical variable can be divided into two distinct groups using a descriptive variable you can assess the likelihood of these groups being different using an **independent groups *t*-test**. This compares the difference in the means of the two groups using a measure of the spread of the scores. If the likelihood of any difference between these two groups occurring by chance alone is low, this will be represented by a large *t* statistic with a probability less than 0.05. This is termed statistically significant.

Alternatively, you might have numerical data for two variables that measure the same feature but under different conditions. Your research could focus on the effects of an intervention such as employee counselling. As a consequence, you would have pairs of data that measure work performance before and after counselling for each case. To assess the likelihood of any difference between your two variables (each half of the pair) occurring by chance alone you would use a **paired *t*-test** (Box 12.16). Although the calculation of this is slightly different, your interpretation would be the same as for the independent groups *t*-test.

Although the ***t*-test** assumes that the data are normally distributed (Section 12.3), this can be ignored without too many problems even with sample sizes of less than 30 (Hays 1994). The assumption that the data for the two groups have the same variance (standard deviation

Box 12.16
Focus on management research

Testing whether two groups are different

Schneider and Cornwell's (2005) paper in the *International Journal of Advertising* is concerned with the practice of placing brand names, logos and products in computer games. In particular, it is concerned with the impact of different placement practices on game players' recall of brand name, logo and product. This, they highlight, is of increasing importance owing to the rapid increase in the cost of producing a top-quality computer game and the need to seek out methods to subsidise these costs, such as through shared marketing and cross-promotional campaigns. In their paper they propose a number of hypotheses regarding the placement of brands using 'banners', the computer game equivalent of displaying a banner at a sporting event. Four of these hypotheses are listed in the subsequent table.

Having collected data by questionnaire from 46 participants on the brands and products they could remember after playing a particular game for a specified period, the hypotheses were tested using paired samples *t*-tests. The results for the first four hypotheses were as follows:

Hypothesis	*t* value	Df	Significance (2-tailed)
Prominent placements will elicit greater recall than subtle placements	5.627	45	<0.001
Prominent placements will elicit greater recognition than subtle placements	9.833	45	<0.001
Experienced players will show greater recall of brand placement than novice players	2.383	44	<0.02
Experienced players will show greater recognition of brand placement than novice players	3.734	44	<0.001

Based on these results, Schneider and Cornwell argued that the banners which had been placed prominently were siginificantly better recalled than those placed subtly. In addition, prominent placements of banners were siginificantly better recognised than subtle placements. This, along with other aspects of their research, was used to provide guidance regarding the characteristics of successful banner placement in computer games.

squared) can also be ignored provided that the two samples are of similar size (Hays 1994). If the data are skewed or the sample size is small, the most appropriate statistical test is the Mann-Whitney *U* Test. This test is the non-parametric equivalent of the independent groups *t*-test (Dancey and Reidy 2008). Consequently, if the likelihood of any difference between these two groups occurring by chance alone is low, this will be represented by a large *U* statistic with a probability less than 0.05. This is termed statistically significant.

To test whether three or more groups are different

If a numerical variable is divided into three or more distinct groups using a descriptive variable, you can assess the likelihood of these groups being different occurring by chance alone by using **one-way analysis of variance** or one-way **ANOVA** (Table 12.5). As you can gather from its name, ANOVA analyses the **variance**, that is, the spread of data values, within and between groups of data by comparing means. The *F* ratio or *F* statistic represents these differences. If the likelihood of any difference between groups occurring by chance alone is low, this will be represented by a large *F* ratio with a probability of less than 0.05. This is termed statistically significant (Box 12.17).

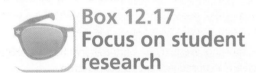

Box 12.17
Focus on student research

Testing whether three (or more) groups are different

Andy was interested to discover whether there were differences in job satisfaction across three groups of employees (managers, administrators, shop floor workers) within a manufacturing organisation. He decided to measure job satisfaction using a tried-and-tested scale based on five questions that resulted in a job satisfaction score (numerical data) for each employee. He labelled this scale 'broad view of job satisfaction'.

After ensuring that the assumptions of one-way ANOVA were satisfied, he analysed his data using statistical analysis software. His output included the following:

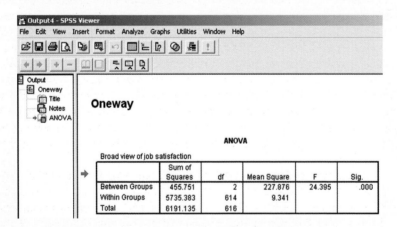

This output shows that the *F* ratio value of 24.395 with 2 and 614 degrees of freedom (df) has a probability of occurrence by chance alone of less than 0.001 if there is no significant difference between the three groups. In his research report Andy concluded that there was:

a statistically significant $[F = 24.39, p < .001]$ difference in job satisfaction between managers, administrators, and shop floor workers.

The following assumptions need to be met before using one-way ANOVA. More detailed discussion is available in Hays (1994) and Dancey and Reidy (2008).

- Each data value is independent and does not relate to any of the other data values. This means that you should not use one-way ANOVA where data values are related in some way, such as the same case being tested repeatedly.
- The data for each group are normally distributed (Section 12.3). This assumption is not particularly important provided that the number of cases in each group is large (30 or more).
- The data for each group have the same variance (standard deviation squared). However, provided that the number of cases in the largest group is not more than 1.5 times that of the smallest group, this appears to have very little effect on the test results.

Assessing the strength of relationship

If your data set contains ranked or numerical data, it is likely that, as part of your exploratory data analysis, you will already have plotted the relationship between cases for these ranked or numerical variables using a scatter graph (Figure 12.12). Such relationships might include those between weekly sales of a new product and those of a similar established product, or age of employees and their length of service with the company. These examples emphasise the fact that your data can contain two sorts of relationship:

- those where a change in one variable is accompanied by a change in another variable but it is not clear which variable caused the other to change, a **correlation**;
- those where a change in one or more (independent) variables causes a change in another (dependent) variable, a cause-and-effect relationship.

To assess the strength of relationship between pairs of variables

A **correlation coefficient** enables you to quantify the strength of the linear relationship between two ranked or numerical variables. This coefficient (usually represented by the letter r) can take on any value between -1 and $+1$ (Figure 12.14). A value of $+1$ represents a perfect **positive correlation**. This means that the two variables are precisely related and that, as values of one variable increase, values of the other variable will increase. By contrast, a value of -1 represents a perfect **negative correlation**. Again, this means that the two variables are precisely related; however, as the values of one variable increase those of the other decrease. Correlation coefficients between -1 and $+1$ represent weaker positive and negative correlations, a value of 0 meaning the variables are perfectly independent. Within business research it is extremely unusual to obtain perfect correlations.

For data collected from a sample you will need to know the probability of your correlation coefficient having occurred by chance alone. Most analysis software calculates this probability automatically (Box 12.18). As outlined earlier, if this probability is very low (usually less than 0.05) then it is considered statistically significant. If the probability is greater than 0.05 then your relationship is not statistically significant.

Figure 12.14
Values of the correlation coefficient

Box 12.18
Focus on student research

Assessing the strength of relationship between pairs of variables

As part of his research project, Hassan obtained data from a company on the number of television advertisements, number of enquiries and number of sales of their product. These data were entered into the statistical analysis software. He wished to discover whether there were any relationships between the following pairs of these variables:

- number of television advertisements and number of enquiries;
- number of television advertisements and number of sales;
- number of enquiries and number of sales.

As the data were numerical, he used the statistical analysis software to calculate Pearson's product moment correlation coefficients for all pairs of variables. The output was a correlation matrix:

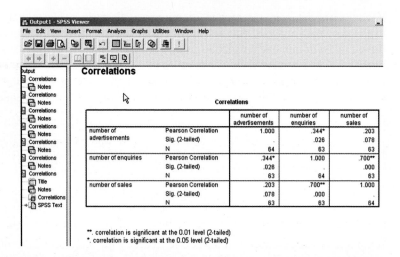

Correlations

		number of advertisements	number of enquiries	number of sales
number of advertisements	Pearson Correlation	1.000	.344*	.203
	Sig. (2-tailed)		.026	.078
	N	64	63	63
number of enquiries	Pearson Correlation	.344*	1.000	.700**
	Sig. (2-tailed)	.026		.000
	N	63	64	63
number of sales	Pearson Correlation	.203	.700**	1.000
	Sig. (2-tailed)	.078	.000	
	N	63	63	64

**. correlation is significant at the 0.01 level (2-tailed)
*. correlation is significant at the 0.05 level (2-tailed)

Hassan's matrix is symmetrical because correlation implies only a relationship rather than a cause-and-effect relationship. The value in each cell of the matrix is the correlation coefficient. Thus, the correlation between the number of advertisements and the number of enquiries is 0.344. This coefficient shows that there is a fairly weak but positive relationship between the number of television advertisements and the number of enquiries. The (*) highlights that the probability of this correlation coefficient occurring by chance alone is less than 0.05 (5 per cent). This correlation coefficient is therefore statistically significant.

Using the data in this matrix Hassan concluded that:

There is a statistically significant strong positive relationship between the number of enquiries and the number of sales ($r = .700$, $p < .01$) and a statistically significant but weaker relationship between the number of television advertisements and the number of enquiries ($r = .344$, $p < .05$). However, there is no statistically significant relationship between the number of television advertisements and the number of sales ($r = .203$, $p > .05$).

If both your variables contain numerical data you should use **Pearson's product moment correlation coefficient** (PMCC) to assess the strength of relationship (Table 12.5). Where these data are from a sample then the sample should have been selected at random. However, if one or both of your variables contain rank data you cannot use PMCC, but will need to use a correlation coefficient that is calculated using ranked data. Such rank correlation coefficients represent the degree of agreement between the two sets of rankings. Before calculating the rank correlation coefficient, you will need to ensure that the data for both variables are ranked. Where one of the variables is numerical this will necessitate converting these data to ranked data. Subsequently, you have a choice of rank correlation coefficients. The two used most widely in business and management research are **Spearman's rank correlation coefficient** (Spearman's rho) and **Kendall's rank correlation coefficient** (Kendall's tau). Where data is being used from a sample, both these rank correlation coefficients assume that the sample is selected at random and the data are ranked (ordinal). Given this, it is not surprising that, whenever you can use Spearman's rank correlation coefficient, you can also use Kendall's rank correlation coefficient. However, if your data for a variable contain tied ranks, Kendall's rank correlation coefficient is generally considered to be the more appropriate of these coefficients to use. Although each of the correlation coefficients discussed uses a different formula in its calculation, the resulting coefficient is interpreted in the same way as PMCC.

To assess the strength of a cause-and-effect relationship between variables

In contrast to the correlation coefficient, the **coefficient of determination** (sometimes known as the **regression coefficient**) enables you to assess the strength of relationship between a numerical dependent variable and one or more numerical independent variables. Once again, where these data have been selected from a sample, the sample must have been selected at random. For a dependent variable and one (or perhaps two) independent variables you will have probably already plotted this relationship on a scatter graph. If you have more than two independent variables this is unlikely as it is very difficult to represent four or more scatter graph axes visually!

The coefficient of determination (represented by r^2) can take on any value between 0 and +1. It measures the proportion of the variation in a dependent variable (amount of sales) that can be explained statistically by the independent variable (marketing expenditure) or variables (marketing expenditure, number of sales staff, etc.). This means that if all the variation in amount of sales can be explained by the marketing expenditure and the number of sales staff, the coefficient of determination will be 1. If 50 per cent of the variation can be explained, the coefficient of determination will be 0.5, and if none of the variation can be explained, the coefficient will be 0 (Box 12.19). Within our research we have rarely obtained a coefficient above 0.8.

Box 12.19
Focus on student research

Assessing a cause-and-effect relationship

As part of her research project, Arethea wanted to assess the relationship between all the employees' annual salaries and the number of years each had been employed by an organisation. She believed that an employee's annual salary would be dependent on the number of years for which she or he had been employed (the independent variable). Arethea entered these data into her analysis software and calculated a coefficient of determination (r^2) of 0.37.

As she was using data for all employees of the firm (the total population) rather than a sample, the probability of her coefficient occurring by chance alone was 0. She therefore concluded that 37 per cent of the variation in current employees' salary could be explained by the number of years they had been employed by the organisation.

The process of calculating coefficient of determination and regression equation using one independent variable is normally termed **regression analysis**. Calculating a **coefficient of multiple determination** (or **multiple regression coefficient**) and regression equation using two or more independent variables is termed **multiple regression analysis**. The calculations and interpretation required by multiple regression are relatively complicated, and we advise you to use statistical analysis software and consult a detailed statistics textbook or computer manual such as Norusis (2007). Most statistical analysis software will calculate the significance of the coefficient of multiple determination for sample data automatically. A very low significance value (usually less than 0.05) means that your coefficient is unlikely to have occurred by chance alone. A value greater than 0.05 means you can conclude that your coefficient of multiple determination could have occurred by chance alone.

To predict the value of a variable from one or more other variables

Regression analysis can also be used to predict the values of a dependent variable given the values of one or more independent variables by calculating a **regression equation**. You may wish to predict the amount of sales for a specified marketing expenditure and number of sales staff. You would represent this as a regression equation:

$$AoS_i = \alpha + \beta_1 ME_i + \beta_2 NSS_i$$

where:

AoS is the Amount of Sales
ME is the Marketing Expenditure
NSS is the Number of Sales Staff
α is the regression constant
β_1 and β_2 are the beta coefficients

This equation can be translated as stating:

$$Amount\ of\ Sales_i = value + (\beta_1 \times Marketing\ Expenditure_i) + (\beta_2 \times Number\ of\ Sales\ Staff_i)$$

Using regression analysis you would calculate the values of the constant coefficient α and the slope coefficients β_1 and β_2 from data you had already collected on amount of sales, marketing expenditure and number of sales staff. A specified marketing expenditure and number of sales staff could then be substituted into the regression equation to predict the amount of sales that would be generated. When calculating a regression equation you need to ensure the following assumptions are met:

- The relationship between dependent and independent variables is linear. **Linearity** refers to the degree to which the change in the dependent variable is related to the change in the independent variables. Linearity can easily be examined through residual plots (these are usually drawn by the analysis software). Two things may influence the linearity. First, individual cases with extreme values on one or more variables (outliers) may violate the assumption of linearity. It is, therefore, important to identify these outliers and, if appropriate, exclude them from the regression analysis. Second, the values for one or more variables may violate the assumption of linearity. For these variables the data values may need to be transformed. Techniques for this can be found in other, more specialised books on multivariate data analysis, for example Anderson (2003).
- The extent to which the data values for the dependent and independent variables have equal variances (this term was explained earlier in Section 12.4), also known as **homoscedasticity**. Again, analysis software usually contains statistical tests for equal

variance. For example, the Levene test for homogeneity of variance measures the equality of variances for a single pair of variables. If **heteroscedasticity** (that is, unequal variances) exists, it may still be possible to carry out your analysis. Further details of this can again be found in more specialised books on multivariate analysis such as Anderson (2003).

- Absence of correlation between two or more independent variables (**collinearity** or **multicollinearity**), as this makes it difficult to determine the separate effects of individual variables. The simplest diagnostic is to use the correlation coefficients, extreme collinearity being represented by a correlation coefficient of 1. The rule of thumb is that the presence of high correlations (generally 0.90 and above) indicates substantial collinearity (Hair *et al.* 2006). Other common measures include the tolerance value and its inverse – the **variance inflation factor** (VIF). Hair *et al.* (2006) recommend that a very small tolerance value (0.10 or below) or a large VIF value (10 or above) indicates high collinearity.
- The data for the independent variables and dependent variable are normally distributed (Section 12.3).

The coefficient of determination, r^2 (discussed earlier), can be used as a measure of how good a predictor your regression equation is likely to be. If your equation is a perfect predictor then the coefficient of determination will be 1. If the equation can predict only 50 per cent of the variation, then the coefficient of determination will be 0.5, and if the equation predicts none of the variation, the coefficient will be 0. The coefficient of multiple determination (R^2) indicates the degree of the goodness of fit for your estimated multiple regression equation. It can be interpreted as how good a predictor your multiple regression equation is likely to be. It represents the proportion of the variability in the dependent variable that can be explained by your multiple regression equation. This means that when multiplied by 100, the coefficient of multiple determination can be interpreted as the percentage of variation in the dependent variable that can be explained by the estimated regression equation. The adjusted R^2 statistic (which takes into account the number of independent variables in your regression equation) is preferred by some researchers as it helps avoid overestimating the impact of adding an independent variable on the amount of variability explained by the estimated regression equation.

The t-test and F-test are used to work out the probability of the relationship represented by your regression analysis having occurred by chance. In simple linear regression (with one independent and one dependent variable), the t-test and F-test will give you the same answer. However, in multiple regression, the t-test is used to find out the probability of the relationship between each of the individual independent variables and the dependent variable occurring by chance. In contrast, the F-test is used to find out the overall probability of the relationship between the dependent variable and all the independent variables occurring by chance. The t distribution table and the F distribution table are used to determine whether a t-test or an F-test is significant by comparing the results with the t distribution and F distribution respectively, given the degrees of freedom and the pre-defined significance level.

Examining trends

When examining longitudinal data the first thing we recommend you do is to draw a line graph to obtain a visual representation of the trend (Figure 12.7). Subsequent to this, statistical analyses can be undertaken. Three of the more common uses of such analyses are:

- to examine the trend or relative change for a single variable over time;
- to compare trends or the relative change for variables measured in different units or of different magnitudes;
- to determine the long-term trend and forecast future values for a variable.

These have been summarised earlier in Table 12.5.

Box 12.20
Focus on student research

Forecasting number of road injury accidents

As part of her research project, Nimmi had obtained data on the number of road injury accidents and the number of drivers breath tested for alcohol in 39 police force areas. In addition, she obtained data on the total population (in thousands) for each of these areas from the most recent census. Nimmi wished to find out if it was possible to predict the number of road injury accidents (RIA) in each police area (her dependent variable) using the number of drivers breath tested (BT) and the total population in thousands (POP) for each of the police force areas (independent variables). This she represented as an equation:

$$RIA_i = \alpha + \beta_1 BT_i + \beta_2 POP_i$$

Nimmi entered her data into the analysis software and undertook a multiple regression. She scrolled down the output file and found the table headed 'Coefficients':

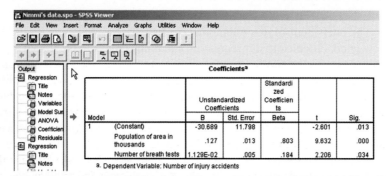

Nimmi substituted the 'unstandardized coefficients' into her regression equation (after rounding the values):

$$RIA_i = -30.7 + 0.01BT_i + 0.13POP_i$$

This meant she could now predict the number of road injury accidents for a police area of different populations for different numbers of drivers breath tested for alcohol. For example, the number of road injury accidents for an area of 500 000 population in which 10 000 drivers were breath tested for alcohol can now be estimated:

$$-30.7 + (0.01 \times 10\,000) + (0.13 \times 500)$$
$$= -30.5 + 100 + 65$$
$$= 135$$

In order to check the usefulness of these estimates, Nimmi scrolled back up her output and looked at the results of R^2, t-test and F-test:

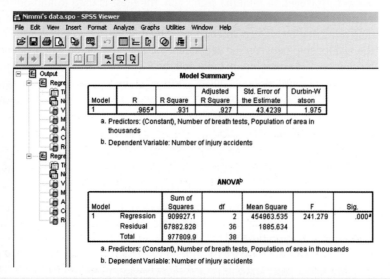

The R^2 and adjusted R^2 values of 0.965 and 0.931 respectively both indicated that there was a high degree of goodness of fit of her regression model. It also means that over 90 per cent of variance in the dependent variable (the number of road injury accidents) can be explained by the regression model. The F-test result was 241.279 with a significance ('Sig.') of .000. This meant that the probability of these results occurring by chance was less than 0.0005. Therefore, a significant relationship was present between the number of road injury accidents in an area and the population of the area, and the number of drivers breath tested for alcohol.

The t-test results for the individual regression coefficients (shown in the first extract) for the two independent variables were 9.632 and 2.206. Once again, the probability of both these results occurring by chance was less than 0.05, being less than 0.001 for the independent variable population of area in thousands and 0.034 for the independent variable number of breath tests. This means that the regression coefficients for these variables were both statistically significant at the $p < 0.05$ level.

To examine the trend

To answer some research question(s) and meet some objectives you may need to examine the trend for one variable. One way of doing this is to use **index numbers** to compare the relative magnitude for each data value (case) over time rather than using the actual data value. Index numbers are also widely used in business publications and by organisations. The *Financial Times* share indices such as the FTSE 100 (Box 12.21, overleaf) and the Retail Price Index are well-known examples.

Although such indices can involve quite complex calculations, they all compare change over time against a base period. The **base period** is normally given the value of 100 (or 1000 in the case of many share indices, including the FTSE 100), and change is calculated relative to this. Thus a value greater than 100 would represent an increase relative to the base period, and a value less than 100 a decrease.

To calculate simple index numbers for each case of a longitudinal variable you use the following formula:

$$\text{index number of case} = \frac{\text{data value for case}}{\text{data value for base period}} \times 100$$

Thus, if a company's sales were 125 000 units in 2007 (base period) and 150 000 units in 2008, the index number for 2007 would be 100 and for 2008 it would be 120.

To compare trends

To answer some other research question(s) and to meet the associated objectives you may need to compare trends between two or more variables measured in different units or at different magnitudes. For example, to compare changes in prices of fuel oil and coal over time is difficult as the prices are recorded for different units (litres and tonnes). One way of overcoming this is to use index numbers (Section 12.4) and compare the relative changes in the value of the index rather than actual figures. The index numbers for each variable are calculated in the same way as outlined earlier.

To determine the trend and forecasting

The trend can be estimated by drawing a freehand line through the data on a line graph. However, these data are often subject to variations such as seasonal variations, and so this method is not very accurate. A straightforward way of overcoming this is to calculate

Box 12.21
Focus on research in the news

FT

Rock faces FTSE 100 exit

The most comprehensive reshuffle of the FTSE 100 index since the aftermath of the dotcom bubble is expected to be announced by index compiler FTSE today.

Seven blue-chip companies, including Northern Rock, the stricken mortgage lender, and Barratt Developments, the housebuilder, could be ejected from the index when the results of the latest quarterly reshuffle are revealed. Punch Taverns and Mitchells & Butlers, the pub operators, Daily Mail & General Trust, the newspaper publisher, DSG International, the high street retailer and Tate & Lyle, the sugar and sweeteners group that has issued several profit warnings, are also likely to lose their places.

The changes broadly reflect the impact of the credit squeeze and the expectation that the UK economy will slow sharply next year, according to analysts. In the past three months, M&B and DSG have both lost almost a quarter of their respective values as investors have fretted about waning consumer confidence, while Barratt shares have tumbled 45 per cent. The last time the FTSE 100 saw such wide-ranging changes was in September 2001 when eight companies left the index. They included IT companies Misys and CMG and telecom companies Energis, Telewest, Colt Telecom and Marconi.

Mike Lenhoff, chief strategist at Brewin Dolphin, said that although consumer-facing stocks were out of favour, further interest rate cuts would help companies such as Barratt. 'If we get the sort of rate cuts that the markets are expecting then the consumer stocks could do really well. This is also where the value lies, given how far some of these stocks have fallen,' he said.

New entrants to the FTSE 100 are expected to include Kelda Group, the water company, FirstGroup, which operates 40 000 yellow school buses in the US, and TUI Group and Thomas Cook, the recently enlarged package tour operators. Cairn Energy, which was demoted from the main index this year, should also join the FTSE 100, along with Admiral, the insurer, and G4S, the security group. Meanwhile, Paragon, the specialist mortgage lender, Pendragon, the UK's largest car dealership, and Luminar, the bar and nightclub operator, are all likely to be demoted from the FTSE 250 mid cap index. Likely replacements include mining group Aricom, which recently switched its listing from Aim, Dignity, the funerals services group, and 888.com, the online gaming company.

Calculated using last night's closing prices, changes to the FTSE indices take effect after the close of business on December 21. An FTSE 100 stock is ejected if it falls to position 111 or below, while a stock must fall below position 376 for demotion from the FTSE 250 index. The changes to the index are subject to ratification by FTSE's review committee.

Source: article by Orr, Robert and Hume, Neil (2007) *Financial Times*, 12 Dec. Copyright © The Financial Times Ltd.

a moving average for the time series of data values. Calculating a **moving average** involves replacing each value in the time series with the mean of that value and those values directly preceding and following it (Morris 2003). This smoothes out the variation in the data so that you can see the trend more clearly. The calculation of a moving average is relatively straightforward using either a spreadsheet or statistical analysis software.

Once the trend has been established, it is possible to forecast future values by continuing the trend forward for time periods for which data have not been collected. This involves calculating the **long-term trend** – that is, the amount by which values are changing each time period after variations have been smoothed out. Once again, this is relatively straightforward to calculate using analysis software. Forecasting can also be undertaken using other statistical methods, including regression analysis.

If you are using regression for your time series analysis, the **Durbin-Watson statistic** can be used to discover whether the value of your dependent variable at time t is related to its value at the previous time period, commonly referred to as $t - 1$. This situation, known as **autocorrelation** or **serial correlation**, is important as it means that the results of your regression analysis are less likely to be reliable. The Durbin-Watson statistic ranges in value from zero to four. A value of two indicates no autocorrelation. A value towards zero indicates positive autocorrelation. Conversely, a value towards four indicates negative autocorrelation. More detailed discussion of the Durbin-Watson test can be found in other, more specialised books on multivariate data analysis, for example Anderson (2003).

12.6 Summary

- Data for quantitative analysis can be collected and subsequently coded at different scales of measurement. The data type (precision of measurement) will constrain the data presentation, summary and analysis techniques you can use.
- Data are entered for computer analysis as a data matrix in which each column usually represents a variable and each row a case. Your first variable should be a unique identifier to facilitate error checking.
- All data should, with few exceptions, be recorded using numerical codes to facilitate analyses.
- Where possible, you should use existing coding schemes to enable comparisons.
- For primary data you should include pre-set codes on the data collection form to minimise coding after collection. For variables where responses are not known, you will need to develop a codebook after data have been collected for the first 50 to 100 cases.
- You should enter codes for all data values, including missing data.
- Your data matrix must be checked for errors.
- Your initial analysis should explore data using both tables and diagrams. Your choice of table or diagram will be influenced by your research question(s) and objectives, the aspects of the data you wish to emphasise, and the scale of measurement at which the data were recorded. This may involve using:
  - tables to show specific values;
  - bar charts, multiple bar charts, histograms and, occasionally, pictograms to show highest and lowest values;
  - line graphs to show trends;
  - pie charts and percentage component bar charts to show proportions;
  - box plots to show distributions;
  - scatter graphs to show relationships between variables.
- Subsequent analyses will involve describing your data and exploring relationships using statistics. As before, your choice of statistics will be influenced by your research question(s) and objectives and the scale of measurement at which the data were recorded. Your analysis may involve using statistics such as:
  - the mean, median and mode to describe the central tendency;
  - the inter-quartile range and the standard deviation to describe the dispersion;
  - chi square, Cramer's V and phi to test whether two variables are significantly associated;
  - Kolmogorov-Smirnov to test whether the values differ significantly from a specified population;
  - *t*-tests and ANOVA to test whether groups are significantly different;
  - correlation and regression to assess the strength of relationships between variables;
  - regression analysis to predict values.
- Longitudinal data may necessitate selecting different statistical techniques such as:
  - index numbers to establish a trend or to compare trends between two or more variables measured in different units or at different magnitudes;
  - moving averages and regression analysis to determine the trend and forecast.

Self-check questions

Help with these questions is available at the end of the chapter.

12.1 The following secondary data have been obtained from the Park Trading Company's audited annual accounts:

Year end	Income	Expenditure
2000	11 000 000	9 500 000
2001	15 200 000	12 900 000
2002	17 050 000	14 000 000
2003	17 900 000	14 900 000
2004	19 000 000	16 100 000
2005	18 700 000	17 200 000
2006	17 100 000	18 100 000
2007	17 700 000	19 500 000
2008	19 900 000	20 000 000

a Which are the variables and which are the cases?

b Sketch a possible data matrix for these data for entering into a spreadsheet.

12.2 a How many variables will be generated from the following request?

Please tell me up to five things you like about this film.   For office use

. . . .   ❏ ❏ ❏

. . . .   ❏ ❏ ❏

. . . .   ❏ ❏ ❏

. . . .   ❏ ❏ ❏

. . . .   ❏ ❏ ❏

b How would you go about devising a coding scheme for these variables from a survey of 500 cinema patrons?

12.3 a Illustrate the data from the Park Trading Company's audited annual accounts (self-check question 12.1) to show trends in income and expenditure.

b What does your diagram emphasise?

c What diagram would you use to emphasise the years with the lowest and highest income?

12.4 As part of research into the impact of television advertising on donations by credit card to a major disaster appeal, data have been collected on the number of viewers reached and the number of donations each day for the past two weeks.

a Which diagram or diagrams would you use to explore these data?

b Give reasons for your choice.

12.5 a Which measures of central tendency and dispersion would you choose to describe the Park Trading Company's income (self-check question 12.1) over the period 2000–2008?

b Give reasons for your choice.

12.6 A colleague has collected data from a sample of 80 students. He presents you with the following output from the statistical analysis software:

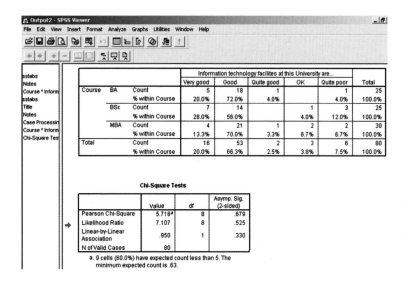

Explain what this tells you about undergraduate and postgraduate students' opinion of the information technology facilities.

12.7 Briefly describe when you would use regression analysis and correlation analysis, using examples to illustrate your answer.

12.8 a Use an appropriate technique to compare the following data on share prices for two financial service companies over the past six months, using the period six months ago as the base period:

	EJ Investment Holdings	AE Financial Services
Price 6 months ago	€10	€587
Price 4 months ago	€12	€613
Price 2 months ago	€13	€658
Current price	€14	€690

b Which company's share prices have increased most in the last six months? (Note: you should quote relevant statistics to justify your answer.)

Review and discussion questions

12.9 Use a search engine to discover coding schemes that already exist for ethnic group, family expenditure, industry group, socio-economic class and the like. To do this you will probably find it best to type the phrase "coding ethnic group" into the search box.

a Discuss how credible you think each coding scheme is with a friend. To come to an agreed answer pay particular attention to:
- the organisation (or person) that is responsible for the coding scheme;
- any explanations regarding the coding scheme's design;
- use of the coding scheme to date.

b Widen your search to include coding schemes that may be of use for your research project. Make a note of the web address of any that are of interest.

12.10 With a friend, choose a large company in which you are interested. Obtain a copy of the annual report for this company. If it is not readily available via the Internet, hard copy can often be obtained from your university library. Examine the use of tables, graphs and charts in your chosen company's report.

    a To what extent does the use of graphs and charts in your chosen report follow the guidance summarised in Box 12.8 and Table 12.2?

    b Why do you think this is?

12.11 With a group of friends, each choose a different share price index. Well-known indices you could chose include the Nasdaq Composite Index, France's CAC 40, Germany's Xetra Dax, Hong Kong's HIS-Hang Seng, Japan's Nikkei Average Index, the UK's FTSE 100 and the USA's Dow Jones Industrial Average Index.

    a For each of the indices, find out how it is calculated and note down its daily values for a one-week period.

    b Compare your findings regarding the calculation of your chosen index with those for the indices chosen by your friends, noting down similarities and differences.

    c To what extent do the indices differ in the changes in share prices they show? Why do you think this is?

12.12 Find out whether your university provides you with access to SPSS. If it does, visit this book's companion website and download the self-teach package and associated data sets. Work through this to explore the features of SPSS.

Progressing your research project

Analysing your data quantitatively

- Examine the technique(s) you are proposing to use to collect data to answer your research question. You need to decide whether you are collecting any data that could usefully be analysed quantitatively.
- If you decide that your data should be analysed quantitatively, you must ensure that the data collection methods you intend to use have been designed to make analysis by computer as straightforward as possible. In particular, you need to pay attention to the coding scheme for each variable and the layout of your data matrix.

- Once your data have been entered into a computer and the dataset opened in your analysis software, you will need to explore and present them. Bearing your research question in mind, you should select the most appropriate diagrams and tables after considering the suitability of all possible techniques. Remember to label your diagrams clearly and to keep an electronic copy, as they may form part of your research report.
- Once you are familiar with your data, describe and explore relationships using those statistical techniques that best help you to answer your research questions and are suitable for the data type. Remember to keep an annotated copy of your analyses, as you will need to quote statistics to justify statements you make in the findings section of your research report.

References

Anderson, T.W. (2003) *An Introduction to Multivariate Statistical Analysis*. New York: John Wiley.

Anderson, D.R., Sweeney, D.J. and Williams, T.A. (1999) *Statistics for Business and Economics* (7th edn). Cincinnati, OH: South-Western College Publishing.

Berman Brown, R. and Saunders, M. (2008) *Dealing with statistics: What You Need to Know*. Maidenhead: McGraw-Hill Open University Press.

Blumberg, B., Cooper, D.R. and Schindler, D.S. (2008) *Business Research Methods*. Maidenhead: McGraw-Hill.

Cohen, L. and Holliday, M. (1996) *Practical Statistics for Students*. London: Paul Chapman.

Curwin, J. and Slater, R. (2007) *Quantitative Methods: A Short Course*. London: Thomson Learning EMEA.

Dancey, C.P. and Reidy, J. (2008) *Statistics Without Maths for Psychology: Using SPSS for Windows* (4th edn). Harlow: Prentice Hall.

deVaus, D.A. (2002) *Surveys in Social Research* (5th edn). London: Routledge.

Diamantopoulos, A. and Schlegelmilch, B.B. (1997) *Taking the Fear Out of Data Analysis*. London: Dryden Press.

Eurostat (2007) 'Environment and energy statistics – data air emissions'. Available at: http://epp.eurostat.cec.eu.int/portal/page?_pageid=1090,30070682,1090_30298591&_dad=portal&_schema=PORTAL [Accessed 16 December 2007.]

Everitt, B.S. and Dunn, G. (2001) *Applied Multivariate Data Analysis* (2nd edn). London: Arnold.

Field, A. (2005) *Discovering Statistics Using SPSS* (2nd edn). London: Sage.

Great Britain Office for National Statistics (2000a) *Standard Occupation Classification Volume 1: Structure and Description of Unit Groups*. London: Stationery Office.

Great Britain Office for National Statistics (2000b) *Standard Occupation Classification Volume 2: The Coding Index*. London: Stationery Office.

Great Britain Office for National Statistics (2002) *Index to the UK Standard Industrial Classification of Economic Activities 2003, UK SIC (2003)*. London: Stationery Office.

Hair, J.F., Black, B., Babin, B., Anderson, R.E. and Tatham, R.L. (2006) *Multivariate Data Analysis* (6th edn). Harlow: Pearson Education.

Harley-Davidson (2007) *Harley-Davidson Inc. 2006 Summary Annual Report*. Available at: http://www.harley-davidson.com/wcm/Content/Pages/Investor_Relations/2006_annual_report_launch.jsp?HDCWPSession=9Sv1LnXZHD7LNcXLTPZ4r2kHNryQn1cjl5hbyQjGtJ8SrswTgltt!1509673641!1097132701&locale=en_US [Accessed 16 December 2007.]

Hays, W.L. (1994) *Statistics* (4th edn). London: Holt-Saunders.

Heath, A., Martin, J. and Beerton, R. (2003) 'Old and new social class measures', in D. Rose and D.J. Pevalin (eds) *A Researcher's Guide to the National Statistics Socio-economic Classification*. London: Sage, pp. 226–43.

Henry, G.T. (1995) *Graphing Data: Techniques for Display and Analysis*. Thousand Oaks, CA: Sage.

Kanji, G.K. (2006) *100 Statistical Tests* (3rd edn). London: Sage.

Kinnear, P.R. and Gray, C.D. (2007) *SPSS 15 Made Simple*. Hove: Psychology Press.

Morris, C. (2003) *Quantitative Approaches in Business Studies* (6th edn). Harlow: Financial Times Prentice Hall.

Norusis, M.J. (2007) *SPSS 15 Guide to Data Analysis*. London: Prentice Hall.

Park, A., Curtice, J., Thomson, K., Phillips, M., Johnson M. and Clery, E. (2007) *British Social Attitudes: 24th Report*. London: Sage.

Push. (2007) 'Push reveals the real costs of higher education'. Available at: http://www.push.co.uk/Document.aspx?id=9E3FCB0D-7275-4BF3-BFA4-8AEEF1D847D1&section=&l2section [Accessed 16 December 2007.]

Robson, C. (2002) *Real World Research* (2nd edn). Oxford: Blackwell.

Rose, D. and Pevalin, D.J. (2003) 'The NS-SEC explained', in D. Rose and D.J. Pevalin (eds) *A Researcher's Guide to the National Statistics Socio-economic Classification*. London: Sage, pp. 28–43.

Schneider, L.-P. and Cornwell, T.B. (2005) 'Cashing in on crashes via brand placement in computer games', *International Journal of Advertising*, Vol. 24, No. 3, pp. 321–43.

Smith, A. (2002) 'The new ethnicity classification in the Labour Force Survey', *Labour Market Trends*, Dec., pp. 657–66.

Snap Surveys (2008) Snap Surveys home page. Available at: http://www.snapsurveys.com [Accessed 1 January 2008.]

Sparrow, J. (1989) 'Graphic displays in information systems: some data properties influencing the effectiveness of alternate forms', *Behaviour and Information Technology*, Vol. 8, No. 1, pp. 43–56.

Sphinx (2008) Sphinx data analysis and survey softwares. Available at: http://www.lesphinx-developpement.fr/en/home/home_sphinx.php [Accessed 1 January 2008.]

Tukey, J.W. (1977) *Exploratory Data Analysis*. Reading, MA: Addison-Wesley.

Yen. T.-Y. and André, P. (2007) 'Ownership structure and operating performance of acquiring firms: the case of English-origin countries', *Journal of Economics and Business*, Vol. 59, No. 5, pp. 380–405.

Further Reading

Berman Brown, R. and Saunders, M. (2008) *Dealing with statistics: What you need to know*. Maidenhead: McGraw Hill Open University Press. This is a statistics book that assumes virtually no statistical knowledge focusing upon which test or graph, when to use it and why. It is written for people who are fearful and anxious about statistics and do not think they can understand numbers!

Blastland, M. and Dilnot, A. (2007) *The Tiger than Isn't*. London: Profile Books. This is a very different type of book on statistics. Rather than explaining how to calculate different statistics it explains how to make sense of the numbers and statistics which we are confronted with in the news media and other publications. It is well worth reading and will almost certainly help you to better understand and interpret numbers and statistics.

Dancey, C.P. and Reidy, J. (2008) *Statistics Without Maths for Psychology: Using SPSS for Windows* (4th edn). Harlow: Prentice Hall. This book introduces key statistical concepts and techniques, avoiding as much maths as possible. It also provides clear descriptions of how to perform statistical tests using SPSS and how to report your results both graphically and in texts.

deVaus, D.A. (2002) *Surveys in Social Research* (5th edn). London: Routledge. Chapters 9 and 10 contain an excellent discussion about coding data and preparing data for analysis. Part IV (Chapters 12–18) provides a detailed discussion of how to analyse survey data.

Field, A. (2005). *Discovering Statistics Using SPSS* (2nd edn). London: Sage. This book offers a clearly explained guide to statistics and using SPSS for Windows. It is divided into four levels, the lowest of which assumes no familiarity with the data analysis software and very little with statistics. It covers inputting data and how to generate and interpret a wide range of tables, diagrams and statistics using SPSS version 13. If you are using an earlier version of SPSS, particularly pre-version 9, be sure to use a book written specifically for that version as there are a number of changes between versions.

Hair, J.F., Black, B., Babin, B., Anderson, R.E. and Tatham, R.L. (2006) *Multivariate Data Analysis*. (6th edn). Harlow: Pearson Education. This book provides detailed information on statistical concepts and techniques. Issues pertinent to design, assumptions, estimation and interpretation are systematically explained for users of more advanced statistical techniques.

Morris, C. (2003) *Quantitative Approaches in Business Studies*. (6th edn). Harlow, Financial Times Prentice Hall. This gives a clear introduction to the use of mathematical and statistical techniques and diagrams in business. Guidance is given on using the Excel spreadsheet.

Case 12
Small business owner managers' skill sets

Since arriving at university, Ishmael had become increasingly interested in small businesses. He had taken all the modules concerned with Small Businesses and Entrepreneurship and chosen to answer a question about small business owner managers for his research project:

'How important do small business owner managers consider the different skill sets needed to run a small business and why?'

Although the project tutor had felt Ishmael's question needed more refinement and suggested that he needed to read widely before collecting any data, Ishmael was pleased with his research question and his method. During his reading to prepare his research proposal he had come across a paper by Brown *et al.* (2006) in the journal *Accounting Forum*. This included, as an appendix, the questions Brown and colleagues had asked small business managers in their questionnaire. He had decided to adapt some of these questions for his own Internet-mediated questionnaire that he administered to small business managers including:

Entrepreneurial Skills					**Exit this survey**

3. How confident are you in your skills in the following areas?

	5 - very confident	4	3	2	1 - not at all confident
Marketing and sales	◡	◡	◡	◡	◡
Interpersonal	◡	◡	◡	◡	◡
Financial/accounts	◡	◡	◡	◡	◡
Managerial	◡	◡	◡	◡	◡
Business planning	◡	◡	◡	◡	◡
IT	◡	◡	◡	◡	◡
Time management	◡	◡	◡	◡	◡
Technical (e.g. plumbing skills for plumber)	◡	◡	◡	◡	◡

4. How important do you think each of the following skills is in running your business at the moment?

	5 - very confident	4	3	2	1 - not at all confident
Marketing and sales	◡	◡	◡	◡	◡
Interpersonal	◡	◡	◡	◡	◡
Financial/accounts	◡	◡	◡	◡	◡
Managerial	◡	◡	◡	◡	◡
Business planning	◡	◡	◡	◡	◡
IT	◡	◡	◡	◡	◡
Time management	◡	◡	◡	◡	◡
Technical (e.g. plumbing skills for plumber)	◡	◡	◡	◡	◡

Source: question layout created by SurveyMonkey.com (2008), Portland, Oregon, USA; author/owner: Ryan Finley. Reproduced with permission

In his initial analysis, Ishmael used SPSS to produce a set of descriptive statistics for each of his questions. For questions three and four these were:

Descriptive Statistics

	N	Minimum	Maximum	Mean	Std. Deviation
3 Confidence in own skills in marketing and sales	96	1	5	3.44	1.074
3 Confidence in own skills in interpersonal	96	2	5	4.06	.723
3 Confidence in own skills in financial/accounts	96	1	5	3.10	.989
3 Confidence in own skills in managerial	96	0	5	3.60	.864
3 Confidence in own skills in business planning	96	1	5	3.17	.959
3 Confidence in own skills in IT	96	1	5	3.39	1.137
3 Confidence in own skills in technical (e.g plumbing skills for plumber)	96	0	5	4.02	1.095
3 Confidence in own skills in time management	96	1	5	3.28	.879
4 Importance of skills in running business-marketing/selling	96	1	5	4.49	.951
4 Importance of skills in running business-interpersonal	96	0	5	4.06	1.177
4 Importance of skills in running business-financial/accounts	96	2	5	3.83	1.002
4 Importance of skills in running business-managerial	96	0	5	3.55	1.141
4 Importance of skills in running business-business planning	96	0	5	4.18	.962
4 Importance of skills in running business-IT	96	0	5	3.35	1.222
4 Importance of skills in running business-technical (e.g. plumbing for plumber)	96	0	5	4.15	1.026
4 Importance of skills in running business-time management	96	1	5	4.05	.863
Valid N (listwise)	96				

He then decided to see if his respondents' perceived confidence in their own skills was related to their perceived importance for each of these skills. Because Ishmael was uncertain as to which statistics to use to examine possible relationships, he used SPSS to both calculate correlation coefficients and to undertake a series of chi square tests:

Correlations

Correlations

		3 Confidence in own skills in marketing and sales	3 Confidence in own skills in interpersonal	3 Confidence in own skills in financial /accounts	4 Importance of skills in running business -marketing /selling	4 Importance of skills in running business -interpersonal	4 Importance of skills in running business -financial /accounts
3 Confidence in own skills in marketing and sales	Pearson Correlation	1	.303**	.056	.241*	−.030	.049
	Sig. (2-tailed)		.003	.590	.018	.770	.636
	N	96	96	96	96	96	96
3 Confidence in own skills in interpersonal	Pearson Correlation	.303**	1	−.068	.047	.119	−.029
	Sig. (2-tailed)	.003		.510	.650	.248	.779
	N	96	96	96	96	96	96
3 Confidence in own skills in financial/accounts	Pearson Correlation	.056	−.068	1	.225*	−.177	−.014
	Sig. (2-tailed)	.590	.510		.028	.084	.891
	N	96	96	96	96	96	96
4 Importance of skills in running business -marketing/selling	Pearson Correlation	.241*	.047	.225*	1	.076	.109
	Sig. (2-tailed)	.018	.650	.028		.463	.292
	N	96	96	96	96	96	96
4 Importance of skills in running business -interpersonal	Pearson Correlation	−.030	.119	−.177	.076	1	.321**
	Sig. (2-tailed)	.770	.248	.084	.463		.001
	N	96	96	96	96	96	96
4 Importance of skills in running business -financial/accounts	Pearson Correlation	.049	−.029	−.014	.109	.321**	1
	Sig. (2-tailed)	.636	.779	.891	.292	.001	
	N	96	96	96	96	96	96

**. Correlation is significant at the 0.01 level (2-tailed).
*. Correlation is significant at the 0.05 level (2-tailed).

Ishmael showed a friend his questionnaire and the SPSS output from his preliminary analysis relating to questions three and four. Over a cup of coffee he asked for advice regarding the analysis of his data. In the subsequent discussion Ishmael emphasised that, as part of the assessment criteria for his research project, he would need to explain why he had chosen to use particular statistics and diagrams.

3 Confidence in own skills in marketing and sales * 4 Importance of skills in running business–marketing/selling

Chi-Square Tests

	Value	df	Asymp. Sig. (2-sided)
Pearson Chi-Square	32.603[a]	16	.008
Likelihood Ratio	22.958	16	.115
Linear-by-Linear Association	5.536	1	.019
N of Valid Cases	96		

a. 20 cells (80.0%) have expected count less than 5.
The minimum expected count is .08.

3 Confidence in own skills in marketing and sales * 4 Importance of skills in running business–interpersonal

Chi-Square Tests

	Value	df	Asymp. Sig. (2-sided)
Pearson Chi-Square	16.662[a]	20	.675
Likelihood Ratio	16.736	20	.670
Linear-by-Linear Association	.087	1	.769
N of Valid Cases	96		

a. 23 cells (76.7%) have expected count less than 5.
The minimum expected count is .04.

References

Brown, R.B., Saunders, M.N.K., and Beresford, R. (2006) 'You owe it to yourselves: the financially literate manager', *Accounting Forum*, Vol. 30, No. 2, pp. 179–91.

SurveyMonkey.com (2008) SurveyMonkey.com. Available at: http://www.surveymonkey.com [Accessed 29 June 2008.]

Questions

1 Ishmael appears uncertain regarding his choice of statistics (the mean and standard deviation) in the first table to describe the responses to questions 3 and 4.
   a How would you advise him?
   b What diagrams would you suggest Ishmael uses to present the data from these questions?
2 Examine the remaining two extracts reporting correlation coefficients and chi square tests. Should Ishmael use either the Pearson's product moment correlation coefficients or the chi square tests as reported in these extracts?
3 Ishmael has decided to undertake further statistical analyses to see if there is any relationship between his respondents' perceived confidence in their own skills and their perceived importance for the same set of skills. Outline the analysis process you would recommend including, if necessary, any further work that might be needed to satisfy your chosen test's assumptions.

Additional case studies relating to material covered in this chapter are available via the book's Companion Website, **www.pearsoned.co.uk/saunders**. They are:

- The marketing of arts festivals
- Marketing a golf course
- The impact of family ownership on financial performance.

Self-check answers

12.1 a The variables are 'income', 'expenditure' and 'year'. There is no real need for a separate case identifier as the variable 'year' can also fulfil this function. Each case (year) is represented by one row of data.

b When the data are entered into a spreadsheet the first column will be the case identifier, for these data the year. Income and expenditure should not be entered with the £ sign as this can be formatted subsequently using the spreadsheet:

	A	B	C
1	Year	Income (£)	Expenditure (£)
2	2000	11000000	9500000
3	2001	15200000	12900000
4	2002	17050000	14000000
5	2003	17900000	14900000
6	2004	19000000	16100000
7	2005	18700000	17200000
8	2006	17100000	18100000
9	2007	17700000	19500000
10	2008	19900000	20000000

12.2 a There is no one correct answer to this question as the number of variables will depend on the method used to code these descriptive data. If you choose the multiple response method, five variables will be generated. If the multiple dichotomy method is used the number of variables will depend on the number of different responses.

b Your first priority is to decide on the level of detail of your intended analyses. Your coding scheme should, if possible, be based on an existing coding scheme. If this is of insufficient detail then it should be designed to be compatible to allow comparisons. To design the coding scheme you need to take the responses from the first 50–100 cases and establish broad groupings. These can be subdivided into increasingly specific subgroups until the detail is sufficient for the intended analysis. Codes can then be allocated to these sub-groups. If you ensure that similar responses receive adjacent codes, this will make any subsequent grouping easier. The actual responses that correspond to each code should be noted in a codebook. Codes should be allocated to data on the data collection form in the 'For office use' box. These codes need to include missing data, such as when four or fewer 'things' have been mentioned.

12.3 a Park Trading Company – Income and Expenditure 2000–08

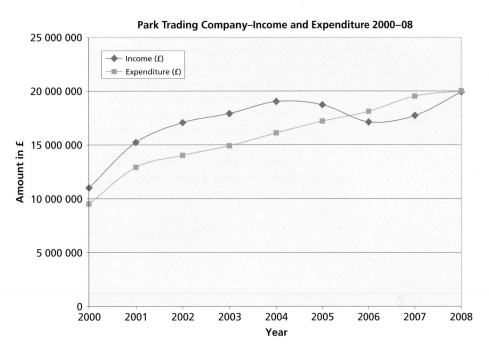

Park Trading Company–Income and Expenditure 2000–08

b Your diagram (it is hoped) emphasises the upward trends of expenditure and (to a lesser extent) income. It also highlights the conjunction where income falls below expenditure in 2006.

c To emphasise the years with the lowest and highest income, you would probably use a histogram because the data are continuous. A frequency polygon would also be suitable.

12.4 a You would probably use a scatter graph in which number of donations would be the dependent variable and number of viewers reached by the advertisement the independent variable.

b This would enable you to see whether there was any relationship between number of viewers reached and number of donations.

12.5 a The first thing you need to do is to establish the data type. As it is numerical, you could theoretically use all three measures of central tendency and both the standard deviation and inter-quartile range. However, you would probably calculate the mean and perhaps the median as measures of central tendency and the standard deviation and perhaps the inter-quartile range as measures of dispersion.

b The mean would be chosen because it includes all data values. The median might be chosen to represent the middle income over the 2000–08 period. The mode would be of little use for these data as each year has different income values.

If you had chosen the mean you would probably choose the standard deviation, as this describes the dispersion of data values around the mean. The inter-quartile range is normally chosen where there are extreme data values that need to be ignored. This is not the case for these data.

12.6 The probability of a chi square value of 5.718 with 8 degrees of freedom occurring by chance alone for these data is 0.679. This means that statistically the association between type of student and their opinion of the information technology facilities is extremely likely to be explained by chance alone. In addition, the assumption of the chi square test that no more than 20 per cent of expected values should be less than 5 has not been satisfied. To explore this lack of association further, you examine the cell values in relation to the row and column totals. For all courses, over 80 per cent of respondents thought the information technology facilities were good or very good. The only course where respondents felt information technology facilities were poor was the BSc, but this represented only three respondents.

12.7 Your answer needs to emphasise that correlation analysis is used to establish whether a change in one variable is accompanied by a change in another. In contrast, regression analysis is used to establish whether a change in a dependent variable is caused by changes in one or more independent variables – in other words, a cause-and-effect relationship. Although it is impossible to list all the examples you might use to illustrate your answer, you should make sure that your examples for regression illustrate a dependent and one or more independent variables.

12.8 a These quantitative data are of different magnitudes. Therefore, the most appropriate technique to compare these data is index numbers. The index numbers for the two companies are:

	EJ Investment Holdings	**AE Financial Services**
Price 6 months ago	100	100.0
Price 4 months ago	120	104.4
Price 2 months ago	130	112.1
Current price	140	117.5

b The price of AE Financial Services' shares has increased by €103 compared with an increase of €4 for EJ Investment Holdings' share price. However, the proportional increase in prices has been greatest for EJ Investment Holdings. Using six months ago as the base period (with a base index number of 100), the index for EJ Investment Holdings' share price is now 140 while the index for AE Financial Services' share price is 117.5.

Get ahead using resources on the Companion Website at:
   www.pearsoned.co.uk/saunders
- Improve your SPSS and NVivo research analysis with practice tutorials.
- Save time researching on the Internet with the Smarter Online Searching Guide.
- Test your progress using self-assessment questions.
- Follow live links to useful websites.

Chapter 13

Analysing qualitative data

Learning outcomes

By the end of this chapter you should be able to:

- identify the main issues that you need to consider when preparing qualitative data for analysis, including when analysing these data using computer aided qualitative data analysis software (CAQDAS);
- transcribe an audio-recorded interview or interview notes and create a data file for analysis by computer;
- recognise the differences between qualitative and quantitative data and understand the implications of this for qualitative data analyses;
- discuss and use deductively based and inductively based analytical approaches to, and procedures for, analysing qualitative data;
- outline reasons for quantifying qualitative data as a means of analysis;
- identify the common functions of CAQDAS and the issues associated with its use.

13.1 Introduction

This chapter is designed to help you analyse the qualitative data that you collect. **Qualitative data** refers to all non-numeric data or data that have not been quantified and can be a product of all research strategies (Section 5.3). It can range from a short list of responses to open-ended questions in an online questionnaire to more complex data such as transcripts of in-depth interviews or entire policy documents. To be useful these data need to be analysed and the meanings understood. Qualitative data analysis procedures assist this, allowing you to develop theory from your data. They include both deductive and inductive approaches and, like the process you use to construct a jigsaw, range from the simple categorisation of responses to processes for identifying relationships between categories.

Until the advent of powerful personal computers and readily available computer aided qualitative data analysis software (**CAQDAS**), qualitative data analysis was undertaken manually. Indeed, it is only comparatively recently that CAQDAS such as NVivo™, ATLAS.ti™, N6™ and HyperRESEARCH™ have begun to be made accessible to students taking undergraduate and masters programmes in universities. Consequently, at an increasing number of universities, it may no longer necessary for you to undertake routine qualitative data management tasks manually such as sorting your data into categories and locating subsets of these data according to specified criteria. However, we would like to sound a note of caution. Whilst the use of analysis software for quantitative data is almost universal, the use of CAQDAS for qualitative data is not so widely practised and the associated software is not always available.

This chapter builds upon the ideas outlined in earlier chapters about data collection. However, unlike Chapter 12, it does not assume that you will necessarily have access to, and will use a computer to organise and analyse your data. Consequently, although we make reference to, and include screenshots of, different software packages in some worked examples, these are used to illustrate generic issues associated with analysis rather than imply that you must use such software. If you wish to develop your skills in one of the more widely used

Nearly all of us have, at some time in our lives, completed a jigsaw puzzle. As children we played with jigsaw puzzles and, as we grew older, those we were able to complete successfully became more complex. Qualitative data analysis can be likened to the process of completing a jigsaw puzzle in which the pieces represent data. These pieces of data and the relationships between them help us as researchers to create our picture, our understanding of what the data is telling us!

When trying to complete a jigsaw puzzle, most of us begin by looking at the picture on the lid of our puzzle's box. Puzzles for which there is no picture are usually more challenging as we have no idea of the picture we are trying to create! Next we empty the pieces out of the box and turn them all picture side up, usually assuming that no pieces are missing! Pieces with similar features such as having an edge or a particular colour are grouped together. Subsequently, we try to fit these similar pieces together. Sometimes we think that two similar pieces should fit together but, in trying to join them, discover that they do not, however hard we try to push them! Other pieces fit together easily. As we progress, the puzzle's picture starts to become clearer to us. Certain pieces, such as those which link different groupings of pieces

The key is for the pieces to be sorted
Source: Marshall Ikonography/Alamy.

together, are extremely important in clarifying the picture. Eventually, we fit the last piece and complete our puzzle. Hopefully, when we look at the picture on the box, it matches perfectly.

CAQDAS packages called NVivo™, a self-teach package is available via our companion website. In addition, books are available that concentrate on specific CAQDAS packages, in particular NVivo™, for example Bazeley (2007).

Within the chapter, therefore, we are concerned with the issues that need to be considered at the planning and analysis stages of your research project and outline a range of analytical procedures. In particular, we discuss:

- the differences between quantitative and qualitative data (Section 13.2);
- preparing your data for analysis, including data transcription and, where appropriate, CAQDAS requirements (Section 13.3);
- the role of theory in qualitative analysis (Section 13.4);
- the natures of qualitative analysis (Section 13.5);
- the use of analytic aids (Section 13.6);
- deductively based analytical procedures (Section 13.7);
- inductively based analytical procedures (Section 13.8);
- using CAQDAS for qualitative analysis (Section 13.9).

13.2 Differences between qualitative and quantitative data

Many authors draw a distinction between qualitative and quantitative research (e.g. Bryman, 1988; Easterby-Smith *et al.* 2008). These are helpful in terms of understanding what is necessary in order to be able to analyse these data meaningfully. Table 13.1 highlights three distinct differences between quantitative and qualitative data. While 'number depends on meaning' (Dey 1993:28), it is not always the case that meaning is dependent on number. Dey (1993:28) points out that 'the more ambiguous and elastic our concepts, the less possible it is to quantify our data in a meaningful way'. Qualitative data are associated with such concepts and are characterised by their richness and fullness based on your opportunity to explore a subject in as real a manner as is possible (Robson 2002). A contrast can thus be drawn between the 'thin' abstraction or description that results from quantitative data collection and the 'thick' or 'thorough' abstraction or description associated with qualitative data (Dey 1993; Robson, 2002; Box 13.1).

The nature of the qualitative data collected has implications for its analysis. During analysis, the non-standardised and complex nature of the data that you have collected will probably need to be condensed (summarised), grouped (categorised) or restructured as a narrative to support meaningful analysis (all discussed later); otherwise the most that may result may be an impressionistic view of what they mean. While it may be possible to make some use of diagrams and statistics at this stage, such as the frequency of occurrence of certain categories of data (Sections 12.3 and 12.4), the way in which you

Table 13.1 Distinctions between quantitative and qualitative data

Quantitative data	Qualitative data
• Based on meanings derived from numbers	• Based on meanings expressed through words
• Collection results in numerical and standardised data	• Collection results in non-standardised data requiring classification into categories
• Analysis conducted through the use of diagrams and statistics	• Analysis conducted through the use of conceptualisation

Sources: developed from Dey (1993); Healey and Rawlinson (1994); authors' experience.

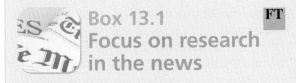

Box 13.1
Focus on research
in the news

FT

Wide range of weapons in analysts' armoury

Luck, astute judgement, clever modelling, visiting department stores and jumping on aircraft – there is no single recipe for predicting a company's earnings or share price. The weapons in the equity analysts' armoury are many and varied. Nevertheless, there are some common techniques that help the best make a more accurate call on the future.

Predicting a company's earnings is a different skill from forecasting how well its shares will perform. It is possible – common even – for an analyst to be a perfect forecaster of a company's numbers but still get its share price wrong. Colin Crook, industrials analyst at UBS, says: 'There's no magic formula. It's just hard work and using experience of what has happened in the past to understand how macro factors interact with how companies operate, and how this feeds through to the reported numbers.' Bruno Paulson, a senior financials analyst at Sanford C. Bernstein, says: 'It's about steering a course between the big picture and attention to detail. When people talk about forecasting accuracy, they generally mean a very short-term activity. When people ask if you got the earnings right, they are normally talking about the quarter just gone rather than your longer term forecasts.'

The new IFRS accounting standards have also introduced much more 'noise' into quarterly earnings statements, and this needs to be factored into forecasts, Mr Paulson says. 'One example of this is the 40 per cent miss by Aegon [the Dutch insurer] in the first quarter, entirely driven by short-term financial variances rather than the underlying business.'

Analysts say the paramount issue with forecasting earnings is good modelling. That does not necessarily mean complex modelling – a model with more parameters is not necessarily any more effective. But it does mean realistic modelling, which requires the analyst to be constantly checking whether the model is consistent with reality, even if in theory its outputs should hold true. 'Some models can become too detailed,' says Mr Crook. 'Models tell you what things should happen; in reality, they often don't. But having a good model enables you to challenge a company's comments when it has an earnings call.'

Another important element is understanding so-called operational gearing: how the interplay between fluctuating revenues and fixed costs determines profit. This is a crucial element of forecasting earnings, and one that analysts admit they frequently get wrong. A fall in revenues of 10 per cent rarely leads to a proportionate drop in earnings. Terry Smith, author of *Accounting for Growth* and chairman of Collins Stewart, the UK stockbroker, says: 'Operational gearing is the single biggest issue . . . [analysts] are appalling at it. They just don't get it.'

The third trick is not to rely too much on guidance from companies themselves. Analysts are often criticised for expecting to be spoon-fed earnings forecasts directly by finance directors in the companies they cover. 'Company guidance often underestimates the impact of key factors, especially at turning points in the earnings cycle,' says Mr Crook. 'Companies usually just don't know what their profits are going to be at the end of the year. We question guidance.' Another analyst, who asked not to be named, agrees, saying: 'I have been given plenty of bum steers by companies about their earnings.'

The fourth element involves being imaginative about what constitutes quantitative research. Top analysts supplement this with more qualitative research. Retail analysts have no excuse for failing to visit companies' stores and the observations made there can be an additional source of quantitative data. But in some industries, the best analysts also take a subjective view on whether products are going to capture consumers' imagination. This is more subjective – for example, judging whether a mobile handset will be popular, or whether a new car is good looking – but it may be just as important as predicting raw material costs. 'You have to put [research from the field] in context. If you fly on an EasyJet plane and it's half empty, that doesn't mean that the same goes for the entire fleet,' says Mr Crook.

○ Box 13.1
Focus on research in
the news *(continued)*

When it comes to predicting share prices, the approaches taken by successful analysts vary considerably, according to each industry's valuation benchmarks. Cyclical industrial companies tend to be priced off sales, whereas the consumer industry relies on earnings multiples and telecoms groups on earnings before interest tax, depreciation and amortisation. Meanwhile, financial stocks are priced relative to their book value.

Strategic questions also carry greater weight in certain industries. For a sector undergoing radical changes, such as media, identifying whether a company has the right strategy may be a more important factor in forecasting its medium-term stock performance than would be the case for a company such as a bank or insurer.

The [2008] credit crunch has prompted many analysts to overhaul their methodologies. Some say that purely quantitative research, which uses sophisticated models to screen sectors for stock tips, has decreased in importance as once-reliable strategies have been undone by the financial turmoil. Moreover, analysts have had to become more co-ordinated in their efforts, as the credit crisis has spread across asset classes and geographies. 'You had to shape yourself to events and the events had more of a global texture than is normally the case,' says the head of research of a large US investment bank of the last nine months [September 2007 to May 2008]. Mr Smith says the best stock pickers not only understand the dynamics of operational leverage, but also financial leverage. He cites the failure of many analysts to spot the latent factors set to weigh on the share price of Ferrovial, the highly geared Spanish infrastructure group, in the wake of its debt-funded purchase of BAA, the UK airports operator, in 2006. While debt was cheap then, greater gearing is risky and increases the return demanded by equity investors. 'They'd see a load of debt and say: "It's cut the company's cost of capital." They forget to factor in that the cost of equity will have gone up,' he says.

Above all, it seems that the best forecasters of both earnings and share prices are those who trust their own experience. Mr Crook says: 'I do think history is a good guide to the future. The cycle happens. Experience definitely helps.'

Mr Paulson adds: 'The key thing is not to panic. Some financials are facing a serious deterioration in their fundamentals, but not all. There was a similar situation in 2002 and 2003 with the fear around the insurers. It is crucial not to be swayed too much by short-term sentiment, as excessive fears in the market can create real opportunities for long-term investors.'

Source: article by Hughes, Chris and Guerrera, Francesco (2008) *Financial Times*, 16 May. Copyright © The Financial Times Ltd.

---

are likely to analyse the qualitative data that you collect is through the creation of a conceptual framework. This may be formulated before, during or after your data collection.

The analysis of qualitative data involves a demanding process and should not be seen as an 'easy option'. Yin (2003) refers to those who leave the data that they have collected unanalysed for periods of time because of their uncertainty about the analytical process required.

Where you have been through the various stages of formulating and clarifying your research topic (Chapter 2), reviewing appropriate literature (Chapter 3), deciding on your research design (Chapter 5), considering access and ethical issues and negotiating the former (Chapter 6) and collecting your data (Chapters 7–11), you clearly will not wish to be halted by an inability to analyse this type of data. Equally you will not wish to be 'marked down' because the analysis of the data collected is perceived to be a weak aspect of your work and one that casts doubt on the thoroughness and validity of the conclusions that you draw from the data.

Indeed, two further aspects arise from this cautionary note. First, you should take the advice of Marshall and Rossman (2006), who include data analysis as one of the issues that you should consider at the time you are formulating a proposal to undertake qualitative research. Second, the process of analysing qualitative data is likely to begin at the same time as you collect these data as well as continue afterwards (Kvale 1996), and this is a matter that we discuss in the following sections, commencing with preparing your data for analysis.

13.3 Preparing your data for analysis

As we have seen in Chapters 8, 9, 10 and 11, qualitative data can be found in many forms. In Chapter 8, when we considered different secondary data, we highlighted how documentary data were available in both written form, including organisational documents, reports, emails and newspapers, and non-written form such as audio- and video-recordings. Subsequently, in Chapter 9, we noted how, in addition to recording your observation on a schedule, it could also be video-recorded. Chapter 10 highlighted the role of audio-recording as well as note taking, emphasising the importance of transcribing both recordings and notes to ensure data were not lost. Finally, Chapter 11, although focusing on collecting quantitative data, noted that open questions could be used to collect qualitative data from respondents, these being recorded in writing by either the respondent or an interviewer. In this section we focus upon the conversion of qualitative data to word-processed text, as this is the form that you are most likely to use in your analysis. As part of this, we discuss the general requirements of CAQDAS packages.

Transcribing qualitative data

In Chapter 11 we emphasised that, in non-standardised (qualitative research) interviews, the interview is normally audio-recorded and subsequently **transcribed**, that is, reproduced as a written (word-processed) account using the actual words. We also emphasised that, as an interviewer, you would be interested not only in what participants said, but in the way they said it as well. This means that the task of transcribing audio-recorded interviews is likely to be time consuming as you will need not only to record exactly what was said and by whom, but also to try to give an indication of the tone in which it was said and the participants' non-verbal communications. You also need to ensure it can be linked to the contextual information that locates the interview (Section 10.4).

Even if you are a touch typist, you will find the task of transcribing an audio-recording extremely time consuming. Most research methods texts suggest that it takes a touch typist between six and ten hours to transcribe every hour of audio-recording. Consequently, it is helpful if your interviews are transcribed as soon as possible after they are undertaken in order to avoid a build-up of audio-recordings and associated transcription work. Fortunately, there are a number of possible ways of reducing the vast amount of personal time needed to transcribe interviews verbatim. These are summarised in Table 13.2 along with some of the associated potential problems. As you will see in Table 13.2, one problem, however you choose to transcribe the data, is making sure that the transcription is accurate by correcting any transcription errors. This process is known as data cleaning. Once this has been done, some researchers send a copy of the transcript to the participant for final checking. Whilst this can be helpful for ensuring factual accuracy, we have found that interviewees often want to correct their own grammar and use of language as well! This is because spoken and written language are very different. For this reason, you need to think carefully before offering to provide each interviewee with a full copy of their transcript.

Each interview you transcribe should be saved as a separate word-processed file. As part of this we recommend that you use a filename that maintains confidentiality and

Table 13.2 Alternative ways of reducing the time needed to transcribe audio-recordings

Alternative	Potential problems
Pay a touch typist to transcribe your audio-recordings	• Expense of paying someone else. • Important data such as pauses, coughs, sighs and the like may not be included. • You will not be familiarising yourself with the data as you are not transcribing it yourself. • The transcription will still require careful checking as errors can creep in.
Borrow a transcription machine with a foot-operated start–play–stop play mechanism	• Although this will allow you to control the audio-recorder more easily, the speed of transcription will still be dependent upon your typing ability. • The transcription will still require careful checking.
'Dictate' your audio-recordings to your computer using voice recognition software	• You will need to discover which voice recognition software works best with your voice. • You will need to 'teach' the voice recognition software to understand your voice. • You will need to listen to and dictate the entire audio-recording. • The transcription will still require careful checking as the software is not entirely accurate.
Only transcribe those sections of each audio-recording that are pertinent to your research (**data sampling**)	• You will need to listen to the entire recording carefully first, at least twice. • You may miss certain things, meaning you will have to go back to the audio-recording later. • Those sections you transcribe will still require careful checking.

preserves anonymity but that you can easily recognise and which codifies important information. When doing this Mark always starts his transcription filenames with the interview number and saves the word-processed transcripts for each research project in a separate subdirectory. Subsequent parts of the filename provide more detail. Thus the file '26MPOrg1.doc' is the transcript of the **26**th interview, **M**ale, **P**rofessional, undertaken at **Org**anisation1. As some CAQDAS programs require filenames of eight or fewer characters, you may need to limit your filenames to this length.

When transcribing interviews and group interviews, you need to be able to distinguish between the interviewer and the participant or participants. This means you need to have clear speaker identifiers such as '17FA' for the seventeenth interviewee who is a Female Administrator. This tends to be more visible in the transcript if they are in capitals (Box 13.2). Similarly, you need to be able to distinguish between any topic headings you use, questions and responses. One way of doing this, dependent upon the precise requirements of your CAQDAS, is to put topic headings in CAPITALS, questions in *italics* and responses in normal font. The most important thing is to be consistent within and across all your transcriptions. Some authors also recommend the use of specific transcription symbols to record intakes of breath, overlapping talk and changes in intonation. A useful list of transcription symbols is provided as an appendix by Silverman (2007).

In a transcription of a more structured interview, you also need to include the question number and the question in your transcription. For example, by including the question number 'Q27' at the start of the question you will be able to search for and find question 27

Box 13.2
Focus on student research

Extract from an interview transcript

Martin had decided to use the code IV to represent himself in the transcripts of his in-depth interviews and 01FS to represent his first interviewee, a female student. By using capital letters to identify both himself and the interviewee Martin could identify clearly where questions and responses started. In addition, it reduced the chance of a mistype in the transcription as identifiers were always a combination of capital letters and

numbers. Martin used transcription symbols such as '(.)' to represent a brief pause and '.hhh' to represent an in breath. He also included brief comments relating to a respondent's actions in the interview transcript. These he enclosed with double parentheses (( )). A brief extract from a transcript follows:

IV: So tell me, why do you use the Student Union Bar?

01FS: Well, erm (.), a lot of my friends go there for the final drink of the evening (.) there is an atmosphere and the drinks are cheap. I don't feel embarrassed to walk in on my own and there's always someone to talk to and scrounge a fag off ((laughs)) . . .

quickly. In addition, by having the full question in your transcript you will be far less likely to misinterpret the question your respondent is answering.

When transcribing audio recordings or your own notes you need to plan in advance how you intend to analyse your transcriptions. If you only have access to a black and white printer, there is little point in using different coloured fonts to distinguish between participants in a group interview or to distinguish non-verbal responses such as nervous laughter in your transcripts as these will be difficult to discern when working from the paper copies. You need to also be careful about using these and other word-processing software features if you are going to analyse the data using CAQDAS. These programs often have precise file formats which can mean that word-processing software features such as **bold** and *italics* generated by your word-processing software will disappear when your data file is imported (Lewins and Silver 2006). For example, although you may transcribe your interviews using a word processor such as Microsoft Word, your chosen CAQDAS package may require this textual data to be saved as a text-only file (.txt) or using rich text format (.rtf), resulting in the loss of some of these features. These are summarised as a checklist in Box 13.3 (see overleaf).

Using electronic textual data including scanned documents

For some forms of textual data such as, for example, email interviews (Section 10.8) or electronic versions of documents (Section 8.2), including organisational emails, blogs and web-based reports, your data may already be in electronic format. Although these data have already been captured electronically, you are still likely to need to spend some time preparing them for analysis. This is likely to involve you in ensuring that, where necessary, the data are:

- suitably anonymised, such as by using separate codes for yourself and different participants;
- appropriately stored for analysis, for example one file for each interview, each meeting's minutes or each organisational policy;
- free of typographical errors that you may have introduced, and, where these occurred, they have been 'cleaned up'.

Box 13.3
Checklist

Transcribing your interviews

✔ Have you thought about how you intend to analyse your data and made sure that your transcription will facilitate this?

✔ Have you chosen clear interviewer and respondent identifiers and used them consistently?

✔ Have you included the interviewer's questions in full in your transcription?

✔ Have you saved your transcribed data using a separate file for each interview?

✔ Does your filename maintain confidentiality and preserve anonymity whilst still allowing you to recognise important information easily?

✔ Have you checked your transcript for accuracy and, where necessary, 'cleaned up' the data?

✔ (If you intend to use CAQDAS) Will the package you are going to use help you to manage and analyse your data effectively? In other words, will it do what you need it to do?

✔ (If you intend to use CAQDAS) Are your saved transcriptions compatible with the CAQDAS package you intend to use, so you will not lose any features from your word-processed document when you import the data?

✔ (If you intend to use CAQDAS) Have you checked your transcript for accuracy and 'cleaned up' the data *prior* to importing into your chosen CAQDAS package?

✔ Have you stored a separate back-up or security copy of each data file on your USB mass storage device or burnt one onto a CD?

Consequently, you are likely to find much of the checklist in Box 13.3 helpful. If you intend to use CAQDAS to help you to manage and analyse documents which are not available electronically, you will need to scan these into your word processing software and ensure they are in a format compatible with your chosen package.

The interactive nature of the process

Data collection, data analysis and the development and verification of propositions are very much an interrelated and interactive set of processes. Analysis occurs during the collection of data as well as after it (Kvale 1996). This analysis helps to shape the direction of data collection, especially where you are following a more inductive, grounded approach (Section 13.7). As propositions emerge from your data, or if you commence your data collection with a theoretical framework or propositions already worked out (Section 13.8), you will seek to test these as you compare them against the cases in your study (Erlandson *et al.* 1993; Glaser and Strauss 1967). The key point here is the relative flexibility that this type of process permits you.

The interactive nature of data collection and analysis allows you to recognise important themes, patterns and relationships as you collect data: in other words, to allow these to emerge from the process of data collection and analysis. As a result you will be able to re-categorise your existing data to see whether these themes, patterns and relationships are present in the cases where you have already collected data. You will also be able to adjust your future data collection to see whether data exist in cases where you intend to conduct your research (Strauss and Corbin 2008).

The concurrent process of data collection and analysis also has implications for the way in which you will need to manage your time and organise your data and related documentation. As we discussed in Section 10.6, it will be necessary to arrange interviews or observations with enough space between them to allow yourself sufficient time to word process a transcript or set of notes, and to analyse this before proceeding to your next data collection session. Where you conduct a small number of interviews in one day, you will need time during the evening to undertake some initial analysis on these before carrying out further interviews. You may also be able to find a little time between interviews to carry out a cursory level of analysis. As part of this we have found it extremely helpful to listen to audio-recordings of interviews we have undertaken while travelling to and from the university. However, there is a clear limit to the value of continuing to undertake interviews or observations without properly analysing these in the manner described earlier.

13.4 Approaches to qualitative analysis

In our discussion of research approaches in Section 4.3 we highlighted how it was possible to approach data collection and analysis from either a deductive or an inductive perspective. Where you commence your research project using a deductive approach you will seek to use existing theory to shape the approach that you adopt to the qualitative research process and to aspects of data analysis. Where you commence your research project using an inductive approach you will seek to build up a theory that is adequately grounded in your data. In this section we discuss the difference between using theory at the start of your research to analyse qualitative data and commencing your research by collecting and exploring your data without a predetermined theoretical or descriptive framework (Yin 2003).

Using a deductive approach

Yin (2003) suggests that, where you have made use of existing theory to formulate your research question and objectives, you may also use the theoretical propositions that helped you do this as a means to devise a framework to help you to organise and direct your data analysis. There is debate about this approach as applied to qualitative analysis. Bryman (1988:81) sums up the argument against it as follows:

> The prior specification of a theory tends to be disfavoured because of the possibility of introducing a premature closure on the issues to be investigated, as well as the possibility of the theoretical constructs departing excessively from the views of participants in a social setting.

If this occurs when you use a theoretical framework to design and analyse your research, you will clearly need to adapt your approach (Box 13.4).

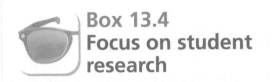

Box 13.4
Focus on student research

Incorporating an inductive approach

Phil commenced a research project by adopting a deductive approach, but found that the theoretical framework he adopted did not yield a sufficiently convincing answer to his research questions and objectives. He, therefore, decided to reanalyse his data inductively. This revealed themes that had not figured prominently in the deductive analysis. A combination of the two approaches generated a more convincing answer to Phil's research questions and objectives.

Even though you may incorporate an inductive approach in your research, commencing your work from a theoretical perspective may have certain advantages. It will link your research into the existing body of knowledge in your subject area, help you to get started and provide you with an initial analytical framework.

To devise a theoretical or descriptive framework you need to identify the main variables, components, themes and issues in your research project and the predicted or presumed relationships between them (Yin 2003). A descriptive framework will rely more on your prior experience and what you expect to occur, although it is of course possible to develop an explanatory framework based on a mixture of theory and your own expectations. You will use this framework as the means to start and direct the analysis of your data.

Using an inductive approach

The alternative to the deductive approach is to start to collect data and then explore them to see which themes or issues to follow up and concentrate on (e.g. Glaser and Strauss 1967; Schatzman and Strauss 1973; Strauss and Corbin 2008; Yin 2003). Yin (2003) believes that this inductive approach may be a difficult strategy to follow and may not lead to success for someone who is an inexperienced researcher. This is likely to be the case where you simply go ahead and collect data without examining them to assess which themes are emerging from the data as you progress. Where you commence your data collection with this type of approach – related initially to an exploratory purpose – you will need to analyse the data as you collect them and develop a conceptual framework to guide your subsequent work. This is also referred to as a grounded approach because of the nature of the theory or explanation that emerges as a result of the research process. In this approach:

- you do not commence such a study with a clearly defined theoretical framework;
- instead you identify relationships between your data and develop questions and hypotheses or propositions to test these;
- theory emerges from the process of data collection and analysis.

You will, however, still need to commence this type of approach with a clear research purpose. To use an inductive approach successfully may involve a lengthy period of time and prove to be resource intensive. It is also likely that this approach will combine some elements of a deductive approach as you seek to develop a theoretical position and then test its applicability through subsequent data collection and analysis. Consequently, while you may commence with either an inductive or a deductive approach, in practice your research is likely to combine elements of both.

In the next section we outline and discuss three types of analytic procedures for analysing data qualitatively. Subsequently, we consider how these different processes are used in as part of deductive and inductive approaches (Sections 13.7 and 13.8).

13.5 Types of qualitative analysis processes

The features of qualitative data outlined in Table 13.1 indicate its diverse nature. To add to this, or because of it, there is no standardised procedure for analysing such data. Despite this, it is still possible to group data into three main types of processes:

- summarising (condensation) of meanings;
- categorisation (grouping) of meanings;
- structuring (ordering) of meanings using narrative.

Figure 13.1
Dimensions of
qualitative
analysis

All of these can be used on their own, or in combination, to support interpretation of your data.

Some procedures for analysing qualitative data may be highly structured, whereas others adopt a much lower level of structure. Related to this, some approaches to analysing qualitative data may be highly formalised such as those associated with categorisation, whereas others, such as those associated with structuring meanings through narrative, rely much more on the researcher's interpretation. As highlighted in the previous section (13.4), a further way of differentiating between procedures is whether they are used deductively or inductively. Some procedures can be used deductively, the data categories and codes to analyse data being derived from theory and following a predetermined analytical framework. Other procedures can commence inductively, without predetermined, or *a priori*, categories and codes to direct your analysis. These means of differentiating qualitative analysis procedures, while not comprehensive, are shown as three dimensions in Figure 13.1.

These means to differentiate qualitative analysis may themselves be problematic when used to map some analytic strategies or procedures. For example, grounded theory analysis procedures (discussed in Section 13.7) may be more or less structured and proceduralised dependent upon the precise grounded theory strategy adopted. However, in general terms the use of these dimensions will allow you to compare different qualitative analysis procedures more easily. Care also needs to be taken in relation to any action that results from a consideration of these dimensions. For example, the use of a procedure that relies on your interpretation should not be seen as implying less analytical rigour (Coffey and Atkinson 1996; Tesch 1990). These three dimensions should not therefore be used to indicate higher quality at one end of a continuum.

Before outlining a number of reasonably distinct ways of analysing qualitative data using inductive or deductive approaches, we discuss the three types of process listed earlier–summarising, categorising and structuring using narrative. We also consider the use of analytic aids such as summaries, self memos and a researcher's diary. Together these processes and aids allow you to interact with your qualitative data in order to:

1 comprehend them;
2 integrate related data drawn from different transcripts and notes;
3 identify key themes or patterns from them for further exploration;
4 develop and/or test theories based on these apparent patterns or relationships;
5 draw and verify conclusions (Kvale 1996; Miles and Huberman 1994).

Summarising data

After you have written up your notes, or produced a transcript, of an interview or observation session, you can also produce a summary of the key points that emerge from undertaking this activity. This summary will compress long statements into briefer statements in which the main sense of what has been said or observed is rephrased in a few words (Kvale 1996). Summarising, therefore, involves condensing the meaning of large amounts of text into fewer words. Through summarising you will become conversant with the principal themes that have emerged from the interview or observation and how

Box 13.5
Focus on student research

Noting an event that affected the nature of data collection

Birjit was facilitating a focus group whose participants were the customers of a large department store. Approximately halfway through the allotted time, an additional participant joined the group. This person almost immediately took control of the discussion, two other participants appearing to become reticent and withdrawing from the group's discussion. Despite this, all Birjit's questions were answered fully and she felt the data she had obtained was valuable. However, she recorded the point at which the new participant joined the group in a post-transcript summary in case any divergence was apparent between the nature of the data in the two parts of the focus group.

you would like to explore these further in forthcoming data collection sessions. You may be able to identify apparent relationships between themes that you wish to note down so that you can return to these to seek to establish their validity. It will also be useful to make some comments about the person(s) you interviewed or observed, the setting in which this occurred and whether anything occurred during the interview or observation that might have affected the nature of the data that you collected (Box 13.5).

Once you have produced a summary of the key points that emerge from the interview or observation and its context, you should attach a copy to the set of your written-up notes or transcript for further reference (Robson 2002).

Qualitative data such as organisational documentation may also be summarised. These data may be an important source in their own right (e.g. using minutes of meetings, internal reports, briefings, planning documents and schedules), or you may use such documentation as a means of triangulating other data that you collect (Section 8.2). Where you use any sort of documentation it is helpful to produce a summary that, in addition to providing a list of the key points it contains, also describes the purpose of the document, how it relates to your work and why it is significant. This type of summary may be useful when you undertake further analysis if you want to refer to sources of data (that is, the document) as well as the way in which your categorical data have been categorised into their component parts.

Categorising data

Categorising data involves two activities: developing categories and, subsequently, attaching these categories to meaningful chunks of data. Through doing this you will begin to recognise relationships and further develop the categories you are using to facilitate this. You will also develop and test propositions, thereby enabling you to draw conclusions as well as analyse quantitatively (see below).

Deriving categories

Categories may be derived from your data or from your theoretical framework (Sections 13.4, 13.6 and 13.8) and are, in effect, codes or labels that you will use to group your data. They provide you with an emergent structure that is relevant to your research project to organise and analyse your data further.

Your identification of categories will be guided by the purpose of your research as expressed through your research question and objectives. Another researcher, for example, with different objectives, may derive different categories from the same data (Dey 1993). It is not that one researcher is right and the other wrong; rather they are interpreting the data differently. Strauss and Corbin (2008) suggest that there are three main sources to derive names for these categories:

- you utilise terms that emerge from your data;
- they are based on the actual terms used by your participants ('*in vivo*' codes); or
- they are derived from terms used in existing theory and the literature.

The categories that you devise need to be part of a coherent set so that they provide you with a well-structured, analytical framework to pursue your analysis. Dey (1993:96–7) states that 'categories must have two aspects, an internal aspect – they must be meaningful in relation to the data – and an external aspect – they must be meaningful in relation to the other categories'. Categories you develop initially, especially where you use an inductive, grounded approach, are likely to be essentially descriptive. As your analysis develops you will develop a more hierarchical approach to the categorisation of your data, whereby some category codes or labels will be developed and used to indicate emerging analytical linkages between, and interpretation of, the data (King 2004; Strauss and Corbin 2008).

'Unitising' data

The next activity of the analytical process, **unitising data** will be to attach relevant 'bits' or 'chunks' of your data, which we will refer to as 'units' of data, to the appropriate category or categories that you have devised. A **unit of data** may be a number of words, a line of a transcript, a sentence, a number of sentences, a complete paragraph, or some other chunk of textual data that fits the category (Box 13.6).

You may use CAQDAS to help you to process your data (Section 13.9) or you may use a manual approach. Where you use the second approach, you can label a unit of data with the appropriate category (or categories) in the margin of your transcript or set of notes (Box 13.6). This may then be copied, cut up and stuck onto a data card, or otherwise transferred, and filed so that you end up with piles of related units of data. When doing this, it is essential to label each unit of data carefully so that you know its precise source (Section 13.3). An alternative is to index categories by recording precisely where they occur in your transcripts or notes (e.g. interview 7, page 2, line 16) on cards headed with particular category labels (Easterby-Smith *et al.* 2008). Undertaking this stage of the analytic process means that you are engaging in a selective process, guided by the purpose of your research, which has the effect of reducing and rearranging your data into a more manageable and comprehensible form.

One way of achieving this reduction and rearrangement of your data, depending on the suitability of the data, is to use one or more of the analytical techniques described by Miles and Huberman (1994). These include a range of different matrices, charts, graphs and networks to use as a means to arrange and display your data. Use of these may allow you to recognise emergent patterns in your data that will provide you with an indication about how to further your data collection. This approach is considered in more detail in Section 13.8.

Recognising relationships and developing categories

Generating categories and reorganising your data according to them, or designing a suitable matrix and placing the data gathered within its cells, means that you are engaging in

Box 13.6
Focus on student research

Interview extract with categories attached

Adrian's research project was concerned with how Human Resource Management professionals from a range of organisations had managed the downsizing process in their own organisation. He derived his initial categories from existing theory in the academic literature and attached them subsequently to units of each transcript. His initial categories were hierarchical, the codes he used being shown in brackets:

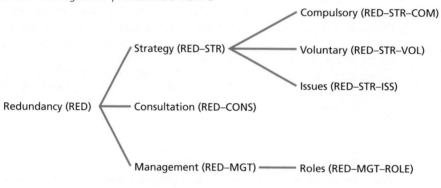

These were then attached to the interview transcript, using sentences as units of data. Like our jigsaw example at the start of this chapter, those units of data that were coded with more than one category suggested interrelationships:

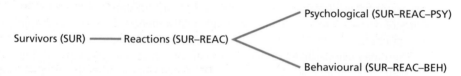

Code	Text	Line
RED–CONS	27MM The first stage is to find out what particular employees	1
	want for themselves and how they want this to happen. Staff are	2
RED–CONS	seen by their line manager and/or a member of personnel.	3
RED–MGT–ROLE	Employees might want to talk to someone from personnel rather	4
	than talk with their line manager – well, you know, for obvious	5
	reasons, at least as they see it – and this would be acceptable to the	6
RED–MGT–VOL	organisation. This meeting provides them with the opportunity to	7
	opt for voluntary redundancy. We do not categorise employees	8
RED–STR–ISS	into anything like core or non-core, although we will tell a group	9
RED–CONS	of employees something like 'there are four of you in this	10
	particular function and we only need two of you, so you think	1
RED–CONS	about what should happen'. Sometimes when we attempt to give	2
	employees a choice about who might leave, they actually ask us to	3
	make the choice. This is one such situation where a compulsory	4
RED–MGT–COM	selection will occur. We prefer to avoid this compulsory selection	5
SUR–REAC–PSY	because of the impact on those who survive – negative feelings,	6
	guilt and so on.	7

Box 13.7
Focus on management research

Assigning data to and developing categories

'After each interview, I transcribed the interview verbatim and filed its material according to the categorisation then in use. The material was typically in the form of paragraphs [that] were cross-classified to several categories. As I filed each statement, I compared it with previous statements in that category and kept running notes on the content of the category. The categories changed over time; some disappeared and were merged under more general titles. Some emerged out of previous categories that became too heterogeneous. Some categories became parts of matched pairs or triads in which any given comment would typically be filed in each constituent category. For example, comments [that] described instances of lax work or bad workmanship also typically mentioned abusive management. Similarly, statements that described devising one's own procedures also typically included statements of satisfaction with the autonomy that provided. This helped to reveal connections between categories.'

Source: Hodson (1991), cited in Erlandson *et al.* (1993:119) *Journal of Contemporary Ethnography.* Copyright © 1991 by Sage Publications, Inc. Reprinted by permission.

---

the process of analysing your data (Dey 1993; Miles and Huberman 1994; Yin 2003). This analysis will continue as you search for key themes and patterns or relationships in your rearranged data. This may lead you to revise your categories and continue to rearrange your data as you search for meaning in your data set. You may decide to 'subdivide or integrate categories as ways of refining or focusing [your] analysis' (Dey 1993:95).

There may be practical reasons for seeking to divide or join your initial categories. Some categories, for example, may attract large numbers of units of data and prove to be too broad for further analysis without being subdivided. You may also gain new insights within existing categories that suggest new ones. Because of this we would strongly recommend you keep an up-to-date definition of each of the categories you are using, so that you can maintain consistency when assigning these to units of data as you continue to undertake interviews or observations (Miles and Huberman 1994). Subsequently you will continue to generate a more hierarchical approach to the categorisation and coding of your data as you move towards the generation of an explanation for the research question and objectives that form the focus of your research.

Developing testable propositions

As you seek to reveal patterns within your data and to recognise relationships between categories, you will be able to develop testable propositions (Box 13.8). The appearance of an apparent relationship or connection between categories will need to be tested if you are to be able to conclude that there is an actual relationship. However, while this is sometimes referred to as 'testing a hypothesis', it is not the same as the statistical hypothesis or significance testing we discussed in relation to quantitative analysis in Section 12.5.

It is important to test the propositions that emerge inductively from the data by seeking alternative explanations and negative examples that do not conform to the pattern or relationship being tested. Alternative explanations frequently exist, and only by testing the propositions that you identify will you be able to move towards formulating valid conclusions and an explanatory theory, even a simple one (Miles and Huberman 1994). Dey (1993:48) points out that 'the association of one variable with another is not sufficient ground for inferring a causal or any other connection between them'. The existence of an

Box 13.8
Focus on students research

Research propositions

During the process of qualitative data analysis a student evaluating the growth of online retailing formulated the following proposition:

Customers' willingness to trust online retailers depends on the ease of use of their website.

A student exploring mortgage borrowers' decision-making drew up this proposition:

Potential mortgage borrowers' choice of lending institution is strongly affected by the level of customer service that they receive during the initial inquiry stage.

Another student investigating cause-related marketing formulated the following proposition:

Companies engaging in cause-related marketing are motivated principally by altruism.

A relationship is evident in each of these propositions. Each was tested using the data that had been collected or that were to be collected.

intervening variable may offer a more valid explanation of an association that is apparent in your data (Box 13.9).

By rigorously testing your propositions against your data, looking for alternative explanations and seeking to explain why negative cases occur, you will be able to move towards the development of valid and well-grounded conclusions. The validity of your conclusions will be verified by their ability to withstand alternative explanations and the nature of negative cases. This important aspect of your analysis is considered further in Sections 13.7 and 13.8.

Box 13.9
Focus on student research

The impact of an intervening variable

Kevin's research project involved looking at the use of subcontractors by an organisation. A relationship appeared to emerge between the total value of contracts a particular sub-contractor had been awarded and the size of that contractor in terms of number of employees; in particular, those contractors with larger numbers of employees had a larger total value of contracts. This could have led Kevin to conclude that the value of work undertaken by a particular sub-contractor was related to that organisation's size and that, in particular, the organisation tended to use sub-contractors with large numbers of employees.

The organisational reality was not so simple. The organisation had originally used over 2500 sub-contractors but had found this exceedingly difficult to manage. To address this issue the organisation had introduced a system of preferred contractors. All 2500 sub-contractors had been graded according to the quality of their work, those whose work had been consistently of high quality being awarded preferred contractor status. This meant that they were invited by the organisation Kevin was researching to tender for all relevant contracts. The intervening variable was therefore the introduction of preferred contractor status dependent upon the quality of work previously undertaken. The fact that the majority of these sub-contractors also had relatively large numbers of employees was not the reason why the organisation had awarded them contracts.

Quantifying your qualitative data

There may be occasions when you decide to quantify some of your qualitative data. This is likely to be the case when you wish to count the frequency of certain events, or of particular reasons that have been given, or in relation to specific references to a phenomenon. These frequencies can then be displayed using a table or diagram (Section 12.3) and can usually be produced using CAQDAS programs and exported to statistical analysis software such as Excel and SPSS. They can also often be exported directly to your word processor.

This approach to describing and presenting your data will provide you with a very useful supplement to the principal means of analysing your qualitative data discussed above. It may also enable you to undertake other quantitative analyses, such as those discussed in Sections 12.4 to 12.6. However, it is indeed a supplementary means of achieving this, and there is clearly only limited purpose in collecting qualitative data if you intend to ignore the nature and value of these data by reducing most of them to a simplified form.

Structuring data using narrative

While categorisation involves the fragmentation of qualitative data to further the process of analysis, some researchers consider the fragmentation of data to be inappropriate. They advocate that researchers should retain the integrity of the data that they collect and commence analysis using verbatim transcripts or complete sets of notes that are produced. Examples of this include phenomenological research (Moustakas 1994) and the life history approach (Musson 2004). Such research is based on individuals' accounts of their experiences and the ways in which they explain these through their subjective interpretations and relate them to constructions of the social world in which they live. This type of analysis commences inductively, and needs to remain sensitive to the social constructions and meanings of those who participate in the research.

The primary method to collect data used in narrative approaches is through in-depth interviews. As part of the interview process, it is likely that participants will provide accounts that, at least in part, take the form of narratives, or stories. You may also deliberately seek to encourage this by asking participants to provide responses in this form. A **narrative** is defined broadly as an account of an experience that is told in a sequenced way, indicating a flow of related events that, taken together, are significant for the narrator and which convey meaning to the researcher (Coffey and Atkinson 1996). It follows that understanding and meaning are likely to be promoted through analysing data in their originally told form rather than by seeking to fragment them through a process of developing categories and coding. This is not to say that such accounts cannot also be subjected to this type of analysis (that is, categorisation). Rather, narrative structuring ensures that the data are organised both temporally and with regard to the social or organisational contexts of the research participant (Kvale 1996). This form of analysis focuses upon the stories told during the interviews, working on their structures and plots. Alternatively, narrative analysis can be used to create a coherent story from the data collected during an interview. Narrative analysis therefore allows the nature of the participants' engagement, the actions that they took, the consequences of these and the relationship events that followed to be retained within the narrative flow of the account without losing the significance of the social or organisational context within which these events occurred.

Narrative structuring, as a story with a beginning, middle and end, usually follows a perceptible structure. Coffey and Atkinson (1996) draw on previous research to outline the structural elements that are often present in narratives. These broadly take the following form:

- What the story is about.
- What happened, to whom, whereabouts and why?
- The consequences that arose from this.
- The significance of these events.
- The final outcome.

Coffey and Atkinson (1996) point out that these elements may not occur in the order listed and may also recur in a given narrative. Whilst structuring using narrative may reduce the amount of interview text, it may also expand it as the narrative of what happened is developed (Kvale 1996).

13.6 Analytical aids

In addition to transcribing your audio-recording or notes, and assigning units of data to appropriate categories, it will also help your analysis if you make a record of additional contextual information (Section 10.4). This will help you to recall the context and content of the interview or observation as well as informing your interpretation as you will be more likely to remember the precise circumstances to which your data relate (Box 13.10). Various researchers have suggested additional ways of recording information that will usefully supplement your written-up notes or transcripts and your categorised data (e.g. Glaser 1978; Miles and Huberman 1994; Riley 1996; Strauss and Corbin 2008). These include:

- interim summaries;
- self-memos;
- a researcher's diary.

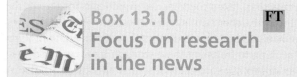

Box 13.10
Focus on research
in the news

FT

Sales manager wins 'The Apprentice'

Recruitment sales manager Lee McQueen emerged victorious from last night's finale of *The Apprentice*, the BBC's popular show about business wannabes.

After 11 weeks, the original 16 candidates had been whittled down to a final four, tasked for last night's programme with creating a new male fragrance and launching it to an audience of 100 industry experts, including top names such as Givenchy and Estée Lauder. Regarded by many as the 'people's choice', Mr McQueen, 30, whose first job was as a catering manager at Harrow School, tested tycoon Sir Alan Sugar's patience when it emerged in last week's episode he had lied about his educational background. Nevertheless, he survived to win the competition.

Sir Alan quickly put the final two contestants out of their misery: 'It's been a long journey as you know, and at this final hurdle I have to make a very serious decision . . . Lee, you're very convincing. You are very, very, very convincing. I've concluded . . . Lee, you're hired!'

Source: article by Patrikarakos, David (2008) *Financial Times*, 12 June. Copyright © 2008 The Financial Times Ltd.

Interim summaries

As your analysis progresses you may wish to write an interim summary of your progress to date. This outlines:

- what you have found so far;
- what level of confidence you have in your findings and conclusions to date;
- what you need to do in order to improve the quality of your data and/or to seek to substantiate your apparent conclusions, or to seek alternative explanations;
- how you will seek to achieve the needs identified by the above interim analysis.

This can become a working document to which you make continued reference as your research project continues to make progress (Robson 2002).

Self-memos

Self-memos allow you to record ideas that occur to you about any aspect of your research, as you think of them. Where you omit to record any idea as it occurs to you it may well be forgotten. The occasions when you are likely to want to write a memo include:

- when you are writing up interview or observation notes, or producing a transcript of this event;
- when you are constructing a narrative;
- when you are categorising these data;
- as you continue to categorise and analyse these data;
- when you engage in writing your research project.

Most CAQDAS programs include some form of writing tool that allows you make notes, add comments or write self-memos as you are analysing your data (Lewins and Silver 2006). This is extremely helpful and, as your self-memos are automatically dated, you can also trace the development of your ideas. Ideas may also occur as you engage in an interview or observation session. In this case you may record the idea very briefly as a margin note and write it as a memo to yourself after the event. Similarly, ideas may occur as you work through a documentary source. It may be useful to carry a reporter's notebook in order to be able to record your ideas, whenever and wherever they occur. When you are undertaking the production of notes, or a transcript, or any aspect of qualitative analysis, the notebook will be ready to record your ideas in.

Self-memos may vary in length from a few words to one or more pages. They can be written as simple notes – they do not need to be set out formally. Miles and Huberman (1994) suggest it will be useful to date them and to provide cross-references to appropriate places in your written-up notes or transcripts, where appropriate. Alternatively, an idea that is not grounded in any data (which may nevertheless prove to be useful) should be recorded as such. Memos should be filed together, not with notes or transcripts, and may themselves be categorised where this will help you to undertake later stages of your qualitative analysis. Memos may also be updated as your research progresses, so that your bank of ideas continues to have currency and relevance (Glaser 1978).

Researcher's diary

An alternative approach to recording your ideas about your research is to keep a researcher's diary. You may of course keep such a diary alongside the creation of self-memos. Its purpose will be similar to the creation of self-memos: to record your ideas and your reflections on these, and to act as an *aide-mémoire* to your intentions about the direction of your research. However, its chronological format may help you to identify the development of certain ideas (such as data categories, propositions or hypotheses) and the way in which your research ideas developed, as well as providing an approach that suits the way in which you like to think (Riley 1996).

13.7 Deductively based analytical procedures

Yin's (2003) preference for devising theoretical propositions prior to data collection as a means to analyse data emphasises a number of specific analytical procedures. This section considers analytical procedures described by Yin (2003) that are particularly applicable to qualitative analysis and examines how the deductive perspective that underpins these impacts upon processes for analysing qualitative data (Section 13.5).

Pattern matching

Pattern matching involves predicting a pattern of outcomes based on theoretical propositions to explain what you expect to find. Using this approach, you will need to develop a conceptual or analytical framework, utilising existing theory, and subsequently test the adequacy of the framework as a means to explain your findings. If the pattern of your data matches that which has been predicted through the conceptual framework you will have found an explanation, where possible threats to the validity of your conclusions can be discounted. There are two variations to this procedure dependent upon the nature of the variables being considered.

The first variation is associated with a set of **dependent** variables where you suggest the likely outcomes arising from another, **independent** variable. For example, based on theoretical propositions drawn from appropriate literature you specify a number of related outcomes (dependent variables) that you expect to find as a result of the implementation of a particular change management programme (independent variable) in an organisation where you intend to undertake research. Having specified these expected outcomes, you then engage in the process of data collection and analysis. Where your predicted outcomes are found, it is likely that your theoretically based explanation is appropriate to explain your findings. If, however, you reveal one or more outcomes that have not been predicted by your explanation, you will need to seek an alternative one (Yin 2003).

The second variation is associated with variables that are independent of each other. In this case you would identify a number of alternative explanations to explain the pattern of outcomes that you expect to find (Box 13.11, opposite). As a consequence, only one of these predicted explanations may be valid. In other words, if one explanation is found to explain your findings then the others may be discarded. Where you find a match between one of these predicted explanations and the pattern of your outcomes you will have evidence to suggest that this is indeed an explanation for your findings. Further evidence that this is a correct explanation will flow from finding the same pattern of outcomes in other similar cases (Yin 2003).

Explanation building

Another pattern matching procedure, which Yin (2003) refers to as a special type, involves an attempt to build an explanation while collecting data and analysing them, rather than testing a predicted explanation as set out above. Yin (2003) recognises that this procedure, which he labels **explanation building**, appears to be similar to grounded theory (and analytic induction) (Section 13.8). However, unlike these, explanation building is designed to test a theoretical proposition, albeit in an iterative manner, rather than to generate theory inductively (Section 13.8). Yin states that his hypothesis-testing approach is related to explanatory case studies, while the hypothesis-generating approach

Box 13.11
Focus on student research

Alternative predicted explanations

The objective of Linzi's research project was to explain why productivity had increased in a case study organisation even though a number of factors had been held constant (technology, numbers of staff employed, pay rates and bonuses, and the order book) during the period of the increase in productivity. She developed two alternative explanations based on different theoretical propositions to explain why this increase in productivity had occurred in the organisation. Her explanations were related to the following propositions:

1 the productivity increase is due to better management, which has been able to generate greater employee commitment, where this proposition is based on theory related to strategic human resource management;
2 the productivity increase is due to fears about change and uncertainty in the future, where this proposition is, in addition, based on theory related to organisational behaviour and the management of change.

These propositions offered her two possible and exclusive reasons why the described phenomenon had occurred, so that where evidence could be found to support one of these, the other, which did not match her outcomes, could be discounted.

developed by Glaser and Strauss (1967) is relevant for exploratory studies. The explanation-building procedure uses the following stages (Yin 2003):

1 Devise a theoretically based proposition, which you will then seek to test.
2 Undertake data collection through an initial case study in order to be able to compare the findings from this in relation to this theoretically based proposition.
3 Where necessary, amend the theoretically based proposition in the light of the findings from the initial case study.
4 Undertake a further round of data collection in order to compare the findings from this in relation to the revised proposition.
5 Where necessary, further amend the revised proposition in the light of the findings from the second case study.
6 Undertake further iterations of this process until a satisfactory explanation is derived.

Impact of a deductive approach on the analysis process

In relation to pattern matching and explanation building, you will still be able to follow the general processes outlined earlier for analysing qualitative data (Section 13.5), with some modification. First, you will be in a position to commence your data collection with a well-defined research question and objectives, and a clear framework and propositions, derived from the theory that you have used. Second, with regard to sampling (Section 7.3), you will be in a position to identify the number and type of organisations to which you wish to gain access in order to undertake data collection. However, non-probability sampling should not be used as an excuse for adopting a less than rigorous approach to selecting sufficient cases to test the propositions that have been advanced and to answer your research question and meet your objectives. Third, the literature that you used and the theory within it will shape the data collection questions that you wish to ask those who participate in your research project (Section 3.2). It is also to be expected that categories for analysis will emerge from the nature of your interview questions. Therefore you will be able to commence data collection with an initial set of categories derived from your theoretical propositions/hypotheses and conceptual framework, linked to your research question and objectives (Miles and Huberman 1994).

Of course, these categories may be subject to change, depending on their appropriateness for the data that your participants provide (Dey 1993). However, where your predicted theoretical explanations appear to fit the data being revealed, your predetermined categories may prove to be useful, subject to some revision and development (Miles and Huberman 1994).

Your use of this deductive approach will also provide you with key themes and patterns to search for in your data. For example, as you carry out your research and conduct analysis through attaching units of data to categories, and examine these for emergent patterns, your analysis will be guided by the theoretical propositions and explanations with which you commenced. Your propositions will still need to be tested with rigour – associated with the thoroughness with which you carry out this analytical process and by seeking negative examples and alternative explanations that do not conform to the pattern or association being tested for.

The use of predicted explanations should mean that the pathway to an answer to your research question and objectives is reasonably defined. The extent to which this is the case will depend on two factors:

- your level of thoroughness in using existing theory to define clearly the theoretical propositions and conceptual framework that will guide your research project;
- the appropriateness of these theoretical propositions and the conceptual framework for the data that you reveal.

The use of a deductive approach is underpinned by the need to specify theoretical propositions before the commencement of data collection and its analysis. Even in explanation building, a theoretically based proposition is suggested initially, although this may be revised through the iterative stages of the process involved. The general processes types outlined earlier for analysing qualitative data will be useful to you in carrying out these deductive analytical procedures. In particular the stages of the process related to summarising and categorising are likely to be more useful where the focus of the summary or of the categories is, at least initially, derived from existing theory.

13.8 Inductively based analytical procedures

This section outlines and briefly discusses a number of inductively based analytical procedures to analyse qualitative data. These are:

- data display and analysis;
- template analysis;
- analytic induction;
- grounded theory;
- discourse analysis;
- narrative analysis.

In practice, however, a number of these analytical procedures combine inductive and deductive approaches to analyse qualitative data, as we discuss.

There may be a number of good reasons for adopting an inductive approach to your research project and the analysis of the data that are revealed. First, as we discussed in Section 13.4, you may commence an exploratory project seeking to generate a direction for further work. Second, the scope of your research may be constrained by adopting restrictive theoretical propositions that do not reflect your participants' views and experience

(Bryman 1988). In this case, the use of a theoretically based approach to qualitative analysis would prove to be inadequate. The use of an inductive approach in such a case should allow a good 'fit' to develop between the social reality of the research participants and the theory that emerges – it will be 'grounded' in that reality. This relationship should also mean that those who participated in the research process would understand any theory that emerges. Third, the theory may be used to suggest subsequent, appropriate action to be taken because it is specifically derived from the events and circumstances of the setting in which the research was conducted. Finally, the theory's generalisability may also be tested in other contexts (e.g. Glaser and Strauss 1967; Strauss and Corbin 2008).

You should not, however, use an inductive approach as a means of avoiding a proper level of preparation before commencing your research project. Researchers who use such an approach do not start to research a subject area without a competent level of knowledge about that area. Their research commences with a clearly defined research question and objectives, even though this may be altered by the nature of the data that they collect. For example, Hodson (1991, cited in Erlandson *et al.* 1993) reported that his initial purpose was focused on organisational sabotage, although the research process led him to develop and seek to verify a hypothesis related to more subtle forms of non-cooperation with an employer. The avoidance of a predetermined theoretical basis in this type of approach is related to the desire to search for and recognise meanings in the data and to understand the social context and perceptions of your research participants. It is not to avoid the burden of producing this before the process of data collection! You will need to compare your explanations with existing theory once these have emerged. The use of an inductive approach may also involve you in a lengthy period of data collection and concurrent analysis in order to analyse a theme adequately or to derive a well-grounded theory. Strauss and Corbin (2008) suggest that this type of approach may take months to complete. This is an important consideration if, like many of our students, your research project is time constrained by a submission date.

Data display and analysis

The data display and analysis approach is based on the work of Miles and Huberman (1994), whose book focuses on the process of 'doing analysis'. For them, the process of analysis consists of three concurrent sub-processes:

- data reduction;
- data display;
- drawing and verifying conclusions.

As part of the process, data reduction includes summarising and simplifying the data collected and/or selectively focusing on some parts of this data. The aim of this process is to transform the data and to condense it. Miles and Huberman outline a number of methods for summarising data, some of which we have already referred to in Section 13.5. These include the production of interview or observation summaries, document summaries, coding and categorising data and perhaps, constructing a narrative.

Data display involves organising and assembling your data into summary diagrammatic or visual displays. Miles and Huberman describe a number of ways of displaying data, and refer to two main families of data display: matrices and networks. Matrices are generally tabular in form, with defined columns and rows, where data are entered selectively into the appropriate cells of such a matrix. A network is a collection of nodes or boxes that are joined or linked by lines, perhaps with arrows to indicate relationships (Box 13.12). The boxes or nodes contain brief descriptions or labels to indicate variables or key points from the data.

Box 13.12
Focus on student research

Using a network to indicate relationships

Eike's research was concerned with the use of internal communication during organisational change. As part of his research, Eike had interviewed both the recipients and implementers of change about different aspects of communication, audio-recording each interview. He had subsequently transcribed these interviews and begun to analyse them using the CAQDAS package ATLAS.ti™. During the first stage of his analysis of the transcripts, Eike used in-vivo codes wherever practicable as his analysis was focused on participants' subjective perceptions of the communication activities. Open coding was used only when a unit of data was considered important but did

not include a term that could be used to label that code.

In the second stage of his analysis, familiarity with his data meant that Eike could now begin to interpret the codes in the context of the communication process as a whole. As part of this stage Eike found it necessary to merge some codes, divide or relabel others as well as create additional codes. He found that CAQDAS helped this process. His increasing familiarity with his data allowed him to begin to develop an understanding of the relationships between different codes. He recorded these relationships between categories using phrases such as 'is part of' and 'is cause of'.

The third stage of his analysis involved searching for patterns in the relationships between different codes. For this he used the theory-building features of ATLAS.ti™ to create a series of network views. In each diagram he used the self-memo feature of the CAQDAS to record his thoughts about the relationships between different codes:

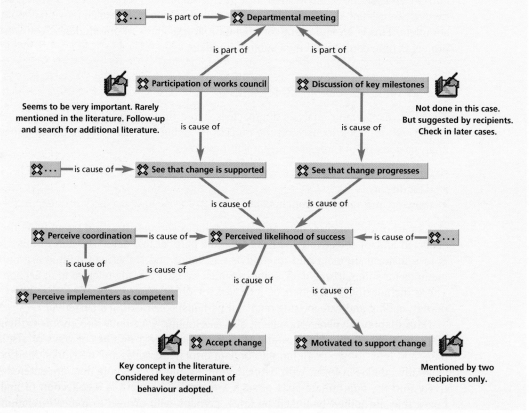

Source: Atlas.ti with permission.

Miles and Huberman (1994) believe that there are a number of advantages associated with using these forms of data display. Qualitative data collection tends to produce hours of audio-recorded interviews or extensive piles of notes (Box 13.16 on page 512). Once these have been transcribed or word-processed, they are generally referred to as 'extended text'. Extended text is considered an unreduced form of display that is difficult to analyse because it is both extensive and poorly ordered. Based on the logic that 'you know what you display', the analysis of data and the drawing of conclusions from these will be helped by using matrices, networks or other visual forms to display reduced or selected data drawn from your extended text. Miles and Huberman argue that these forms of display are relatively easy to generate, can be developed to fit your data specifically, and will help you develop your analytical thinking as you work through several iterations to develop a visual form that represents your data well.

Recognising relationships and patterns in the data, as well as drawing conclusions and verifying these, are helped by the use of data displays. A display allows you to make comparisons between the elements of the data and to identify any relationships, key themes, patterns and trends that may be evident. These will be worthy of further exploration and analysis. In this way, the use of data displays can help you to interpret your data and to draw meaning from it. As is illustrated in Box 13.12, some CAQDAS packages, including ATLAS.ti™, allow you to represent your data graphically (Lewins and Silver 2006).

Use of data display and analysis can provide you with an appropriate set of procedures to analyse your qualitative data, or alternatively one or more of the techniques that Miles and Huberman outline may be useful as part of your approach to analysing this type of data. They describe the analysis of qualitative data as an interactive process, and in this sense their approach includes many aspects of analysis that complement the generic processes outlined in Section 13.5. Their approach is a systematic and structured one, and they recognise that the procedures that they outline are often associated with a fairly high level of formalisation (Box 13.13, overleaf). However, unlike grounded theory, the exact procedures to be followed within their framework of data reduction, display and conclusion drawing and verification are not specified. Miles and Huberman refer to their work as a 'sourcebook', and as such they offer a number of possible techniques that may be appropriate within their overall approach. If you intend to use this book we suggest you take care in identifying what is useful for you in the context of your own research question and objectives.

Data display and analysis is suited to an inductive strategy to analyse qualitative data, although it is also compatible with a more deductive strategy. Miles and Huberman's (1994) book is useful both for its overall discussion of the analysis of qualitative data and in relation to the many suggestions relating to particular aspects of, and techniques for, the successful conduct of this process.

Template analysis

This sub-section is based on the work of King (2004). He describes and discusses a procedure to analyse qualitative data known as template analysis. A **template** is essentially a list of the codes or categories that represent the themes revealed from the data that have been collected. Like the data display approach just discussed, template analysis combines a deductive and an inductive approach to qualitative analysis in the sense that codes can be predetermined and then amended or added to as data are collected and analysed.

King (2004) provides a number of ways of differentiating template analysis from procedures used in a grounded theory strategy, which he says it resembles. Grounded theory, as we discuss later in this section, does not permit the prior specification of any codes to analyse data, holding as it does to a more purely inductive analytical approach as far as is

Box 13.13
Focus on management research

Resistance to information technology implementation

Lapointe and Rivard (2005) used data from three longitudinal case studies of hospitals' electronic medical records (EMRs) systems to examine models of resistance to information technology. EMRs are computer-based systems that allow access to patients' records at all times from different locations to retrieve data, observe treatment programmes or obtain test results. In each of the three cases, Lapointe and Rivard focused on the implementation process from EMR software selection to its installation and use by the hospital's physicians. Data were collected from three sources:

- direct observation over a period of days at each site observing how each EMR was used;
- system and project documentation, minutes of committee meetings, memoranda and letters;
- 43 semi-structured interviews with physicians (15), nurses (14) and managers (14).

One of the researchers subsequently produced and coded complete transcripts using the CAQDAS program NUD*IST™ (subsequently developed as N6). Extracts of data from each of the cases were subsequently coded by other researchers to ensure validity

of the coding process. This initial coding was based upon an analysis of the resistance to IT literature and 'allowed for the identification of behaviours, precursors, threats, subject, and objects of resistance' (Lapointe and Rivard 2005:470). As part of this process, the coding structure was modified where it was felt it did not adequately represent the data.

Data analysis was conducted in two stages:

1 *within* each of the three cases to provide a rich understanding of the case and allow unique patterns within each case to emerge;
2 *across* the three cases to search for common patterns and unique features.

The first stage used data reduction and presentation techniques, creating separate tables to distinguish between different periods of resistance. Units of each transcript that reported specific resisting behaviours were identified and examined to establish the object of these behaviours, their associated threats and the conditions in which they had occurred. Similar behaviours were then clustered together, providing clear chains of evidence.

For the second stage, a number of categories of resisting behaviours were selected. Each of these was explored across the cases to identify similarities and differences between them. Through this a general explanation that could be applied to all cases was developed. Based on these analyses Lapointe and Rivard were able to develop a model that they argued both explained the dynamics of group-level resistance and showed how these emerged from individual resistance behaviours over time.

practically possible. Grounded theory is also more structured than template analysis, specifying a set of procedures that must be used (Strauss and Corbin 2008). In this sense King (2004) comments that grounded theory is much more prescriptive whilst template analysis is similar to the data display and analysis approach in that it offers a more flexible route to analysis, which would allow you to amend its use to the needs of your own research project.

Like the general approach to categorising data outlined earlier in Section 13.5, template analysis involves developing categories and attaching these to units of data. Data are coded and analysed to identify and explore themes, patterns and relationships. The template approach allows codes and categories to be shown hierarchically to help this analytical process. In Box 13.14 a hierarchical relationship is shown between the codes listed, there being (in the example) three levels of codes and greater depth of

Box 13.14
Focus on student research

Part of an initial template to analyse an advertising campaign's impact

Joss had been asked to analyse the impact of a recent advertising campaign. Using her interview topic guide, she used the main questions to set higher-order codes (shown in CAPITALS). Subsidiary questions and probes were used to generate lower-order codes, shown in lower case and italic script. An extract of her initial template follows:

1 CONTEXTUAL FACTORS
   1 Reasons for campaign

   2 Environment
      1 Political
      2 Economic
      3 Socio-cultural
      4 Technological
      5 Legal
   3 Nature of the product
      1 Cost
      2 Features
      3 Target groups
2 NATURE OF THE CAMPAIGN
   1 Media
   2 Coverage
3 AWARENESS BY TARGET GROUPS AND OTHERS
   1 Those in target groups
   2 Others

analysis being indicated by the lower-level codes shown towards the right-hand side of the template. Codes are also grouped together in levels 2 and 3 to show how higher-order codes are constituted.

As data collection proceeds, your template will be subject to revision as part of the process of qualitative analysis. The process of analysing interview transcripts or observation notes will lead to some of the codes being revised and even changes to their place or level in the template hierarchy. This process will also involve unitising data according to the list of codes currently in use. Where you consider introducing a new code or altering the level of an existing code in the template, you will need to verify this action and explore its implications in relation to your previous coding activity. This is usually more straightforward using CAQDAS (Lewins and Silver 2006). As part of this, it is helpful to use self-memos to remind you later of the reasons for these changes.

King (2004) outlines four ways in which a template may be revised:

- insertion of a new code into the hierarchy as the result of a relevant issue being identified through data collection for which there is no existing code;
- deletion of a code from the hierarchy if it is not needed;
- changing the scope of a code, that is altering its level within the hierarchy;
- reclassifying a code to a different category.

The issue or theme indicated by a lower-order code may assume a greater importance than expected once data collection and analysis occurs. For example, in Box 13.14, the third-level code 'Features' may prove to be of greater importance in relation to the research project and therefore require to be reclassified as a level 1 code or category. Equally, the analytical relevance of some higher-order codes may be restricted in practice so that they are reclassified at a lower level as a subset of another higher-order code. A template may also be modified when a code originally included as a sub-category of one higher-order code is reclassified as a sub-category of another as you begin to immerse yourself in your transcripts more fully.

The template may continue to be revised until all of the data collected have been coded and analysed carefully. It will therefore serve as an analytical procedure through which to devise an initial conceptual framework that will be subsequently revised and then finalised as a means to represent and explore key themes and relationships in your data. Using a template will also help you to select key themes to explore and to identify emergent issues that arise through the process of data collection and analysis that you may not have intended to focus on as you commenced your research project (King 2004).

Analytic induction

Analytic induction is an inductive version of the explanation-building procedure outlined earlier in Section 13.7 (Yin 2003). Johnson (2004:165) defines **analytic induction** as 'the intensive examination of a strategically selected number of cases so as to empirically establish the causes of a specific phenomenon'. As an inductively led approach to analyse qualitative data, it therefore commences with a less defined explanation of the phenomenon to be explored, which is not derived from existing theory. This explanation (sometimes termed a proposition) is then tested through a case study that is selected purposively (Section 7.3) to allow the phenomenon to be explored. Given the loosely defined nature of the explanation it is likely either that the explanation will need to be redefined or that the scope of the phenomenon to be explained will need to be narrowed. Adopting one of these courses of action leads to a redefinition (of the phenomenon or its explanation) and the need to explore a second case study that will also be selected purposively. Where the explanation appears to be confirmed, you may either cease data collection on the basis that you believe that you have found a valid explanation or seek to test the explanation in other purposively selected cases to see whether it is still valid. Where the explanation is not adequate, it will again be necessary to revise it and to test this in the context of another purposively selected case. This process may continue until a refined explanation is generated that reasonably explains the phenomenon in relevant cases where you collected and analysed data.

As an inductive and incremental way of collecting and analysing data qualitatively this process has the capability of leading to the development of well-grounded explanations. In this way, analytic induction encourages the collection of data that are thorough and rich and based on the explored actions and meanings of those who participate in this process, whether through in-depth interviews or observation, or some combination of these methods. However, it has been evaluated in different ways in relation to the nature of the explanations that are likely to be produced. On the one hand, it has been claimed that thorough and rigorous use of analytic induction may lead to unassailable explanations where all negative cases are either accounted for by the final revised explanation or excluded by redefining the phenomenon being studied (Johnson 2004; Kidder 1981). On the other hand, analytic induction has been criticised because it seeks to find an explanation for the necessary conditions that exist in cases where a phenomenon occurs, whereas there may well be other cases where the same conditions exist but the phenomenon does not occur. For example, an explanation may be developed to explain the conditions that exist in cases where organisational theft occurs, whereas there are likely to be other cases where the same conditions apply but where such theft may or may not occur. In this way, it would also be necessary to study a range of cases where such conditions apply, having identified these, to find out whether the phenomenon (theft) also exists in all or only some of these cases (Johnson 2004). Such an approach is likely to be highly time consuming and resource intensive and therefore perhaps suitable only for major research projects.

Grounded theory

Grounded theory has already been outlined briefly as a strategy in Section 5.3. Within this strategy specific analysis procedures are used to build an explanation or to generate a theory around the core or central theme that emerges from your data. Some prominent advocates of grounded theory state fairly precise procedures to be followed in relation to each of the stages of the categorising data process that was outlined in general terms in Section 13.5 In this way, the grounded theory of Strauss and Corbin (2008) is structured and systematic, with set procedures to follow at each stage of analysis. Where you do not pay particular attention to the nature of the procedures outlined for grounded theory, you may not produce a research report that is sufficiently rigorous to substantiate the explanation or theory that you are seeking to advance.

In the grounded theory of Strauss and Corbin (2008) the disaggregation of data into units is called **open coding**, the process of recognising relationships between categories is referred to as **axial coding**, and the integration of categories to produce a theory is labelled **selective coding**. We shall briefly outline each of these in turn, drawing on the work of Strauss and Corbin (2008). Within grounded theory, choice of cases through which to gather data and refine concepts is termed 'theoretical sampling' (Glaser and Strauss 1967; Strauss and Corbin 2008). In this way, sampling is purposive (Section 7.3), where critical cases are chosen to further the development of concepts and categories and to explore relationships between these to develop a theory. Underpinning this is the process of 'constantly comparing' the data being collected with the concepts and categories being used, so as to aid the process of developing an emerging theory that will be thoroughly grounded in that data. Theoretical sampling continues until 'theoretical saturation' is reached. This occurs when data collection ceases to reveal new data that are relevant to a category, where categories have become well developed and understood and relationships between categories have been verified (Strauss and Corbin 2008).

Open coding

Open coding is similar to the unitisation and categorisation procedures outlined in Section 13.5. The data that you collect will be disaggregated into conceptual units and provided with a label. The same label or name will be given to similar units of data. However, because this research process commences without an explicit basis in existing theory, the result may be the creation of a multitude of conceptual labels related to the lower level of focus and structure with which you commence your research (Box 13.15). The emphasis in this grounded theory approach will be to derive meaning from the subjects and settings being studied. In Section 13.5 we stated that a unit of data might relate to a few words, a line, a sentence or number of sentences, or a paragraph. The need to understand meanings and to generate categories to encompass these in a grounded theory approach is likely to lead you to conduct your early analysis by looking at smaller rather than larger units of data. The resulting multitude of code labels will therefore need to be compared and placed into broader, related groupings or categories. This will allow you to produce a more manageable and focused research project and to develop the analytical process

Strauss and Corbin (2008) suggest that there are three main sources to derive names for these categories: you utilise terms that emerge from your data; they are based on actual terms used by your participants ('*in vivo*' codes); or they come from terms used in existing theory and the literature. However, Strauss and Corbin counsel against names being derived from existing theory and literature in a grounded approach. This is because their use in the written account of your research may lead readers to interpret these

Box 13.15
Focus on student research

Using OPEN CODING

As part of her studies, Maureen had become particularly interested in the difficulties her fellow students faced in writing. In preparation for a class exercise, her research methods tutor had asked each student to describe in writing how they prepared to write. As part of this they were instructed to pay particular attention to the details of the process. Each transcript was word-processed and imported into the CAQDAS package NVivo™. Open codes were applied to each transcript using the CAQDAS package NVivo™ as illustrated in the extract shown.

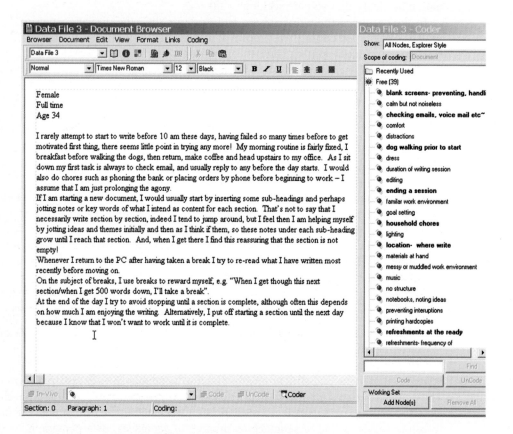

Based upon their subsequent analysis, Maureen and her colleagues developed the theory that, when writing, students performed a series of rituals which they believed influenced their writing process positively.

according to their prior understanding of such theoretical concepts rather than the particular meaning now being placed on such terms.

The categorisation that you derive from your data will indicate significant themes and issues and help you to consider where data collection should be focused in the future. In conjunction with this, it will also help you to develop a sharper focus in relation to your research question. The nature of this research approach will inevitably mean that your initial research question will be broadly focused, although still within manageable exploratory confines. As you develop a narrower focus through this process, you will be able to refine and limit the scope of your research question (Strauss and Corbin 2008).

Axial coding

This stage refers to the process of looking for relationships between the categories of data that have emerged from open coding. It indicates a process of theoretical development. As relationships between categories are recognised, they are rearranged into a hierarchical form, with the emergence of subcategories. The essence of this approach is to explore and explain a phenomenon (the subject of your research project, or one of them) by identifying what is happening and why, the environmental factors that affect this (such as economic, technological, political, legal, social and cultural ones), how it is being managed within the context being examined, and what the outcomes are of the action that has been taken. Clearly, there will be a relationship between these aspects, or categories, and the purpose of your analysis will be to explain this.

Once these relationships have been recognised, you will then seek to verify them against actual data that you have collected. Strauss and Corbin (2008) recommend that you undertake this by formulating questions or statements, which can then be phrased as hypotheses, to test these apparent relationships. As you undertake this process you will be looking for evidence that supports these 'hypotheses' and for negative cases that will demonstrate variations from these relationships.

Selective coding

Strauss and Corbin (2008) suggest that after a lengthy period of data collection, which may take several months, you will have developed a number of principal categories and related subcategories. The stage that follows is called 'selective coding'. This is intended to identify one of these principal categories, which becomes known as the central or core category, in order to relate the other categories to this with the intention of integrating the research and developing a grounded theory (Strauss and Corbin 2008). In the previous stage the emphasis was placed on recognising the relationships between categories and their subcategories. In this stage the emphasis is placed on recognising and developing the relationships between the principal categories that have emerged from this grounded approach in order to develop an explanatory theory.

Implications of using grounded theory

A number of implications have emerged from this brief outline of the main procedures involved in the use of grounded theory. These may be summed up by saying that the use of a grounded theory strategy will involve you in processes that will be time consuming, intensive and reflective. Before you commit yourself to this strategy, you will need to consider the time that you have to conduct your research, the level of competence you will need, your access to data, and the logistical implications of immersing yourself in such an intensive approach to research (Box 13.16, overleaf). There may also be a concern that little of significance will emerge at the end of the research process, and this will be an important aspect for you to consider when determining the focus of your research if you use a grounded theory and the prescribed analysis procedures.

Discourse analysis

Discourse analysis is a general term that covers an extremely wide variety of approaches to the analysis of language in its own right and is concerned with how and why individuals' language is used by individuals in specific social contexts. In particular, it explores

Box 13.16
Focus on management research

Organisational culture change in grocery retailing

In their 2003 *Journal of Management Studies* paper, Ogbonna and Wilkinson report on the impact of a programme of culture change on managers in a leading grocery retail chain employing over 100 000 people in approximately 160 UK stores, the majority of which were superstores. Qualitative data were gathered from three sources:

- organisational documents, such as internal memoranda, internal consultancy reports, copies of staff attitude surveys, internal records and press cuttings;
- observation of managers' behaviours at two series of training and team-building events;
- 30 in-depth face-to-face interviews with 15 middle managers (each was interviewed twice), an additional in-depth face-to-face interview with a

director and observations at six of the largest superstores identified as flagship stores.

This resulted in over 400 pages of reports, change manuals and other organisational documents as well as over 300 pages of verbatim transcribed interview data.

Data analysis commenced by coding the organisational documents and interview transcripts into theoretically derived categories. These focused 'on the espoused rationale for change, the changing nature of managerial roles, the level of culture change advocated, the approaches adopted, the intended and unintended impacts of change, and the tensions and contradictions which characterized change' (Ogbonna and Wilkinson 2003:1158). The authors suggest that the subsequent process of developing categories, linkages, relationships and sub-dividing categories was undertaken in a manner similar to Strauss and Corbin's grounded theory.

Based on their analyses Ogbonna and Wilkinson concluded that, in this case, changes in managerial behaviour were related more to surveillance and direct control, including the threat of sanction, rather than to any real change in managerial values.

how language (discourse) in the form of talk and text both constructs and simultaneously reproduces and/or changes the social world rather than using it as a means to reveal the social world as a phenomenon (Phillips and Hardy 2002). The focus is therefore on identifying how this reproduction or change occurs. Given these concerns, you will not be surprised that researchers using discourse analysis usually adopt a subjectivist ontology (Section 4.2). In choosing a discourse analysis approach you would explore the use of language in specific contexts such as holiday brochures to construct a social reality of a package holiday or the minutes of meetings to reflect the meaning of the meeting from the perspective of the chairperson. Although there are many forms of discourse analysis (Dick, 2004), within this sub-section we concern ourselves with one, critical discourse analysis.

Critical discourse analysis assumes that the constructions that individuals make operate not only in a sense-making way but also reproduce or challenge the underlying ideological belief systems of society at large (Dick 2004). Consequently, different discourses will produce different explanations of the same practice such as a meeting, a holiday or a day at work. They will also produce different versions of the same concept. For example, the discourse related to the norms of behaviour that are expected in a classroom are likely to differ between students attending primary school, secondary school and university. In addition, the concept of being a student in a classroom can only be constructed in those societies where some form of organised education exists.

The data that are analysed in critical discourse analysis are texts but can be, as discussed in Section 13.3, collected from a wide variety of sources. Within this, Dick (2004) argues that for some research it is useful to identify specific contexts such as the career identities of graduates or the resistance to diversity initiatives in a particular type of organisation. Interview data are transcribed in full prior to analysis and, as the focus is content, Dick (2004) advises that there is no need to indicate pauses or overlaps between speakers (Box 13.2 earlier). She also suggests that it may be possible to use data sampling rather than transcribe and analyse entire interviews (Table 13.2). Once data have been collected, they can be analysed qualitatively, using the procedures outlined in Section 13.5, through a three-dimensional analytical framework. This analyses each discourse from the perspectives of its being (Figure 13.2):

- text;
- discursive practice;
- social practice.

It is this final dimension, social practice, that is likely to reveal where discourses are multiple and contradictory. The extent to which the text defends a particular position provides a clear indication as to the degree to which that position is contested. Where positions are challenged or defended vigorously with the text, these are examples of hegemonic struggle where two or more ideologies compete for dominance.

Discourse analysis, therefore, focuses on understanding how language is used to construct and change aspects of the world. This means it encourages you not to accept your research data at face value. Its main disadvantages are that it is time consuming and requires considerable experience before you feel comfortable with the process. In addition, it is a contentious method which is subject to much debate (Dick 2004).

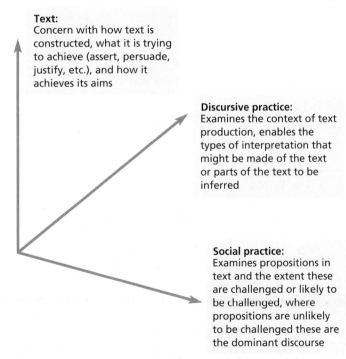

Figure 13.2 A three-dimensional analytical framework for critical discourse analysis

Narrative analysis

Depending on the nature of your research question and objectives, the data collection methods used and the data that are produced, narrative may be suitable for you to use. It may be used either as the principal means to analyse your qualitative data, or as a complementary means. In this way, narrative analysis may be used as a means to explore linkages, relationships and socially constructed explanations that naturally occur within narrative accounts, where fragmentation of these into categories and themes would therefore be rendered unnecessary. The structural elements that are present in narratives may also help you to analyse each narrative account and perhaps to compare the course of events in different narratives where there is likely to be some analytical benefit in comparing these.

Stories and story telling have become more frequently used in recent years in organisational research although they are still in their infancy (Gabriel and Griffiths 2004). Stories have been defined as narratives which have both plots and characters and generate emotion in the story teller and their audience using elaboration and poetic licence (Gabriel 2000). For data collected as stories through, for example, semi or unstructured interviews, requirements for accuracy are often less important than the points that are made and what these points symbolise, and how they illuminate particular issues such as organisational politics, culture and change (Gabriel and Griffiths 2004). Consequently, whilst such narratives may not always present facts, they provide meaning to the facts.

13.9 Using CAQDAS for qualitative analysis

The use of CAQDAS offers a number of advantages in relation to the analytical procedures we have been discussing. In particular, when used systematically, it can aid continuity and increase both transparency and methodological rigour. These latter points were summarised by one of our students as 'it forces you to do your analysis properly!' However, the use of this type of software may be problematic, not least due to its not being available at some universities!

The literature that evaluates CAQDAS raises a number of issues associated with its use. While there are a number of different CAQDAS programs available, these vary in relation to the type of facilities that they offer and, therefore, potentially in their usefulness for different analytic situations. Consequently, you need to develop some familiarity with a range of programs to be able to evaluate their applicability for the particular analyses you wish to undertake. At the same time, it is likely that only one or perhaps two of these programs will be available for you to explore and evaluate in your university. Lewins and Silver (2006:1) summarise this situation, stating:

> It is not always easy to visualise exactly what a CAQDAS package offers when exploring it for the first time yourself. Equally when asking someone else for their opinion, it is not always easy to know which questions you should be asking. Most of the software packages we are aware of and discuss regularly are excellent products in one way or several! Sometimes you choose a package that is already *in situ* and make good use of it – but if you have a choice about which software to purchase for your research project, you may be in some uncertainty about how to proceed.

Functions

Despite differences between CAQDAS programs, the basic ways in which they can facilitate your qualitative data analysis are similar. Lewins and Silver (2006) summarise these as:

- *Structure of work:* ability to store or provide connections between all data files within the research project;
- *Closeness to data and interactivity:* almost instantaneous access to all your data once it has been introduced;
- *Explore the data:* text search tools enable a word, a phrase or a collection of words to be searched and retrieved within context;
- *Code and retrieve:* complete freedom over the use of inductive, deductive or a combination of coding schema to code, retrieve, recode and output data;
- *Project management and data organisation:* powerful means to manage the research project as a whole and organise your data. Data organisation allows you to focus on subsets of data;
- *Searching and interrogating:* on basis of language used, including automatically coding data, on basis of relationships between codes, for different units of data to build hypotheses and theorise;
- *Writing memos, comments, notes, etc.* to record thoughts systematically in relation to the data;
- *Output:* reports allowing you to view material in hard copy or export it to other applications such as word processors and spreadsheets as well as produce tabular reports.

What is not apparent from this list is that the functions contained in some CAQDAS packages are better at supporting certain types of qualitative data analysis procedures than others. This means that you may need to experiment with more than one package before you find the CAQDAS that meets your needs. Your final choice of CAQDAS package will be dependent on a range of factors, including, not least, the relative benefits you will gain relative to the time you need to invest to learn a CAQDAS program. These factors are summarised in Box 13.17 as a checklist.

Box 13.17
Checklist

Choosing a CAQDAS package

- ✔ How much data do you have that needs to be analysed qualitatively?
- ✔ How important are these data, relative to other data you have collected for your research project?
- ✔ How much time do you have to learn how to use the package?
- ✔ How much support is available in your university to help you learn to use the package?
- ✔ What is the operating system of your computer?
- ✔ How much memory does your computer have?
- ✔ How much time do you have to undertake your analysis?
- ✔ Do you want software that will allow you to take an inductive (or a deductive) approach to your analysis?
- ✔ Do you want a package that will help you manage your thinking and allow you to develop your own codes?
- ✔ Do you want a package that will allow you to explore the way language is used in your data?
- ✔ Do you want a package that allows you display relationships within your data diagrammatically?
- ✔ Do you want a package that will allow you to quantify your data?

Table 13.3 Internet addresses for a range of selected CAQDAS developers

Name	Internet address	Brief comments
ATLAS.ti	http://www.atlasti.de	Windows version only, offers great flexibility
HyperRESEARCH	http://www.researchware.com	Windows and MAC versions, simple to use
MAXqda2	http://www.maxqda.de	Windows version only, intuitive, easy to get to grips with
NVivo	http://www.qsrinternational.com/	Windows version only, very powerful software, large range of searching possibilities
QSR N6	http://www.qsrinternational.com/	Windows version only, excellent range of search tools

Sources: developed from Lewins and Silver (2006); authors' experiences

Exploring the latest versions of CAQDAS

Published information about CAQDAS programs is likely to become out of date fairly quickly. Fortunately, there is a wealth of up-to-date information available from the CAQDAS Networking project's website hosted by the University of Surrey.[1] If you are considering using CAQDAS, we would strongly recommend a visit to this website which, in addition to a wealth of useful articles, also contains web links to commercial software producers' sites including downloadable demonstration versions of the software. We would also advise you to explore the Internet sites of CAQDAS producers to obtain details and demonstrations of the latest versions of these packages and the features that they offer. Some of those most widely used are listed in Table 13.3.

13.10 Summary

- Qualitative data are non-numerical data that have not been quantified. They result from the collection of non-standardised data that require classification and are analysed through the use of conceptualisation.
- Qualitative analysis generally involves one or more of: summarising data, categorising data and structuring data using narrative to recognise relationships, develop and test propositions and produce well-grounded conclusions. It can lead to reanalysing categories developed from qualitative data quantitatively.
- The processes of data analysis and data collection are necessarily interactive.
- There are a number of aids that you might use to help you through the process of qualitative analysis, including interim summaries, self-memos and maintaining a researcher's diary.
- Qualitative analysis procedures can be related to using either a deductively based or an inductively based research approach.
- The use of computer-assisted qualitative data analysis software (CAQDAS) can help you during qualitative analysis with regard to project management and data organisation, keeping close to your data, exploration, coding and retrieval of your data, searching and interrogating to build propositions and theorise, and recording your thoughts systematically.

---

[1]The Internet address for the CAQDAS Networking Project is http://caqdas.soc.surrey.ac.uk/

Self-check questions

Help with these questions is available at the end of the chapter.

13.1 Why do we describe qualitative analysis as an 'interactive process'?

13.2 What types of data will you need to retain and file while you are undertaking qualitative research?

13.3 How would you differentiate between a deductive and an inductive analytical approach?

13.4 What are the main implications of using a deductive analytical approach for the way in which you conduct the process of qualitative analysis?

13.5 What are the main implications of using an inductive analytical approach for the way in which you conduct the process of qualitative analysis?

Review and discussion questions

13.6 With a friend, obtain a transcript of an interview that has already been undertaken. If your university subscribes to online newspapers such as ft.com, these are a good source of business-related transcripts. Alternatively, typing 'interview transcript' into a search engine such as Google will generate numerous possibilities on a vast range of topics!

    a With your friend, decide on the unit of analysis you wish to use. We suggest you use either lines or paragraphs and subsequently agree on a coding template.

    b Independently, apply your template to your transcript, using it to code your data units.

    c How well did your coding template work?

    d To what extent does your coding differ from that of your friend?

    e Why do you think this is?

13.7 Visit one of the CAQDAS websites listed in Table 13.3. Find and download a demonstration version of the CAQDAS package and explore its features. How useful do you think this will be for analysing your research data?

13.8 Find out whether your university provides you with access to the NVivo™ CAQDAS. If it does, visit this book's companion website and download the self-teach package and associated data sets. Work through this to explore the features of NVivo™.

Progressing your research project

Analysing your data qualitatively

- Undertake and audio-record an initial semi-structured or in-depth interview related to your research project, transcribe this interview, and make a few copies of your transcript. Alternatively obtain a copy of a relevant document.

- Decide whether it is most appropriate to summarise, categorise or develop a narrative using your data in order to answer your research question.

- Where a summary is most appropriate develop this, ensuring you also include contextual data.

- Where a narrative is most appropriate, develop this paying particular attention to the temporal order and the organisational and social contexts.

- Where categorising is most appropriate and your research project is based on a deductive approach, develop a provisional set of categories from your research question and objectives,

▶ Progressing your research project (continued)

conceptual framework, research themes and initial propositions. Produce a description of each of these categories. Evaluate these categories to see whether they appear to form a coherent set in relation to the aim of your research.

- Using one of your transcripts, attempt to allocate units of data to appropriate categories by using CAQDAS or writing their code labels alongside the text in the left-hand margin. Again, evaluate this provisional set of categories and modify any that appear to be inappropriate.

- Where categorising is most appropriate and your research project is based on an inductive approach, work through one of the transcript copies and seek to identify categories related to your research purpose. Allocate units of data to appropriate categories by using CAQDAS or writing appropriate code labels for these categories alongside the text in the left-hand margin. List these categories and their labels and produce a description for each of the categories that you have devised.

- Once you have allocated units of data to the set of categories, use the CAQDAS program to organise your data by different categories. Alternatively, cut out the units of data related to different categories and transfer them to an appropriately labelled index card (reference to the interview, location of the text in the transcript and the date and so forth). Read through the units of data within each category.

- Analyse these data by asking questions such as: What are the points of interest that emerge within each category? How will you seek to follow these up during your next data collection session? How does the material that has been revealed through this interview relate to any theoretical explanation or initial propositions with which you commenced your data collection? Are any connections evident between the categories?

- Produce a summary of the interview and attach it to a copy of the transcript. Memo any ideas that you have and file these.

- Repeat the procedures for the remaining qualitative data as appropriate and revise your ideas as necessary.

References

Bazeley, P. (2007) *Qualitative Data Analysis with NVivo.* London: Sage.

Bryman, A. (1988) *Quantity and Quality in Social Research.* London: Unwin Hyman.

Coffey, A. and Atkinson, P. (1996) *Making Sense of Qualitative Data.* Thousand Oaks, CA: Sage.

Dey, I. (1993) *Qualitative Data Analysis.* London: Routledge.

Dick, P. (2004) 'Discourse analysis', in C. Cassell and G. Symon (eds). *Essential Guide to Qualitative Methods and Analysis in Organizational Research.* London: Sage, pp. 203–13.

Easterby-Smith, M., Thorpe, R. and Jackson, P. (2008) *Management Research: An Introduction* (3rd edn). London: Sage.

Erlandson, D.A., Harris, E.L., Skipper, B.L. and Allen, S.D. (1993) *Doing Naturalistic Inquiry.* Newbury Park, CA: Sage.

Gabriel, Y. (2000) *Storytelling in Organizations: Facts, Fictions Fantasies.* Oxford: Oxford University Press.

Gabriel, Y. and Griffiths, D.S. (2004) 'Stories in Organizational Research', in C. Cassell and G. Symon (eds) *Essential Guide to Qualitative Methods and Analysis in Organizational Research.* London: Sage, pp. 114–126.

Glaser, B. (1978) *Theoretical Sensitivity: Advances in the Methodology of Grounded Theory*. Mill Valley, CA: Sociology Press.

Glaser, B. and Strauss, A. (1967) *The Discovery of Grounded Theory*. Chicago, IL: Aldine.

Healey, M.J. and Rawlinson, M.B. (1994) 'Interviewing techniques in business and management research', in V.J. Wass and P.E. Wells (eds) *Principles and Practice in Business and Management Research*. Aldershot: Dartmouth, pp. 123–45.

Hodson, R. (1991) 'The active worker: compliance and autonomy at the workplace', *Journal of Contemporary Ethnography*, Vol. 20, No. 1, pp. 47–8.

Johnson, P. (2004) 'Analytic induction', in C. Cassell and G. Symon (eds) *Essential Guide to Qualitative Methods and Analysis in Organizational Research*. London: Sage, pp. 165–79.

Kidder, L.H. (1981) 'Qualitative research and quasi-experimental frameworks', in M.B. Brewer and B.E. Collins (eds) *Scientific Enquiry and the Social Sciences.* San Francisco, CA: Jossey Bass, pp. 226–56.

King, N. (2004) 'Using templates in the thematic analysis of text', in C. Cassell and G. Symon (eds) *Essential Guide to Qualitative Methods in Organizational Research*. London: Sage, pp. 256–70.

Kvale, S. (1996) *InterViews*. Thousand Oaks, CA: Sage.

Lapointe, L. and Rivard, S. (2005) 'A multilevel model of resistance to information technology implementation', *MIS Quarterly*, Vol. 29, No. 3, pp. 461–91.

Lewins, A. and Silver, C. (2006) 'Choosing a CAQDAS package – 5th edition', CAQDAS Networking Project Working Paper. Available at: http://caqdas.soc.surrey.ac.uk/ChoosingLewins&SilverV5July06.pdf [Accessed 18 June 2008.]

Marshall, C. and Rossman, G.B. (2006) *Designing Qualitative Research* (4th edn). Thousand Oaks, CA: Sage.

Miles, M.B. and Huberman, A.M. (1994) *Qualitative Data Analysis* (2nd edn). Thousand Oaks, CA: Sage.

Moustakas, C. (1994) *Phenomenological Research Methods*. Thousand Oaks, CA: Sage.

Musson, G. (2004) 'Life histories', in C. Cassell and G. Symon (eds) *Essential Guide to Qualitative Methods in Organizational Research*. London: Sage, pp. 34–44.

Ogbonna, E. and Wilkinson, B. (2003) 'The false promise of organizational culture change: A case study of middle managers in grocery retailing', *Journal of Management Studies,* Vol. 40, No. 5, pp. 1151–78.

Phillips, N. and Hardy, C. (2002) *Discourse Analysis: Investigating Processes of Social Construction*. London: Sage.

Riley, J. (1996) *Getting the Most from your Data: A Handbook of Practical Ideas on How to Analyse Qualitative Data* (2nd edn). Bristol: Technical and Educational Services Ltd.

Robson, C. (2002) *Real World Research* (2nd edn). Oxford: Blackwell.

Schatzman, L. and Strauss, A. (1973) *Field Research: Strategies for a Natural Sociology*. Englewood Cliffs, NJ: Prentice-Hall.

Silverman, D. (2007) *A Very Short, Fairly Interesting and Reasonably Cheap Book about Qualitative Research*. London: Sage.

Strauss, A. and Corbin, J. (2008) *Basics of Qualitative Research* (3rd edn). Thousand Oaks, CA: Sage.

Tesch, R. (1990) *Qualitative Research: Analysis Types and Software Tools.* New York: Falmer.

Yin, R.K. (2003) *Case Study Research: Design and Methods* (3rd edn). Thousand Oaks, CA: Sage.

Further reading

Cassell, C. and Symon, G. (eds) (2004) *Essential Guide to Qualitative Methods and Analysis in Organizational Research*. London: Sage. This edited work contains an excellent range of chapters related to analytical strategies.

Dey, I. (1993) *Qualitative Data Analysis*. London: Routledge. Provides a very thorough discussion of the stages of qualitative analysis without being bound to any of the approaches referred to in the sources below.

Lewins, A. and Silver, C. (2006) 'Choosing a CAQDAS package – 5th edition', CAQDAS Networking Project Working Paper. Available at: http://caqdas.soc.surrey.ac.uk/ChoosingLewins&SilverV5July06.pdf [Accessed 18 June 2008.] This working paper provides an excellent summary of types of software for managing qualitative data. It covers both code-based theory-building and text retrievers and text based managers software.

Miles, M.B. and Huberman, A.M. (1994) *Qualitative Data Analysis* (2nd edn). Thousand Oaks, CA: Sage. Provides an excellent source of reference to the elements involved in qualitative research as well as offering a number of particular techniques that may help you to analyse your data.

Strauss, A. and Corbin, J. (2008) *Basics of Qualitative Research* (3rd edn). Newbury Park, CA: Sage. Provides a very thorough introduction to the grounded theory approach.

Yin, R.K. (2003) *Case Study Research: Design and Methods* (3rd edn). Thousand Oaks, CA: Sage. Chapter 5 very usefully examines analytical strategies and procedures based on a deductive approach.

Case 13
The influence of film on tourist decision making

Lord of the Rings Scenery – Mount Ngauruhoe from Whakapapa, New Zealand
Source: © Mark Saunders 2008.

Sarah had always had a keen interest in movies and when choosing a topic for her final research project in her tourism course she decided she wanted to investigate the concept of film induced tourism. She had read articles by authors such as Beeton (2005), Hudson and Ritchie (2006) and Grihault (2007) which had fuelled her interest further. These articles seemed to take an approach of focusing on marketing and other business related aspects on the importance of film induced tourism to a destination. From her early reading, Sarah felt she wanted to look at other avenues of interest to her. She decided that she wanted to investigate the reasons why some people were influenced by films in choosing their holiday destinations.

Sarah arranged a meeting with her project tutor to discuss her ideas and the approach she should take. She explained the reasons for wanting to concentrate on the tourists themselves and investigate what it was about movies that influenced some people in their decision-making. She felt further investigation of these issues could be very relevant and useful to tourist organisations wanting to utilise film to promote their areas, providing them with a better understanding of what was happening. Her project tutor responded by commenting that her research ideas sounded interesting and relevant but that she really needed to think about how she was going to collect the data.

Sarah carried out some additional reading on qualitative methods. Some early work on the use of online mechanisms such as blogs, wiki's and forums by O'Connor and Madge (2003), Oravec (2004), Sauer *et al.* (2005), Cohen and Krishnamurthy (2006) and Pan *et al.* (2007) caught her attention. In her reading and investigations she found that blogs (e.g. travelblog.org), message boards (e.g. TripAdvisor) and public-access video sites (e.g. YouTube) had become commonplace. Tourists now used these 'informal online environments' to publish details of their holidays, their experiences and their views (good or bad), both textually and visually (in the form of photographs or digital video clips). This provided a new and sometimes very rich source of information for other travellers and in some ways helps to make more tangible something which is inherently intangible. Sarah felt here was clearly an opportunity to use such a mechanism for her research. She thought that setting up a blog would be both an innovative and very appropriate mechanism to gather opinion from a truly international perspective for her study and allow her to ask questions of tourists whose thoughts, feelings and opinions had been influenced by films.

She investigated ways to set up a blog and found that it could be done quite easily with no real knowledge of website design required, with many websites offering a facility to set one up for free. Initially Sarah explained her ideas to her project tutor who thought the technique was both relevant and innovative and that she had shown initiative in both looking for another way to obtain the data she needed and in carrying out some research to back up use of such a technique. Sarah's project tutor advised her to conduct more research on carrying out online qualitative data collection and methods of analysing such data before designing and setting up her actual blog.

In Sarah's reading she found that qualitative data collection methods can provide a very rich source of data if collected carefully and analysed properly. She quickly realised that the strength of using a blog and its success would be dependent on exactly how she asked the questions, gathered the data and how it was then analysed. In relation to blogs Sarah found that Oravec (2004: 238) states '. . . weblogs allow individuals considerable personal leeway to link various resources and convey descriptive and evaluative commentary in the context of streams of personal reflections'. This was exactly what Sarah wanted – a forum or platform for people to comment and share their multiple subjective opinions on her topic. As she was using the Internet it would also be global, anyone from anywhere in the world would be able to contribute. After gaining the final go ahead from her tutor, Sarah set up her blog on film induced tourism on the Internet.

Through her reading, Sarah realised an issue with using blogs (as with traditional websites) was that people have to know it's out there. If they do not, no one will know of the blogs existence, no one might visit it and, therefore, no one would post their thoughts, comments and opinions. If this happened, she would have no useful data. This was something she would have to address if her use of a blog as a main data-collection method was to be successful. Another key challenge she faced was analysing the data which the blog generated in an appropriate and meaningful way. Both Sarah and her project tutor felt that blog research was an innovative and effective method to capture the kind of data required for her study. Clearly though (as with many data collection methods), there were still inherent challenges to be overcome.

When it had been established for a period, people gradually began to visit the blog. With comments steadily being posted Sarah's first task – in analysis terms – was to classify her data into meaningful categories which she derived from the respondents' comments. Bloggers mentioned such aspects as which film(s) they felt had influenced their travels and also referred to aspects such as scenery, music, emotion, nostalgia and the like as key factors from the film that motivated them. Sarah used these as codes or labels to help her group the data she was receiving. The next stage was to 'unitise' the data. This involved Sarah attaching relevant 'chunks' or 'units' of data to the categories she had drawn up (such as film examples, motivating factors). This enabled her to begin to reduce and rearrange the mass of blog data into a form that was more manageable and usable. Sarah also used this process to draw up grids for further analysis and visual representation.

Analysis grid: movie factors that influence visitation

Respondent	Characters	Scenery	Narrative or story	Actors or actresses	Music or film score	Emotional attachment	Nostalgia	Other
lindsay		✓						
Lisa M		✓				✓		
the meadester		✓			✓			
rachel london						✓		
zeni	✓	✓	✓		✓		✓	
francesco		✓						
katieshaw						✓		
samanthaj						✓		
yoshikuni		✓	✓					
james cooke								✓
esmie		✓						
kerry t		✓						
steve w	✓	✓	✓					
kristy bull		✓	✓					
marcushog	✓		✓					
markc	✓		✓					
geoffdowl					✓			
newjack		✓	✓		✓			

References

Beeton, S. (2005) *Film-Induced Tourism*. Clevedon: Channel View Publications.

Cohen, E. and Krishnamurthy, B. (2006) 'A short walk in the Blogistan', *Computer Networks*, Vol. 50, pp. 615–30.

Grihault, N. (2007) 'Set-jetting tourism – international', *Mintel Reports*, March, pp. 1–45.

Hudson, S. and Ritchie, J.R.B. (2006) 'Promoting destinations via film tourism: An empirical identification of supporting marketing initiatives, *Journal of Travel Research*, Vol. 44, May, pp. 387–96.

O'Connor, H. and Madge, C. (2003) 'Focus groups in cyberspace: using the Internet for qualitative research', *Qualitative Market Research: An International Journal*, Vol. 6, No. 2, pp. 133–43.

Oravec, J.A. (2004) 'Incremental understandings: warblogs and peaceblogs in peace education', *Journal of Peace Education*, Vol. 1, No. 2, pp. 225–38.

Pan, B., MacLaurin, T. and Crotts, J.C. (2007) 'Travel blogs and the implications for destination marketing', *Journal of Travel Research*, Vol. 46, Aug. pp. 35–45.

Sauer, I.M., Bialek, D., Efimova, E., Schwartlander, R., Pless, G. and Neuhaus, P. (2005) '"*Blogs*" and "*wikis*" are valuable software tools for communication within research groups', *Artificial Organs*, Vol. 29, No. 1, pp.82–9.

Questions

1 In order for her to get the data she needs, people will have to make comments on Sarah's film-tourism blog. How will Sarah ensure that people know about and find her blog so that they can keep posting comments and ensure that such comments will keep steadily coming through?

2 Sarah has begun to analyse the data that she is getting through her blog. How should she continue this process? Some sample data is shown in the blog screenshot opposite as well as the sample analysis grid, and further selected quotes are listed below:

Desert Rose said. . .

> For me its very much the scenery that grabs me. Fiji looked so fabulous in the Blue Lagoon that I just had to go there…and Ko Samui is still very much on my list after seeing The Beach. I also want to visit Prague and I think part of that is that I've been exposed to many scenes of the city in lots of recent movies. So whether its natural or man-made, its the scenery that gets me.

Kerry said…

> The different films which influenced me to visit Japan brought different factors into play I feel. With The Last Samurai and to some degree Memoirs of a Geisha it was the natural scenery that took my breath away. With Lost in Translation, in particular, and also Memoirs it was the urban scene and modern culture that influenced me strongly. As a result, I visited both urban and natural settings during my trip to experience the different scenery and culture the country had to offer.

Sun Burst said…

> Factors for me – mainly the story and to some extent the characters as part of that. A good story that hits home, something that really gets to me in some way and makes a lasting impact or impression. You then leave the cinema thinking about the film and maybe the seeds have then been planted to visit the place – to go there and experience or feel part of the story.

3 What methods could Sarah employ to take her initial blog research further, disaggregate comments more and delve into the topic in even greater depth?

Additional case studies relating to material covered in this chapter are available via the book's Companion Website, **www.pearsoned.co.uk/saunders.** They are:

- Communicating bad news at Abco
- Paying for competence at Investco
- Internet abuse in universities.

Self-check answers

13.1 There are a number of reasons why we may describe qualitative analysis as an 'interactive process'. Analysis needs to occur during the collection of data as well as after it. This helps to shape the direction of data collection, especially where you are following a grounded-theory approach. The interactive nature of data collection and analysis allows you to recognise important themes, patterns and relationships as you collect data. As a result, you will be able to re-categorise your existing data to see whether these themes, patterns and relationships are present in the cases where you have already collected data. In addition, you will be able to adjust your future data collection approach to see whether they exist in cases where you intend to conduct your research.

13.2 You will generate three broad types of data that you will need to retain and file as the result of undertaking qualitative research.

The first of these may be referred to as raw data files. These are your original notes and audio-recordings made during the conduct of interviews or observations, or from consulting documentation. In addition, you will also retain transcripts and written-up notes of interviews and observations, although these may also be contained in a computer file.

The second of these is analytical files containing your categorised data. Alternatively, this may contain your summary or your narrative. These may of course also be contained in a computer file.

The third of these may be referred to as a supporting file, or indeed it may be different files, containing working papers, self-memos, interim reports and so forth. Again, these may also be contained in a computer file. You are well advised to keep all of this until the end of your research project.

Eventually you will create a fourth file – containing your finished work!

13.3 A *deductive* analytical approach is one where you will seek to use existing theory to shape the approach that you adopt to the qualitative research process and to aspects of data analysis. An *inductive* analytical approach is one where you will seek to build up a theory that is adequately grounded in a number of relevant cases. The design of qualitative research requires you to recognise this choice and to choose an appropriate approach to guide your research project.

13.4 There are a number of implications of using a deductive analytical approach for the way in which you conduct the process of qualitative analysis:

- You will be in a position to commence your data collection with a well-defined research question and objectives and a clear framework and propositions, derived from the theory that you will have used.
- With regard to sampling, you will be in a position to identify the number and type of organisations to which you wish to gain access in order to undertake data collection to answer your research question and meet your objectives.

- The use of literature and the theory within it will shape the data collection questions that you wish to ask those who participate in your research project.
- You will be able to commence data collection with an initial set of categories derived from your theoretical propositions/hypotheses and conceptual framework linked to your research question and objectives.
- This approach will provide you with key themes and patterns to search for in your data, and your analysis will be guided by the theoretical propositions and explanations with which you commenced.

13.5 The main implications of using an inductive analytical approach for the process of qualitative analysis are likely to be related to:

- managing and categorising a large number of code labels, which are likely to emerge from the data that you collect;
- working with smaller rather than larger units of data;
- recognising significant themes and issues during early analysis to help you to consider where data collection should be focused in the future;
- recognising the relationships between categories and rearranging these into a hierarchical form, with the emergence of sub-categories;
- seeking to verify apparent relationships against the actual data that you have collected;
- understanding how negative cases broaden (or threaten) your emerging explanation;
- recognising the relationships between the principal categories that have emerged from this grounded approach in order to develop an explanatory theory;
- being rigorous in your use of the procedures that are advocated in order to be able to produce a research report that contains findings that are sufficiently 'grounded' to substantiate the analysis or theory that you are seeking to advance.

Get ahead using resources ont the Companion at:
www.pearsoned.co.uk/saunders

- Improve your SPSS and NVivo research analysis with practice tutorials:
- Save time researching on theInternet with the Smarter Online Searching Guide.
- Test your progress using self-assessment questions.
- Follow live links to useful websites.

Chapter 14

Writing and presenting your project report

Learning outcomes

By the end of this chapter you should be able to:

- view the writing of the final project report as an exciting prospect;
- write in such a way that you can reflect on all you have learned while conducting the research;
- write a final project report that presents an authoritative account of your research;
- adopt an appropriate format, structure and style for the final project report;
- differentiate between a project report and a consultancy report;
- ensure that your report meets the necessary assessment criteria;
- plan and design an oral presentation of your report.

14.1 Introduction

Some of you may view the process of writing your **project report** and presenting it orally as an exciting prospect. However, it is more likely that you will approach this stage of your research with a mixture of resignation and trepidation. This is a great pity. We believe that writing about your work is the most effective way of clarifying your thoughts. This suggests that writing should not be seen as the last stage of your research but thought of as something that is continuous throughout the research process.

Writing is a powerful way of learning (Griffiths 1993). Most teachers will tell you that the best way to learn is to teach. This is because of the necessity to understand something thoroughly yourself before you can begin to explain it to others. This is the position you are in as the writer of your project report. You have to explain a highly complex set of ideas and facts to an audience that you must assume has little or no knowledge of your subject. There is another problem here, which has a parallel with teaching. Often, the more familiar you are with a subject, the more difficult it is to explain it to others with no knowledge of that subject. You will be so familiar with your subject that, like the teacher, you will find it difficult to put yourself in the place of the reader. The result of this is that you may fail to explain something that you assume the reader will know. Even worse, you may leave out important material that should be included.

However, why do most of us view writing with such concern? Veroff (2001) argues that much of this is rooted in the experience we have of writing. Many of us are afraid of exposing our efforts to an audience that we feel will be more likely to criticise than encourage. In our education much of our writing has been little more than rehashing the ideas of others. This has taught us to think of writing as a boring, repetitive process. Some of us are impatient. We are unwilling to devote the time and energy (and inevitable frustration) that is needed for writing.

This fear of criticism is captured perfectly by Richards (1986), who recites the story of being asked by the distinguished sociologist Howard Becker to adopt his method of sitting down and writing what came into her head about the research she had done without even consulting her notes. Her fears of producing poor-quality material, which would be derided by colleagues who saw her work, are described vividly. It is a fear most of us experience.

We agree with Phillips and Pugh (2005), who note that writing is the only time when we really think. This suggests that writing your project report is something that should not be left until every other part of your research has been completed. However, there will be more on that in the next section.

We all write a lot more than we think. We email; send endless numbers of text messages on our mobile phones; add comments to conversations on web pages. Now many of us are becoming 'bloggers'. A **blog**, or **web log**, is a written account of a mixture of what is happening in a person's life and what is happening on the Internet, published on the Internet. It's a kind of hybrid diary/guide website, although there are as many unique types of blogs as there are people.

Blogging is an exciting way to publish on the Internet. You can share pictures, video, links, documents, newsletters, opinions and more, with family and friends. You can have a website without being a webmaster. There is no HTML to learn and no new software to download and install. Unlike traditional websites, web logs give you the opportunity to connect with others because they are a conversation rather than a billboard. You post content – others can post their responses. Moreover, privacy is not an issue. You control who is authorised to view personal photos or confidential documents by placing them in a private

An everyday scene in New York, which could be the content of a photo blog
Source: © Ben Saunders 2008.

viewing area. Blogging will even allow you to ban undesirable users.

You can compose blogs on any topic you choose: travel (see photo), your hobby, photography, your family or even your research project! Above all, it's a great way to get writing!

For many of us the fear of making an oral presentation is even more daunting. As we note in Section 14.7, some of this apprehension can be overcome by thorough preparation. But at least you have the consolation of knowing that you will be an expert in your topic.

In this chapter we begin (Section 14.2) by looking at issues concerned with getting started in the writing process including the importance of generating a plan. Sections 14.3 and 14.4 are devoted to the core issues of writing your project report – structure and content and explain the differences between a project report and a consultancy report. We then consider the topic of writing style (Section 14.5) before examining how to meet the assessment criteria (Section 14.6). The chapter ends (Section 14.7) with a look at the preparation and delivery of the oral presentation.

14.2 Getting started with writing

If writing is synonymous with thinking, it follows that writing is something you should do throughout the whole research process. Chapter 2 emphasises the need for clear ideas in writing about research questions and objectives. If you have done this already you will know the difficulty of committing your vague ideas to paper and amending them continually until they express your ideas with brevity, clarity and accuracy. However, there is no reason why your research proposal and plan should be the last writing you do before you finally write up your research in the project report. We encourage you to write as a continual process throughout the research.

Many researchers find it helpful to write the literature review early on in their research. This has clear benefits. It gets you writing on a part of the research process that necessarily comes early in that process. Also, it focuses your thinking on the way in which the literature will inform the research strategy you adopt. You will be pleased you wrote this part of the report when the time pressure is on as the submission deadline for your report approaches. Do not worry that early writing of the literature review means that subsequently published relevant literature is ignored in your review. It can always be incorporated at a later date. This is one of the advantages of using word processing, a topic that we shall cover later in this section.

Having discouraged you from thinking of writing as a process you leave until the end of your research, this section goes on to consider a number of practical hints to assist you to get started.

Create time for your writing

Writing is not an activity that can be allocated an odd half-hour whenever it is convenient. It requires sustained concentration. The amount of time needed to make real progress in your writing is dependent on the way in which you prefer to work. Most people find that it takes at least a day to write about 2000 words, but we all work in different ways. Once some people have started, they prefer to continue until they drop from exhaustion! Others like to set a strict timetable where three or four hours a day are devoted to writing. Whichever category you are in, make sure that you have time for writing allocated in your diary. We have found that it is helpful to have blocks of time where writing can take place on successive days. This ensures a degree of continuity of ideas, which is not as easy if you keep having to 'think your way back' into your research.

Write when your mind is fresh

We have emphasised so far in this chapter that writing should be a highly creative process. It is important, therefore, that you write at the time of day when your mind is at its freshest. All of us have jobs to do during the day that require little or no creativity. Arrange your day so that the uncreative jobs are done in the time when you are at your least mentally alert.

Find a regular writing place

Most of us have one place where we do our writing. It is so important that we often cannot write in unfamiliar surroundings. If this is the case with you it is essential that you combine this psychological comfort with a few practical features of your writing place that will enhance your productivity. One of the most important of these is to ensure that you are not interrupted. A simple 'do not disturb' sign on the door usually works wonders. You may, like Phil, find a telephone-answering service useful. Remove all distractions, such as television, magazines and computer games, from the room. It may be that you need background noise, even your MP3 player, to help you concentrate. One person's distractions are another person's necessities. What is important is to know what distracts you and to remove those distractions.

Set goals and achieve them

This is the height of self-discipline. Most writers set themselves targets for the period of writing. Usually this is a set number of words. It is better to be realistic about these goals. If you are too ambitious the quality of your work may suffer as you rush to meet the goal. You may be as self-disciplined as Mark, who sets himself sub-goals during the day and rewards the achievement of these goals with coffee breaks. What is important is that you see this as entering into a contract with yourself. If you break this contract by not meeting your goal, you are the one who should feel guilty. You may like to enter into a similar arrangement with a close friend on the understanding that each of you will insist on the other meeting your goals.

Use word processing

Word processing has revolutionised writing (Box 14.1). There are still some who prefer to write longhand before word-processing the final report. However, for those of us who 'think onto the screen' the main advantage of word processing is that it enables us to keep

---

Box 14.1
Focus on student research

Using word processing to transcribe field notes to the final project report

Phil made interview notes in longhand during the interviews that he conducted with managers about the pay system in their organisations. He was particularly careful to note verbatim especially relevant comments from the managers.

Phil ensured that he word-processed these notes, either on his laptop on the return train journey at the end of the day, or at home in the evening.

When writing the project report, Phil found the word-processed notes invaluable. He wanted to use some of the verbatim quotes to illustrate key arguments that he was developing from the data. He was able to insert many of these into the report, thus saving time and ensuring accuracy of transcription.

amending copy without having to fill the waste paper basket with numerous unsatisfactory attempts. In addition, word processing enables you to keep updating your project report as you develop new ideas or become dissatisfied with old ones. There is, however, a potential problem here. The ease with which you can keep inserting and deleting text means that relevant 'flagging' material will need to be changed. At its simplest, this may be the contents page or the announcement at the beginning of a chapter that the chapter will cover certain ground. However, it is just as likely to be an obscure reference buried in the text to a table that you have deleted, thus making the reference redundant.

Two other advantages of word processing may have occurred to you. First, most packages have a word count facility. You can use this to check your progress towards the word goal you have set yourself for the writing session. The second advantage is the readability statistics that are a feature of Microsoft Word. This allows you to check not only spelling, but also the average number of sentences per paragraph and words per sentence. To do this click on the 'Tools' menu, click 'Options...', and then click the 'Spelling & Grammar' tab. Select the 'Check grammar with spelling' and the 'Show readability statistics' check boxes and click on 'OK'. Next time you click on 'Spelling & Grammar' Word will display readability statistics.

The necessity of keeping back-up copies of your work should go without saying. However, do learn from the experience of one of our students, who lost all his research material as a consequence of not keeping adequate back-up copies. This led to him having to abandon his research project completely.

Generate a plan

Few of us can sit down and write without a lot of thought and planning. We all have our own systems for doing this. However, most people find it essential to construct a plan before they start writing. Veroff (2001) describes the 'clustering' method. This may be familiar to you. The method's stages are:

1 Write the main topic in the middle of a sheet of paper.
2 Jot down the other ideas that occur to you at other points on the page.
3 As the page begins to fill, relationships between the ideas suggest themselves and lines between the ideas may be drawn.
4 This allows you to group the ideas into discrete but related 'chunks', which enables you to devise an outline structure for a section, or chapter.

This chapter started out as just such a pencilled plan written on four pieces of A4 held together with sticky tape. It is essential to get your ideas into some form of order at the outset. This will give you encouragement to start writing.

Finish the writing session on a high point

Many writers prefer to finish their writing session while they are in the middle of a section to which they will look forward to returning. This eases the way in next time. The worst thing you can do is to leave a complex section half completed. It will be difficult to pick up the threads.

Get friends to read your work

Writing is creative and exciting, but checking our work is not. The importance of getting someone else to read through your material cannot be over-emphasised. Your project tutor should not be the first person who reads your report, even in its draft form.

Ask your friend to be constructively critical. Your friend must be prepared to tell you about things in the text that are not easy to understand – to point out omissions, spelling, punctuation and grammatical errors. Overall, your friend must tell you whether the piece of writing makes sense and achieves its purpose.

This is not an easy process for you or your critical friend. Most of us are sensitive to criticism, particularly when the consequence of it is the necessity to do a lot more work. Many of us are also hesitant about giving criticism. However, if your project report does not communicate to the reader in the way it should, you will get it back for revision work in the long run. It is much better to try to ensure that this does not happen.

14.3 Structuring your project report

Suggested structure

Most writers agree with Robson (2002) on the general structure to adopt for a project report that is the end product of your research. This is:

- Abstract
- Introduction
- Literature review
- Method
- Results
- Discussion
- Conclusions
- References
- Appendices.

However, this suggested structure should not inhibit you from adopting something different. The structure outlined above fits the deductive approach particularly closely. It assumes that the literature was reviewed to establish the current state of knowledge on the topic and this informed the method adopted. Reporting the findings in a factual manner gives rise to a detailed consideration of what these findings mean to the specific piece of research that has been conducted and to the current state of knowledge on the topic. However, if your research is essentially inductive, it may be that you prefer to structure the report in a different way. You may prefer to tell your story (that is, to explain your conclusions) in the early part of the report. This may include a clear explanation of how this story relates to the existing literature on the topic. This could be followed by a detailed explanation of how you arrived at these conclusions (a combination of an explanation of method adopted and findings established). The precise structure you adopt is less important than the necessity for your reader to be absolutely clear about what you are saying and for you to meet the assessment criteria.

Phillips and Pugh (2005) note that these general sections can be sub-divided into one or more relevant chapters depending on the topic and the way in which you want to present your particular **storyline**. This is a vital point. Your structure should have a logical flow. Your readers should know the journey on which they are being taken, and should know at all times the point in the journey that has been reached. Above all, the structure you adopt should enable your reader, having read the report, to identify the storyline clearly.

We shall now explain how to distinguish between these broad sections by outlining their purpose and content.

The abstract

The **abstract** is probably the most important part of your report because it may be the only part that some will read. It is a short summary of the complete content of the project report. This enables those who are not sure whether they wish to read the complete report to make an informed decision. For those who intend to read the whole report the abstract prepares them for what is to come. It should contain four short paragraphs with the answers to the following questions:

1 What were my research questions, and why were these important?
2 How did I go about answering the research questions?
3 What did I find out in response to my research questions?
4 What conclusions do I draw regarding my research questions?

The academic publisher, Emerald, gives advice to potential academic authors on how to compile an abstract. This is shown in Box 14.2. Although referring to academic journal articles (papers), it is useful to consider in terms of preparation of your research report and any subsequent publication.

Smith (1991) lists five principles for the writing of a good abstract. He argues that:

1 It should be short. Try to keep it to a maximum of two sides of A4. (Some universities stipulate a maximum length, often 300–500 words.)
2 It must be self-contained. Since it may be the only part of your project report that some people see, it follows that it must summarise the complete content of your report.
3 It must satisfy your reader's needs. Your reader must be told about the problem, or central issue, that the research addressed and the method adopted to pursue the issue. It must also contain a brief statement of the main results and conclusions.

Box 14.2
Focus on management research

Advice on the preparation of an abstract for publication

Abstracts should contain no more than 250 words. Write concisely and clearly. The abstract should reflect only what appears in the original paper.

Purpose of this paper
What are the reason(s) for writing the paper or the aims of the research?

Design/methodology/approach
How are the objectives achieved? Include the main method(s) used for the research. What is the approach to the topic and what is the theoretical or subject scope of the paper?

Findings
What was found in the course of the work? This will refer to analysis, discussion, or results.

Research limitations/implications (if applicable)
If research is reported on in the paper, this section must be completed and should include suggestions for future research and any identified limitations in the research process.

Practical implications (if applicable)
What outcomes and implications for practice, applications and consequences are identified? Not all papers will have practical implications but most will. What changes to practice should be made as a result of this research/paper?

What is original/value of paper
What is new in the paper? State the value of the paper and to whom.

Source: From Emerald Group Publishing (2008) 'How to . . . write an abstract'. From The Emerald website, http://info.emeraldinsight.com/authors/guides/abstracts.htm. Reproduced with permission.

4 It must convey the same emphasis as the project report, with the consequence that the reader should get an accurate impression of the report's contents from the abstract.

5 It should be objective, precise and easy to read. The project report contents page should give you the outline structure for the abstract. Summarising each section should give you an accurate résumé of the content of the report. Do ensure that you stick to what you have written in the report. The abstract is not the place for elaborating any of your main themes. Be objective. You will need to write several drafts before you eliminate every word that is not absolutely necessary. The purpose is to convey the content of your report in as clear and brief a way as possible.

Writing a good abstract is difficult. The obvious thing to do is to write it after you have finished the report. We suggest that you draft it at the start of your writing so that you have got your storyline abundantly clear in your mind. You can then amend the draft when you have finished the report so that it conforms to the five principles above. Box 14.3 is a good example of an abstract that meets most of the criteria for an effective abstract that we list above.

Box 14.3
Focus on management research

Abstract from a refereed journal article on the changing travel behaviour of Austria's ageing population and its impact on tourism

As the population of the Western world is ageing, the importance of seniors for the tourism economy is growing. Seniors are expected to be an important future market. Thus, overall leisure behaviour in general, and travel and tourism behaviour in particular, are analysed for the example of the Austrian market.

A focus group was conducted with participants aged 55+, where their leisure and travel habits as well as preferences were investigated.

The results showed that leisure and travelling played a major role in the participants' lives. Additionally, the participants did not change their travel behaviour considerably when entering retirement status. While they changed their preferences to longer stays and to travelling off-season, their preferences considering holiday destinations, mode of transport or distance of travel did not change significantly. The assumption that travel behaviour and travel preferences are acquired over a longer time span during the life of tourists and, therefore, will not change considerably when retiring can be confirmed for the participants of the focus group.

It can be concluded that future senior tourists will differ from today's travelling seniors in their travel behaviour and their preferences. A larger sample and more detailed research concerning the actual motivation and preferences of Austrian holiday travellers, as well as the factors influencing them, are necessary in order to be able to react adequately to future demands of senior tourists.

The paper contributes to a better understanding of the importance of and attitude towards leisure and tourism in the growing senior market. Based on the results of a focus group, it serves as a basis for further research in the field.

Source: Möller, C., Weiermair, K. and Wintersberger, E. (2007) 'The changing travel behaviour of Austria's ageing population and its impact on tourism', *Tourism Review*, 62 (3/4), pp. 15–20.

The introductory chapter

The **introduction** should give the reader a clear idea about the central issue of concern in your research and why you thought that this was worth studying. It should also include a full statement of your research question(s) and research objectives. If your research is based in an organisation, we think that it is a good idea to include in this chapter some details of the organisation, such as its history, size, products and services. This may be a general background to the more specific detail on the research setting you include in the method chapter. It is also important to include in this chapter a 'route map' to guide the reader through the rest of the report. This will give brief details of the content of each chapter and present an overview of how your storyline unfolds.

This will usually be a fairly brief chapter, but it is vitally important.

The literature review

Chapter 3 deals in detail with the writing of a literature review. All that it is necessary to comment on here is the position of this chapter in the project report. We suggest that this is placed before the methodology chapter.

The main purposes of your literature review are to set your study within its wider context and to show the reader how your study supplements the work that has already been done on your topic. The literature review, therefore, may inform directly your research questions (see Box 14.4) and any specific hypotheses that your research is designed to test. These hypotheses will also suggest a particular research approach, strategy and data collection techniques. If, on the other hand, you are working inductively (that is, from data to theory) your literature review may serve the purpose of illuminating and enriching your conclusions.

The title of your literature review chapter should reflect the content of the chapter. It may draw on one of the main themes in the review. We recommend that you do not call it simply 'literature review'. It may be that your literature is reviewed in more than one chapter. This would be the case, for example, where you were using more than one body of literature in your research.

Box 14.4
Focus on student research

Using the literature review to inform the research questions

Guiyan was a Chinese student studying for an MA in a UK university. In her research dissertation she was interested to know whether Chinese managers would be able to conduct performance appraisal schemes effectively in China with Chinese employees. She was aware that there were certain aspects of Chinese culture that would make this difficult. Guiyan studied two bodies of literature: that relating to the managerial skills of performance appraisal, and a second concerned with the effects of Chinese culture on the ways in which Chinese managers manage their employees. She presented both in a literature review

chapter. She structured her chapter around three questions:

1 What are the key skills needed by managers to conduct performance appraisal effectively?
2 What are the most important aspects of Chinese culture which impact upon on the ways in which Chinese managers manage their employees?
3 To what extent will the aspects of Chinese culture, explained in the answer to question 2, affect the ability of Chinese managers to conduct performance appraisal effectively?

From this, Guiyan developed a theoretical proposition that supported her initial idea that certain aspects of Chinese culture would make the conduct of performance appraisal by Chinese managers with Chinese employees difficult. She was then ready to move on to her method chapter, which was an explanation of the way in which she would test her theoretical proposition.

The method chapter

This should be a detailed chapter giving the reader sufficient information to make an estimate of the reliability and validity of your methods. Box 14.5 provides a useful checklist of the points that you should include in the method chapter.

Box 14.5 Checklist

Points to include in your method chapter

Setting
- ✔ What was the research setting?
- ✔ Why did you choose that particular setting?
- ✔ What ethical issues were raised by the study, and how were these addressed?

Participants
- ✔ How many?
- ✔ How were they selected?
- ✔ What were their characteristics?
- ✔ How were refusals/non-returns handled?

Materials
- ✔ What tests/scales/interview or observation schedules/questionnaires were used?
- ✔ How were purpose-made instruments developed?
- ✔ How were the resulting data analysed?

Procedures
- ✔ What were the characteristics of the interviewers and observers, and how were they trained?
- ✔ How valid and reliable do you think the procedures were?
- ✔ What instructions were given to participants?
- ✔ How many interviews/observations/questionnaires were there; how long did they last; where did they take place?
- ✔ When was the research carried out?

Source: developed from Robson (2002) *Real World Research* (2nd edn). Oxford: Blackwell. Reproduced with permission.

The results chapter(s)

It may well be that your report will contain more than one results chapter. The question you should ask yourself is: 'Is more than one results chapter necessary to communicate my findings clearly?'

The results chapter or chapters are probably the most straightforward to write. It is your opportunity to report the facts that your research discovered. This is where you will include such tables and graphs that will illustrate your findings (do not put these in the appendices). The chapter may also contain verbatim quotes from interviewees, or sections of narrative account that illustrate periods of unstructured observation. This is a particularly powerful way in which you can convey the richness of your data. It is the qualitative equivalent of tables and graphs. Often, a short verbatim quote can convey with penetrating simplicity a particularly difficult concept that you are trying to explain. Do not be afraid to capture precisely what the interviewee said. Slang and swear words are often the most revealing, and provide amusement for the reader!

There are two important points to bear in mind when writing your results. The first is to stress that the purpose is to present facts. It is normally not appropriate in this chapter to begin to offer opinions on the facts. This is for the following chapter(s). Many of us become confused about the difference between findings and the conclusions drawn from these which form the basis of the discussion and conclusions chapters. One way of overcoming the confusion is to draw up a table with two columns. The first should be headed 'What I found out' and the second 'What judgements I have formed as a result of what I found out'. The first list is entirely factual (e.g. 66 per cent of respondents indicated they preferred to receive email messages rather than paper memos) and therefore the content of your findings chapter. The second list will be your judgements based on what you found out (e.g. it appears that electronic forms of communication are preferred to traditional) and therefore the content of your conclusions section.

The second point links to the first. Drawing up a table will lead you to a consideration of the way in which you present your findings. The purpose of your project report is to communicate the answer to your research question to your audience in as clear a manner as possible. Therefore you should structure your findings in a clear, logical and easily understood manner. There are many ways of doing this. One of the simplest is to return to the research objectives and let these dictate the order in which you present your findings. Alternatively, you may prefer to report your findings thematically. You could present the themes in descending order of importance. Whichever method you choose should be obvious to the reader. As with the literature review, the chapter(s) devoted to research should be titled in an interesting way that reflects the content of findings.

The clarity of your findings should be such that they may find their way into a news report similar to that in Box 14.6.

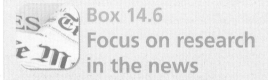

Box 14.6
Focus on research in the news

Report concludes that privacy rights 'fragile' in 2007

Threats to personal privacy got more severe in 2007, a report has claimed. Compiled by Privacy International and the Electronic Privacy Information Center the report details global trends in privacy protection and surveillance.

It found that in 2007 more nations than ever ranked as places where surveillance had become 'endemic'. The move toward greater surveillance had left the fundamental right to a private life 'fragile and exposed', the report said.

The 1000 page report from the two campaigning groups details what governments, companies and lobby groups have done in the past 12 months to defend or dismantle privacy online or offline. Overall, wrote the report's authors, privacy protection 'worsened' during 2007. As in previous years, the report found no nation which consistently tried to uphold privacy or gave substantial help, legislative or otherwise, to protect personal data.

Greece topped the table of 47 countries ranked in the report and was the only one that was identified as having 'adequate safeguards against abuse'. Most countries surveyed were classed as having 'some safeguards but weakened protections' or a 'systemic failure' to defend citizens' private lives. In 2007 the survey found surveillance 'endemic' in nine countries – compared to five in 2006. The nine were – England, Wales, Malaysia, China, Russia, Singapore, Taiwan, Thailand and the USA.

The report said that greater scrutiny of citizens grew out of two trends – government efforts to beef up national security and a burgeoning industry built around surveillance or the data it collects. It noted that action by lobby groups or campaigners to protect privacy were 'marginal' and added that any substantive effort to fight back could struggle against the complex and diverse threats ranged against privacy.

Source: derived from BBC News Online, 31 Dec. 2007.

The discussion chapter

Findings presented without reflective thought run the risk of your reader asking 'so what?': what meaning do these findings have for me?; for my organisation?; for professional practice?; for the development of theory? So the main focus of the discussion chapter is on the interpretation of the results that you presented in the previous chapter. You should state the relation of the findings to the goals, questions and hypotheses that you stated in the introductory chapter. In addition, the discussion chapter will benefit from a consideration of the implications of your research for the relevant theories which you detailed in your literature review. It is usual to discuss the strengths, weaknesses and limitations of your study. However, it is not a good idea to be too modest here and draw attention to aspects of your research which you may consider to be a limitation but that the reader has not noticed!

The discussion chapter is where you have the opportunity to shine. It will show the degree of insight that you exhibit in reaching your conclusions. However, it is the part of the report that most of us find difficult. It is the second major opportunity in the research process to demonstrate real originality of thought (the first time being at the stage where you choose the research topic). Because of that, we urge you to pay due attention to the discussion chapter. In our view it should normally be at least as long as your results chapter(s). Crucially, here you are making judgements rather than reporting facts, so this is where your maturity of understanding can shine through.

The conclusion chapter

This should be a conclusion to the whole project (and not just the research findings). Check that your work answers the questions in Box 14.7.

Box 14.7
Do your conclusions answer these questions?

✔ Did the research project meet your research objectives?
✔ Did the research project answer your research questions?
✔ What are the main findings of the research?

✔ Are there any recommendations for future action based on the conclusions you have drawn?
✔ Do you have any overall conclusions on the research process itself?
✔ Where should further research be focused? (Typically this will consider two points: firstly, new areas of investigation implied by developments in your project, and secondly parts of your work which were not completed due to time constraints and/or problems encountered.)

You may find that the clearest way to present your conclusions is to follow a similar structure to the one used in your findings section. If that structure reflects the research objectives then it should make certain that your conclusions would address them. Drawing up a matrix similar to that in Figure 14.1 may help you in structuring your

Figure 14.1
Using a matrix in the planning of the content for the results and conclusions chapters

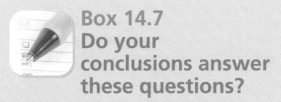

Research questions	Results (what factual information did I discover in relation to the specific research questions?)	Conclusions (what judgements can I make about the results in relation to the specific research questions?)
What are the operational differences between different shifts in the production plant?	Cases of indiscipline in the last six months have been twice as frequent on the night shift as on the day shift	The night shift indiscipline problems may be due to the reluctance of operators to work on this shift

findings and conclusions. The result should be a clear statement of conclusions drawn similar to that shown in Box 14.8 (opposite).

You may also have a final section in your conclusion chapter(s) called '**discussion**'. Alternatively, you may make this a separate chapter with this general heading. Here you would turn to your conclusions and ask such questions as: 'What does this mean?' 'What are the implications for organisations?' 'What are the implications for the current state of knowledge of the topic?' 'How does it add to the literature?' 'What are the implications for future research?' The conclusions chapter should not include new material but the discussion may do so, as long as it is germane to the point you are making about your conclusions.

An alternative approach to the matrix is to draw a 'mind map' (see Section 2.3), which places the findings randomly on a blank page and links conclusions to these findings by way of lines and arrows. For some of you this may be a more creative approach, which enables you to associate groups of findings with conclusions and vice versa.

Answering the research question(s), meeting the objectives and, if appropriate, supporting or otherwise the research hypotheses is the main purpose of the conclusions chapter. This is where you will consider the findings presented in the previous chapter. You should also return to your literature review and ask yourself 'What do my conclusions add to the understanding of the topic displayed in the literature?'

It may be that there are practical implications of your findings. In a management report this would normally form the content of a chapter specifically devoted to recommendations. We suggest that you check with your project tutor whether this is expected. In the reports that students are required to prepare on some professional courses this is an important requirement. For academic degree programmes it is often unnecessary.

Even if you do not specify any practical implications of your research you may comment in the conclusions chapter on what your research implies for any future research. This is a logical extension of a section in the conclusions chapter that should be devoted to the limitations of your research. These limitations may be the size of sample, the snapshot nature of the research, or the restriction to one geographical area of an organisation. Virtually all research has its limitations. This section should not be seen as a confession of your weaknesses, but as a mature reflection on the degree to which your findings and conclusions can be said to be the 'truth'.

References

A range of conventions are used to reference the material of other writers' material that you have cited in your text. Appendix 1 illustrates three of the most popular of these, the Harvard, footnotes and American Psychological Association (APA) systems. However, we suggest that you consult your project tutor about the system that is appropriate for your project report, as many universities require their own variation of these systems.

It is a good idea to start your references section at the beginning of the writing process and add to it as you go along. It will be a tedious and time-consuming task if left until you have completed the main body of the text. If you do leave it until the end, the time spent on compiling the reference section is time that would have been better spent on checking and amending your report.

At the start of your report you must acknowledge all those who have contributed to your research (including your project tutor!). In addition, you should ensure that you have cited in your reference section all those sources to which you have referred in the text. In order to avoid charges of plagiarism you should ensure that all data and material taken verbatim from another person's published or unpublished written or electronic

Box 14.8
Focus on management research

Psychological and behavioural drivers of online clothes purchasing

Goldsmith and Flynn (2006) studied selected demographic and psychological characteristics that lead consumers to buy clothing online. They surveyed 805 consumers who described their online clothing buying as well as how innovative and involved they were for clothing and fashion, how innovative they were with regard to buying on the Internet, and how much they purchased clothing through catalogues.

The resulting article is structured along the classic lines of introduction, literature review, hypotheses, research method, results and discussion. We summarise here their discussion section to give you an understanding of the character of their conclusions.

The purpose of Goldsmith and Flynn's study was to assess the relative influence of several key variables on the amount of online clothing buying. The data analysis revealed that three demographic variables (age, sex and income) played a relatively minor role in explaining online clothing buying. Better predictors were an enthusiasm and venturesomeness for online buying in general and a history of buying clothes from catalogues. Fashion innovativeness was weakly related to online buying, but fashion involvement was not. It appears that being an Internet innovator and an experienced catalogue shopper are more predictive of online clothing shopping than an interest in fashion.

Goldsmith and Flynn's discussion section is based on the implications of their findings. These are summarised below.

First, being a catalogue shopper, a consumer with a previous history of shopping from home, is a significant predictor of shopping online. This is probably due to a general propensity or affinity for direct buying, but might also be due to the presence of many catalogue retailers on the web. If a shopper has experience with a direct merchant it is a smaller leap of faith to move from catalogue to online shopping with the same retailer. So the Land's End catalogue buyer might be easily encouraged to buy from Land's End online. It is also possible that circumstances leading one to buy via catalogues, such as time pressure or limited access to stores, would also lead to online purchasing.

Second, because innovativeness for online shopping predicts online clothing purchase, Goldsmith and Flynn conclude that shopping via the Internet is in its earlier stages of the diffusion process. If online shopping were more broadly diffused, innovators would not be so heavily represented among such shoppers. They conclude that as innovators are an important buying group, this implies that the phenomenon will grow in the future.

Third, the enduring involvement in a product category does not necessarily predict more buying of that category through a new medium. While personal importance of fashion is linked to more buying in that category, being a 'clotheshorse' was not a good indicator of shopping for clothing online. Increased shopping via the Internet appears to be better predicted by the tendency to be a home shopper than by strong interest in the product category. E-commerce clothing managers would do well to focus more effort on wooing Internet innovators than fashion innovators.

Fourth, the likelihood of a consumer shopping from home and their venturesomeness with regard to new shopping media seem to be the most prominent factors predicting online shopping. This is important because individual differences in these areas trump product-category-related differences in predicting medium choice. The implications are straightforward. Catalogue shoppers are likely to be the same as online shoppers. Catalogue managers should work to encourage their customers to migrate to the web.

Goldsmith and Flynn point out that their findings are limited by the sample and measures used. Studies of other populations of consumers using other measures should be done to confirm and expand these results. Another limitation lies in the self-report nature of the shopping variables that might introduce measurement error into the data. However, they claim that their findings do contribute to our understanding of online clothing shopping, and future studies can build on these results to complete this picture.

work is explicitly identified and referenced to its author. This also extends to work which is referred to in the written work of others. Even if this work is not quoted verbatim, the originator should be cited in your references. If you are in any doubt about this it is important that you consult your tutor. The proliferation of online material now is such that all academic institutions are very mindful of plagiarism.

Appendices

In general, **appendices** should be kept to the minimum. If they are so important that your reader's understanding of the points you are making in the text makes their inclusion in the report necessary, then they should be in the main body of the text. If, on the other hand, the material is 'interesting to know' rather than 'essential to know' then it should be in the appendices. Often students feel tempted to include appendices to 'pad out' a project report. Resist this temptation. Your readers will not be reading your report for leisure reading. They will be pressed for time and will probably not look at your appendices. Your project report will stand or fall on the quality of the main text. However, your appendices should include a blank copy of your questionnaire, interview or observation schedule. Where these have been conducted in a language different from that in which you write your submitted project report you will need to submit both this version and the translation.

The management report

You may have wondered why we made no reference to recommendations in the report structure. In the typical **management report** or consultancy report (discussed later) this may be the most important section. The hard-pressed executive reading your report may turn to your recommendations first to see what action needs to be taken to tackle the issue.

Whether you include a recommendation section depends on the objectives of your research. If you are doing exploratory research you may well write recommendations, among which will be suggestions for the pursuit of further research. However, if your research is designed to explain or describe, recommendations are less likely. For example, the research question 'Why do small engineering companies in the UK reinvest less of their profits in their businesses than their German counterparts?' may imply clear points for action. However, strictly speaking, recommendations are outside the scope of the research question, which is to discover 'Why?' not 'What can be done about it?' The message is clear. If you want your research to change the situation that you are researching, then include the need to develop recommendations in your research objectives.

Length of the project report

You will probably have guidelines on the number of words your project report should contain. Do stick to these. However interesting your report, your tutors will have others to read, so they will not thank you for exceeding the limit. Indeed, if you can meet your research objectives fully in a clear and absorbing report that is significantly shorter than the word limit, the good mood in which you put your tutors may be reflected in a higher grade. Reports that exceed the word limit are usually excessively verbose. It is more difficult to be succinct. Do not fall into the trap of writing a long report because you did not have the time to write a shorter one.

14.4 Organising the project report's content

Choosing a title

This is the part of the project report on which most of us spend the least time. Yet it is the only knowledge that many people have of the project. Day and Gastel (2006) comment that a good title is one that has the minimum possible number of words that describe accurately the content of the paper. Try choosing a title and then ask a colleague who knows your subject what they think the title describes. If their description matches your content then stick with your title.

Tell a clear story

Be prepared for your project tutor to ask you 'What's your main storyline?' Your storyline (your central argument or thesis) should be clear, simple and straightforward. It should be so clear that you can stop the next person you see walking towards you and tell that person what your project report's storyline is and he or she will say 'Yes, I understand that'. This is where writing the abstract helps. It forces you to think clearly about the storyline because you have to summarise it in so few words.

A simple format for developing the storyline is shown in Figure 14.2.

Another way of checking to see whether your storyline is clear is to 'reason backwards'. An example of this may be a report that ends in clear recommendations for action. Start by explaining your recommendations to the manager who, for example, may have to spend money on their implementation. This invites the question from that manager: 'What makes you recommend this action?' Your answer should be: 'I came to the conclusion in my report that they are necessary.' The follow-up question from the manager here could be: 'On what basis do you draw these conclusions?' Here your answer is, of course, on the findings that you established. The next question asked by the manager is: 'How did you arrive at these findings?' in response to which you explain your method. The

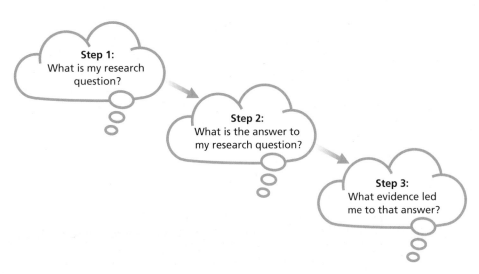

Figure 14.2 A format for developing the storyline

Souce: developed from Raimond (1993:175) *Management Project: Design, Research and Presentation.* Reproduced with permission of Thompson Publishing Services.

manager may counter by asking you why she should take any notice of your findings. The response to this is that you took care to design a research strategy that would lead to valid and reliable findings. Moreover, that research strategy is based on clear research objectives and a detailed review of the relevant literature.

Such 'reasoning backwards' is a useful check to see not only whether your storyline is clear but also that it stands up to logical analysis.

Helping the reader to get all the information out

Dividing your work

One of us once received the first draft of a twenty-thousand-word project report that had virtually no divisions except the chapters. It was like looking at a road map that did not include any road numbers or towns. It was just as difficult to find your way around that report as it would be to journey between two cities using a townless road map. The content of the project report seemed fine. However, it was hard to be sure about this because it was so difficult to spot any gaps in the ground it covered. What was needed were some signposts and some town names. Do not think about how you can put in all your information. Instead, concentrate on helping the reader to get all the information out (Box 14.9).

The message is simple. Divide your work in such a way that it is easy for readers to find their way round it and for them always to be clear where they are, where they have come from, and where they are going.

To do this you may find it helpful to return to the matrix idea in Figure 14.1. You will see that each column of the matrix represents the broad content of a chapter. The cells indicate the way in which the chapters may be divided. Each division may have a sub-division.

We hope that you have noticed that we have employed a similar system in this book. However, this book is printed in more than one colour. The equivalent would be that each chapter section is identified by bold upper-case letters. The sub-headings are bold lower-case, and further divisions of the subsection content are denoted by bold, lower-case italics. Smith (1991) explains various ways of organising and signposting text. It is not important which way you do this as long as your approach is consistent and it helps the reader around the report and matches the ways specified by your examining institution.

Previewing and summarising chapters

A further way in which you can signpost your work is to 'top and tail' each chapter. This is to include a few words at the beginning of the chapter (Smith 1991) that provide a

---

Box 14.9
Focus on student research

Developing a storyline

Step 1

I wanted to know whether, as the literature suggested, organisational structures are determined by their strategies.

Step 2

The answer is that organisation structures are in part determined by strategies and in part by *ad hoc* factors that owe little to strategy considerations.

Step 3

I based this answer on interviews with senior managers in three large UK organisations and examination of the minutes of meetings at which structural issues were discussed. The particular focus was on the removal of management positions.

description of how the chapter is to contribute to answering the research question, the methods used in this part of the study, and the points that are covered. At the end of each chapter it is useful if the reader has a brief summary of the content of the chapter and a very brief indication of how this content links to the following chapter. This may seem like repetition. However, it helps the reader on her or his journey through your report and ensures that you, the writer, are on the correct road.

Tables and graphics

Your reader will find your project report more accessible and easier to read if you present some of your data and ideas in tables and graphics. It is not only numerical data that can be presented in tables. You can also present ideas that can be easily compared. Table 13.1 is an example of this.

Do not be tempted to put your numerical tables in the appendices. They will probably be some of your most important data. Include them and comment on them in the text. Your commentary should note the significance of the data in the tables. It should not simply describe the table's contents.

Section 12.3 has detail on the presentation of tables and diagrams.

A final note of caution should be sounded. To avoid confusing your reader, do make sure that, wherever possible, you have introduced the table or diagram before it appears in the text.

One report?

Many researchers of management topics face the dilemma of having to write for more than one audience. In addition to the academic audience, who possibly will mark and grade the report for a degree or a diploma, it may be necessary to prepare a report for the management of the employing organisation, or, indeed, a non-employing organisation both of whom who will be interested in the practical benefit that the report promises. This raises the thorny question, 'For whom should the report be written?'

Many people have resolved this dilemma by writing two reports: one for each audience. The academic report will usually be much longer and contain contextual description that the organisational audience does not require. Similarly, those managers reading the report will probably be less interested in the literature review and the development of theory than the academic audience. If the research question did not imply the necessity for recommendations for future action, these may need to be written for the organisational version. The content of this chapter concentrates on the academic report. However, in the sub-section below we include a brief discussion on consultancy reports.

Fortunately, the advent of word processing makes the job of compiling more than one report quite easy. Some careful cutting and pasting will be necessary. However, what should always be kept in mind is the audience that each specific report is addressing. Take care not to fall between two stools. Write each report for its audience in style and content.

The consultancy report

Here we assume that the report that you write for the management of the employing organisation, or a non-employing organisation, follow the same format. For this reason we refer to both as **consultancy reports**.

Advice from the Institute of Management Consultancy (now the Institute of Business Consulting) suggests that a number of key questions need to be asked before the consultancy report is planned. Among these are: what information does management expect?; with what level of detail?; how much knowledge does management already have?; for what purpose will the report be used?; who will read it? Another fundamental question is: what key messages and recommendations do you want to impart? To be consistent with the main thrust of this chapter a report structure such as:

- Executive summary
- Introduction
- Results
- Conclusions
- Recommendations

is the most straightforward.

There is, however, an alternative structure which, arguably, is simpler and delivers the message more forcibly. In this you start with your main message and then provide the information that supports it. This second structure, will, however, involve you in more alteration of the academic report you have written.

Decisions about what to include in (and, just as importantly, to exclude from) the report requires ruthlessness. Only information that is essential to management should go in the main body of the report; any information that is 'important' or 'of interest' should be relegated to appendices. Additional detail, for example figures, references or diagrams are all examples of 'important' information. The Institute of Management Consultancy suggests that you should put yourself in the reader's shoes. The management reader will be short of time and want only essential detail. That said, the management reader will be interested in the background to the project and in how you carried out the research. But the main purpose of the report will be to tell management your recommendations. Recommendations equate with action, and managers are paid to act! As with the academic report, division of the report content into logical sections with clear sub-headings will lead management through the report and show them where to find specific topics.

The executive summary is likely to be the part of the report on which managers will concentrate. It is important that it can stand alone and that it contains real information, including hard facts and figures. If your report includes recommendations, the executive summary should make it clear what these are and include their implications, values and costs. As with the abstract, the executive summary should be short (no more than two pages) and designed to get your main message across.

Two final points about the writing style of the consultancy report. The reader will not appreciate long words, complicated language, 'management speak' or a multitude of acronyms and abbreviations. If it is necessary to use complex technical terms, make sure you provide a glossary in the appendix.

Finally, it is more appropriate to use the first person in the consultancy report. Language like 'it was found', 'it is estimated', 'it is recommended' does not sound more professional; it simply depersonalises your report and makes it less accessible. Be bold and put yourself at the heart of your writing!

As well as presenting two written reports you may have to present your report orally. In the next two sections we address the writing of reports, and in the final section (14.7), we turn our attention to their oral presentation.

14.5 Developing an appropriate writing style

Much of your concern in writing your project report will be about what you write. In this section of the chapter we ask you to think about the way you write. Your writing style is just as important as the content, structure and layout of your report. That said, it is often observed that good writing cannot substitute for flawed thinking (Phillips and Pugh 2005). In fact, the clearer the writing the more flawed thinking is exposed. However, poor writing can spoil the effect of good-quality thought.

Clarity and simplicity

> The . . . lack of ready intelligibility [in scholarly writing], I believe, usually has little or nothing to do with the complexity of the subject matter, and nothing at all to do with profundity of thought. It has to do almost entirely with certain confusions of the academic writer about his own status . . . To overcome the academic prose you first of all have to overcome the academic pose . . .
>
> Wright Mills (1970:239–40)

Each Christmas, Mark accompanies his Christmas cards with a family newsletter. It is written in a simple, direct and friendly manner that is easy and enjoyable to read. Few of the project reports we read are written in such a simple, direct manner. They are more elaborate in their explanation: they use difficult words where Mark's family newsletter would use simple ones. They adopt the academic pose.

Phil tells a story that reinforces the point made by Wright Mills in the above quotation. He was asked by a student to comment on her thesis in progress, which was about the impact of a particular job advertising strategy. He thought that it was written in an over-elaborate and 'academic' way. After many suggestions for amendments Phil came across a sentence that explained that the strategy his student was studying 'was characterised by factors congruent with the results of a lifestyle analysis of the target market'. Phil thought that this was too wordy. He suggested making it simpler. His student examined the sentence at length and declared she could see no way of improving it. Phil thought that it could say 'it was a strategy that matched the lifestyles of those at whom it was aimed'. His student protested. She agreed it was shorter and clearer but protested that it was less 'academic'. We think that clarity and simplicity are more important than wishing to appear academic. Your project report is a piece of communication in the same way as Mark's Christmas newsletter.

Phillips and Pugh (2005) advise that you should aim to provide readers with a report that they cannot put down until 2.00 a.m. or later for fear of spoiling the flow. (If you are reading this chapter at 2.30 a.m. we have succeeded!)

Write simple sentences

A common source of lack of clarity is the confusing sentence (see Box 14.10). This is often because it is too long. A simple rule to adopt is: one idea – one sentence. Mark reads his work out loud. If the sentences are too long, he runs out of breath! This is another useful guide to sentence length.

Avoid jargon

Jargon should not be confused with technical terminology. Some technical terms are unavoidable. To assist your reader, it is best to put a glossary of such terms in the appendices. However, do not assume that your reader will have such a full knowledge as you of the subject and, in particular, the context. Here, and in all cases, try to put yourself in the position of the reader. Phil makes this point to students who use organisations as vehicles to write assignments. He asks them to 'mark' past (anonymous) assignments. They are usually horrified at the assumptions that their fellow students make about the tutor's prior knowledge.

Box 14.10
Focus on student research

Writing clearer sentences

Consider the following sentence.

While it is true to say that researchers have illusions of academic grandeur when they sit down to write their project report, and who can blame them because they have had to demonstrate skill and resilience to get to this point in their studies, they nonetheless must consider that writing a project report is an exercise in communication, and nobody likes reading a lot of ideas that are expressed in such a confusing and pretentious way that nobody can understand them, let alone the poor tutor who has to plough through it all to try and make some sense of it.

There appear to be at least six separate ideas in this sentence. It contains 101 words (when marking, we sometimes come across sentences with over 150!). In addition, it contains a common way of introducing multiple ideas into a sentence: the embedded clause. In the sentence above the embedded clause is '. . . and who can blame them because they have had to demonstrate skill and resilience to get to this point in their studies,...' The give-away is the first word in the sentence: 'While'. This invites an embedded clause. The point here is that potentially rich ideas get buried away in the literary undergrowth. Dig them up and replant them. Let them flourish in a sentence of their own.

The sentence needs to be clearer and simpler. However, it should not lose any of its meaning. Halving the number of words and dividing up the sentence into smaller clearer sentences results in the following:

Researchers have illusions of academic grandeur when they write their project report. This is understandable. They have demonstrated skill and resilience to reach this point in their studies. However, writing a project report is an exercise in communication. Nobody likes confusing and pretentious writing that is difficult to understand. Pity the tutor who has to make sense of it.

What can be avoided is the sort of jargon that *The New Oxford English Dictionary* (1998) defines as 'gibberish' and 'debased language'. You will know the sort of phrases: 'ongoing situation'; 'going down the route of'; 'at the end of the day'; 'the bottom line'; 'at this moment in time'. It is not just that they are ugly but they are not clear and simple. For example, 'now' is much clearer and simpler than 'at this moment in time'.

Beware of using large numbers of quotations from the literature

We believe that quotations from the literature should be used infrequently in your project report. Occasionally we receive draft projects that consist of little more than a series of quotations from books and journal articles that a student has linked together with a few sentences of her or his own. This tells us very little about the student's understanding of the concepts within the quotations. All it shows is that he or she has looked at the book or journal article and, it is hoped, can acknowledge sources correctly! In addition, by using quotations in this way the student's line of argument tends to become disjointed and less easy to follow. It is therefore usually better to explain other people's ideas in your own words.

That is not to say that you should never use quotations. As you have seen, we have used direct quotations from other people's work in this book. Rather we would advise you to use them sparingly to create maximum impact in supporting your storyline.

Check your spelling and grammar

Spelling is still a problem for many of us, in spite of the word processing software's spelling check facility. It will not correct your 'moral' when you wished to say 'morale' or sort out when you should write 'practise' rather than 'practice'. This is where the friend who is reading your draft can help, provided that friend is a competent speller. Tutors tend to be more patient with errors of this kind than those that reflect carelessness. However, the point remains that spelling errors detract from the quality of your presentation and the authority of your ideas.

Avoiding common grammatical errors

Grammatical errors threaten the credibility of our writing. In Table 14.1. we outline 10 of the most common errors, most of which, with some careful checking, can be avoided.

It is not our intention here to conduct an English grammar lesson. Some of the common errors in Table 14.1 are self-explanatory.

You may argue that the **split infinitive** is not often thought of as an error these days. However, 'to boldly go' ahead with your project report ignoring this rule risks irritating your reader – something you can ill afford to do. You want the reader to concentrate on your ideas.

Day's 'dangling participle' warning is amusingly illustrated by the draft questionnaire shown to us by a student. This asked for 'the amount of people you employ in your organisation, broken down by sex'. We wrote on our copy: 'We haven't got people in that category: they've not got the energy when they work here!' (Remember that when writing your questionnaire!)

Some of the more obvious grammatical errors you can spot by reading your text aloud to yourself. You need not know the grammatical rules; they often just sound wrong.

Table 14.1 Ten common grammatical errors

Often we write	The correct way is
1 Each pronoun should agree with **their** antecedent.	Each pronoun should agree with **its** antecedent.
2 Just between you and I, case is important.	Just between you and **me**, case is important.
3 A preposition is a poor word to end a sentence **with**	A preposition is a poor word **with which** to end a sentence.
4 Verbs **has** to agree with their subject.	Verbs **have** to agree with their subject.
5 Do not use **no** double negatives.	Do not use double negatives.
6 Remember **to never split** an infinitive.	Remember **never to split** an infinitive.
7 When dangling, do not use participles.	Do not use dangling participles.
8 Avoid clichés like the plague.	To avoid clichés like the plague!
9 Do not write a run-on sentence it is difficult when you got to punctuate it so it makes sense when the reader reads what you wrote.	Do not write a run-on sentence. It is difficult to punctuate it so that it makes sense to the reader.
10 The data **is** included in this section.	The data **are** included in this section.

Source: developed from Day (1998:160).

Person, tense and gender

Traditionally, academic writing has been dry and unexciting. This is partly because the convention has been to write impersonally, in the past **tense** and in the **passive voice** (e.g. 'interviews were conducted following the administration of questionnaires').

The writer was expected to be distanced from the text. This convention is no longer as strong. It is a matter of preferred style rather than rules. The research approach that dominates your methods may dictate your choice of **personal pronoun**. Section 4.2 notes that one feature of positivism is that 'the researcher is independent of, and neither affects nor is affected by, the subject of the research'. It follows from this that an impersonal style is more appropriate. By contrast, Section 9.2 notes that the participant observer 'participates in the daily life of people under study'. The researcher is an intrinsic part of the research process. Use of the first person seems more logical here. However, style is important. Use of the term 'the author' sounds too impersonal and stilted. In contrast, excessive use of 'I' and 'we' may raise questions in your readers' minds about your ability to stand outside your data and to be objective.

Day (1998) identifies rules for the use correct use of tense. He suggests that you should normally use the present tense when referring to previously published work (e.g. Day identifies) and the past tense when referring to your present results (e.g. I found that . . .)'. Although he notes exceptions to this rule, it serves as a useful guide.

Day and Gastel (2006) and Becker (2008) both stridently attack the passive voice (it was found that) and champion the use of the **active voice** (I found that). Certainly, it is clearer, shorter and unambiguous. It is a good idea to check with your project tutor here which is most likely to be acceptable.

Finally, a note about the use of language that assumes the gender of a classification of people. The most obvious example of these is the constant reference to managers as 'he'. Not only is this inaccurate in many organisations, it also gives offence to many people of both sexes. Those offended will probably include your readers! It is simple enough to avoid (e.g. 'I propose to interview each executive unless he refuses' becomes 'I propose to interview each executive unless I receive a refusal') but often less easy to spot. The further reading section in the first draft of this chapter referred to Becker as a 'master craftsman'. These notes on language and gender prompted us to change it to 'an expert in the field'. Appendix 4 gives more detailed guidance on the use of non-discriminatory language.

It is a good idea to be aware of any specific discriminatory or potentially insulting concepts, terms and expressions which may be used in your research due to the particular context of the research (e.g. the industry or organisation in which you work). If your work has an international dimension, it is also a good idea to be aware of any country-specific or national guidelines on the non-discriminatory use of language.

Preserving anonymity

You may have given the participants (and the organisations) from whom you collected data an undertaking that you would not disclose their identity in anything you write. In this case you will need to conceal their identity in your project report. The usual way of doing this is to invent pseudonyms for organisations and not to name individual participants. This should not detract from the impact of your report.

Similarly, your sponsoring organisation(s) may have requested sight of your report before it is submitted. Should there be misgivings about the content of the report you should be able to alleviate these by the use of pseudonyms. This is usually a better option than significant text changes.

The need for continual revision

Adrian asked a group of undergraduate students how many of them did more than one draft of their assignment papers. He did not expect that many would reply that they did.

What he did not predict was that many of them had not even thought that this was necessary.

Submitting the first attempt is due partly to the heavy assessment loads on many courses, which means that students are constantly having to 'keep up with the clock'. On part-time courses, students these days have so many demands in their daily work that writing an assignment just once is all that is possible. This is the way most of us learned to write at school. The paper is usually seen only by the teacher. The arrangement is a private one.

However, project reports are different. They will be seen by an audience much wider than one tutor. They will usually be lodged in the library to be read by succeeding students. You will be judged on the quality of your work. For that reason we urge you most strongly to polish your work with successive drafts until you are happy that you can do no better.

The final version of this chapter (which, incidentally, even for the first edition of this book, was read by five people and was the last of seven or eight drafts) contains guidelines that you can use to evaluate your first draft. These are summarised in the checklist in Box 14.11.

Having been through this checklist you may decide to make minor alterations to your text. On the other hand you may rewrite sections or move sections within chapters to other chapters. Keep asking yourself 'How can I make the reader's task easier?'

After each successive draft do leave a space of time for your thoughts to mature. It is amazing how something you wrote a few days before will now make no sense to you. However, you will also be impressed with the clarity and insight of some passages.

Having completed a second draft you may now feel confident enough to give it to your colleague or friend to read. Ask your reader to use the checklist above, to which you can add specific points that you feel are important (e.g. are my arguments well reasoned?).

Box 14.11 Checklist

Evaluating your first draft

✔ Is there a clear structure?
✔ Is there a clear storyline?
✔ Does your abstract reflect accurately the whole content of the report?
✔ Does your introduction state clearly the research question(s) and objectives?
✔ Does your literature review inform the later content of the report?
✔ Are your methods clearly explained?
✔ Have you made a clear distinction between findings and conclusions in the two relevant chapters?

✔ Have you checked all your references and presented these in the required manner?
✔ Is there any text material that should be in the appendices or vice versa?
✔ Does your title reflect accurately your content?
✔ Have you divided up your text throughout with suitable headings?
✔ Does each chapter have a preview and a summary?
✔ Are you happy that your writing is clear, simple and direct?
✔ Have you eliminated all jargon?
✔ Have you eliminated all unnecessary quotations?
✔ Have you checked spelling and grammar?
✔ Have you checked for assumptions about gender?
✔ Is your report in a format that will be acceptable to the assessing body?

14.6 Meeting the assessment criteria

Your readers will be assessing your work against the assessment criteria that apply to your research programme. Therefore, it is essential that you familiarise yourself with these criteria. Easterby-Smith *et al.* (2008) cite Bloom's (1971) well-known taxonomy of educational objectives to illustrate the level that project reports should meet. At the lower levels project reports should show knowledge and comprehension of the topic covered. At the intermediate levels they should contain evidence of application and analysis. Application is thought of as the ability to apply certain principles and rules in particular situations. Your method section should be the principal vehicle for demonstrating application. Analysis may be illustrated by your ability to break down your data and to clarify the nature of the component parts and the relationship between them. Whatever your assessment criteria, it is certain that you will be expected to demonstrate your ability at these lower and intermediate levels.

The higher levels are **synthesis** and **evaluation**. Rowntree (1987:103) defines synthesis as 'the ability to arrange and assemble various elements so as to make a new statement or plan or conclusion – a unique communication'. The emphasis put on conclusions and, in particular, on the development of a storyline in your project report suggests that we feel that you should be showing evidence of synthesis. Evaluation refers to 'the ability to judge materials or methods in terms of internal accuracy and consistency or by comparison with external criteria' (Rowntree 1987:103). You have the chance to show this ability in the literature review and in the awareness of the limitations of your own research (see Section 14.3).

In summary, we think that each of the levels of educational objectives should be demonstrated in your project report.

14.7 Oral presentation of the report

Many students, particularly on professional courses, have to present their project report orally as part of the assessment process. The skills required here are quite different from those involved with writing. We discuss them here under three headings: planning and preparation; the use of visual aids; and presenting.

Planning and preparing

We make no apology for starting this section with the trainer's old adage 'Failing to prepare is preparing to fail'. Your assessors will forgive any inadequacies that stem from inexperience, but they will be much less forgiving of students who have paid little attention to preparation. You can be sure of one thing about insufficient preparation: it shows, particularly to the experienced tutor.

All presentations should have clear aims and objectives. This is not the place to analyse the difference between these. Suffice to say that your aim should be to give the audience members an overview of your report in such a way that it will capture their interest. Keep it clear and simple. By doing so you will meet the most basic assessment criterion: that some time later the tutor in the audience can remember clearly your main project storyline. Your objectives are more specific. They should start you thinking about the interests of your audience. These should be phrased in terms of what it is you want your audience members to be able to do after your presentation. Since your presentation will usually be confined to the imparting of knowledge, it is sufficient to phrase your objectives in terms of the audience members being able, for example, to define, describe, explain or clarify. It is a good idea to share the objectives with your audience members so they know about the journey on which they are being taken (Box 14.12).

Setting clear objectives for your presentation leads you neatly to deciding the content. This should be straightforward because your abstract should serve as your guide to the content. After all, the purpose of the abstract is to give the reader a brief overview of the report, which is precisely the same purpose as the presentation. How much detail you go into on each point will be determined largely by the time at your disposal. But the audience member who wants more detail can always ask you to elaborate, or read it in the report.

The final point to note here is to think about the general approach you will adopt in delivering your presentation. It is a good idea to involve the audience members rather than simply tell them what it is you want them to know. Thirty minutes of you talking at the audience members can seem like an age, for you and sometimes for them! Asking them to ask questions throughout the presentation is a good way of ensuring that the talk is not all in one direction. Rarely will tutors miss the opportunity of asking you to 'dig a little deeper' to test your understanding, so don't worry that no questions will arise. However, you must be careful to ensure that you do not let questions and answers run away with time. The more you open up your presentation to debate, the less control you have of time. In general we do not think it is a good idea to attempt to emulate tutors and turn your presentation into a teaching session. We have seen students set the audience mini-exercises to get them involved, but often these tend to fall flat. Play to your strengths and enjoy the opportunity to share your detailed knowledge with an interested audience.

Using visual aids

Now another old adage: 'I hear and I forget, I see and I remember' (Rawlins 1999:37). The use of **visual aids** will do more than enhance the understanding of your audience. It will help you to look better prepared and therefore more professional. It is unlikely that you will have the time to use elaborate media such as video or photographic slides, and often your subject matter will not lend itself to their use. So we shall confine our discussion here to the use of more prosaic media such as the overhead projector and the whiteboard.

A simple set of slides will perform the same function as a set of notes, in that it will ensure that you do not forget key points, and will help you to keep your presentation on track. You will know the material so well that a key point noted on the overhead will be enough to trigger your thought process and focus the attention of the audience. Key points will also ensure that you are not tempted to read a script for your presentation, something that will not sustain the attention of your audience for very long.

The use of Microsoft **PowerPoint**™ has revolutionised the preparation of overhead projector transparencies. It is now easy to produce a highly professional presentation, which can include simple illustrations to reinforce a point or add a little humour. You may have the facility to project the slides direct to a screen using a computer, which clearly adds to the degree of professionalism (Box 14.12). This allows you electronically to reveal each point as you talk about it while concealing forthcoming points. Alternatively, you may need to print the slides from PowerPoint and copy these to acetates and show them using an overhead projector. The latter method means that you must ensure that your slides are numbered and kept in a neat pile when shown, otherwise you will be searching for the correct slide to show at a particular time. PowerPoint also allows you to print miniature versions of your slides as handouts (Version 5, Box 14.12) which is a very useful *aide-mémoire* for the audience.

Box 14.12
Focus on student research

Presenting the objectives for a project

Phil created the following slides as part of a lecture on project presentation. To help give a professional appearance to his slides, he used the Microsoft PowerPoint™ program. This allows you to produce various designs of slide to meet your purpose, examples of which are shown in the following versions:

Version 1: Standard PowerPoint slide

Objectives for a presentation

- Describe the purpose of the research project.

- Explain the context in which the research project research was set.

- Identify the research strategy adopted and the reasons for its choice.

- List the main findings, conclusions and recommendations flowing from the research.

- *N.B. Detail related to the specific project may be added.*

Version 2: PowerPoint slide using design template

Objectives for a presentation

- Describe the purpose of the research project.

- Explain the context in which the research project research was set.

- Identify the research strategy adopted and the reasons for its choice.

- List the main findings, conclusions and recommendations flowing from the research.

N.B. Detail related to the specific project may be added.

Version 3: PowerPoint slide using more colour

Objectives for a presentation

■Describe the purpose of the research project.

■Explain the context in which the research project research was set.

■Identify the research strategy adopted and the reasons for its choice.

■List the main findings, conclusions and recommendations flowing from the research.

n.b. Detail related to the specific project may be added.

Version 4: PowerPoint slide with photograph inserted

Objectives for a presentation

- Describe the purpose of the research project.

- Explain the context in which the research project research was set.

- Identify the research strategy adopted and the reasons for its choice.

- List the main findings, conclusions and recommendations flowing from the research.

- *N.B. Detail related to the specific project may be added.*

Version 5: PowerPoint slide with space for audience to add notes

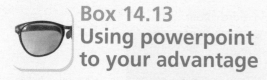

Box 14.13
Using powerpoint to your advantage

Let's face it, PowerPoint presentations can be dull and boring! But we all continue to rely on them to deliver information. Harvard University psychology professor Stephen Kosslyn (2007) in his new book, *Clear and to the Point* has some useful tips on keeping the audience awake.

Kosslyn's main points are:

Keep it simple. Don't include so much information that the audience loses the thread of your argument. Kosslyn thinks that telling them too much will leave them overwhelmed, disoriented and irritated. The rule of thumb: an effective presentation is organised around a central message, everything you include should reinforce that message. If in doubt, leave it out.

Tell them what they need to know. Don't assume too much knowledge on the part of the audience. Too many bullet points and too much industry jargon may confuse your message. Your audience will spend its time trying to decipher your "code" rather than listening. Be clear. Don't treat listeners like insiders unless they are.

Know the audience. Tailor the material to fit the audience's interests and concerns. A listener who feels personally connected with the material will be more likely to consider it and remember it. People will listen and remember only if you're telling them something they want to know.

Use visuals only to clarify. PowerPoint has so many clever features that we are all tempted to overdo the charts, graphs and other visual attractions. Less is more.

Give the audience time to digest. Build in breaks. Use relevant anecdotes (or even jokes) to lighten the content-heavy parts of your presentation. This will give your audience the opportunity to digest the details. The rule of thumb: make sure your interjections help illustrate your point, and don't run the risk of offending your audience.

Source: article by Loeb, Marshall (2007) *Colorado Spring Gazette*, 23 Sept. Available online at: http://www.gazette.com/articles/audience_27641 article.html/information_powerpoint.html.

You may want to supplement your pre-prepared slides with the use of the whiteboard. This may be useful for explaining points in relation to questions you receive. A word of warning here: ensure that you use dry markers that can be wiped from the board. A vain attempt to erase the results of a permanent pen in front of your audience will do nothing to enhance your confidence. Ensuring that you have dry wipe markers (use only black and blue pens – red and green are too faint), and checking computers and overhead projectors before the presentation, serve to emphasise the need for careful preparation.

Making the presentation

The first thing to say here is: don't worry about nerves. As Janner (1984:15) says: 'Confidence comes with preparation, practice and training.' Your audience will expect you to be a little nervous. Indeed, without some nervous tension before your presentation it is unlikely you will do yourself justice. Be positive about your presentation and your report. Trial your presentation on a friend to ensure that it flows logically and smoothly and that you can deliver it in the allotted time. In our experience most students put too much material in their presentations, although they worry beforehand that they have not got enough.

It is important that your presentation has a clear structure. We can do no better than repeat the words of a famous evangelist: when asked how he held the attention of his audience, he replied 'First I tell them what I'm going to say, then I say it, then I tell them what I've said' (Parry 1991:17). Parry (1991) notes that audiences like to know where they are going, they like to know how they are progressing on the journey, and they like to know when they have arrived.

Finally some practical points that will help.

- Think about whether you would prefer to sit or stand at the presentation. The former may be better to foster debate, the latter is likely to give you a sense of 'control' (Rawlins 1999). Which one you choose may depend upon the circumstances of the presentation, including the approach you wish to adopt, the room layout, the equipment you are using and your preferred style.
- Consider how you will deal with difficult questions. Rehearse these and your answers in your mind so that you can deal with them confidently during the presentation.
- Avoid jargon.
- Check the room before the presentation to ensure you have everything you need, you are happy and familiar with the layout, and all your equipment is working.

14.8 Summary

- Writing is a powerful way of clarifying your thinking.
- Writing is a creative process, which needs the right conditions if it is to produce successful results.
- Your project report should have a clear structure that enables you to develop a clear storyline.
- Your report should be laid out in such a way that your reader finds all the information readily accessible.
- You should try to develop a clear, simple writing style that will make reading the report an easy and enjoyable experience.
- Spelling and grammatical errors should be avoided.
- Do not think of your first draft as your last. Be prepared to rewrite your report several times until you think it is the best you can do.
- Failing to prepare for your presentation is preparing to fail.
- Visual aids will enhance the understanding of your audience and lend your presentation professionalism.
- Remember: tell them what you're going to say, say it, then tell them what you've said.

Self-check questions

Help with these questions is available at the end of the chapter.

14.1 Your project tutor has returned your draft project report with the suggestion that you make a clearer distinction between your results and your conclusions. How will you go about this?

14.2 Why is it considered good practice to acknowledge the limitations of your research in the project report?

14.3 Look again at the quote from Wright Mills cited early in Section 14.5. Rewrite this so that his idea is communicated to the reader in the clearest way possible.

14.4 There are other problems that must be avoided when repositioning sections of your report in the redrafting processes. What are they?

14.5 Look at the PowerPoint slide below and comment on any weaknesses.

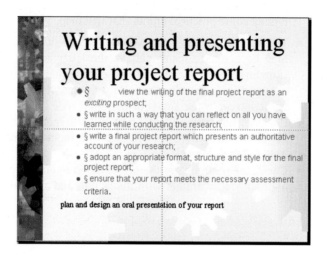

Review and discussion questions

14.6 Draft a plan for your dissertation, show it to your friends and compare your plan with those they have drafted. Explain the reason for any differences between your plan and those of your friends.

14.7 Look through several of the refereed academic journals that relate to your subject area. Choose an article that is based upon some primary research and note the structure of the article. Decide whether you agree with the way in which the author has structured the article and think of ways in which you may have done this differently.

14.8 Share pieces of your writing with a group of your friends. Look at the example in Box 14.10 and subject all the pieces to the 'write clearer sentences' test.

Progressing your research project

Writing your project report

- Design a clear structure for your report that broadly fits the structure suggested in Section 14.3. Ensure that the structure you design accommodates a clear storyline and meets the expectations of your audience.

- Write the report's abstract. Remember that you will need to rewrite this when you have finished your first draft.

- Compile the main body of the report. How will you ensure that the literature review relates to the following chapters? What method will you adopt to make the distinction between result and conclusions?

- Give your report the 'reader-friendly' test to ensure that the style is easy to read and free from avoidable errors.

References

BBC News Online (2007) 'Privacy rights 'fragile' in 2007', 31 Dec. Available at: http://news.bbc.co.uk/1/hi/technology/7165778.stm [Accessed 24 May 2008.]

Becker, H. (2008) *Writing for Social Scientists*. Chicago, IL.:University of Chicago Press.

Bloom, B. (ed.) (1971) *Taxonomy of Educational Objectives: Cognitive Domain*. New York: McKay.

Day, R. (1998) *How to Write and Publish a Scientific Paper* (5th edn). Phoenix, AZ: Oryx Press.

Day, R. and Gastel. B. (2006) *How to Write and Publish a Scientific Paper* (6th edn). Cambridge: Cambridge University Press.

Easterby-Smith, M., Thorpe, R. and Jackson, P. (2008) *Management Research* (3rd edn). London: Sage.

Emerald Group Publishing (2006) 'Writing for an Emerald publication: instructions for writing a structured abstract'. Available at: http://info.emeraldinsight.com/authors/guides/abstracts.htm [Accessed 25 May 2008.]

Goldsmith, R. and Flynn, L. (2006) 'Psychological and behavioral drivers of online clothing purchase', *Journal of Fashion Marketing and Management*, Vol. 8, No. 1, pp. 84–95.

Griffiths, M. (1993) 'Productive writing', *The New Academic*, Autumn, pp. 29–31.

Janner, G. (1984) *Janner on Presentations*. London: Business Books Ltd.

Kosslyn, S. (2007) *Clear and to the Point: 8 Psychological Principles for Compelling PowerPoint Presentations*. New York: Oxford University Press.

Möller, C., Weiermair, K. and Wintersberger, E. (2007) 'The changing travel behaviour of Austria's ageing population and its impact on tourism', *Tourism Review*, Vol. 62, Nos. 3/4, pp. 15–20.

Parry, H. (1991) *Successful Business Presentations*. Kingston-upon-Thames: Croner.

Pearsall, J. (ed.) (1998) *The New Oxford English Dictionary*. Oxford: Oxford University Press.

Phillips, E.M. and Pugh, D.S. (2005) *How to get a PhD* (3rd edn). Maidenhead: Open University Press.

Raimond, P. (1993) *Management Projects: Design. Research and Presentation*. London: Chapman & Hall.

Rawlins, K. (1999) *Presentation and Communication Skills: A Handbook for Practitioners*. London: Emap Healthcare Ltd.

Richards, P. (1986) 'Risk', in H. Becker, *Writing for Social Scientists*. Chicago, IL: University of Chicago Press, pp. 108–20.

Robson, C. (2002) *Real World Research* (2nd edn). Oxford: Blackwell.

Rowntree, D. (1987) *Assessing Students: How Shall We Know Them?* (revised edn). London: Harper & Row.

Smith, C.B. (1991) *A Guide to Business Research*. Chicago, IL: Nelson-Hall.

Veroff, J. (2001) 'Writing', in K. Rudestam and R. Newton. R. (eds), *Surviving your Dissertation* (2nd edn). Newbury Park, CA: Sage.

Wright Mills, C. (1970) 'On intellectual craftsmanship', in C. Wright Mills, *The Sociological Imagination*. London: Pelican.

Further reading

Becker, H. (2008) *Writing for Social Scientists*. Chicago, IL: University of Chicago Press. This is a highly readable book, full of anecdotes, from an expert in the field. It is rich in ideas about how writing may be improved. Most of these have been developed by Becker from his own writing and teaching. Such is the emphasis that Becker puts on rewriting that the title would more accurately be 'Rewriting for Social Scientists'.

Day, R. and Gastel, B. (2006) *How to Write and Publish a Scientific Paper* (6th edn). Cambridge: Cambridge University Press. This takes the reader through the whole process, with a host of useful advice. It is funny and irreverent but none the less valuable for that!

Fisher, C. (2004) *Researching and Writing a Dissertation*. Harlow: FT Prentice Hall. Chapter 6 has lots of useful tips for the writing-up process.

Rawlins, K. (1999) *Presentation and Communication Skills: A Handbook for Practitioners*. Basingstoke: Palgrave MacMillan. A very useful and practical guide for the inexperienced.

Smith, C.B. (1991) *A Guide to Business Research*. Chicago, IL: Nelson-Hall. Chapters 7–10 provide an excellent introduction to writing for business and management researchers.

Case 14
James' consultancy report on managers' financial information needs

Radisson Hotel, St Petersburg
Source: Alex Segre/Alamy

James, the Area Financial Controller (London) in the Europe, Middle East & Africa (EMEA) region of an international hotel group, is currently studying for a part-time Masters degree. As part of the programme, he is required to complete a consultancy project for an in-house client within his own organisation.

Aware of James' ongoing studies, the Regional Vice-President (Finance), who is based in Brussels, telephoned with the following proposition:

> James, we've been set a new five-year bottom-line profit target of €300 m for the region. As part of the strategy to achieve the target we need to improve our financial management decision-making at the hotel property level – would you like to get involved with this in relation to your Masters consultancy project?

From James' point of view, the Vice-President's request for the assignment was timely for two reasons. Firstly, it fitted conveniently with the need to develop a consultancy project for his studies. Secondly, he had already been stimulated by the work of Graham and Harris (1999) on *Developing a Profit Planning Framework* for another major international hotel chain to begin his own assessment and testing of the practicability of applying marginal analysis in one of his London hotels. Consequently, after discussion with his project tutor, James accepted the Regional Vice-President's short brief. This stated:

> In the light of current best practice, assess the financial reporting for decision-making at the properties in the region and submit a report to me recommending the future financial information needs of managers, together with a training and development strategy to support the implementation of your recommendations.

After discussing his ideas and agreeing a suitable consultancy proposal with his project tutor, James made a formal presentation to the Regional Vice-President's EMEA Financial Management Board in Brussels. Whilst the proposal included the purpose of the investigation and a method for determining the current and future financial information needs of managers, the core of the proposal was the implementation of marginal accounting techniques across the EMEA region, adapted from Graham and Harris' (1999) conceptual framework. The Board liked the presentation and asked James to commence the assignment.

With the guidance of his project tutor, James began work by spending time in the university library getting to grips with books and articles relating to the theory and application of marginal accounting techniques and searching the Internet for possible accounting firm and hospitality consulting firm reports on implementing the techniques in hotels. He also began reading Wickham and Wickham's (2008) *Management Consulting* and Thomas' (2003) *High-Performance Consulting Skills* in order to gain an understanding of what the consulting process entailed. Concurrently with the desk research, he arranged interview visits to a number of department managers across the EMEA region to discover their opinions as to the relevance of the financial information they were receiving for day-to-day decision-making purposes.

Analysis of James' interview responses revealed a mismatch between the information being produced by the hotel property financial controllers and the type of decisions being taken by managers; in effect, financial controllers were producing reports by departments whilst managers were making decisions by market segment. James realised this situation was primarily due to the accounting systems being used in the hotel industry. Most hotel companies use the *Uniform System of Accounts for the Lodging Industry* (2006), the industry standard based on the traditional departmental method of operating hotels, i.e. rooms (bedrooms), food (restaurants) and beverage (bars). Whilst *USALI* is a widely accepted hotel accounting system, its emphasis is on controlling and reporting (the past) to the corporate hierarchy rather than producing information for decision making (for the future), so was not conducive to achieving the VP's objective of improving decision-making at the properties. In fact, this was the very reason James had been investigating and assessing the case for marginal analysis in the company. Marginal analysis, he believed, could provide an important first step along the road to providing more relevant financial information for managers' routine, day-to-day, decision-making. Thus, it became clear to James that both the hotel property financial controllers and department managers should produce (financial controllers) and use (department managers) marginal accounting information in reports for routine decision-making.

Having completed the interviews, analysed the responses and read the relevant books, articles and consulting surveys, James felt that he was ready to begin the task of drafting his report for the VP's Financial Management Board in Brussels. To assist him in the design and preparation of a suitable report, James had made reference to Sally Garratt's (1991) *How to be a Consultant* and Calvert Markham's (1997) *Practical Management Consultancy*. He made an appointment with his project tutor to show him his primary and secondary findings and to ask his advice on the structure, content and layout of the report. Among other issues, James' tutor emphasised that a critical element of report writing was to address the 'brief' and reflect on the 'audience'.

References

Garratt, S. (1991) *How to Be a Consultant*. Aldershot: Gower.

Graham, I. and Harris, P. (1999) 'Development of a profit planning framework in an international hotel chain: A case study', *International Journal of Contemporary Hospitality Management*, Vol. 11, No. 5, pp. 198–208.

Hotel Association of New York City (2006) *Uniform System of Accounts for the Lodging industry*. East Lansing: American Hotel and Lodging Educational Institute.

Markham, C. (1997) *Practical Management Consultancy* (3rd edn). Milton Keynes: Accountancy Books (ICAE&W).

Thomas , M. (2003) *High-Performance Consulting Skills*. London: Thorgood.

Wickham, P. and Wickham, L. (2008) *Management Consulting: Delivering an Effective Project* (3rd edn). Harlow: Pearson Education.

Questions

1 Draft an outline structure of headings that would be broadly suitable for the main body of a consultancy report for James' client (including James' report) and explain the purpose of such a report.

2 Outline the content that you would expect James to include under each of the 'main headings' you have proposed for the report.

3 Outline the purpose and content of an 'executive summary' in a consultancy report.

Additional case studies relating to material covered in this chapter are available via the book's Companion Website, **www.pearsoned.co.uk/saunders**. They are:

- Writing Lata's project report
- Amina's story
- Akasma's draft disappointment.

Self-check answers

14.1 This is easier said than done. Start by going through your results chapter, continually asking yourself 'Did I find this out?' You will probably weed out a lot of things that you have thought about that are related to points you found out. These belong in the conclusions (or discussion) chapter.

Now turn to the conclusions chapter, asking yourself the question: 'Is this a reflection of what I found out?' If the points are a repeat of what you covered in your findings section, then cut them out and make sure you write reflections on the findings.

14.2 It shows that you have thought about your research design. It demonstrates that you have insight into the various ways of pursuing research. Remember that there is no perfect research design. Look again at Section 5.4. This asked the question, 'How do you know that the answer to the research question(s) is the correct one?' The answer, of course, is that in the literal sense of the question you cannot know. All you can do is reduce the possibility of getting the answer wrong.

14.3 Academic writing is often difficult to understand. This is not usually because the subject matter is complex or the thoughts profound. It is because the writer thinks it necessary to write in an 'academic' way.

14.4 The 'road map' you announced in the introduction may not now be correct. The previews and summaries at the beginning and end of the relevant chapters may need changing. A more serious potential problem is that the storyline may be altered. This should not be the case. Nonetheless, it is important to reread the whole report to ensure that the repositioning does not alter its sense of coherence.

14.5.1 Well, it looks a bit of a mess! The title is too big: it is out of proportion to the rest of the text. Not all the points are 'bulleted', and the spaces between the bullet and text are not consistent. There are three different fonts and, most importantly, there is too much text on the slide. All of these faults are easily rectifiable. It is worth playing around with it and making a few mistakes – it's a good way of learning!

Get ahead using resources on the Companion Website at:
www.pearsoned.co.uk/saunders

- Improve your SPSS and NVivo research analysis with practice tutorials.
- Save time researching on the Internet with the Smarter Online Searching Guide.
- Test your progress using self-assessment questions.
- Follow live links to useful websites.

Bibliography

A

Ackroyd, S. and Hughes, J. (1992) *Data Collection in Context* (2nd edn). London: Longman.

Adams, G. and Schvaneveldt, J. (1991) *Understanding Research Methods* (2nd edn). New York: Longman.

American Psychological Association (2005) *Concise rules of the APA style*. Washington, DC: American Psychological Association.

Anderson, D.R., Sweeney, D.J. and Williams, T.A. (1999) *Statistics for Business and Economics* (7th edn). Cincinnati, OH: South-Western College Publishing.

Anderson, T.W. (2003) *An Introduction to Multivariate Statistical Analysis*. New York: John Wiley.

B

Ball, A. and Seal, W. (2005) 'Social justice in a cold climate: could social accounting make a difference?', *Accounting Forum*, Vol. 29, No. 4, pp. 455–73.

Barnett, V. (1991) *Sample Survey Principles and Methods*. London: Edward Arnold.

Baruch, Y. (1999) 'Response rates in academic studies – a comparative analysis', *Human Relations*, Vol. 52, No. 4, pp. 421–38.

BBC News Online (2005) 'South Korean dies after games session'. Available at: http://news.bbc.co.uk/1/hi/technology/4137782.stm [Accessed 21 May 2008.]

BBC News Online (2007) *'Privacy rights "fragile" in 2007'*, 31 Dec. Available at: http://news.bbc.co.uk/1/hi/technology/7165778.stm [Accessed 24 May 2008.]

Becken, S. (2007) 'Tourist perception of international air travel's impact on global climate and potential climate change policies', *Journal of Sustainable Tourism*, Vol. 15, No. 4, pp. 351–60.

Becker, H. (2008) *Writing for Social Scientists*. Chicago, IL: University of Chicago Press.

Beeton, S. (2005) *Film-Induced Tourism*. Clevedon: Channel View Publications.

Bell, E. and Bryman, A. (2007) 'The ethics of management research: an exploratory content analysis', *British Journal of Management*, Vol. 18, No. 1, pp. 63–77.

Bell, J. (2005) *Doing your Research Project* (4th edn). Buckingham: Open University Press.

Bendoly, E. and Swink, M. (2007) 'Moderating effects of information access on project management behavior, performance and perceptions', *Journal of Operations Management*, Vol. 25, pp. 604–22.

Bennett, R. (1991) 'What is management research?', in N.C. Smith and P. Dainty (eds) *The Management Research Handbook*. London: Routledge: pp. 67–77.

Berman Brown, R. and Saunders, M. (2008) *Dealing with statistics: What you need to know*. Maidenhead: McGraw-Hill Open University Press.

Bhaskar, R. (1989) *Reclaiming Reality: A Critical Introduction to Contemporary Philosophy*. London: Verso.

Bloom, B. (ed.) (1971) *Taxonomy of Educational Objectives: Cognitive Domain*. New York: McKay.

Blumberg, B., Cooper, D.R. and Schindler, P.S. (2008) *Business Research Methods*. (international student edn). Maidenhead: McGraw-Hill Education.

Boddy, C. (2005) 'A rose by any other name may smell as sweet but "group discussion" is not another name for "focus group" nor should it be', *Qualitative Market Research*, Vol. 8, No. 3, pp. 248–55.

Bolugan, J. and Hailey, V.H. (2004) *Exploring Strategic Change*, (2nd edn). Harlow: Prentice Hall.

Bouma, G. and Atkinson, G. (1995) *A Handbook of Social Science Research: A Comprehensive and Practical Guide for Students* (2nd edn). Oxford: Oxford University Press.

Bourque, L.B. and Clark, V.A. (1994) 'Processing data: the survey example', in M.S. Lewis-Beck, *Research Practice*. London: Sage, pp. 1–88.

Bradley, N. (1999) 'Sampling for Internet surveys: an examination of respondent selection for Internet research', *Journal of the Market Research Society*, Vol. 41, No. 4, pp. 387–95.

Brandsen, T. and Pestoff, V. (2008) 'Co-production, the third sector and the delivery of public services', *Public Management Review*, Vol. 8, No. 4, pp. 493–501.

Brannick, T. and Coghlan, D. (2007) 'In defense of being native the case for insider academic research', *Organizational Research Methods*, Vol.10, No.1, pp. 59–74.

Bray, R. (2005) 'Survey probes shift to airline e-ticketing', *Financial Times*, 8 Sept.

British Psychological Society (1988) 'Guidelines for the use of non-sexist language', *The Psychologist*, Vol. 1, No. 2, pp. 53–4.

British Psychological Society (2004) 'Style Guide'. Available at: http://www.bps.org.uk/publications/submission-guidelines/submission-guidelines_home.cfm [Accessed 21 June 2008.]

British Sociological Association (2004a) 'Language and the BSA: Sex and Gender'. Available at: http://www.britsoc.co.uk/equality/ [Accessed 21 June 2008.]

British Sociological Association (2004b) 'Language and the BSA: Non-disablist'. Available at: http://www.britsoc.co.uk/equality/ [Accessed 21 June 2008.]

British Sociological Association (2005) 'Language and the BSA: Ethnicity and Race'. Available at: http://www.britsoc.co.uk/equality/ [Accessed 21 June 2008.]

Brown, R.B., Saunders, M.N.K. and Beresford, R. (2006) 'You owe it to yourselves: the financially literate manager', *Accounting Forum*. Vol. 30, No. 2, pp. 179–91.

Bryman, A. (1989) *Research Methods and Organisation Studies*. London: Unwin Hyman.

Bryman, A. (2006) 'Editor's introduction: mixed methods research', in A. Bryman (ed.). *Mixed Methods: Volume 1*. London: Sage, pp. XXV–LII.

Bryman, A. (2006) 'Integrating quantitative and qualitative research: how is it done?', *Qualitative Research*, Vol. 6, pp. 97–113.

Bryman, A. (2007) 'The research question in social research: what is its role?', *International. Journal of Social Research Methodology*, Vol. 10, No. 1, pp. 5–20.

Bryson, B. (1995) *Made in America*. London: Minerva.

Buchanan, D., Boddy, D. and McAlman, J. (1988) 'Getting in, getting on, getting out and getting back', in A. Bryman, A. (ed.) *Doing Research in Organisations*. London: Routledge, pp. 53–67.

Burke, M. (2007) 'Making choices: research paradigms and information management: Practical applications of philosophy in IM research', *Library Review*, Vol. 56, No. 6, pp. 476–84.

Burnes, B. (2005) 'Complexity theories and organizational change', *International Journal of Management Reviews*, Vol. 7, No. 2, pp. 73–90.

Burrell, G. and Morgan, G. (1982) *Sociological Paradigms and Organisational Analysis*. London: Heinemann.

Buzan, T. (2006) *The Ultimate Book of Mind Maps*. London: Harper Thorsons.

C

Campbell, D.J., Moore, G. and Shrives, P.J. (2006) 'Cross-sectional effects in community disclosure', *Accounting, Auditing and Accountability Journal*, Vol. 19, No. 1, pp. 96–114.

Cane, A. (2007) 'You don't need to be a mechanic to drive a car', *Financial Times*, 12 Feb.

Carroll, L. (1989) *Alice's Adventures in Wonderland*. London: Hutchinson.

Carson, D., Gilmore, A., Perry, C. and Grønhaug, K. (2001) *Qualitative Marketing Research*. London: Sage.

Cheng Shu-Li. Olsen W., Southerton. D. and Warde A. (2007) 'The changing practice of eating: evidence from UK time diaries: 1975 and 2000', *British Journal of Sociology*, Vol. 58, No. 1, pp. 39–61.

Clausen, H. (1996) 'Web information quality as seen from libraries', *New Library World* 97: 1130, pp. 4–8.

Clennell, A. (2002) 'How Brunel lobby came off the rails', *The Guardian*, 25 Nov.

Clough, P. and Nutbrown, C. (2002) *A Student's Guide to Methodology*. London: Sage.

Coghlan , D. and Rashford, N.S. (2006) *Organizational Change and Strategy: An Interlevel Dynamics Approach*. Abingdon: Routledge.

Coghlan , D. and Shani A.B. (Rami) (2008) 'Insider Action Research: The Dynamics of Developing New Capabilities', in P. Reason and H. Bradbury (eds). *Handbook of Action Research* (2nd edn). London: Sage, pp. 643–455.

Coghlan , D. and Brannick, T. (2005) '*Doing Action Research in Your Own Organization* (2nd edn). London: Sage.

Cohen, E. and Krishnamurthy, B. (2006) 'A short walk in the Blogistan', *Computer Networks*, Vol. 50, pp. 615–30.

Cohen, L. and Holliday, M. (1996) *Practical Statistics for Students*. London: Paul Chapman.

Collis, J. and Hussey, R. (2003) *Business Research: A Practical Guide for Undergraduate and Postgraduate Students* (2nd edn). Basingstoke: Palgrave Macmillan.

Coomber, R. (1997) 'Using the Internet for survey research', *Sociological Research Online*, Vol. 2, No. 2. Available at: http://www.socresonline.org.uk/socresonline/2/2/2.html [Accessed 20 April 2008.]

Cooper, C., Taylor, P, Smith, N. and Catchpowle, L. (2005) 'A discussion of the political potential of Social Accounting', *Critical Perspectives on Accounting*, Vol. 16, No. 7, pp. 951–74.

Cooper, D.R. and Schindler, P.S. (2008) *Business Research Methods* (10th edn). Boston, MA and Burr Ridge, IL: McGraw-Hill.

Cooper, J. (2002) *Great Britons, the Great Debate*, London: National Portrait Gallery.

Corbetta, P. (2003) *Social Research: Theory, Methods and Techniques*. London: Sage.

Cowton. C.J. (1998) The use of secondary data in business ethics research. *Journal of Business Ethics*. Vol. 17, No. 4, pp. 423–34.

Creswell, J. (2002) *Qualitative, Quantitative, and Mixed Methods Approaches* (2nd edn). Thousand Oaks, CA: Sage.

Creswell, J. (2007) *Qualitative inquiry and Research Design: Choosing among Five Approaches* (2nd edn). Thousand Oaks, CA: Sage.

Cully, M. Woodland, S. O'Reilly, A and Dix, G. (1999). *Britain At Work: As Depicted by the 1998 Workplace Employee Relations Survey.* London: Routledge.

Curran, J. and Blackburn, R.A. (2001) *Researching the Small Enterprise.* London: Sage.

Curwin, J. and Slater, R. (2007) *Quantitative Methods: A Short Course.* London: Thomson Learning EMEA.

D

Dale, A., Arber, S. and Procter, M. (1988) *Doing Secondary Research.* London, Unwin Hyman.

Dale. P. (2004) *Guide to Libraries and Information Units in Government Departments and Other Organisations* (4th edn). London: British Library Publishing.

Dancey, C. P. and Reidy, J. (2008) *Statistics Without Maths for Psychology: Using SPSS for Windows* (4th edn). Harlow: Prentice Hall.

Davies. J. (2001) 'International comparisons of labour disputes in 1999', *Labour Market Trends*, Vol. 109, No. 4, pp. 195–201.

Day, R. (1998) *How to Write and Publish a Scientific Paper* (5th edn). Phoenix, AZ: Oryx Press.

Day, R. and Gastel. B. (2006) *How to Write and Publish a Scientific Paper* (6th edn). Cambridge: Cambridge University Press.

Deakins, D. and Freel, M. (2003) *Entrepreneurship and Small Firms.* Maidenhead, Berkshire: McGraw-Hill Education.

Deegan, C., M. Rankin and Tobin J. (2002) 'An examination of the corporate social and environmental disclosures of BHP from 1983–1997: A test of legitimacy theory', *Accounting, Auditing and Accountability Journal*, Vol. 15, No. 3, pp. 312–43.

Deegan, C., Rankin, M. and Voght, P. (2000) 'Firms' disclosure reactions to major social incidents: Australian evidence', *Accounting Forum*. Vol. 24, No. 1, pp. 101–30.

Dees, R. (2003) *Writing the Modern Research Paper* (4th edn). Boston, MA: Allyn and Bacon.

Delbridge, R. and Kirkpatrick, I. (1994) 'Theory and practice of participant observation', in V. Wass and P. Wells (eds), *Principles and Practice in Business and Management Research*. Aldershot: Dartmouth, pp. 35–62.

Denscombe, M. (2007) *The Good Research Guide* (3rd edn). Buckingham: Open University Press.

Denyer, D. and Neely, A. (2004) 'Introduction to special issue: Innovation and productivity performance in the UK', *International Journal of Management Reviews*, Vol. 5/6, Nos. 3 and 4, pp. 131–5.

Denzin, N. (1989) *The Research Act: A Theoretical Introduction to Sociological Methods* (3rd edn). Englewood Cliffs, NJ: Prentice-Hall.

deVaus, D.A. (2002) *Surveys in Social Research.* (5th edn). London: Routledge.

Diamantopoulos, A. and Schlegelmilch, B.B. (1997) *Taking the Fear Out of Data Analysis.* London: Dryden Press.

Dickmann M. and Doherty, N. (2008) 'Exploring the Career Capital Impact of International Assignments within Distinct Organizational Contexts', *British Journal of Management*, Vol. 19, No. 2, pp. 145–61.

Dillman, D.A. (2007) *Mail and Internet Surveys: The Tailored Design Method.* (2nd edn 2007 update). Hobeken, NJ: Wiley.

Ditton, J. (1977) *Part-Time Crime: An Ethnography of Fiddling and Pilferage.* London: Macmillan.

Dobson, P. (2002) 'Critical realism and information systems research: why bother with philosophy?' Available at: http://informationr.net/ir/7-2/paper124.html [Accessed 27 May 2008.]

Dochartaigh, N.O. (2002) *The Internet Research Handbook: A Practical Guide for Students and Researchers in the Social Sciences.* London: Sage.

'Dragons' Den' (2007) Series 5, Episode 1, 'Beach Break Live', British Broadcasting Corporation Television broadcast, 15 Oct. Available at: http://www.bbc.co.uk/dragonsden/series5/episode1.shtml [Accessed 8 June 2008.]

Dwivedi, M. (2006) Travel Tales from India. Taj Mahal, Agra: Shatabdi to Shatabdi One Day Trip 23 July 2006. Available at: http://www.gonomad.com/traveltalesfromindia/labels/Agra.html [Accessed 31 Jan. 2008.]

Dyer, O. (2003) 'Lancet accuses AstraZeneca of sponsoring biased research', *British Medical Journal*, Vol. 327, No. 1, p. 1005.

E

Easterby-Smith, M., Thorpe, R., Jackson, P. and Lowe, A. (2008) *Management Research* (3rd edn). London: Sage.

Economic and Social Data Service (2007) 'A step by step ESDS guide to: archiving and reusing data: consent issues'. Available at: http://www.esds.ac.uk/support/E8.asp [Accessed 6 April 2008.]

Eden, C. and Huxham, C. (1996) 'Action research for management research', *British Journal of Management*, Vol. 7, No. 1, pp. 75–86.

Edwards, P., Roberts, I., Clarke, M., Di Giuseppe, C., Pratap, S., Wentz, R., and Kwan, I. (2002) 'Increasing response rates to postal questionnaires: systematic review', *British Medical Journal*, No. 324, May, pp. 1183–91.

Edwards, T., Tregaskis, O., Edwards, P., Ferner, A., Marginson, A. with Arrowsmith, J., Adam, D., Meyer, M. and Budjanovcanin, A. (2007) 'Charting the contours of multinationals in Britain: Methodological challenges arising in survey-based research', Warwick papers in Industrial Relations No. 86. Available at: http://www2.warwick.ac.uk/fac/soc/wbs/research/irru/wpir/ [Accessed 2 February 2008.]

ELC International (2007) *Europe's 15000 Largest Companies* (31st edn). Oxford: ELC International.

Ellis, P.D. (2005) 'Market orientation and marketing practice in a developing economy', *European Journal of Marketing*, Vol. 39, Nos. 5/6, pp. 629–45.

Emerald Group Publishing (2006) 'Writing for an Emerald publication: instructions for writing a structured abstract'. Available at: http://info.emeraldinsight.com/authors/guides/abstracts.htm [Accessed 25 May 2008.]

European Commission (2007) 'Eurostat – structural indicators'. Available at: http://epp.eurostat.ec.europa.eu/portal/page?_pageid=1133,47800773,1133_47802558&_dad=portal&_schema=PORTAL [Accessed 27 November 2007.]

Eurostat (2007) 'Environment and energy statistics–data air emissions'. Available at: http://epp.eurostat.cec.eu.int/portal/page?_pageid=1090, 30070682,1090_30298591&_dad=portal&_schema=PORTAL [Accessed 16 December 2007.]

Eurostat (2008a) *Europe in Figures: Eurostat Yearbook 2008*. Luxembourg: Office for Official Publications of the European Communities.

Eurostat (2008b) Eurostat home page. Available at: http://epp.eurostat.ec.europa.eu/portal/page?_pageid=1090.30070682.1090_33076576&_dad=portal&_schema=PORTAL [Accessed 23 May 2008.]

Eurostat (2008c) 'Harmonized Indices of Consumer Prices'. Available at: http://epp.eurostat.ec.europa.eu/portal/page?_pageid=1073,46587259&_dad=portal&_schema=PORTAL&p_product_code=KS-QA-08-024 [Accessed 29 June 2008.]

Everitt, B.S. and Dunn, G. (2001) *Applied Multivariate Data Analysis* (2nd edn). London: Arnold.

Eysenbach, G. and Till, J.E. (2001) 'Ethical issues in qualitative research on internet communities', *British Medical Journal*, 323:7321, pp. 1103–5.

F

Festinger, L. (1957) *A Theory of Cognitive Dissonance*. Stanford, CA: Stanford University Press.

Field, A. (2005) *Discovering Statistics Using SPSS* (2nd edn). London: Sage.

Financial Times (2003) 'George Lucas is a god in Britain. Literally', 14 Feb.

Fink, A. (2003a) *How to Ask Survey Questions* (2nd edn). Thousand Oaks, CA: Sage.

Fink, A. (2003b) *The Survey Handbook* (2nd edn). Thousand Oaks, CA: Sage.

Fisher, C. (2007) *Researching and Writing a Dissertation for Business Students* (2nd edn). Harlow: Financial Times Prentice Hall.

Foddy, W. (1994) *Constructing Questions for Interviews and Questionnaires*. Cambridge: Cambridge University Press.

Fukami, C. (2007) 'The third road', *Journal of Management Education*, Vol. 31, pp. 358–64.

G

Gall, M.D., Gall, J.P. and Borg, W. (2006) *Educational Research: An Introduction* (8th edn). New York: Longman.

Garratt, S. (1991) *How to Be a Consultant*. Aldershot: Gower.

Gay, G., Schelluch, P. and Baines, A. (1998) 'Perceptions of messages conveyed by review and audit reports', *Accounting, Auditing and Accountability Journal*, Vol. 11, No. 4, pp. 472–94.

Geiger, S. (2007) 'Exploring night-time grocery shopping behaviour', *Journal of Retailing and Consumer Services*, January, pp. 24–34.

Ghauri, P. and Grønhaug, K. (2005) *Research Methods in Business Studies: A Practical Guide* (3rd edn). Harlow: Financial Times Prentice Hall.

Gibb, F. (1995) 'Consumer group accuses lawyers of shoddy service', *The Times*, 5 Oct. 1995.

Gibbons, M.L., Limoges, H., Nowotny, S., Schwartman, P., Scott, P. and Trow, M. (1994) *The New Production of Knowledge: The Dynamics of Science and Research in Contemporary Societies*. London: Sage.

Gill, J. and Johnson, P. (2002) *Research Methods for Managers* (3rd edn). London: Sage Publications.

Glaser, B. and Strauss, A. (1967) *The Discovery of Grounded Theory*. Chicago, IL: Aldine.

Goldsmith, R. and Flynn, L. (2006) 'Psychological and behavioral drivers of online clothing purchase', *Journal of Fashion Marketing and Management*, Vol. 8, No. 1, pp. 84–95.

Goulding, C. (2002) *Grounded Theory: A Practical Guide for Management. Business and Market Researchers*. London: Sage.

Grande, C. (2007) 'Star performers on back of the internet', *Financial Times*, 14 Apr.

Grande, C. (2007) 'TNS warns over the reliability of data collected online', *Financial Times*, 4 Sept.

Gray, R.H., Kouhy, R. and Lavers, S. (1995) 'Corporate social and environmental reporting: a review of the literature and a longitudinal study of UK disclosure', *Accounting, Auditing & Accountability Journal*, Vol. 8, No. 2, pp. 47–77.

Great Britain Office for National Statistics (2000a) *Standard Occupation Classification Volume 1: Structure and Description of Unit Groups*. London: Stationery Office.

Great Britain Office for National Statistics (2000b) *Standard Occupation Classification Volume 2: The Coding Index.* London: Stationery Office.

Great Britain Office for National Statistics (2002) *Index to the UK Standard Industrial Classification of Economic Activities 2003, UK SIC (2003).* London: Stationery Office.

Greenhalgh, T. (1997) 'Papers that summarise other papers (systematic reviews and meta-analyses)', *British Medical Journal*, Vol. 315, pp. 672–5.

Griffiths, M. (1993) 'Productive writing', *The New Academic*, Autumn, pp. 29–31.

Grihault, N. (2007) 'Set-jetting Tourism – International', *Mintel Reports*, Mar., pp. 1–45.

Guba, E. and Lincoln, Y. (1994) 'Competing paradigms in qualitative research', in N.K. Denzin and Y.S. Lincoln (eds) *Handbook of Qualitative Research.* London: Sage, pp. 105–17.

Guest, G., Bunce, A. and Johnson, L. (2006) 'How many interviews are enough? An experiment with data saturation and validity', *Field Methods*, Vol. 18, No. 1, pp. 59–82.

Gummesson, E. (2000) *Qualitative Methods in Management Research* (2nd edn). Thousand Oaks, CA: Sage.

H

Habrakan, A., Schmitz, R. and van Tilberg, P. (2008) 'Searching the World Wide Web: a basic tutorial', Available at: http://www.tilburguniversity.nl/ services/library/instruction/www/onlinecourse [Accessed 21 May 2008.]

Hahn, H. (2008) 'Harley Hahns Internet Yellow Pages', Available at: http://www.harley.com/yp/home.html [Accessed 20 May 2008.]

Hair, J.F., Black, B., Babin, B., Anderson, R.E. and Tatham, R.L. (2006) *Multivariate Data Analysis* (6th edn). Harlow: Pearson Education.

Hakim, C. (1982) *Secondary Analysis in Social Research.* London: Allen & Unwin.

Hakim, C. (2000) *Research Design: Successful Designs for Social and Economic Research* (2nd edn). London: Routledge.

Harley-Davidson (2007) 'Harley-Davidson Inc. 2006 Summary Annual Report'. Available at: http://www.harley-davidson.com/wcm/Content/Pages/Investor_Relations/2006_annual_report_launch.jsp?HDCWPSessi on=9Sv1LnXZHD7LNcXLTPZ4r2kHNryQn1cjl5hbyQjGtJ8 SrswTgltt!1509673641!1097132701&locale=en_US [Accessed 16 December 2007.]

Harrison, R. T. and Mason, C. M. (1992) 'International perspectives on the supply of informal venture capital', *Journal of Business Venturing*, Vol. 7, No. 6, pp. 459–75.

Hart, C. (1998) *Doing a Literature Review.* London: Sage.

Harvard College Library (2006) 'Interrogating Texts: 6 Reading Habits to Develop in Your First Year at Harvard'. Available at: http://hcl.harvard.edu/research/guides/lamont_handouts/interrogatingtexts.html [Accessed 20 May 2008.]

Hays, W.L. (1994) *Statistics.* (4th edn). London: Holt-Saunders.

Healey, M.J. (1991) 'Obtaining information from businesses', in M.J. Healey (ed.) *Economic Activity and Land Use.* Harlow: Longman, pp. 193–251.

Healey, M.J. and Rawlinson, M.B. (1993) 'Interviewing business owners and managers: a review of methods and techniques', *Geoforum*, Vol. 24, No. 3, pp. 339–55.

Healey, M.J. and Rawlinson, M.B. (1994) 'Interviewing techniques in business and management research', in V.J. Wass, V.J. and P.E. Wells (eds) *Principles and Practice in Business and Management Research.* Aldershot: Dartmouth, pp. 123–46.

Heath, A., Martin, J. and Beerton, R. (2003) 'Old and new social class measures', in D. Rose and D.J. Pevalin (eds) *A Researcher's Guide to the National Statistics Socio-economic Classification.* London: Sage, pp. 226–43.

Hedrick, T.E., Bickmann, L. and Rog, D.J. (1993) *Applied Research Design.* Newbury Park, CA: Sage.

Henry, G.T. (1990) *Practical Sampling.* Newbury Park: CA: Sage.

Henry, G.T. (1995) *Graphing Data: Techniques for Display and Analysis.* Thousand Oaks, CA: Sage.

Heron, J. (1996) *Co-operative Inquiry: Research into the Human Condition.* London: Sage.

Hewson, C., Yule, P., Laurent, D. and Vogel, C. (2003) *Internet Research Methods: A Practical Guide for the Social and Behavioural Sciences.* London: Sage.

Hodgkinson, G.P., Herriot, P. and Anderson, N. (2001) 'Re-aligning the stakeholders in management research: lessons from industrial, work and organizational psychology', *British Journal of Management*, Vol. 12, Special Issue, pp. 41–8.

Hodgson, P. (2005) 'The first step in restoring public trust in statistics', *Financial Times*, 1 Dec.

Hofstede, G. (2001) *Culture's Consequences: Comparing Values, Behaviours, Institutions and Organisations Across Nations* (2nd edn). London: Sage.

Hofstede, G.H. (1980) *Culture Consequences: International Differences in Work-related Values.* London: Sage.

Hotel Association of New York City (2006) *Uniform System of Accounts for the Lodging Industry.* East Lansing: American Hotel and Lodging Educational Institute.

Howe, K. (1988) 'Against the quantitative-qualitative incompatibility thesis – or Dogmas die hard', *Educational Researcher*, Vol. 17, No. 8, pp. 10–16.

Hudson, S. and Ritchie, J.R.B. (2006) 'Promoting destinations via film tourism: An empirical identification of supporting marketing initiatives', *Journal of Travel Research*, Vol. 44, May, pp. 387–96.

Huff, A., Tranfield, D. and van Aken, J. (2006) 'Management as a design science mindful of art and surprise. A conversation between Anne Huff, David Tranfield, and Joan Ernst van Aken', *Journal of Management Inquiry*, Vol. 15. No. 4, pp. 413–24.

Huff, A.S. and Huff, J.O. (2001) 'Re-focusing the business school agenda', *British Journal of Management*, Vol. 12, Special Issue, pp. 49–54.

I

Idea Works (2008) 'Methodologist's Toolchest Ex-sample'. Available at: http://www.ideaworks.com/mt/exsample.html [Accessed 2 February 2008.]

Idea Works (2008) 'Methodologist's Toolchest Features'. Available at: http://www.ideaworks.com/mt/index.html [Accessed 19 May 2008.]

Information Commissioners Office (2008) Freedom of Information Act. Available at: http://www.ico.gov.uk/what_we_cover/freedom_of_information.aspx [Accessed 23 May 2008.]

Inspiration (2008) Inspiration homepage. Available at: http://www.inspiration.com [Accessed 21 May 2008.]

Ipsos MORI (2007) 'What do we really think about counterfeiting?' Available at: http://www.ipsos-mori.com/content/what-do-we-really-think-about-counterfeiting.ashx [Accessed 9 June 2008.]

J

Jacob. H. (1994) 'Using published data: errors and remedies', in M.S. Lewis-Beck. (ed.) *Research Practice*. London: Sage and Toppan, pp. 339–89.

Jankowicz, A.D. (2005) *Business Research Projects* (4th edn). London: Thomson Learning.

Janner, G. (1984) *Janner on Presentations*. London: Business Books Ltd.

Johnson, J.M. (1975) *Doing Field Research*. New York, Free Press.

Johnson, P. and Clark, M. (2006) 'Mapping the terrain: an overview of business and management research methodologies', in P. Johnson and M. Clark. (eds). *Business and Management Research Methodologies*. London: Sage.

Johnson, S. (2008) 'FSA warns on derivatives dangers', *Financial Times*, 11 Feb.

K

Kahn, R. and Cannell, C. (1957) *The Dynamics of Interviewing*. New York and Chichester: Wiley.

Kanji, G.K. (2006) *100 Statistical Tests* (3rd edn). London: Sage.

Kay, J. (2007a) 'How I did it' books give me a sinking feeling', *Financial Times*, 28 Aug.

Kay, J. (2007b) 'Research that aids publicists but not the public', *Financial Times*, 30 Oct.

Keaveney, S.M. (1995) 'Customer switching behaviour in service industries: an exploratory study', *Journal of Marketing*, Vol. 59, No. 2, pp. 71–82.

Kellerman, B. (2007) 'What Every Leader Needs to Know About Followers', *Harvard Business Review*, Vol. 85, No. 12, pp. 84–91.

Kelly, G.A. (1955) *The Psychology of Personal Constructs*. New York: Norton.

Kerlinger, F. and Lee, H. (2000) *Foundations of Behavioral Research* (4th edn). Fort Worth, TX: Harcourt College Publishers.

Kersley, B., Alpin, C., Forth, J., Bryson, A., Bewley, H., Dix, G. and Oxenbridge, S. (2006) *Inside the Workplace: Findings from the 2004 Workplace Employment Relations Survey*. London: Routledge.

Kervin, J.B. (1999) *Methods for Business Research* (2nd edn). New York: HarperCollins.

Kindberg, T., Spasojevic, M., Fleck, R. and Sellen, A. (2005) 'The ubiquitous camera: An in-depth study of camera phone use'. Available at: http://www.informatics.sussex.ac.uk/research/groups/interact/publications/ubiquitousCamera.pdf [Accessed 19 May 2007.]

King, N. (2004) 'Using interviews in qualitative research', in C. Cassell and G. Symon (eds) *Essential Guide to Qualitative Methods in Organizational Research*. London: Sage, pp. 11–22.

King, S.A. (1996) 'Researching internet communities: proposed ethical guidelines for the reporting of results', *The Information Society*, Vol. 12, No. 2, pp. 119–27.

Kingsbury, P. (1997) *IT Answers to HR Questions*. London: Institute of Personnel and Development.

Kinnear, P.R. and Gray, C.D. (2007) *SPSS 15 Made Simple*. Hove: Psychology Press.

Kosslyn, S. (2007) *Clear and to the Point: 8 Psychological Principles for Compelling PowerPoint Presentations*. New York: Oxford University Press.

Kotabe, M. (1992a) 'A Comparative Study of US and Japanese Patent Systems', *Journal of International Business Studies*, Vol. 23, No. 1, pp. 147–68.

Kotabe, M. (1992b) 'The Impact of Foreign Patents on National Economy: A Case of the US, Japan, Germany and Britain', *Applied Economics*, Vol. 24, pp. 1335–43.

Kozinets, R. (2002) 'The field behind the screen: using netnography for marketing research in online communities', *Journal of Marketing Research*, Vol. 39, No. 1, pp. 61–72.

Kozinets, R.V. (2006) 'Netnography 2.0', in R.W. Belk (ed.). *Handbook of Qualitative Research Methods in Marketing*. Cheltenham: Edward Elgar Publishing, pp. 129–42.

Krueger, R.A. and Casey, M.A. (2000) *Focus Groups: A Practical Guide for Applied Research* (3rd edn), Thousand Oaks, CA: Sage.

L

Langer, R. and Beckman, S.C. (2005) 'Sensitive research topics: netnography revisited. *Qualitative Market Research*', Vol. 8, No. 2, pp. 189–203.

Lavrakas, P.J. (1993) *Telephone Survey Methods: Sampling, Selection and Supervision*. Newbury Park, CA: Sage.

Lee, N. and Broderick, A. (2007) 'The past, present and future of observational research in marketing', *Qualitative Market Research*, Vol. 10, No. 2, pp. 121–29.

Lee, R.M. (1993) *Doing Research on Sensitive Topic*, London: Sage.

Lemelson-MIT Program (2007) 'Art Fry and Spencer Silver'. Available at: http://web.mit.edu/invent/iow/frysilver.html [Accessed 19 December 2007.]

Library Association (2005) *Libraries in the United Kingdom and Republic of Ireland*. London: Library Assocation.

Lichtenstein, S., Williamson, K. and Sturt, C. (2006) 'Understanding consumer adoption of Internet banking: an interpretive study in the Australian banking context', *Journal of Electronic Commerce Research*, Vol. 7, No. 2, pp. 50–66.

M

Mackenzie, K.D. (2000a) 'Knobby analyses of knobless survey items, part I: The approach', *International Journal of Organizational Analysis*, Vol. 8, No. 2, pp. 131–54.

Mackenzie, K.D. (2000b) 'Knobby analyses of knobless survey items, part II: An application', *International Journal of Organizational Analysis*, Vol. 8, No. 3, pp. 238–61.

Mann, C. and Stewart, F. (2000) *Internet Communication and Qualitative Research: A Handbook for Researching Online*. London: Sage.

Markham, C. (1997) *Practical Management Consultancy* (3rd edn). Milton Keynes: Accountancy Books (ICAE&W).

Marshall, C. and Rossman, G.B. (1999) *Designing Qualitative Research* (3rd edn). Thousand Oaks, CA: Sage.

Marshall, C. and Rossman, G.B. (2006) *Designing Qualitative Research* (4th edn). Thousand Oaks, CA: Sage.

Mason, C.M. & Harrison, R.T. (1997) 'Developing the informal venture capital market in the UK: Is there still a role for public sector business angel networks?', *Small Business Economics*, Vol. 9, No. 2, pp. 111–23.

Maylor, H. and Blackmon, K. (2005) *Researching Business and Management*. Basingstoke: Palgrave Macmillan.

McKenzie, E. (2003) *Guide to Libraries in Key UK Companies*. London: British Library.

McMillan, E. (2004) *Complexity, Organizations and Change*. London: Routledge.

McNeill, P. (2005) *Research Methods* (3rd edn). London: Routledge.

McNiff, J. with Whitehead, J. (2000) *Action Research in Organizations*. London: Routledge.

Meyer, H., Kay, E. and French, J. (1965) 'Split roles in performance appraisal', *Harvard Business Review*, Vol. 43, No. 1, pp. 123–29.

Michael Peel, M. and Timmins, N. (2007) 'Watchdog in call for criminal sanctions', *Financial Times*, 22 Nov.

Miller, D., Le Breton-Miller, I. and Scholnick, B. (2008) 'Stewardship versus stagnation: An empirical comparison of small family and non-family businesses', *Journal of Management Studies,* Vol. 45, No.1, pp. 51–78.

Miller, D.C. and Salkind, N.J. (eds) (2002) *Handbook of Research Design and Social Measurement* (6th edn). Thousand Oaks, CA: Sage.

Miller, R.L (2007) *Researching Life Stories and Family Histories*. London: Sage.

Millward, N., Stevens, M., Smart, D. and Hawes, W.R. (1992) *Workplace Industrial Relations in Transition*. Aldershot: Dartmouth.

MindGenius (2008) MindGenius homepage. Available at: http://www.mindgenius.com/website/presenter. aspx?type=doc&uri=/home.htm#topofpage [Accessed 21 May 2008.]

Mingers, J. (2000) 'What is it to be critical? Teaching a critical approach to management undergraduates', *Management Learning*, Vol. 31, No. 2, pp. 219–37.

Mintzberg, H. (1973) *The Nature of Managerial Work*. New York: Harper & Row.

Mintzberg, H. and Waters, J. (1989) 'Of strategies, deliberate and emergent', in D. Asch and C. Bowman (eds) *Readings in Strategic Management*. Basingstoke: Macmillan Education, pp. 4–19.

Mitchell, V. (1996) 'Assessing the reliability and validity of questionnaires: an empirical example', *Journal of Applied Management Studies*, Vol. 5, No. 2, pp. 199–207.

Möller, C., Weiermair, K. and Wintersberger, E. (2007) 'The changing travel behaviour of Austria's ageing population and its impact on tourism', *Tourism Review*, Vol. 62, Nos. 3/4, pp. 15–20.

Moody, P.E. (1988) *Decision Making: Proven Methods for Better Decisions* (2nd edn). Maidenhead, McGraw-Hill.

Morgan, S.J. and Symon, G. (2004) 'Electronic interviews in organizational research', in C. Cassell and G. Symon (eds), *Essential Guide to Qualitative Methods in Organizational Research*. London: Sage, pp. 3–33.

Morris, C. (2003) *Quantitative Approaches in Business Studies* (6th edn). Harlow: Financial Times Prentice Hall.

Morris, T. and Wood, S. (1991) 'Testing the survey method: continuity and change in British industrial relations',

Work Employment and Society, Vol. 5, No. 2, pp. 259–82.

Mullins, L. (2002) *Management and Organisational Behaviour* (6th edn). Harlow: Financial Times Prentice Hall.

Murray, A., Sinclair, D., Power, D. and Gray, R. (2006) 'Do financial markets care about social and environmental disclosure? Further evidence from the UK', *Accounting, Auditing & Accountability Journal*, Vol. 19, No. 2, pp. 228–55.

Mychasuk, E. and Terazono, E. (2008) 'Sir Adrian's thorn', *Financial Times*, 29 May.

N

Naipaul, V.S. (1989) *A Turn in the South*. London: Penguin.

Nando's (2008) 'Talk to us'. Available at: http://www.nandos.co.uk/faq/CU/Contact_Us.html# [Accessed 27 April 2008.]

National Patient Safety Agency (2007) *Defining Research* (Issue 3). London, National Patient Safety Agency.

Neuman, W.L. (2005) *Social Research Methods* (6th edn). London: Pearson.

Neville, C. (2007) *The Complete Guide to Referencing and Avoiding Plagiarism*. Maidenhead: Open University Press.

North, D.J., Leigh, R. and Gough, J. (1983) 'Monitoring industrial change at the local level: some comments on methods and data sources', in M.J. Healey (ed.) *Urban and Regional Industrial Research: The Changing UK Data Base*. Norwich: Geo Books, pp. 111–29.

Norusis, M.J. (2007) *SPSS 15 Guide to Data Analysis*. London: Prentice Hall.

O

O'Connor, H. and Madge, C. (2003) 'Focus groups in cyberspace: using the Internet for qualitative research', *Qualitative Market Research: An International Journal*, Vol. 6, No. 2, pp. 133–43.

Office for National Statistics (2001) '200 years of the census'. Available at: http://www.statistics.gov.uk/census2001/bicentenary/pdfs/200years.pdf [Accessed 23 May 2008.]

Office for National Statistics (2007a) 'Annual Survey of Hours and Earnings (ASHE) 2007 Results'. Available at: http://www.statistics.gov.uk/statBase/product.asp?vlnk=13101 [Accessed 21 May 2008.]

Office for National Statistics (2007b) 'Family spending – A report on the expenditure and food survey'. Available at: http://www.statistics.gov.uk/StatBase/Product.asp?vlnk=361 [Accessed 23 May 2008.]

Office for National Statistics (2007c) 'Labour force survey'. Available at: http://www.statistics.gov.uk/StatBase/Source.asp?vlnk=358&More=Y [Accessed 23 May 2008.]

Office for National Statistics (2007d) 'Social trends'. Available at: http://www.statistics.gov.uk/statbase/Product.asp?vlnk=5748&More=Y [Accessed 21 May 2008.]

Office for National Statistics (2008) 'Annual abstract of statistics'. Available at: http://www.statistics.gov.uk/statbase/Product.asp?vlnk=94&More=Y [Accessed 23 May 2008.]

Okazaki, S. and Mueller, B. (2007) 'Cross-cultural advertising research: where we have been and where we need to go', *International Marketing Review*, Vol. 24, No. 5, pp. 499–518.

Okumus, F., Altinay, L. and Roper, A. (2007) 'Gaining access for research: Reflections from experience', *Annals of Tourism Research*, Vol. 34, No. 1, pp. 7–26.

Oppenheim, A.N. (2000) *Questionnaire Design, Interviewing and Attitude Measurement* (new edn). London: Continuum International.

Oravec, J.A. (2004) 'Incremental understandings: warblogs and peaceblogs in peace education', *Journal of Peace Education*, Vol. 1, No. 2, pp. 225–38.

Orr, R. and Hume, N. (2007) 'Rock faces FTSE 100 exit', *Financial Times* 12 Dec.

Owen, D. (2008) 'Adventures in social and environmental accounting and auditing research: A personal reflection', in C. Humphrey and B. Lee (eds) *The Real Life Guide to Accounting Research*. Oxford: Elsevier/CIMA.

P

Palmer, M. (2008) 'BT keeps an eye on surfing habits in quest for better advert targeting', *Financial Times*, 24 May.

Pan, B., MacLaurin, T. and Crotts, J.C. (2007) 'Travel blogs and the implications for destination marketing', *Journal of Travel Research*, Vol. 46, Aug., pp. 35–45.

Park, A., Curtice, J., Thomson, K., Phillips, M., Johnson, M. and Clery, E. (2007) *British Social Attitudes: 24th Report*. London: Sage.

Park, C. (2003) 'In other (people's) words: plagiarism by university students – literature and lessons', *Assessment & Evaluation in Higher Education*, Vol. 28, No. 5, pp. 471–88.

Parry, H. (1991) *Successful Business Presentations*. Kingston-upon-Thames: Croner.

Patten, D.M. (1992) 'Intra-industry environmental disclosure in response to the Alaskan oil spill: A note on legitimacy theory', *Accounting, Organisations and Society*, Vol. 17, pp. 471–75.

Patton, M.Q. (2002) *Qualitative Research and Evaluation Methods* (3rd edn). Thousand Oaks, CA: Sage.

Patzer, G.L. (1996) *Using Secondary Data in Market Research: United States and World-wide.* Westport. CT: Quorum Books.

Pearsall, J. (ed.) (1998) *The New Oxford English Dictionary.* Oxford: Oxford University Press.

Penn, R. (2005) 'Football spectators in English and Italian stadia'. Available at: http://www.maths.lancs.ac.uk/~penn/papers/roger/FootballSpectators/Football_Spectators_in_English_and_Italian_Stadia.html [Accessed 24 May 2008.]

Peters, T. and Waterman, R. (1982) *In Search of Excellence.* New York: Harper & Row.

Pettigrew, A.M (2001) 'Management research after modernism', *British Journal of Management*, Vol. 12(S), pp. 61–70.

Phillips, E.M. and Pugh, D.S. (2005) *How to get a PhD* (4th edn). Maidenhead: Open University Press.

Powney, J. and Watts, M. (1987) *Interviewing in Educational Research.* London: Routledge and Kegan Paul.

Punch, M. (1993) 'Observation and the police: the research experience', in M. Hammersley, *Social Research: Philosophy. Politics and Practice.* London: Sage, pp. 181–99.

Push (2007) 'Push reveals the real costs of higher education'. Available at: http://www.push.co.uk/Document.aspx?id=9E3FCB0D-7275-4BF3-BFA4-8AEEF1D847D1&section=&l2section [Accessed 16 December 2007.]

Q

Quinton, S. and Smallbone, T. (2005) 'The troublesome triplets: issues in teaching reliability, validity and generalisation to business students', *Teaching in Higher Education*, Vol. 10, No. 3, pp. 299–311.

R

Raimond, P. (1993) *Management Projects.* London, Chapman & Hall.

Rawlins, K. (1999) *Presentation and Communication Skills: A Handbook for Practitioners.* London: Emap Healthcare Ltd.

Reichardt, C. and Rallis, S. (1994) 'Qualitative and quantitative inquiries are not incompatible: A call for a new partnership', in C. Reichardt and S. Rallis (eds). *The Qualitative-Quantitative Debate: New Perspectives.* San Francisco: Jossey-Bass.

Reichman, C.S. (1970) *Use and Abuse of Statistics.* New York: Oxford University Press.

Remenyi, D., Williams, B., Money, A. and Swartz, E. (1998) *Doing Research in Business and Management: An Introduction to Process and Method.* London: Sage.

Research Randomizer (2008) Research Randomizer. Available at: http://www.randomizer.org/index.htm [Accessed 20 March 2008.]

Riach, K. and Wilson, F. (2007) 'Don't screw the crew: Exploring the rules of engagement in organisational romance', *British Journal of Management*, Vol. 18, No.1, pp. 79–92.

Richards, P. (1986) 'Risk', in H. Becker, *Writing for Social Scientists.* Chicago, IL: University of Chicago Press, pp. 108–20.

Robson, C. (2002) *Real World Research* (2nd edn). Oxford: Blackwell.

Rogelberg, S.G. and Stanton, J.M. (2007) 'Understanding and dealing with organizational survey nonresponse', *Organizational Research Methods*, Vol. 10, pp. 195–208.

Rogers, C.R. (1961) *On Becoming a Person.* London: Constable.

Rose, D. and Pevalin, D.J. (2003) 'The NS-SEC explained', in D. Rose and D.J. Pevalin (eds) *A Researcher's Guide to the National Statistics Socio-economic Classification.* London: Sage, pp. 28–43.

Rosen, M. (1991) 'Breakfast at Spiros dramaturgy and dominance', in P. Frost, L. Moore, M. Louis, C. Lundberg and J. Martin (eds) *Reframing Organisational Culture.* Newbury Park, CA: Sage, pp. 77–89.

Rousseau, D. (2006) 'Is there such a thing as "evidence-based management"?', *Academy of Management Review*, Vol. 31, No. 2, pp. 256–69.

Rowntree, D. (1987) *Assessing Students: How Shall We Know Them?* (revised edn). London: Harper & Row.

Roy, D. (1952) 'Quota restriction and goldbricking in a machine shop', *American Journal of Sociology*, Vol. 57, pp. 427–42.

S

Sadri, G. and Marcoulides, G.A (1997) 'An examination of academic and occupational stress in the USA', *International Journal of Educational Management*, Vol. 11, No. 1, pp. 32–43.

Sauer, I.M., Bialek, D., Efimova, E., Schwartlander, R., Pless, G. and Neuhaus, P. (2005) '"Blogs" and "wikis" are valuable software tools for communication within research groups', *Artificial Organs*, Vol. 29, No. 1, pp. 82–9.

Saunders, M., Lewis, P. and Thornhill, A. (2007) *Research Methods for Business Students* (4th edn). Harlow: FT Prentice Hall.

Saunders, M.N.K. and Lewis, P. (1997) 'Great ideas and blind alleys? A review of the literature on starting research', *Management Learning*, Vol. 28, No. 3, pp. 283–99.

Scandura, T.A. and Williams, E.A. (2000) 'Research Methods in Management Current Practices, Trends, and Implications for Future Research', *Academy of Management Journal*, Vol. 43, No. 6, pp. 1248–64.

Schein, E. (1999) *Process Consultation Revisited: Building the Helping Relationship.* Reading, MA: Addison-Wesley.

Schein, E.H. (2004) *Organizational Culture and Leadership* (3rd edn). San Francisco, CA: Jossey-Bass.

Schneider, L.-P. and Cornwell, T.B. (2005) 'Cashing in on crashes via brand placement in computer games', *International Journal of Advertising*, Vol. 24, No. 3, pp. 321–43.

Schraeder, M. and Self, D. (2003) 'Enhancing the success of mergers and acquisitions: An organisational culture perspective', *Management Decision*, Vol. 41, No. 5, pp. 511–22.

Schrauf, R.W. and Navarro, E. (2005) 'Using Existing Tests and Scales in the Field', *Field Methods*, Vol. 17, No. 4, pp. 373–93.

Searcy, D.L. and Mentzer, J.T. (2003) 'A framework for conducting and evaluating research, *Journal of Accounting Literature*', Vol. 22, pp. 130–67.

Sekaran, U. (2003) *Research Methods for Business – A Skill Building Approach* (4th edn). New York: John Wiley & Sons.

Serwer, A. (2001) 'P&G's covert operation: an intelligence-gathering campaign against Unilever went way too far', *Fortune Magazine*, 17 Sept. Available at: http://money.cnn.com/magazines/ fortune/fortune_archive/2001/09/17/310274/index.htm [Accessed 11 April 2008.]

Shapiro, D., Kirkman, B. and Courtney, H. (2007) 'Perceived causes and solutions of the translation problem in management research', *Academy of Management Journal*, Vol. 50, No. 2, pp. 249–66.

Sharp, J., Peters, J. and Howard, K. (2002) *The Management of a Student Research Project* (3rd edn). Aldershot: Gower.

Silverman, D. (2007) *A Very Short, Fairly Interesting and Reasonably Cheap Book about Qualitative Research.* London: Sage.

Smircich, L. (1983) 'Concepts of culture and organisational analysis', *Administrative Science Quarterly*, Vol. 28, No. 3, pp. 339–58.

Smith, A. (2002) 'The new ethnicity classification in the Labour Force Survey', *Labour Market Trends*, December, pp. 657–66.

Smith, C.B. (1991) *A Guide to Business Research.* Chicago, IL: Nelson-Hall.

Smith, H. (1981) *Strategies of Social Research: The Methodological Imagination* (2nd edn). Englewood Cliffs, NJ: Prentice-Hall.

Smith, N.C. and Dainty, P. (1991) *The Management Research Handbook.* London: Routledge.

Snap Surveys (2008) 'Snap Surveys: the complete survey solution'. Available at: http://www.snapsurveys.com [Accessed 20 April 2008.]

Sparrow, J. (1989) 'Graphic displays in information systems: some data properties influencing the effectiveness of alternate forms', *Behaviour and Information Technology*, Vol. 8, No. 1, pp. 43–56.

Sphinx Development (2008) Sphinx Development. Available at: http://www.sphinxdevelopment.co.uk/ [Accessed 20 April 2008.]

Sphinx (2008) 'Sphinx data analysis and survey softwares'. Available at: http://www.lesphinx-developpement.fr/en/home/home_sphinx.php [Accessed 1 January 2008.]

Srivastava, S. (2007) 'Green supply-chain management: A state-of-the-art literature review', *International Journal of Management Review*, Vol. 9, No. 1, pp. 53–80.

Starkey, K. and Madan, P. (2001) 'Bridging the relevance gap: aligning stakeholders in the future of management research', *British Journal of Management*, Vol. 12, Special Issue, pp. 3–26.

Starr, R. and Fernandez, K. (2007) 'The mindcam methodology: Perceiving through the natives eye', *Qualitative Market Research*, Vol. 10, No. 2, pp. 168–82.

Stewart, D.W. and Kamins, M.A. (1993) *Secondary Research: Information Sources and Methods* (2nd edn). Newbury Park, CA: Sage.

Stokes, D. and Bergin, R. (2006) 'Methodology or "methodolatry"? An evaluation of focus groups and depth interviews', *Qualitative Market Research*, Vol. 9, No. 1, pp. 26–37.

Strauss, A. and Corbin, J. (2008) *Basics of Qualitative Research* (3rd edn). Thousand Oaks, CA: Sage.

Stutely, M. (2003) *Numbers Guide: The Essentials of Business Numeracy.* London: Bloomberg Press.

Suddaby, R. (2006) 'From the editors: what grounded theory is not', *Academy of Management Journal*, Vol. 49, No. 4, pp. 633–42.

SurveyMonkey.com (2008) SurveyMonkey.com. Available at: http://www.surveymonkey.com [Accessed 29 June 2008.]

Suthersanen, U. (2006) Utility Models and Innovation in Developing Countries, UNCTAD-ICTSD: Geneva.

Sutton, R. and Staw, B. (1995) 'What theory is not', *Administrative Science Quarterly*, Vol. 40, No. 3, pp. 371–84.

Sweet, C. (2001) 'Designing and conducting virtual focus groups', *Qualitative Market Research*, Vol. 4, No. 3, pp. 130–35.

Sydney Morning Herald (2008) 'Revealed: the most violent pubs and club', 11 Mar.

Sykes, W. (1991) 'Taking stock: issues from the literature in validity and reliability in qualitative research', *Journal of Market Research Society*, Vol. 33, No. 1, pp. 3–12.

T

Tasci, A.D.A. and Gartner, W.C. (2007) 'Destination image and its functional relationships', *Journal of Travel Research*, Vol. 45, No. 4, pp. 413–25.

Tashakkori, A. and Teddlie, C. (1998) *Mixed Methodology: Combining Qualitative and Quantitative Approaches.* Thousand Oaks, CA: Sage.

Tashakkori, A. and Teddlie, C. (eds) (2003) *Handbook of Mixed Methods in Social and Behavioural Research.* Thousand Oaks, CA: Sage.

Taylor, B. (2007) 'More poll questions than answers'. Available at: http://news.bbc.co.uk/1/hi/scotland/6264483.stm [Accessed 14 April 2008.]

Tharenou, P., Donohue, R. and Cooper, B. (2007) *Management Research Methods.* Melbourne: Cambridge University Press.

The Stationery Office (1998) *Data Protection Act 1998.* London: Stationery Office.

The Suzy Lamplugh Trust (2006) 'Personal Safety Alone in the Workplace'. Available at: http://www.suzylamplugh.org/files/pdfs/guidance%20pdfs/aloneinworkplace.pdf [Accessed 4 April 2008.]

Thomas, M. (2003) *High-Performance Consulting Skills.* London: Thorgood.

Thornhill, A., Saunders, M.N.K. and Stead, J. (1997) 'Downsizing, delayering but where's the commitment? The development of a diagnostic tool to help manage survivors', *Personnel Review*, Vol. 26, No. 1/2, pp. 81–98.

Torrington, D. (1991) *Management Face to Face.* London: Prentice Hall.

Tranfield, D. and Denyer, D. (2004) 'Linking theory to practice: a grand challenge for management research in the 21st century?', *Organization Management Journal*, Vol. 1, No. 1, pp. 10–14.

Tranfield, D. and Starkey, K. (1998) 'The nature, social organization and promotion of management research: towards policy', *British Journal of Management*, Vol. 9, pp. 341–53.

Tranfield, D., Denyer, D. and Smart, P. (2003) 'Towards a methodology for developing evidence-informed management knowledge by means of systematic review', *British Journal of Management*, Vol. 14, No. 3, pp. 207–22.

Tucker, C. and Lepkowski, J.M. (2008) 'Telephone survey methods: adapting to change', in J.M. Lepkowski, C. Tucker, J.M. Brick, E.D. De Leeuw, L. Japec, P.J. Lavrakas, M.W. Link and R.L. Sangster, *Advances in Telephone Survey Methodology.* Hoboken, NJ: Wiley, pp. 3–28.

Tukey, J.W. (1977) *Exploratory Data Analysis.* Reading, MA: Addison-Wesley.

U

UK Data Archive (2008) UK Data Archive. Available at: http://www.data-archive.ac.uk/ [Accessed 23 May 2008.]

Usunier, J.-C. (1998) *International and Cross-Cultural Management Research.* London: Sage.

V

Valck, K., Langerak, F., Verhoef, P.C. and Verhoef, P.W.J. (2007) 'Satisifaction with virtual communities of interest: Effect of members' visit frequency', *British Journal of Management*, Vol. 18, No. 3, pp. 241–56.

Van De Ven, A. and Johnson, P. (2006) 'Knowledge for theory and practice', *Academy of Management Review*, Vol. 31, No. 4, pp. 802–21.

Van Osnabrugge, M. and Robinson, R.J. (2000) *Angel Investing: Matching Start-up Funds with Start-up Companies – The Guide for Entrepreneurs, Individual Investors, and Venture Capitalists.* San Francisco: Jossey-Bass.

Veroff, J. (2001) 'Writing', in K. Rudestam and R. Newton (eds) *Surviving your Dissertation* (2nd edn). Newbury Park, CA: Sage.

W

Walker, A. (2002) *Living in Britain: Results from the 2000 General Household Survey.* London: Stationery Office.

Walker, R. (1985) *Doing Research: A Handbook for Teachers.* London: Methuen.

Wallace, M. and Wray, A. (2006) *Critical Reading and Writing for Postgraduates.* London: Sage.

Walliman, N. (2005) *Your Research Project: A Step by Step Guide for the First-Time Researcher* (2nd edn). London: Sage.

Wass, V. and Wells, P. (1994) 'Research methods in action: an introduction', in V.J. Wass and P.E. Wells (eds) *Principles and Practice in Business and Management Research.* Aldershot: Dartmouth, pp. 1–34.

Wells, P. (1994) 'Ethics in business and management research', *in* V.J. Wass and P.E. Wells (eds) *Principles and Practice in Business and Management Research.* Aldershot: Dartmouth, pp. 277–97.

Westfall, R.D. (1997) 'Does telecommuting really increase productivity? Fifteen rival hypotheses', AIS Americas Conference, Indianapolis, IN, 15–17 Aug.

Wheatley, R. (2000) *Taking the Strain. A Survey of Managers and Workplace Stress.* London: Institute of Management.

Whetten, D. (1989) 'What constitutes a theoretical contribution?', *Academy of Management Review*, Vol. 14, No. 4, pp. 490–5.

Whyte, W. (1955) *Street Corner Society* (2nd edn). Chicago, IL: University of Chicago Press.

Wickham, P. and Wickham, L. (2008) *Management Consulting: Delivering an Effective Project* (3rd edn). Harlow: Pearson Education.

Wikipedia (2008) Wikipedia home page. Available at: http://www.wikipedia.org [Accessed 21 May 2008.]

Williams, C.S. and Saunders, M.N.K. (2006) 'Developing the Service Template: From measurement to agendas for improvement', *Service Industries Journal*, Vol. 26, No. 5, pp. 1–15.

Willimack, D.K., Nichols, E. and Sudman, S. (2002) 'Understanding unit and item nonresponse in business surveys', in D.A. Dillman, J.L. Eltringe, J.L. Groves and R.J.A. Little (eds) *Survey Nonresponse*. New York: Wiley Interscience, pp. 213–27.

Witmer, D.F., Colman, R.W. and Katzman, S.L. (1999) 'From paper and pen to screen and keyboard: towards a methodology for survey research on the Internet', in S. Jones (ed) *Doing Internet Research*. Thousand Oaks, CA: Sage, pp. 145–62.

Wolf, A. (2007) 'People have a tendency to assume that quantitative data must be out there on the web waiting to be found', *The Times Higher Education Supplement*, 12 Oct. Available at: http://www.timeshighereducation.co.uk/story. asp?sectioncode=26&storycode=310797 [Accessed 23 May 2008.]

Wright Mills, C. (1970) 'On intellectual craftsmanship', in C. Wright Mills, *The Sociological Imagination*. London: Pelican.

Y

Yang, D. (2008) 'Pendency and grant ratios on invention patents: A comparative study of the US and China', *Research Policy*. Available at: http://dx.doi.org/10.1016/j.respol.2008.03.008 [Accessed 14 May 2008.]

Yen, T.-Y. and André, P. (2007) 'Ownership structure and operating performance of acquiring firms: the case of English-origin countries', *Journal of Economics and Business*, Vol. 59, No. 5, pp. 380–405.

Yin, R.K. (2003) *Case Study Research: Design and Method* (3rd edn). London: Sage.

Z

Zikmund, W.G. (2000) *Business Research Methods* (6th edn). Fort Worth, TX: Dryden Press.

Appendix 1 Styles of referencing

Preferred styles of referencing differ both between universities and between departments within universities. Even styles that are in wide use such as 'Harvard' vary in how they are used in practice by different institutions. When this is combined with the reality that some lecturers apply an adopted style strictly, whilst others are more lenient, it emphasises the need for you to use the precise style prescribed in your assessment criteria. Within business and management, two referencing styles predominate, the Harvard style and the American Psychological Association (APA) style, both of which are author-date systems. The alternative, numeric systems, are used far less widely.

Four points are important when referencing:

- Credit must be given when quoting or citing other's work.
- Adequate information must be provided in the reference to enable that work to be located.
- References must be consistent and complete.
- References must be recorded using precisely the style required by your university.

Author-date systems

The Harvard style

Referencing in the text

The Harvard style is an author-date *system*, a variation of which we use in this book. It appears to have its origins in a referencing practice developed by a professor of anatomy at Harvard University (Neville 2007) and usually uses the author's name and year of publication to identify cited documents within the text. All references are listed alphabetically at the end of the text. Common variations within the Harvard style which are applied consistently include (Neville 2007):

- Name(s) of authors or organisations may or may not be in UPPER CASE.
- Where there are more than two authors, the names of the second and subsequent authors may or may not be replaced by *et al.* in *italics*.
- The year of publication may or may not be enclosed in (brackets).
- The title of the publication may be in *italics* or may be <u>underlined</u>.

The style for referencing work in the text is outlined in Table A1.1.

Referencing in the references or bibliography

In the references or bibliography the publications are listed alphabetically by author's name, and all authors' surnames and initials are normally listed in full. If there is more than one work by the same author, these are listed chronologically. The style for referencing work in the references or bibliography is outlined in Table A1.2. While it would be impossible for us to include

Table A1.1 Using the Harvard style to reference in the text

To refer to	Use the general format	For example
A single author	(Surname year)	(Saunders 2007)
Dual authors	(Surname and Surname year)	(Saunders and Thornhill 2006)
More than two authors	(Surname *et al.* year)	(Lewis *et al.* 2004)
Work by different authors generally	(Surname year, Surname year) in alphabetical order	(Cassell 2004, Dillman 2000, Robson 2002)
Different authors with the same surname	(Surname Initial year)	(Smith J 2008)
Different works by the same author	(Surname year, year) in ascending year order	(Saunders 2004, 2005)
Different works by the same author from the same year	(Surname year letter), make sure the letter is consistent throughout	(de Vita 2006a)
An author referred to by another author where the original has not been read (*secondary reference*)	(Surname year, cited by Surname year)	(Granovetter 1974, cited by Saunders 1993)
A corporate author	(Corporate name year)	(Harley-Davidson Inc. 2008)
A newspaper article with no obvious author	(Newspaper name year)	(The Guardian 2008)
Another type of work with no obvious author	(Publication title year)	(Labour Market Trends 2005)
An Internet site	(Source organisation year)	(Financial Times 2008)
A television or radio programme	(Television or radio programme series title year)	(Today Programme 2008)
A commercial DVD or video that is part of a series	(DVD or video series title year)	(The Office Series 1 and 2 2005)
A commercial DVD or video that is not part of a series	(DVD or video title year)	(One Flew Over the Cuckoo's Nest 2002)
A work for which the year of publication cannot be identified	(Surname or Corporate name nd), where 'nd' means no year	(Woollons nd)
	(Surname or Corporate name c. year) where 'c.' means circa	(Hattersley c. 2004)
A direct quotation	(Surname or Corporate name, year, p. ###) where 'p.' means 'page' and ### is the page in the original publication on which the quotation appears	'Whenever an employee's job ceases to exist it is potentially fair to dismiss that person.' (Lewis *et al.* 2003, p. 350)

Table A1.2 Using the Harvard style to reference in the references or bibliography

To reference		Use the general format	For example
Books, chapters in books and brochures	Book (first edition)	Surname, Initials. and Surname, Initials. (year). *Title.* Place of publication: Publisher.	Berman Brown, R. and Saunders, M. (2008). *Dealing with statistics: What you need to know.* Maidenhead: Open University Press.
	Book (other than first edition)	Surname, Initials. and Surname, Initials. (year). *Title.* (# edn) Place of publication: Publisher.	Morris, C. (2003). *Quantitative approaches to business studies.* (6th edn). London: Financial Times Pitman Publishing.
	Book (no obvious author)	Corporate name or Publication name. (year). *Title.* Place of publication: Publisher.	Mintel Marketing Intelligence. (1998). *Designerwear: Mintel marketing intelligence report.* London: Mintel International Group Ltd.
	Chapter in a book	Surname, Initials. and Surname, Initials. (year). *Title.* Place of publication: Publisher. Chapter #.	Robson, C. (2002). *Real World Research.* (2nd edn). Oxford: Blackwell. Chapter 3.
	Chapter in an edited book containing a collection of articles (sometimes called a reader)	Surname, Initials. (year). Chapter title. In Initials. Surname and Initials. Surname (eds) *Title.* Place of publication: Publisher. pp. ###-###.	King, N. (2004). Using templates in the thematic analysis of text. In C. Cassell and J. Symon (eds) *Essential guide to qualitative methods in organizational research.* London: Sage. pp. 256–270.
	Dictionary and other reference books where is an author or editor and referring to particular entry	Surname, Initials. (year). *Title.* (# edn). Place of Publication: Publisher. pp. ###–###.	Vogt, W.P. (2005). *Dictionary of statistics and methodology: a nontechnical guide for the social sciences.* (3rd edn). Thousand Oaks, CA: Sage. pp. 124–5.
	Dictionary and other reference books where no author or editor and referring to particular entry	*Title.* (year). (# edn). Place of Publication: Publisher. pp. ###–###.	*The right word at the right time.* (1985). Pleasantville, NY: Readers Digest Association. pp. 563–4.
	Brochure	Corporate name or Publication name. (year). *Title.* Place of publication: as for author.	Harley-Davidson Europe. (2007). *2008 make every day count.* Oxford: Harley-Davidson Europe.
	Republished book	Surname, Initials. and Surname, Initials. (year). *Title.* Place of publication: Publisher (originally published by Publisher year).	Marshall, J.D. (1981). *Furness and the industrial revolution.* Beckermont: Michael Moon (originally published by Barrow Town Council 1958).
Journal and magazine articles	Journal article (originally printed but same as found online)	Surname, Initials. and Surname, Initials. (year). Title of article. *Journal name.* Vol. ##, No. ##, pp. ###–####.	Storey, J., Cressey, P., Morris, T. and Wilkinson, A. (1997). Changing employment practices in UK banking: case studies. *Personnel Review.* Vol. 26, No. 1, pp. 24–42.

Table A1.2 (continued)

To reference		Use the general format	For example
	Journal article only published online	Surname, Initials. and Surname, Initials. (year). Title of article, *Journal name*, Vol. ##, No. ##, pp. ###–###. Available at http:// www. remainderoffullInternetaddress/ [Accessed day month year].	Illingworth, N. (2001). The Internet matters: exploring the use of the Internet as a research tool. *Sociological Research Online*, Vol. 6, No. 2. Available at http://www.socresonline.org.uk/6/2/ illingworth.html [Accessed 20 Mar. 2002].
	Journal article for which corrected proofs are available online but which is still to be published	Surname, Initials. and Surname, Initials. (year). Title of article, *Journal name*. Available at http://www. fulldoiInternetaddress/ [Accessed day month year].	Yang, D. (2008). Pendency and grant ratios on invention patents: A Comparative Study of the US and China, *Research Policy*. Available at http://dx.doi.org/10.1016/j.respol.2008. 03.008 [Accessed 14 May 2008].
	Magazine article (no obvious author)	Corporate name or Publication name. (year). Title of article. *Magazine name*. Vol. ##, No. ## (or day month), p. ###.	Quality World. (2007). Immigration abuse. *Quality World*. Vol. 33, No 12, p. 6.
Government publications	Parliamentary papers including acts and bills	Country of origin. (year) *Title*. Place of publication: Publisher.	United Kingdom. (2005). *The Prevention of Terrorism Act*. London: The Stationery Office.
	Others (with authors)	As for books	As for books
	Others (no obvious authors)	Department name or Committee name. (year). *Title*. Place of publication: Publisher.	Department of Trade and Industry. (1992). *The Single Market: Europe Open for Professions, UK Implementation*. London: HMSO.
Newspapers, including CD-ROM databases	Newspaper article	Surname, Initials. and Surname, Initials. Title of article. *Newspaper name*, day month year, p. ## (where known).	Hawkes, S. Umbro slashes England shirt production. *The Times*. 24 Nov. 2007, p. 63.
	Newspaper article (no obvious author)	Newspaper name. Title of article, day month year, p. ## (where known).	The Times. Business big shot Steve Mankin, 24 Nov. 2007, p. 63.
	Newspaper article (from CD-ROM database, no obvious author)	Newspaper name. Title of article, day month year, [CD-ROM]. p. ## (where known).	Financial Times. Recruitment: lessons in leadership: moral issues are increasingly pertinent to the military and top corporate ranks, 11 Mar. 1998. [CD-ROM]. p. 32.
Other CD-ROM publications	CD-ROM	Surname, Initials. and surname, initials. (year). *Title of CD-ROM*. [CD-ROM]. Place of publication: Publisher.	Friedman, M., Friedman, R. and Adams, J. (2007). *Free to chase*. [CD-ROM]. Ashland, OR: Blackstone Audiobooks.

Table A1.2 *(continued)*

To reference		Use the general format	For example
	CD-ROM, no obvious author	Title of CD-ROM. (year). [CD-ROM]. Place of publication: Publisher.	Encarta 2006 Encyclopaedia. (2005). [CD-ROM]. Redmond, WA: Microsoft.
Unpublished conference papers		Surname, Initials. and Surname, Initials. (year). *Title of paper.* Unpublished paper presented at 'Conference name'. Location of conference, day month year.	Saunders, M.N.K., Thornhill, A. and Evans, C. (2007). *Conceptualising trust and distrust and the role of boundaries: an organisationally based exploration.* Unpublished paper presented at 'EIASM 4th Workshop on Trust Within and Between Organisations'. Amsterdam, 25–26 Oct. 2007.
Letters, personal emails and electronic conferences/ bulletin boards	Letter	Sender's Surname, Sender's Initials. (year). Unpublished letter to Recipient's Initials. Recipient's Surname re. Subject matter, day, month, year	Saunders, J. (2008). Unpublished letter to M.N.K. Saunders re. French Revolution, 10 Sept. 2008.
	Personal email	Sender's surname, Sender's initials. (year). Email to recipient's initials. recipient's surname re. Subject matter, day month year.	McPartlin, A. (2008). Email to M.N.K. Saunders re. Reviewers' feedback, 23 Nov. 2008.
	Blog	Owner's Surname, Owner's Initials. (year of posting). Specific subject. *Title of Blog.* Day Month Year (of posting). Avalable at http://www.remainderoffullInternetaddress/ [Accessed day month year].	Bonham-Carter, D. (2007) Career Change Questionnaire. *David's life coaching blog.* 10 Dec 2007. Available at http://www.davidbonham-carter.com/2007/12/career-change-questionnaire.html [Accessed 11 Dec. 2007].
	Discussion list email (where emailer known)	Sender's Surname, Sender's Initials. (year of posting). Re. Subject of discussion. Posted day month year. Sender's email address. [Accessed day month year].	Manno, D.F. (2007). Re. I got an email solicitation. Posted 6 Dec 2007. Survey Pro or Con? dfma...@mail.com [Accessed 10 Dec. 2007].
	Internet site/specific site pages	Source organisation. (year). *Title of site or page within site.* Available at http://www.remainderoffullInternetaddress/ [Accessed day month year].	European Commission. (2007). *Eurostat – structural indicators.* Available at http://epp.eurostat.ec.europa.eu/portal/page?_pageid=1133,47800773, 1133_47802558&_dad=portal&_schema=PORTAL [Accessed 27 Nov. 2007].
	Internet reports and guides	Surname, Initials. and Surname, Initials. (year). *Title of report.* Available at http://www.remainderoffullInternetaddress/ [Accessed day month year].	Browne, L. and Alstrup, P. (eds.) (2006). *What exactly is the Labour Force Survey?* Available at http://www.statistics.gov.uk/downloads/theme_labour/What_exactly_is_LFS1.pdf [Accessed 25 Dec. 2007].

Table A1.2 *(continued)*

To reference		Use the general format	For example
	Internet reports and guides (no author)	Organisation name. (year). *Title of report.* Available at http://www .remainderoffullInternetaddress/ [Accessed day month year].	Department for Transport. (2007). *Adding capacity at Heathrow airport: consultation document.* Available at http://www.dft.gov.uk/consultations/ open/heathrowconsultation/ consultationdocument/ [Accessed 25 Dec. 2007].
Audio-visual material	Television or radio programme	*Programme title.* (year of production). Transmitting organisation and nature of transmission, day month year of transmission.	*The Today Programme.* (2008). British Broadcasting Corporation Radio broadcast, 6 Apr. 2008.
	Television or radio programme that is part of a series	*Series title.* (year of production). Episode. episode title. Transmitting organisation and nature of transmission, day month year of transmission.	*The Money Programme.* (2007). Episode. Last orders for Guinness. British Broadcasting Corporation Television broadcast, 11 Dec. 2007.
	Commercial DVD	*DVD title.* (Year of production). [DVD]. Place of publication: Publisher.	*Bruce Springsteen Live in New York City* (2003). [DVD]. New York: Sony.
	Commercial DVD that is part of a series	*DVD series title* (Year of production) Episode. Episode title. [DVD]. Place of publication: Publisher.	*The Office Complete Series 1 and 2 and the Christmas Specials.* (2005). Episode. Series 1 Christmas Special. [DVD]. London: British Broadcasting Corporation.
	Audio CD	Surname, Initials. or Artist. or Group. (year). *Title of CD.* [Audio CD]. Place of Publication: Publisher.	Goldratt, E.M. (2005). *Beyond the goal.* [Audio CD]. Buffalo NY: Goldratt's Marketing Group.

Notes: Where date is not known or unclear, follow conventions outlined towards the end of Table A1.1.

Email addresses should not be included except when they are in the public domain. Even where this is the case, permission should be obtained or the email address replaced by '. . .' after the fourth character, for example: 'abcd...@isp.ac.uk'.

an example of every type of reference you might need to include, the information contained in this table should enable you to work out the required format for all your references. If there are any about which you are unsure, Colin Neville's (2007) book *The Complete Guide to Referencing and Avoiding Plagiarism* is one of the most comprehensive sources we have found.

For copies of journal articles from printed journals that you have obtained electronically via the Internet it is usually acceptable to reference these using exactly the same format as printed journal articles (Table A1.2), provided that you have obtained and read a facsimile (exact) copy of the article. Exact copies of journal articles have precisely the same format as the printed version, including page numbering, tables and diagrams. They are usually obtained by downloading the article via the Internet as a .pdf file that can be read on the screen and printed using Adobe Acrobat Reader. The Adobe Acrobat Reader can be downloaded free of charge from: http://www.adobe.com/

Finally, remember to include a, b, c etc. immediately after the year when you are referencing different publications by the same author from the same year. Do not forget to ensure that these are consistent with the letters used for the references in the main text.

The American Psychological Association (APA) style

The *American Psychological Association style* or *APA style* is a variation on the author-date system. Like the Harvard style it dates from the 1930s and 1940s, and has been updated subsequently. The latest updates are outlined in the latest edition of the American Psychological Association's (2005) *Concise rules of the APA style*, which is likely to be available for reference in your university's library.

Relatively small but significant differences exist between the Harvard and APA styles, and many authors adopt a combination of the two styles. The key differences are outlined in Table A1.3.

Table A1.3 Key differences between Harvard and APA styles of referencing

Harvard style	APA style	Comment
Referencing in the text		
(Lewis 2001)	(Lewis, 2001)	Note punctuation
(Williams and Saunders 2006)	(Williams & Saunders, 2006)	'&' not 'and'
(Saunders *et al.* 2005)	(Saunders, Skinner & Beresford, 2005)	For first occurrence if three to five authors
(Saunders *et al.* 2005)	(Saunders *et al.*, 2005)	For first occurrence if six or more authors
(Saunders *et al.* 2005)	(Saunders *et al.*, 2005)	For subsequent occurrences; note punctuation
Referencing in the references or bibliography		
Berman Brown, R. and Saunders, M. (2008). *Dealing with statistics: What you need to know.* Maidenhead: Open University Press.	Berman Brown, R. & Saunders, M. (2008). *Dealing with statistics: What you need to know.* Maidenhead: Open University Press.	Note use of 'and' and '&'

Numeric systems

Referencing in the text

When using *a* Numeric system such as the Vancouver style, references within the project report are shown by a number that is either bracketed or in superscript. This number refers directly to the list of references at the end of the text, and it means it is not necessary for you to include the authors' names or year of publication:

'Research[1] indicates that . . .'

[1]Ritzer, G. *The McDonaldization of Society.* (revised edn). Thousand Oaks, CA, Pine Forge Press; 1996.

Referencing in the references

The references list sequentially the referenced items in the order they are referred to in your project report. This means that they are unlikely to be in alphabetical order. When using the Numeric system you need to ensure that:

- The layout of individual references is that prescribed by the style you have adopted. This is likely to differ from both the Harvard and APA styles (Table A1.3) and will be dependent upon precisely which style has been adopted. The reference to Ritzer's book in the previous sub-section follows the Vancouver style. Further details of this and other numeric styles can be found in Neville's (2007) book.
- The items referred to include only those you have cited in your report. They, therefore, should be headed 'References' rather than 'Bibliography'.
- Only one number is used for each item, except where you refer to the same item more than once but need to refer to different pages. In such instances you use standard bibliographic abbreviations to save repeating the reference in full (Table A1.4).

Table A1.4 Bibliographic Abbreviations

Abbreviation	Explanation	For example
Op. cit. *(opere citato)*	Meaning 'in the work cited'. This refers to a work previously referenced, and so you must give the author and year and, if necessary, the page number.	Robson (2002) *op. cit.* pp. 23–4.
Loc. cit. *(loco citato)*	Meaning 'in the place cited'. This refers to the same page of a work previously referenced, and so you must give the author and year.	Robson (2002) *loc. cit.*
Ibid. (ibidem)	Meaning 'the same work given immediately before'. This refers to the work referenced immediately before, and replaces all details of the previous reference other than a page number if necessary.	*Ibid.* p. 59.

References

American Psychological Association (2005) *Concise Rules of the APA Style*. Washington, DC: American Psychological Association.

Neville, C. (2007) *The Complete Guide to Referencing and Avoiding Plagiarism*. Maidenhead: Open University Press.

Further Reading

American Psychological Association (2005) *Concise Rules of the APA Style*. Washington, DC: American Psychological Association. The most recent version of this manual contains full details of how to use this form of the author–date system of referencing as well as how to lay out tables, figures, equations and other statistical data. It also provides guidance on grammar and writing.

Neville, C. (2007) *The Complete Guide to Referencing and Avoiding Plagiarism*. Maidenhead: Open University Press. This book provides a comprehensive, up-to-date discussion of the layout required for a multitude of information sources including those from the Internet. It includes guidance on the Harvard, American Psychological Association, numerical and other referencing styles as well as a chapter on plagiarism.

Appendix 2 Calculating the minimum sample size

In some situations, such as experimental research, it is necessary for you to calculate the precise minimum sample size you require. This calculation assumes that data will be collected from all cases in the sample and is based on:

- how confident you need to be that the estimate is accurate (the level of confidence in the estimate);
- how accurate the estimate needs to be (the margin of error that can be tolerated);
- the proportion of responses you expect to have some particular attribute.

Provided that you know the level of confidence and the margin of error, it is relatively easy to estimate the proportion of responses you expect to have a particular attribute. To do this, ideally you need to collect a pilot sample of about 30 observations and from this to infer the likely proportion for your main survey. It is therefore important that the pilot sample uses the same methods as your main survey. Alternatively, you might have undertaken a very similar survey and so already have a reasonable idea of the likely proportion. If you do not, then you need either to make an informed guess or to assume that 50 per cent of the sample will have the specified attribute – the worst scenario. Most surveys will involve collecting data on more than one attribute. It is argued by deVaus (2002) that for such multi-purpose surveys you should determine the sample size on the basis of those variables in the sample that are likely to have the greatest variability.

Once you have all the information you substitute it into the formula,

$$n = p\% \times q\% \times \left[\frac{z}{e\%} \right]^2$$

where

n is the minimum sample size required

$p\%$ is the proportion belonging to the specified category

$q\%$ is the proportion not belonging to the specified category

z is the z value corresponding to the level of confidence required (see Table A2.1)

$e\%$ is the margin of error required.

Table A2.1 Levels of confidence and associated z values

Level of confidence	z value
90% certain	1.65
95% certain	1.96
99% certain	2.57

Box A2.1
Focus on student research

Calculating the minimum sample size

To answer a research question Jon needed to estimate the proportion of a total population of 4000 home care clients who receive a visit from their home care assistant at least once a week. Based on his reading of the research methods literature he decided that he needed to be 95 per cent certain that his 'estimate' was accurate (the level of confidence in the estimate); this corresponded to a z score of 1.96 (Table A2.1). Based on his reading he also decided that his 'estimate' needed to be accurate to within plus or minus 5 per cent of the true percentage (the margin of error that can be tolerated).

In order to calculate the minimum sample size, Jon still needed to estimate the proportion of respondents who received a visit from their home care assistant at least once a week. From his pilot survey he discovered that 12 out of the 30 clients receive a visit at least once a week – in other words, that 40 per cent belonged to this specified category. This meant that 60 per cent did not.

Jon substituted these figures into the formula:

$$n = 40 \times 60 \times \left(\frac{1.96}{5}\right)^2$$

$$= 2400 \times (0.392)^2$$

$$= 2400 \times 0.154$$

$$= 369.6$$

His minimum sample size, therefore, was 370 returns.

As the total population of home care clients was 4000, Jon could now calculate the adjusted minimum sample size:

$$n' = \frac{369.6}{1 + \left(\dfrac{369.6}{4000}\right)}$$

$$= \frac{369.6}{1 + 0.092}$$

$$= \frac{369.6}{1.092}$$

$$= 338.46$$

Because of the small total population, Jon needed a minimum sample size of only 339. However, this assumed he had a response rate of 100 per cent

---

Where your population is less than 10 000, a smaller sample size can be used without affecting the accuracy. This is called the *adjusted minimum sample size* (Box A2.1). It is calculated using the following formula:

$$n' = \frac{n}{1 + \left(\dfrac{n}{N}\right)}$$

where
n' is the adjusted minimum sample size
n is the minimum sample size (as calculated above)
N is the total population.

Reference

deVaus, D.A. (2002) *Surveys in Social Research* (5th edn). London: Routledge.

78 41	11 62	72 18	66 69	58 71	31 90	51 36	78 09	41 00
70 50	58 19	68 26	75 69	04 00	25 29	16 72	35 73	55 85
32 78	14 47	01 55	10 91	83 21	13 32	59 53	03 38	79 32
71 60	20 53	86 78	50 57	42 30	73 48	68 09	16 35	21 87
35 30	15 57	99 96	33 25	56 43	65 67	51 45	37 99	54 89
09 08	05 41	66 54	01 49	97 34	38 85	85 23	34 62	60 58
02 59	34 51	98 71	31 54	28 85	23 84	49 07	33 71	17 88
20 13	44 15	22 95	98 97	60 02	85 07	17 57	20 51	01 67
36 26	70 11	63 81	27 31	79 71	08 11	87 74	85 53	86 78
00 30	62 19	81 68	86 10	65 61	62 22	17 22	96 83	56 37
38 41	14 59	53 03	52 86	21 88	55 87	85 59	14 90	74 87
18 89	40 84	71 04	09 82	54 44	94 23	83 89	04 59	38 29
34 38	85 56	80 74	22 31	26 39	65 63	12 38	45 75	30 35
55 90	21 71	17 88	20 08	57 64	17 93	22 34	00 55	09 78
81 43	53 96	96 88	36 86	04 33	31 40	18 71	06 00	51 45
59 69	13 03	38 31	77 08	71 20	23 28	92 43	92 63	21 74
60 24	47 44	73 93	64 37	64 97	19 82	27 59	24 20	00 04
17 04	93 46	05 70	20 95	42 25	33 95	78 80	07 57	86 58
09 55	42 30	27 05	27 93	78 10	69 11	29 56	29 79	28 66
46 69	28 64	81 02	41 89	12 03	31 20	25 16	79 93	28 22
28 94	00 91	16 15	35 12	68 93	23 71	11 55	64 56	76 95
59 10	06 29	83 84	03 68	97 65	59 21	58 54	61 59	30 54
41 04	70 71	05 56	76 66	57 86	29 30	11 31	56 76	24 13
09 81	81 80	73 10	10 23	26 29	61 15	50 00	76 37	60 16
91 55	76 68	06 82	05 33	06 75	92 35	82 21	78 15	19 43
82 69	36 73	58 69	10 92	31 14	21 08	13 78	56 53	97 77
03 59	65 34	32 06	63 43	38 04	65 30	32 82	57 05	33 95
03 96	30 87	81 54	69 39	95 69	95 69	89 33	78 90	30 07
39 91	27 38	20 90	41 10	10 80	59 68	93 10	85 25	59 25
89 93	92 10	59 40	26 14	27 47	39 51	46 70	86 85	76 02
99 16	73 21	39 05	03 36	87 58	18 52	61 61	02 92	07 24
93 13	20 70	42 59	77 69	35 59	71 80	61 95	82 96	48 84
47 32	87 68	97 86	28 51	61 21	33 02	79 65	59 49	89 93
09 75	58 00	72 49	36 58	19 45	30 61	87 74	43 01	93 91
63 24	15 65	02 05	32 92	45 61	35 43	67 64	94 45	95 66
33 58	69 42	25 71	74 31	88 80	04 50	22 60	72 01	27 88
23 25	22 78	24 88	68 48	83 60	53 59	73 73	82 43	82 66
07 17	77 20	79 37	50 08	29 79	55 13	51 90	36 77	68 69
16 07	31 84	57 22	29 54	35 14	22 22	22 60	72 15	40 90
67 90	79 28	62 83	44 96	87 70	40 64	27 22	60 19	52 54
79 52	74 68	69 74	31 75	80 59	29 28	21 69	15 97	35 88
69 44	31 09	16 38	92 82	12 25	10 57	81 32	76 71	31 61
09 47	57 04	54 00	78 75	91 99	26 20	36 19	53 29	11 55
74 78	09 25	95 80	25 72	88 85	76 02	29 89	70 78	93 84

Source: from Morris, C. (2003) *Quantitative Approaches in Business Studies* (6th edn). Reproduced by permission of Pearson Education Ltd.

Reference

Morris, C. (2003) *Quantitative Approaches in Business Studies* (6th edn). Harlow: FT Prentice Hall.

Appendix 4 Guidelines for non-discriminatory language

Writing in a non-discriminatory manner is important in all areas of business and management. For example, in Section 14.5 we noted how the use of language that assumes the gender of a group of people, such as referring to a clerical assistant as 'she', not only is inaccurate but also gives offence to people of both sexes. Similar care needs to be exercised when using other gender-based terms, referring to people from different ethnic groups, and people with disabilities. Without this, the language used may reinforce beliefs and prejudices, as well as being oppressive, offensive, unfair or even incorrect. The impact of this is summarised clearly by Bill Bryson (1995:425) in his book, *Made in America*, when he observes: '... at the root of the bias-free language movement lies a commendable sentiment: to make language less wounding or demeaning to those whose sex, race, physical condition or circumstances leave them vulnerable to the raw power of words'.

Therefore, although the task of ensuring that the language you use is non-discriminatory may at first seem difficult, it is important that you do so. Some universities have developed their own guidelines, which are available via their intranet or the Internet. However, if your university has not developed its own guidelines, we hope those in this appendix will help you to ensure that your language is not discriminatory.

Guidelines for gender

When referring to both sexes, it is inappropriate to use the terms 'men' or 'women' and their gender-based equivalents; in other words, do not use gender-specific terms generically. Some of the more common gender-neutral alternatives are listed in Table A4.1.

Guidelines for ethnicity

Attention needs to be paid when referring to different ethnic groups. This is especially important where the term used refers to a number of ethnic groups. For example, the term 'Asian' includes a number of diverse ethnic groups that can be recognised with the terms 'Asian peoples' or 'Asian communities'. Similarly, the diversity of people represented by the term 'Black' can be recognised by referring to 'Black peoples' or 'Black communities'. Where possible, the individual groups within these communities should be identified separately.

'Black' as a term used to be regarded as offensive. More recently it has acquired connotations of unity against racism and has been reclaimed as a source of pride and identity (British Sociological Association 2005). 'Afro-Caribbean' is a term that is also associated with a commitment to anti-racism and is used to describe black people from the Caribbean islands. Increasingly, hyphenated terms such as 'Black-British' or 'African-American' are being used to refer to second- or third-generation people, many of whom have been born in a country but wish to retain a sense of their origins.

Table A4.1 Gender-specific terms and gender-neutral alternatives

Gender-specific term	Gender-neutral alternative
chairman	chair, chairperson
Dear Sir	Dear Sir/Madam
disseminate	broadcast, inform, publicise
forefathers	ancestors
foreman	supervisor
layman	lay person
man	person
man hours	work hours
mankind	humanity, humankind, people
man-made	manufactured, synthetic
manning	resourcing, staffing
manpower	human resources, labour, staff, workforce
master copy	original, top copy
masterful	domineering, very skilful
policewoman/policeman	police officer
rights of man	people's/citizens' rights, rights of the individual
seminal	classical, formative
women	People
working man/working woman	worker, working people

Source: developed from British Psychological Society (1988); British Sociological Association (2004a). Reproduced with permission. You can find the latest BPS advice on gender-specific terms and gender-neutral alternatives in its *Style Guide* (2004), available at: http:// www.bps.org.uk/publications/submission-guidelines/submission-guidelines_home.cfm. Advice on sex-specific language can be found on pp. 35–6 in the guide.

If you are unsure of the term to use, then ask someone from the appropriate community for the most acceptable current term. Alternatively, consult a more comprehensive text such as the British Sociological Association's (2005) guidelines which are available via the Internet.

Guidelines for disability

Disability is also an area where terminology is constantly changing as people voice their own preferences. Despite this, general guidelines can be offered:

- Avoid the use of medical labels as they promote the view of disabled people as patients.
- Where it is necessary to refer to a person's medical condition, make the person explicit (see Table A4.2).
- Where referring to historical and some contemporary common terms, place speech marks around the term.

Table A4.2 Disablist terms and non-disablist alternatives

Disablist term	Non-disablist alternative
the blind	blind and partially sighted people, visually impaired people
cripple	mobility impaired person
the deaf	deaf or hard of hearing people
the disabled, the handicapped, invalid	disabled people, people with disabilities, employees with disabilities
dumb, mute	person with a speech impairment
epileptic, epileptics	person who has epilepsy
handicap	disability
mentally handicapped	person with a learning difficulty or learning disability
mentally ill, mental patient	mental health service user
patient	person
spastic	person who has cerebral palsy
wheelchair-bound	wheelchair user
victim of, afflicted by, suffering from, crippled by	person who has, person with

Source: developed from British Sociological Association (2004b). Reproduced with permission.

There are non-disablist alternatives for the more common disablist terms. These are summarised in Table A4.2. However, if you are unsure of the term to use, ask someone from the appropriate group for the most acceptable current term.

References

British Psychological Society (1988) 'Guidelines for the use of non-sexist language', *The Psychologist*, Vol. 1, No. 2, pp. 53–4.

British Psychological Society (2004) 'Style Guide'. Available at: http://www.bps.org.uk/publications/submission-guidelines/submission-guidelines_home.cfm [Accessed 21 June 2008.]

British Sociological Association (2004a) 'Language and the BSA: Sex and Gender'. Available at: http://www.britsoc.co.uk/equality/ [Accessed 21 June 2008.]

British Sociological Association (2004b) 'Language and the BSA: Non-disablist'. Available at: http://www.britsoc.co.uk/equality/ [Accessed 21 June 2008.]

British Sociological Association (2005) 'Language and the BSA: Ethnicity and Race'. Available at: http://www.britsoc.co.uk/equality/ [Accessed 21 June 2008.]

Bryson, B. (1995) *Made in America*. London: Minerva.

Glossary

50th percentile The middle value when all the values of a variable are arranged in rank order; usually known as the median.

A

abstract (1) Summary, usually of an article or book, also containing sufficient information for the original to be located. **(2)** Summary of the complete content of the project report.

access (1) The process involved in gaining entry into an organisation to undertake research. **(2)** The situation where a research participant is willing to share data with a researcher. *See also* cognitive access, continuing access, physical access.

action research Research strategy concerned with the management of a change and involving close collaboration between practitioners and researchers. The results flowing from action research should also inform other contexts.

active response rate The total number of responses divided by the total number in the sample after ineligible and unreachable respondents have been excluded. *See* ineligible respondent, unreachable respondent.

active voice The voice in which the action of the verb is attributed to the person. For example, '*I* conducted interviews'.

alternative hypothesis Testable proposition stating that there no significant difference or relationship between two or more variables. Often referred to as H_a *See also:* hypothesis, null hypothesis.

analysis The ability to break down data and to clarify the nature of the component parts and the relationship between them.

analysis of variance Statistical test to determine the probability (likelihood) that the values of a numerical data variable for three or more independent samples or groups are different. The test assesses the likelihood of any difference between these groups occurring by chance alone.

analytic induction Analysis of qualitative data that involves the iterative examination of a number of strategically selected cases to identify the cause of a particular phenomenon.

analytic reflection The process of enquiry often used in the participant as observer role whereby key informants are encouraged to reflect analytically on the processes in which they are involved. This stems from the fact that research subjects know the identity of the researcher and, consequently, the researcher asks questions of those subjects promoting in the research subjects the process of analytic reflection. *See also* participant as observer.

anonymity The process of concealing the identity of participants in all documents resulting from the research.

ANOVA *See* analysis of variance.

appendix A supplement to the project report. It should not normally include material that is essential for the understanding of the report itself, but additional relevant material in which the reader may be interested.

application The ability to apply certain principles and rules in particular situations.

applied research Research of direct and immediate relevance to practitioners that addresses issues they see as important and is presented in ways they can understand and act upon.

archival research Research strategy that analyses administrative records and documents as principal source of data because they are products of day-to-day activities.

asynchronous Not undertaken in real time, working offline.

attribute variable Variable that records data about respondents' characteristics, in other words things they possess.

autocorrelation The extent to which the value of a variable at a particular time (t) is related to its value at the previous time period ($t - 1$).

axial coding The process of recognising relationships between categories in grounded theory.

axiology A branch of philosophy that studies judgements about the role of values.

B

bar chart Diagram for showing frequency distributions for a categorical or grouped discrete data variable, which highlights the highest and lowest values.

base period The period against which index numbers are calculated to facilitate comparisons of trends or changes over time. *See also* index number.

basic research Research undertaken purely to understand processes and their outcomes, predominantly in universities as a result of an academic agenda, for which the key consumer is the academic community.

behaviour variable Variable that records what respondents actually do.

bibliographic details The information needed to enable readers to find original items consulted or used for a research project. These normally include the author, date of publication, title of article, title of book or journal.

bibliography Alphabetical list of the bibliographic details for all relevant items consulted and used, including those items not referred to directly in the text. The university will specify the format of these.

blog Usually refers to a written account of a mixture of what is happening in a person's life and what is happening on the Internet, published on the Internet.

Boolean logic System by which the variety of items found in a search based on logical propositions that can be either true or false can be combined, limited or widened.

box plot Diagram that provides a pictorial representation of the distribution of the data for a variable and statistics such as median, inter-quartile range, and the highest and lowest values.

brainstorming Technique that can be used to generate and refine research ideas. It is best undertaken with a group of people.

broker *See* gatekeeper.

C

CAQDAS Computer Aided Qualitative Data Analysis Software.

case (1) Individual element or group member within a sample or population such as an employee. **(2)** Individual unit for which data have been collected.

case study Research strategy that involves the empirical investigation of a particular contemporary phenomenon within its real-life context, using multiple sources of evidence.

categorical data Data whose values cannot be measured numerically but can either be classified into sets (categories) or placed in rank order.

categorising The process of developing categories and subsequently attaching these categories to meaningful units of data. *See also* unitising, units of data

category question Closed question in which the respondent is offered a set of mutually exclusive categories and instructed to select one.

causal relationship Relationship between two or more variables in which the change (effect) in one variable is caused by the other variable(s).

census The collection and analysis of data from every possible case or group member in a population.

central limit theorem The larger the absolute size of a sample, the more closely its distribution will be to the normal distribution. *See* normal distribution.

central tendency measure The generic term for statistics that can be used to provide an impression of those values for a variable that are common, middling or average.

chat room An online forum operating in synchronous mode. *See also* synchronous.

chi square test Statistical test to determine the probability (likelihood) that two categorical data variables are associated. A common use is to discover whether there are statistically significant differences between the observed frequencies and the expected frequencies of two variables presented in a cross-tabulation.

classic experiment Experiment in which two groups are established and members assigned at random to each. *See also* experiment, experimental group.

closed question Question that provides a number of alternative answers from which the respondent is instructed to choose.

cluster sampling Probability sampling procedure in which the population is divided into discrete groups or clusters prior to sampling. A random sample (systematic or simple) of these clusters is then drawn.

codebook Complete list of all the codes used to code data variables.

code of ethics Statement of principles and procedures for the design and conduct of research. *See also* privacy, research ethics, research ethics committee.

coding *See* axial coding, categorising, open coding, selective coding, unitising data

coefficient of determination *See* regression coefficient.

coefficient of multiple determination *See* multiple regression coefficient.

coefficient of variation Statistic that compares the extent of spread of data values around the mean between two or more variables containing numerical data.

cognitive access The process of gaining access to data from intended participants. This involves participants agreeing to be interviewed or observed, within agreed limits. *See also* informed consent.

cohort study Study that collects data from the same cases over time using a series of 'snapshots'.

collinearity The extent to which two or more independent variables are correlated with each other. Also termed multicollinearity.

comparative proportional pie chart Diagram for comparing both proportions and totals for all types of data variables.

compiled data Data that have been processed, such as through some form of selection or summarising.

complete observer Observational role in which the researcher does not reveal the purpose of the research activity to those being observed. However, unlike the complete participant role, the researcher does not take part in the activities of the group being studied.

complete participant Observational role in which the researcher attempts to become a member of the group in which research is being conducted. The true purpose of the research is not revealed to the group members.

computer-aided personal interviewing (CAPI) Type of interviewing in which the interviewer reads questions from a computer screen and enters the respondent's answers directly into the computer.

computer-aided telephone interviewing (CATI) Type of telephone interviewing in which the interviewer reads questions from a computer screen and enters the respondent's answers directly into the computer.

conclusion The section of the project report in which judgements are made rather than just facts reported. New material is not normally introduced in the conclusion.

confidentiality Concern relating to the right of access to the data provided by the participants and, in particular the need to keep these data secret or private.

consent *See* implied consent, informed consent.

consent form Written agreement, signed by both parties in which the participant agrees to take part in the research and gives there permission for data to be used in specified ways.

construct validity Extent to which your measurement questions actually measure the presence of those constructs you intended them to measure.

consultancy report *See* management report.

content validity *See* face validity.

contextual data Additional data recorded when collecting primary or secondary data that reveals background information about the setting and the data collection process.

contingency table Technique for summarising data from two or more variables so that specific values can be read.

continuing access Gaining agreed research access to an organisation on an incremental basis.

continuous data Data whose values can theoretically take any value (sometimes within a restricted range) provided they can be measured with sufficient accuracy.

control group Group in an experiment that, for the sake of comparison, does not receive the intervention n which you are interested. *See also* experiment, experimental group.

controlled index language The terms and phrases used by databases to index items within the database. If search terms do not match the controlled index language, the search is likely to be unsuccessful.

controls to allow the testing of hypotheses Ways of being sure that the outcome being measured (the dependent variable) is caused by the predicted phenomena alone (the independent variable) rather than extraneous unpredicted variables.

convenience sampling Non-probability sampling procedure in which cases are selected haphazardly on the basis that they are easiest to obtain. *See also* non-probability sampling.

correlation The extent to which two variables are related to each other. *See also* correlation coefficient, negative correlation, positive correlation.

correlation coefficient Number between -1 and $+1$ representing the strength of the relationship between two ranked or numerical variables. A value of $+1$ represents a perfect positive correlation. A value of -1 represents a perfect negative correlation. Correlation coefficients between -1 and $+1$ represent weaker positive and negative correlations, a value of 0 meaning the variables are perfectly independent. *See also* negative correlation, Pearson's product moment correlation coefficient, positive correlation, Spearman's rank correlation coefficient.

coverage The extent to which a data set covers the population it is intended to cover.

covering letter Letter accompanying a questionnaire, which explains the purpose of the survey. *See also* introductory letter.

covert research Research undertaken where those being researched are not aware of this fact.

Cramer's V Statistical test to measure the association between two variables within a table on a scale where 0 represents no association and 1 represents perfect association. Because the value of Cramer's V is always between 0 and 1, the relative strengths of significant associations between different pairs of variables can be compared.

creative thinking technique One of a number of techniques for generating and refining research ideas based on non-rational criteria. These may be, for example, biased heavily in favour of the individual's preferences or the spontaneous ideas of the individual or others. *See also* brainstorming, Delphi technique, relevance tree.

criterion-related validity Ability of a statistical test to make accurate predictions.

critical case sampling A purposive sampling method which focuses on selecting those cases on the basis of making a point dramatically or because they are important. *See also* purposive sampling.

critical incidence technique A technique in which respondents are asked to describe in detail a critical incident or number of incidents that is key to the research question. *See also* critical incident.

critical incident An activity or event where the consequences were so clear that the respondent has a definite idea regarding the effects.

critical (literature) review Detailed and justified analysis and commentary of the merits and faults of the literature within a chosen area, which demonstrates familiarity with what is already known about your research topic.

critical realism The epistemological position that what we experience are sensations, the images of the things in the real world, not the things directly. *See also* direct realism, realism.

cross-posting Receipt by individuals of multiple copies of an email, often due to the use of multiple mailing lists on which that individual appears.

cross-sectional research The study of a particular phenomenon (or phenomena) at a particular time, i.e. a 'snapshot'.

cross-tabulation *See* contingency table.

D

data Facts, opinions and statistics that have been collected together and recorded for reference or for analysis.

data display and analysis A process for the collection and analysis of qualitative data that involves three concurrent subprocesses of data reduction, data display, and drawing and verifying conclusions.

data matrix The table format in which data are usually entered into analysis software consisting of rows (cases) and columns (variables).

data requirements table A table designed to ensure that, when completed, the data collected will enable the research question(s) to be answered and the objectives achieved.

data sampling The process of only transcribing those sections of an audio-recording that are pertinent to your research, having listened to it repeatedly beforehand.

data saturation The stage when any additional data collected provides few, if any, new insights.

debriefing Providing research participants with a retrospective explanation about a research project and its purpose where covert observation has occurred.

deception Deceiving participants about the nature, purpose or use of research by the researcher(s). *See also* informed consent, research ethics.

decile One of 10 sections when data are ranked and divided into 10 groups of equal size.

deductive approach Research approach involving the testing of a theoretical proposition by the employment of a research strategy specifically designed for the purpose of its testing.

deliberate distortion Form of bias that occurs when data are recorded inaccurately on purpose. It is most common for secondary data sources such as organisational records.

delivery and collection questionnaire Data collection technique in which the questionnaire is delivered to each respondent. She or he then reads and answers the same set of questions in a predetermined order without an interviewer being present before the completed questionnaire is collected.

Delphi technique Technique using a group of people who are either involved or interested in the research topic to generate and select a more specific research idea.

deontological view View that the ends served by research can never justify research which is unethical.

dependent variable Variable that changes in response to changes in other variables.

descriptive data Data whose values cannot be measured numerically but can be distinguished by classifying into sets (categories).

descriptive observation Observation where the researcher concentrates on observing the physical setting, the key participants and their activities, particular events and their sequence and the attendant processes and emotions involved.

descriptive research Research for which the purpose is to produce an accurate representation of persons, events or situations.

descriptive statistics Generic term for statistics that can be used to describe variables.

descripto-explanatory study A study whose purpose is both descriptive and explanatory where, usually, description is the precursor to explanation.

deviant sampling *See* extreme case sampling.

dichotomous data Descriptive data that are grouped into two categories. *See also* descriptive data.

direct realism The epistemological position that what you see is what you get: what we experience through our senses portrays the world accurately. *See also* critical realism, realism.

discourse analysis General term covering a variety of approaches to the analysis of language in its own right. It explores how language constructs and simultaneously reproduces and/or changes the social world rather than using it as a means to reveal the social world as a phenomenon.

discrete data Data whose values are measured in discrete units and therefore can take only one of a finite number of values from a scale that measures changes in this way.

discussion The section of the project report in which the wider implications of the findings (and conclusions) are considered.

dispersion measures Generic term for statistics that can be used to provide an impression of how the values for a variable are dispersed around the central tendency.

dissertation The usual name for research projects undertaken as part of undergraduate and taught masters degrees. Dissertations are usually written for an academic audience.

documentary secondary data Written documents such as notices, minutes of meetings, diaries, administrative and public records and reports to shareholders as well as non-written documents such as tape and video recordings, pictures, films and television programmes.

Durbin–Watson statistic Statistical test to measure the extent to which the value of a dependent variable at time t is related to its value at the previous time period, $t - 1$ (autocorrelation). The statistic ranges in value from zero to four. A value of two indicates no autocorrelation. A value of towards zero indicates positive autocorrelation. A value towards four indicates negative autocorrelation. *See also* autocorrelation.

E

ecological validity A type of external validity referring to the extent to which findings can be generalised from one group to another. *See also* external validity.

electronic interview An Internet- or intranet-mediated interview conducted through either a chat room, Internet forum, web conferencing or email. *See also* email interview, chat room, Internet forum.

electronic questionnaire An Internet- or intranet-mediated questionnaire. *See also* Internet-mediated questionnaire, intranet-mediated questionnaire.

element Individual case or group member within a sample or population such as an employee.

email interview A series of emails each containing a small number of questions rather than one email containing a series of questions.

epistemology A branch of philosophy that studies the nature of knowledge and what constitutes acceptable knowledge in a field of study.

ethics *See* research ethics, research ethics committees, code of ethics.

ethnography Research strategy that focuses upon describing and interpreting the social world through first-hand field study.

evaluation The process of judging materials or methods in terms of internal accuracy and consistency or by comparison with external criteria.

experiential data Data about the researcher's perceptions and feelings as the research develops.

experiential meaning The equivalence of meaning of a word or sentence for different people in their everyday experiences.

experiment Research strategy that involves the definition of a theoretical hypothesis; the selection of samples of individuals from known populations; the allocation of samples to different experimental conditions; the introduction of planned change on one or more of the variables; and measurement on a small number of variables and control of other variables. *See also* control group, experimental group.

experimental group Group in an experiment that receives the intervention in which you are interested. *See also* control group, experiment.

expert system Computer-based system that contains much of the knowledge used by experts in a specific field and is designed to assist non-experts in problem solving.

explanation building Deductive process for analysing qualitative data that involves the iterative examination of a number of strategically selected cases to test a theoretical proposition.

explanatory research Research that focuses on studying a situation or a problem in order to explain the relationships between variables.

exploratory data analysis (EDA) Approach to data analysis that emphasises the use of diagrams to explore and understand the data.

exploratory study Research that aims to seek new insights into phenomena, to ask questions, and to assess the phenomena in a new light.

external researcher Researcher who wishes to gain access to an organisation for which she or he does not work. *See also* access, internal researcher.

external validity The extent to which the research results from a particular study are generalisable to all relevant contexts.

extraneous variable Variable that might also cause changes in a dependent variable, thereby providing an alternative explanation to your independent variables. *See* dependent variable, independent variable.

extreme case sampling A purposive sampling method which focuses on unusual or special cases. *See also* purposive sampling.

F

face validity Agreement that a question, scale, or measure appears logically to reflect accurately what it was intended to measure.

filter question Closed question that identifies those respondents for whom the following question or questions are not applicable, enabling them to skip these questions.

focus group Group interview, composed of a small number of participants, facilitated by a 'moderator', in which the topic is defined clearly and precisely and there is a focus on enabling and recording interactive discussion between participants. *See also* group interview.

follow-up Contact made with respondents to thank them for completing and returning a survey and to remind non-respondents to complete and return their surveys.

forced-choice question *See* closed question.

forum *See* Internet forum.

free text searching Feature that allows searching of an entire database rather than just those terms included in the controlled index language.

frequency distribution Table for summarising data from one variable so that specific values can be read.

functionalist paradigm A philosophical position which is concerned with a rational explanation of behaviours and institutions such as why a particular organisational problem is occurring in terms of the functions they perform.

fundamental research *See* basic research.

G

Gantt chart Chart that provides a simple visual representation of the tasks or activities that make up a project, each being plotted against a time line.

gatekeeper The person, often in an organisation, who controls research access.

general focus research question Question that flows from the research idea and may lead to several more detailed questions or the definition of research objectives.

generalisability The extent to which the findings of a research study are applicable to other settings.

generalisation The making of more widely applicable propositions based upon the process of deduction from specific cases.

Goldilocks test A test to decide whether research questions are either too big, too small, too hot or just right. Those that are too big probably demand too many resources. Questions that are too small are likely to be of insufficient substance, while those that are too hot may be so because of sensitivities that may be aroused as a result of doing the research.

grammatical error Error of grammar that detracts from the authority of the project report.

grey literature *See* primary literature.

grounded theory Research strategy in which theory is developed from data generated by a series of observations or interviews principally involving an inductive approach. *See also* deductive approach, inductive approach.

group interview General term to describe all non-standardised interviews conducted with two or more people.

H

habituation Situation where, in observation studies, the subjects being observed become familiar with the process of observation so that they take it for granted. This is an attempt to overcome 'observer effect' or reactivity.

haphazard sampling *See* convenience sampling.

heterogeneous sampling A purposive sampling method which focuses on obtaining the maximum variation in the cases selected. *See also* purposive sampling.

heteroscedasticity Extent to which the data values for the dependent and independent variables have unequal variances. *See also* variance.

histogram Diagram for showing frequency distributions for a grouped continuous data variable in which the area of each bar represents the frequency of occurrence.

homogeneous sampling A purposive sampling method which focuses on selecting cases from one particular subgroup in which all the members are similar. *See also* purposive sampling.

homoscedasticity Extent to which the data values for the dependent and independent variables have equal variances. *See also* variance.

hypothesis (1) Testable proposition stating that there is a significant difference or relationship between two or more variables. Often referred to as H_1 *See also:* alternative hypothesis, null hypothesis. **(2)** Testable proposition about the relationship between two or more events or concepts.

I

idiomatic meaning The meaning ascribed to a group of words that are natural to a native speaker, but which is not deducible from the individual words.

implied consent Position achieved when intended participants are fully informed about the nature, purpose and use of research to be undertaken and their role within it, but their consent to participate, is inferred from their participating in the research, such as by responding to a questionnaire. *See also* informed consent.

independent groups *t*-test Statistical test to determine the probability (likelihood) that the values of a numerical data variable for two independent samples or groups are different. The test assesses the likelihood of any difference between these two groups occurring by chance alone.

independent variable Variable that causes changes to a dependent variable or variables.

in-depth interview *See* unstructured interview.

index number Summary data value calculated from a base period for numerical variables, to facilitate comparisons of trends or changes over time. *See also* base period.

inductive approach Research approach involving the development of a theory as a result of the observation of empirical data.

ineligible respondent Respondent selected for a sample who does not meet the requirements of the research.

inference, statistical *See* statistical inference.

informant interview Interview guided by the perceptions of the interviewee.

informant verification Form of triangulation in which the researcher presents written accounts of, for example, interview notes to informants for them to verify the content. *See also* triangulation.

informed consent Position achieved when intended participants are fully informed about the nature, purpose

and use of research to be undertaken and their role within it, and where their consent to participate, if provided, is freely given. *See also* deception, implied consent.

integer A whole number.

intelligence gathering The gathering of facts or descriptive research.

inter-library loan System for borrowing a book or obtaining a copy of a journal article from another library.

internal researcher Person who conducts research within an organisation for which they work. *See also* cognitive access, external researcher.

internal validity Extent to which findings can be attributed to interventions rather than any flaws in your research design.

Internet forum Commonly referred to as web forums, message boards, discussion boards, discussion forums, discussion groups and bulletin boards. Usually only deal with one topic and discourage personal exchanges.

Internet-mediated questionnaire Questionnaire administered electronically using the Internet.

interpretive paradigm A philosophical position which is concerned with understanding the way we as humans make sense of the world around us.

interpretivism The epistemological position that advocates the necessity to understand differences between humans in their role as social actors.

inter-quartile range The difference between the upper and lower quartiles, representing the middle 50% of the data when the data values for a variable have been ranked.

interval data Numerical data for which the difference or 'interval' between any two data values for a particular variable can be stated, but for which the relative difference can not be stated. *See also:* numerical data.

interview schedules *See* structured interviews.

interviewee bias Attempt by an interviewee to construct an account that hides some data or when she or he presents herself or himself in a socially desirable role or situation.

interviewer bias Attempt by an interviewer to introduce bias during the conduct of an interview, or where the appearance or behaviour of the interviewer has the effect of introducing bias in the interviewee's responses.

interviewer-administered questionnaire Data collection technique in which an interviewer reads the same set of questions to the respondent in a predetermined order and records his or her responses. *See also* structured interview, telephone questionnaire.

intranet-mediated questionnaire Questionnaire administered electronically using an organisation's intranet.

introduction The opening to the project report, which gives the reader a clear idea of the central issue of concern of the research, states the research question(s) and research objectives, and explains the research context and the structure of the project report.

introductory letter Request for research access, addressed to an intended participant or organisational broker/gatekeeper, stating the purpose of the research, the nature of the help being sought, and the requirements of agreeing to participate. *See also* covering letter, gatekeeper.

intrusive research methods Methods that involve direct access to participants, including qualitative interviewing, observation, longitudinal research based on these methods and phenomenologically based approaches to research. *See also* access, cognitive access.

investigative question One of a number of questions that need to be answered in order to address satisfactorily each research question and meet each objective.

J

journal *See* professional journal, refereed academic journal.

judgemental sampling *See* non-probability sampling.

K

Kendall's rank correlation coefficient Statistical test that assesses the strength of the relationship between two ranked data variables, especially where the data for a variable contain tied ranks. For data collected from a sample, there is also a need to calculate the probability of the correlation coefficient having occurred by chance alone.

key word Basic term that describes the research question(s) and objectives, which can be used in combination to search the tertiary literature.

knobs Processes that establish and define a causal and functional relationship between the process cause and its outcome.

Kolmogorov–Smirnov test Statistical test to determine the probability (likelihood) that an observed set of values for each category of a variable differs from a specified distribution. A common use is to discover whether a sample differs significantly from the population from which it was selected.

kurtosis The pointedness or flatness of a distribution's shape compared with the normal distribution. If a distribution is pointier or peaked, it is leptokurtic and the kurtosis value is positive. If a distribution is flatter, it is platykurtic and the kurtosis value is negative. *See also* normal distribution.

L

law of large numbers Samples of larger absolute size are more likely to be representative of the population from which they are drawn than smaller samples and, in particular, the mean (average) calculated for the sample is more likely to equal the mean for the population, providing the samples are not biased.

lexical meaning The precise meaning of an individual word.

Likert-style rating scale Scale that allows the respondent to indicate how strongly she or he agrees or disagrees with a statement.

linearity Degree to which change in a dependent variable is related to change in one or more independent variables. *See also* dependent variable, independent variable

line graph Diagram for showing trends in longitudinal data for a variable.

list question Closed question, in which the respondent is offered a list of items and instructed to select those that are appropriate.

literature review *See* critical (literature) review.

longitudinal study The study of a particular phenomenon (or phenomena) over an extended period of time.

long-term trend The overall direction of movement of numerical data values for a single variable after variations have been smoothed out. *See also* moving average.

lower quartile The value below which a quarter of the data values lie when the data values for a variable have been ranked.

M

management report Abbreviated version of the project report, usually written for a practitioner audience. Normally includes a brief account of objectives, method, findings, conclusions and recommendations.

Mann-Whitney *U* Test Statistical test to determine the probability (likelihood) that the values of a ordinal data variable for two independent samples or groups are different. The test assesses the likelihood of any difference between these two groups occurring by chance alone and is often used when the assumptions of the independent samples *t*-test are not met.

matrix question Series of two or more closed questions in which each respondent's answers are recorded using the same grid.

maximum variation sampling *See* heterogeneous sampling.

mean The average value calculated by adding up the values of each case for a variable and dividing by the total number of cases.

measurement validity The extent to which a scale or measuring instrument measures what it is intended to measure.

median The middle value when all the values of a variable are arranged in rank order; sometimes known as the 50th percentile.

method The techniques and procedures used to obtain and analyse research data, including for example questionnaires, observation, interviews, and statistical and non-statistical techniques.

methodology The theory of how research should be undertaken, including the theoretical and philosophical assumptions upon which research is based and the implications of these for the method or methods adopted.

minimal interaction Process in which the observer tries as much as possible to 'melt into the background', having as little interaction as possible with the subjects of the observation. This is an attempt to overcome observer effect. *See also* observer effect.

mixed-method research Use of quantitative and qualitative data collection techniques and analysis procedures either at the same time (parallel) or one after the other (sequential) but not in combination.

mixed-methods approach General term for approach when both quantitative and qualitative data collection techniques and analysis procedures are both used in a research design.

mixed-model research Combination of quantitative and qualitative data collection techniques and analysis procedures as well as combining quantitative and qualitative approaches in other phases of the research such as research question generation.

mode The value of a variable that occurs most frequently.

modal group The most frequently occurring category for data that have been grouped.

Mode 1 knowledge creation Research of a fundamental rather than applied nature, in which the questions are set and solved by academic interests with little, if any, focus on exploitation of research by practitioners.

Mode 2 knowledge creation Research of an applied nature, governed by the world of practice and highlighting the importance of collaboration both with and between practitioners.

Mode 3 knowledge creation Research growing out of Mode 1 and Mode 2 whose purpose is 'to assure survival and promote the common good at various levels of social aggregation' (Huff and Huff 2001:S53).

moderator Facilitator of focus group interviews. *See also* focus group, group interview.

mono method Use of a single data collection technique and corresponding analysis procedure or procedures.

moving average Statistical method of smoothing out variations in numerical data recorded for a single variable over time to enable the long-term trend to be seen more clearly. *See also* long-term trend.

multicollinearity *See* collinearity.

multi-method Use of more than one data collection technique and corresponding analysis procedure or procedures.

multi-method qualitative study Use of more than one quantitative data collection technique and corresponding quantitative analysis procedure or procedures.

multi-method quantitative study Use of more than one qualitative data collection technique and corresponding qualitative analysis procedure or procedures.

multiple bar chart Diagram for comparing frequency distributions for categorical or grouped discrete or continuous data variables, which highlights the highest and lowest values.

multiple-dichotomy method Method of data coding using a separate variable for each possible response to an open question or an item in a list question. *See also* list question, open question.

multiple line graph Diagram for comparing trends over time between numerical data variables.

multiple methods Use of more than one data collection technique and analysis procedure or procedures.

multiple regression analysis The process of calculating a coefficient of multiple determination and regression equation using two or more independent variables and one dependent variable. For data collected from a sample, there is also a need to calculate the probability of the regression coefficient having occurred by chance alone. *See also* multiple regression coefficient, regression analysis, regression equation.

multiple regression coefficient Number between 0 and +1 that enables the strength of the relationship between a numerical dependent variable and two or more numerical independent variables to be assessed. The coefficient represents the proportion of the variation in the dependent variable that can be explained statistically by the independent variables. A value of 1 means that all the variation in the dependent variable can be explained statistically by the independent variables. A value of 0 means that none of the variation in the dependent variable can be explained by the independent variables. *See also* multiple regression analysis.

multiple-response method Method of data coding using the same number of variables as the maximum number of different responses to an open question or a list question by any one case. *See also* list question, open question.

multiple-source secondary data Secondary data created by combining two or more different data sets prior to the data being accessed for the research. These data sets can be based entirely on documentary or on survey data, or can be an amalgam of the two.

multi-stage sampling Probability sampling procedure that is a development of cluster sampling. It involves taking a series of cluster samples, each of which uses random sampling (systematic, stratified or simple).

N

narrative account The researcher's detailed account of the research process, written in much the same style as that used by an investigative journalist.

narrative analysis The collection and analysis of qualitative data that preserves the integrity and narrative value of data collected, thereby avoiding their fragmentation.

naturalistic Adopting an ethnographic strategy in which the researcher researches the phenomenon within the context in which it occurs.

negative correlation Relationship between two variables for which, as the values of one variable increase, the values of the other variable decrease. *See also* correlation coefficient.

negative skew Distribution of numerical data for a variable in which the majority of the data are found bunched to the right, with a long tail to the left.

netiquette General operating guidelines for using the Internet, including not sending junk emails.

nominal data *See* descriptive data.

non-maleficence Avoidance of harm.

non-parametric statistic Statistic designed to be used when data are not normally distributed. Often used with categorical data. *See also* categorical data.

non-probability sampling Selection of sampling techniques in which the chance or probability of each case being selected is not known.

non-random sampling *See* non-probability sampling.

non-response When the respondent refuses to take part in the research or answer a question.

Non-response bias bias in findings caused by respondent refusing to take part in the research or answer a question.

non-standardised interview *See* semi-structured interview, unstructured interview.

normal distribution Special form of the symmetric distribution in which the numerical data for a variable can be plotted as a bell-shaped curve.

notebook of ideas Technique for noting down any interesting research ideas as you think of them.

null hypothesis Testable proposition stating that there is no significant difference or relationship between two or more variables. Often referred to as H_0. *See also:* alternative hypothesis, hypothesis.

numerical data Data whose values can be measured numerically as quantities.

numeric rating scale Rating scale that uses numbers as response options to identify and record the respondent's response. The end response options, and sometimes the middle, are labelled.

O

objectivism An ontological position that asserts that social entities exist in a reality external to, and independent of, social actors concerned with their existence. *See also* ontology, subjectivism.

objectivity Avoidance of (conscious) bias and subjective selection during the conduct and reporting of research. In some research philosophies the researcher will consider that interpretation is likely to be related to a set of values and therefore will attempt to recognise and explore this.

observation The systematic observation, recording, description, analysis and interpretation of people's behaviour.

observer as participant Observational role in which the researcher observes activities without taking part in those activities in the same way as the 'real' research subjects. The researcher's identity as a researcher and research purpose is clear to all concerned. *See also* participant as observer.

observer bias This may occur when observers give inaccurate responses in order to distort the results of the research.

observer effect The impact of being observed on how people act. *See also* habituation, reactivity.

observer error Systematic errors made by observers, as a result of tiredness, for example.

one-way analysis of variance *See* analysis of variance.

online questionnaire Data collection technique in which the questionnaire is delivered via the Internet or an intranet to each respondent. She or he then reads and answers the same set of questions in a predetermined order without an interviewer being present before returning it electronically.

ontology Branch of philosophy that studies the nature of reality or being. *See also* axiology, epistemology.

open coding The process of disaggregating data into units in grounded theory.

open question Question allowing respondents to give answers in their own way.

operationalisation The translation of concepts into tangible indicators of their existence.

opinion variable Variable that records what respondents feel about something or what they think or believe is true or false.

optical mark reader Data input device that recognises and converts marks on a data collection form such as a questionnaire into data that can be stored on a computer.

ordinal data *See* ranked data.

P

paired *t*-test Statistical test to determine the probability (likelihood) that the values of two (a pair of) numerical data variables collected for the same cases are different. The test assesses the likelihood of any difference between two variables (each half of the pair) occurring by chance alone.

paradigm A way of examining social phenomena from which particular understandings of these phenomena can be gained and explanations attempted.

parametric statistic Statistic designed to be used when data are normally distributed. Used with numerical data. *See also* numerical data.

participant The person who answers the questions, usually in an interview or group interview.

participant as observer Observational role in which the researcher takes part in and observes activities in the same way as the 'real' research subjects. The researcher's identity as a researcher and research purpose is clear to all concerned. *See also* observer as participant.

participant information sheet Information required by gatekeepers and intended participants in order for informed consent to be given.

participant interview Interview directed by the questions posed by the interviewer, to which the interviewee responds. *See also* respondent interview.

participant observation Observation in which the researcher attempts to participate fully in the lives and activities of the research subjects and thus becomes a member of the subjects' group(s), organisation(s) or community. *See also* complete observer, complete participant, observer as participant, participant as observer.

participant researcher *See* internal researcher.

passive voice The voice in which the subject of the sentence undergoes the action of the verb: for example, 'interviews were conducted'.

pattern matching Analysis of qualitative data involving the prediction of a pattern of outcomes based on theoretical propositions to seek to explain a set of findings.

Pearson's product moment correlation coefficient Statistical test that assesses the strength of the relationship between two numerical data variables. For data collected from a sample there is also a need to calculate the probability of the correlation coefficient having occurred by chance alone.

percentage component bar chart Diagram for comparing proportions for all types of data variables.

percentile One of 100 sections when data are ranked and divided into 100 groups of equal size.

personal data Category of data, defined in law, relating to identified or identifiable persons.

personal entry Situation where the researcher needs to conduct research within an organisation, rather than rely on the use and completion of self-administered, postal questionnaires or the use of publicly available secondary data. *See* access.

personal pronoun One of the pronouns used to refer to people: I, me, you, he, she, we, us, they, him, her, them.

phenomenology Research philosophy that sees social phenomena as socially constructed, and is particularly concerned with generating meanings and gaining insights into those phenomena.

Phi Statistic to measure association between two variables using a scale between -1 (perfect negative association), through 0 (no association) to $+1$ (perfect association).

physical access The initial level of gaining access to an organisation to conduct research. *See also* cognitive access, continuing access, gatekeeper.

pictogram Diagram in which a picture or series of pictures are used to represent the data proportionally.

pie chart Diagram frequently used for showing proportions for a categorical data or a grouped continuous or discrete data variable.

pilot test Small-scale study to test a questionnaire, interview checklist or observation schedule, to minimise the likelihood of respondents having problems in answering the questions and of data recording problems as well as to allow some assessment of the questions' validity and the reliability of the data that will be collected.

population The complete set of cases or group members.

positive correlation Relationship between two variables for which, as the value of one variable increases, the values of the other variable also increase. *See also* correlation coefficient.

positive skew Distribution of numerical data for a variable in which the majority of the data are found bunched to the left, with a long tail to the right.

positivism The epistemological position that advocates working with an observable social reality. The emphasis is on highly structured methodology to facilitate replication, and the end product can be law-like generalisations similar to those produced by the physical and natural scientists.

postal questionnaire Data collection technique in which the questionnaire is delivered by post to each respondent. She or he then reads and answers the same set of questions in a predetermined order without an interviewer being present before returning it by post.

PowerPoint™ Microsoft computer package that allows the presenter to design overhead slides using text, pictures, photographs etc., which lend a professional appearance.

practitioner-researcher Role occupied by a researcher when she or he is conducting research in an organisation, often her or his own, while fulfilling her or his normal working role.

pragmatism A position that argues that the most important determinant of the research philosophy adopted is the research question, arguing that it is possible to work within both positivist and interpretivist positions. It applies a practical approach, integrating different perspectives to help collect and interpret data. *See also* interpretivism, positivism.

pre-coding The process of incorporating coding schemes in questions prior to a questionnaire's administration.

predictive validity *See* criterion-related validity.

preliminary search This way of searching the literature may be a useful way of generating research ideas. It may be based, for example, on lecture notes or course textbooks.

preliminary study The process by which a research idea is refined in order to turn it into a research project. This may be simply a review of the relevant literature.

pre-set codes Codes established prior to data collection and often included as part of the data collection form.

pre-survey contact Contact made with a respondent to advise them of a forthcoming survey in which she or he will be asked to take part.

primary data Data collected specifically for the research project being undertaken.

primary literature The first occurrence of a piece of work, including published sources such as government white papers and planning documents and unpublished manuscript sources such as letters, memos and committee minutes.

primary observation Observation where the researcher notes what happened or what was said at the time. This is often done by keeping a research diary.

privacy Primary ethical concern relating to the rights of individuals not to participate in research and to their treatment where they agree to participate. *See also* research ethics, informed consent.

probability sampling Selection of sampling techniques in which the chance, or probability, of each case being selected from the population is known and is not zero.

probing questions Questions used to further explore responses that are of significance to the research topic.

professional journal Journals produced by a professional organisation for its members, often containing articles of a practical nature related to professional needs. Articles in professional journals are usually not refereed.

project report The term used in this book to refer generally to dissertations, theses and management reports. *See also* dissertation, management report, thesis.

pure research *See* basic research.

purposive sampling Non-probability sampling procedure in which the judgement of the researcher is used to select the cases that make up the sample. This can be done on the basis of extreme cases, heterogeneity (maximum variation), homogeneity (maximum similarity), critical cases, or typical cases.

Q

qualitative data Non-numerical data or data that have not been quantified.

qualitative interview Collective term for semi-structured and unstructured interviews aimed at generating qualitative data.

qualitise Conversion of quantitative data into narrative that can be analysed qualitatively.

quantifiable data *See:* numerical data.

quantitative data Numerical data or data that have been quantified.

quantitise Conversion of qualitative data into numerical codes that can be analysed statistically.

quantity question Closed question in which the respondent's answer is recorded as a number giving the amount.

quartile one of four sections when data are ranked and divided into four groups of equal size. *See also* lower quartile, upper quartile.

questionnaire General term including all data collection techniques in which each person is asked to respond to the same set of questions in a predetermined order. *See also* delivery and collection questionnaire, interviewer-administered questionnaire, online questionnaire, postal questionnaire, self-administered questionnaire.

quota sampling Non-probability sampling procedure that ensures that the sample represents certain characteristics of the population chosen by the researcher.

R

radical change A perspective which relates to a judgement about the way organisational affairs should be conducted and suggests ways in which these affairs may be conducted in order to make fundamental changes to the normal order of things.

radical humanist paradigm A position concerned with changing the status quo, of existing social patterns.

radical structuralist paradigm A position concerned with achieving fundamental change based upon an analysis of underlying structures that cannot be easily observed, for example organisational phenomena as power relationships and patterns of conflict.

random sampling *See* simple random sampling.

range The difference between the highest and the lowest values for a variable.

ranked data Data whose values cannot be measured numerically but which can be placed in a definite order (rank).

ranking question Closed question in which the respondent is offered a list of items and instructed to place them in rank order.

rating question Closed question in which a scaling device is used to record the respondent's response. *See also* Likert-type rating scale, numeric rating scale, semantic differential rating scale.

ratio data Numerical data for which both the difference or 'interval' and relative difference between any two data values for a particular variable can be stated. *See also:* numerical data.

rational thinking technique One of a number of techniques for generating and refining research ideas based on a systematic approach such as searching the literature or examining past projects.

raw data Data for which little, if any, data processing has taken place.

reactivity Reaction by research participants to any research intervention that affects data reliability. *See also* habituation, observer effect.

realism The epistemological position that objects exist independently of our knowledge of their existence. *See also* critical realism, direct realism.

re-coding The process of grouping or combining a variable's codes to form a new variable, usually with less detailed categories.

reductionism The idea that problems as a whole are better understood if they are reduced to the simplest possible elements.

refereed academic journal Journal in which the articles have been evaluated by academic peers prior to publication to assess their quality and suitability. Not all academic journals are refereed.

references, list of Bibliographic details of all items referred to directly in the text. The university will specify the format required.

regression analysis The process of calculating a regression coefficient and regression equation using one independent variable and one dependent variable. For data collected from a sample, there is also a need to calculate the probability of the regression coefficient having occurred by chance alone. *See also* multiple regression analysis, regression coefficient, regression equation.

regression coefficient Number between 0 and +1 that enables the strength of the relationship between a numerical dependent variable and a numerical independent variable to be assessed. The coefficient represents the proportion of the variation in the dependent variable that can be explained statistically by the independent variable. A value of 1 means that all the variation in the dependent variable can be explained statistically by the independent variable. A value of 0 means that none of the variation in the dependent variable can be explained by the independent variable. *See also* regression analysis.

regression equation Equation used to predict the values of a dependent variable given the values of one or more independent variables. The associated regression coefficient provides an indication of how good a predictor the regression equation is likely to be. *See* regression coefficient.

regulatory perspective A perspective that seeks to explain the way in which organisational affairs are regulated and offer suggestions as to how they may be improved within the framework of the way things are done at present.

relevance tree Technique for generating research topics that starts with a broad concept from which further (usually more specific) topics are generated. Each of these topics forms a separate branch, from which further sub-branches that are more detailed can be generated.

reliability The extent to which data collection technique or techniques will yield consistent findings, similar observations would be made or conclusions reached by other researchers or there is transparency in how sense was made from the raw data.

representative sample Sample that represents exactly the population from which it is drawn.

representative sampling *See* probability sampling.

research The systematic collection and interpretation of information with a clear purpose, to find things out. *See also* applied research, basic research.

research approach General term for inductive or deductive research approach. *See also* deductive approach, inductive approach.

research ethics The appropriateness of the researcher's behaviour in relation to the rights of those who become the subject of a research project, or who are affected by it. *See also* code of ethics, privacy, research ethics committee.

research ethics committee Learned committee established to produce a code of research ethics, examine and approve or veto research proposals and advise in relation to the ethical dilemmas facing researchers during the conduct and reporting of research projects. *See also* code of ethics.

research idea Initial idea that may be worked up into a research project.

research objectives Clear, specific statements that identify what the researcher wishes to accomplish as a result of doing the research.

research philosophy Overarching term relating to the development of knowledge and the nature of that knowledge in relation to research.

research population Set of cases or group members that you are researching.

research question One of a number of key questions that the research process will address. These are often the precursor of research objectives.

research strategy General plan of how the researcher will go about answering the research question(s).

respondent The person who answers the questions usually either in an interview or on a questionnaire. *See also* participant.

respondent interview Interview directed by the questions posed by the interviewer, to which the interviewee responds. *See also* participant interview.

response bias *See* interviewee bias.

response rate *See* active response rate.

review article Article, normally published in a refereed academic journal, that contains both a considered review of the state of knowledge in a given topic area and pointers towards areas where further research needs to be undertaken. *See also* refereed academic journal.

review question Specific question you ask of the material you are reading, which is linked either directly or indirectly to your research question. *See also* research question.

S

sample Sub-group or part of a larger population.

sampling fraction The proportion of the total population selected for a probability sample.

sampling frame The complete list of all the cases in the population, from which a probability sample is drawn.

saturation *See* data saturation.

scale Measure of a concept, such as customer loyalty or organisational commitment, created by combining scores to a number of rating questions.

scale item Rating question used in combination with other rating questions to create a scale. *See* rating question, scale.

scale question *See* rating question.

scatter graph Diagram for showing the relationship between two numerical or ranked data variables.

scatter plot *See:* scatter graph.

scientific research Research that involves the systematic observation of and experiment with phenomena.

search engine Automated software that searches an index of documents on the Internet using key words and Boolean logic.

search string Combination of key words used in searching online databases.

secondary data Data used for a research project that were originally collected for some other purpose. *See also* documentary secondary data, multiple source secondary data, survey-based secondary data.

secondary literature Subsequent publication of primary literature such as books and journals.

secondary observation Statement made by an observer of what happened or was said. By necessity this involves that observer's interpretations.

selective coding The process of integrating categories to produce theory in grounded theory.

self-administered questionnaire Data collection technique in which each respondent reads and answers the same set of questions in a predetermined order without an interviewer being present.

self-coded question Question each respondent codes her or himself as part of the process of recording their answer.

self-selection sampling Non-probability sampling procedure in which the case, usually an individual, is allowed to identify their desire to be part of the sample.

semantic differential rating scale Rating scale that allows the respondent to indicate his or her attitude to a concept defined by opposite adjectives or phrases.

semi-structured interview Wide-ranging category of interview in which the interviewer commences with a set of interview themes but is prepared to vary the order in which questions are asked and to ask new questions in the context of the research situation.

sensitive personal data Category of data, defined in law, that refers to certain specified characteristics or beliefs relating to identified or identifiable persons.

serial correlation *See* autocorrelation.

shadowing Process that the researcher would follow in order to gain a better understanding of the research context. This might involve following employees who are likely to be important in the research.

significance testing Testing the probability of a pattern such as a relationship between two variables occurring by chance alone.

simple random sampling Probability sampling procedure that ensures that each case in the population has an equal chance of being included in the sample.

snowball sampling Non-probability sampling procedure in which subsequent respondents are obtained from information provided by initial respondents.

social constructionism Research philosophy that views the social world as being socially constructed.

social norm The type of behaviour that a person ought to adopt in a particular situation.

socially desirable response Answer given by a respondent due to her or his desire, either conscious or unconscious, to gain prestige or appear in a different social role.

source questionnaire The questionnaire that is to be translated from when translating a questionnaire.

Spearman's rank correlation coefficient Statistical test that assesses the strength of the relationship between two ranked data variables. For data collected from a sample, there is also a need to calculate the probability of the correlation coefficient having occurred by chance alone.

split infinitive Phrase consisting of an infinitive with an adverb inserted between 'to' and the verb: for example, 'to readily agree'.

stacked bar chart Diagram for comparing totals and subtotals for all types of data variable.

standard deviation Statistic that describes the extent of spread of data values around the mean for a variable containing numerical data.

statistical inference The process of coming to conclusions about the population on the basis of data describing a sample drawn from that population.

statistical significance The likelihood of the pattern that is observed (or one more extreme) occurring by chance alone, if there really was no difference in the population from that which the sample was drawn.

storyline The way in which the reader is led through the research project to the main conclusion or the answer to the research question. The storyline is, in effect, a clear theme that runs through the whole of the project report to convey a coherent and consistent message.

stratified random sampling Probability sampling procedure in which the population is divided into two or more relevant strata and a random sample (systematic or simple) is drawn from each of the strata.

structured interview Data collection technique in which an interviewer physically meets the respondent, reads them the same set of questions in a predetermined order, and records his or her response to each.

structured methodology Data collection methods that are easily replicated (such as the use of an observation schedule or questionnaire) to ensure high reliability.

subject directory Hierarchically organised index categorised into broad topics, which, as it has been compiled by people, is likely to have its content partly censored and evaluated.

subject or participant bias Bias that may occur when research subjects are giving inaccurate responses in order to distort the results of the research.

subject or participant error Errors that may occur when research subjects are studied in situations that are inconsistent with their normal behaviour patterns, leading to atypical responses.

subjectivism An ontological position that asserts that entities are created from the perceptions and consequent actions of those social actors responsible for their creation. *See also* ontology, objectivism.

survey Research strategy that involves the structured collection of data from a sizeable population. Although the term 'survey' is often used to describe the collection of data using questionnaires, it includes other techniques such as structured observation and structured interviews.

survey-based secondary data Data collected by surveys, such as by questionnaire, which have already been analysed for their original purpose.

symbolic interactionism Social process through which the individual derives a sense of identity from interaction and communication with others. Through this process of interaction and communication the individual responds to others and adjusts his or her understandings and behaviour as a shared sense of order and reality is 'negotiated' with others.

symmetric distribution Description of the distribution of data for a variable in which the data are distributed equally either side of the highest frequency.

symmetry of potential outcomes Situation in which the results of the research will be of similar value whatever they are.

synchronous Undertaken in real time, occurring at the same time.

synthesis Process of arranging and assembling various elements so as to make a new statement, or conclusion.

systematic review A process for reviewing the literature using a comprehenisve pre-planned search strategy. There are clear assessment criteria for selection of articles to review, articles are assessed on the quality of research and findings, individual studies are synthesised using a clear framework and findings presented in a balanced, impartial and comprehensive manner.

systematic sampling Probability sampling procedure in which the initial sampling point is selected at random, and then the cases are selected at regular intervals.

T

table Technique for summarising data from one or more variables so that specific values can be read. *See also* contingency table, frequency distribution.

tailored design method Approach to designing questionnaires specifying precisely how to construct and use them; previously referred to as the 'total design method'.

target questionnaire The translated questionnaire when translating from a source questionnaire.

teleological view View that the ends served by research justify the means. Consequently, the benefits of research findings are weighed against the costs of acting unethically.

telephone questionnaire Data collection technique in which an interviewer contacts the respondent and administers the questionnaire using a telephone. The interviewer reads the same set of questions to the respondent in a predetermined order and records his or her responses.

template analysis Analysis of qualitative data that involves creating and developing a hierarchical template of data codes or categories representing themes revealed in the data collected and the relationships between these.

tense The form taken by the verb to indicate the time of the action (i.e. past, present or future).

tertiary literature source Source designed to help locate primary and secondary literature, such as an index, abstract, encyclopaedia or bibliography.

theory Formulation regarding the cause and effect relationships between two or more variables, which may or may not have been tested.

theory dependent If we accept that every purposive decision we take is based on the assumption that certain consequences will flow from the decision, then these decisions are theory dependent.

thesis The usual name for research projects undertaken for Master of Philosophy (MPhil) and Doctor of Philosophy (PhD) degrees, written for an academic audience.

time error Error, usually associated with structured observations, where the time at which the observation is being conducted provides data that are untypical of the time period in which the event(s) being studied would normally occur.

time series Set of numerical data values recorded for a single variable over time usually at regular intervals. *See also* moving average.

transcription The written record of what a participant (or respondent) said in response to a question, or what participants (or respondents) said to one another in conversation, in their own words.

triangulation The use of two or more independent sources of data or data-collection methods within one study in order to help ensure that the data are telling you what you think they are telling you.

t-test *See* independent groups *t*-test, paired *t*-test.

Type I error Error made by wrongly coming to the decision that something is true when in reality it is not.

Type II error Error made by wrongly coming to the decision that something is not true when in reality it is.

typical case sampling A purposive sampling method which focuses on selecting those cases on the basis that they are typical or illustrative. *See also* purposive sampling.

U

uninformed response Tendency for a respondent to deliberately guess where they have sufficient knowledge or experience to answer a question.

unitising data The process of attaching relevant 'bits' or 'chunks' of your data to the appropriate category or categories that you have devised.

unit of data A number of words, a line of a transcript, a sentence, a number of sentences, a complete paragraph, or some other chunk of textual data that fits the category.

unreachable respondent Respondent selected for a sample who cannot be located or who cannot be contacted.

unstructured interview Loosely structured and informally conducted interview that may commence with one or more themes to explore with participants but without a predetermined list of questions to work through. *See also* informant interview.

upper quartile The value above which a quarter of the data values lie when the data values for a variable have been ranked.

V

validity (1) The extent to which data collection method or methods accurately measure what they were intended to measure. **(2)** The extent to which research findings are really about what they profess to be about. *See also* construct validity, criterion related validity, ecological validity, face validity, internal validity, measurement validity, predictive validity.

variable Individual element or attribute upon which data have been collected.

variance Statistic that measures the spread of data values; a measure of dispersion. The smaller the variance, the closer individual data values are to the mean. The value of the variance is the square root of the standard deviation. *See also* dispersion measures, standard deviation.

variance inflation factor (VIF) Statistic used to measure collinearity. *See* collinearity.

VIF *See* variance inflation factor.

visual aid Item such as an overhead projector slide, whiteboard, video recording or handout that is designed to enhance professional presentation and the learning of the audience.

W

web log *See* blog.

weighting The process by which data values are adjusted to reflect differences in the proportion of the population that each case represents.

Index

Page numbers in **bold** refer to glossary entries.
50th percentile (median) 444, 445, 446, **587**

C

S